Pugilistica: The History of British Boxing Containing Lives of the Most Celebrated Pugilists; Full Reports of Their Battles from Contemporary Newspapers, with Authentic Portraits, Personal Anecdotes, and Sketches of the Principal Patrons of the Prize Ring

Henry Downes Miles

PUGILISTICA

THE HISTORY
OF
BRITISH BOXING

FIRST FIGHT OF SPRING AND LANGAN, ON WORCESTER RACE COURSE, January 24th, 1824. *See* page 25.

VOL. II.

Frontispiece

PUGILISTICA

THE HISTORY

OF

BRITISH BOXING

CONTAINING

LIVES OF THE MOST CELEBRATED PUGILISTS; FULL REPORTS OF THEIR BATTLES
FROM CONTEMPORARY NEWSPAPERS, WITH AUTHENTIC PORTRAITS, PERSONAL
ANECDOTES, AND SKETCHES OF THE PRINCIPAL PATRONS OF THE PRIZE
RING, FORMING A COMPLETE HISTORY OF THE RING FROM FIG
AND BROUGHTON, 1719-40, TO THE LAST CHAMPIONSHIP BATTLE
BETWEEN KING AND HEENAN, IN DECEMBER 1863

BY HENRY DOWNES MILES

EDITOR OF "THE SPORTSMAN'S MAGAZINE." AUTHOR OF "THE BOOK OF FIELD SPORTS,"
"ENGLISH COUNTRY LIFE," ETC., ETC.

VOLUME TWO

Edinburgh

JOHN GRANT

1906

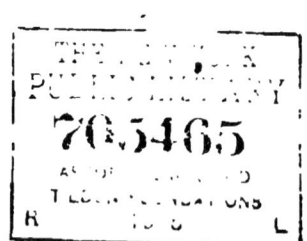

TO

THE HONOURABLE ROBERT GRIMSTON,

THE CONSTANT AND LIBERAL PATRON AND UPHOLDER

OF

THE ATHLETIC SPORTS AND MANLY EXERCISES OF THE PEOPLE,

THESE RECORDS OF THE

COURAGE, SKILL, FORBEARANCE AND FORTITUDE

OF

BRITISH BOXERS

ARE APPROPRIATELY DEDICATED BY

THE AUTHOR.

Wood Green, August, 1880.

PREFACE TO VOLUME II.

THE favour with which the first volume of PUGILISTICA has been received gives the author encouraging hope that the present instalment of his history will prove yet more interesting and acceptable.

The two periods comprised in these pages embrace the lives of several of the most skilful and courageous boxers who have illustrated the art of attack and defence. In the first, we have the battles of Spring (Thos. Winter), John Langan, Ned Painter, Oliver, Neat of Bristol, Thomas Hickman, Dan Donnelly, and Carter, with minor stars in an Appendix. In the second, Jem Ward, Peter Crawley, Tom Cannon, Josh. Hudson, Ned Neale, Ned Baldwin, Young Dutch Sam, Alec Reid, Tom Gaynor, Bishop Sharpe, Brown of Bridgnorth, and Sampson of Birmingham. Dick Curtis, Barney Aaron, Harry Jones, and light-weights forming the Appendix.

The third and concluding volume, commencing with Bendigo (William Thompson), will include the Decline and Fall of the P.R., with occasional flickerings of its olden fire, till its final expiry in the doings of Tom Sayers, John Camel Heenan, and Tom King.

Wood Green, August, 1880,

THOMAS WINTER (SPRING), CHAMPION.

From a Drawing by GEORGE SHARPLES *in 1822.*

PUGILISTICA:

THE HISTORY OF BRITISH BOXING.

PERIOD V.—1814 TO 1824.

FROM THE CHAMPIONSHIP OF TOM SPRING TO THAT OF JEM WARD.

CHAPTER I.

TOM SPRING (CHAMPION).—1814–1824.

A NEW era in boxing arose about the period of Spring's appearance and Tom Cribb's later battles, of which Thomas Winter (Spring) was the exponent, and of which school Jem Ward (in the next Period), Peter Crawley, Ned Neale, Jem Burn, Baldwin, Young Dutch Sam, and others, with numerous light weights, carried out the exemplification and practice. This we shall have ample occasion to notice in the coming chapters; for the present we will address ourselves to the milling career of Thomas Spring.

Thomas Winter, who adopted the name of Spring on his appearance in the ring as a professor, was born at Fownhope, Herefordshire, February 22nd, 1795. His fighting weight thirteen stone two pounds; later, thirteen stone four pounds; height, five feet eleven and a-half inches.

The relations and connexions of Thomas Winter, at Hereford and in the neighbourhood, were respectable; and when he tried his "'prentice han'," at the age of seventeen, in battle with Hollands, a big countryman of some provincial repute, he won by science and steadiness. He thus gained a name in the immediate neighbourhood of Mordeford, where he was in service with a butcher, who was in after life a firm friend and an admirer of Tom's prowess.

Two years afterwards (in 1814), one Henley, a local celebrity, challenged

Tom for three sovereigns a-side. This also came off at Mordeford, when in eleven rounds Henley was satisfied that he had found his master in the youth whom he had challenged to the fray.

Spring two years afterwards made his way to the metropolis. Here he met one Stringer, a Yorkshireman, from Rawcliffe, renowned for its "paddocks." Stringer was under the wing of Richmond, and was proposed as a "trial horse" for the young aspirant Spring. The battle took place at Moulsey, September, 9, 1817. We take the contemporary report as giving the first impressions produced on those who did not foresee the brilliant career of the youthful débutant.

The appearance of Stringer was athletic and big, but by no means fresh, and his cut of countenance was rough and weatherbeaten. He was an ugly looking customer in more than one sense. Spring looked boyish, not more than 21 years of age, and in some points he was thought to resemble the late Jem Belcher, but on a larger scale. The men, it appears, were about equal in weight—Stringer thirteen stone seven pounds, Spring thirteen stone two pounds. Both men were about six feet in height, and formidable fellows. The stakes were forty guineas and a purse given by the P. C. (Pugilistic Club). Stringer was waited upon by Richmond and Shelton; Spring was seconded by Tom Owen and Parish, the Waterman. Two to one was asked upon Spring; but seven to four was the current betting against Stringer.

THE FIGHT.

Round 1.—Stringer, on setting-to, placed himself in a better attitude than was expected. He also made two feints. Some blows were exchanged; in closing, both down.

2.—In this round the superiority of science was evident on the part of Spring. In closing he fibbed his opponent severely, and in struggling for the throw, both went down, Stringer uppermost.

3.—This round was courageously fought. It was curious to observe the left hand of Stringer pushing, as it were, against his opponent, with his right close upon it. Yorky did not appear wholly without judgment, though many of his blows were made at random. Both were down. The odds had now risen rapidly upon Spring.

4.—Stringer rushed in with all the impetuosity of a bull, seized hold of his adversary improperly, and sent him down. Loud cries of "foul," "fair," etc. occurred. But the fight was suffered to proceed, it being attributed more to want of knowledge than to absolute design.

5.—Strength, activity, and science were now pre-eminent on the part of Spring,

and, at this early stage of the fight, it was almost certain how it must end. Spring kept hitting his opponent completely away, but still he returned desperately, till he was at length hit down.

6.—This was also a desperate round. The men stood up to each other, and hammered away like a couple of blacksmiths, but Spring had the best of it. The latter nobly disdained taking an advantage when Stringer was on the ropes, and let him go down without extra punishment. Great applause from all parts of the ring.

7.—The determination of Stringer was truly astonishing; he bored in regardless of the consequences. In passing Spring he got a tremendous nobber, and was ultimately sent down.

8.—Nothing but milling, till they closed, and both down.

9.—On setting-to Yorky received a facer, which nearly turned him round, but he recovered himself, and planted a good hit. In closing, Stringer got his arms round his opponent's body, but he could not prevent Spring from administering some heavy punishment. The Yorkshireman, however, obtained the throw, and fell with all his weight upon Spring.

10.—Stringer fought with so much desperation that he almost laid himself down, he appeared so exhausted.

11.—The Yorkshireman could not protect his head from the repeated shots of his opponent. In closing, both down, but Spring uppermost.

12.—Both men exhibited severe marks of the other's handy-work. The claret was flowing copiously. Both down. A quarter of an hour had elapsed.

13.—A short but sharp round, till both on the ground.

14.—Stringer was rather conspicuous in this round. He bored Spring to the ropes, where much struggling took place before they went down.

15.—Stringer was hit down at the ropes. Great applause.

16.—This was as terrible a round as any in the fight. One minute passed in hard milling, without intermission, till Spring got the best of it, when Stringer went down and fell upon his hands.

17.—The conduct of Spring was again truly brave. He had Stringer in a situation that he might have punished him till he was tired, but he let him down amidst the loudest shouts of approbation. Bravo, Spring!

18.—Stringer kept fighting till he fell.

19.—The game displayed by the Yorkshireman was equal to anything ever seen; notwithstanding the severe milling he received, he came laughing up to the scratch. But his head was never out of chancery in this round. Both down.

20.—The men upon setting-to went as eagerly to work as if the fight had just commenced. Hit for hit were reciprocally given, till, in closing, both had enough of it, and went down.

21.—Equally desperate with any of the preceding rounds. Richmond now loudly observed to Stringer "to fight his own way." The Yorkshireman went down covered with claret.

22.—Spring took the lead in this round in an eminent degree. He fibbed Stringer terribly, till he slipped through his hands.

23.—The courage of the Yorkshireman was truly fine, and had he possessed science equal to his opponent the termination of the battle would have been doubtful. The men fought like lions, till they both fell out of the ropes. Loud shouting.

24.—Spring again behaved handsomely to Stringer. Many of the spectators called out to "take the Yorkshireman away." (Three to one on Spring.)

25.—A more determined round was never fought. In a rally, both men were hit to a stand still; they at length got away from each other, when Stringer rushed in and got his arms round his opponent's body, but, ultimately, he was so severely fibbed that he went down exhausted.

26.—On setting-to, Stringer merely exchanged a blow and went down.

27.—Stringer in endeavouring to bore in upon his adversary ran himself down.

28.—Stringer now made a last and desperate effort. His seconds kept as it were urging him forward, telling him "to hold up his head." He continued to fight till he was sent down.

29th and last.—This round was, in point of execution, the severest ever seen. Stringer received so tremendous a hit in his body, from the right hand of his opponent, that he was only prevented in the act of falling on his face by a quick repetition of it, which caught Yorky's nob, and instantly floored him on his back! He was carried out of the ring by his seconds in a state of stupor. The battle lasted thirty-nine minutes.

REMARKS.—A more determined man was never witnessed than Stringer proved himself. He put in some desperate blows, and his confidence never forsook him; indeed he laughed several times. On being asked how he felt himself within the last two rounds, he observed, "he was as hearty as a buck!" As a "Receiver General" he stands almost without an equal. It was a truly desperate fight, and might stand comparison with the battle between Symonds and George Maddox. Stringer was most ably seconded by Richmond and Shelton. His nob was completely metamorphosed. Stringer looks like a man of forty, and, it would seem, he has commenced pugilist too late in the day to attain any celebrity. He is able to beat any rough commoner. From the exhibition of Spring in this battle, he bids fair to put all the "big ones" upon the alert. It is true, he wants improvement in his mode of fighting; nevertheless, he displayed those sound requisites, which, when united with experience, must ultimately constitute him a first-rate boxer. His strength is unquestionable; his game by no means doubtful; and he possesses a tolerably good knowledge of the science. Spring was not once distressed throughout the above battle. He never bobbed his head aside to avoid the coming blow, but stood firm as a rock, and stopped or parried. His generous behaviour also to Stringer, in four or five instances, when he might have administered additional punishment, was so manly and humane that it cannot be passed over, nor ought it to be forgotten. Spring has a prepossessing appearance, is well made, and weighs more than fourteen stone.* Both of the above boxers have stood at the Royal Academy, as "studies" for the artists. The frame of Stringer is considered to possess great anatomical beauty.

* This is an error of the reporter's. Spring has told us he was thirteen stone, nett, when he met Stringer.

Spring, anxious to obtain a high situation on the milling list, and to lose his time no longer with rough commoners, without hesitation challenged Ned Painter for 100 guineas a-side, which was as unhesitatingly accepted. It was thought a bold attempt on the part of Spring, and to show more of ambition than sound judgment. This match occasioned much conversation in the milling circles; but Painter was decidedly the favourite. Some difficulty occurred in making the stakes good on the part of Spring, many of his promised backers being found absent at the appointed time. A gentleman, however, stepped forward and made up the deficiency, to prevent disappointment.

The sun had scarcely shed his beams over the metropolis, on Wednesday morning, the 1st of April, 1818, when the roads leading to Mickleham Downs, near Leatherhead, in Surrey, were thronged with vehicles of every description, full of amateurs hastening to the appointed spot to enjoy scientific pugilism, it being the first "big fight" in the season. The Bonifaces along the road were rather taken by surprise, it being April Fool-day, but as soon as they got hold of the right scent, the "dashing system" was put into requisition, and the "cooling article" was most liberally added, in order to prevent the amateurs from getting the fever, or over-heating their frames from too copious draughts of ardent spirits. The "knowing ones" were perfectly satisfied that Painter must win, and seven to four were the odds sported; but the admirers of youth, supported by science, strength, and pluck, added to the chance of long odds, proved eager takers.

The situation of the ring was truly picturesque and delightful, commanding an uninterrupted view of diversified scenery for sixty miles. Some fir trees contiguous to it had an animated appearance from the numerous spectators mounted upon their boughs. At a little after one, Painter and Spring appeared in the outer ring. and, upon meeting, shook hands in a cordial and true Englishman-like manner. Spring threw his hat first in the ring; Painter immediately followed the same line of conduct. A half-past one the men set-to; Painter was seconded by Tom Belcher and Harry Harmer; Spring by Cribb and Byrne. Seven to four current, and two to one against Spring. Gully kept the time.

THE FIGHT.

Round 1.—The attitude of Spring was firm —his body far back, and his length of arm rendered him difficult to be got at. They sparred for three minutes without a hit being exchanged; Spring appeared tired and put down his hands. He then, in planting a blow, hit short; more long sparring occurred, when some hits were exchanged, and Painter received a blow on the side of his throat that sent him staggering, and, in falling, the back of his head and part of his shoulder came in violent contact with one of the stakes. The shock was heard by all the spectators. This round occupied six minutes—Spring received great applause.

2. The time-keeper, it appears, from this circumstance, thought his occupation was at an end; and Mr. Jackson also deemed it next to an impossibility for the fight to proceed. Painter seemed completely stupefied from the effects of this accident, and Belcher lifted him up with the heaviness of a log of wood; nevertheless he came to his time. In fact it appeared more from instinct than meeting his man under the influence of intellect. A swelling, the bigness of an egg, had now risen on his head, and the skin on his shoulder was cut. Spring again hit short, when Painter planted a sharp facer with his left hand. More long sparring occurred—some blows were exchanged—when Painter received a hit and slipped down. Shouting and applause. The long odds at this early stage of the fight were on the totter.

3.—The idea of a smashing fight was now at an end, and the Randall and Belasco system seemed to be the order of the day. It was more a display of science than of milling. Spring planted a blow and got away. Painter made a hit, but Spring followed him over the ring. Two sharp counter hits occurred in the body. Spring laughed, and gave Painter a nobber, and got away dexterously. Painter made play and put in a severe facer; some blows were exchanged—and in closing, the latter endeavoured to "weave" his antagonist, but, in struggling, the strength of Spring prevailed. He not only held Painter's hands, but extricated himself in gallant style, and planted a hit on him as he was going down. Great applause, and the long odds completely floored; in many parts of the ring it was now even betting. Twenty-one minutes had elapsed. Painter, while sitting upon his second's knee, confusedly inquired, "what is it?" just coming to his recollection; having fought the last two rounds in total ignorance. Harmer then informed him of the accident he had experienced, when Painter complained of his shoulder.

4.—Long sparring again occurred. Some hits were exchanged. In closing, Spring held his opponent's hand (called Tom Owen's stop, and first introduced by that boxer). Both down, but Spring uppermost.

5.—The forte of Painter seemed to have materially changed. There was more of science exhibited than work performed. The claret scorned to make its appearance. In closing, Spring threw Painter.

6. For "Big Ones," there was nothing like going to work, and a long fight was contemplated by all the spectators. Two severe counter-hits occurred. Painter hit short, when Spring returned a sharp blow on his mouth. In closing Spring got Painter down. Applause. (The first six rounds occupied half an hour.)

7. Painter commenced this round by planting a blow on the head, and one on the body of his opponent. But in closing Spring fell heavily upon him.

8. This was also a good round. Painter put in three facers, and got away. In closing, both hung on the ropes, and went down.

9. This round was the best display by Painter throughout the fight. He planted several facers with success, and one was so severe, that, had it not been for the ropes, Spring must have gone down. In closing, both down.

10. Spring hit short several times, and Painter planted a good nobber, but, in return, he received some sharp hits, so that he turned round and went down. Great applause for Spring.

11.—The manliness of conduct exhibited in this round by Spring received thunders of applause. Painter endeavoured to punish Spring in the act of closing; but the latter, instead of holding him up, as he might have done, let his man down, and put up both his hands. "Bravo, Spring!" and he now became, in a great measure, the favourite. The knowing ones began to look queer.

12.—The same manly conduct again exhibited on the part of Spring.

13.—Painter hit down.

14.—Blow for blow, but Painter down.

15.—Spring slipped, but hit Painter again to grass.

16.—Spring hit down by a complete body-blow. "Well done, Painter," from his friends.

17.—Painter got a blow on the mouth, when he went down, but appeared to slip.

18.—The left hand of Spring was used with success; and his science and length gave him great advantages. Painter down.

19 to 24.—Painter was evidently much distressed, and went down in all these rounds. He frequently hit himself down.

25.—Spring, although he occasionally hit short, planted some heavy chopping blows on the arms and shoulders of Painter, which, added to the accident, tended, in a great measure, to disable his efforts. The latter, on going in, was hit down, Caleb Baldwin now loudly offered five guineas to one on Spring.

26.—Painter was so weak that he hit himself down.

27.—Spring's left hand caught Painter as he was coming in, and the latter fell on his face.

28 to 31, and last.—Description is not necessary for these rounds. Painter was completely exhausted, and he resigned the contest in one hour and twenty-nine minutes; nothing but the highest state of condition could have enabled him to last such a length of time.

REMARKS.—Spring turned out a much better man than he was previously rated; though it was still urged that he was not a hard hitter. Painter did not complain of the punishment he received, but of the excruciating pain of his head, and the impractica-bility he experienced of using his shoulder to any advantage. The gameness of Painter was too well known to need comment. Spring used his left hand well, and got away with ease and dexterity; he also displayed cool-ness and command of temper. Spring's body was rather marked; his peepers somewhat damaged; he was also distressed a little at one period of the fight, but soon recovered, and kept the lead. On being declared the victor, Cribb took him up in his arms and carried him round the ring, amidst loud huzzas.

So anxious were the friends of Painter for a second trial of skill with Spring, that they put down a deposit the same week, and on the 14th of April increased it to £40, to fight on August 7th, 1818, for 100 guineas a-side, it being specially named in the articles that the ring should have nly *eight* stakes.

Spring was now doomed to receive a slight check to his ambition in his second contest with Painter, on the 7th of August, 1818, at Russia Farm, when our hero lost the battle. This unexpected defeat weighed severely on Spring's mind. (See the life of NED PAINTER, *post.*)

In consequence of the friends of Shelton forfeiting to Spring, a match was proposed between Oliver and Spring; but the bad state of Oliver's hand prevented it. The backers of Spring, it appears, were determined to give him an opportunity of reinstating himself, and he was matched against Carter, who had, for two years, challenged all England as champion. The stakes were £50 a-side, and a £50 purse to be given by the Pugilistic Club. The odds were high in favour of Carter, and the backers of Spring asked two to one. The above battle was decided on the 4th of May, 1819, at Crawley Down, immediately after Randall and Martin had left the ring. Carter was seconded by Oliver and Donnelly; and Spring was attended by Cribb and Shelton. Generally speaking, it was thought a hollow thing; and Carter was estimated so extravagantly that three to one was betted upon the combatants setting to.

THE FIGHT.

Round 1—Carter entered the ring with great self-importance, smiling contemptu-ously upon his opponent, and indicating by his gestures that he had a mere nothing to contend with. Both the combatants appeared in good condition, particularly Spring. Upon shaking hands, Carter did not, as hereto-fore, let fly with his left hand, and both men sparred for an opening. Spring, at length, planted a hit on Carter's right shoulder. All eyes were fixed upon the *soi-disant* Champion, to see him go to work, almost expecting him to annihilate his oppo-nent. A long pause occurred, and the men appeared more like statues than living pu-gilists in actual combat. Spring broke from his position, and planted another hit upon Carter's shoulder. The latter endeavoured to make a blow with his left, which was well stopped by Spring, who also fought his way into a close; Carter got him on the ropes, where a terrible struggle occurred for the throw, and, amidst much hissing and hooting. Carter got Spring down.

2.—Long sparring, when Spring put in a facer. The intent of Carter seemed upon hugging more than hitting, and at the ropes, he endeavoured to throw Spring. The latter, however, proved the stronger, and Carter was undermost. Loud shouting, and "Well done, Spring!"

3.—Spring made a hit, when Carter got away. The former followed to the ropes, and felt for his nob, till the hugging system commenced, and both went down. (Hissing.)

4.—The amateurs were astonished at the

hard fighting of Carter, who seemed to have no relish for anything but hugging his opponent on the ropes till both were down.

5.—Spring put in several hits; in struggling Carter was undermost.

6.—Both down; but Spring decidedly the better man, he gave the Lancashire hero some sharp hits.

7.—Spring took the lead in good style, when Carter in a manner turned away from the blows, and fell down. Spring pointed at him with contempt; the "Champion" was loudly hissed.

8.—Disgust and murmuring were expressed all round the ring at the conduct of Carter. Manliness and courage were displayed by Spring, and he hit Carter out of the ring, but fell on one knee.

9 to 11.—The finish of all these rounds consisted in struggling at the ropes, and the backs of the men were scored.

12.—Spring put in a good nobber without any return, and also threw Carter.

13 to 15.—These rounds were principally hugging; Spring made several hits, yet went down weak.

16.—This was rather a sharp round, and Carter made some return. Spring hit his opponent to the ropes, and also broke away from a close. He renewed the attack sharply, till both went down.

17.—Carter made a good hit with the left, and threw Spring.

18.—It was evident to all the spectators that Spring had rapidly improved; he stopped the left hand of Carter with the greatest ease. This being the peculiar forte of the Carlisle Champion he could do nothing with his right hand, and was foiled. Spring fought manfully, planted three good hits, and sent Carter down.

19 and 20.—Spring took the lead; but in struggling, both down.

21.—Spring put in a heavy hit on Carter's nose, with his left hand, and also threw him. "Well done, Spring!" and ten to eight offered upon the latter.

22.—Spring hit Carter on the side of the nob, punished him at the ropes, and broke away from a close. Spring hit Carter down, who instantly got up, but Spring fell from caution or weakness.

23.—Spring slipped in making a blow.

24.—The conduct of Carter in this round created great disapprobation. It seemed as if he was fighting a bear instead of a man. He ran sharply in with his head lowered into Spring's body, when the latter paid him well over the nob for it. But in closing the hissing was very loud, and a distinguished amateur called out to several persons, that Carter was "going."

25.—Spring planted some hits and got away. In struggling at the ropes, when Carter was receiving punishment, he exclaimed, "What are you at?"

26.—It was plain that Carter meant to tire his opponent, or win the contest by hugging. A terrible struggle occurred, when the ropes were broken, and both went down.*

27 and 28—Both down. Spring hit Carter down at the ropes.

29.—This was a good round on the part of Spring. He planted two facers sharply. The claret was now seen issuing from Carter's mouth, and his mug damaged.

30.—Spring hit Carter on the nob, but in struggling both went over the ropes. (Thirteen to five on Spring.)

31.—The right eye of Carter was rather damaged. Spring hit and broke away. He, however, punished Carter down, and fell.

32.—Carter sat cross-legged upon his second's knee. Spring hit, and followed him over the ring. In struggling at the ropes. Carter exclaimed, "Let go." Both down.

33 to 35.—Spring worked hard in all these rounds; took the lead from his hitting; but went down from his exertions.

36.—This was a severe round, and Carter was hit out of the ropes. Loud shouting; and "Bravo, Spring! Where's the Champion now?"

37.—Spring made a good hit, but went down from weakness.

38.—Carter hit down at the ropes.

39.—Spring shewed good science; he hit and broke away, and planted a blow on Carter's nose. Both down.

40.—After some exchanges, Spring was hit sharply, and fell upon his head. He was extremely weak, and his friends felt alarmed that he was falling off; the odds got down upon him.

41.—Spring, in a struggle, fell upon Carter, which appeared to shake him to pieces.

42.—Spring made a hit upon Carter's nose, but was too weak to follow up this advantage. In closing, on the ropes, both down.

43.—Both down.

44.—The right eye of Carter was nearly closed; but Spring was still weak, and went down from a slight hit.

45 to 49.—Both down in all these rounds. Hugging was the leading feature; but whenever Spring could extricate himself he did, and administered punishment to his opponent.

50.—Spring hit Carter out of the ropes but, to the astonishment of the spectators, h got up with the utmost sang froid.

51.—Carter tried to make a hit with his right hand, but it was stopped. After a few exchanges, Spring went down very weak.

* This resembled the much-discussed round in Heenan and Sayers' fight at Farnborough, where the Yankees claimed a "foul" because the ropes were lowered when Heenan was throttling the English Champion. The twenty-eighth rule of the P.R., which governs this case, authorises the referee to have the men separated, or the ropes cut, to prevent a fatal result. This the American party ignored or were really ignorant of.—Ed. PUGILISTICA.

One hour and twenty-five minutes had passed, and severity of punishment was not visible, to any extent, on either side.

52.—Spring now went in, hitting and following Carter closely, till he punished him down. ("Bravo, Spring! the Champion's not in Carlisle now.")

53.—Hugging again till both down. (Murmuring in all parts of the ring; and three and four to one betters lamenting their want of discrimination in backing a man who seemed to have no fight left in him.)

54.—Carter nearly received his quietus in this round. Spring hit him on the head so strongly that he went down like a shot. [Thunders of applause; and a guinea to a shilling offered.]

55.—Carter came in a tottering state to the scratch, but was hit down. Ten to one.

56.—This was the most interesting part of the combat; Carter, to the astonishment of the ring, commenced fighting with his left hand, and made two hits, but was sent down. ("Go it, Spring, you have not a minute to lose. Give such a Champion a finisher!")

57.—Carter again floored.

58.—Carter struggling at the ropes, where he positively hung by both his hands, Spring punishing him on the ribs till he went down. Carter never returned a blow in this round.

59.—Spring went in, and planted a nobber that sent Carter down like a log. His seconds pulled him up, and held his head. A hundred to five. The burst of applause beggars description.

60.—It astonished the ring to see Carter come again, and, from his recovery, fears were still entertained for Spring.—Carter seemed anxious to win, and commenced hitting. He also made a desperate struggle at the ropes till he went down.

61.—Prejudice was aroused against Carter from all parts of the ring, owing to the overbearing consequence which he had assumed since his "hugging" victory at Carlisle.—

Carter commenced fighting, but went down from a slight hit; in fact, he almost laid himself down.

62.—In this round Spring was quite the hero. He nobbed and bodied Carter so severely, that the latter could not lift his arms. (Any odds.)

63.—Carter was sent down, with striking marks of punishment about his head and body.

64.—Carter appeared to get round, made a hit, but was sent down.

65.—Carter put in two left-handed hits, but Spring went in manfully, and got him down.

66.—In closing, both down.

67.—Carter now tried his left hand; but in closing he received a heavy fall. Spring fell on him. "It is all up;" was the cry.

68.—Carter hit first with his left hand. Both down.

69.—Spring was now very weak, but he went in and punished Carter in all directions, till both went down.

70.—The fight was now drawing fast to an end. Carter was so confused and weak that he was hit to the ropes, where he stood still to receive, till he made a trifling struggle, when both went down.

71.—This was a strange and severe round; Carter endeavoured to make some hits; but, in closing, he received such a fall, with Spring upon him, that when time was called, he could not come again. One hour and fifty-five minutes had elapsed.

REMARKS.—If Spring had been a *punishing* hitter, he *must* have won it in half the time. He, however, displayed not only consummate tactics in the offensive, but his defensive movements elicited general applause. Although never rash, he never shrunk from his work, and this triumphant defeat of the braggadocio north-countryman placed him on a pinnacle of fame.

Spring, in company with Cribb, now set out on a sparring tour in the west, in which a friendship was cemented which lasted for life, to the credit of both parties. Bill Neat (who had beaten the game Tom Oliver in the previous year, July 10, 1818) was picked out by the Bristolians for a match with "Young Spring" for 100 guineas a-side, and half-way between Bristol and London was named as the ground, articles signed, and £50 made good on September 6th, for a fight on the 6th of October following. But a certificate from Bristol, dated September 19th, 1819, states that "Neat, from a fall, having broken his right arm, twelve months must elapse before he will be well." Spring complained, and justly, of not receiving forfeit in this case, as he had been put to considerable expenses, and Neat's accident (generally supposed not to be a fracture at all) was occasioned by his imprudently running, for a wager, down a steep hill, known as King's Weston.

The friends of Oliver now made a deposit of five sovereigns, but in the same month of October Spring received that as a forfeit.

On the 20th December, 1819, Spring being at Belcher's, and Ben Burn in a depreciatory humour, "my uncle" offered to post £20 and meet Spring at Wimbledon Common next morning at one o'clock. Both men were there to time. Eales and an amateur seconded Spring; Richmond and Scroggins Uncle Ben. The affair was a burlesque, though Ben fought in a most manly style. Spring was certainly out of condition, and remarkably cautious. He hit heavily, but seldom, and never gave away a chance. Poor Ben, with the exception of one slight success in a scramble, when he caught Spring over the right eye (the same optic that suffered in his fight with Painter), never got on to his man. On the contrary, Spring hit him when and where he pleased for eighteen minutes, when, at the end of the eleventh round, the second big Yorkshireman whom Tom had manipulated, was thoroughly finished off. Not more than 200 persons were present; but the Commissary and the stakes, with many of the P. C., were there, and formed the ring.

A third match with Painter ended in a forfeit on the part of Painter's friends, who preferred a match with Oliver for the same amount as a safer investment.

In consequence of this forfeit "Uncle Ben," who didn't at all stomach his thrashing by a man who, according to some of the connoisseurs of the old ding-dong school, "couldn't hit a dent in a pound of butter," now determined, for the greater glory of the house of Burn, to match Bob Burn against his conqueror for £100 a-side. This ended for a time curiously. Spring was out of health, and, not to give a chance away, his backers forfeited the £100 rather than risk a contest. A second match was soon made, and on the 16th of May, 1820, the men met on Epsom Downs.

The morning was stormy, yet the string of vehicles emulated a Derby Day. The ring was delightfully situated, having the hill on the northern side of it, from which hundreds viewed the battle without the inconvenience of a crowd.

Burn had risen in the esteem of the amateurs from a slashing set-to with Larkin, and some Fives Court displays. Spring also was notoriously unwell, and a strong prejudice existed against his "finishing" or "punishing" abilities. These circumstances induced most of the sporting men to hedge their bets, and take the odds upon Burn. Indeed, in a few instances, the odds were now laid upon the latter; five to four on the ground was thinly sported on Spring, the takers snapping at it instantly.

Burn appeared first, and threw his hat into the ring, attended by his seconds, Larkin and Randall, and kept walking up and down for some minutes before his adversary entered the ropes. Spring at length showed, followed by Cribb and Shelton; when the latter observed to Spring, "Mind, Tom, that you throw your hat into the ring so that it does not blow out," the incident having an evil augury, as several pugilists had been defeated when their hats had taken flight. Spring took the hint, and his castor remained firm in the ring. Randall (for Burn) then tied his colours (green) to the stakes, and the blue kerchief of Spring was immediately added to them. Upon the Commander-in-Chief ordering the sports to commence, the two umpires and the referee (an honourable baronet) wished to impress upon the minds of the seconds and bottle-holders, "That the watch would be held by them only on the following consideration:—That upon the men setting-to, the seconds were to retire to the corners of the ring, and if any one of them spoke to the combatants, that moment the watch would be thrown down. Much irritation had been occasioned by such conduct on both sides at previous fights. It was highly improper, unfair and unmanly; and also in direct opposition to the rules of Broughton, who was looked up to as the father of the Prize Ring." These remarks were emphatically repeated, and throughout the fight were strictly attended to.

THE FIGHT.

Round 1.—On stripping, we were told that Burn was a stone less in weight than when he fought Shelton; his condition was nevertheless as fine as art and nature could exhibit. In fact, his proper pitch had been ascertained, and Burn flattered himself that he was man enough for anything on the fighting list. Spring did not appear on the ground till the last minute; and it was thought by many that he would forfeit a second time, owing to his not being well. On stripping, though he appeared better than was expected from the rumours which had gone forth, it was evident that he was not in fighting trim. After some little sparring Burn endeavoured to put in two hits, right and left, somewhat confidently, which Spring scientifically stopped. A pause. Spring very neatly put in a facer, and got away. Burn gave two blows without effect. More sparring. Spring again gave a nobber, and got away. Some little fighting now occurred, and several good hits were exchanged, from one of which, a right-handed blow, Burn went off his balance, and fell on his hands. (A roar of approbation. "Burn can't win it!" Seven to four; several were bold enough to offer two to one.)

2.—This round was short, but decisive, and the takers of the odds looked blue. Burn thrust out his left hand, pawing, as it were, when he was returned upon by Spring right and left. The latter, however, got a small taste over his left ogle, and a bump soon rose. In an exchange of blows, Burn again went down from a hit on the side of his head. (Tumultuous applause, and "The big one can't fight," was the cry. Two to one nearly current.)

3.—This round quite satisfied the judges that if Spring had been well he must have won the battle in a canter. He hit Burn staggering all over the ring, followed him up, and gave the big one pepper at the ropes, till he went down. (Another Babel shout, and four to one was offered.)

4.—The claret was plain enough now on the mug of Burn. Spring put in a heavy claim on his opponent's victualling office, and got away cleverly. Some sharp exchanges occurred, in which Spring received a nobber or two, and not light ones; but Burn was sent staggering and staggering, till he ultimately went down. (More betters than takers.)

5.—Spring showed great weakness; but he also showed that he knew the advantages of science, and from science alone he could win, and reduce the strength of his opponent. Burn planted a most desperate hit on the side of Spring's head; and so keenly did it operate, as a sort of scalping touch, that the hair instantly flew off, and the place was bare. Spring, however, conked his opponent, when they closed, and, in a severe struggle for the throw, Spring broke away and hit Burn down. ("Bravo! well done, Spring; it's all your own.")

6.—Burn had been hit or went down in all the preceding rounds; and in this Spring fell upon his adversary heavy, after an exchange of several blows. It was here again asserted that, notwithstanding the punishment Spring had administered to his opponent, it might be seen he was not a hard hitter, from the little effects visible. Perhaps this may be more of a theoretical than a practical prejudice against Spring.

7.—The latter put in a sharp bodier with his left hand, and got away; but in an exchange of blows afterwards, Burn gave Spring a heavy one on his ear. In struggling for the throw, Burn appeared much distressed, but both men fell out of the ropes.

8.—This was rather a dangerous round to Spring, and he might have lost the battle from it, although it was in his favour. Some severe blows passed on both sides, when the combatants fought their way to the ropes, and got entangled in so curious a manner that it appeared so difficult to the spectators that "Go down, Spring," was the cry. The struggle to get the best of the throw was severe indeed; they grappled at each other's hand, and if Shelton had not held up the rope, they were so entangled that the men must have been parted; however, by a strong effort they got away from this dilemma into the middle of the ring, when Spring hit Burn well as he was falling, but Spring also fell upon his head. (Loud shouting for Spring.)

9.—The preceding struggle had distressed Spring so much, that in setting-to he put down his hands quite exhausted; nevertheless, it turned out a severe round, and Spring jobbed his opponent so severely that, in closing, Burn was so confused that he caught hold of Spring's nose. (Great disapprobation.) In going down Burn was undermost.

10.—The left eye of Burn was rather damaged, and Spring made play in good style. Burn scarcely ever went to work till he was nobbed into it; and then he made some good counter-hits. This was rather a sharp round; but in going down Spring was undermost.

11.—After some exchanges, Spring's left ear showed marks of punishment. Sparring for wind, when Spring got a facer. The latter again showed bad condition, and stood still for a short period; but Burn did not turn it to account. However, after a hit or two, Spring fell down, his head upon his arm. Some slight fears were here entertained that the strength of Burn might tire out Spring.

12 to 14.—In all these rounds the fighting was on the part of Spring. Most certainly the latter never fought so well in any of his battles as in the present. He put in several hits, and got away with great agility.

15.—In this round Spring did as he pleased with his opponent; Burn's body and head were quite at his service, and it was evident the battle must soon end. In going down Burn was also undermost. Any odds; but it was all up. Here Burn informed his second that Spring was too strong for him.

16.—In this round Burn was hit sharply; and in going down his left leg fell under him, and great fears were entertained it was broken. ("Spring for ever," and twenty to one; indeed it was thought Burn would not come again.)

17.—Burn endeavoured to show fight, but he was again sent down at the ropes, and £10 to a crown was offered.

18 and last.—Burn was soon down, and Spring proclaimed the conqueror. Tom walked out of the ring with apparent ease, and with very few marks.

REMARKS.—Although this was pronounced a bad fight, Spring is justly entitled to much praise, from his good style of fighting, and the skill he displayed in not going "to work" too rashly, from his bad condition. Had Spring been as well as he ought, the battle must have been over in half the time. It, however, was the general opinion of the fancy, that Burn, previous to the contest, could not be disposed of in half an hour, and numerous bets were made to that effect. The judges too insisted that Spring was not a hard hitter, and they did so at the conclusion of this battle; but he repeated his blows so often on the nob of his opponent that they ultimately proved effectual. Burn, after the first round, appeared to have lost confidence. Gameness alone will not reach the top of the tree. Spring behaved bravely to his opponent, and was much applauded. He had Burn at the ropes in a defenceless state, but he saw the battle was his own, and he lifted up his hands and walked away. If it be admitted that Spring was not a hard hitter, it cannot be denied that he possessed a superior knowledge of fighting, and was too difficult a man for Burn to get at.

A match was on the *tapis* between Spring and Sutton, the Black, but it went off.

In consequence of some dispute about impropriety of conduct, between Spring and Josh. Hudson, after the battle of Cooper and Shelton, at Moulsey Hurst, on Tuesday, June 27, 1820, a purse of £20 was immediately subscribed by the amateurs for Spring and Hudson to fight. Both men accepted the offer without the least hesitation; more especially as an amateur offered £5 to Hudson, if he would only fight one round with Spring. Five or six rounds, however, were sharply contested, in which Joshua drew the cork of his antagonist, but on his getting the worst of it, Hudson pocketed the £5, and Turner judiciously took him out of the ring. This was the fourth battle on that day. Spring looked upon this £20 as a sweetener for his recent losses on Shelton, whom he had backed. The dispute in question, it seems, was owing to Spring refusing to admit Hudson into the room where Shelton had been put to bed.

During the time Spring was at Norwich, when Painter fought with Oliver, five guineas a-side were deposited for a match between the Gas-Light Man and our hero. The backers of Hickman, however, did not come forward at the appointed time, in London, to make the stakes good, when the £5 was forfeited to Spring.

The friends of Oliver, anxious to keep the game alive, made a match for £100 a-side with Spring.

Thus the game Tom Oliver was pitched upon to try to check the upward career of Spring, and the stakes, 200 sovereigns, were made good over a jolly dinner at Belcher's, and the day fixed for February 20, 1821. Accordingly, as this was the first spring meeting of gymnastic sports for the year, at daybreak on the following morn the Western Road was all bustle. It was a prime turn-out of the swells; upwards of nine noblemen were present; but it was a "big fight," and that is sure to bring them to the ring. Salt Hill was the place first named; but a hint from the beaks removed it early in the morning, and the ring was again formed at about two miles from Arlington Corner. Here the magistrates again interfered, it is said, at the request of a lady of rank, whose sons were great supporters of this British sport, and the "beaks" were not to be gammoned into good humour, although Oliver had made his appearance in the ring. The bustle and confusion created to be off instanter was truly laughable, and the "devil take the hindmost" was the order of the day. But in a few minutes the scene was truly delightful. It was a perfect steeple chase. The string of carriages for miles winding round the road, the horsemen galloping and leaping over the hedges, the pedestrians all on the trot, and the anxiety displayed on every countenance to arrive in time, all following the Commander-in-Chief and Bill Gibbons with the stakes.   The surprise occasioned in the villages through which his motley group passed, the children out of doors at the farm houses shouting, the "Johnny Raws" staring, the country girls grinning, the ould folks wondering what was the matter, and asking if the French were coming, the swells laughing and bowing to the females, and all the fancy, from the pink on his " bit of blood," down to the toddler, full of life and spirits, formed a most interesting picture.   At length Hayes was reached, and the ring formed without delay.   Oliver threw his hat into the ring about six minutes to three, followed by Tom Owen, in his white topper, and Richmond.   Spring appeared shortly afterwards, repeating the token of defiance, attended by the Champion of England and Painter.   The colours, yellow for Oliver, and blue for Spring, were tied to the stakes.   On meeting in the ring, the combatants shook hands together in true British style, and Spring asked Oliver how he did ?   " Pretty bobbish," said Oliver, smiling ; " very well."

THE FIGHT.

Round 1 —On stripping, both men appeared in excellent condition, and each asserted he was never better, if so well, in his life.   Oliver looked rather pale, and Spring had a small flush on his cheeks. Oliver made an offer to hit, when Spring got away.   Oliver made a hit, which Spring stopped neatly.   Spring endeavoured to put in a blow, which Oliver parried.   A pause, and great caution on both sides.   They smiled at each other's attempts, as much as to say, " I am prepared."   Some little time occurred in sparring, when the long reach of Spring enabled him to make a hit.   Oliver returned, when some exchange of blows at the corner of the ropes produced a struggle, and they both went down in a sort of scramble, Oliver on his back, and Spring nearly by his side.   (" Bravo !" from the Westminster boys ; " Oliver must win it."   Indeed, Oliver appeared to have the good wishes of the old fanciers.)

2.—Spring missed a hit. A pause. Spring got away from a heavy blow ; in fact, the latter showed excellent science, and Oliver found his opponent a most difficult man to get at.   In a close, Oliver was completely hit down, from a severe blow on the side of his head. (Loud shouting for Spring, and " That's the way to win.")

3.—The mouth of Oliver was cut. Spring got away with great dexterity ; indeed, it was thought by the real judges of pugilism, at this early stage of the battle, that it was likely to be a long fight, but that Spring would win it.   Oliver again down.

4.—In closing, a struggle took place, and Spring was undermost. (Loud shouting from Oliver's backers, and the Westminster lads in an uproar.)

5.—Spring got away from every blow in the first part of the round.   Oliver planted a left-handed body hit.   In a severe struggle for the throw at the ropes, Oliver caught hold of the rope, but Spring got him down heavily, and they rolled over each other.

6.—This round the fight had nearly been at an end.   Spring not only took the lead in first-rate style, but put in two heavy body blows, and fell heavily upon Oliver.   His head lolled upon his shoulder, and when time was called, he could scarcely hear the vociferation of his seconds, " Tom, Tom ! be awake, my boy !" the spectators crying out, " It's all up."   Indeed it appeared so, and many of the anxious betters, who had their money upon Spring, and not wishing to give half a chance away, thought it a very long half minute before " time " was called.

7.—The sudden start of Oliver, on recovering his recollection, the animated expression of his eyes, and putting himself in an attitude to meet his opponent, was one of the finest specimens of true courage ever witnessed ; he, however, was soon sent down. (" He's a brave creature ;" " he's an extraordinary man ;" " he's the gamest creature in the world ;" were the general expressions all over the ring.)

8.—Oliver very queer.   Spring punished him about the head till he was again undermost, and received another fall.   (" It's all over now—Oliver cannot recover these falls," was the general opinion ; and two to one, or, in fact, any odds.)

9.—Oliver floored from a severe nobber. Great shouting for Spring.   The game displayed by Oliver astonished all the ring.

10.—Oliver again thrown, and Spring fell heavily on him.

11 to 17.—Oliver recovered, it is true, in some degree, from the severity of the fall which he received in the sixth round; but he could make no change; in fact, the chance was decidedly against him. In this round, Spring punished Oliver till he went down. The truth was, Oliver could not get at Spring.

18.—This was a sharp round, and Oliver exerted himself to win, but without effect. It was thought Spring had hit Oliver foul, but it was a blow he put in as Oliver was going down. Spring, in finishing this round, put in some tremendous body blows, after the quick manner of Randall.

19.—Clark, the friend of Oliver, now thinking that Oliver could not win, went into the ring and threw up his hat; but Oliver would continue the fight till he was hit down. Oliver might be said to be dragged up by his second, Tom Owen, who exerted himself to the utmost degree to bring the old Westminster hero through the piece. Richmond also paid every attention, but the fight was completely out of him, and the persons at the outer ring left their places.

20.—Oliver went up resolutely to Spring, determined to make a change in his favour; but it was only to receive punishment; he was again down.

21.—When time was called, Oliver not coming up directly, Spring was told that it was all over, and had got hold of his coat to put it on, when Oliver again showed fight, and was terribly hit about the head and body, till he measured his length. ("Take him away; he can't win it.")

22 and 23.—These rounds were fought in the greatest confusion. The ring being flogged out, the time-keeper taking refuge in the rope ring, with two or three other swells, till the rounds were finished. Oliver was now quite exhausted, but positively refused to give in.

24, 25, and last.—All these rounds were fought in the greatest confusion, and when Spring had got Oliver at the ropes, and might have fibbed him severely so as to put an end to the battle, some person cut the ropes, which let Oliver down easy. Oliver contended every inch of ground, although so much distressed: at length he was so much punished that he could not leave the knee of his second when time was called. It was over in fifty-five minutes.

REMARKS.—It is but common justice to Spring to assert, that he won this battle three times before it was over. It is true that he had no right to give a chance away, either against himself or his backers; but he plainly saw that the battle was his own; he fought without grumbling, and in acting so honourably, nay, generously, to a fine, high-couraged, game opponent, that Oliver should not have to say, "that he had not every opportunity to win, if he could." What was more important, however, it prevented any thing like a wrangle being attempted. Spring, by his superior mode of fighting this day, raised himself highly in the estimation of the Fancy in general; in fact, the ring was much surprised that Oliver could do nothing with him. The prejudice which so long remained against Spring in respect to his not being a hard hitter, was removed in this battle. Oliver was most terribly punished; while Spring, on the contrary, had not the slightest mark on his face. The bravery of Oliver, and his exertions to win, were above all praise. Spring, in the style of a true Briton, "when the battle is ended, the heart of a lamb," called to see Oliver, on the Friday after the fight, when they shook hands with each other in the same style of friendship as heretofore. Oliver then told Spring that he had entertained an opinion, before the fight, he was the stronger man; but that Spring was too long for him.

On Tom Cribb's retirement from the arena, Spring considered himself champion; and soon after his conquest over Oliver, in order that it might not afterwards be brought against him that he had left the prize ring silently, he offered, by public advertisement, March 25, 1821, a challenge to all England for three months. This challenge not having been accepted, although he offered to fight Neat for £500 a-side, on August 19, nearly five months after the period stated, he entered into articles of agreement of a more tender kind, and made a match "for better or for worse." We wish that our personal reminiscences did not unpleasantly remind us that, as regards the lady she was all "worse," and never showed signs of "better." He then commenced proprietor of the Weymouth Arms Tavern, in Weymouth Street, Portman Square. Spring's opening dinner took place on Thursday, the 6th of December, 1821. The swells mustered numerously round Mr. Jackson who presided upon this occasion; and 140 persons sat down to a prime dinner, served up, in excellent style, by Spring in person. The evening was dedicated to harmony and good-fellowship.

After the sport at Moulsey, on Wednesday, June 12th, 1822, the great match was made between Spring and Neat, subject to the following articles :

" *Red Lion, Hampton, June* 12, 1822.

" Mr. Elliott, on the part of Thomas Spring, and Thomas Belcher, on the part of William Neat, have deposited £50 a-side, to make a match on the following terms :—W. Neat agrees to fight T. Spring on Tuesday, the 26th of November next, for a stake of £600 (£300 a-side). in a twenty-four foot ring, half-minute time. The place to be named by Mr. Jackson. within forty miles of London, on the Bristol road, and the umpires to be chosen on the ground. The second deposit, upon the above conditions, £100 a-side, to be made at T. Spring's, Weymouth Arms, Weymouth Street, on the 12th of July, between the hours of four and eight o'clock. The deposit to be forfeited by the defaulter. The remainder of the stakes to be made good at T. Belcher's, the Castle Tavern, Holborn, on the 12th of November. Mr. W. S. has received, and is answerable for, the deposit of £100."

On the 12th of November a sporting dinner took place at Belcher's, to make the stakes good between Neat and Spring,. Belcher, on the part of Neat, completed the stakes of £200 ; but Mr. Elliott, the backer of Spring, did not appear, when the chairman reluctantly declared the deposit down, £150, to be forfeited to Neat.

At a sporting dinner at the One Tun, on the Friday following, November 16th, Spring informed the company that he would have attended at the Castle Tavern, on the day appointed, but his backer wished him not to leave the country on any account, as he might take cold—Mr. Elliott asserting he would make it all right. He (Spring) was now ready to make a new match for £200 a-side, for the 10th of December.

At Harry Holt's opening dinner, at the Golden Cross, Cross Lane, Long Acre, on Friday, November 22nd, 1822, the president informed Mr. Belcher, that if the stakeholder of the £150 was indemnified, the forfeiture of that sum by the backer of Spring (Mr. Elliott) would be given up to Neat. Mr. Belcher replied, he should receive a guarantee. The president then observed that the sporting world in general were anxious to have it decided which was the best man between Spring and Neat ; and that the former could be backed for £200 a-side, to fight in the course of a fortnight. Mr. Belcher, in reply, stated, that Neat, since the match had been broken off, had conducted himself more like a bird out of cage than anything else ; the " gaily circling glass " had been continually up to his mouth ; the result was, he could not answer for his condition, and he would not make the match so soon as a fortnight : it ought to be, at least, a month. Neat had left London for Bristol, and he had no doubt, from his gay disposition, was playing the same sort of game there; but he would write to him immediately, and whatever answer Neat returned as to time, he would then make a fight.

Spring addressed the meeting and said he was certain that Neat was in as good condition as himself. He had fretted considerably about the match being off: and this, added to his participation of "Life in London," since his training had been so abruptly brought to an end, it might be fairly stated that he was on a par with his opponent. But, to show how anxious he was for a fight, and that the sporting world should decide which was the best man, he would extend the time to next Tuesday three weeks: that was meeting Mr. Belcher half way. (Loud cheers, and "Well said," "Manly," etc., from all parts of the room.) Not a day after that time would he agree to fight Neat; he should then quit the prize ring for ever, to attend to his family and business, in order to make up for his loss of time, and great expenses in which he had been involved, owing (unfortunately for himself) to the desertion of his backer, when so many gentlemen who were present at that meeting, had they been acquainted with the circumstances, would have stepped forward to make the match.

The Fives Court was well attended on Thursday, November 28, 1823, in order to give the game Bob Purcell a turn. Carter and Spring ascended the stage together. The latter pugilist addressed the spectators, previously to his setting-to, nearly in the following words:—"Gentlemen, I feel much disappointment in the match being off between myself and Neat. I hope he will get the forfeit of £150. He is most certainly entitled to it. It was no fault of mine the match did not take place; and to show that I meant fighting, I gave a week, then a fortnight, longer to Mr. Neat than I first intended, and am now ready to make the match for £200 a-side." (Applause.) Mr. Belcher observed, "Gentlemen, I am here for Neat; and all I can say, is this—if any gentleman will indemnify me for the £150, I will make a match immediately; but on no other account." Spring, in reply, stated, "that it could not be expected he should indemnify Mr. Belcher, but he was ready to put down any sum required immediately. ("Bravo!—that looks like fighting.") He, however, would not make a match after that day —he had lost too much time already, and he was determined to follow his business in future, and to take his leave of the prize ring; therefore, the match must now be made, or never." "Very fair," from all parts of the Court. The set-to between Spring and Carter proved attractive and good.

Three months elapsed in idle reports respecting another match between Spring and Neat, when the following articles were drawn, which set the fancy on the *qui vive*: —

" *Castle Tavern, Holborn, Wednesday, March 12, 1823.*

" William Neat agrees to fight Thomas Spring for £200 a-side, in a twenty-four feet ring, half-minute time. To be a fair stand-up fight; to take place on Tuesday, the 20th day of May. The money to be placed in the hands of Mr. Jackson. The place and distance from London to be left entirely to Mr. Jackson. An umpire to be chosen by each party, and a referee to be named on the ground. £50 a-side is now deposited in the hands of Mr. Jackson. £50 a-side more to be deposited on Monday, the 31st of March, at Mr. Belcher's, Castle Tavern; and the remainder of the stakes of £100 a-side to be completed on Monday, the 5th of May, also at Mr. Belcher's. The above stakes to be put down between the hours of eight and eleven o'clock on each evening. The above deposit, or deposits, to be forfeited, in case of either party not appearing on the specified evenings to make the money good."

T. Belcher signed on the part of W. Neat, and a well known gentleman amateur for T. Spring. Witness, P. E.

We preserve a little bit of justice's justice which we think here was indisputably, impartially, and rightfully administered. Spring went into training at Brighton; he was accompanied by Tom Shelton, the latter being under articles to fight Josh. Hudson.

On Friday, April 4, 1823, a fight took place on the Downs, beyond the race-hill, between Daniel Watts and James Smith, the one a bricklayer's labourer, the other a sawyer, and both residing in the place. An immense concourse of spectators assembled on the ground, which was just without the boundaries of the parish of Brighton, and in that of Ovingdean.

One of the men engaged in this contest, Smith, having died from congestion of the brain, Sir David Scott, a local magistrate, issued warrants for the apprehension of many parties present; and on the following morning, in consequence of information that Spring and Shelton, the celebrated pugilists, had borne an active part in the fight, they were also taken up, and brought before Sir David Scott, at a special sitting held at the New Inn. Considerable difficulty was experienced in procuring evidence, every one being anxious to conceal that he had been present; but at length several persons were found, whose testimony was in substance as follows:—That there was a person on horseback keeping the ring, and that Spring and Shelton, on foot, assisted, with whips in their hands, to keep the people back; and it was further proved that Spring had also a watch in his hand during the fight. On the strength of this evidence, Sir David Scott considered them to be accessories, having both acted in the capacity of ring-keepers, and one of them in that of time-keeper; he therefore ordered them to find bail, to keep the peace for twelve months. They both urged that they had come from London only on Tuesday or Wednesday, and that the match was made up several days before, so that they were totally ignorant of it until after their arrival at Brighton. Shelton also said, that in London, on occasions of this sort, when proceedings are taken against the principals, the umpires are never affected; but Sir David cut this argument short, by saying, that he could not consent to be guided by the practice or decisions of other magistrates, on any case that might come before him. They were unable to find bail, and were kept for a few days, at a public-house, in custody of one of the headboroughs.

Two other men, named Hazledean and Sherwood, one acting as bottle-holder to Smith, and the other as Watts's second, were each ordered to find bail for twelve months.

Spring and Shelton, after being in custody for a week, in default of procuring the bail required of them, were liberated by Sir David Scott, on entering into their own recognizances, £100 each, to be of good behaviour for twelve months.

To all which we should merely say, with the Cornish jury, " Sarve them right." They were imprudent, as men in training, and his worship leniently administered the law.

Tom Cribb had a jolly party at his tavern on Monday, May 3, 1823, as also had Tom Belcher. Spring was Cribb's hero; Neat, the attractive man at the Castle Tavern. The stakes were made good for £200 a-side, and were deposited in the hands of Mr. Jackson. Spring in the course of the evening made his bow to the company; he was well received, and his health drank with great spirit. The same compliment was also paid to Neat in his absence. Mr. Belcher gave up £15 to Spring, respecting Neat's forfeit at Bristol; therefore all disputes concerning money matters were settled. Spring offered to bet £100, according to Neat's challenge; but Belcher said, " he had no authority to put down any money then; however, on the morning of fighting, Neat should bet him the £100." " No!" replied Spring, " I am ready to bet the £100 now; but I shall have something else to do on the morning of the fight." Both the principals were extremely fond of the match, and both Spring and Neat displayed the highest confidence in the event. Even betting was about the state of the thing. Spring, within the last few days, got up for choice. At Bristol the odds were high upon Neat.

Within a few days of the appointed time some of the magistrates of Berks, Wilts, and Somerset, displayed bad taste by issuing their documents to prevent an exhibition of this branch of the "fine arts" at any of the places recited. Mr. Jackson's "chateau" at Pimlico was literally besieged by Corinthians on the Saturday previous to the fight, May 17, 1823; and the whole of the night his knocker was in motion, so numerous were the enquiries after the mill. At length the mist was dispelled; the office being given for Weyhill, Hampshire. The inns were immediately scoured for places by the stage-coaches, and, at peep of day on Monday morning the roads from Gloucester, Newbury, Winchester, Bristol, Southampton, London, etc., were covered with vehicles of every description. By five o'clock in the afternoon not a bed could be procured at Andover, although a sovereign per head was offered. The "flooring" system was obliged to be adopted by many "downy" ones, and a carpet was considered a luxury. The principal taverns at Andover were filled with persons of the highest quality in the kingdom, and men and horses were obliged to put up with any shelter that could be got for money. The little towns and villages contiguous to Andover were equally overflowing with company, and thousands were on the road all night. The Mayor and Corporation of Andover, it seems, were "ear-wigged" to spoil the sport, but possessed too much sense to mulct the inhabitants of the neighbourhood.

Hinckley Down, where the battle took place, is delightfully picturesque. A hill at the back of the field formed an amphitheatre, not unlike Epsom race-course, and upwards of thirty thousand spectators had a fine view of the fight. The ring, under the superintendence of Mr. Jackson, was excellent. At one o'clock, Neat, arm-in-arm with his backer, Mr. Harrison, and Belcher, followed by Harmer, threw up his hat in the ropes amidst thunders of applause. About ten minutes afterwards Spring, with his backer, Mr. Sant, and Painter appeared, Cribb waiting for them. Spring very coolly walked up to the ropes, and dropped his beaver within them. He then shook hands with Neat, saying, "I hope you are well." "I am very well, thank you; I hope you are," was the reply of Neat. Spring was rather the favourite on the ground. The colours, an orange-yellow for Neat, were tied to the stakes by Belcher; the blue, for Spring, placed over them by Tom Cribb. Before the battle, Mr. Jackson entered the ring and addressed the spectators :— "Gentlemen, I have to inform you that no persons but the umpires and referee can be stationed close to the ropes; I have therefore to request that every gentleman will retire to some distance from the ring; and also, if necessity requires it, that you will give me your assistance to keep the ground clear, to prevent confusion, and to have a fair fight. I have refused to be referee, that I may walk about and attend to the ring." (Bravo! and applause.) This address had the desired effect—the gentlemen retired to their places, the good consequences of which were that every individual had an uninterrupted view of the fight, and not the slightest disorder occurred. Oh, *si sic omnes !*

THE FIGHT.

Round 1.—The interesting moment had now arrived, all doubts and fears as to a fight were at an end, and the ability of Spring to obtain the Championship was about to be put to the test. Hands were crossed and shaken, in token that no animosity existed. To describe the intense interest of this vast assemblage is impossible. Spring was fine as a star, strong as an ox, light and active as a deer, and confident as a lion. His condition was tip-top; and in truth, could not be better; his weight thirteen stone, three pounds. Neat was equally an object of admiration; his partisans were highly delighted with his appearance, and his frame was pronounced to have fully answered the good effects of training. Indeed, two finer young men could not have been opposed to each other, or a more equal match made: Neat having slightly the advantage in weight over his rival. Spring, cool, collected, firm, and confident, appeared to meet his renowned and formidable opponent, who had obtained so much fame by his conquest over the terrific Gas-light Man. Neat, equally confident—nay, more so, if his countenance bespoke his mind—thought it presumption for any boxer on the list to dispute his right to the title of Champion. A pause of two minutes occurred in looking at each other—dodging about for two minutes longer—Spring then let fly with his left hand, but no mischief done. Neat missed the body of his opponent with his right hand. Another long pause. Neat aimed a tremendous blow with his right, which Spring stopped in great style. (Applause from all parts of the ring.) A pause. Neat again attempted his favourite slaughtering hit, which Spring parried, smiling and nodding at his opponent. (Loud shouts of approbation from the spectators.) Spring put down his hands, but Neat did not avail himself of the chance. Spring immediately made himself up in one of the finest attitudes for administering punishment ever witnessed, and endeavoured to plant a hit with his right hand, which Neat stopped in the most scientific manner. (The Bristolians shouting in turn, "Bravo, Neat!" in fact applause from all parts of the ring.) Neat missed the body of Spring with his left. Spring now went to work, some blows were exchanged, but Spring's hits were so severe that Neat turned round. ("What do you think of that 'ere for light-hitting?" a Cockney cove observed to a Bristol man who sat close to him.) They followed each other over the ring, when Spring, in retreating from some well-meant heavy blows, got into a corner close against the stake, feeling with his heel whereabouts he was situated; ("Now's the time," cried Tom Belcher;) but the defensive position of Spring was so excellent that he was not to be got at without great danger, which Neat perceiving did not get near enough to do anything like execution. Spring fought his way out à la Randall; a close ensued, when Neat had nearly got Spring off his legs; but in struggling for the throw, Spring, with the utmost agility, turned Neat over in his arms and sent him on the ground, falling upon him. Between nine and ten minutes had elapsed. (The chaff-cutters from the Long Town were now roaring with delight—"Spring for ever—for anything—he can fight for a day and a night into the bargain." Seven to four on Herefordshire.

2.—The superiority displayed by Spring in the preceding round rather alarmed the backers of Neat. They did not expect it. The "lady's-maid fighter," as he had been libelled—the "china-man," as he had been designated—the "light tapper," as he had been termed—thus to set at defiance the slaughtering hitter Neat; nay more, to turn the scales and take the lead of him, operated severely on their feelings. A long pause occurred. Spring stood as firm as a rock, Neat unable to get at him; he, however, endeavoured to plant a hit, but it fell short. Both men now made themselves up for mischief, and counter-hits followed. Spring's right went in so severely over Neat's eye that the claret followed instantly. Spring exclaimed, "First blood, Neat." This touch confused the Bristol hero a little; but he tried to give his opponent a heavy blow, which fell short. Spring, in return, gave him so sharp a nobber, that Neat looked round, and was nearly going down.—(Disapprobation.) The latter collected himself, and showed fight, when Spring fought his way into a close, fibbed Neat with the utmost ease, and sent him down. (The applause was like the roar of artillery. Two to one, and "Neat has no chance—it's all up with him." Spring, while sitting on his second's knee, observed to Painter, smiling, "It is as right as the day; I would not take £100 to £1, and stand it—he can't hit me in a week.")

3.—The only chance now left to save a transfer of the Bristolians' coin to the Metropolitan pockets, it would seem, was one of those silencing hits by which Neat had acquired his milling fame, so as to spoil Spring's science, reduce his confidence, and take the fight out of him. All the backers of Neat were on the gaze in anxious expectation to see the "slogger" put in, which was to relieve their fears, and produce a change in their favour. Shyness on both sides. Spring endeavoured to plant a heavy right-handed hit, which Neat stopped cleverly. (Great applause, and "Well done, Neat.") The latter smiled at this success, and Spring observed, "Well stopped!" Rather a long pause. The toes of the combatants were close together, and Spring not to be gammoned off his guard. Some blows were at length exchanged, and Spring received so heavy a hit on his ribs, that his face for the instant bespoke great pain, and his arms dropped a little; but, in closing, Spring had decidedly the advantage; and, in going down, Neat was undermost. (The Springites were now as gay as larks, offering to back their man to any amount.)

4.—Neat, instead of going up and fighting at the head of his opponent, where at least, he might have had a chance of planting some of his tremendous blows, showed no signs of going in to fight. Standing off to a superior, fine scienced boxer like Spring, almost reduced it to a certainty, that in the event he must be beaten. In his character as a heavy-hitting pugilist his strategy ought to have been to smash his shifty opponent. He could not get an opening at his length to put in any effective blows; in fact, he could not break through the guard of Spring. Neat endeavoured to plant a severe blow, which Spring stopped with the utmost ease. (Great applause; and "You'll break his heart, Tom, if you go on in that way.") Neat missed the body of Spring with his left hand. (Laughing, and "It's of no use" from the crowd.) A short rally near the ropes, in which Spring had the best of it, and, in struggling for the throw, Neat experienced a tremendous fall, added to the whole weight of Spring on his body. (Shouting like thunder from thirty thousand persons.)

5.—Neat informed Belcher (while sitting on Harmer's knee) that his arm was broken; it was, however, previously evident to every disinterested spectator, that Neat had not a shadow of chance. Neat made another stop; some blows were exchanged, and a slight rally took place; Neat broke away, the latter gave Spring a slight hit, and was going down, but he resumed his attitude. (Disapprobation.) Spring, to make all safe, was in no hurry to go to work; another pause ensued. Neat, as he was in the act of falling, received a hit, when Spring added another one on his back. (The umpires called out to Belcher, and told him "It was a stand-up fight; and Neat must take care what he was about." "I assure you, gentlemen," replied Mr. Jackson, "Neat received a blow." Here Martin offered, in a very loud manner, that he would bet £1,000 to £100 on Spring. During this round, Belcher came to the side of the ropes, and in a low tone of voice told Mr. Jackson, that Neat's arm was "fractured." "I perceive it," replied Mr. J., "but I shall not notice it to the other side.")

6.—Neat hit short at Spring's body with his left hand; holding his right in a very different position from the mode when the battle commenced. The Bristol hero was piping, and betraying symptoms of great distress. Neat, however, gave a bodier to his opponent and also made a good stop; but in a rally he received several blows, and ultimately went down,

7.—Spring was as fresh as if he had not

been fighting; and, although it was now a guinea to a shilling, and no chance of losing, yet Spring was as careful as if he had had a giant before him. The latter got away from a blow. ("We can fight for a week in that manner," said Belcher. "Yes," replied Painter; "but we have got the general." Neat received a severe hit on his head, and fell down on his knees. The shouts of joy from the partisans of Spring, and roars of approbation from the spectators in general beggared description.)

8th and last.—Neat endeavoured to plant a heavy blow on the body of Spring, but the latter jumped away as light as a cork. A pause. Spring was satisfied he had won the battle. Spring put in a hit on Neat's face; and when the latter returned, he again got away. In an exchange of blows, Neat was hit down. When time was called Neat got up and shook hands with Spring, and said his arm was broken, and he could not fight any more. The battle was at an end in thirty-seven minutes.

REMARKS.—We must admit that, as championship contests, there was certainly a different colouring visible in the fights between Gull and Gregson, and Cribb and Molineaux; to witness two big ones opposed to each other for upwards of half an hour, and no mischief done, was not likely to give satisfaction to the old-fashioned admirers of milling. But the torrent of opinion was so strong in favour of Neat, both in Bristol and London, on account of his tremendous hitting, as to carry away like a flood all kind of calculation on the subject. Spring was to have been smashed, and nothing else but smashed. One hit was to have spoilt the science of Spring: two were to have taken the fight completely out of him; and the third to have operated as a *coup de grace*. Then why did not Neat smash Spring, as he did the Gas? We will endeavour to answer the question for the fallen Neat. Because he had a man of his own size and weight, a boxer of superior talent to himself, pitted against him: one that was armed at all points, and not to be diverted or frightened from his purpose. His blows were not only stopped, but all his efforts to break through the guard of his antagonist were rendered of no avail. Hence it was that the fighting of Neat appeared so defective in the eyes of his friends and backers. He was out-generalled; and the fine fighting of Spring laughed to scorn all the much-talked-of tremendous hitting of his opponent. In truth, Neat could not plant a single effective hit. In the fourth round, Neat asserted his arm received a serious injury, and one of the small bones was broken; but we have no hesitation in asserting, that Spring had won the battle before it occurred. Spring triumphantly disproved the current libel on his character, that "he could not make a dent in a pound of butter." To give punishment, and to avoid being hit, is deemed the triumph of the art of boxing. Randall was distinguished for this peculiar trait in all his battles, Spring adopted the same mode, and by so doing he did not disgrace his character as a boxer: on the contrary, he showed himself a safe man to back, and reduced success to a certainty. Spring called on Neat after the battle, whom he found in bed, and his arm put to rights by a surgeon. The latter said, " I am not beaten, but I lost the battle by the accident." Spring generously made Neat a present of ten pounds. Spring arrived in town on Wednesday night, but he did not sport the colours of his adversary until after he had quitted the town of Andover, and received the shouts and smiles attendant on victory from the populace in all the towns through which he passed. He had a slight black mark on his eye, and his arm in a sling, one of the bones of his right hand having received an injury.

The abrupt conclusion of the battle produced sensations among the backers of Neat not easily described, and such coarse expressions were uttered by the disappointed ones as we cannot give place to in print. The Bristolians were outrageous in the extreme; a few of them positively acted like madmen; others were dejected and chapfallen. Neat was thought to be invulnerable by his countrymen, and also by the majority of sporting people throughout the kingdom. A few silly persons, in their paroxysm of rage and disappointment, pronounced the above event a cross.

We feel anxious for the honour of the ring, and no exertions on our part shall be wanting to preserve it. Tom Belcher and Neat both courted inquiry on the subject. It was the expressed opinion of a spectator of the fight, that "if Neat had possessed four arms instead of two, he never could have conquered Spring."

It is utterly impossible to describe the anxiety which prevailed in the metropolis to learn the event of the battle on Tuesday evening, May 20, 1823. Belcher's house was like a fair; Randall's crowded to suffocation; Holt's not room for a pin; Harmer's overflowing; Shelton's like a mob; Eales' overstocked; and Tom Cribb's crammed with visitors. Both ends of the town, East and West, were equally alive, and profited by the event. Hampshire had not had such a turn since the day when Humphries and Mendoza fought at Odiham. Thus was good derived by thousands of persons not in any way connected with the event. Several wagers were won in London after eight o'clock at night on Spring—so high did Neat stand in public opinion.

At Shelton's benefit, May 22nd, 1823, after several spirited bouts, Spring was loudly called for; he addressed the assemblage in the following terms :— " Gentlemen, I return you my sincere thanks for the honour you have done me to-day, and I hope my future conduct will equally merit your kind attention. I promised to set-to with Shelton; but having met with an accident (his hand was tied up with a handkerchief), I trust you will excuse me; at all other times, you will find me willing and ready to obey your commands." Shelton returned thanks; and Belcher likewise informed the audience that his benefit took place on Tuesday, May 27, when Neat would be present, in order to convince the amateurs that his arm was broken in the fight with Spring. The latter received from Mr. Jackson the £200 of the battle-money as the reward of victory. Mr. Jackson also publicly declared, for the satisfaction of the sporting world, that, in company with two eminent surgeons, he had seen Neat; and those two gentlemen had pronounced the small bone of his arm to have been broken.

Spring now paid a visit to his native place. Fortune had favoured him, and he was not unmindful of old friends. Here he was also not only remembered, but respected; and a cup, made by Messrs. Grayhurst and Harvey, of the Strand, was presented to him. This cup, known as "the Hereford Cup." The inscription and description are as follows:—

"1823.
TO THOMAS WINTER,
Of Fownhope, in the County of Hereford,
This Cup was presented,
By his Countrymen of the Land of Cider,
In Token of their Esteem for the Manliness and Science
Which, in many severe Contests in the Pugilistic Ring,
Under the name of
SPRING,
Raised him to the proud Distinction of
THE CHAMPION OF ENGLAND."

The inscription is surrounded by a handsome device of apples, etc., at the bottom of which is the representation of two game-cocks at the close of a battle, one standing over the other. On the other side of the cup is a view of the P. R., with two pugilists in attitudes. Upon the top or lid of the cup is a cider-barrel placed on a stand. The inside is gilt; and it is large enough to hold a gallon of "nectar divine." It has two elegantly chased handles, and a fluted pedestal.

About this period a new milling star arose in the west, in the person of Jack Langan; and during a tour in the north of England some correspondence took place between them, which is not worth reprinting. On Thursday, October 23, 1823, at the Castle Tavern, Holborn, Belcher, on the part of Langan, deposited £50 towards making a match for £300 a-side with Spring. On the articles being completed, Spring offered £100 to £80, p. p., that he won the battle. Monday, December 1, 1823, the backers of the "Big Ones" dined together at the Castle Tavern, Holborn, but neither Spring nor Langan showed upon the occasion. However, when time was called by the president of the D. C., the blunt was ready. The Ould Champion (Tom Cribb) who attended on the part of his boy, Spring, said that he had only one hundred pounds to put down; while, on the behalf of Langan, Belcher insisted that the spirit of the articles required £150, and he was ready to put down £150 for Langan. The question was fairly discussed by the meeting; and the president decided in favour of the majority—that if £100 a-side were put down, the articles would be complied with. The Ould Champion rose with some warmth, and said, "He was not particular, and if the other party wished it, he would make the £300 a-side good immediately; or he would increase the match between Langan and Spring up to 1,000 guineas. He (Tom Cribb) was quite certain that Langan meant fighting, and if the latter wished to increase the stakes, he and his party had an opportunity of doing it."

On Thursday, January 1, 1824, the whole of the stakes of £600 were made good over a sporting dinner at Tom Cribb's. When time was called, Belcher showed at the mark on the part of Langan, and put down £150. Cribb also, for his boy Spring, instantly fobbed out £150. At the head of the table, before the president, was placed the "Ould Champion's" silver cup, and Spring's cup was also seen before the deputy-president. The John Bull fighter was present, and, by way of keeping the game alive, offered to give two guineas to fight Langan, let him win or lose, for £200 a-side; and likewise, that he would take ten guineas for £200 a-side with Spring. The true courage of Josh. Hudson was greatly admired, and loudly applauded. The dinner was good, the wines were excellent, and the company separated well pleased with their evening's entertainment. Spring was decidedly the favourite, at two to one; two and a half to one was also betted; and in one instance £300 to £100 was laid. In consequence of Langan being a complete stranger to the sporting world the fancy were inclined to bet the odds, instead of taking them.

The sight at Worcester on Wednesday, January 7, 1824, was beyond all former example. Upwards of thirty thousand persons were present; nay, several calculators declared, to the best of their belief, that not less than fifty thousand people were assembled. Proprietors of splendid parks and demesnes; inmates from proud and lofty mansions; groups from the most respectable dwellings; thousands from the peaceful cot; and myriads from no houses at all—in a word, it was a conglomeration of the fancy. Peers, M.P.s, yokels of every cast, cockneys, and sheenies throwing "away their propertiah" without a sigh that it cost so much "monish" to witness the grand mill. The roads in every direction round Worcester beggared description. The adventures at the inns would furnish subjects for twenty farces, and the company in the city of Worcester was of so masquerading a character as to defy the pen; even the pencil of a George Cruikshank would be at fault to give it effect. The grand stand was filled to an overflow in every part, with two additional wings or scaffolds erected for the occasion. Ten shillings were paid for the admission of each person. The masts of the vessels in the river Severn, which flowed close behind, moored on each side of the stand, were overloaded with persons; and even temporary scaffolds, about two stories high, outside of the wagons, were filled by anxious spectators, regardless of danger, so great was the public curiosity excited by this event. Let the reader picture to himself a spacious amphitheatre, encircled by wagons, an outer roped ring within for the many-headed, who stood up to their knees in mud. What is termed the P. C. Ring was raised about two feet from the ground, covered with dry turf, with a cart-load of sawdust sprinkled over it. The race-course was so intolerably bad and full of slush that all the scavengers and mudlarks from the metropolis could not have cleansed it in a week. Outside the wagons the ground displayed one complete sheet of water; and several lads, who were jolly enough to save a few yards of ground by jumping over ditches, measured their lengths in the water, receiving a complete ducking, to the no small amusement of the yokels. What will not curiosity do? Here swells were seen sitting down in the mud more coolly than if lolling on a sofa. Not a place could be obtained in the stand after ten o'clock. The city of Worcester was full of gaiety early in the day; the streets were filled by the arrival of coaches and four, post-chaises, mails, and vehicles of every description, blowing of horns, and the bells ringing. A Roman carnival is not half so hearty a thing as a prize-fight used to be when the people's hearts were in it.

Spring rode through the town in a stylish barouche and four (Colonel Berkeley's) about twelve o'clock. The postilions were in red, and everything *en suite*. He arrived on the ground by half-past twelve, amidst the shouts of the spectators, and drove close up to the ropes in a postchaise. He threw his hat into the ring, accompanied by Tom Cribb and Ned Painter. He was dressed with striking neatness. At this period all were on the look-out for Langan, but a quarter of an hour had elapsed, and no Langan—half an hour gone, and no Paddy—three quarters over, and still no Irish Champion in sight. Spring pulled out his watch, and said, "It is time." In the *midst* of the hour, waiting for the arrival of Langan, the right wing belonging to the stand gave way, and fifteen hundred persons, at least, were thrown in a promiscuous heap. It was an awful moment. To give any description of the feelings of the spectators baffles attempt. Spring turned pale, and said, "How sorry I am for this accident." In a few minutes composure was restored, it being ascertained that nothing material had occurred, except a few contusions, and some of the persons limping away from the spot. "Thank God!" ejaculated Spring, "I would not have had it happen while I was fighting for a hundred thousand pounds!" The John Bull boxer had now become impatient, and exclaimed, "This is strange! Where's my man?" "I'll bet ten to one," said a swell, "he don't mean to come at all." "I'll take it, sir," said an Irishman, "a thousand times over." "No," was the reply—"I meant I would take it." The stakes would certainly have been claimed by Spring, but no precise time was specified in the articles. It was, as the lawyers say, a day in law—meaning "any time within the day:" the time had not been mentioned in black and white. Nearly an hour had elapsed, when several voices sung out from the stand, "Josh. Hudson! Josh. Hudson! Langan wishes to see you." The John Bull fighter bolted towards the place like lightning, and in a few minutes afterwards shouts rending the air proclaimed the approach of the Irish Champion. He did not, like most other boxers, throw his castor up in the air, but in the most modest way possible leaned over the ropes and laid it down. He immediately went up and shook hands with Spring. The latter, with great good nature, said, "I hope you are well, Langan." "Very well, my boy; and we'll soon talk to each other in another way." The men now stripped, when Reynolds went up to Spring, and said, "I understand you have got a belt on, and whalebone in it; if you persist in fighting in such belt, I shall put one on Langan." Spring replied (showing a belt such as are worn by gentlemen when riding), "I have always fought in this, and shall now." "Then," replied Reynolds (putting on a large belt, crossed in various parts with a hard substance), "Langan shall fight in this." "No, he won't," said Cribb; "it is not a fair thing." "Never mind," urged Spring, "I'll take it off;" which he did immediately. Josh. Hudson and Tom Reynolds were the seconds for Langan, and the Irish Champion declared he was ready to go to work. The colours were tied to the stakes; and, singular to state, black for Langan, which he took off his neck; and blue for Spring. "This is new," said Josh.; "but nevertheless, the emblem is correct as to milling (laughing); it is black and blue; I'll take one hundred to one, we shall see those colours upon their mugs before it is over." The time was kept by Lord Deerhurst, afterwards Earl of Harrington, who was also Spring's umpire, while Sir Harry Goodricke was umpire for Langan; Colonel Berkeley acted as referee. Five to two, and three to one on Spring.

THE FIGHT.

Round 1.—On stripping, the bust of Langan was much admired for its anatomical beauty; his arms also were peculiarly fine and athletic; and his nob looked like a fighting one. His legs were thin; his knees very small, and his loins deficient as to strength. It was evident he had been reduced too much in training. Langan did not exceed twelve stone four pounds, and was nearly two inches shorter than his opponent. Spring was in fine condition; cool and confident, and a stone heavier than his adversary. On placing themselves in attitude, the advantages were manifest on the side of the English Champion. The combatants kept at a respectful distance from each other; both on the look-out for an opening. Spring at length made a hit, which Langan stopped with skill. The Champion slowly advanced, and Langan kept retreating, till he was near the stake at the corner of the ring. At this instant the position of Langan was not only fine but formidable, and Spring did not view it with contempt. The latter let fly right and left, and Langan's left ogle received a slight touch. Spring got away from a heavy body blow. A pause. An exchange of blows, but no mischief done; Langan broke ground well. Another pause. Langan again in the corner, smiling, in a position armed at all points; Spring's eye measuring his opponent, but hesitating to go in. Langan endeavoured to plant a body blow with his left hand, when Spring jumped away as light as a cork. Here Langan put his thumb to his nose, by way of derision. The latter stopped Langan's left hand. "Fight away, Jack," said Josh Hudson, "he can't hurt nobody." Some blows were exchanged sharply, when the John Bull fighter, and Tom Reynolds, exclaimed, "First blood!" "No," replied Spring. "Yes," urged Hudson, "it is on your lip." A long pause. Langan made a good stop with his right hand. Some hits passed between the combatants, when they closed, and a severe struggle ensued to obtain the throw; both down, but Langan uppermost. This round occupied nine minutes. "This battle will not be over in half an hour," said a good judge.

2.—It was seen, in this early stage of the battle, that Langan would require heavy work to take the fight out of him. Spring was very cautious, and appeared as if determined not to receive any of Paddy's clumsy thumps. A long pause. Langan hit Spring with his left hand on the body. The latter planted a tremendous facer on the top of Langan's nose, that produced the claret; but the Irishman shook it off. Science displayed on both sides. After a long pause Spring put down his hands. The English Champion appeared to have made up his mind not to be hit, but to be liberal in the extreme—to give and not to take. Langan again displayed skill in stopping. (At this juncture the left

wing of the temporary scaffold erected for the accommodation of the spectators, gave way with a tremendous crash, and upwards of one thousand persons, from the height of thirty feet, were precipitated one upon the other in one confused mass. The countenance of Spring, whose face was towards the accident, underwent that sort of sensation which did honour to his feelings and to his heart—he appeared sick with affliction at the circumstance, put up his hands, indicating that his mind was perplexed whether he should quit the ring or proceed with the battle.) Langan received a heavy blow on his left eye; and both went down in a close.

3.—Both cautious. Spring put down his hands. Langan tried his left hand twice; but Spring jumped away. "Take care of your plum-pudding, boy!" said Josh, "he's coming." In closing Langan went down.

4.—The slightest offer on the part of Langan to make a hit never escaped the wary eye of Spring, and the latter got away with the utmost dexterity and ease; Langan followed his opponent to the ropes; but Spring stopped a heavy hit. In closing, at the corner of the ropes, both went down, but Langan uppermost.

5.—This was a short round. The Irish Champion ran in, hit Spring, and also bored him down. "You have got the great man down, at all events," said Josh.

6.—Langan's left peeper was nearly closed; but, in struggling for the throw, Spring went down heavily on his head.

7.—Twenty-five minutes had elapsed, and nothing like mischief to either combatant had yet taken place. A long pause. Langan made two good stops, when he run in, and by dint of strength got Spring on the ropes; a severe struggle took place till both down. The spectators were now getting close to the ropes; and the whips were hard at work, to keep the space allotted to the boxers.

8.—Langan received a nobber without giving any return. Another tedious pause. Spring, as lively as an eel, jumped backwards from a hit. Pause the second. The attitudes of the men were considered peculiarly fine at this instant. Langan appeared formidable. The English Champion put in two facers left and right. Langan could not reach the body of Spring effectually: the left hand of the latter could not get home. In struggling for the throw Langan was undermost.

9.—The science and patience displayed by Spring rendered him a truly troublesome, nay, a very tiresome customer to Langan. The Irish Champion threw Spring in good style.

10.—Spring waiting at his leisure for Langan to commence hitting. Langan, however, was not to be gammoned to go in, without something like a chance offering itself. Spring put in a slight nobber, which produced an exchange of blows. A very long pause. Langan's left hand touched the body of his opponent. This was a tedious round. In struggling at the ropes, both down, but Spring uppermost.

11.—Without the Irish Champion ran in he could not make a hit to a certainty. Both down, Langan undermost.

12.—Spring got away from almost every blow aimed at him. In closing, Spring was thrown heavily.

13.—Langan came to the scratch smiling, and said, "You see I am always ready." Spring jumped two yards back from a body blow. An exchange of hits but no mischief. Spring was again thrown.

14.—In all the preceding rounds, though Langan had received several nobbers, he was not in the slightest degree reduced as to courage. On the contrary, he was as gay as a lark Langan observed to Spring, "My boy, I can fight for a week." "Yes," said Josh, "for a month, if you get no heavier blows than you have received already. I'm sure it is not safe to the Champion; his honours are shaking, if not upon the go." Langan was thrown.

15.—Langan's nose was pinked a little, and his left eye swelled up. In closing, both down.

16.—The length of Spring enabled him to make a hit without any return. The caution manifested by the English Champion perfectly satisfied the spectators that he meant to give, but not to take. Langan, by strength alone, got his opponent down.

17.—After looking at each other for some time, Langan bored in. At the ropes both were down, Spring undermost.

18.—This was a tedious round. Nothing done. Both down.

19.—"Go to work, Spring," from several spectators. "All in good time," replied Tom. "Never fear," said Langan, "I am ready for anything," An exchange of blows; but the combatants were out of distance. Both down.

20.—Langan could not reach Spring effectively at the scratch; he therefore bored in. At the ropes Spring tried the weaving system till both were upon the ground.

21.—Langan threw Spring out of the ropes; and, with much jocularity and good nature, observed, laying hold of Spring's arm, "If I sent you down, I have a right to pick you up!" ("Bravo! What a strange fellow!")

22.—Both down, Spring uppermost.

23.—Langan stopped several blows skilfully; but he was not tall enough for his opponent. In closing, Spring went down heavily, and Langan upon him.

24.—Spring put in a body hit. In closing, both down.

25.—Spring was undermost in the fall.

26.—This was a good round, in comparison with several of the preceding sets-to. Langan again put out his strength, and Spring was undermost on the ground.

27.—The Irish Champion ran his opponent completely down.

28.—One hour and fourteen minutes had elapsed, and the Irish Champion still as good as gold. Langan took the lead rather in this round. He planted a couple of hits, and also threw Spring.

29.—Langan, it was thought, had decidedly the best of this round also. He hit Spring; and, in closing, a severe struggle took place; but ultimately Langan threw Spring over the ropes. ("Bravo, Langan.")

30.—Of no consequence. Both down.

31.—In this round, Spring was thrown upon his head. ("How well the Irishman throws," was the remark.)

32.—In several of the preceding rounds Spring planted some facers; but they were not heavy enough to take the pluck out of Langan. ("How bad Spring fights to-day." was the observation of an old backer of the English Champion. This was not the fact; Spring appeared to fight with more caution than usual; the blows of Langan were to be avoided at all events, if the battle was to be made perfectly safe to Spring. The truth was, that Langan's right hand was dangerous, and a well-directed blow, at a proper distance, on the mark, or on the nob, might have reduced the science of Spring.) Langan napped a facer; but Spring was undermost in the fall.

33.—The left hand of the Irish Champion told on his opponent's body. Several blows passed, and Langan put in a hit on the side of Spring's head. Both down, Langan undermost.

34.—Langan went sharply up to Spring, but he received a nobber and went down.

35.—The Irish Champion, as fresh as a daisy, appeared at the scratch. In closing at the ropes Spring endeavoured to fib his opponent till both went down. The ring was in much confusion, and the P.C. men had their work to do to keep it clear.

36.—If Spring did not please the multitude by his smashing qualities, his backers expressed themselves well pleased with the caution he displayed. Lots of blunt, as to long odds, had been sported upon the English Champion; but his friends began to be somewhat apprehensive that the strength and throwing of Langan, might tire out Spring. Some exchanges, but both down.

37.—Langan hit Spring slightly. On the whole this might be termed a fighting round. In closing, a desperate struggle took place; Spring undermost.

38.—This was also an excellent fighting round. Langan laughed at Spring, saying, "You have done nothing yet!" "All in good time," replied Spring, "I shall do it at last." Langan planted two blows on the side of Spring's head; but the Irishman wanted length to do severe mischief. Both fell, and Cribb, in the bustle, was also on the ground.

39.—Spring gave his opponent a noser, when a few hits passed till both went down.

40.—Langan received another nobber. Both down.

41.—This was a tedious round; neither combatant would go to work for some time. In closing, Spring obtained the fall, and was uppermost.

42.—Langan kept trying his left hand, in order to punish Spring's body; but the latter got away so cleverly, that the blows of the Irish Champion were not effective. Spring undermost in the throw.

43.—A desperate trial of strength on the part of Langan to obtain the fall, which the Irish Champion ultimately accomplished, Spring being undermost.

44.—Langan planted two body blows with his left hand. Langan was thrown; and Spring fell upon his knees

45.—Spring cautious; Langan full of spirits. (Most of the fighting men exclaimed, "He is the best Irishman ever seen in the ring. He is the gamest man alive!" Here Martin observed to a Corinthian, "What a pity it is that the backers of Langan had no more judgment than to place him in opposition to Spring.") Spring had the best of this round, and Langan was fibbed down at the ropes.

46.—Langan made a hit. An exchange of blows, but the Irish Champion slipped and went down.

47.—The ring was getting worse every round. In closing, both down.

48.—The men had not room for their exertions. The spectators were close upon the combatants, and the utmost disorder prevailed. In closing, Langan threw Spring.

49.—Some severe struggling; the English Champion fibbing Langan till he went down.

50.—The face of Spring did not exhibit any marks of punishment, but the left hand of Langan had told now and then upon his body. The English Champion appeared getting weak from the struggles, and from several heavy falls. Both down.

51.—The rounds were now short—the crowd pressing upon the men at every step they took. Spring received a heavy hit on the side of his head. In closing, both went down.

52.—Close quarters. An exchange of blows; both again down.

53.—Langan hit Spring, and also got him down.

54.—The English Champion had no room now to jump away from his antagonist. Spring, in closing, fibbed Langan down.

55.—Struggling for the throw, but Langan undermost.

56.—The outer roped ring had been for the last hour in the greatest disorder. The constables' long poles were useless; the whips of the fighting men were of no avail; and the mob was now close up to the ring. Spring put in the most hits on the nob of his opponent; but the strength of Langan in getting

Spring down surprised every one present. Both down.

57.—Spring received a fall, and Langan upon him.

58.—So much disorder now prevailed, that it was difficult for those persons who were placed only at a few yards' distance from the ring to see the fight. Langan on the ground, and undermost

59.—Spring had not room to display his science, but he endeavoured to hit Langan as the latter rushed in. Spring had the worst of the throw.

60.—Cribb, at this instant, was so pressed upon by the crowd, that, in a violent rage, he declared he would give a floorer to any person who stood in his way. "Here's a pretty go!" said Tom, "a set of fellows with books and pencils in their hands, pretending to be reporters. A parcel of impostors! I don't care; I'll hit any body." One of the umpires, a noble lord, was hit with a shillelah by a rough Patlander, who was attempting to get a little space for Langan, and when informed that he was behaving rude to a nobleman, "Devil may care," says Pat; "all I want is fair play for Jack Langan. There's no difference here: lords are no better than commoners. Faith! I can't distinguish them one from another, at all, at all!") Langan ran in and gave Spring a blow on the head: but, in struggling for the throw, the Irish Champion was undermost.

61.—When time was called, "Here we are," said Langan. Spring had only time to make a hit, when Langan bored in; but Spring again had the best of the throw, Langan being undermost.

62.—Nothing. Langan bored Spring down.

63.—Spring had decidedly the best of this round. He made several hits; and Langan received an ugly throw.

64.—"Go to work, Erin-go-bragh! Spring has no hits left in him. You must win it," said Josh. Langan followed this advice, and some sharp work was the result. Spring could not retreat. Fighting till both down.

65.—("Go in, Jack," said Josh, "as you did the last time, and you will soon spoil his fine science." Langan rushed in, but Spring avoided his blow. In closing, the struggle to obtain the throw was violent in the extreme, but Langan got it; Spring came down on his back, and Langan on him, and the breath of the Champion was nearly shaken out of his body. Spring was picked up by Cribb in a weak state, and looked extremely pale. Here two or three persons hallooed out six to four on Langan, but the confusion was so great that no bets could be made.)

66.—In this round the English Champion put in a tremendous nobber, and also fibbed Langan down. ("That's a settler," said a bystander. "Indeed it is not," replied a Paddy, "Spring will not settle his account this time." (Laughing.) "Where's Jack Randall?" says Josh; "here's a countryman for you! Spring's tired of it. He can't hit a dent in a pound of butter." "Well done, Josh," said Spring, smiling, "chaff away. I'll give you all you can do, except winning." "We can't lose it," replied the John Bull fighter.)

67.—Spring was still cautious: he would not give a chance away. Both down.

68.—Langan's left hand told on Spring's body; but the Irish Champion received a nobber for it. Langan seemed determined to have Spring down, at all events. The struggle for the throw was severely contested; Langan got Spring undermost.

69.—Short; a hit or two passed, when both were down.

70.—Langan's face looked the worse for the battle, but his eye retained all its fire and animation; the other peeper had been nearly darkened for an hour and a half. "I am sure," said Josh, "that Langan has made a contract with Spring for seven years; this is a fine specimen of one of his fighting days." Both men were getting weak, but Langan always got up when time was called, saying, "I am ready!" In the throw, Langan was undermost.

71.—The ring was now in confusion; yet some of the sharpest rounds were fought. Spring received another fall, and was undermost.

72.—The general opinion in the twenty-four foot ring (which was nothing else but a crowd), appeared to be, that Spring would win; nevertheless the countenances of Spring's backers indicated it was not quite safe. Spring had no room to get away. Colonel Berkeley, the referee, said, "I am so disgusted with the treatment I have experienced, that I will give up the watch. Here is no ring. It is impossible to stand still a second, without being assailed with a cut from a whip, or a blow from a stick, and no good done either." In no fight whatever was there such a scene of confusion in the space allotted for the men to fight. In closing, both down. During the time Spring was on Painter's knee, Sampson, Oliver and Israel Belasco, were giving advice. "Hallo!" said Josh, "do you call this fair play? How many seconds is Spring to have?" and, snatching a whip out of a bystander's hand, endeavoured to whip out the ring, followed by Oliver. "Only give us a chance," cried Josh, "and we can't lose it." Nothing foul appeared to be attempted on the part of Spring or on the side of Langan. The constables were mixed in the mob, struggling for breath; the fighting men hoarse with calling out, "Clear the ring," and dead beat from the exertions they had made. Nothing less than a company of Horse Guards could have made out a ring at this period, so closely jammed were the spectators.

73.—The courage, confidence, and good spirits displayed by Langan, excited the admiration of every beholder. He was too short in the arm for Spring: he could not reach his head without rushing in to mill.

Langan left his second's knee rather weak; in closing, he was fibbed severely by Spring, who was well assured he had not a minute to lose. The English Champion was cool, felt his situation, and his knowledge and experience in the prize-ring gave him the advantage when the nicety of the thing was required.

74.—On Langan placing himself in attitude, "Go and fight," said Cribb to Spring; when the Champion went to work without delay, and Langan received a heavy blow in the middle of his head, and went down. ("Twenty to one," said a swell, "he'll not come again.")

75.—The Irish Champion appeared the worse for the last round, and, on his appearing at the scratch, Spring commenced the attack, when Langan returned with great spirit; but Spring had decidedly the best, and Langan was fibbed down, his face covered with claret. ("Take the brave fellow away." "I will not be taken away—who dare say so?" exclaimed Langan.)

76.—Spring was now determined to lose no time, and again went to work; but Langan showed fight, and struggled to obtain the throw: both down. ("Take him away!" Langan's head rested on his second's shoulder till time was called. The Springites roared out—"It's as right as the day. Ten pounds to a crown the battle is over in five minutes.")

77th and last.—Langan came up quite groggy, but full of pluck. Spring now administered heavy punishment with both hands, and Langan fell quite exhausted, Reynolds had great difficulty in getting him from the ground; he was in a state of stupor, and his eye closed. Several gentlemen said, "Do not let the brave fellow fight any more; Reynolds, take him away; it is impossible he can meet Spring any more." When time was called, Langan was insensible—and Josh. Hudson gave in for him. Half a minute after, Langan opened his eyes, still sitting on the knee of his second. When he was told that the fight was over, he said, "His second had no right to give in for him. He could fight forty more rounds." "Don't leave the ring, Spring," several persons cried out. Cribb told Langan, "The battle was over;" and Painter observed, "Don't let so good a man be killed; he does not know what he is talking about!" The umpire was asked for his decision, and he said, "Langan did not come when time was called; therefore he had lost the battle, according to the rules of pugilism." Upon this answer, and decision of the umpire, Spring left the ring, amidst the shouts of the populace, Langan roaring out, "I am not beaten—clear out the ring—I can fight for four hours." In the course of a few minutes, he left the ring, and, as he approached the Grand Stand, he was received with applause, and jumped over some ropes in his way with agility. The battle lasted two hours and twenty-nine minutes.

REMARKS.*—In consequence of the breaking in of the ring, the struggles, and repeated falls of the men, it is impossible for any reporter to be strictly accurate as to the precise rounds fought. The battle would have terminated much sooner could Spring have used his left hand effectively, but after the eighth round he could only use it defensively, having injured his knuckles by bringing them in violent contact with Langan's nut. He has, however, proved himself one of the safest boxers ever known, and as Dusty Bob observes, "never gives a chance away." Another circumstance that retarded the final issue was the destruction of the inner ring; the combatants were so closely surrounded that they had no room for action. which was greatly to the disadvantage of Spring, whose fine science was set at nought in such close quarters. Langan has proved himself a perfect glutton, and the best big Irishman that ever appeared in the P.R. He has hitherto been unknown to the London Ring, and the wonder is, how such a novice could make so long a stand against the best man in it, and his superior in weight by nearly half a stone." The remarks conclude with some observations upon the persons who had erected stands for the spectators, which, although the charges were exorbitant, were so insecure as to cause serious injuries to many of their customers. Not less than twenty persons were seriously injured, many having broken bones, while an equal number were more or less bruised. After deducting sufficient to pay the ringkeepers, out of the money collected for admission to the ring, there remained £200, which was divided equally between Spring and Langan. At the conclusion of the fight, Cribb said to Langan, "You are a brave man indeed." "I never saw a better," replied Painter. Even betting occurred several times in the fight for small sums; and six to four was offered on Langan in light bets, after the fight had lasted two hours.

A voluminous paper war followed this fight, stimulated by "the historian," who at this period edited a weekly, called *Pierce Egan's Life in London.* The "milling correspondence," as it was termed, became as verbose and inconsequential as diplomatic circular notes or the "protocols" on the Schleswig-Holstein question. Langan, Spring, Tom Reynolds, Josh. Hudson, and Cribb, by their amanuenses, or self-appointed secretaries, figured in print in what they would have called in their vernacular, the "'fending and proving" line; but the great gun was Tom Reynolds, primed and charged by Pierce himself. The very reading of his letters, and weary reading they were, reminds us of the Bastard Falconbridge's description of the magniloquent citizen of Angiers :—

> " He speaks plain cannon, fire, and smoke, and bounce;
> He gives the bastinado with his tongue;
> Our ears are cudgelled; not a word of his
> But buffets better than a fist of France.
> Zounds! I was never so bethump'd with words
> Since I first called my brother's father 'dad.'"

Reynolds proved too much in these letters (several of which serve to "pad" out the bulk of "Boxiana") by charging conduct upon men whose whole life gave the lie to such imputations.

On the 19th of February, 1824, Langan had a bumper benefit at the Tennis Court, and, at its close, thus addressed the audience :—"Gentlemen, I thank you for the honour you have conferred upon me, and I beg to assure you, on the honour of an Irishman (placing his hand on his breast), if I have

* Though this report is mainly from Pierce Egan's text, it is not his writing; these "remarks" are from the pen of Mr. Vincent Dowling, and appeared in *Bell's Life in London,* of January 11, 1824.

the good fortune again to enter the ring, that no effort shall be wanting on my part to make it a more pleasant and agreeable 'mill' than the last in which I was engaged. Gentlemen, I am ready to fight any man who calls himself Champion of England, for any sum, from three hundred to a thousand, upon a boarded stage, like this, in the same way as Cribb fought Molineaux."

This challenge produced the following epistle from Spring to the Editor of *Pierce Egan's Life in London* :—

"SIR,

"Your paper, and others of the public journals, have of late teemed with idle correspondence on the subject of my fight with Langan. Of Langan I have nothing to say, but that I consider him a brave fellow in the ring, and a good fellow out of it; but in order to put an end to all further chaffing, and to bring our matters to a clear understanding, I have only this to observe : Langan, at his own benefit, publicly stated that "he was ready to fight any man who called himself Champion of England, on a stage, for from £300 to £1,000." Now, I have been pronounced the character he describes, and I am ready to fight Langan, or any other man, for £500, in a roped ring on the turf, or for £1,000 in any way that himself or his friends may think proper to suggest—on an iron pavement if they choose. This is my final answer to all challenges ; and I shall be at the Fives' Court to-morrow, at Turner's benefit, and come to the scratch if called.

"I am, sir, yours most respectfully,

"THOMAS W. SPRING.

"*February* 24, 1824."

This was followed by a letter (bearing internal marks of proceeding from the pen of Tom Reynolds) magniloquently entitled—

"THE IRISH CHAMPION'S DECLARATION TO THE SPORTING WORLD.

"GENTLEMEN,

"Mr. Spring, in his letter, speaks of his wish to avoid 'chaffing, and bring matters to a right understanding' between him and me. To show you, therefore, the chaffing is not on my side, and that I am really anxious to have matters clearly understood, I beg leave to submit the following facts to your judgment :—

"When I challenged him in Manchester, for £100 a-side, he pretended to treat my offer with contempt (though he had never, but in one instance, fought for more), and named £500 as the least stake, a sum three times greater than any for which he had contended. But though he was afterwards shamed into agreeing for £300 a-side, yet he calculated on my inability to raise so much ; and, to prevent my doing so, he and his friends, besides throwing other obstacles in my way, contrived to induce the gentleman who agreed to put down the whole sum for me to withdraw his patronage, so that it was with the utmost difficulty I raised the battle money.

"As to the battle, it is needless to repeat that I have good reasons to complain of the treatment I experienced. Every unprejudiced witness will bear me out in this, and my friends are so satisfied with my conduct, that they are ready to back me against Spring for £500, on a stage, which they think the only way of guarding against a repetition of unfair treatment. But when Spring finds me thus supported, he raises his demand to £1,000, on the ground that I challenged him to fight for any sum from £300 to £1,000. My words were, that I would fight him for from £300 to £500, or for £1,000, if I were backed, and I do not deny them ; for if I had £100,000 I would confidently stake it. But £500 is a sum between £300 and £1,000 ; and if I could get backed for £1,000, I should rejoice at it, as it would at once do away with this excuse of Spring. I think, however, that it will not tell much for his credit, if he continues to reject the £500, which I can command, and £50 of which I am ready to lay down at Belcher's, to make the match, any time he thinks proper. I believe nine out of ten in the sporting world will agree that Spring cannot honourably refuse this proposal, were it only to meet the complaint of foul play, which I am justified in making with regard to the former battle.

" But he also pledged himself, when he received the championship, to imitate the donor's conduct. Then why not redeem his pledge, or resign the gift?

" He says that he does not wish to enter the ring again. This is mere shuffling. He ought not to hold a situation for which he has no taste : he cannot, in justice, have the honour without the danger. If he will not fight, then let him resign the championship to one that will—to a man who will not want to make a sinecure of the title, and will always be ready to fight for a stake of £500.

" Permit me again to repeat that I am ready to make a match to fight Spring for £500 a-side, within a hundred miles of London, on a stage * similar to the one on which Cribb and Molineaux fought. Sparring exhibitions I cannot attend till I set-to for my friend Reynolds, on the 17th of March.

"I am, gentlemen, your very obedient servant,

"JOHN LANGAN.

" *Castle Tavern, Holborn, February 26.*"

This letter produced its desired effect, for next week Spring thus addressed the several sporting editors :—

" Sir,

" I can bear the bullying of this Langan no longer, but will, by the consent of my friends, meet him upon the terms demanded in his last letter. I will be at Cribb's on Tuesday evening next, at eight o'clock, to stake £100, and settle the business at once.

" I am, sir, yours, etc.,

" T. W. SPRING.

" *84, High Street, Marylebone.*"

Langan accepted Spring's invitation, and honest Tom Cribb's crib, on Tuesday, February 24, 1824, at a very early period of the evening was crowded, not a seat to be had for begging or praying, for love or money. The house was not one-third big enough, and hundreds of persons went away angry and disappointed. Tom Belcher first made his appearance, followed by Langan, in a military cloak ; the rear was brought up by the president of the Daffy Club. The street door was immediately closed, to prevent an improper rush, and a sentinel was placed at the door of the stairs. The Irish Champion seated himself in the first floor, and drank Spring's health in

* " FIGHTING UPON A STAGE.—Some little difference of opinion having existed upon the merits of the case between Langan and Spring, the majority of the supporters of pugilism assert, according to milling precedents, that if Spring intended to retain the title of Champion, he could, nay, he ought not to have refused to fight Langan upon a stage, as the following circumstances support the claim of Langan. It appears that Jack Bartholomew thought he had not fair play in the ring when he fought with Jem Belcher ; and upon Bartholomew's soliciting Belcher to give him a chance upon a stage, he replied, " Any where ; a saw-pit, if you like." Again, when Molineaux entertained an opinion that he had not justice done him in a ring with Cribb, the latter veteran answered the request of the man of colour, with a smile upon his face, " Yes, upon a stage, the top of a house, in a ship, or in any place you think proper." It is likewise insisted upon by the admirers of boxing that the advantages are all upon the side of Spring. He is the tallest, the heaviest, and the longest man, with the addition of his superior science into the bargain. Most of the prize battles formerly were fought upon stages—Tom Johnson with Perrins, Big Ben with Jacombs, and George the brewer with Pickard; Johnson with Ryan, Johnson also with Big Ben, Mendoza with Humphries, Ward with Mendoza, Tom Tyne with Earl, etc. It is also worthy of remark, that none of the above stages were covered with turf. The only instance that bears upon the point respecting "turf," is the stage which was erected at Newbury, upon which Big Ben and Hooper were to have fought. This was covered with turf, but the magistrates interfered ; the fight was removed to some miles distant. Big Ben and Hooper fought on the ground in a ring."—PIERCE EGAN.

a glass of wine, the company, in return, drinking the health of Langan. Spring, on being informed Langan had arrived, sent word to the Irish Champion that he was ready. Cribb, who was very lame, hobbled up stairs to meet his old opponent, and to " argufy the topic" in a parliamentary style, across the table. Belcher then produced a draft of the articles which, he said, Langan was prepared to sign. These articles were as follows:—

" *Memorandum of an Agreement entered into between Thomas Winter Spring and John Langan at Thomas Cribb's, Panton Street, on the 2nd of March,* 1824.

" It is hereby agreed between Thomas Winter Spring and John Langan to fight, on a twenty-four feet stage, on Tuesday, the 8th of June, 1824, for £500 a-side, to be a fair stand-up fight, half minute time ; umpires to be chosen by each party, and a referee to be chosen on the ground by the umpires. The fight to take place within one hundred miles of London, and the place to be named by Mr. Jackson. The men to be in the ring between twelve and one o'clock, unless prevented by magisterial interference. Fifty pounds of the money are now deposited in the hands of the stake-holder, Mr. —— ; £50 more to be deposited, on the 17th of March, at Mr. John Randall's, Hole-in-the-Wall, Chancery Lane ; £200 to be deposited at Mr. Thomas Cribb's, on the 1st of May ; and the remainder of the £500 to be made good at Mr. Thomas Belcher's, at the Castle Tavern, Holborn, on the 1st of June ; and in case of failure on either side, the money deposited to be forfeited.

" The stage to be boarded with deal planks, at least three inches thick, and to be six feet from the ground, without turf. The bottle-holders and seconds to retire to the corners of the ring when the men shall have set-to, and not to approach the combatants till one or both of them shall be down.

" The expenses of the stage to be equally borne by each of the men."

To these conditions Spring took exceptions ; first, expressing his desire that the present deposit should be £100 instead of £50 ; this objection, after a few remarks, he waived. He then objected to the day named for the fight to take place, proposing the 25th of May instead of the 8th of June ; and, lastly, he insisted that the second £50 should be deposited on the 13th of March, instead of the 17th, upon the ground that the 17th had been appointed for Reynold's benefit, and he did not wish to lend himself to this additional attraction to the public. A good deal of discussion followed, but, finally, there was mutual concession, Spring agreeing to fight on the 8th of June, and Langan agreeing to make his second deposit on the 13th instead of the 17th of March. All difficulties thus cleared away, there were one or two verbal alterations made in the articles ; and a paragraph was added, by which it was agreed, " that when the whole of the money was made good, it should be deposited in the hands of Mr. Jackson."

Spring, in alluding to the expense of erecting the stage, said he thought it but fair, as this was Langan's fancy, that he should bear the whole expense. To which Langan replied, " See, now, Tom ; say nothing about that, for if I win, and I think I will, I'll bear the whole expense of the stage myself. (Loud cheers.) But that's neither here nor there ; I hope the best man will win ; and though we are going to fight, it's myself that would go a hundred miles to serve you, for I have no antipathy or ill-blood towards you whatever."

The president of the Daffy Club was then appointed stakeholder. The articles having been signed and witnessed, and everything relative to the pugilistic tourney having been settled comfortably on both sides, Langan and his friends made their bows, and returned to finish the evening at Belcher's (the Castle).

Spring and Langan, according to the articles, met on Saturday evening, the 13th of March, at Randall's, and made £100 a-side good towards the completion of the stakes of 1,000 sovereigns. They met like good fellows, brave men, and personal friends. In the course of the evening Langan proposed the health of Spring. He also rebuked several of his partisans, who frequently shouted out, "Well done, Langan!" "Bravo, Jack!" etc. "I hate these sort of remarks," said the Irish Champion; "they are calculated to make ill-blood and provoke animosity, which it is my most sincere wish to prevent, if possible. All I want is, that we may meet as friends, and have a comfortable, pleasant mill on the 8th of June!" Sixty to forty was offered by a gentleman from Yorkshire upon Spring. "I will bet £70 to £40," said the latter. "I'll take it, Tom," replied Langan; and before they separated, Spring betted with Langan £580 to £168, that he should win the battle. The evening was spent with the utmost good humour by all parties.

Spring's benefit at the Fives Court on Tuesday, June 1, 1824, not only produced a bumper, but the body of the Court was crowded, the gallery overloaded even to danger; the little room, "the swells' retreat," once secure from the vulgar eye and intrusion of commoners, was now full of all sorts, and Earls, Right Honourables, Honourables, and M.P.'s, were squeezed together, without complaint, quite satisfied with obtaining only now and then a glimpse of the stage. In fact, numbers of persons could not be admitted, and the doors were closed to prevent accidents from the pressure of the multitude. Spring addressed the populace in the street from one of the windows in the Fives Court.

In the evening a dinner was held at the Castle Tavern, Holborn, at which fifty-two gentlemen were present. The chair was taken by Mr. Rayner (well known for his excellent performances of Tyke, Giles, Fixture, etc.), and the deputy-chair ably filled by the President of the Daffy Club. When "time" was called, Spring, supported by his backer and Cribb, appeared and posted the money. Loud approbation was expressed when it was announced that £1,000 were deposited in the hands of the stake-holder. Langan was present for a short time. The dinner was excellent, and the wines pronounced of the first quality. Four to one was betted on Spring!

The second great match was fixed for Tuesday, June 8, 1824, and Warwick, in the first instance, was the place decided upon, but Chichester was the "latest intelligence." Some hundreds were "thrown out" by the change. Nevertheless, the capital of Sussex was overflowing with company so soon as it was known to be the right scent. Spring arrived at the Swan Hotel in the course of Monday, in company with his backer, Mr. Sant; they were received with loud cheers. Colonel O'Neil, Langan, Tom Belcher, and company, arrived nearly at the same time at the Dolphin Hotel, and were equally well received.

The cause of the change was, Mr. Hewlings, of the Swan Inn, Chichester, having undertaken to give the men £200, and having intimated that there would be no interruption. The spot chosen for the trial of strength was admirably adapted for the purpose; it was a field about three miles from the city, one side of which was bordered by the Canal, and it was only approachable by means of a drawbridge, over which all must necessarily pass to the ring side, and at which a toll was imposed on all comers. The bridge was called Birdham Bridge. The moment the farmers in the neighbourhood were informed of the gratification which awaited them, they volunteered their wagons to form the outer ring, an offer which was at once accepted by Mr. Hewlings, who appears to have taken the whole management on himself, and in the course of Monday, the day prior to the fight, no less than fifty-three large wagons were arranged in a circle round the spot on which, in the course of the day, the stage was erected. This stage was six feet from the ground, and was planked with three-inch deal. Round it were fixed strong posts, to which three rows of stout rails were fastened; these and the posts were rounded, so as to diminish as much as possible any injury to the combatants. During Monday afternoon Chichester presented an extraordinary appearance, and was as crowded as one is accustomed to see it during the Goodwood meeting, and all day the windows were filled with anxious spectators on the look out for a peep at the combatants.

In London, as soon as it was generally known that Chichester was the centre of attraction, there was a simultaneous move to secure places in the coaches going either to that city, or to Brighton or Portsmouth. Many persons, unable to obtain places, and equally unable to afford posters, had to betake themselves to their ten toes, so determined were they not to miss the treat. As the evening advanced, the curiosity of the Chichester folks was more or less gratified by the arrival of Cribb, Oliver, Jack Martin, Dick Curtis, Ben Burn, Randall, Painter, Jack Scroggins, and a long list of pugilists of note. Post-chaises and carriages and four poured rapidly into the town : every inn was soon crowded to an overflow, and soon every corner was filled. Spring and his friends arrived at the Swan Inn about half past seven o'clock, and were received with loud cheers. He was in excellent health and spirits, and seemed delighted at his cordial reception. Langan was not long after him, and took up his quarters at the Dolphin. He, like Spring, was warmly cheered. He was in high spirits, laughed heartily, and appeared to be in excellent condition. Some doubts having been expressed by the friends of Langan as to the good faith of Mr. Hewlings, who had promised the men £200 to fight near Chichester, that gentleman at once posted half the money in responsible hands, to be paid to the loser, and it was agreed that the winner should receive his £100 as soon as the contest was over. In the course of the evening a little money was invested at three to one on Spring.

On the morning of fighting the bustle was redoubled in Chichester, and the excitement appeared to extend to Bognor, Portsmouth, and other places in the neighbourhood. Both men rose in excellent spirits, and thoroughly up to the mark. Spring's weight was about thirteen stone four pounds, while Langan was at least a stone under that amount, and by many it was considered he had drawn it too fine. About eleven o'clock a move commenced towards the ground, and on the arrival of the public at the before-named bridge, it was found that some of the milling gentry had planted themselves at the entrance, where they extorted sums varying from 2s. 6d. to 5s. from every one who passed, thus forestalling Mr. Hewlings, who had hired the field and erected the stage at his own expense, depending on the toll at the bridge for his reimbursement. Of course much indignation was excited by this conduct, but on the arrival of Mr. Jackson everything was set right, and a settlement made with Mr. Hewlings.

At length, everything being arranged, Mr. Jackson, who acted as Commander-in-Chief, directed that the men should be brought forward.

A few minutes before one o'clock, Spring, arm-in-arm with his backer and a baronet, made his way through the crowd towards the stage, and was received with loud huzzas, Cribb and Painter close behind him. Spring threw up his hat, which alighted upon the stage, then ascended the ladder and jumped over the rails.

While Spring was taking off his boots, Cribb and Ned Painter put on knee-caps, made of chamois leather and stuffed with wool. It having been circulated in Ireland that Painter used his knee against Langan when he was on the ground, in the fight at Worcester, a sergeant-major in a marching regiment, quartered at Norwich, and occasionally visiting the house of

Painter, observed, "By J——s, Mr. Painter, I'll take care you do not hurt Langan this time with your knees: I'll have a couple of knee-caps made for you both, and if you mean to give Jack fair play, I insist that you wear them during the battle." The sergeant had them made according to his own order, and as Painter and Cribb always were lovers of fair play, both these pugilists, with the utmost good humour, placed the caps, tied with a narrow blue ribbon, round their knees.

Langan shortly followed, under the patronage of Colonel O'Neil. Belcher, Harmer, and O'Neil (not "Ned," of Streatham), his bottle-holder, were in attendance. The Irish champion ascended the stage, and in a modest manner dropped his hat within the rails. He was prepared for action; but the Champion not being ready, he walked up and down the boards with the utmost composure.

A black silk handkerchief was placed loosely round Langan's neck, which, we understand, was tied by the delicate hands of the lady of a gallant Irish Colonel O'B——, before he left the inn, at which the lady stopped in her journey to the Isle of Wight. Mrs. O'B—— offered him a green handkerchief, as a token of his country; but Langan politely refused, saying, "I am not of importance enough to make it a national affair: I do not wish it, indeed, madam; it is merely to decide which is the best man; therefore, if you please, I prefer a black one, having fought under that colour." Mrs. O'B——, on tying it round his neck, romantically exclaimed, "You are Irish: colour is immaterial to a brave man: glory is your only object. Go, then, and conquer!" Langan returned thanks very politely for the attention paid to him, and the good wishes of the lady. Everything being ready, the colours, dark blue with bird's eye for Spring, black for Langan, were tied to the stage, and Mr. Jackson arranged the spectators round the ring in an orderly and comfortable manner. Betting two to one, and five to two, at the beginning of

THE FIGHT.

Round 1.—Spring never looked so big, nor so well, in any of his previous contests; he appeared perfectly at his ease: coolness sat upon his brow, and his deportment altogether was a fine personification of confidence: indeed, it was observed by a noble lord, "There is something about the person of the Champion, if not truly noble, yet manly and elegant." Langan also looked well; his face exhibited a tinge of the sun, and his frame was robust and hardy; his loins appeared smaller than in his former contest. His countenance was as pleasant as his opponent's, and his eyes sparkled with fire and animation. Previous to setting-to, Langan went up to Spring, opening his drawers, and observed, "See, Tom, I have no belt about me;" the Champion immediately followed his example, and said (also opening his drawers), "Nor I neither, Jack!" This circumstance elicited great applause from all parts of the ring. "Well done, Langan; bravo, Spring!" Spring now shook his brave opponent by the hand. Cribb laid hold of Tom Belcher's fist, and Ned Painter shook the bunch of fives of big Paddy O'Neil (shortly afterwards beaten by "my nevvy," Jem Burn.*) The men placed themselves in attitude. The glorious moment had arrived, and the seconds, in compliance with the articles, retired to the corners of the stage. This time Langan stood up within the reach of his adversary, and it was pleasing to witness the activity displayed by the combatants moving over the stage to obtain the first hit. A stand still, stedfastly looking at the eyes of each other; at length Langan made an offer, which Spring stopped well. The Champion made a hit, which told slightly on Langan's nob; the latter fought his way into a close, in which Spring endeavoured to fib his antagonist. Here the struggle began for the throw—it was desperate; the art of wrestling was not resorted to by either of the boxers, and main strength was the trial. Langan broke from the arms of Spring, and a stand still was the result. Langan observed, "First blood, Tom;" which slightly appeared at the corner of Spring's mouth. The Irish Champion made a good stop, but was blowing a little. Spring planted another facer, when Langan fought his way into a close: a desperate struggle ensued: fibbing was again attempted, when Langan went down on his knees. Spring patted the Irish Champion on the back with the utmost good humour, as much as to say, "You are a brave fellow," (A thundering report of approbation, and "Well done, Spring!") Four minutes and a few seconds. The referee, on being asked who drew the first blood, replied, "He did not see any on Spring; but he saw a little on the left cheek of Langan, just under his eye."

2.—Langan made play; but Spring, with the nimbleness of a harlequin showed the utility of a quick step. The Irish Champion made a rush, when they were again entangled for a short time, until Langan broke away. A pause: breath wanted: and consideration necessary. Langan gave Spring a facer with his right hand, and tried to repeat the dose; another quick movement prevented it, Spring smiling. A little bit of in-fighting: a desperate struggle for the throw: downright strength, when Spring went down, Langan falling heavily upon him. ("Bravo, Langan!")

3.—The attitudes of the combatants were interesting, and both extremely cautious. Spring got away from one intended for his nob. The science displayed on both sides was so excellent in stopping, that in the ecstacy of the moment the Commander-in-Chief† loudly exclaimed, "Beautiful." Another skilful stop by Spring; and one by Langan. "Well done: good on both sides," observed Mr. Jackson. Langan planted a hit. A pause. ("Fight, Langan," from Belcher, "you have all the best of it.") Spring drove Langan to the corner, but the hero of the black fogle got out of danger in style. He made also an excellent

stop while on the retreat: Langan made himself up to do mischief, and Spring received loud applause for stopping a tremendous hit. The Champion also bobbed his nob aside, in the Dutch Sam style, from what might have been a floorer. The Champion again broke ground, and bobbed cleverly away from the coming blow. Spring now took the lead famously. He planted a facer without any return; repeated the dose, and administered a third pill. Langan again got out of the corner, by fighting up like a trump. A short stand still. Heavy counter hits. A pause: Spring made another facer; a stand still. The Champion stopped well, and also drove Langan into the corner, but the hero of the black wipe would not be detained; he fought his way out manfully, and, in closing, though the struggle was terrible, Spring obtained the throw. (Loud applause.) This round occupied nearly seven minutes. The left hand of Spring was already going, if not gone.

4.—The "good bit of stuff from ould Ireland" endeavoured to take the lead, and had the best of this round; he fought first. He planted one or two hits, and not light ones either, and would have kept it up, but Spring said "it wouldn't do," and stopped him. In fact, this was a well-contested round on both sides; and Langan, after a terrible try for it, got Spring down. (Applause.)

5.—The left ear of Langan was much swelled; he was also piping. The superior science of Spring enabled him to get away from a number of heavy blows. Langan followed his opponent, trying to do something. Two counter-hits, which reminded both the men they were milling; the claret ran from Spring's nose. Spring planted a facer; and after a determined struggle on both sides, as Langan was going down, the Champion cleverly caught him a hard blow on the nose. ("That's the way, Spring; you'll soon win it.")

6.—A stand-still for a short time—Spring always taking his time to do his work. Counter-hits that were a little too much for the combatants. Langan began to shift: indeed, Spring had drawn his claret liberally. Both down, Spring uppermost.

7.—This was a bustling round. Langan stopped well. Counter-hits, and good ones. The stopping on both sides was excellent, and obtained loud applause. "Be ready, my boy," said Belcher, "fight first; he can't hurt you!"—"Walker," replied Tom Cribb; "gammon him to that if you can." Langan followed the advice of his able second, put a tremendous hit under Spring's left ogle, and tried to repeat it, but it was "no go." A pause. Spring planted a facer; Langan got away from another intended for him. The left hand of Spring told well on his opponent's body: he also planted three facers without

* See Life of JEM BURN, Period VI., Chapter VI.　　　　　† Mr. John Jackson.

any return. Counter-hits, of no consequence to any but the receivers; the hero of the black fogle touched Spring's body with his left hand. A stand still. "Keep up your head, Langan." Spring followed his opponent, administering pepper, and Langan's face clareted. Langan endeavoured to put in a heavy blow, but the harlequin step of Spring prevented it. Langan napped two or three hits in succession; in fact, he was quite groggy; nevertheless he fought like a man, was mischievous, and gave Spring a nobber. In closing, Spring could not throw him, when they separated; in closing again, after another struggle, Langan received a topper as he was staggering and going down.— (Great applause. "It won't last long—five to two, and three to one, Spring will win it in a few rounds;" the backers of the Champion were smiling, and said, "It is all right.")

8.—Belcher got his man up very heavily, but on his being placed at the scratch, he showed fight and got away from a hit. However, Spring had decidedly the best of the round, and Langan was thrown. Twenty-six minutes.

9.—This was also a short round, but against the Irish Champion. Spring planted two or three nobbers, and also got his opponent down.

10.—It was evident to every one that Langan up to this time had had the worst of it, and the general opinion was, that he must lose the battle. Spring planted two successive blows, without any return. Langan was getting better, and made an exchange of blows with some effect. Belcher again cried out, "Fight, Jack." In struggling for the throw, Paddy O'Neil sung out, "Give him a back fall, Jack, but don't hurt him;" and, sure enough, Mr. Spring did receive a back fall.

11.—Langan was now fast recovering his second wind and went to work. An exchange of blows; a pause. Langan planted a slight body hit with his left hand. Counter-hits. Langan down, Spring on him.

12.—In the struggle for the throw, Spring was undermost. ("Bravo, Langan!") The head of the Champion had an ugly knock against the lower rail of the stage.

13.—Spring proved himself a most difficult boxer to get at; however, Langan got in a body blow. In closing, both down, Spring uppermost.

14.—Spring getting weak, Langan improving: so said the most experienced judge of boxing belonging to the P.C. Indeed, it is accounted for without difficulty; as a superior fighter Spring ought not to have wrestled so much with his opponent. The strongest man in the world must have felt weakness had he been engaged in such violent pulling, hauling, grappling, and catching hold of each other's hands. This round was little more than a struggle for the throw; Langan undermost.

15.—It was now known to all the ring that the left hand of Spring was gone; indeed, it was swelled and puffed like a blister. Langan planted a left-handed blow, but Spring stopped his right. In closing, the struggle was great, and, as Langan was going down, Spring hit his nob. ("Foul, foul!" It was unintentional on the part of Spring; he was in the act of hitting, and, therefore, it could not be decided wrong.)*

16.—Under all circumstances, Langan was a troublesome customer. The remarks made by some persons were, that he did not fight well, though they were compelled to allow that he was an extraordinary game man. The counter-hits in this round were again well placed; but it was regretted, by several sporting men, to see such numerous struggles. Yet, to their credit be it spoken, neither of the men wished to go down unhandsomely, which accounts for so much wrestling. Both went down together; Langan patted the back of Spring with the utmost good humour, both smiling.

17.—The fine science of Spring was again exhibited in skilfully stopping his opponent; but, in closing, he received a dangerous cross-buttock, which shook him terribly, and his legs rebounded from the ground. (A cheering burst of applause for Langan.)

18.—The manner with which Langan had got round did not look very promising for the backers of Spring. The Irish Champion went resolutely in, and planted two hits. In closing, Spring tried the fibbing system, when Langan broke away. Both combatants in turn retreated from the blows of each other. Both down.

19.—The Champion showed weakness: it would have been singular if he had not. He bobbed his head aside from a tremendous right-handed blow of Langan's, which might have settled the account in favour of the hero of the black fogle; however, he closed the round by throwing Langan cleverly.

20.—Spring stopped several blows, and the Irish Champion was thrown violently on his head; Spring also fell heavily on him. Forty-five minutes had elapsed. ("That fall is a settler: he can't fight above another round or two.")

21.—Spring nobbed his opponent. A severe struggle took place at the corner of the stage, and some fears were expressed that the men might fall through the rails upon the ground. Langan received another heavy fall.

22.—Langan, according to the advice of Belcher, fought first, but his efforts were stopped, and he again went down, Spring uppermost. During the time the Champion was sitting on the knee of his second, he

* So says the reporter. It would, however, be fair, even if intentional, for any man is entitled to hit another "going down," but of course, not when "down."—Ed. PUGILISTICA.

nodded, and gave a smile to his friends, intimating " It was all right."

23.—This was a short round, and Spring fibbed Langan down severely, to all appearance, yet, on being picked up and placed on his second's knee, when asked to have some brandy and water by Belcher, who told Harmer, who was below the stage, to hand it up, Langan said, "Stop a bit, Harry; only keep it cool." The president of the Daffy Club, who was standing close by at the time, observed, "What a strange fellow!"

24.—After three heavy falls in succession, and severe fibbing, Langan came to the scratch as if nothing serious had happened; he contrived to put in a body blow, but was thrown.

25.—Spring, although he had got the lead by his superior science and length, was determined not to give a chance away, and was as cautious as when he first commenced the battle. He retreated from Langan's blows, planted some returns with success, and ultimately Langan was down.

26.—Langan made play, but Spring was too wary. Both down, Spring uppermost.

27.—The Champion was evidently distressed, and his right hand also getting bad. Some exchanges took place; but, in a trifling struggle at the corner of the stage, it appeared to Spring's umpire that Langan went down without a blow, when he observed to Belcher, "Tell your man not to go down without a blow, or I shall notice it." " I assure you, gentlemen," replied Tom, "blows had passed in the round, and it could not be termed going down without a blow, according to the rules of fighting." Blows certainly had passed between the combatants.

28.—Langan walked up to the umpire, and said, "Sir, I did not go down." Time had been called, when Cribb sung out, " Why don't you come to the scratch? what manœuvres are you about, Mr. Belcher?" " I want nothing but fair play," replied Tom; "lick us fairly, and I shall be satisfied." Langan again made play, but was thrown.

29. — Spring planted a heavy facer. ("That's a little one for us, I believe," said Cribb; "our hands are gone, are they?" Laughter.) Langan was thrown heavily.

30.—It was quite clear that Langan could not get the lead, yet he was not to be viewed with indifference; he was still dangerous, as a throw might win the battle. Both down, Spring undermost.

31.—This round, more particularly at this stage of the fight, exalted the character of Langan as one of the gamest of men. Langan planted a body blow, but napped three facers in succession. A pause. Langan received a heavy body blow, seemed exhausted, and fell on his latter end.

32.—This round it was thought would have proved the quietus of Langan. He was thrown heavily, and his head touched the lower rail. (" That's a finisher!" "He'll not come again," were the remarks of the spectators.)

33.—Spring's conduct towards Langan was generous and manly, and deservedly applauded. Langan rushed in and made a blow at his opponent, which Spring parried, then, laying hold of Langan, let him down without punishment.

34. — Langan's determination not only astonished the amateurs, but a little alarmed the backers of Spring. Without an accident it was booked almost to a certainty that Spring must win; still an accident might happen. Langan could not persuade himself that anything alive could master him. His backers were aware of his opinion, and therefore would not oppose his resolution. The Irish Champion had again the worst of it, and went down very much distressed. One hour and seven minutes had elapsed, therefore all the bets that Spring proved the conqueror in an hour were lost.

35.—This was a milling round. Langan would not go away, although hit staggering: he went down as if he would not have been able to come again. (Four to one on Spring.)

36.—This was ditto, with repeated, if not increased, punishment; yet Langan returned, and Spring, with a caution that all his backers must give him credit for, got away when anything like a heavy blow was levelled at him. Langan fell exhausted. (" Take the brave fellow away. Where are his backers?" "Very good, indeed," replied Belcher; "you are not hurt yet, Jack; and Spring's hands are too far gone to hurt you now." " I will not give in," said Langan; " I shall win it.")

37.—Langan fought this round better than any of the spectators could anticipate. He planted a couple of hits; it is true they were not effective, but it showed the fight was not out of him. The Irish Champion fought under the black flag, "death or victory," and went down, out-fought at all points.

38. — Belcher brought his man to the scratch, nay, almost carried him,* when, singular to relate, game-cock like, all his energies appeared to return, and he commenced milling like a hero. Spring planted four blows without any return, and Langan went down.

39.—Langan was again down.

40.—The hero of the black fogle showed fight till he went down quite exhausted.

41.—A short round, but it was surprising to witness the strength exhibited by Langan in the struggle for the throw. Both down, when Spring patted him on the back.

42.—Langan was undermost in this round,

---

* The more humane provisions of the "New Rules," do not allow this conduct on the part of the second. By rule 9, the man must rise from the knee of his bottle-holder and walk unaided to the scratch to meet his opponent.—Ed. PUGILISTICA.

but Spring really had his work to do to place his opponent in that situation.

43.—Langan again undermost, and Spring fell heavily upon him.

44.—Spring planted a facer, but met with a return. In struggling for the throw, Langan took hold of the drawers of Spring, when Cribb and Painter called out "Let go his drawers." Langan immediately relinquished his hold. The Irish Champion was thrown.

45.—Langan hit Spring on the side of his head, and fought well in an exchange of blows. Spring, however, obtained the throw.

46.—It was astonishing, after getting the worst of it in the previous rounds, to witness the resolute manner in which Langan contested this round. He was still dangerous in the exchanges, and, in struggling, both fell upon the stage. Langan undermost.

47.—Langan, on being placed at the scratch, was ready for the attack. In a short time, after struggling, both went down. (The John Bull fighter roared out—"I'm sorry for you, Tom Belcher; you will certainly be 'lagged' if you don't take your man away." "Well done, Josh," replied Belcher, "that comes well from you; but we shall win it; Spring can't hurt a mouse now.") Langan took a little brandy and water.

48.—Spring exhibited weakness, but threw Langan.

49.—Langan still made a fight of it, to the surprise of all. In an exchange of blows, however exhausted the brave boy from Paddy's land appeared to be, Spring used his harlequin step to prevent accidents. In struggling for the throw, both down.

50.—Langan again showed himself ready at the scratch. "My dear boy," said Belcher, "it's all your own if you will but fight first." Langan put in a body blow, and also countered with his opponent, but had the worst of it, and went down.

51.—Seeing is believing; but to the reader who has perused the whole of the above rounds, it must almost appear like romance to state, that Langan held Spring for a short time against the rails to get the throw, till they both went down, and Spring fell on him.

52.—Spring stopped a blow, and also got away from another; ultimately Langan was hit down.

53.—Langan went to work and hit Spring on the nose; but the Champion returned the favour, with interest, by nobbing his brave adversary down. ("Is there anything the matter with that hand, I should like to know? Lord! how Spring did hit him in the middle of the head!" exclaimed Cribb.)

54.—"'Pon my soul, it's no lie!" Langan threw Spring cleverly. Great applause followed this momentary turn. ("He's an extraordinary fellow," said Mr. Jackson; "he is really a very good man.")

55.—Spring again had all the best of this round; but Langan kept fighting till he went down.

56.—This round, it was thought, had settled the business. Langan exchanged several blows, but, in closing, Spring hit up terrifically on the face of his opponent, who went down like a log of wood.

57.—Langan commenced milling, and planted a blow on the side of Spring's head! "Do that again," said Belcher. Langan endeavoured to follow the directions of his master, but the Champion got away. Spring now hit him staggering, repeated the dose, and Langan went down.

58.—This was a good round, considering the protracted period of the battle. Langan returned some blows till he went down.— ("Take him away,"—"He has no chance.")

59.—Langan appeared so exhausted that every round was expected to be the last. He went down from a slight hit, little more than a push.

60.—"Wonders will never cease!" said a cove who had lost a trifle that Langan was licked in forty minutes—"why he has got Spring down again; it's not so safe to the Champion as his friends may think."

61.—Langan was now as groggy as a sailor three sheets in the wind, and a slight blow sent him down. "I never saw such a fellow," said Jack Randall; "he'll fight for a week! He don't know when to leave off."

62.—The distress exhibited by Langan was so great that every time he went down it was thought he could not again toe the scratch. If the spectators did not think Langan dangerous, Spring got away from all his hits, to prevent anything being the matter. Langan was once more sent down.

63.—Langan, still determined to have a shy for the £500, made a hit at Spring, but was shoved, rather than hit, down.

64.—For the last fifteen minutes it was next to an impossibility Spring could lose, yet, contrary to all calculations on the subject, Langan still contested the fight. The hands of Spring were in such an inefficient, not to say painful, state, that he could not hit. Here was the danger, as it was possible that he might be worn out, but his caution and generalship did everything for him. Langan was so distressed that a slight touch on his arm sent him down. A good blow must have put an end to the fight, but Spring could not hit effectively.

65.—Langan, when at the scratch, not only showed fight, but hit Spring on the head; the latter, however, had the best of the round, though Langan got the throw, Spring undermost. ("Where's the brandy?" said Belcher. "Here it is," replied Tom Cribb; "a brave fellow shall not want for anything in my possession." "Bravo!" cried Belcher; "that's friendly, and I won't forget it.")

66.—The chance was decidedly against the Irish Champion; nevertheless, he attempted to be troublesome to his opponent. Spring put in a nobber, and also threw him.

67.—Exchange of blows. A pause. Langan

on the totter, but he planted two slight hits on the Champion's face. Spring followed him up, and gave Langan two blows, one in the body and one in the head, which dropped the hero of the black fogle.

68.—The bravery of Langan was equal to anything ever witnessed in the prize ring. The hands of Spring were in such a swollen state that he could scarcely close them, and most of his blows appeared to be open-handed. Langan was hit down. ("Take him away!" "Do you hear what they say, Jack?" said Belcher. "Yes," replied Langan: "I will not be taken away; I can win it yet.")

69.—In struggling for the throw, Langan's head fell against the rails. Both down.

70.—Langan again napped on the nobbing system, and was sent down. One hour and forty-two minutes had elapsed. (Loud cries of "Take him away!")

71.—The backers of Spring were anxious to have it over; and the spectators in general cried out, on the score of humanity, that Langan ought not to be suffered to fight any more. Colonel O'Neil, the friend and backer of the Irish Champion, assured the umpire that he did not want for humanity; and he was well satisfied in his own mind that, from the tumefied state of Spring's hands, no danger could arise. Langan was fighting for £200 of his own money, therefore he had no right to interfere; he had, previous to the fight, left it in the hands of his skilful second, Belcher, who, he was certain, would not suffer the fight to last longer than was safe to all parties. Langan, after a short round, was sent down.

72.—Langan was brought to the scratch by Belcher, who said, "Fight, my dear boy; Spring can't hurt you." Langan, with undaunted resolution, plunged in to hit his opponent; but, after receiving more punishment, was sent down. (Repeated cries of "Take him away!")

73.—It was now evident to all persons that Langan, while he retained the slightest knowledge of what he was about, would not give in. Spring fibbed Langan as severely as he was able, to put an end to the fight, till he went down. (Here Jack Randall came close to the stage, and said, "Tom Belcher, take him away; he cannot win it now." "He says he will not, Jack, and that he can fight longer," replied Tom Belcher.)

74.—This round was a fine picture of resolution under the most distressing circumstances. Langan, without the slightest shadow of a chance, seemed angry that his limbs would not do their duty; he came again to the scratch, and, with true courage, fought till he was sent down. While sitting on the knee of his second, Cribb thus addressed him: "You are a brave man, Langan!" "A better was never seen in the prize ring,"

rejoined Painter; "but you can't win, Langan; it is no use for you to fight, and it may prove dangerous." "I *will* fight," said Langan; "no one shall take me away."

75.—When time was called, Langan was brought to the scratch, and placed himself in attitude. He attempted to hit, when Spring caught hold of him and again fibbed him. ("Give no chance away now," said Cribb; "you must finish the battle.") Langan went down quite stupid. ("Take him away!" from all parts of the ring.)

76 and last.—Strange to relate, Langan again showed at the scratch; it might be asserted that he fought from instinct. It did not require much punishment, at this period, to send the brave Langan off his legs; and, to the credit of Spring be it recorded, he did his duty towards his backers as a fighting man, and acted so humanely towards an opponent, that, to the end of life, Langan had the highest respect for him as a man. Langan put up his arms in attitude, but they were soon rendered useless, Spring driving him down without giving punishment. When time was called, Langan was insensible to the call, and thus, after a contest of one hour and forty-nine minutes, the hat was thrown up, and Spring was declared the conqueror, amidst the loudest shouts of approbation. Mr. Jackson and Mr. Sant immediately ascended the stage. Mr. Sant congratulated Spring on his victory, but concluded, "If you ever fight again, I will never speak to you any more, Tom; I never saw such bad hands in any battle." Spring replied, "Sir, I never will." He then left the knee of his second, and went up to Langan, and laid hold of his hand. The Irish Champion had not yet recovered, but on opening his eyes, he asked in a faint tone, "Is the battle over?" "Yes," replied Belcher. "Oh dear!" articulated Langan. Spring immediately shook his hand again, and said, "Jack, you and I must be friends to the end of our lives; and anything that is within my power, I will do to serve you. When I see you in town I will give you £10."

REMARKS.—This contest was one of the fairest battles ever witnessed. The principals had twenty-four square feet for their exertions, without the slightest interruption throughout the mill. The seconds and bottle-holders did their duty like men; they remained as fixtures during the whole of the fight, except when the rounds were at an end, and their assistance became necessary.* The umpires were gentlemen—an Englishman for Spring, and an Irishman for Langan—and they both did their duty. They watched every movement of the men, that nothing like foul play should be attempted on either side, and had the satisfaction of feeling there was no difference of opinion

* This is negatived by round thirty-eight of the report: see also the notes. — Ed.
PUGILISTICA.

between them in any instance whatever, and therefore no necessity to call on the referee. Langan was beaten against his will; and the conduct of Belcher deserves the highest praise as a second: he stuck to his man; and we must here observe that his humanity ought not to be called in question. He was anxious that no reports should reach Ireland, or be scattered over England, that he had given in for his man. Langan, previous to the battle, requested, nay, insisted, that neither his bottle-holder nor second should take upon themselves that decision, which, he declared, only rested in his own bosom. They complied with it. After thirty minutes had elapsed, it appeared to be the general opinion of the ring, by the advantages Spring had gained, that the battle would be decided in forty minutes; but at that period Langan recovered, and Spring became weaker, and the best judges declared they did not know what to make of it. The strength of Langan, certainly for several rounds, did not make it decidedly safe for Spring. The superior science of Spring won him the battle; and this confirmed a cele-

brated tactician in the memorable observation that he "always viewed Tom as an artificial fighter—he meant that he had no 'natural' hits belonging to him; and hence always placed him in the highest place on the boxing list." So Tom Spring overcame the defects of nature, and, without what are vulgarly called great "natural" capabilities for fighting, has become the Champion of England. He is the greatest master of the art of self-defence, and, if he could not hit hard himself, almost prevented others from hitting him at all. His stopping in this battle was admirable, and he continually got out of danger by the goodness of his legs. Always cool and collected, he proved himself one of the safest men in the P. R. to back, because he could not be gammoned out of his own mode of milling. Before the company quitted the ground £50 were collected for Langan, which was afterwards increased three-fold. Spring was much bruised by his falls on the stage, and complained of them as his principal inconvenience. He now announced, a second time, his retirement from the ring.

Spring beat all the men he ever fought with in the prize ring; and in the whole of his contests lost but one battle. It is a curious coincidence, that on Whit-Tuesday, 1823, he defeated the formidable Neat, near Andover, and on Whit-Tuesday, 1824, he overcame the brave Langan. Spring, therefore, won three great battles in one twelvemonth, and one thousand pounds into the bargain; for instance—

With Neat	£200
With Langan	300
Ditto	500
	£1,000

On Spring's return to the Swan Hotel, Chichester, he was received by the shouts of the populace all along the road; the ladies waving their handkerchiefs at the windows as he passed along. Langan, so soon as he had recovered a little from the effects of the battle, left the stage amidst loudly expressed approbation: "You are an extraordinary fellow, Langan," "A brave man," etc. The Irish Champion, accompanied by Belcher and his backer, also received great applause on his return to the Dolphin, in Chichester. Spring was immediately put to bed, and bled, and a warm bath prepared for him. His hands were in a bad state, and his face exhibited more punishment than appeared upon the stage, yet he was cheerful, and quite collected. The same kind attention was paid to Langan; and on being asked how he felt himself? he replied, "Very well; I have lost the battle, but it is owing to my want of condition; I am not quite twelve stone; I have been harassed all over the country; I have travelled two hundred and sixty miles within the last two days; I was feverish, and on the road instead of my bed on Saturday night; I wanted rest." After making his man comfortable, Belcher, accompanied by his bottle-holder, and also Colonel O'Neil, in the true spirit of chivalry, all rivalry now being at an end, paid a visit to the bedside of Spring. Here all was friendly, as it should be, and all parties were only anxious for the recovery of both the pugilists. "How is Langan?" said Spring to Belcher. "He is doing well," replied Tom. "I am glad of it," said Spring. "We have had a fair fight, we have been licked, and I am satisfied," observed Belcher. All parties shook hands over the bed of the conqueror. On leaving Spring, Mr. Sant, followed by Tom Cribb and Ned Painter, immediately returned with Colonel O'Neil to the bedside of Langan. Mr. Sant observed, "Well Langan, how do you do—do you know me? You can't see me." "Yes, sir," replied the fallen hero. "I am Spring's backer," said Mr. Sant, "but, nevertheless, your friend." "I am obliged to you, sir," answered Langan; "if it was not for such gentlemen as you in the sporting world, we should have no fights. Indeed, Spring is a smart, clever fellow, and I wish him well." "That is liberal," said Painter; "I am happy to hear one brave man speak well of another." The visitors now retired, and left Langan to repose.

Spring left his bed early in the evening; and his first visit he paid to Langan, at the Dolphin; they met like brave men, and on taking his departure he shook Langan by the hand, leaving ten pounds in it.

The Champion left Chichester at eight o'clock on Wednesday morning, in an open barouche, accompanied by Mr. Sant. He was cheered out of the town by the populace; and, on his entrance into the metropolis, he was also greeted with loud marks of approbation.

We here close the unstained and untarnished career of Tom Spring, as a pugilist; if we wished to point a moral to his brother professors, a better proof that "honesty is the best policy," than the esteem which Spring earned and held throughout his long career, could not be desired. This respect has exhibited itself in several public testimonials, to say nothing of innumerable private marks of respect. Spring, who had been keeping a house, the Booth Hall, in the city of Hereford, on the retirement of Tom Belcher became land-lord of the Castle, in Holborn; and, as the present seems the most fitting opportunity for a brief sketch of this head-quarters of sporting, we shall make no apology for here introducing a brief history of this once noted sporting resort.

The Castle Tavern was first opened as a sporting house about seventy years ago, by the well-known Bob Gregson; and designated, at that period, "Bob's Chop House." (See GREGSON, *ante*.)

The Castle Tavern was viewed as a "finger-post" by his countrymen, as the "Lancashire House;" and considered by them a most eligible situation to give their Champion a call on their visits to the metropolis. It is rather singular that Bob Gregson rose, in the estimation of the sporting world, from defeat; he fought only four battles in the P. R., and lost them all. Indeed, Bob's character as a boxer reminds us of the simile used in the House of Commons, by Charles James Fox, who observed of the fighting Austrian General, Clairfait, who had been engaged in one-and-twenty battles in the cause of his country, that he might be compared to a drum, for he was never heard of but when he was beaten. Just so with Gregson. Nevertheless, the Castle Tavern rose rapidly into note, soon after Bob showed himself the landlord of it.

In mine host's parlour, or little snuggery, behind the bar—considered a sort of *sanctum sanctorum*, a house of lords to the fancy, where commoners never attempted to intrude upon the company—Gregson carried on a roaring trade. "Heavy wet," or anything in the shape of it, except at meal-times, was entirely excluded from this "Repository of Choice Spirits," where Champagne of the best quality was tossed off like ale, Madeira, Claret, Hock, and other choice wines, handed about, while Port and Sherry were the common drink of the snuggery. It might be invidious, if not improper, to mention the names of the visitors who spent an hour or two, on different occasions, in this little spot, famed for sporting, mirth, harmony, and good fellowship; let it suffice, and with truth, to observe, that persons of some consequence in the state were to be seen in it, independent of officers, noblemen, actors, artists, and other men of ability, connected with the "upper ten thousand." John Emery, distinguished as a comedian on the boards of Covent Garden, and a man of immense talent in every point of view, spent many of his leisure hours in "the snuggery." George Kent, the ring reporter, was also eminent here for keeping the game alive. He was of a gay disposition, fond of life in any shape; when perfectly sober one of the most peaceable men in the kingdom, and an excellent companion, but, when he got a little liquor in his noddle, a word and a blow were too often his failings, and which came first doubtful. The late Captain D—, connected with one of the most noble families in the kingdom, and one of the highest fanciers in the sporting world, in consequence of being six feet four inches and a half in height, was likewise a great frequenter of the "Repository of Choice Spirits." Numerous others might be noted, but these three will be sufficient as a sample of tl.e company to be met with in Bob Gregson's snuggery—where there was wit at will, the parties sought out each other to please and be pleased, "Dull Care" could never obtain a seat, and fun to be had at all times. Sporting was the general theme, but not to the exclusion of the topics of the day. Heavy matches were made here; and certainly the period alluded to may be marked as the "Corinthian age of the Fancy."

The sun, for a time, shone brilliantly over this Temple of the Fancy; but poor Bob, like too many of his class, did not make hay while it was in his power. The scene changed, the clouds of misfortune overwhelmed him, and, in 1818, the Lancashire hero was compelled to take a voyage on board his Majesty's "Fleet," not only for the recovery of his health, but to obtain a certificate against future attacks of the enemy. Thus ended the reign of Bob Gregson, at the Castle Tavern, Holborn.

For a few months a sort of stoppage occurred at the Castle; the sporting world was missing, and comparative silence reigned throughout the house, when the sprightly, stylish, well-conducted Tom Belcher, in the summer of 1814 (under the auspices of his sincere friend, and almost father, Mr. John Shelton), appeared in the character of landlord. The house had undergone repairs; the rooms were retouched by the painter; elegance and cleanliness, backed by civility, became the order of the day, and a prime stock of liquors and wines was laid in. Tom's opening dinner was completely successful, and the Fancy immediately rallied round a hero who had nobly contended for victory in thirteen prize battles. Tom was considered the most accomplished boxer and sparrer of the day; and the remembrance, likewise, that he was the brother of the renowned Jem Belcher, were points in themselves of great attraction in the sporting world. The Castle again became one of the most favourite resorts of the Fancy in general.

During the time Tom Belcher was the landlord of the Castle Tavern the famous Daffy Club was started by Mr. James Soares.

During the principal time of Tom's residence at the Castle, the members of the sporting world were in "high feather." Patrons "came out" to give it support. No man knew better how to get up a purse, make a match, or back a man, than Tom Belcher. He was always smart, and exemplarily well dressed, whenever he made his appearance in the ring, upon a race-course, or indeed in any situation before the public. Belcher was a keen observer of society: he measured his way through life, and every step he took turned to good account. He had lots of sporting dinners, numerous gay little suppers, and plenty of matches on the board to excite the attention of the fancy. "The Daffy Club" became very popular in the sporting world, and for a long time was crowded to excess; indeed,

" Fortune seem'd buckled to his back! "

Everything went right; Tom stuck to the Castle—he was always to be found at his post; and the Castle in turn fortified him at all points; and although Tom was prompt at times to lay a heavy bet, prudence was generally at his elbow to prevent him from getting out of his depth. Tom was far from a gambler; the hazard table had no charms for him, and he scarcely ever sported a shilling, except upon a horse-race or a fight. His principal style of betting was, to use his own words, "Blow my dicky, I'll bet a guinea and a goose!" and if he did not like to make a bet, he would observe, " I'll leave it all to the cook!"

Tom Belcher, after fourteen years' residence at the Castle Tavern, was enabled, by his civil conduct, attention to business, and good luck, to retire from the busy world. If Tom did not retire in a "shower of gold," he, nevertheless, put by a good quantity of the "sweeteners of life," to render his retreat to the country safe and pleasant.

At this juncture Tom Spring, who had not only been losing his time amongst his countrymen at the Booth Hall, in the city of Hereford, but, what was worse, his hard-earned money, was determined, when the opportunity offered, to have another "shy" in London: therefore, after several sets-to had taken place between the "two Toms," the match was made, the money posted, and Tom Spring appeared in the character of "mine host," at the Castle Tavern, Holborn.

The subject of this memoir did not enter upon his new capacity without possessing the highest claims to the notice of the patrons of boxing, from his victorious career; and no man, from his general conduct and deportment, was considered by the sporting world so eligible in every point of view to succeed Tom Belcher.

With the close of Spring's life the glories of the Castle were extinguished; but ere we chronicle this event we will pause to notice the testimonials with which his many admiring friends at various times presented him

The first was a vase in silver, entitled " The Hereford Cup," of the weight of fifty ounces. The inscription on this local mark of esteem from the inhabitants of his native place sufficiently explains the motive of its donors. Its presentation and inscription will be found at page 23.

In the following year (1824), after his first battle with Langan, some Manchester sporting men, out of respect to his honour, integrity, and noble maintenance of the English championship against all comers, decided upon their testimonial in the form of a silver vase, of elegant proportions and massive weight. This, called "The Manchester Cup," also decorated Tom's buffet on public and festive occasions. It was thus inscribed:—

"This Cup was presented to
THOMAS WINTER SPRING
By a Party of his Friends in Manchester,
Not only for the Upright and Manly Conduct uniformly displayed by him in the Prize Ring,
But also as a Man,
And as a Sincere Token of the Esteem
In which they hold his Private Character.
Manchester, 12th of April, 1824."

The third and most valuable public testimonial (for Tom had many gifts of snuff-boxes, canes, pencil-cases, etc., from private friends), was known as "The Champion Testimonial," and consisted of a noble tankard in silver, of the capacity of one gallon, or six bottles of wine, with a lining of 450 sovereigns, the balance of a subscription of over £500 raised by the ex-Champion's friends. The tankard, which was executed by Messrs. Hunt and Roskell, is a beautiful work of art, ornamented with chased bands of leaves of the British oak and English rose. The cover was surmounted by a bold acorn, the outer edge having, in raised letters, "THE SPRING TESTIMONIAL." On the shield it bears the inscription:—

"Presented
By Public Subscription to
THOMAS WINTER SPRING,
EX-CHAMPION OF ENGLAND,
In Testimony of the Sincere Respect in which he is held
For his Pure and Honourable Conduct
During his Long and Unblemished Career
In Public and Private Life.
1846."

After an excellent dinner (on Tuesday, May 19, 1846), presided over by the editor of *Bell's Life in London* (Vincent George Dowling, Esq.), the Chairman took occasion thus to allude to the letters of various distant subscribers: "Every letter he had seen bore testimony to the public and private worth of Spring, and spoke of him as a man whose unblemished integrity, benevolence of heart, urbanity of disposition, and unquestionable courage, entitled him to the highest praise. In all and every of these sentiments he concurred. From the first hour he had known him he had watched his conduct, and he could conscientiously say that in his opinion a more honest or a more high-principled man did not exist. But in whatever light he might regard this testimony towards Spring, it had a higher value in his eyes, as being the representative of those sentiments of admiration with which the feelings of honour and honesty were regarded by every class of the community. It was a proof that such qualities were not overlooked, and he only regretted that every pugilist in England could not be assembled in that room to witness the fruits of a career distinguished by these virtues, as it would afford them the best encouragement to persevere in the same course, and probably elicit similar marks of favour." After some further laudatory remarks, the Chairman presented the testimonial, with an earnest belief that it would be received with becoming sentiments of gratitude, and in the hope that Spring might long live to see it grace his table, in addition to his other cups, as a sterling representative of his merits, and of the sincere respect to which he had entitled himself.

After a short pause Spring rose, almost overpowered by his feelings. He knew not, he said, how to express in words the overflowing sentiments of gratitude with which his heart was bursting. He had certainly endeavoured through life to steer the straightforward and honest course, and when he looked inwardly he could not charge himself with ever having given ground for shaking the confidence of his friends (hear). Still he could not persuade himself he was better than other men, or that he had entitled himself to this magnificent token of public favour—for public it was, arising as it had from the spontaneous contribution of a large and mixed portion of his countrymen— to whom he could not say how sincerely he was obliged, or how deeply sensible he was of their munificent liberality. When he received the cup presented to him at Manchester, and subsequently that given to him by his friends in Herefordshire, both of which were then on the table, and when to these were added other tokens, less in value, but not less dearly appreciated, he could not but feel proud; but when these were followed by the testimonial now presented to him, he candidly confessed the fondest wishes of his ambition had been realised. He should indeed cherish it with a becoming sense of its intrinsic and representative value, and would, in the closing years of his life, look back to this day as one of surpassing interest to himself and to all those who were dear to him. Here Spring could no longer sustain his self-possession, and placing his hand on the tankard with deep emotion, he concluded by saying, "I can only thank you, and all else I might say I must leave to your own hearts to imagine." (Loud and continued cheers.)

Caunt, Ned Neale, Frank Redmond, Johnny Broome, Owen Swift, Dan Dismore, Joe Phelps, etc., were among the pugilists present; and Mr. Sant, one of the earliest backers and a constant friend of Tom Spring, after a warm eulogy on mine host, proposed "The Subscribers to the Testimonial."

TOM SPRING'S MONUMENT IN

From this period to that of his death, on the 20th of August, 1851, Spring dispensed the hospitalities of the Castle, never losing a friend, except by the hand of death.   In his later days, family difficulties, and too great a confidence in self-styled friends, who induced him to execute turf commissions, and when the thing went wrong were absentees or defaulters, added to his embarrassments.   Still he held on, universally respected by all who knew him until his 56th year, when pale death struck him down somewhat suddenly, the blow being dealt through a heart disease of some years' standing. His funeral took place with becoming solemnity on Sunday, the 25th of August, 1851, his remains being followed by several mourning coaches and other carriages to the grave.   In the first carriage were his only surviving son, Melchior Winter; Mr. Price, of Hereford, his solicitor and executor; his firm friend, Mr. Elbam, of Piccadilly; and the writer of these pages. Poor Tom lies buried in the Norwood Cemetery, beneath the monument which we have here engraved.   "Peace be to his manes!"   Few men who have led a public life have less reason to dread the last call of "Time," than Thomas Winter Spring.

CHAPTER II.

JOHN LANGAN, THE IRISH CHAMPION—1819–1824.

JOHN LANGAN, one of the bravest of pugilists—and whose fortune it was to find his ambition foiled when struggling to the topmost round of the ladder, by the superior skill of Tom Spring, the English Champion—well deserves a chapter in the History of Pugilism. As the author of "Boxiana" was not only the countryman but the personal friend of Langan, we shall accept, with a few alterations and additions, the biography of "the Irish Champion," as we find it in that work; and for the further reason that it is, in its earlier pages, a lively and amusing specimen of "the historian's" apocrypha.

John Langan was born in the month of May, 1798, at Clondalton, in the county Kildare. Ireland was then in the full blaze of insurrection, and Pierce Egan tells us "that young Paddy had scarcely become one of his father's family five minutes, before his ears were saluted by a tremendous fire of musketry from a party of United Men who were attempting to get possession of a powder-mill situated within fifty yards of his daddy's mud edifice. Mrs. Judy O'Shaughnessy, his nurse, had her own way of explaining this as rather ominous that little Jack Langan was born to make a noise in the world. The early years of little Jack passed as is usual with lively urchins, until his father left Clondalton, and settled in the suburbs of Dublin, at a place called Ballybough Lane, adjoining that beautiful spot of freedom known as Mud Island.

Langan had always a taste for milling; and his turns up at school (?), says Pierce Egan, would fill a moderate volume. In company with two of his school-fellows, he discovered a bird's nest; but as the birds were not fledged, it was unanimously agreed to leave it till a more convenient opportunity. The boys played truant one afternoon, and went in search of the bird's nest, and the eldest lad claimed for his share the top bird, which is generally considered the cock. Langan protested against such choice, and a battle decided

JOHN LANGAN (IRISH CHAMPION).

it; but, after a fight of an hour's duration, in which Jack proved the conqueror, the only recompense he got for the scratches and loss of claret, was, upon examining the nest, that the birds had fled during the row.

On the borders of the Dublin canal, when only thirteen years of age, he thought himself man enough to enter the lists with a strong youth of eighteen years of age; in fact, he stood forward as champion for his friend, who had received a blow from the youth. In forty-five minutes, against weight, length, and height, Langan proved the conqueror.

Shortly after the above battle, Jack persuaded his father to let him go to sea, and, ultimately, he was bound apprentice to Messrs. Dunn and Harris, of Dublin. Langan sailed for Oporto and Lisbon, in the New Active, Captain M'Carthy. In Bull Bay, Lisbon, in spite of the stiletto used by two Portuguese, he made the cowards run before him; but Jack received a scratch or two on his body from their knives. His courage, however, did not desert him for an instant, though he was attacked in such an assassin-like manner.

On Langan's passage home, he severely drubbed one of his messmates, of the name of Dunn, who had taken liberties with the fame of Ould Ireland. "Erin-go-Bragh!" said Jack Langan, after giving Mr. Dunn a receipt in full of all demands, then retired to his berth to take his grog, singing—

> " St. Patrick is still our protector,
>   He made us an Island of Saints,
> Drove out snakes and toads like a Hector,
>   And ne'er shut his eyes to complaints:
> Then if you would live and be frisky,
>   And never die when you're in bed,
> Arrah! come to Ireland and tipple the whiskey,
>   And live ten years after you're dead!!!"

Like all new schemes and occupations, a sailor's life, for a short period, was highly relished by Langan; some terrible gales of wind, however, and a tremendous storm or two, on his return to Ireland, showed the other side of the picture so emphatically, that Jack spoke to his ould dad to get his indentures from the captain, as he had a great wish to try his fortune on shore. Old Langan accomplished this circumstance for his darling boy; and Jack was bound apprentice to a sawyer. Langan soon became a proficient in his business, and arrived at the climax of his trade, a top-sawyer; but he was anxious to get a cut above the pit, and turn his hand to another account. Although but fifteen years of age, our hero had a taste for milling; he was fond of fighting, but not quarrelling; yet he was always ready to punish impudence and insolence, whenever rude fellows crossed his path.

> " From little causes great events arise!"

Throwing snow-balls at each other, near the Dublin canal, produced a most determined mill between Jemmy Lyons, a Hibernian pugilist, and Jack Langan. It was a cool situation for a fight, but warm work while it lasted; and Jack's blows were put in so fast and hard upon the face of Paddy Lyons, for the space of twenty-five minutes, that he cried out "Enough! too much!" This turn-up was without any precision as to time: it was pelt away, till Jemmy was carried off the ground. "By St. Patrick," said Jack Riley (the friend of Lyons) to Langan, "you shall get a good bating for all your luck this time; and if you will meet me in Cannon's Quarry, I will soon make you cry quarter." "And is it to me you mane, Misther Riley, that is to ask you for quarter? Well, come on, and we'll soon see all about it," replied Langan. Riley was the hero of the Mud-Island, in the milling way. In Cannon's Quarry, Langan so served out Riley, that when he was taken home to Mud Island he was so spoilt as to be scarcely recognisable by his most intimate acquaintance.

Langan was now viewed as a "striking" object in Mud-Island; Jack, however, was too good-humoured a fellow to be anything like a terror to the peaceable inhabitants of that happy spot. Pat Macguire had a great desire to take the shine out of Langan, and boasted that he would be "number one" in the Island. "So you shall," replied our hero, "if you can." But poor Pat Macguire reckoned his chickens before they were hatched; for, in the short space of ten minutes, his peepers were darkened, his nose swelled up to the size of two, his ivories dancing, and the whole of his face the picture of agony and distress. Soon after poor Pat was undressed and put to bed, he exclaimed, "By J——s, those blows I got from Jack Langan are more like the kicks of a horse than the thumps of a man."

Michael Angin, who had some notions of boxing, was completely satisfied in a single round with Langan, at Clontarf. A tremendous nobber put Mike's head in chancery. On returning to his mother's cabin, she saluted him with "Arragh! Mike, my jewel, what have you got in your mouth, that makes you look so ugly?" "It's Jack Langan's fist, mother. I am almost choked," replied Angin, hoarse as a raven. "Take it out, my darlint," said his parent; "sure it is no good to anybody!"

Robert Titford, Dan Henigan (brother of the boxer of that name), and Jem Turner, were, in succession, disposed of with apparent ease by our hero. In short, he had no competitor amongst the boys, and therefore we will take leave of his early turn-ups, for battles of a more manly description.

Langan had a desperate battle with a man of the name of Hemet: the latter person struck the father of our hero. "I will make you repent your conduct, you blackguard," said Jack. "A boy like you?" replied Hemet;

"I'll kick your breech, if you give me any more of your prate." Young Langan, as we have before mentioned, was fond of milling; but in defence of his father felt doubly armed; and in the course of thirty minutes Hemet was glad to acknowledge the boy was his master.

One Savage, a man weighing about eleven stone, and twenty-one years of age, had behaved unhandsomely to Jack three years previously to the period when the following circumstances transpired. Langan, although not more than sixteen years old, entertained an opinion that he was able to take the field against Savage, and challenged him without hesitation. Savage, with the utmost contempt, accepted the challenge, and agreed to fight on the banks of the Dublin canal. A few friends on each side attended to see fair play. The battle was long, and well-contested; but night coming on, as neither of the combatants would agree to surrender, it was deemed expedient according to the laws of honour, to fight it out, and therefore candles* were introduced. But, before the glims required topping, Langan floored his opponent, by a wisty-castor upon the jugular, and Savage was carried home amidst the lamentations of his friends, and the regret of Langan. Savage was washed and laid out by his lamenting associates, and everything comfortable prepared to "wake" him. The body was surrounded by about forty old women and men, smoking and drinking, and bewailing his loss, interspersed every now and then with some prime fil-la-loos. "Arrah! my dear Jemmy, why did you put your head in the way of Jack Langan's fist?"

In the midst of this beautiful solemnity, to the great surprise and confusion of the company present, Mr. Savage waked himself, but, before he could enquire into the particulars how he came into this strange situation, the whole assembly brushed off with terror, leaving the corpse to explain his position in the best manner he could.

Good as Langan had proved himself in the above contest, Paddy Moran challenged our hero. The latter proposed to fight Jack upon the real principles of milling—for love, glory, and honour. Blunt was out of the question, for the best of all reasons—Moran had nothing in the funds. "You shall be accommodated," replied Langan; "it shall be for love, glory, and honour." It was a severe battle for fourteen rounds, and although Moran was compelled to submit to defeat, he proved himself a brave man, and Langan's nob received some ugly visitations during the fight.

Moran's brother called Langan out to meet him in the field of battle, the following week. Our hero, fresh as a daisy, and gay as a lark, accepted the

* This reminds us of a duel which was fought at Liverpool some years since by the light of lamps, between a volunteer colonel and the aide-de-camp of a royal duke.

challenge with the utmost alacrity and when "Time" was called, proved himself ready.   Moran's brother likewise proved a man of excellent courage, but he had nothing like so good a chance as his relative.   After a few rounds, Langan became the conqueror, without a mark the worse for his encounter. Norman, a pugilist distinguished in Dublin, seconded Moran's brother against Jack; but his conduct appearing questionable, Langan sent a challenge to Norman.

Norman accepted the challenge, but requested to name Sunday for the time of combat.   To this request Langan positively refused; upon any other day, he said he should be happy to wait upon his opponent.   After some little "blowing up" on the subject, it was agreed that the battle should take place on the following Thursday.   Norman, who was a deep covey, and wishing to turn everything to a good account in which he was engaged, gave out the mill would take place on the Sunday.   He was a proprietor of jaunting cars, and every one of his vehicles was engaged for the fight.   Some hundreds of the Fancy were completely hoaxed by being collected together within a short distance of Old Langan's cottage.   Young Jack did not make his appearance, to the astonishment of the spectators; when Norman cut a great bounce, and, offered to put down twenty pounds to back himself—well knowing Langan would not be present; expressing his surprise at the absence of Langan, who, he told the crowd, had made a promise to meet him.   The news was soon brought to Jack of the trick played off by Norman.   He instantly started off to the public-house, where Norman was swallowing the whiskey like water; rejoicing how he had done the flats that day.   Langan, with more courage than prudence, without hesitation, told Norman he had conducted himself like a blackguard.   Norman, surrounded by his father, brothers, and friends, fell upon Langan before he was scarcely withinside the door, and, with the aid of whips, sticks, etc., so punished him that if a few of his supporters had not rushed in, Langan might have been found as "dead as door nail."   Jack was picked up insensible, taken home, and put to bed.

Thursday, the day appointed for the mill, drew on rapidly, when our hero sent to Norman, trusting that he would not fail in being true to his time. This Langan did, against the advice of his friends.   Jack could hardly lift his right hand to his head, from a blow he had received among the mob of unmanly fellows, in the interest of Norman, nevertheless he met his man on the North Strand, near Clontarf.   The car-keeper was seconded by Pat Halton and Cummings; and Langan by two tight boys belonging to the "Island of Mud."   The battle lasted above an hour, because Langan could not punish Norman with his right, but, even in this crippled state he had so much the best of the fight, that Norman's friends, who were by far the most numerous, seeing that he must lose, rushed in, separated the combatants, saved their blunt, and put an end to the mill. Langan was exceedingly vexed that he was prevented from dressing his antagonist as he deserved. In a few days after this affair, about five o'clock in the morning, Jack was roused from his bed by a violent knocking at the door. Between sleeping and waking, with peepers neither open nor shut, he came down in his shirt to see what was the matter. On opening the door, Jack believed he was dreaming, for, strange to relate, he beheld Norman stripped, and in a fighting attitude. "By J——s," said Norman, "I have been uneasy all night. I could not sleep, Jack, so I thought you and I could amuse ourselves very agreeably; besides having the day before us." "Is it a day you said?" replied Langan; "by the Saint of Ould Ireland, I'll settle your impertinence in a few minutes; before I return to roost and finish my rest, I'll pay you, Misther Norman, for calling me up." Langan ran over to the stream opposite his father's cabin, and washed his face. "Now," said he, "I'm ready; take care of yourself." The novelty of this battle was, that no umpires, bottle-holders, nor seconds on either side, were engaged. In the short space of four rounds, it was all over. Norman napt it in such first-rate style, that he laid on the ground like a calf, so completely satisfied, that he never requested a third battle. Langan at that period did not weigh more than ten stone three pounds,* while Norman weighed thirteen stone seven pounds.

It was impossible for Langan to remain idle with such a reputation, as some one or other was continually offering himself to his notice. Slantlea, a hardy fellow, offered his services to Jack, which were accepted without a single murmur. But to ensure success, the night before the battle, Langan was introduced by a friend to the late Sir Daniel Donnelly. The advice of the Irish (whiskey-punch) Champion was asked as to the best mode of training. "Is it training you mane?" replied Sir Dan, with a smile upon his comical mug; "by the okey, I never troubled myself much about that training, d'ye see, which the fellows in the Long-town make so much bother about. But, nevertheless, I will give my opinion as to what I think necessary to be done upon such occasions. First of all, you must take off your shirt, Jack Langan, then walk up and down the room briskly, and hit well out with both hands, as if you intended giving your opponent a snoozing without asking for his night-cap. Jump backwards and forwards one hundred times at least; and then to find out if the wind is good, for being out of breath in fighting, my

---

* This is most unlikely; Langan was, we should say, never under eleven stone seven pounds to ten pounds from the time he was a grown man.—Ed. PUGILISTICA.

boy, is not a very comfortable thing for a distressed man. Now, Jack," says Sir Dan, it being then about twelve o'clock at night, "you must go home directly, and drink half a gallon of the sourest butter-milk you can get, and then go to bed. At five o'clock, not a minute after five o'clock in the morning, you must get up, and run three or four miles, and at every mile you must swig, not whiskey, by J——s, but a quart of spring water. Mind, now Langan, do as I tell you." Jack thanked Sir Daniel for his friendly advice, and started off to procure the butter-milk; but felt extremely mortified after knocking up all the dairymen in the neighbourhood, that he was not able to buy more than three pints. At five o'clock in the morning, although Langan had scarcely had an hour or two of rest, he jumped out of bed to finish his training. To make up for the deficiency of butter-milk, our hero drank a greater proportion of water. The time appointed for the fight to take place was six o'clock; but Jack, in his eagerness to train, was nearly half an hour behind his time. His antagonist was upon leaving the ground, when Langan mounted the brow of a hill, in sight of the ring, quite out of breath, and dripping with perspiration, roared out as loud as he was able, "Don't go yet, man, I'll be wid you in a jiffy!" The ring was again formed, and Langan. hot as fire, stripped for action cool as a cucumber.

Slantlea began well: he took the lead, gave Langan several clumsy thumps, and had decidedly the best of the Irish Champion for the first four rounds. He sent Langan down three times by nobbing hits; and the friends of the former laughed heartily at the idea of his paying off Slantlea for waiting for him. "You have got your master now, Jack, before you." "Be aisy," replied Langan; "I have trained by the advice of Dan Donnelly; I'm sure I'll bate any opponent; only look, I'm just going to begin!" and letting fly his left hand in full force upon Slantlea's head, the latter fell as if he had been shot. Poor Slantlea never recovered from the effects of this blow; but he proved himself a game man for thirteen rounds, when he received a finisher. It was over in thirty-five minutes.

A porter of the name of Dalton, employed at the Irish Custom-house—a Josh. Hudson in nature, but so fond of milling that hardly a fellow round the Custom-house dared look at him—challenged Langan. "By the powers of Moll Kelly," said Dalton, "he shall find he will have something more to do in bating me than he had with Slantlea." The battle took place in Gloucester-fields. Dalton pelted away like a bull-dog for four rounds, but Langan put an end to his ferocity in the course of three more. At the expiration of twenty-five minutes Dalton was rendered as harmless as a mouse.

Pat Halton, at this period, was called "Donnelly's boy;" in fact, he was the avowed pupil of the late Irish Knight of the Sod. Langan and Halton met at Donnelly's house, and a match was made between them, to fight at Ballinden-Scorney, in the county of Wicklow. On the day appointed, a great muster of the Fancy took place; but the multitude was compelled to separate by the horse-police, and to cross the water to form a new ring. During the interregnum, Halton went into a public house, kept by one Maguire, and took a glass of liquor. When he was called out to meet Langan, he complained that the liquor he had drunk was bad, and had made him so unwell that he was not able to fight. Langan, of course, claimed the money, but the stake-holder would not part with it. However, by way of some compensation to our hero, the subscription money, £19, which had been collected from the spectators for the privilege of the inner ring, was given to him. This disappointment produced "lots of grumbling," until a new match was made. Langan full of gaiety, fond of company, and much caressed by his friends, lived freely till his money was nearly gone, when he was called upon once more to enter the ring with Halton. Jack had not above a day to prepare himself, while it was said that Halton had been training upon the sly, at Bray. "Devil may care," replied Langan, when he was told of it; "I am ready, even without butter-milk, this time."* On the Curragh of Kildare this battle took place. It is but fair to state, that the mill between Langan and Halton has been differently reported; but we are credibly informed that the following account is a correct outline:—Coady and Norman were the seconds for Halton, and Grace and a countryman for Langan. It was for £50 a-side. The first five rounds were manfully contested on both sides; but upon Halton being floored by a tremendous blow on his head, he became very shy afterwards, and did not like to meet his man; he kept retreating, and getting down in the best manner he could. Upwards of sixty minutes had elapsed, and it rained all the time; Halton went down from a flooring hit, and could not come to the scratch when time was called. This created a disturbance, the ring was in disorder, and when Halton came to, he said he was not licked. The backers of Langan insisted upon the money being given up; but Donnelly, whose word was law at that time, asserted that his boy had not lost the battle, and no individual being found on the ground to contradict or dispute the assertion of that mighty chief, the parties separated very much dissatisfied at the non-decision of the contest!

A short time afterwards, Langan met with Donnelly at the Cockpit, and

* This sort of balderdash abounds in Pierce Egan's (or rather, we suspect, Tom Reynolds') Sketches of Irish Boxers in "Boxiana." We let it stand here as something to provoke a smile.—Ed. PUGILISTICA.

remonstrated with him on the impropriety of his conduct, in being the cause of withholding the stakes from our hero. Some high words passed between them, when Langan, with more courage than prudence, thus addressed the chief of Ireland—"I know, Dan;—no, I do not know, Dan, neither—but I think, you could bate me; yet I will hold you a wager, that you do not lick me in half an hour, and I will have a turn-up with you directly in the Cock-pit." Donnelly did not appear inclined for a mill; and, after considerable chaffing about the merits of the battle, Langan received the money.

Our hero was now an object of envy in Dublin. Carney, a boat-builder, a fine strapping fellow, and a milling cove into the bargain, challenged Jack Langan for £50 a-side. It was accepted without delay, and at a place called Saggert, in the county of Wicklow, they met to decide which was the best man. Donnelly was present. Langan had for his seconds Plunket and Malone. While they were beating out the ring, Langan employed himself by using a pickaxe, digging out the scratch. Carney asked Malone, "What Jack was doing?" "Doing, man," replied Malone; "don't you know? Why Langan is one of the most industrious fellows alive; he not only manes to bate you, but afterwards to bury you: he digs graves for all the men that he fights with!" Carney turned pale at the recital; his knees trembled, and he seemed frightened almost out of his wits. His second, however, cheered him up a little, by telling Carney not to mind such trash.* Carney mustered up courage, and commenced the battle well, and with a terrifying blow made Langan kiss his mother earth. A louder fil-la-loo from Carney's party was never heard at any fight, and he tried to repeat the dose in the second round, but Langan was too clever—he made a tie of it with his opponent, and Carney found himself at full length upon the turf. In the third round Langan put in such a teazer, in the middle of his adversary's nob, that his eyes rolled about with astonishment, and he put up his hand to feel if his head had not taken flight from his shoulders, as he lay prostrate on the ground. This blow put an end to the fight; and Cummins, a potato factor, and second to Carney, fell foul of Plunket, as a signal for a riot. The ring was broken, and Langan cruelly treated. Twenty thousand persons were present. By this stratagem Langan did not get a farthing for the battle, which ended in a most terrible uproar.

Langan challenged Cummins for his foul conduct, although the potato merchant weighed fifteen stone. The latter, in answer, said he would not disgrace himself by fighting in a public ring. In the course of a month

---

* The reader should also take the advice of Carney's second, and "not mind such trash."
—Ed, PUGILISTICA.

Langan went to Palmerston Fair, to buy a horse for his father, when he accidentally met with Cummins, who had several fellows with him. The potato factor observed to Langan, " You had the impudence some time ago to challenge me (then giving Langan a blow); there, take that for your prate." " Well," replied Jack, " I did; and only come out and let us have fair play, and I will give you what you deserve in a few minutes." Langan and Cummins immediately repaired to the outside of the fair, and, although Langan was alone, in the course of ten rounds he punished Paddy Cummins so severely that he could not forget for six months he had been well thrashed at Palmerston Fair. We now come to the first authenticated combat of Jack Langan.

Owen M'Gowran, a native of the fighting locality of Donnybrook, and a boxer of considerable note, was matched against Langan, for 100 guineas a-side. The contest came off on Wednesday, May 29, 1819, on the Curragh of Kildare.

The crowd assembled was immense : vehicles of every kind were put in requisition, and by twelve o'clock the Curragh exhibited as motley a concourse as could be imagined. The country boys from the adjacent counties, Wicklow and Kildare, who love a bit of sport of this kind as well as the best of the fancy, assembled in great numbers, and all repaired to take their places at that natural and beautiful amphitheatre, known by the name of " Belcher's Valley."* In the centre flat, surrounded entirely by rising hills, a twenty-four feet ring was erected, well corded in—the amateurs paying 5s. for front seats—while the uplands were covered with spectators. About twenty-five minutes before one o'clock Langan entered the ring, attended by his second, Halton, with Norman as his bottle-holder; immediately after, Owen M'Gowran, attended by Kearney as his second, with his bottle-holder, advanced to the scene of action. The combatants stripped, both apparently in good condition; they shook hands with the greatest cordiality, and at eighteen minutes before one o'clock the fight commenced, at minute time. Betting five to four on Langan, the favourite.

THE FIGHT.

Round 1.—The first round commenced with cautious sparring, each man waiting for his adversary ; both made play right and left, then closed, and, after some hugging, both fell, M'Gowran under. (Betting rising in favour of Langan.)

2.—Each advanced cautiously to meet his adversary, warily sparring ; at last Langan made a feint, which gave him an opening, and he hit M'Gowran a chopper over his right eye, which drew first blood. This blow had a great effect throughout the fight.

* The place where Tom Belcher defeated Dogherty, and which has ever since been called after the former celebrated pugilist. See BELCHER (TOM), vol. i., p. 160.

They closed and fell together. (Four to one on Langan.)

3.—The combatants came up with much caution, and sparred à *la distance*. Some smart hitting took place, but not severe; the hits were followed up until they closed and fell, Langan under.

4.—Much sparring, counter-hits, but no great punishment. M'Gowran staggered and fell.

5.—Similar fighting. M'Gowran grassed, but not by a clean knock-down.

6.—Like the two former at the beginning. Both closed and fell, Langan under. (Bets still the same.)

7.—This might be said to have commenced the fight in earnest; both came up determined, and desperate hard hitting took place. Each stood well up, and received and paid in prime style—no flinching. After very severe hitting, they closed and both fell together.

8.—Both went in, showing much pluck, stood fairly up, and fought hard. Langan grassed his man again, although he seemed to have got much the worst of the hitting. (Bets even.)

9.—Both determined milled away rapidly, and there was good in-fighting. They closed with equal advantage, and both went down together.

10.—The combatants seemed cautious from the effects of the last round, and made much play, hitting wide. At last they closed more lovingly, when Langan was hit down, but not cleverly. (Cries of "Owen for ever!" from the surrounding heights.)

11.—Very severe fighting, at the close of which M'Gowran was hit down.

12.—A desperate rally commenced, and any science that either had heretofore shown was here out of the question: they stood close in, and hit as hard as they could; at last they clenched. Both fell, M'Gowran under.

13.—Both came up to the scratch more cautiously, making play, the effects of the last round being visible on both. Some counter-hitting, but weak. The men parted, but neither down.

14.—Owen placed a tremendous blow on Langan's left side. The latter grunted; and, in a close, both fell, Langan under. (Loud cheering. Betting changed in favour of M'Gowran.)

15.—Some severe fighting, which ended in M'Gowran's falling. (Betting again even.)

16.—Good play on both sides: closed and parted; set-to again; much fighting, chiefly body blows. Langan hit over the ropes.

17.—Langan stood to his man with spirit, and planted a severe facer, which uncorked the claret from M'Gowran's nose. Both down, M'Gowran under.

18.—Both very queer in the bellows; closed and parted; came up again—a desperate rally; parted again; time counted.

19.—Both came up refreshed, and made play; desperate fighting. Langan hit over the ropes, and grassed the third time. ("Huzza for Paddy M'Gowran.")

From the twentieth to twenty-sixth round similar fighting. Both appeared much exhausted, and little science displayed.

27.—Much hard hitting. Langan hit over his adversary's right eye, as in the second round; M'Gowran's claret puzzling him, he fell much exhausted.

The combatants fought to the thirty-fifth round, during which time M'Gowran was much punished. He came in time to the thirty-sixth round, but finding that he had so thorough-bred a customer to deal with, gave up in a manly style. The fight lasted an hour and forty-seven minutes.

Langan, by his conquest over M'Gowran, was placed at the top of the tree, in Dublin, as a pugilist. He threw down the glove to all Ireland, but no boxer thought it would fit him. The gauntlet, therefore, remained untouched, and Langan was hailed as Champion by the warm-hearted boys of the sod. His friends, however, wished him to have a shy in the London Ring; but, while he was undecided as to his future steps, a larger field presented itself for the exertions of our hero.

Colonel Mead was raising a regiment in Dublin, to join the Independents in South America, during which time the Colonel became acquainted with Langan, and he roused in his breast so strong a sympathy for the American sons of liberty, that Langan resolved to give his bunch of fives a holiday for a short period, and to take up the cause of the Independents with his sword. Jack sailed from Liverpool, with that ill-fated expedition, in the Charlotte Gambier brig, in company with another vessel, named La Force. Langan, being a smart, lively fellow, was made a serjeant, as an earnest of his patron's future intentions. During the voyage, the privations which the crew endured were extremely severe; but by the really patriotically inclined adventurer they were borne without a murmur, while those individuals who embarked to obtain wealth by their speculation—the thoughts of the gold and silver mines, those precious metals, which their minds had flattered them might be had for carrying away—pursued their voyage without grumbling, in hopes that they would be paid for their troubles at last. Indeed, so strongly did the accumulation of riches operate upon some of their feelings, that several of the crew employed themselves in making canvass bags, out of old sail-cloth, to hold the dollars and doubloons.

The first place this expedition touched at was St. Michael's. Colonel Mead, in a conversation with the British Consul, mentioned Langan as a pugilist; when the latter gentleman expressed a wish to witness an exhibition of sparring. Langan immediately complied with the request of the British Consul, and on board of the Charlotte Gambier some sets-to occurred. The superiority of Langan was so great, in point of scientific movements, over the hardy and brave sailors, that he disposed of five or six in the style of an auctioneer knocking down a lot of sundries. From the Azores they sailed to Tobago. In this island Langan's brother died, who once belonged to Admiral Nelson's ship, the Victory. The brother of Langan was on board when the gallant Admiral died at Aboukir Bay.*

The expedition then made for the island of St. Marguerite, which was made the depôt, but more correctly speaking, the grave of the European troops. Landed at St. Marguerite, the anticipation of wealth and glory vanished, and the truth presented itself. Owing to the state of starvation, the badness of the food, and the unwholesomeness of the climate, the men, one after the other, sunk into the grave. Langan, with a constitution unbroken, defied all the horrors by which he was surrounded, and never enjoyed a better state of health. He was always foremost in giving assistance to his sick comrades, and never complained of being unwell for a single day. To describe the sufferings of this wretched, ill-fated band, is impossible; the officers did not experience any kinder treatment than the men. It was nothing uncommon to meet with superior officers, with scarcely any covering upon their backs, ragged as beggars, an old blanket thrown across their emaciated frames, with holes made to admit their head and arms.

* Our friend the historian of "Boxiana," here makes a sad mess of it. The Victory was not at Aboukir Bay at all; Nelson's ship at the battle of the Nile (Aboukir) was the Vanguard. Every schoolboy knows the hero died off the coast of Spain, about sixty miles west of Cadiz, October 21 1805, after the "crowning victory" off Cape Trafalgar.—Ed. PUGILISTICA.

The proverb says that "hunger will force its way through stone walls."
Langan, who had been without food for a considerable time, in company with
Captain Collins and Major Brian, were compelled to compromise their feelings, and went seven miles up the country one night to pay their respects to
an inviting pig. The residence of this four-footed beauty had been marked
down in the course of the day, and the spot was soon recognised in the dark.
Our hero, who did not want for science in flooring an opponent, was quite at
a loss to quiet a pig: coaxing proved fruitless, and the pig made so much
noise that its owner was instantly alarmed for the safety of his inmate, and a
party sallied out well armed to shoot the abductors. Langan, at this juncture,
had got hold of the pig's leg by way of a parley; but his companions catching a glimpse of the farmers, who were approaching in battle array, and
being unarmed, made their escape. Running away from the scene of action
was so contrary to the feelings of our hero, that he hesitated for a moment
whether he should show fight or bolt; but ten to one being rather too much
odds for Jack, he plunged into the nearest thicket and laid himself down.
In this situation he waited their approach, and heard his pursuers thrust
their rifles, with a sword affixed to the end, into every bush and thicket
which they supposed able to conceal a man. When Langan's pursuers
approached the place where he had hid himself, they thrust the rifle, with
the sword, into the thicket several times without doing him the slightest
injury; but the last push wounded Langan in the leg. His game was put
to the test. To cry out would have cost him his life; silence, therefore, was
his only security. The armed band now retired, concluding the borrowers of
the pigs had made good their retreat. When the coast was clear, Langan
hobbled from his place of concealment, and joined his companions in safety.

It ought to have been mentioned, that soon after Langan's arrival at
St. Marguerite, Colonel Mead mentioned his prowess in the milling line to
Admiral Bryan, who had a *penchant* for fistic exercises. The admiral's boatswain, Jack Power, bore a high character for his thumping qualities, and was
anxious to have a trial of skill with our hero. The boatswain waited upon
Langan with proposals for a match; he was received by the latter with
a hearty welcome, and the match made without delay. Three days only
were allowed for training; at the expiration of which a proper place was
selected for the mill, and a tolerably good ring made, although not so tight
and compact as the Commissary-general of England, Bill Gibbons, might have
produced. At the coolest period of the day, the combatants, attended by
their respective friends, appeared; the "legion" of course attended to have
a peep at the triumph of their countryman. For the first five rounds the

boatswain took the lead: his constitution was excellent, and his shipmates backed him to win. Jack was floored several times, and napt lots of punishment, but his pluck never deserted him; his superior science enabled him to get out of trouble, and his goodness upon his legs ultimately decided the battle in his favour. The natives appeared highly pleased with the manly exhibition; and it is to be sincerely wished that they had also profited by such a display of true courage over the stiletto and knife, those treacherous weapons being generally used among the natives, the legitimate use of the bunch of fives being unknown to them. This conquest tended to increase Langan's popularity, and also to establish his character as an out-and-outer among the islanders.

At this period Langan's rank was Quarter-master Sergeant; promotion had been promised to him on the first opportunity, but in consequence of the gross mismanagement of the funds, and the neglect which had occurred in the hospital department, Jack resolved to quit the service. Langan, therefore, left St. Marguerite, and worked his passage to Trinidad, in company with several officers and men, whose military ardour was damped by the want of funds and clothing, and the dreary prospects of the expedition.

At Trinidad Jack found employment in a coaster, the property of a Mr. Jewel, a merchant in the island. Some months were passed by Langan in this new mode of life, when he came alongside of a Bristol man of the name of Newton, who had milled several of Jack's shipmates. Meantime another boxer arrived at Trinidad, with whom Jack was compelled to enter the lists without delay; but Jack polished off "Mr. Newcome" in such quick and decisive style that the backers of Newton became alarmed; they possessed influence enough, however, to induce the governor to draw his bets upon the intended match, and in all probability, by so doing, not only saved the honour of Newton, but also their pockets. Soon after the above circumstance Jack sailed for Cork, on board of the Guadaloupe, of Greenock: after a most favourable voyage he arrived at Cork in safety. It is impossible to depict his feelings on his once more beholding his beloved country; the ideas and anticipated delight of "sweet home!" formed altogether a most agreeable contrast with the difficulties and privations he had experienced in less hospitable climes.

Langan's stay in Cork was very short, and Dublin soon became the object of his attention; at the latter famed city, he began the world again in the character of a publican; an employment for which it should seem that nature had peculiarly adapted him. He was a lively fellow over his glass, possessing a fund of wit and humour well calculated to amuse; not forgetting, at the same time, that Jack was seconded by a fair stock of muscle and bone, to keep up good discipline amongst disorderly or rum customers. Thus we perceive our hero changing from one tutelary divinity to another, discarding Mars to worship at the shrine of Bacchus! The jolly god was delighted at receiving the devoirs of such a votary, showering upon him his benign influence, and, for two years, Langan carried on a roaring trade, in King Street, at the sign of the Irish Arms, which bears the following motto :—

> "Quiet when stroked;
> Fierce when provoked!"

The attentions of our hero had hitherto been paid to Mars and Bacchus; in fact, so exclusively, that Venus and Cupid were determined to resent the insult and contempt offered to their power, through the person of Miss Katty Flynn. Miss Katty was of true Hibernian genealogy; her father was a dairyman, and the fair daddles of Katty, it is said, were often employed in churning of butter.

> "Most people fall in love some time or other,
> 'Tis useless, when the flame breaks out, trying it to smother;"

and so it appeared with poor Katty. Amongst her numerous elegant customers was the funny, joking, gay Jack Langan. Katty endeavoured to smother the unruly flame, but all-powerful love prevailed, and upon every succeeding visit at Jack's crib it increased like an oil-fed blaze. The cream of her dairy was continually offered as a present to our hero to embellish his tea tackle; in addition to which, lots of new-laid eggs, lumps of butter, and oceans of milk; a dietary, according to Lord Byron, of the most dangerous excitement to amatory ideas. Jack's counsel urged in his defence, that instead of being the seducer, he was the seduced: and it would be a perversion of justice if he was not placed as the payee, instead of the payer, for endeavouring to impart comfort and consolation to the love-stricken damsel. But despite the sophistry of his learned counsel, the jury were ungallant enough to award damages against him of One Hundred Pounds. This circumstance, combined with the treachery of a friend, compelled Jack once more to quit Ireland, and try his luck in England. A few fleeting hours enabled our hero to lose sight of the Pigeon-house, and the charms of Miss Katty Flynn, and he landed in a whole skin at Liverpool, where he was not long before he found himself seated snugly in Bob Gregson's hostelrie.

Under this friendly roof he rested himself for a few days. Jack then started for Manchester, in which place Pat Crawley had the honour of entertaining the aspiring Irish hero, at the Three Tuns Tavern. At Oldham Jack followed the occupation of a sawyer, and Tom Reynolds, like the celebrated Peter Pindar, who discovered Opie in a saw-pit, found Langan in a similar situation. "Come up, Jack," says Tom, "and I'll soon make a top-sawyer of you." Langan obeyed the summons; and after comparing notes together, and having a small wet, Reynolds and Langan became inseparable friends, setting-to together, both in private and public, for their mutual advantage. Things went on in this way for a few months, when Matthew Vipond, alias Weeping, a Manchester man, well known as a good bit of stuff, entered the lists with the Irish Champion, on Wednesday, April 30, 1823. The celebrity of the pugilists drew together five thousand persons. The battle was fought between Buxton and Bakewell, in a field called Lydia's Island, and certainly a better place could not be wished for—it was a perfect amphitheatre, and every person was near enough to the ring to have a distinct view of the men, when seated on the ridges of the surrounding eminences. The ring, which was a roped one of twenty-four feet square, being formed, Vipond first entered it, and threw up his golgotha; a few minutes after Langan made his *entrée*, and hoisted his also in the air. The Manchester man was seconded by two amateurs, the Irishman by Reynolds and Halton. Ned Turner and Bob Purcell also attended. About two o'clock the men peeled, shook each other by the fives, and the mill commenced.

THE FIGHT.

Round 1.—The men came to the scratch with good humour painted on their mugs, and after gathering up and breaking ground for a few seconds, Vipond made play, but was stopped and hit in a style by no means expected. Vipond got in at last, closed, and gave the Hibernian his first welcome to English ground by a sort of cross-buttock.

2.—Vipond came up, bleeding from the left ogle, not quite so confident, but nothing loth, and wishing to pay with interest the favour received; but, alas! he was not the first man disappointed in good intentions, for he was met in so tremendous a manner by Pat's right hand on the temple, that he was sent to the ground as if kicked by a horse. (Ten to one on Pat.)

3.—The Patlanders in the last and in this round seemed frantic with joy; hats went up in the air, and all roaring out for the darling boy. Bob Purcell called out to Reynolds, "Blow my dickey, Tom, if you don't keep the Murphy back he will kill his man, and you'll get lagged." This had no effect on Tom, for he sent Langan in to

Vipond, who was staggering from the effects of the blow in the last round. Paddy brought him to his recollection by a blow at the victualling office, and following it up with another for the box of knowledge, Matthew went down before he received, and Langan fell also from over-reaching himself.

4.—Vipond came to the scratch with far different spirits to those he started with: he was nervous in the extreme, and a person might easily guess that if he had known as much before as he did then he would have left Mr. Irishman for somebody else. Vipond's ivory box was visited by Pat's left mawley; by a ditto from the right, on the old sore on the temple, he went down, and the amateurs thought he would not come again. Langan during this round, and, in fact, all the others, was laughing.

5.—It was astonishing how willingly Vipond came to the scratch; but though he made some excellent hits, none of them told, they were so well stopped. Unfortunately for Matthew there was a kind of magnetic attraction between Paddy's left hand and the Lancashire man's frontispiece, which kept the claret continually streaming, and before the round was half over, Matthew seemed as if sprinkled by a mop. This was the busiest and the longest round in the fight; it ended by their getting entangled at the ropes, and both were down in a struggle for the throw.

6.—Vipond toed his mark, but in such a manner that any odds might be had against him. The only surprise was that he came at all, for he had had enough to satisfy an out-and-outer, without the slightest chance of winning. Langan, in commencing this round, nobbed him two or three times, and then let go a good one at the mark, but as the hit was going in, Vipond struck Langan's wrist downwards, which caused the blow to fall below the waistband. This the seconds thought to take some advantage of, by saying the blow was below the line prescribed by the laws of fighting, and a complete standstill took place, until the umpires declared they saw nothing unfair, and desired the fight to proceed.

7.—The time-keepers called time, but Vipond seemed to hang fire. The moment he got on his legs, Reynolds sent Langan to him, and Matthew went to grass.

8.—Matthew, to tell the truth, did not like the suit; and we must say he had no reason. When his second lifted him up to take him to the scratch, he declared he had been struck foul in the sixth round, and disregarding the direction of the umpires, declined fighting any more. Time was called, but Matthew slipped under the ropes and left the ring. Victory was then proclaimed for Langan in a shout that rent the skies.

REMARKS.—This fight excited more interest in Lancashire and the surrounding counties, than anything of the kind that has happened in the recollection of the oldest man. It was a kind of duel between England and Ireland—the English free in backing Vipond, the Irish almost offended if any doubt was expressed against Paddy. Langan stood five feet ten inches; Matthew, five feet eleven inches and three-quarters, about ten pounds the heavier, and a most powerful man. It was, as long as it lasted, a lively fight; but Vipond certainly had no chance of winning. The Irishman was (a wonder for that nation) cool and deliberate. Independent of that, he was quick on his legs, hit hard, and used both hands. As a proof of the inequality of the men, Pat had not the slightest visible mark of injury about him when the contest ended. At the time the row ensued, and Vipond had left the ring, a man called Rough Robin, about fifteen stone, entered the ropes, and challenged Pat for any money. Langan offered to fight that instant for £5, or anything else; but simple as Robin looked, he had good sense enough to take a second thought, and said he would train first. At the conclusion, Langan was exultingly carried by the boys of Shillelah on their shoulders to his carriage, and left the ground. The following certificate of the umpires was considered sufficient to satisfy all parties as to any doubt which they might have at the time respecting the alleged foul blow:—

"CERTIFICATE.

"This is to certify that Messrs. Swiney and Cope, being appointed umpires in the fight between Langan and Vipond, declare that the fight was fairly won by Langan.
                                   "W. SWINEY,
                                   "ENOS COPE.
"Buxton, April 30th, 1823."

Langan, after his conquest over Vipond, left Lancashire for the Emerald Isle, to exonerate his bail; honesty being at all times his polar star. He had scarcely landed in Dublin, when he was compelled to spend his time in the Marshalsea, in consequence of not being able to raise the sum of money necessary to repair Miss Katty's damages. Langan ultimately got out of his love adventure by the adverse party not opposing his discharge at the Insolvent Court; nevertheless, this bit of a love affair made great havoc in his cash account. Shortly after our hero's liberation from durance vile, he received a letter from Tom Reynolds, informing Jack that Rough Robin could be backed against him in Manchester. He lost no time in obeying the summons; but to his great regret, he found out it was "no go"—the Rough One did not appear at the scratch. Langan issued a challenge to all the Lancashire boys, but without the desired effect, and the Irish Champion could not pick up a customer. A sporting friend recommended Langan to visit Ned Painter, at Norwich, and under his auspices to enter the P. R. Jack would readily have availed himself of his advice, but Tom Reynolds, under whose guidance he was at that time, wished Langan to have a shy with Josh Hudson, at Doncaster Races, for a subscription purse—the John Bull Fighter having announced himself ready to meet any boxer at that sporting town. Many slips, however, happen between the cup and the lip; the manager of the Manchester Theatre had engaged Spring and Cribb for a sparring exhibition; the placards announced Spring as the Champion of England, and stated, at the same time, that the latter celebrated pugilist was ready to fight any man in the world. Langan conceived that the validity of Spring's title to the championship at least demanded a trial, and therefore, without hesitation, challenged Tom Spring for £100. This, in the first instance, was refused by Spring, but after several negotiations upon the subject, a match was made for six hundred sovereigns, and the battle took place at Worcester, on Wednesday, January 7, 1824, as may be seen detailed in the preceding chapter.

Langan, accompanied by Reynolds, appeared in London a few days after his defeat at Worcester, and exhibited the art of self-defence at the Surrey Theatre. He was warmly received by the Sporting World.

Thinking he was not fairly treated in his fight at Worcester, Langan entered into a second match for 1,000 sovereigns.

For the details of this gallant contest we must also refer to the memoir of the victor. To the minutiæ there given we must here add a few proofs from contemporary publications of the deservedly high position in which Langan's gallant conduct placed him with the public at large and sporting men generally.

Spring, it cannot be denied, received considerably more punishment in this battle than in any of his previous contests. This speaks for itself, and refutes the imputation of Langan being a bad fighter. The hero of the black fogle hit hard at a greater distance than most boxers. Mr. Jackson went round the ring and collected several pounds for Langan; and in the course of a few minutes, as a proof of how high the Irish Champion stood in the opinion of the amateurs, Pierce Egan collected on the stage, from a few gentlemen, £12 16s., of which sum Mr. Gully subscribed five sovereigns. The following letter from John Badcock (the Jon Bee of Sporting Literature) forms a fitting accompaniment to the appended verses in praise of Langan :—

" Well, sir, there is redemption in Gath, and the Philistines are discomfited, the Puritans overthrown, the Parliament of the Barebones dissolved, the opponents of the fancy defeated in their designs, the impugners of manhood laughed into scorn. There have now been no beaks, no × ×'s, like clouds and storms upon the pugilistic hemisphere; we have had a noble,

manly, fair British fight—the flag of the P. R. is again triumphant, and the colours of both
the combatants covered with glory. The conqueror has reaped new laurels, the conquered
has renewed and refreshed his : Spring has been truly triumphant, but Langan is not disgraced—as the old Major says, 'quite the contrary.'
"You have acted, and you have written nobly, sir, about the discomfited son of Erin : you
have rendered unto Cæsar Cæsar's goods. I am an Englishman, and I love, I reverence,
the land of mawleys and roast beef; but I can respect our brethren of the Union, and speak
well of the country of shillelahs and potatoes. The hero of the sable banner shall yet be a
conqueror—'quoit it down, Bardolph !'—and so, my jolly Daffs, let us have a stave for the
Black Fogle.
                                                "JOHN OF CORINTH.

                          "THE BLACK FOGLE.
          "'Hic Niger est, hunc tu Romane caveto.'—*Old Classics.*
      "'He sports a black flag, ye millers beware of him.'—*Modern Classical Translation.*

            "Hail to brave Pat ! though he's had a sound thumping,
                Long life to the Champion from Ireland so dear;
            Strike up, ye fancy coves, and be all jumping,
                To give the brave Paddy a benefit clear,
                      Crest of John Langan—
                      Faith, 'tis a queer 'un,
            A fogle of sable as black as can be,
                      And he hath stuck to it,
                      Though without luck to it—
            Whack for the fogle and Jack Langan's spree !

            "Oh ! 'tis a colour that ne'er shall grow whiter,
                The blues and the yellows may flaunt it amain,
            But the black flag that waves for the Paddy Bull fighter,
                If torn a small bit shall not nourish a stain,
                      Hudson may puff away,
                      Sampson may blarney gay,
            Still 'tis no Gaza to yield to his blow ;
                      Shelton may shake a fist,
                      Ward he may try a twist,
            And be one in chancery if he does so.

            "Drink, Paddies, drink, to your hero from Erin !
                While manhood shall flourish, and true friendship thrive,
            So long for your Champion his ensign be wearing,
                'Tis defended and held by a good bunch of fives.
                      While the ring flourishes,
                      And Erin nourishes
            Freedom and fancy and true sporting joys,
                      The black flag shall have a toast,
                      The P. R. shall ever boast
            The fogle of sable and Langan, my boys !"

Langan took a benefit at the Fives Court on Thursday, July 1, 1824,
when that popular place of amusement was crowded to suffocation, and
numbers went away disappointed, not being able to procure admittance.
Hundreds of amateurs were quite satisfied at getting a short peep now and
then at the stage, and a great number of persons left the Court without being
able, with all their efforts, to obtain a single glimpse of the sparring; indeed,
it was such an overflow as almost to render the safety of the spectators
doubtful. The sets-to were generally good.
    Loud cheers greeted the appearance of Spring, and also Langan, upon the
stage. Neither of the heroes had yet recovered from the effects of their then

recent contest. The set-to was a fac-simile of the battle in Chichester, the length of Spring giving him the advantage; it, however, gave general satisfaction. At the conclusion Langan addressed the audience in the following words:

"Gentlemen.—The first wish nearest my heart, is to return thanks for the kindness and attention I have received in this country. I trust you will believe me, when I say, that I do not appear here in anything like a national point of view. There is no man loves Ireland and her sons better than I do. My pretensions are to show as a man among pugilists, and to contend for the Championship of England. I will contend with honour, and that shall be my pride, or I should be undeserving of that patronage which you so liberally bestowed upon me. When I met the Champion of England at Manchester, my friends backed me for the sum which was asked, £300. I would be proud to have my name enrolled in history amongst those brave champions; Jem Belcher, Pearce (the Game Chicken), John Gully, Cribb, and Tom Spring. I am now willing to accept a challenge to fight any man in England—to fight for that proud and enviable title, for the sum asked of me by Spring—£300."

Jem Ward then mounted the stage, and said he was willing to fight Langan for 200 sovereigns.

Langan—I'll accept your challenge if you'll make it 300, but I'll not fight for less—it would be beneath the dignity of the distinction at which I aim, to fight for a smaller sum.

Ward—I am willing to fight for £300 if my friends will make up the sum.

Here the matter ended, and nothing decisive was done.

The Irish hero arrived in Bristol, on his way to Dublin, on the 11th of July, 1824, but the packet not being ready to sail, he immediately set off by the steam-boat for Tenby, in Wales, in order to meet with the steam-packet for Waterford. In his journey through Pembroke and Milford he met with a very kind reception from the Welsh people. Langan put up at the Nelson's Hotel, in Milford. Crowds of people surrounded the house during his stay; and the sailors, who were wind-bound, came on shore, along with the crews of two revenue cutters, just to get a peep at the Irish milling cove. The inhabitants of Tenby wished him to spar for a benefit, and some gentlemen amateurs offered him their assistance, but Langan refused to accept their kind offer, on account of his father's illness. He sailed in the Ivanhoe steam-packet for Waterford, on the 14th.

In the second fight with Spring, our hero, during one of his severe falls on the stage, injured his shoulder so seriously, that upon Langan's application

to Mr. Cline, the celebrated surgeon, the latter gentleman informed him he
must not fight for a twelvemonth.   In consequence of this advice, Langan
kept aloof from the prize-ring, and went on a sparring tour, in various parts
of England, with Spring; paid a visit to Dublin, Cork, and various other
parts of Ireland, with great success, and likewise went on a similar expedition with Peter Crawley to Liverpool, Manchester, etc.   Jack improved considerably during his practice with the late ponderous host of the French
Horn.

Lots of letter writing passed between Langan and Shelton on the subject
of a fight, but it all ended in smoke.   Ward and our hero had also a few
words on the subject of a mill, but no battle was the result.   For several
months after Langan's fight with Spring, the pain in his shoulder operated
as a great drawback to his exertions in setting-to.   Jack could not hit out
with effect.

We copy the following letter from a Dublin journal, to show the feelings
of our hero upon the subject of a challenge :

"*To the Editor of* FREEMAN'S JOURNAL.

"SIR,

"May I request you will contradict a statement which appeared in your paper of Saturday,
in a letter signed 'Paul Spencer,' in which it is stated that during my stay in Cork I was
challenged to fight an English soldier for £150, and that I did not accept the challenge.
I have not been challenged by any person whatsoever, and therefore the statement in the
letter signed 'Paul Spencer' is utterly without foundation.   There are certain persons in
Dublin with whom I would not associate, and who, in consequence, have felt a soreness that
fully accounts for the occasional squibs which now and then appear in print to my prejudice,
and which I hold in the utmost contempt.

"I remain your obedient servant,

"JOHN LANGAN.

"*April 22, 1826.*"

For some months Langan was completely lost sight of by the London
Fancy; at length he was heard of as the proprietor of a snug public-house in
Liverpool.   Here his lively disposition, civility of demeanour, industry, and
attention gained him hosts of friends.   Langan sang a tolerably good song,
and told a story well.   He was the first to prevent a brawl, the last to
provoke any one, or to suffer any one to be insulted in his house, and ever
ready to lend a hand to any one in distress—colour, country, or profession
disregarded.   He gained the esteem of all who knew him; he accumulated
money, and took an hotel, which he termed St. Patrick's, at Clarence Dock,
from whence he after some years retired with an ample fortune.   At his
house he had a large room; in this place he nightly placed beds of clean
straw, rugs, etc.; it was a nightly refuge for every Irishman that chose to
apply.   Let the tongue be but tipped with a bit of the brogue, "Come in and
welcome," said Langan, "only, lads, let me take away your reaping hooks

and shillelahs—there is a clean bed, a warm rug, and lashings of potatoes, for the honour of the land we all come from." This Langan did, unaided by any subscription, for years. Such a fact needs no comment. We could enumerate a hundred acts of his charity—he did not wait to be asked.

Here, for many years, he lived honoured, respected, and prosperous; but latterly his health failed, and he retired from the bustle of business to a house at Five Lanes End, Cheshire, where, on the 17th of March (St. Patrick's Day), in the year 1846, he departed this life, aged forty-seven.

It was with deep regret that we heard of the demise of the brave, the good Jack Langan. Brave he was, as his conduct in conflict showed; good he was, as perpetual acts of benevolence proved. He was a boxer, a prize-fighter—no matter, a profession never yet disgraced a man, if he took care not to disgrace the profession. Langan, though poorly educated was a man of superior mind; he was, to speak of them generally, better educated than the class with whom his name was associated; and in power of observation, acuteness of reasoning, was, in fact, far above many who walk in higher places.

The sun never rose on a braver or a better man; and hundreds of poor Irishmen have cause to bless his memory. One of those domestic afflictions that are utterly beyond remedy increased the maladies to which he had been long subject, and we fear we may, to use a common but expressive phrase, say that he died of a broken heart.

"Light lie the earth on his grave."

CHAPTER III.

NED PAINTER—1813–1820.

EDWARD PAINTER was known to the past and to not a few of the present generation, as a worthy specimen of the English boxer—a race of men, we fear, well nigh extinct. To the first, as one of the gamest of pugilists that ever pulled off a shirt; to the second, as a respectable and worthy tradesman resident in Norwich, but ever and anon visiting his old friends and patrons in the great metropolis, when some "event" occurred, in which those he knew in former days required a hand; or when some public or charitable object could be assisted by "Old Ned's" showing with Tom Spring, Peter Crawley, Jem Ward, one or other of the distinguished "big 'uns," who were contemporary with his ring career.

Ned Painter was born at Stratford, Lancashire, within four miles of Manchester, in March, 1797, and, as a young man, followed the calling of a brewer. His connexions were respectable, and young Ned bore the character of a well-behaved, civil fellow. A difference with a big fellow in the brewery, one Wilkins, led to a blow from that personage, and its return by the youthful Ned. A cartel from Wilkins was boldly answered by Painter, and they met in due form in the yard of the Swan Inn, Manchester, when Ned so quickly polished off the "big one" that he gave in after a very few minutes. Ned's master, who was a spectator of the affair, complimented him for his courage and skill, and, as Ned himself said, gave him the idea of his own boxing qualities. Accordingly, when Jack Carter, "The Lancashire Champion," as he vauntingly called himself, was exhibiting in Manchester, in 1811, Painter, at the solicitation of his friends, was induced to offer himself for a set-to. The specimen he gave with the gloves confirmed their good opinion that he was the "right stuff," but required a little more polish to spar with a full-blown "professional." Painter, at this time, was in his twenty-fourth year, his weight thirteen stone, his height five feet nine inches and three quarters, and his bust, when stripped, an anatomical study

NED PAINTER, of Norwich.

From a Drawing by George Sharples, 1824.

for symmetry and strength.   Few men, at this time, or in after years, could
throw half a hundred-weight near to the distance to which Painter could sling
it with comparative ease.   Our hero, thus qualified, presented himself to his
fellow countryman, Bob Gregson, at the Castle, as an aspirant for fistic fame.
Bob, at this time, was a sort of Mæcenas of millers, as boxers were then
termed, and his house the mart for match-making.   He welcomed the arrival
of this promising young Lancastrian, and soon found him an opponent in one
Coyne,* an Irish boxer from Kilkenny, six feet in height, and fourteen stone
in weight, who also ambitioned a name.   The articles fixed 40 guineas a-side
as the stake, and the men met at St. Nicholas, near Margate (in the same
ring as Harmer and Ford), August 23, 1813.   Painter was attended by his
friend Bob Gregson, and Joe Clark; Coyne was esquired by Joe Ward and
Hall.   The men lost little time in preliminary sparring, and, considering the
size of the Hibernian, Painter's confidence was more conspicuous than his
science   He went up to the head of Paddy, and put in one-two, but got it
heavily in return, and as the rally went on the weight and length of Coyne
bored him gradually back on to the ropes, where he escaped cleverly, and
"upper-cut" his opponent amidst some applause.   Another rally and both
napped it heavily; the round ending in Painter down, but the larger share of
punishment certainly to Coyne, whose appearance excited much amusement.
His arms were unusually long and lathy, and his face long also, with sharp-
cut features and a prominent "cut-water;" indeed, after a little of Painter's
painting, it is compared by the reporter to that of the Knight of La Mancha—
he of "the woeful countenance;" the swinging of his arms, too, resembled
that of the windmill sails so unsuccessfully attacked by Cervantes' hero.   The
mill, however, went on merrily, Painter receiving far more than he need
have received, but for his eagerness to "polish off" his man triumphantly.
Paddy was game as a pebble; but Painter, by his skill, gradually obtained a
decided lead, and ended each round by milling poor Coyne to grass.   After
forty minutes, during the latter part of which time Coyne acted as "receiver
general," Painter was hailed the conqueror.

Alexander, known as "The Gamekeeper," who had, a short time before,
defeated the game Jack Ford, at Hayes Common, now challenged Painter,
and the match was made for 60 guineas a-side.   The Fancy betted two to one
on Alexander!   The battle came off at Moulsey Hurst, on Saturday, the 20th
of November, 1813.   Gregson and Tom Owen were the knowing seconds
to Painter; Old Joe Ward and the veteran Paddington Jones attended to the

* Pierce Egan makes, reason unknown, this man's name "Cohen."   He was afterwards
beaten by Davis (the navigator), and is rightly indexed as Coyne in "Fistiana."

Gamekeeper. At one o'clock the men stood up, there being scarcely a point to choose, in height, weight, or length of arm.

THE FIGHT.

Round 1.—Painter gave evidence of improvement, and immediately went to work with both hands. The Gamekeeper, equally on the alert, hit Painter on the head. Some blows were exchanged, when Alexander went down, from a slip on his knee.

2.—Some caution before blows were exchanged. Alexander did not show himself off in the superior style which had been anticipated. Painter proved himself an equal, if not a superior fighter to his opponent. They fought their way into a close, and in going down, the Gamekeeper was undermost. (Five to two now vanished, and level betting was the truth.)

3.—Both on their mettle. Heavy exchanges occurred in a sharp rally. Painter was thrown.

4. Milling, without ceremony, hit for hit. This was the evenest and best contested round in the fight. The Gamekeeper planted a desperate blow on Painter's ear that staggered him. Both their nobs, from heavy punishment, were metamorphosed. The claret was first seen on Alexander's face. Painter went down from a slip. Great applause.

5.—Both distressed at the scratch. The efforts of the last round had winded them. Alexander was soon down. (Betting now took a turn, and Painter was the favourite.)

6.—The superiority was now decidedly on the part of Painter. Alexander endeavoured to keep pace with his opponent, but had the worst of it at every move. In closing the Gamekeeper was thrown.

7.—Alexander took the lead in this round. He nobbed Painter twice under the ear, without return. Both down.

8.—Both combatants appeared to have out-fought themselves, and sparred for wind. In closing, both down, but Painter uppermost.

9.—It was now a blinking concern, both their peepers being materially damaged. The Gamekeeper's right hand appeared to have given way, and he made his blows at random. Painter took the lead in fine style, and finished the round by flooring his adversary. This was the first knock-down blow.

10.—Painter still kept the advantage, but in closing both down.

11.—Alexander contested his ground ably, but Painter had the best of the hitting. In struggling to obtain the throw the latter experienced a severe cross-buttock.

12.—It was altogether a sporting fight; another change had taken place, and the Gamekeeper appeared the freshest man. Alexander commenced play with increased spirit. A desperate rally took place, in which Painter received a severe blow again under his ear, and he was ultimately thrown.

13.—The Gamekeeper kept the advantage, and also brought into play his left hand, which had hitherto been neglected. Painter exhibited great weakness, and Alexander improved this opportunity with considerable skill by putting in some good blows, and ultimately obtained the throw. Alexander was again the favourite in point of betting.

14.—One of Painter's eyes was completely closed, and the Gamekeeper did everything in his power to put the other into a state of darkness, but in this attempt he was floored so severely by Painter that he went down nob foremost.

15.—In favour of Painter; but both down, and Alexander undermost.

16 to 20.—These rounds were in favour of Alexander, who fought with his left hand at Painter's half-closed eye. The latter stood up manfully to his opponent, but seemed incapable of hitting effectively. Alexander was best in wind and strength, and was booked as the winning man. (Three to one was boldly offered in his favour).

21 and last.—Such is the uncertainty of war, that although victory seemed within the grasp of Alexander, yet from a straight well-directed hit at the "mark," Painter was announced the conqueror in a twinkling. It positively electrified the "knowing ones" (who had just before sported the odds against Painter), to see Alexander stagger away from his opponent. The Gamekeeper fell heavily and could not be brought to time. The battle continued for near forty minutes.

REMARKS.—This was a proud day for the Lancashire fancy, and Bob Gregson felt considerable exultation in having produced a hero who bid fair to obtain a high place on the roll of fame. Painter was brought home to the Castle Tavern with the honours of a triumphal entry.

Painter, from this conquest, was deemed a match for Tom Oliver; but here the smiles of conquest deserted our hero, who experienced a most gallant defeat. For an account of this memorable battle, see Life of OLIVER, Chapter IV.

For a purse of 50 guineas, without training, Painter entered the lists with Shaw, the life-guardsman, at Hounslow Heath, on April 18, 1815. Nothing but true courage could have induced Painter to contend with an opponent so much his superior in every point. Shaw was upwards of six feet in height, and above fifteen stone in weight. Having the advantages, also, of military exercise every day, a good knowledge of pugilistic science, frequent practice with the gloves, and so confident of success, that he had challenged all England. Painter, on the contrary, was a debtor in the Fleet, and had only obtained a day-rule. The odds, in consequence, were two to one on the life-guardsman. Cribb and Oliver seconded Painter. The latter set-to with great gaiety, and the soldier did not appear to have much the best of him, but the length and weight of Shaw ultimately prevailed, and numerous terrible hits were exchanged. It was piteous to view the punishment Painter received, and the game he exhibited astonished every one present. The long arms of Shaw were truly formidable, and he stood over Ned, planting his blows with confidence. Painter received ten knock-down blows in succession; and, although requested to resign the battle, not the slightest chance appearing in his favour, he refused to quit the ring till nature was exhausted. The battle lasted twenty-eight minutes.

At Carter's benefit, at the Fives Court, on Tuesday, March 11, 1816, Oliver and Painter set-to; the latter boxer was considered to have rather the best of it, and, in one instance, Painter hit Oliver away from him with such violence against the rail of the stage, that it was broken. This circumstance occasioned considerable conversation among the amateurs; and, at a sporting dinner which occurred soon after at Belcher's, the friends of Painter, in order that he might have a chance to recover his lost laurels, subscribed £100 towards a second combat. It was generally thought that Painter was much improved from frequent practice with Carter, in their sparring tour in various parts of England and Ireland, and it was argued that it was during his "noviciate" he was defeated by Oliver. The following challenge was, in consequence, sent by Painter:—

"*Castle Tavern, Holborn, March* 21, 1817.

"E. Painter's compliments to Mr. T. Oliver, and challenges him to fight, on Thursday, the 22nd day of May next, in a twenty-four feet ring, half-minute time between each round, a fair stand-up fight, for one hundred guineas a-side. The place to be appointed by and stakes deposited with Mr. Jackson, who, Mr. Painter understands, is willing to contribute a purse of twenty-five guineas to make up the one hundred. An early answer is requested."

The following answer was returned:—

"Tom Oliver, with compliments to Mr. Painter, informs him he has received his most welcome challenge to fight him. Oliver certainly cannot refuse to fight him on the day appointed. but requests it to be understood, he will not fight for a smaller stake than £100 a-side, independent of the purse which may be thought proper to be given by the Club.

"Oliver also begs leave to inform Mr. Painter, he agrees to his own proposal, that is, to make it a stand-up fight, in a twenty-four feet ring, at half-minute time between each round; and also the place to be appointed by Mr. Jackson; and, if it meets his pleasure (which it does his most unexceptionably) to deposit the whole stakes in his hands. Your early answer to the above terms is requested, in order that he may apprise his friends to come and make a deposit. They will either meet you at my house, or he will meet you and them at Mr. Thomas Belcher's, in Holborn, at his."

"Peter P. Weston —22nd March, 1817."

———

"Mr. Painter has to inform Mr. Oliver, that having waited upon Mr. Jackson with the above reply, it is contrary to the rules of the Pugilistic Club to give a purse of twenty-five guineas when the battle money amounts to £100.

"*Castle Tavern, March 24, 1817.*"

The following articles were, at length, most amicably agreed to:—

"*Castle Tavern, April* 10, 1817

"Thomas Oliver and Edward Painter agree to fight, on the 19th of May next, for 100 guineas a-side, in a twenty-four foot ring, a fair stand-up fight, half-minute time. The fight not to take place within twenty-five miles of London. Twenty guineas are deposited in the hands of Mr. Belcher, which deposit is to be forfeited, if the whole of the money is not made good on the 2nd May, at T. Oliver's, Great Peter-street, Westminster. The men to be in the ring precisely at one o'clock.

"THOMAS OLIVER, HIS ✕ MARK.
"EDWARD PAINTER."

"Witnessed by T. W. and J. H."

The stakes were made good as stipulated, and the odds were six to four on Oliver. The sporting world, however, experienced great disappointment from the unexpected interruption of the fight. Oliver, from an information laid against him at Worship Street, Moorfields, was brought from Riddles-down, where he was in training, to the above police-office, and bound over to keep the peace for a twelvemonth, himself in £200, and two sureties in £100 each. Both combatants felt equally mortified in being thus defeated without a blow. A trip to Calais was talked of among the swells, as the only safe mode of evading this untoward circumstance. Oliver and Painter were both eager for the fray, and "Mossoo" might be treated to an opportunity of witnessing *le boxe Anglaise*.

To keep the game alive, a match was proposed between Painter and Sutton, a strong, bony, long-armed, man of colour, aged twenty-seven years, who made a début in the ring, on the casual offer of a purse, at Coombe Warren, on May 28, 1816, with an old black man. From his sets-to, soon afterwards, with Cooper and Oliver, at the Fives Court, it was thought he displayed capabilities; and his fight with Robinson, at Doncaster, not only confirmed this opinion, but produced him numerous patrons. He also fought a man of the name of Dunn, for an hour and seven minutes, at Deptford, with success. Sutton was well known to be a desperate punisher, without fear, possessing great strength, a penetrating eye to direct his efforts, and tolerably well thought of by the milling fraternity. He and Painter met on Wednesday, the 23rd of July, 1817, at Moulsey Hurst, and boxing annals do not record a greater exhibition of pugilistic heroism. Painter was finally defeated, after a battle of forty-eight minutes, which was "anybody's fight" up to the last round. Painter strained every nerve to turn the chance in his favour, but in vain. He fought till nature refused to second his will; and more sincere regrets were never expressed at the defeat of any pugilist, for Ned had earned hosts of friends by his inoffensive disposition and respectful demeanour in society.

It was not to be expected that so courageous a boxer as Ned Painter had proved himself to be should "rest and be thankful" under the dark shade of this black defeat. Accordingly he at once demanded of his sable victor another trial, which Harry Sutton most cheerfully granted, nothing doubting to score another win. Bungay, in Suffolk, was the spot pitched upon, and the stake 100 guineas. On the morning of the 7th of August, 1818, the rendezvous being the ancient city of Norwich, whence Painter was backed, the amateurs were in motion, and not a coach, chaise, cart, or any sort of vehicle whatever, could be had, all having been previously engaged for the mill. Notwithstanding the rainy state of the weather, myriads of pedestrians were pouring in from all parts of the county, and by twelve o'clock not less than 15,000 persons had assembled upon Bungay Common. The ring was formed in a superior style to those made at Moulsey or Shepperton. Besides the enclosed quadrangle of twenty-four feet for the combatants to engage in, an outer roped ring was placed, leaving a clear space of twenty yards for those persons connected with the fighting men to walk round without confusion. Outside this stood the pedestrians several rows deep; and three circles of wagons surrounded the whole, giving the ring the appearance of an amphitheatre. Every person could see with the utmost ease, and all was conducted with good order. The spectators were unusually silent for such an occasion, though the combatants were much applauded upon entering the ring. Painter was seconded by Tom Belcher and Harry Harmer; Sutton attended by Tom Owen and Richmond. About ten minutes after one the men shook hands and set-to. Five and six to four upon Sutton.

THE FIGHT.

Round 1.—The fine condition of Painter attracted the attention of every eye, and the formidable bulk of Sutton was equally imposing. Nine minutes elapsed before a hit occurred, during which much science was displayed. The Black, it seems, had undergone some previous rehearsals, and his "cue" was "steady," which was given to him by his second, Tom Owen, in order not to make the first blow. The attack, however, was begun from Sutton, which Painter returned by a right handed hit at the Black's nob. A rally followed, and Painter's superior skill milled the man of colour most successfully. Painter at length got away, when a second rally occurred, and Sutton was floored by a right handed hit on his jaw. The first blood was, however, drawn by Sutton, slightly, from Painter's nose. (Great applause.)

2.—The science of Painter was much admired, and the knowledge of boxing displayed by Sutton far above mediocrity. Painter planted, with much adroitness, a severe bodier, and got away, the Black following; but he received a facer, till Painter made a sudden stand, and again floored the nigger. (Six to four against Sutton.)

3.—The success of Painter rendered it necessary for Sutton to alter his previously planned system; and Owen, upon the alert, like a skilful general, loudly observed to Sutton "to fight his own way!" This hint was enough, and the man of colour went to work without loss of time. He endeavoured to plant a terrible blow with his left hand, which Painter stopped in a scientific manner. The Black now seemed determined on doing some execution, and Painter appeared equally resolute. They stood up to each other as if insensible to the effects of punishment, exchanging hits with all the celerity of blacksmiths striking at an anvil, till they became exhausted, when Painter was thrown in closing. In this round the advantages were considered on the side of Sutton; but the claret run down in a stream from his left eye. The nob of Painter was rather damaged, and one of his ogles slightly marked. (Even betting.)

4.—The man of colour seemed bent on milling, and rallied in a most heroic style. Finer courage or greater resolution could not be witnessed. The gameness of Sutton was the object of admiration from all the spectators, and the true bottom exhibited by Painter equally impressive. It is impossible to particularise the blows that passed between them in this round, more than to observe that they were dreadful indeed. Sutton not only received a severe bodier, but so tremendous a blow on his nob that it was distinctly heard all over the ground. Painter went down easy.

5.—Half a minute was too short apparently for the men to come up to the scratch anything like themselves, and both commenced sparring to recover wind. The Black at length made play, but out of distance, and got again severely nobbed. He, without dismay, fought his way manfully in, although he had the worst of the punishment. One of Painter's listeners received a heavy hit, and, in closing, he was thrown.

6.—Sutton's nob, from the milling it had undergone, and the singular contrast of the red streams upon his coal black phiz, would have been a fine subject for the strong imagination of a Fuseli. Some reciprocal hitting occurred, when Painter's back was accidentally turned for an instant upon his opponent, but he soon righted himself, and

in a sharp contested rally planted a good blow on the head of Sutton. In closing, Painter went down.

7.—In this round the superiority of fighting was decidedly on the side of Painter, who, with much skill put in a "winder," and also planted a severe blow on his opponent's punished head. The men opposed each other like lions, till Painter fell, rather exhausted from the exertions he had made. Sutton was equally distressed, and staggered like a drunken man. He appeared scarcely to know where he was.

8 to 10.—The fine condition of Painter was manifest in these rounds, and he recovered himself with advantage in all of them. His improved science was evident.

11.—Sutton proved himself a troublesome customer to be got rid of, and in the most manly style he endeavoured to get a change in his favour. The head of the Black, terrific to view, was again punished; but the left ear of Painter received so sharp a hit that the blood ran down his back. In closing, both down. It was evident Sutton was beaten, and Tom Belcher went up and asked the question, but the seconds of the Black reproved him for the interference.

12.—In this round Painter astonished his most intimate friends, from the superiority of science he exhibited. Sutton had no chance left him now but desperation, and he bored in, regardless of the consequences. His nob came in contact with the left hand of Painter, and the claret followed profusely. Still the gameness of Sutton was not to be denied, and he contended bravely. Painter, in getting away from his impetuosity, found himself awkwardly situated against the stakes of the ring, when he fought his way out in the Randall style, and extricated himself from his perilous position cleverly. He also showed the advantage of giving, and the art of not receiving. The Black's nob was again punished out of all shape, and fibbed so sharply that the claret flowed from his ear. It was a terrible round, and Sutton was all but done.

13.—The Black was nothing else but a "good one," or he never could have met his man again. In fact he appeared stupid as to scientific movements, but, nevertheless, rushed at his opponent pell mell. Painter, quite collected, stopped the desperation of the Black with the utmost ease, and nobbed him at will. Painter received a chance hit upon his cheek, but in return he floored Sutton. The Black was now so dead beat that he resigned the contest in a whisper to his seconds. He was requested to try two rounds more, which he gamely did, but it was only to add to his punishment. At the end of the fifteenth round he could scarcely articulate in reply to Belcher, who had crossed the ring, "he would fight no more."

REMARKS. — One hour and forty-two minutes had elapsed, and a braver or a more manly battle does not stand recorded in the annals of pugilism. Sutton weighed thirteen stone nine pounds, being two pounds heavier than his opponent; he was also about three inches taller; his arms too were considerably longer than Painter's. Several of the spectators were so pleased with the manliness displayed by the combatants, that, in the impulse of the moment, they drew Painter and his seconds off the ground in their post-chaises into the town of Bungay, where females were seen waving their handkerchiefs from the windows as he passed through the streets to the inn. From the superior style with which this victory was gained Painter raised himself high in the opinion of the sporting world. True, that to good condition and active and careful training, he was much indebted for conquest, opposed to a man of almost Herculean strength and pluck. His first battle lost with Sutton proceeded greatly from a deficiency of tone in the system, but he was now able to face his man for an hour and forty-two minutes without difficulty; whereas, in his former contest with this sombre hero his distress was so great that he could not lift up his hands. At Bungay he came into the ring so confident in mind and firm in his person that he took the fight out of Sutton at an early part of the battle. It was good training that enabled him to do this. Painter, it was remarked, could have fought much longer had it proved necessary. The advantages of a scientific second were manifest throughout the fight, from the improved system of tactics pursued by Painter upon this occasion. "Gladiator in arena capit consilium," was said two thousand years ago, and Tom Belcher being at Painter's elbow, the defensive plan was acted upon with judgment and success; indeed, according to the expressed opinion of many of the best informed, the prompt advice and superior skill of Belcher tended in an eminent degree, in addition to the tractability of disposition and courage of Painter, to ensure victory. Comparison proves the fact. The latter, in his second contest, hit and got away; while in his first battle he went in boldly, opposing strength to strength; hence he was defeated, the length and weight of Sutton overpowering him. In the character of a second, from his experience and practice as a scientific pugilist, Tom Belcher, if not superior, was not excelled by any boxer. The result of this contest completely deceived the knowing ones, as the odds were greatly in favour of Sutton previous to the fight; and Oliver, the conqueror of Painter, backed the Black freely on the ground, so sure was the event considered.

Painter called, the morning after the battle, upon Sutton and left him a *douceur*. The sporting people of Norfolk, it appears, were highly gratified at the manner in which the battle between Painter and Sutton was conducted. Belcher, Harmer, Richmond, Owen, Oliver, etc., exhibited at the Norwich Theatre in the evening, after the battle, and their efforts to amuse were respectably attended.

We have noticed Painter's athletic capabilities; he, about this time, proved winner in several foot races. In a trial of strength in a field belonging to the White Hart, Commercial Road, Stepney, March 21, 1817, Painter undertook, for a wager of 10 guineas, a dozen of wine, and a good dinner for twelve, to throw half a hundred-weight against a gentleman of the name of Donovan, of immense Herculean proportions, and renowned for his prodigious strength. Mr. Donovan called on Painter to "set" a throw, which he did (with his coat on). The distance, though unfortunately not recorded, was so great that Mr. Donovan, after every preparation, could not touch it by eighteen inches and a half. "Painter," adds the report, "has, as yet, beaten every competitor in this feat, from England, Scotland, and Ireland." A fine athletic young man, called "Spring," was matched by Scroggins to run the distance of five miles against Painter, for 10 guineas. It was a hasty bet on the part of the latter, and undertaken without training. The race was decided on the 7th of November, 1817, from the four mile stone on the Essex road. Painter merely jogged on before Spring at starting, when the latter took the lead, and kept it for nearly two miles and a half, the distance of running out, Painter keeping close at his elbow, compelling Spring, as it were, to use his best speed. Painter now shot by him like an arrow, touched the handkerchief first, and returned to run the two miles and a half in. Spring was so dead beat, and out of wind, at the corner of White Post Lane, three miles and a half, that he could proceed no farther. Painter continued to run in gallant style, at the rate of ten miles an hour, and arrived at the place of starting at the expiration of thirty-five minutes and a half. This great feat for "a big one" like Painter, was loudly cheered on his touching the winning post.

At this period a young "big one" from Herefordshire, whose career was destined to be of the brightest, had just arrived in the metropolis, determined, as he himself declared, to go in for the Championship. The friends of Painter thought that Ned was the very man to check his aspiring flight, and a match was made for 100 guineas, when Painter was defeated by the future champion, on Mickleham Downs, in thirty-one rounds, occupying eighty-nine minutes, giving reason to many of the "knowing ones" to remember their lack of wisdom on the 1st of April, 1818, as will be found in full under the memoir of Tom Spring, in the first Chapter of this Period.

The friends of Painter were not satisfied that their man was defeated upon his merits, and made another match for 100 guineas a-side so early as April 10, at the Castle Tavern, Holborn, each party depositing 10 guineas. The contest to take place on Friday, the 7th of August, 1818. Tom Belcher took an active part in making this match, feeling confidence in Painter. Nearly four months was allowed him to recover from his accident, and it was also inserted in the articles, that the ring should be made with eight instead of twelve stakes. The betting immediately commenced at six and seven to four on Spring. It also continued in favour of the latter during the time of training. The former backers of Spring betted upon him freely; even many of Painter's friends changed sides.

The fight took place on a piece of ground called Russia Farm, four or five miles from Kingston, and was well attended. Painter had for his seconds Belcher and Harmer; Spring was waited on by Cribb and Clark.

THE FIGHT.

Round 1.—Both the combatants stripped with great confidence. Painter, attributing his loss of the last battle to an accident, appeared to feel that he had an opportunity to recover his blighted laurels. Spring, equally satisfied that his victory was due to his superior science. seemed conscious that conquest would again crown his efforts, but in less time. Great caution was observed on both sides, and between four and five minutes elapsed in endeavouring to gain the first advantage. when Spring made play, but Painter stopped his left in good style. Painter now appeared bent on mischief, and skilfully measured his distance, making a feint with his left hand, and, with a tremendous right-handed blow over Spring's eye. not only produced the claret copiously, but floored him like a shot. This decided two events upon which many wagers were depending, namely, first blood and first knock-down blow. Loud shouting from the Castle side of the question; the betting was reduced to even, and Painter much fancied.

2.—The last blow might be said almost to have made the fight Painter's own. Spring was evidently confused from its great severity, and the claret running down in streams, Painter lost no time, but endeavoured to improve his success, and immediately went to work. Some slight hits were exchanged, and in struggling for the throw, Painter went down undermost.

3.—Spring showed that he did not mean to let Painter have it all his own way, and gave the latter a heavy nobber. Exchanges, and both down.

4.—A short but sharp round. In throwing Spring proved that he was the stronger man.

5.—Two nobbing counter hits, that made both men go back a little. In closing. Painter got his opponent's nob under his left arm, and endeavoured to fib him, but Spring, with much dexterity, stopped Painter's hand, and ultimately threw the latter heavily. (Bravo, Spring!)

6.—This was a most manly round. Reciprocal hitting occurred. The punishment was heavy, but Spring had rather the best of it, and got Painter down.

7 and 8.—The combatants were both rather winded, and became cautious of getting into work. Slight exchanges till both were down.

9.—This was nothing else but a fighting round. Hit for hit occurred, till at the close of a rally Spring received a terrible blow upon his ear, that brought the claret freely. Spring reeled from its severity, and Painter was the favourite at seven to four. Spring went down to avoid a close.

10.—Spring came staggering to the scratch, evidently suffering from the last hit. He, however, went to work in the most gallant style, and in a rally gave Painter "pepper;" but the latter got away scientifically. In a close, Painter was thrown,

11 to 13.—Spring had the worst of these rounds, nevertheless he displayed great game.

14.—In this round the turn was on the side of Spring; he had not only the best of the hitting, but knocked Painter off his legs. ("Do that again, Spring, and you'll win it.")

15 to 22.—Painter decidedly took the lead in all these rounds. A tremendous rally occurred, when Painter finished the round by fibbing Spring down.

23 to 30.—It was almost a certainty that Spring must lose the battle; he was getting worse every round, but his game was of the first quality.

31.—This round, it was thought, would have finished the contest. Spring received a tremendous hit on his jaw, and went down exhausted. "It was all up," was the cry, any odds upon Painter, and even that Spring did not again come to the scratch.

32 to 42 and last.—Spring was satisfied that he could not win, yet, like a brave man, he was determined to continue the battle while a chance remained. He came up for ten rounds, but could not plant effectively. He was hit on the ear in the last round, and fell dead to time. He did not give in; that is, he did not say No. It was over in one hour and four minutes.

REMARKS.—Painter displayed great coolness and judgment in this fight, and having so able a general as Tom Belcher for his second, was greatly in his favour. Spring never recovered the severity of the blow on his eye in the first round, but his game was of so staunch a quality that his fame rose by defeat, and the loss of the battle was attributed to the chance of war.

Painter now publicly declared that he would not fight any more prize battles. Indeed, he took his farewell of the ring, with a benefit at the Fives Court, in a combat with Richmond, on Monday, the 7th of September, 1818. Spring was extremely anxious for another trial; but Painter positively refused. After spending a few months at Lancaster, and not finding a house in London to suit him, Painter left the metropolis, and commenced publican, in Lobster Lane, Norwich, under the most flattering auspices of the sporting people of the above ancient city. Here Painter enjoyed a quiet life, till the following circumstance, in November, 1819, put him " on the fret."

Some aspersions having been made upon the character of his first battle with Spring, at Mickleham Downs—indeed, an influential amateur having declared it to have been a cross—Painter indignantly repelled the accusation. He immediately set off for London, determined to undergo the most rigid examination by the supporters of the P. R. In the fight in question, in the second round, Painter received a knock-down blow, and, in falling, his head not only came in contact with one of the stakes of the ring, but his shoulder also received a violent contusion. He, however, continued the battle for one hour and twenty-five minutes; but, retiring from the contest without much punishment, gave rise to the report in question. Painter, at the time, procured the assistance of one of the most eminent surgeon in the kingdom, Mr. Cline, (a gentleman totally unconnected with the sporting world) to reduce the fracture. On Thursday, November 5, 1819, an application was made to Mr. Cline as to the fact, when he immediately wrote a certificate, which stated the injury Painter had received on the curve of the shoulder bone had rendered him incapable of using his arm at the time specified. This document was put into the hands of the members of the P. C., and the result was satisfactory. Ned's integrity was declared to be without a stain.

The following paragraph appeared on November 21, "The amateurs of Norwich will back Painter for 100 guineas, or more, and also give a purse of £50, if Spring will contend with Ned at Norwich. The patrons of the science, also, will give Spring £20 towards his expenses."

In consequence of this challenge, a match was made between Spring and Painter, on the Tuesday following, at Cribb's, the Union Arms, Oxendon Street, "to fight on the second Tuesday in February, in a twenty-four feet ring, thirty miles from London. An umpire to be chosen by each party, and Mr. Jackson as the referee; fifty guineas a-side to be completed in the course of three weeks at Cribb's, and the remaining fifty at Harmer's the last Tuesday in January, or the deposit money to be forfeited."

The friends of Painter, however, forfeited to Spring, or rather, the gentleman who somewhat hastily put down the £5. In consequence, however, of a challenge that Tom Belcher would back Oliver against Painter for £100 a-side, within thirty miles of London, and deposit £20, pp., the gage was taken up with great spirit by the sporting men of Norwich, which led to the following articles of agreement:—

"Castle Tavern, May 20, 1820.

"Edward Painter agrees to fight Thomas Oliver for a purse of 100 guineas, on Monday, the 17th July, within twenty miles of the city of Norwich. To be a fair stand-up fight, in a twenty-four feet ring, half-minute time. An umpire to be chosen by each party, and a referee selected on the ground by the umpires. Ten pounds a-side are deposited in the hands of **Mr. Soares, and the** remaining ten pounds a-side to be made good at the Castle Tavern, on **Monday, May 29,** between the hours of seven and eleven o'clock. The forty **pounds to be placed in the hands of Mr. Jackson.** Either party declining the contest to **forfeit the deposit money;** but if a fight takes place, Oliver to draw the £40. The purse to be given **by the Pugilistic Club at Norwich.** The place of fighting to be left in writing **for Oliver and his friends, at the house of Mr. Painter,** on the Saturday previous to the battle. **The gate-money to be divided between Oliver and Painter,** and their respective seconds and **bottle-holders. The purse** to be placed in the hands of a banker previous to the day of fighting.

"Signed, in behalf of PAINTER,   C. T.
"For OLIVER,   T. BELCHER."

The betting was six to four on Painter. He was decidedly the favourite in the metropolis; but in Norwich, long odds were laid on him. So great was the interest that, for a week before the fight, numerous parties left London daily to be sure of witnessing the battle. The stage coaches, besides a variety of vehicles from London, were filled inside and out for some days previous to the appointed time; and small groups of persons mustered of an evening in the streets of Norwich to hail the arrivals. In short, the ancient city appeared as much alive upon the subject as on the eve of an election. This sensation was also felt for miles around Norwich. The spot selected for the combat was North Walsham, sixteen and a half miles from the above city; and so little apprehension was entertained of the fight being interfered with, that a stage was built upon the ground for the accommodation of the spectators. In short, this fistic tournay engrossed the conversation in Norwich.

On Monday, July 17, 1820, every vehicle in Norwich was engaged to go to the scene of action. People were in motion by four o'clock in the morning; and in the streets which tended towards the place of contest the doors and windows of the houses displayed groups, eager to witness the departure. The road to North Walsham, which is delightful and picturesque, was thronged with carriages, equestrians, and pedestrians. To give some idea of the appearance the route presented, it may be mentioned that at least twelve hundred vehicles, of various descriptions, are ascertained to have passed over Coltishall Bridge. By ten o'clock, North Walsham was literally crammed with strangers; and the arrival of persons, continued up to two o'clock, from all the roads leading to the fight, baffled description.

In the field, a stage of a hundred yards in length was erected for spectators; and a circle of about sixty wagons was formed round the outer roped ring, at about ten yards distance from it, which were also filled with spectators. In the space between the outer and inner ropes some few persons were likewise admitted. The ring was similar to that of the Pugilistic Club, and the stakes were also of the same colour. Upon the whole, it was better made, and the accommodation it afforded to the spectators, as well as to the combatants, was superior to the London ring. £50 were collected at the gate (the pedestrians being made to tip), and the stage produced £80. The greatest order prevailed; the decorum of the thing was kept up by Shelton, Randall, Turner, Scroggins, Eales, Josh. Hudson, Harmer, Purcell, Teasdale, etc. And the immense concourse of assembled faces above faces, rising in amphitheatric tiers, formed an extraordinary and an interesting sight.

About a quarter before one o'clock, Oliver, dressed in white trowsers, a black waistcoat, and a green great coat, made his appearance, and threw up his hat, followed by the Champion of England (Cribb) and Belcher. A clapping of hands took place. Some little time elapsed, and Painter not making his appearance, Cribb asked one of the Norwich Committee where Painter was? The question had scarcely escaped the lips of Cribb when enthusiastic shouts announced the approach of Painter. Upon throwing up his hat the shouting was universal; the clapping of hands, and the noise of upwards of thirty thousand persons, was like a roar of artillery. Painter was without his coat, and on his entering the ring he immediately and cordially shook hands with Oliver. Spring and Paul attended upon Painter.

Some demur took place respecting the division of what is termed the gate-money,* Oliver claiming half the cash taken for admissions upon the stage, and also the money collected in the sixty wagons upon the ground. This claim was resisted by the Norwich Committee, who insisted that the stage and wagons were an entire gift to Painter. Here Cribb offered to bet a guinea that no fight would take place. The articles were now resorted to, and a gentleman from London, one of the umpires, decided that, according to the articles, Oliver was not entitled to the stage or the wagons, although the latter did offer to pay half of the expenses. This knotty point being settled, the scratch was made, and a toss-up took place between Cribb and Spring for the shady side of the ring, which was won by the latter. The combatants then stripped. The colours, yellow for Painter, and blue for Oliver, were tied to the stakes; the ceremony of all the parties shaking hands was not forgotten. The moment so long wished-for had now arrived, and the boxers prepared to set-to. Five-and-a-half to four were the real odds upon the ground.

---

* Respecting the division of the "gate-money," Mr. Jackson's opinion was, "that all moneys taken upon the ground, in point of right and justice, belong to both of the combatants, who are the primary cause of the multitude assembling, and therefore ought to be fairly divided between them, without any reservation whatever."

THE FIGHT.

Round 1.—Oliver appeared in good condition. He fought in striped silk stockings; and the symmetry of his form was not only attractive to the amateur, but the lovers of anatomy had before them a capital subject in the action and development of his muscles. Painter was also in tip-top trim, and though he had been reduced in training nearly two stone, he was effective for every purpose. On the men placing themselves in fighting attitudes, caution was the order of the day. After eyeing each other for about a minute, Oliver made an offer to hit, when Painter got away; Oliver in turn now got away from a hit made by Painter. Oliver hit short. Painter endeavoured to put in a tremendous hit, which was stopped in first rate style by his opponent. Painter got away from another hit. Oliver stopped a heavy hit, and gave a loud "ahem." The combatants seemed tired of holding up their arms, and stood still and looked at each other, and after a pause Painter put in a tremendous hit on Oliver's neck. Painter ran in to follow up his success, but Oliver stopped him with the accuracy of a Randall. Some heavy hits were exchanged, and in closing Painter endeavoured to fib Oliver, when the latter in the first style of the pugilistic art, broke away from him, (Applause.) Both were piping a little, and Oliver gave Painter a slight tap on the body. Each in turn stopped scientifically. Painter put in two hits, and after severe exchanges the men again broke away. Oliver hit Painter on the nose, when the combatants fought into another close, and Painter again attempted the weaving system, when Oliver used Tom Owen's stop for a short period, till Painter got away in gallant style. Each man now made himself up for tremendous hitting, and the stopping was admirable on both sides. Painter put in another severe hit on Oliver's cheek. The men closed, and in a struggle for the throw, Oliver got Painter down. Rather better than ten minutes had elapsed.

2.—First blood was now decided, as it was seen trickling from Painter's nose. Oliver endeavoured to plant a nobber, which Painter stopped, and laughed at him. This second round was longer than the first, but the caution and mode of fighting was exactly the same. Oliver got a hit on the nose; he also broke away from a close in great style, and gave Painter so severe a blow on his right cheek, that red ink was the result. Oliver put down his hands, and both seemed exhausted from the length of the round. In closing, Painter weaved down Oliver at the ropes. The applause was loud. Twenty-four minutes had now elapsed.

3.—Oliver appeared rather to more advantage; he nearly closed Painter's right eye, and to prevent being fibbed held his hand at the ropes, and ultimately got him down.

4.—This was a sharp set-to. Hard exchanges; both down very much distressed.

5.—Oliver hit Painter's left cheek, and produced the claret in a twinkling; but, in a short rally, Oliver, from a tremendous hit on the side of the head, went down. Twenty-nine minutes.

6 and 7.—Both piping a little. Oliver broke away from the weaving, but after some sharp exchanges, both went down in struggling for the throw. Thirty-seven minutes.

8.—One minute, and no hit made. Oliver at length put in a sharp facer, which was returned in a counter by Painter. A long pause. Oliver met Painter in the front of the head, as he was coming in to mill. Severe exchanges, till both down. The Norwich people were silent, and exhibited symptoms of fear for the result.

9.—Painter's right eye was rather troublesome to him, and he put up his finger; but he hit Oliver hard upon the side of his head. Some sharp blows passed, to the advantage of Oliver, who now with great force floored Painter.

10.—Oliver had rather the best of this round; but, in struggling for the throw, Painter fell upon him so heavily, that the wind seemed shaken out of him.

11.—Oliver made a good hit; but at the ropes he was again down. It was still thought he would win it, by the Londoners.

12 and last.—Oliver made play, put in a sharp facer, and got away; in fact, he generally showed fight first. Two terrible counter hits occurred, and both the combatants went back. Some sharp blows passed, when Painter followed up Oliver to the ropes, where the latter received a tremendous blow upon his temple, that floored him. When time was called, he could not appear at the scratch. The hat was, therefore, thrown up, and the victory proclaimed for Painter.

REMARKS.—When Oliver recovered from the state of insensibility into which the last blow had thrown him, he rose (as if from a trance) from his second's knee, and going up to Painter, said—"I am ready to fight." "No," said Painter, "I have won the battle;" upon which Oliver, in the utmost astonishment, asked his second why he had not picked him up sooner? The reply was, "Why, Tom, I could not wake you." Painter walked two or three times round the ring after the fight, and then returned to North Walsham. Oliver, after resting himself on his second's knee for about a minute, dressed himself, put the yellow handkerchief round his neck, and sat himself down upon some straw to see the next fight. Oliver has declared to several of his friends since, that the

blow operated upon him like a shock of lightning, rendering him totally insensible. Oliver's
face bore scarcely any marks of punishment.
Painter, in point of appearance, had received
most about the head; but neither could be
said to be much hurt. Painter showed great
activity and goodness upon his legs, and

stopped in good style. The Londoners were
much mortified at this "chance blow," as
they termed it. Oliver appeared greatly
dejected at losing the battle; but the punishment the combatants received was so light
for such heavy men, that they were up at an
early hour next morning to breakfast.

It is remarkable that Painter, at the first attempt, was defeated by Oliver,
Sutton, and Spring, but that in each case on demanding another trial, he
reversed the verdict, and proved the conqueror in all three instances.

At a public dinner at North Walsham, after the battle, Painter, on his
health being drunk, repeated the declaration he had made, previous to his
encounter with Oliver, that he would never fight again; and this resolution
he adhered to.

Painter now lived retired from the ring, but was a publican for many
years at the Anchor, in Lobster Lane, Norwich; he afterwards removed to
the Market Place, and died in that city on the 19th of September, 1853.

CHAPTER IV.

TOM OLIVER (COMMISSARY-GENERAL OF THE P. R.)—1811–1831.

TOM OLIVER, originally a member of the most ancient of callings—a gardener—lives in the memory of hundreds of modern ring-goers as the civil, active, diligent, and respectable *custos* of the P. R. ropes and stakes; enjoying in a green old age, despite occasional twinges of the gout, the post of "Commissary," assisted latterly in his duties by his son Fred, also known as a pedestrian. Tom, who was a fine specimen of manhood, entered the ring somewhat late in life. An anecdote is preserved that his first appearance in the ring was owing to his accidentally witnessing the battle between Silverthorne and Dogherty, at Coombe Warren, in January, 1811, where Tom was engaged in digging and planting. He is said to have remarked on their display—"Well, if you call this prize-fighting, I'll be hanged if I don't think I could fight a little," and he determined to put his abilities to the test of experiment. At his début Tom received the appellation of "The Battersea Gardener," from his general place of employment; he was, however, born at Breadlow, in Buckinghamshire, in June, 1789. He left his native place a mere boy, and lived in the service of Mr. Baker, a gardener at Millbank. Here he made his first attempt at milling, with one Kimber, a stonemason from Walham Green. The battle took place in the dominions of old Caleb Baldwin, Tothill Fields, Westminster, for a couple of guineas a-side. Oliver was seconded by Silverthorne and Byrne. It was a heavy fight for an hour and forty minutes, when Oliver's strength and game prevailed, and he was hailed the conqueror.

Oliver's second engagement also took place in Tothill Fields, with a fighting man denominated "Hopping Ned." The sum fought for was four guineas a-side. Oliver, rather diffident of his own abilities, when pitted against a scientific pretender, proposed that the loser should receive two guineas by way of consolation for defeat; but Ned, confident in his own prowess, scouted the idea, and declared the entire sum should go to the conqueror, which was ultimately agreed to.   But such is the uncertain fate of war, that "Hopping Ned," who had congratulated himself with what ease and dexterity he would serve out the Gardener, was, in the short space of a quarter of an hour, so completely milled out of all conceit of his fighting, that he was reluctantly compelled to cry, enough !   He was convinced of his error by retiring severely punished, without the benefit of the two "quid." Oliver was so much in obscurity at this period that the fighting men present seemed rather shy in seconding him, and a novice must have performed that office, if Silverthorne and old Dick Hall had not appeared, and stepped forward to bring their friend through the piece.

On the 2nd of June, Oliver fought with Harry Lancaster, at Newman's Meadow, near the turnpike, at Hayes, Middlesex, for a subscription-purse of twenty guineas.   Caleb Baldwin seconded Oliver, and Paddington Jones attended upon Lancaster.   Harry, who had a sparring reputation, cut a sorry figure before Oliver.   In fact, on the part of Lancaster, it was a most contemptible fight.   Oliver was everything, and in the short space of eighteen minutes was proclaimed the conqueror.   So easy a thing did it appear to the spectators, that it was the general opinion Oliver could have won without taking off his clothes.

Oliver, somewhat more experienced, next entered the prize-ring with Ford, for a subscription-purse of twenty guineas to the winner, and five guineas to the loser, on the 6th of October, 1812, at Greenford Common, Middlesex.   Caleb Baldwin and Silverthorne were his seconds; and Tom Jones and Joe Norton officiated for Ford.   The latter was deficient in weight, but considered the most effective boxer.   Little more was known of "The Gardener" than that he was a good man; but an opinion was entertained that his milling abilities were rather moderate.   He was slow in hitting, and not looked upon as anything of a punisher.   Previous to the battle it was even betting.   During a contest of two hours and ten minutes, his patience, courage, science, and fortitude, were completely put to the test.   It was not only a battle of experience, but a proper day of trial to him; and it will hereafter be seen that he completely profited by it.   To detail the numerous rounds would be superfluous, but the odds changed several times during the fight.   Ford, in the fifth round, put in a tremendous blow on Oliver's eye, which nearly closed it up; this raised the betting six to four on Ford.   From the tenth to the fifteenth round Oliver took the lead, when Ford, recovering from his weakness, again kept the advantage for some time.   It might be said to be reciprocal fighting for about an hour and a quarter, when Ford felt

TOM OLIVER.
From a Drawing by WAGEMAN.

.

convinced that every art and stratagem must be adopted. Oliver received heavy punishment in the face repeatedly, and had few opportunities of returning, as Ford generally fell on making a hit. Every manœuvre was practised to tire out "The Gardener;" but he at length triumphed over all the shifting, notwithstanding he was nearly blind the last half hour of the battle. The game of Oliver claimed universal praise; for few men possess fortitude enough to have endured such an irritating opponent. They were both terribly punished.

From the sound pugilistic qualities developed by Oliver, he became an interesting article to the Fancy, and the afterwards renowned George Cooper (see *ante*, p. 303, vol. i.), was selected as a competitor for a subscription-purse, at Moulsey Hurst, on May 15, 1813. Bill Gibbons and Caleb Baldwin were seconds to Oliver; Richmond and Jones for Cooper. Betting six to four on "The Gardener."

THE FIGHT.

Round 1.—Milling seemed determined upon by both, and set in with unusual severity. The Gardener, in putting in a right-handed hit, met with a severe return, and a good rally followed. The men closed, but soon broke away, and again rallied courageously, when Cooper put in a severe blow upon the neck of his adversary, who gallantly returned. Strength was now resorted to, when Oliver went down. So severe a first round has seldom been witnessed.

2.—Cooper hit his opponent on the head, who not only returned severely, but also threw him. The odds rose considerably, and a few offered two to one on Oliver.

3.—A better round was never seen, nor was greater courage ever displayed by pugilists. Both combatants full of gaiety showed themselves off to great advantage; and a great many hard blows were exchanged. Towards the close of the round Cooper suffered severely from the fibbing he received from Oliver, who got his head under his left arm.

4.—The scene was now materially changed, and Cooper played his part with so much judgment, that it became even betting. In a desperate rally, Cooper planted a terrible hit, and as Oliver was going in to return the favour, Cooper measured his distance so accurately, that he again hit Oliver between his jaw and ear with such tremendous force, that he went down as if he were "finished." Cooper took the lead most decidedly in this round.

5.—The admirers of bravery and manhood were anxiously interested. Each man claimed equal attention. If the one was brave, the other proved himself equally courageous. But Cooper appeared to have the advantage also in this round, from the great facility with which he used both hands. He hit Oliver to the ropes, where he was thrown. Betting stationary.

6.—This round was bravely contested. A severe rally took place, but terminated in favour of Cooper, who got his man down. Notwithstanding the manhood displayed by Oliver, it was evident he had not got the better of the severe blow he received in the fourth round.

7.—Cooper put in a tremendous blow upon Oliver's eye, just as he commenced a rally. This round was also bravely fought. Several heavy hits were exchanged, when Oliver was thrown.

8.—A small change took place. Cooper seemed rather distressed, and Oliver appeared getting fresh. A long and hammering rally occurred, but Oliver had the best of it, and Cooper went down exhausted.

9.—Cooper now showed he was no stranger to the science, and adopted his master's (Richmond's) plan of hitting and getting away. He, with much adroitness, put in a body blow and got away, but the Gardener was not to be had upon this spoiling suit; by watching the manœuvres of the enemy with vigour and caution, and by his prudence, he gained the best of the round, and threw his man.

10.—Cooper now appeared much fatigued, yet his game was good. Oliver, perceiving the chance was in his favour, lost no time in going-in, when Cooper was levelled. Oliver, the winning man, five to one.

11.—Oliver showed himself a cool and steady fighter, possessing good judgment, and determined resolution. He was now winning fast, and again sent his man down.

The exertions of Cooper were manly and firm, but his strength was so reduced that he could not check the successful career of his antagonist.

12.—Cooper now only stood up to receive punishment. He was so much exhausted, that his blows produced no effect upon Oliver.

13 and last.—It was pitiable to view the gameness of Cooper induce him to make another effort, as he was now so beaten that he could not deliver a blow, whereupon Oliver was declared the conqueror, in seventeen minutes.

REMARKS.—Two such boxers do not often meet, and, it might be observed, it was the best and most evenly contested battle that had been witnessed for a long time. Bravery and science marked both men's efforts. The game of Oliver was clearly manifested with Ford, but his marked improvement in science claimed peculiar attention. He was cool, steady, and confident, and used both his hands with much greater facility than heretofore. The severe checks he received from Cooper in the fourth, fifth, and sixth rounds, enough to terrify most men, did not deter Oliver from persevering until he became the conqueror.

Cooper, although defeated, must be viewed as a pugilist of no common pretensions. He is a diffident young man, and this operated as a sort of drawback to him during the mill. It was his second attempt, he having but a short time previously defeated Harry Lancaster. Cooper is a first-rate pugilist, a hard and quick hitter, and possesses courage of the finest quality, with science that gives him a good place among the list of prime boxers.

Oliver acquired considerable fame in conquering Cooper, and was deemed an equal match for Painter, who had distinguished himself by two recent conquests, and was looking forward to the highest honour of the ring. When this match was first made known, Painter, being the heavier man, was rather the favourite, but on the night previous to the battle, the odds had changed eleven to eight on Oliver.

On Tuesday, May 17, 1814, they met at Shepperton-Range, for a purse of £50, given by the Pugilistic Club, to be contended for in a twenty-four feet ring. Oliver was seconded by the Champion and Clark, and Bob Gregson officiated for his friend and countryman, Painter. At one o'clock they set-to.

THE FIGHT.

Round 1.—Upon stripping, the clear appearance of Oliver satisfied every one that he had been trained to the highest pitch of condition; and his arms, from their muscular form, were a study for the anatomist. Painter was equally conspicuous; two finer young men never entered the ring. The anxious moment had arrived, and the spectators were watching with eagerness for the first advantage. Oliver commenced the attack by making play with his left hand, which was returned by Painter, but too short to do execution. The men rallied with high spirit and determination, during which sharp facers were exchanged and the claret was first seen trickling down Painter's chin. In endeavouring to put in a right-handed blow, Painter, not being correct in his distance, missed his man, which brought them to a close, when Oliver immediately got his opponent's nob under his left arm, fibbed him cleverly, and ultimately threw him. More anxiety displayed than betting.

2.—Most determined resolution appeared on both sides; indeed, the spectators were aware, from the character of the men, that victory would not be obtained by either at an easy rate. Oliver, with much dexterity, put in a severe hit upon Painter's mug, who returned sharply with his right. A desperate rally now commenced, when it was perceived that Painter left his head unprotected. Oliver, awake to every chance, punished his opponent's nob terribly with his left; but Painter, with considerable adroitness and execution, planted a blow on the cheek of Oliver, that instantly sent him down. Its effect was not unlike the kick of a horse. Even betting.

3.—From such a tremendous hit it was truly astonishing to see Oliver so ready to time. Painter, somewhat flattered by his last effort, made play, but his distance proved incorrect. Oliver returned by planting a heavy blow in his face. A rally now followed, in which so much determination was exhibited, as to excite surprise in the most experienced pugilists. It lasted more than two minutes, without advantage to either combatant. If courage was at any time portrayed, no boxers in the world ever put in a higher claim to it than Painter and Oliver, who undauntedly stood up to each other, giving blow for blow, till accuracy of stopping and force of hitting had left them both. A pause ensued. The skill of Oliver at length obtained the advantage. He adopted the Cribb system of milling on the retreat, and punished his opponent's nob heavily, till Painter fought his way in to another rally, which, if possible, was more determined and severe than the first. This second rally seemed rather in favour of Painter, who hit tremendously, but he was checked in the midst of his career by a severe body blow, that nearly sent him down. He, however, collected himself a little, and continued fighting till he fell from weakness. A more thorough milling round is not to be met in the annals of pugilism, and there was more execution done in it than in many fights of an hour's length. Indeed, it was enough to finish most men. It lasted four minutes and a half, and twelve seconds, all fighting !

4.—On this round the fate of the battle hung. Skill was now required to recover from the severe winding each had experienced in those two desperate rallies. Oliver, convinced that systematic precaution was necessary, again successfully adopted milling on the retreat. He nobbed his opponent with his left hand, as Painter incautiously followed, literally throwing away most of his blows, which, had they reached their destination, must have done execution. Painter was evidently distressed by this retreating system, but at length got in a tremendous right-handed hit upon Oliver's eye, and appeared getting more fresh in his wind. A spirited rally took place, when some heavy blows were exchanged, but Painter fell exhausted. Two to one was loudly vociferated upon Oliver.

5.—Oliver kept the advantage of his system of fighting, reducing the strength of his opponent in almost every round. He hit Painter repeatedly without receiving a return, and his left hand was continually at work. Painter still kept pursuing Oliver, although so heavily hit at every step, and he at length fell upon his face.

6.—This round was rather more evenly contested, and, in rallying, Painter put in several good hits both right and left, when he fell from weakness.

7.—It was now demonstrable which way the battle would terminate. Oliver appeared so much at home that he punished his opponent in any direction he thought proper. Painter did everything that a game man could, but he was so exhausted that in making a hit he fell on one knee. Three to one, but no takers.

8 and last.—Painter was done up, and Oliver finished the contest in prime style, by meeting his antagonist in every way that he presented himself; and, finally, with a right-handed blow, knocked him down. Painter could not be brought to time. They were both punished heavily. Oliver's body showed marks of some punishment, and both his eyes were in mourning.

REMARKS.—Upon Oliver's being declared the conqueror, Cribb took him up in his arms and carried him round the ring in triumph, when he received universal applause, and he deserved it.

In conquering Painter he defeated a hero of the first mould, whose fine game and true courage were never excelled. But game alone will not win in opposition to superior science, though it may prolong the battle. Painter suffered severely from his distances proving incorrect. During the battle he missed nineteen hits; and, in one round, Oliver put in five severe blows on the head, without receiving a single hit in return. Oliver is a fine looking young man, and weighed, in the above fight, twelve stone, seven pounds, and is in height five feet nine inches and three quarters. In every battle he has successively risen in fame and shown more science; but with Painter, however desperately contested, it appears, that he felt within himself less danger of being beaten than in any of his other five. In the early part of his training (for which he was indebted to the peculiar skill, care, and attention of Captain Barclay), the severity of fatigue he experienced rendered him unwell, but when his pitch was correctly ascertained, his constitution was so finely and vigorously tempered, so much spirit, lightness, and sound stamina were infused into his frame, that it was thought he could have fought an hour without much difficulty. It is astonishing what confidence men are taught to feel, from the superior system of training pursued by Captain Barclay.

In fighting Kimber, Oliver appeared a mere novice; in his battle with "Hopping Ned," he was a promising tyro; with Harry Lancaster, he rose above the thumping commoner; when he fought Ford, he showed that he had good stuff in him, and proved himself a staunch tough man; in his severe conflict with Cooper, he was an improving and steady boxer; while against Painter, he proved his claim to the appellation of a first-rate pugilist. It was from this progressive state of pugilistic acquirement, and Oliver's superiority over Painter, that he was considered equal to anything upon the list. Not even the Champion was excepted; in fact, so high were his capabilities rated, that before Carter offered himself as a customer, Oliver had displayed great anxiety to enter the lists with Tom Cribb; and it appears that some conversation had passed between those mighty heroes of the fist, as to the propriety of a meeting to decide the subject.

Tom had at this juncture touched the culminating point of his pugilistic eminence. He was now a publican, and his house, the Duke's Head, in Peter Street, Westminster, was looked upon as head-quarters of the Fancy of that special district. Tom had inherited the title and dominion of the renowned Caleb Baldwin, and was regarded as the hero and champion of Westminster. It is but justice to observe, that contemporary prints bear testimony to the personal civility and general good behaviour of Oliver as a public man, and of his disposition as "truly inoffensive;" a general characteristic of steady and unflinching courage. After a couple of years of "minding the bar," Tom accepted the challenge of Jack Carter, "the Lancashire hero," who, at this period, boldly claimed the Championship. The game battle near Carlisle, October 4, 1816, in which Oliver fell gloriously, although at one period three to one was laid in his favour, will be found in the Life of CARTER, Chapter VIII. of this Period. (Page 170.)

Tom now returned to serving his customers, and again nearly two years' peaceful interval was spent by Tom in "minding his own business," when some of the friends of Bill Neat, of Bristol, of whom hereafter, offered to make a match with Oliver, for 100 guineas a-side, to fight on the 10th of July, 1818, within thirty miles of London. The invitation was accepted, and the articles signed, betting being, at first, in favour of Oliver. The tremendous hitting of Neat knocked the game Tom off his legs, and into a state of obliviousness, after an hour's hard up-hill fighting. See NEAT, Chapter V. of this Period.

On the 28th May, 1819, Oliver was at Epsom, enjoying the racing, when a purse of £50 being to be fought for, and Kendrick, the Black, expressing a desire to "try for it," Tom agreed to be his opponent, as he expressed it, "to keep his hand in." About six o'clock, accordingly, when the last race was over, a ring was formed near the starting post, and surrounded quickly by several thousands of spectators. Oliver showed first, attended by Tom Cribb and Randall, while Carter and Richmond waited on the Black.

THE FIGHT.

In the first round, the Black threw Oliver; and in the fifth he also fibbed him sharply. In a few other instances he had the best of the rounds, but not enough to turn the battle in his favour, or to influence the betting. Massa did not attempt to hit, but he stopped extremely well, and rushed in for a close. When he was forced into a rally, too, he fought with some determination. Oliver not only threw Massa in great style twice, but he went down very heavily in the hitting. The Black did not exhibit much signs of punishment, but would have left off earlier than he did, had his second not induced him to try it on a little longer. He was at length hit down by a tremendous facer, which so satisfied him that he would not again appear at the scratch. Little, if any, betting occurred, as the £50 was considered a present for Oliver. Some few wagers took place that it would be over in thirty minutes. It was not, however, won with that ease which had been anticipated, and it was asserted, that if Massa had been in better condition, and had possessed the advantages of patronage, he might have proved a troublesome customer. As it was, the battle lasted one hour and a quarter, during which thirty rounds were fought.

Favoured by adventitious circumstances, and puffed with praise, Dan Donnelly, the Irish Champion, now appeared upon the scene with "A Manifesto to the Milling World," which will be found in his memoir, Chapter VIII. of this Period. Accordingly at Jack Martin's benefit, April 20, 1819, Oliver challenged Donnelly for 100 guineas a-side, when Randall declared he was authorised to accept it. That day six weeks was named as the time of battle, the articles signed at Dignam's, the Red Lion, Houghton Street, Clare Market, and the battle came off at Crawley Hurst, thirty miles from London, on Wednesday, July 21, 1819, as fully detailed in the Life of Dan Donnelly, post.

Shelton, who had risen high in the opinion of his friends, from his conquest of Big Bob Burn, was soon matched against Oliver for 100 guineas a-side, and the battle came off at Sawbridgeworth, Herts., twenty-seven miles from London, on Thursday, January 13, 1820. Shelton was the favourite, partly owing to Oliver's recent defeat. At a few minutes before one o'clock Oliver threw his hat into the ring (which was swept, and strewed with sawdust), and was soon followed by Shelton. The look of Oliver was firm and collected, and smiling confidence sat on his brow. He fought under the "yellow-man," à la Belcher, and was going to tie his colours himself to the stakes, but Randall took them out of his hand, and placed them on the ropes. After some little time Spring covered Oliver's colours with the blue handkerchief. The time was announced for the men to strip, notwithstanding a heavy fall of snow. Randall and Tom Callas waited upon Oliver, and Spring and Turner seconded Shelton. The latter had his right wrist tied with a small piece of his colours, part of a blue handkerchief. This was done in order to give a security to his wrist, which had received a severe injury from a cut with a glass rummer about eight months previous to the fight. In tossing for the choice of side, Oliver was the winner. The men then shook hands and set-to for

THE FIGHT.

Round 1.—Shelton, being the best two-handed fighter on the list, and the hardest hitter, it was expected that he would go to work immediately; but there was a drawback to his efforts in Oliver's attitude and guard, and great caution was the prominent feature; he, however, made two feints, but Oliver stopped him. Shelton made another attempt without effect, as Oliver got away. Sparring with great caution. Some exchange of blows now occurred, and a trifling rally. Counter hits, which operated upon both their mugs, and a tinge of claret was seen upon the mouth of Oliver, when Shelton observed, "First blood, Tom." Oliver, in great style, stopped right and left the hits of Shelton, and returned a severe body blow. Shelton showed also some science in stopping, but Oliver planted two severe facers right and left. Some exchanges took place, and in a sort of close both men went down, Shelton undermost. The round occupied seven minutes. (Loud shouting in favour of Oliver.)

2.—Oliver put in a severe facer without any return. Shelton seemed rather confused at the superior tactics displayed by his opponent, and absolutely stood still from the severity of a blow he received on his ribs. He, however, recovered from his stupor, and with more fury than science attacked Oliver till the latter went down. ("Well done, Shelton! Bravo!")

3.—In this round the spectators were astonished at the excellence of Oliver. Some smart exchanges took place, when the latter not only damaged Shelton's right ogle, but hit him severely in the throat, followed him and ultimately floored him.

4.—The fine fighting of Shelton could not be perceived. Oliver put in such a tremendous facer that Shelton put down his hands and retreated. The latter, rather angry, endeavoured to plant a heavy hit on the tender ear of Oliver, but he stopped him on his elbow, laughing at him. Shelton received some more facers, and Oliver ultimately got him down. ("That's the way, Oliver; go it, my old Westminster trump, we shall have another jubilee yet in the dominions of old Caleb.")

5.—Shelton went down, but it appeared more from the slippery state of the ground than the hit.

6.—Shelton put in a sharp nobber; but in return his upper works were peppered, and he was again down. Shelton's right eye was nearly gone, and Oliver smiled with confidence.

7.—Shelton threw his opponent, and appeared the stronger man.

8.—This was a well-contested round. Shelton's face now exhibited the handywork of his opponent. He went down, and Oliver fell upon him, but threw up his arms.

9.—Oliver's right hand would be nobbing Shelton; but the latter made a desperate return on Oliver's already cut mouth that fetched the claret copiously. Shelton endeavoured to repeat this electrifying touch, but Oliver stopped him neatly Shelton then closed, pelting away, and in struggling made a jump to get his opponent down. Both fell, Oliver undermost.

10. — Oliver commenced this round by planting two facers, right and left, and also put in a bodier, without a return Shelton, however, gallantly fought his way into a sharp rally, and some severe exchanges occurred, when the men broke away. In closing again, both down, but Shelton undermost. ("Bravo!" from all parts of the ring; "good on both sides.") More real courage could not be witnessed.

11.—The scene was now rather changed, and some little danger was apprehended from Shelton's not only nobbing his opponent, but by a well gathered hit having floored Oliver like a shot. Randall and Callas lost not a moment in getting Oliver up; but when placed on his second's knee his head lolled on one side, and he appeared lost to what was going forward. In fact, it seemed as if the game Oliver could not recover, although Randall kept telling him to look about and recollect himself, calling out. "Tom! Tom!" Shelton's friends, who had previously been as if frozen, now jumped about and began to bet without hesitation.

12.—Shelton satisfied the spectators that his nob was screwed on the right way; he immediately went to work with Oliver, and again got him down. (Ten to one on Shelton.)

13.—Oliver was very bad, but his game brought him through it, and he came up better than was expected. Shelton did not wait for his coming up to the scratch, but was going to attack him, when Randall reminding him of it, he struck the Nonpareil, saying, "I'll lick you as well; don't talk to me about the scratch." Randall very properly passed it over, observing, "It was the first time he ever received a hit without returning it." Shelton, however, made a bold attack upon Oliver, but the latter caught him at the ropes, and in the Randall style fibbed him till he went down. The joy of the Westminster boys cannot be described.

14.—The fibbing system was repeated till Shelton went down.

15.—Shelton in going down received a sharp facer in falling.

16.—It was singular to observe that Shelton could not stop Oliver's right hand. A smart rally occurred, when the men broke away. Shelton was ultimately hit down. (This change surprised every one. Oliver was again the favourite, seven to four.)

17.—Shelton went down as quickly as he could in this round, and Oliver behaved generously.

18.—This was a gallant round; both men fought like lions, and displayed heroism that called forth the loudest approbation from all parts of the ring. Both down.

19.—Shelton passionately ran in, but went down. (Disapprobation.) Both his peepers were much damaged.

20.—Oliver, who had hitherto been considered a slow fighter, evinced considerable quickness; and as Shelton was coming in with a tremendous hit he was stopped by Oliver, who, in finishing the round, hit Shelton down. (The Westminster boys offered to sport their last brown on their old favourite, Oliver.)

21.—This round was decidedly in favour of Oliver; in fact, he had it all his own way, till Shelton was hit down, when Oliver, with much manliness, stepped over him. This conduct was received as it deserved; Oliver was loudly cheered.

22.—Shelton got away with much dexterity from a body blow aimed by Oliver; but turned to and fought like a hero, till he went down in a distressed state.

23.—Here the warmth of Shelton's feelings was evident; he rushed in to mill Oliver, regardless of consequences, till he went down.

24.—Shelton hit Oliver on the mouth, which operated forcibly, and made a change again in Shelton's favour; but the bravery of Oliver was not to be overcome, and he sent Shelton down, although obliged to go down himself. With much honour he endeavoured not to fall upon his opponent. ("Bravo, Oliver! you are a noble fellow, and an honour to the ring.")

25.—This was a most singular round. Shelton was hit off his balance, and went round like a whirligig. Oliver did the same: their backs came against each other. They recovered themselves, and made some good exchanges, till Shelton went down.

26.—Shelton was floored from a flush hit on his nose.

27.—Oliver again hit Shelton in the face as he was falling; but Oliver was in the act of giving and could not help it. It was not an intentional blow. However, loud cries of "Foul, foul!" "Fair, fair!" occurred; and on Shelton's asking the umpires if it was not foul, it was deemed fair, the hit not being intentional.

28.—This was a most courageous round, and Shelton did all that a brave man could do to win. The hits on both sides were

terrific, till Shelton retreated from the heavy punishment dealt out to him, followed by Oliver all over the ring. He caught Shelton, in the act of falling, under his arm, carrying him a considerable way, then generously letting him go down easily. (Tumultuous applause for Oliver.)

29.—Another fine round—all hitting and no flinching. Both down, but Shelton undermost. When the combatants were on the knees of their seconds, Shelton said to Oliver, "Let them chaff (meaning the seconds), but you and I, Tom, will do what is right." "Certainly," replied Oliver.

30.—Shelton still proved himself a dangerous customer; he went up to Oliver, planting some hard blows, till he was hit away. In struggling, both down.

31.—It was not long before Shelton was floored.

32.—Shelton put in a good nobber; but Oliver soon returned two facers, right and left, and Shelton went down on his knee.

33.—Oliver observed to his opponent, "Tom, I have got you now," and instantly went to work, till Shelton went down much distressed.

34.—Shelton got wild, and ran after Oliver, till he was stopped by a flush hit and went down exhausted.

35.—Shelton had now lost his self-possession, but still he was dangerous, for Oliver received a nobber that moved him from the ground. Shelton ran all over the ring after Oliver, while the latter kept getting away, putting in a hit now and then, and laughing till Shelton ran himself down. (Any odds. "It's all your own, but be steady.")

36.—It was sad to see the state of Shelton; he hit at random and was as groggy as a Jack tar three sheets in the wind. He received a hit on his head, and fell.

37.—Notwithstanding the groggy state of Shelton, Oliver would not give a chance away, but kept at a distance, planting his hits in a winning manner, till Shelton went down. While the latter was on the knee of his second, Callas went up to Shelton and asked him if he would fight any more. Spring was irritated with Callas, and a row had nearly been the result. (Odds were now out of the question.)

38.—The opponents of Shelton could not but compliment his bravery, as he came up like a man, although reeling to and fro; he, nevertheless, made a hit, till he was sent down at the ropes.

39 and last.—On time being called, Shelton got up, but he reeled and could not steady himself at the scratch. Some interference took place, and Oliver was declared the conqueror. The latter jumped up for joy. He immediately left the ring, and did not appear much punished about the face, except his mouth. Shelton was shortly afterwards led out of the ring; his face was much peppered. It was over in fifty-one minutes.

REMARKS.—The game of Oliver brought him through triumphantly, to the surprise and expense of the knowing ones, many of them paying dearly for their mistake. The conduct of Oliver was a perfect specimen of a thorough-bred Englishman, and finer courage was never displayed, nor more manliness and generosity. The "stale one," as Tom was termed, defeated in style a much better fighter than himself. Shelton, on being stopped, appeared to lose his confidence, although he took a great deal of punishment, and exerted himself even after his last chance was gone. The success of Oliver was greatly due to the able seconding of Randall, whose advice at critical periods was invaluable. Shelton fell with honour, for a more gallant battle could not be fought. On being put to bed at Harlow, Shelton said, "My heart is not beat, that's as good as ever; but I'm sorry for those who have backed me." On Shelton's return to town a medical certificate was shown to the effect that two of his ribs were broken.

Shelton solicited his friends to allow him another chance with Oliver for £100; and they not only presented him with a handsome gratuity, but proposed to post the money for a new trial; but this was interfered with by the match we are about to notice. Although Tom Spring had been beaten in a second battle by Painter (August 7, 1818), that excellent judge, Tom Belcher, contrasting the styles of the men, declared he thought Oliver a good match for the Norwich hero, whom, as we have already seen, he had defeated four years previously, and purposed to back him for £100. The friends of Painter, though refusing Spring a new trial, thought the present "a good thing," and Painter sharing their opinion, articles were quickly agreed on. See Life of PAINTER, in the preceding chapter. In this fight, at North Walsham, near Norwich, July 17, 1820, Oliver suffered defeat. Still his friends adhered to him, and that their confidence was not withdrawn a striking instance was soon given. Tom Spring—although he had beaten in succession Henley, Stringer, Ned Painter (and been beaten in turn by him), and afterwards conquered Carter (who had beaten Oliver), Ben. Burn, Bob Burn, and Josh. Hudson—was declared by many to be "a sparring hitter," and it was urged that this "fine fighting" would never dispose of the gallant Tom. At any rate opinions differed, and accordingly Oliver was backed for 100 guineas, the tourney to take place on February 20, 1821. How Oliver struggled against length, weight, skill, and superior judgment, is told in the memoir of SPRING, his conqueror, whose merits Oliver, during his long life, has often warmly descanted upon. He once said to us, "It's no use arguing—Spring was too long, too clever, and too strong for any of us. I tried his strength, but found out my mistake. Lord bless you, he never let nobody see *how much he could fight till it was wanted*, then he just served out the quantity. He had *a head for fighting, and a man only wins by chance if he hasn't a head.*" Oliver experienced this, and acknowledged it. His argument, however, received an adverse illustration shortly afterwards, when he met Hickman, the Gas-light man, as yet unconquered, on Tuesday, June 12, 1821, at Blindlow Heath, Surrey, and was defeated in nine rounds. Oliver was virtually beaten in the first round. He was stale, slow, and could not in any way parry the onslaught of his opponent; yet here again he kept untarnished his fame as a courageous man. See HICKMAN, *post*, Chapter VI.

Tom seems, like many other high-couraged men, not to have been at all conscious of the important axiom that "youth will be served," and once again, for his last appearance but one, made a match with a powerful young boxer, Bill Abbott, for the trifling sum of ten guineas. The affair was considered a "bubble," and that a forfeit must follow. Abbott, however, meant it, and so did Oliver, and they met November 6, 1821, on Moulsey Hurst, when Oliver was beaten by a heavy hit under the ear in the thirtieth round, the odds immediately before the blow being four to one on him. How this fight was lost and won will be seen under ABBOTT in the Appendix to Period VI., Abbott's last fight being in 1832.

Years now rolled by, and Tom was generally known and respected. Being appointed to the charge of the ropes and stakes of the P. R., he was a constant attendant at the ring-side as commissary, and at sparring benefits. At length, in 1834, the "old war-horse" was neighed to by another old charger, no other than "Uncle Ben" (Burn). "My Nevvy" (Jem Burn) had removed from the Red Horse, Bond Street, to the Queen's Head, Windmill Street, Haymarket, and there the commissary, "Mine Uncle," and many of the old school, as well as the aspirants of the new school, nightly held their merry meetings, and talked over "deeds that were done and the men who did them," with an occasional interlude of a new match between the active pugilistic practitioners of the day. For a long time "Uncle Ben" had amused himself and the listeners by somewhat disparaging opinions, not of Tom's game, but of what he called his "wooden fighting," and at length, half in jest, half in earnest, Tom, in his matter-of-fact style, informed "Mine Uncle," that his opinion of the family was that they had produced only one "fighting man among the lot," and he was his very good friend Jem Burn. This was "most tolerable, and not to be endured;" and "my Nevvy," who loved a bit of fun, "as an alderman loves marrow," tarred on the old uns by siding with the Commissary. Ben. hereupon produced his pouch, and offered to post a deposit to meet the veteran in battle array. The joke went on, but the old heroes were in earnest, and meant the thing they said. Articles were drawn, and the day fixed for Tuesday, the 28th of January, 1834. Oliver having won the toss, he named Coombe Warren as the place of rendezvous, and on Monday evening Uncle Ben took his departure from his training quarters at Finchley to the Robin Hood, at Kingston Bottom, where he arrived safe and sound, in the full anticipation of covering himself with

glory on the ensuing day.   Oliver, who was not so fortunate in patrons, had
not the advantage of training beyond what he could obtain by his daily
walks from his own domicile in Westminster, and on Thursday morning took
the road towards the appointed place in a cab, accompanied by the Deputy
Commissary, Jack Clarke, who had the care of the ropes and stakes.   He
made a halt at the same house as "my Uncle," only occupying a separate
apartment.

The crowd assembled in front of the Robin Hood at twelve o'clock would
have been characterised by Dominie Sampson as "prodigious!" and it was
not till "the office" was given that the ring had been formed by Deputy
Commissary Clarke in a field at the back of Coombe Wood, that a move took
place and the blockade of the Robin Hood was raised.   The moment the
where was known, a simultaneous toddle took place up the hill, and the ring
was shortly surrounded by an extensive circle of panting prads and loaded
vehicles; but scarcely had the anxious coves time to congratulate themselves
on having obtained a good berth, when a "Conservative" beak, one of the
enemies of the sports of the people, who had stolen from his counter in
the town of Kingston, attended by a noted distributor of religious tracts,
poked his ill-omened visage into the ring, and addressing Jack Clarke, who
was viewing his handiwork with the eye of an accomplished artist, said,
"My good man, you have your duty to perform and I have mine; I am a
magistrate, and will not permit any fight to take place in this county, and I
trust I shall not be molested."   Jack looked as civil as a gipsy at the tusks
of a farm-yard dog; but he was too good a judge to "kick against the
pricks."   He saw it was no go, and assuring his worship he was as safe
as if he were wrapped up in a ball of his own flannel, he saw him safely
through the surrounding multitude.   An immediate retreat was beaten up
the main road, and Jack lost no time in undoing what he had done, and
packing his traps, as before, under the wings of a cab, with which he
followed his friends.

A consultation now took place as to what was to be done.   Some were for
a flight to Hayes, in Kent, while others looked towards Middlesex, and at
last the latter course was taken, and "to Hampton" was the word of command.   The cavalcade set off helter-skelter, taking the course over Kingston
Bridge, to the unexpected but great satisfaction of the toll-keepers, who were
thus put into a good thing, not improbably for good reasons, by the pious
Kingston beak.   But here a new difficulty and some jarring arose, for the
cabs in those early days not being entitled to go more than eight miles from
London without paying an additional duty of 1s. 9d. to the excise, the

impost was demanded, and the gate shut till it was exacted. The stoppage produced not only great resistance, but much ill-blood, and at one time there was a string of not less than three hundred carriages on the stand-still, all impatient, and each fresh cabman producing fresh arguments in favour of a right of passage. At last foul means took the place of fair: the gate was opened by the "friends of liberty," and away went the whole line pell-mell, many of them not even condescending to pay the ordinary toll. Thus the imprudent resistance (when the number of the cab might have been sufficient) led to the loss of much which would otherwise have been bagged to the positive advantage of the Trust. The way was now clear to Hampton, with the exception of a few accidents by "flood," for the waters being out on the road between Hampton Court and the Bell, many immersions took place; and, in not a few instances, "old Father Thames," with the pertinacity of an exciseman, walked through the bottoms of those drags which happened not to be at least two feet from the surface of his waters. These were, however, "trifles light as air," and in due course the motley assemblage were collected round the roped arena once more, a convenient field having been found, of which possession was taken without the ceremony of saying to the proprietor, "by your leave." All now went smoothly; the men arrived on the field "ripe for action;" and by a quarter to three o'clock the dense mass was all alive for the commencement of business, a straw rick in the vicinity affording ample material for forming a dry resting-place for the "Corinthians" close to the stakes. Such was the crowd, however, that great difficulty was experienced in preserving order, and hundreds were altogether shut out from a view of the sport which they had encountered so many difficulties to witness. At ten minutes to three the men entered the ring; Oliver attended by Frank Redmond and Owen Swift, and Burn by Young Dutch Sam and Anthony Noon. Oliver sported a bird's eye blue, and Burn a yellow man, which were tied to the stakes in due form. Burn, on entering the ring, seemed to be a good deal excited, and some thought he had been sitting too near the brandy bottle; but his subsequent conduct showed that he had lost nothing by the aid of artificial spirit. Oliver was quiet and easy in his manner; and although he was aware of the importance of the contest upon which he was about to enter, exhibited as much coolness as if he were engaged in his ordinary occupation of Commissary. He wore a tarpaulin hat, which gave him much the appearance of a veteran tar, instead of a veteran of the boxing school. On stripping, it was clear that Burn had the advantage of height and weight, as well as in freshness, although his flesh shook within his skin, as if the latter had been made too large, or the former had shrunk from its natural rotundity, the inevitable effect of training upon an old frame. Oliver looked sleek, and in good case. He was, however, stiff in the pins, which, although not "gummy," as might have been expected from his frequent attacks of the gout, wanted that elasticity of muscle requisite to the display of activity, an important essential in getting away from the rush of a heavy and determined antagonist, as he discovered in the course of the mill. The odds on setting-to were six and seven to four on Oliver.

THE FIGHT.

Round 1.—The men eyed each other à la distance, Oliver smiling, Ben as serious as Newton solving a problem in astronomy, their hands well up, and Tom waiting for the attack; but Ben was in no hurry. Tom tried a feint—no go; Ben steady. After a short pause Ben let out his left, caught Tom on the canister, and stopped the counter with his right. Neat stopping, followed by counter hits with the left, which raised a blush on the cheek of each. Good straight hitting and stopping, and no flinching. Tom caught Ben on the pimple with his left, but had it on the mark from Ben's left in return. A sharp rally, give and take in good style; no getting away or mincing matters, it was all hard work. Both became flushed and got to a close, but little was done at infighting; mutual efforts to chop and fib, when they broke away. Ben was all alive, and popped in his left straight as an arrow on Tom's mouth. Tom returned, but was short. (Cries of "First blood" from Sam, and Tom showed claret from the mouth.) Burn again put in his left, and stopped the counter. Oliver was slow, but sure, and stealing a march, gave Ben a poke on the snout. Ben had him on the noddle in return. Oliver threw in a blow on Ben's ribs with his right, but he was rather short. Ben countered on his pimple; good manly fighting, and neither retreated an inch. Ben flung out his left as swift as lightning, and catching Oliver between the chin and the lip, gave him a "snig," from which the blood flowed copiously. ("No mistake about blood now," cried the Burnites, while Sam said "it was a certainty." "Aye," cried Ben exultingly, "I can lick him and Tom Spring in the same ring!") Oliver smiled, but was not dismayed; he went to his man and tried his left, but was short. Hit for hit, and no dodging. The men stood like Trojans, fearless of consequences, depending solely on science in stopping or hitting. A spirited rally and some heavy exchanges, when Oliver put in his left upon Ben's throat, and downed him in good style. This was "trick and tie," first blood for Ben and first knock down for Tom. The friends of the latter, who were not prepared for so

admirable a display on the part of Burn, revived. The round lasted eleven minutes, all fighting, and both were a little fagged.

2.—Ben came up as confident as ever, while Tom smiled as if unshaken in his own good opinion. After a short pause Ben caught Oliver a swinging hit with his right on the side of the head, just above the ear. Tom popped in his left twice on Ben's smelling bottle and cigar trap, drawing blood from the latter. Some good manly hits and neat stopping, when both closed, but in the struggle neither could do much. They appeared to be incapable of getting the lock or giving a cross-buttock. Each fibbed by turns, and at last Oliver succeeded in getting Ben down and falling upon him. Both got up bleeding, and the spectators were agreeably surprised by the manly and straightforward manner in which the men continued the contest.

3.—Oliver came up a little groggy on his pins, but ripe for action. He let go his left, but Burn stopped him beautifully, and made a pretty counter in return. A brisk rally, in which heavy hits were exchanged, and Burn was again floored with a poke as he was on the retreat. This was given as a second knock-down blow.

4.—Again did Burn show his generalship by stopping Oliver's left; but it was now seen that the knuckles of his right hand were gone, and that he did not keep up his arm so well as at starting. Oliver saw the opening, and "flared up" with his left so quickly and effectually that he cut Ben between the eyes, and down came the claret in a stream. Still Ben showed no symptoms of fear. Counter hitting; the men firm to the scratch and no denial. ("Remember his ribs," cried Frank Redmond to Tom.) No sooner said than done, and whack went Tom's right on the appointed spot. Ben did not like this, but he fought manfully, and the counter hitting and stopping was of the first order. Again did Oliver plant on the sore ribs, but had it on the nob for his pains. Ben's right continued low, and a job on the snout reminded him of his negligence; but this memorandum was not sufficient. Oliver again hit with his left: he received in return; but in the next broadside Ben went down. (Oliver's friends now became satisfied that "all was right," and cheered him accordingly.)

5.—Both men came up somewhat exhausted, for there was no breathing time taken on either side. Ben tried his left, but was stopped; and the return from Tom's left on his knowledge box was neat, though with little severity. Oliver again dropped heavily on Ben's ribs with his right and no return. A splendid rally, in which the "old uns" fought with signal bravery. Tom, however, had the advantage of hitting, as Ben's right kept dropping, in spite of hints from Sam to keep it up. The jobbing with the left was effective on both sides; but in the end, after a desperate rally, in which both were piping and weak, and yawing like a ship in a storm, Uncle Ben dropped exhausted.

6 and last.—Notwithstanding Ben's distress in the last round he came up with unshrinking bravery, although looking blue. And "now came the tug of war," for, in point of punishment, the men were pretty much on a par, and all seemed to depend on their physical strength. Ben's right guard still drooped, and Oliver commenced by giving him a job with his left. Ben was not idle, and returned; repeated counter hits were given, and Oliver delivered both right and left with precision, although not with much force; still the blows told on a man already on the go, and at last, in the close, both went down, Ben under. It was now all over, and, on time being called, Ben was declared incapable of coming again. Oliver, who had every reason to be glad his labours were brought to a conclusion, was immediately hailed as the victor, amidst the shouts of his friends; but he was some time before he was sufficiently master of his motions to quit the ring. Burn received every attention from his "Nevvy," and complained that he felt the effects of a rupture, under which he had been long labouring. It was this which induced Jem Burn not to let him get up for another round, though he wished it. The fight lasted exactly twenty-four minutes.

REMARKS.—This affair surprised and delighted the old ring goers, for all anticipated, from the age of the combatants, that it would be a "muffish" affair, and especially as Ben had never had a very high reputation for game. It was admitted on all hands, however, that few more manly fights had been witnessed, and that no men, considering their capabilities, could have conducted themselves better. There was no cowardly retreating or flinching on either side, nor any of those hugging manœuvres which are so foreign to fair stand-up fighting. We doubt whether "Uncle Ben" ever showed to so much advantage; and, in defeat, he had at least the consolation of having convinced his friends that his pretensions to the character of a "foighting" man were not altogether without foundation. Tom has lost all that fire for which he was formerly distinguished, and of course much of his vigour, for his blows were not delivered with severity; nevertheless, he vindicated his character as a thorough game man, and to that quality his success may be in a great measure ascribed. for the punishment he received, would have more than satisfied many younger men. The betting was not heavy, and those who lost were perfectly satisfied Ben had done his best, both for himself and them. Nature, and not his will, forcing him to say "enough."

This was Tom's "last bumper at parting" with the active practice of pugilism, though up to a very recent period, when succeeded by his son, Fred. Oliver, the veteran Tom was rarely, despite his periodical visitations of his old enemy the gout, absent from his post whenever the P. R. ropes and stakes were in requisition. The civility, respectful attention, and forbearing good humour (often under circumstances of the utmost provocation) of Oliver we can personally bear testimony to. He was emphatically "the right man in the right place;" even-tempered, firm, obliging, yet undismayed by the most demonstrative of "roughs," Tom preserved his dignity, and commanded order by his quiet, inoffensive, yet determined mode of doing what he considered to be his "duty." During his latter years, "Old Tom" vegetated as a fruiterer and greengrocer in Pimlico and Chelsea, where he brought up a family, as a fine specimen of lusty old age, and of the days when we may say of the ring, "there were giants in the land." Tom finally "threw up the sponge," June, 1864, at the ripe age of 75.

CHAPTER V.

BILL NEAT, OF BRISTOL—1818-1823.

At one period this weighty and hard-hitting specimen of the Bristol school bid fair to attain the topmost round of the ladder to pugilistic fame. Neat was born on the 11th of March, 1791, in Castle Street, of respectable hard-working parents, and was known to his townsmen for many years of his youth and manhood as a man of prodigious strength of arm, temperate habits, and extreme personal civility. A finer young fellow, "take him for all in all," could not be met with in a day's walk in a populous city. His height was five feet eleven inches and a half; his weight, in training, thirteen stone seven pounds. He had arrived at the age of twenty-seven before London heard of his provincial reputation, a fight with one Churchill, a maltster, weighing fourteen stone, being his only recorded battle. This was a somewhat curious affair. It was admitted that Churchill could not beat Neat, but the latter, for a trifling wager, offered to thrash Churchill "in ten minutes!" The cash was posted, and the combat came off, Churchill fighting with "yokel desperation." Nevertheless, Neat lost his money by not hitting his opponent out of time in the ridiculously short space stipulated by the agreement. However, the powers displayed by Neat led to some conversation, in which a Bristol amateur offered to find 100 guineas for Neat, if he chose to meet Tom Oliver, then in the city on a sparring tour. Neat, who was as brave as he was powerful, closed with the offer.

Bristol, since the appearance of the renowned Jem and Tom Belcher in the metropolitan prize-ring, followed in rapid succession by the never-defeated Game Chicken, the truly brave Gully, and the staunch and often-tried Champion of England, Tom Cribb, not only attained a high character for pugilistic excellence, but was denominated the "nursery of British boxers." Neat was brought forward under those advantages; and although he could not boast of the experience of

" Battles bravely fought, and hardly won!"

yet his qualifications were so promising, his patronage so high and imposing,

BILL NEAT.

that with the improving value of ten weeks' training under the immediate auspices and tuition of Cribb, the advice of Gully, and the generally sound judgment of Captain Barclay, he soon became the favourite; the Bristolians anxiously anticipating, through the exertions of this new candidate for milling fame, to realize the days of another Jem Belcher.

Oliver, nothing loth, accepted the cartel, and the subjoined articles were drawn up:—

"W. Neat engages to fight Thos. Oliver on the 10th of July, 1818, within thirty miles of London, for 100 guineas a-side. A fair stand-up fight, in a twenty-four feet ring. Mr. Jackson to name the place. The whole of the money to be made good on the 23rd of May. Neat not to exceed thirteen stone seven pounds. Ten guineas a-side are now deposited.

"Witness, W. TRAST."

Upon the deposit being made, the odds were decidedly in favour of Oliver; but previous to the day of battle, they changed to five to four on Neat; the good judges observing that if freshness, length, strength, and height were points towards victory, Neat, who possessed them all, ought to win the fight. The latter, however, sustained some drawback from being an entire stranger to the London fancy.

In opposition to these pretensions, Oliver, the darling of Westminster, who had bravely conquered, in succession, Kimber, Hopping Ned, Harry Lancaster, Ford, Cooper, and the determined Painter—but who was rather cast in the shade from his defeat at Carlisle by Carter, if not considered to have received a check to the championship of England—again presented himself to the attention of the amateurs. Many of the old fanciers were partial to Oliver; and if some of them thought him slow, others viewed him as sure, and the odds against him were taken with much confidence. Previous to the fight the betting varied repeatedly, and on Thursday evening both Oliver and Neat were favourites in turn; it might almost be termed even betting.

Not a bed could be had at any of the villages at an early hour on the preceding evening; and Uxbridge was crowded beyond all precedent. At four o'clock in the morning vehicles of every description were in motion; and the road from Hyde Park Corner to Gerrard's Cross was one cloud of dust. The ring was formed upon one of the most delightful spots the eye of a landscape painter could imagine. The scenery was truly picturesque. Bulstrode House, the seat of the late Duke of Portland, was on the left of it; the foliage of the trees, the verdure of the ground, the swelling eminences, and the grandeur of the prospect, rendered the *tout ensemble* captivating, and the company congratulated each other on the excellent choice which had been made for the display of gymnastic sports. Yet before an entrance could be gained to this elysium of the fancy a handsome tip was demanded at the gate, guarded by more heads than were in the possession of Cerberus of old. But such is the uncertainty of human affairs, in an instant this enchanting scene was changed; all was anxiety and suspense—the stakes were pulled up, the carriages rolled off with the utmost celerity, and the bustling scene became as it were a desert. A magistrate had fixed his paw upon Neat, and no milling could be permitted in Buckinghamshire on that day. Cerberus had now taken flight from the gate, and lots of Johnny Raws stood laughing at the flats who had been drawn of their tin. Rickmansworth, nine miles off, was the scent, and the string of carriages on the road exceeded all calculation. In a field, within a mile of the above place, the ring was again formed; and a few minutes before three Neat appeared and threw up his hat. Oliver immediately followed, bowing to the spectators, and was received with great applause. The latter, on stripping, showed good condition, and was seconded by Tom Jones and Clark; Cribb and Tom Belcher performing that office for Neat. Cribb tied the yellow colours of his man to the stakes, and Jones placed the blue handkerchief of Oliver upon them. Lord Yarmouth, Sir Henry Smith, and a long *et cetera* of amateurs, were round the ring. The ceremony of shaking hands took place, and at three o'clock the fight commenced. Neat five and six to four the favourite.

THE FIGHT.

Round 1.—On setting-to, Neat looked formidable. His attitude was springy and ready for quick action. His legs, decorated with silk stockings, not only evinced fine form, but vast strength; and his arms were equally sinewy. Upon the whole, he had the appearance and make of what is generally considered a prize pugilist. He had also excellent symmetry. Both were anxious to commence in good style, and some sparring occurred. Neat hit short, and Oliver planted the first blow. Some hits were exchanged, and Oliver put in a body hit and got away; however, in following his opponent, he received a blow, and, slipping at the same time, went down. Two minutes and a half had elapsed.

2.—It was evident that experience was on the side of Oliver; but the right arm of Neat was truly dangerous. Oliver put in a bodier, and Neat returned short. The combatants then got into a sharp rally, which terminated with Oliver fibbing down his opponent. (Great applause.) The claret was now seen on the mouth and neck of Neat.

3.—Oliver again made a hit on the body, which Neat returned short with his left hand. Oliver also planted successfully several body blows, and Neat frequently missed in return. Some good counter hits occurred. Oliver followed Neat closely up; some exchanges took place, when Neat turned round and went down from a hit. (Slight disapprobation.)

4.—Oliver found his opponent was a novice, and felt confident of success. This was the longest round in the fight, displaying the various tactics and style of fighting of both the combatants: it may serve as a sort of criterion for the whole battle, and save much of the minute routine of the rounds. Oliver, with much gaiety, planted a severe facer, and Neat in return hit short. Oliver gave another facer. Neat, with his right hand, gave Oliver a tremendous blow under his ear that seemed to send his head from his shoulders, the claret flowing copiously, and a large lump instantly rose. Oliver here showed a good acquaintance with the science, and fought better than usual; he frequently planted body hits and facers without experiencing returns, and broke away in good style. Oliver was tired and put down his hands. Several counter hits occurred. Neat put in a severe body blow, when Oliver soon afterwards was observed to spit, as if his inside had suffered. Oliver made a good right-handed hit, and stopped a tremendous blow with his left. Several other incidents also occurred in Oliver's favour. The latter again spat, and, in a rally, both went down from exhaustion. The round lasted eight minutes. (Six to four on Oliver.)

5.—The hands of Oliver were covered with claret from the work he had done upon his opponent's mug. Oliver took the lead, and finished the round by sending Neat down. (Shouts, and three to one on Oliver.)

6.—Oliver planted a good facer, and counter hits again took place. This was a singular round. Oliver followed Neat to the ropes, and, in a sort of souffle, caught the latter by the thighs, when Neat fell, and Oliver also went down. Both exhibited severe marks of punishment: Neat's mouth was open, and he appeared distressed. Oliver was now decidedly the favourite.

7.—This round had nearly decided the fight. Oliver went down like a dead man from a tremendous right-handed blow under the ear. His senses were completely hit out of him; and Jones, by extraordinary exertions, placed him on the bottle-holder's knee and used every means to recover him again to meet his opponent. ("Time, time," was loudly vociferated from all parts of the ring, and many persons with stop-watches in their hands insisted a minute had elapsed.)

8.—Oliver's second at length brought him forward, with his arm round his body, up to the scratch, when the bottle-holder on Neat's behalf, insisted on his letting go his man. Oliver, staggering, put himself in position to fight, when he was immediately floored.

9.—Time was again called by the spectators, on the difficulty of Oliver's coming to the mark. The latter was evidently stupefied, and was again hit down. (Ten to one on Neat, and hats were thrown up.)

10.—The gameness of Oliver astonished the oldest amateur; and he now so far recovered himself as to have the best of it, and fibbed his opponent down at the ropes. (Great applause.)

11.—Oliver kept the lead, and not only gave a staggering hit to Neat, but caught him again as he was falling.

12.—Oliver in this round was everything. His science in getting away was excellent: he gave his opponent a severe facer, a blow on the eye, and finally floored him, Neat frequently hitting short. ("Bravo, Oliver!" and the odds rising rapidly.)

13.—Neat gave Oliver, in following him, a tremendous right-handed hit on his mouth, so that his upper works were in a complete state of chaos. Neat, notwithstanding this superiority, went down, and it was loudly asserted without a blow. It occasioned marks of disapprobation. (£100 to £5 was offered on Oliver, but no one took it.)

14.—Oliver, after having the best of the round, threw Neat.

15.—Neat hit down, and Oliver fell upon him.

16.—Oliver planted a severe blow under the left ear of his opponent, who went down much distressed.

17.—Oliver made a hit, but Neat stopped it with much dexterity; counter hits, yet Neat was floored.

18.—Neat made three blows, but went down.

19.—Oliver floored his opponent, but was, nevertheless, punished in the round.

20.—Neat's right hand was at work, and Oliver quickly followed him up till he went down.

21.—Oliver floored his antagonist, and fell upon him, and hit Neat in the face as he was in the act of falling upon him. (This produced "Foul, foul," from the friends of Neat.)

22.—Oliver received a hit from Neat, when the latter fell. (Hissing.)

23.—Oliver, in closing, fell upon his opponent.

24.—Neat planted some sharp blows; but Oliver had the best of the round, when Neat went down. ("Bravo, Oliver! well done, Tom!" and the betting greatly in his favour.)

25.—Neat, it appeared, now felt the use of his right arm, and with two blows, right and left-handed, not only sent Oliver staggering away, but hit him down like a shot. (The hats were again thrown up, and the odds had all vanished.)

26.—It was evident Oliver could not recover from the severe effects of the last round. ("Time" was again loudly vociferated; and he came up staggering, only to be hit down.)

27.—Neat again went to work, and planted more tremendous blows; but, in closing, Neat was undermost.

28.—Oliver, game to the last, and more than anxious that his backers should not find fault with him, contended for victory as if the fate of an empire hung upon the event. The stunning blows he had received had put aside all his science, and he now incautiously followed his opponent, who, with his right hand, gave Oliver the *coup de grace*, which took him off his legs in a singular manner: he fell flat on his back as senseless as a log of wood. "Time" was called, but the brave Oliver heard not the sound. One hour and thirty-one seconds had elapsed.

REMARKS. — Neat, notwithstanding the decisive victory he obtained over Oliver, appeared little more than a novice in scientific boxing. It is true, he might be improved under the tuition of skilful and accomplished boxers, for he possesses a requisite above all that teaching can achieve, namely, "one hit with his right hand, given in proper distance, can gain a victory, and three of them are positively enough to dispose of a giant." Neat hits from the shoulder with an astonishing and peculiar force; and, in one instance, the arm of Oliver received so paralyzing a shock in stopping the blow, that it appeared almost useless. The admirers of fine fighting are decidedly of opinion that

Neat has no such pretensions; but as a hard hitter (of steam-engine power), it is asserted there is nothing like him on the present list. He fought very awkwardly; and had he used his right hand to advantage in the early part of the fight, in all probability it must have been over in a few rounds; but it should be recollected it was his first appearance in the London ring. One word for the brave but fallen Oliver before these remarks are closed. He fought like a hero; and the courage of human nature was never witnessed in a higher point of view than exhibited by him in this contest. The battle was never safe to him, notwithstanding his exertions were more scientific than in any of his previous fights. It was also far from being safe to Neat till the twenty-fifth round. The latter was in bad condition, while Oliver could not be finer; but a chance blow from Neat can floor one hundred to one in a twinkling, although he is a round hitter.

Oliver, although defeated, was not disgraced; on the contrary, it was asserted that he had fixed his claims more strongly upon the amateurs in general by his brave conduct. In eight battles he had proved himself a good man—six of them he won. It was upon the whole a good fight; but Oliver was too slow for an active man like Neat. Several minutes elapsed before Oliver recovered sensibility, and his situation for a short period was thought to be critical. He was bled in the ring, and Neat shook hands with him. He was taken from the scene of action in a landau, and every attention paid to him that humanity could suggest. Neat was also assisted to his vehicle in a very distressed state, his face completely altered from the severity of punishment it had undergone.

Neat did not remain long in the metropolis; and, in his way home, he called at Sam Porch's booth, at Lansdown Fair, where the latter, in honour of the victory of his countryman, had for his sign portraits of Neat and Oliver in battle. The amateurs who made the match for Neat now suggested to him the propriety of taking a benefit in London, which the latter rather reluctantly complied with. However, he again arrived in the metropolis; and on Tuesday, the 23rd of February, 1819, the Fives Court was respectably attended for his benefit. Neat, followed by Shelton, attracted considerable attention. It was Neat's first appearance with the gloves at the Fives Court; his severity of hitting in the ring had been previously ascertained, and his knowledge of the science was now only to be developed. He proved quick in his movements, and stopped with skill, and the set-to, upon the whole, was entitled to praise. It is true that Shelton planted the most nobbing hits, and one on the mouth told rather heavily; but a bodier from Neat out-valued the whole of them in calculation and effect, and seemed to operate so sharply upon the frame of his opponent that the interior appeared in sudden motion. Shelton evinced improvement, and was pronounced to have rather the best of this bout. Richmond and Harmer showed the advantages of science: their play was light and pleasing to the amateur. Neat and Harmer wound up the sports of the day in a light contest, when the former complained of not being able to return thanks as he wished, being no orator   Cribb, Oliver, Randall, Reynolds, Owen, and Gregson were present, but did not exhibit. It appeared that one of the small tendons of Neat's right arm had been injured, which prevented him from using it with any strength or activity, and three months must elapse, it was said, before a cure could be pronounced, or Neat returned fit for service.

In calculating his loss of time, the neglect his business sustained at home, and his expenses in London, it is said Neat scarcely cleared himself by this appeal to the patronage of the public.

Cribb and Spring being on a sparring tour, and making Bristol in their route, a match for 100 guineas a-side was made between Neat and Spring, and £50 a-side put down at the Greyhound Inn, Broadmead, Bristol. The fight to take place on the 6th of October, 1819, half way between Bristol and London; but, in consequence of Neat's breaking his arm while in training, this match was off, not only to the chagrin of both the combatants, but to the great disappointment of the sporting world.

Symptoms of a "screw being loose" between the Champion of England and Neat, the following appeared in most of the London newspapers :—

"TO MR. T. CRIBB.

"I observed in a report of the sparring match for the benefit of Harry Harmer, that you, being flushed by the juice of the grape, took an opportunity of paying me a compliment, which I did not expect you had liberality enough to do; namely, that 'Neat was the best of the bad ones,' and that 'you would fight him for from £500 to £1,000.' In answer to which, I inform you that I will fight you as soon as you like (the sooner the better) for from a glass of gin to £200.

                                                       "WILLIAM NEAT.

   "*All Saints' Lane, Bristol, August* 14, 1820."

Neat's next match was with the terrific "Gas" for 100 guineas a-side, and the spot fixed was Newbury, Berks. On Monday, December 11, 1821, the day before the fight, as soon as daylight peeped, the bustle on the road to Maidenhead was tremendous. Nothing particular, however, occurred, except the staring of the good people of Reading at the fancy as they passed through that place. At the entrance of the town of Newbury a strong muster of the yokels stationed themselves throughout the whole of the day grinning at the Londoners as they arrived. Indeed, the road on Monday, and all night, up to Tuesday morning at twelve o'clock, from the metropolis, was thronged with vehicles of every description. The roads leading from Oxford, Gloucester, etc., and likewise from Bristol, were in the same state with persons anxious to reach the rallying point, Newbury. All the inns were filled, and the beds engaged some days previous: it was a prime benefit to the town.

About three o'clock in the afternoon, Hickman, with his backer and Spring, in a barouche and four, with Shelton outside, drove rapidly through the town, the Gas-light Man laughing and bowing, on being recognised and cheered by the populace, till they alighted at the Castle, Speen Hill. Here he was visited by numerous gentlemen, to all of whom he declared his confidence of success, and that victory would crown his efforts in a short time. After the bustle of the day was over, the President of the Daffy Club took the chair at the Three Tuns, in the Market-place, Newbury, which, as soon as the office had been given, became the head quarters. Thither the swells and the sporting men mustered round the holder of the stakes. It was a complete betting stand, and numerous wagers were made on the coming event. In consequence of the Newmarket people, with Mr. Gully and Mr. Bland at their head, taking Neat, the odds fell on the Gas: a few persons who were funking a little got off some of their money, but the principal part of the fancy stood firm, and many of them laid it on thicker, although Mr. Gully, in the most candid manner, declared his opinion, that if a fine, young, strong, fourteen stone man could not defeat a twelve stone boxer, then there was no calculation on prize milling." Tuesday morning, long before the darkness had cleared off, presented a scene to the Johnny Raws, in the numerous arrivals from London, most of them having been on the road all night, with their peepers half open and their tits almost at a standstill. About ten o'clock Newbury presented an interesting appearance. The inhabitants were all out of doors; the windows of the houses crowded with females, anxiously waiting to witness the departure of the fancy to the mill. Indeed it was a lively picture—barouches and four, curricles, post-chaises, gigs, carts, stage-coaches, wagons, myriads of yokels on horseback, chaw-bacons scampering along the road, Corinthians and bang-up lads tooling it along.

The fun and gig was kept up by the lads till Hungerford Downs, the wished-for spot, appeared in sight. It was a delightfully fine morning, the sun adding splendour to the scene, giving the whole a most picturesque appearance. The prospect was quite attractive. A charming country on both sides of the road; the town of Hungerford at a distance, with the spire of the church; the ring on the Downs, surrounded with wagons and coaches, marquees, etc., rising grandly like an amphitheatre, formed so pleasing a feature as to render description no easy task. The spot was selected under the judicious management of Mr. Jackson, and the ring was so well arranged that 25,000 persons, who were present, had an excellent sight of the battle. Not the slightest accident occurred, and the whole was conducted with the greatest decorum. It was curious to witness the anxiety displayed by this great assemblage of persons, waiting with the utmost patience, without the slightest murmur, for two hours, the ring having been formed so early as eleven o'clock.

At a few minutes after one, Neat, arm-in-arm with his backer and Belcher, appeared in the outer space, and threw up his hat, but the sun being in his eyes it did not reach its intended destination, when Belcher picked it up and threw it in the ring. Shortly afterwards the Gas, in a white topper, supported by his backer and Shelton, repeated the token of defiance, and entered the ring sucking an orange. He immediately shook hands with Neat, saying, " How are you ?" Mr. Jackson was the referee. Belcher and Harmer were the seconds for Neat, and Spring and Shelton for the Gas. The odds had completely changed on the preceding evening ; and on the ground Neat was backed five to four, besides numerous even bets, and being taken for choice. Upwards of £150,000, it is calculated, eventually changed owners on this battle. The Gas weighed twelve stone, Neat nearly fourteen. The colours, deep blue for Gas, and the Bristol yellow man for Neat, were tied to the stakes.

THE FIGHT.

Round 1.— Both men appeared in the highest condition ; in fact the backers of Neat and Gas asserted that they were to all intents and purposes fit for milling. The frame of Neat was a fine study ; and the comparison between the pugilists was remarkable. The Gas, on placing himself in attitude, surveyed his opponent from head to foot, and Neat was equally on the alert. Hickman kept dodging about in order to get an opening to plant a determined hit ; but Neat was too leary to be had upon this suit, and whenever the Gas moved, he likewise altered his position. On Neat's preparing to give a blow, the Gas, smiling, drew himself back ; but immediately afterwards, as if resolutely making up his mind to do some mischief, he went right bang in, and with his right hand put in a nobber, Neat retreating. Hickman planted a second blow on his shoulder ; he also put in a third hit upon Neat's left eye, and, elated with his success, he was on the rush to place a fourth blow, when Neat stopped him with a tremendous hit on his throat, which made the Gas stagger a little. Hickman, however, undismayed, attacked Neat with great activity, and the result was, the Bristol hero went down (more from a slip than the severity of the blow) between the legs of Hickman, the Cockneys shouting for joy, and the regular fanciers declaring " it was all right, and that Gas would win it easy." (Seven to four on Gas.)

2.—Hickman came laughing to the scratch,

full of confidence ; but on his endeavouring to plant his tremendous right-handed hit on the throat of his antagonist, the length of Neat prevented it, and the blow alighted on his shoulder. The Gas again endeavoured to make it, when the Bristol hero gave Hickman so hard a blow on his box of ivories that he chattered without talking, and went back from his position as if he could not keep it ; he also was compelled to make a pause before he again commenced the attack. The Gas got away smiling from a left-handed hit, when he rushed in with uncommon severity, and, after an exchange of blows, they both went down, Neat undermost. (Another loud shout for Hickman, the odds rising on him, and " he'll win it to a certainty," was the cry.) While sitting on the knee of his second the Gas winked to his friends, as much as to give the office " it was all right."

3.—If the backers of the Gas could not see the improvement of the Bristol hero, Hickman was satisfied that he had a dangerous customer before him, and found that the length of arm possessed by his opponent rendered it highly necessary for him to act with great caution ; he, therefore, on coming to the scratch, made a pause, and did not appear, as heretofore, eager to go to work. Neat was all caution and steadiness, and determined to wait for his opponent ; the Gas, in consequence, was compelled to make play, and he planted a sharp hit on Neat's head, and, laughing, nodded at him.

Encouraged by this success, he was about furiously to repeat the dose, when Neat caught him with his left hand on his nob, which sent the Gas down on his knee; but his courage was so high and good, that he jumped up and renewed the fight like a game cock, till he was hit down by another tremendous blow. (The Bristolians now took a turn with their chaffers, and the shouting was loud in the extreme. The partisans of the Gas-light Man were rather on the fret, and several of them had "got the uneasiness.")

4.—It was now discovered by the knowing ones that they had not consulted Cocker; it was also evident (but rather too late to turn it to their advantage) that Neat was as quick as his opponent, a better in-fighter, with a tolerable knowledge of the science, and not such a roarer as he had been said to be. The severe nobbers the Gas had received in the preceding round had chanceried his upperworks a little, and, on his appearing at the scratch, he again made a pause. He saw the length of his opponent was difficult to get within; and he also saw that, if he did not commence fighting, Neat was not to be gammoned off his guard for a month. Hickman went in resolutely to smash his opponent, but he was met right in the middle of his head with one of the most tremendous right-handed blows ever witnessed, and went down like a shot. (The Bristolians now applauded to the echo, and the London "good judges," as they had previously thought themselves, were on the funk. "How do you like it?" said one of the swells, who was pretty deep in it. "Why," replied the other, "that blow has cost me, I am afraid, a hundred sovereigns.")

5.—Gas came up an altered man; indeed, a bullock must seriously have felt such a blow. He stood still for an instant, but his high courage would not let him flinch; he defied danger, although it stared him in the face, and, regardless of the consequences, he commenced fighting, made some exchanges, till he went down from a terrible hit in the mouth. (The Bristol boys hoarse with shouting, and the faces of the backers of Gas undergoing all manner of contortions. "That's the way," said Tom Belcher. "It's all your own. You'll win it, my boy: only a little one now and then for the Castle.")

6.—The mouth of the Gas was full of blood, and he appeared almost choking when time was called. He was getting weak; he, nevertheless, rushed in and bored Neat to the ropes, when the spectators were satisfied, by the superiority displayed, that Neat was the best in-fighter. He punished Gas in all directions, and finished the round by grassing him with a belly puncher that would have floored an ox. This hit was quite enough to have finished the pluck of two good men. (The long faces from London were now so numerous, that no artist could have taken their likenesses. The Bristolians

were roaring with delight "Did'nt I tell thee what he could do? The Gas is sure to go out now!" "Not this time," replied a few out-and-outers from the Long Town, who endeavoured to face it out in favour of Hickman, while anything like a chance remained.)

7.—Spring and Shelton were very attentive to their man, and led him up to the scratch at the sound of time. The Gas was sadly distressed, and compelled to pause before he went to work; but Neat waited for him. The Gas was about to make play, when Belcher said to Neat, "Be ready, my boy, he's coming." The Bristol hero sent the Gas staggering from him by a nobber, but Neat would not follow him. On the Gas attempting to make a hit, Neat again put in a tremendous blow on his mouth that uncorked the claret in profusion. The Gas recovered himself to the astonishment of all present, went to work, and, after some desperate exchanges, sent Neat down. This change produced a ray of hope on the part of his backers, and "Bravo, Gas! you're a game fellow, indeed." The anxiety of Tom Belcher to be near his man, occasioned Shelton to remark to Mr. Jackson, that if Tom did not keep away from Neat, according to his order, he should likewise keep close to the Gas. "Tom," said Shelton, "you had better come and fight for Neat."

8.—The Gas, laughing, commenced the attack, but received such a giant-like blow on his right eye that he was convulsed; such were the terrific effects of this hit, that Hickman, after standing motionless for about three seconds, appeared to jump off the ground, his arms hanging by his sides, when he went down like a log on his back, and the shock was so great that his hands flew up over his head: he was totally insensible; so much so that Shelton and Spring could scarcely get him off the ground. The whole ring seemed panic-struck. Spring, vociferating almost with the voice of a Stentor to awake him from his stupor, with the repeated calls of "Gas! Gas! Gas!" The head of Hickman had dropped upon his shoulder. The spectators left their places and ran towards the ropes, thinking it was all over; indeed, the anxiety displayed, and the confusion which occurred in whipping out the ring, had such an effect that several persons observed a minute had passed away. On time being called, the Gas opened one eye wildly, for he had now only one left, the other being swelled and bleeding copiously.

9.—The battle was now decidedly Neat's own, and every eye was on the stretch, in expection of the Bristol hero going in to administer the *coup de grace*. An experienced boxer of the London ring would have taken advantage of this circumstance, and not have given the chance away; but Neat, in the most manly manner, waited for Hickman at the scratch till the Gas felt himself enabled to renew milling. On recovering, he shook himself, as it were, to remove the effects of the overpowering stupor under which he laboured, and every person seemed electrified with his manner. He commenced the attack with much activity, and, after an exchange of blows, strange to say, sent Neat down. (Loud shouts of applause, and the whole ring expressing their admiration at the almost invincible courage Hickman possessed.)

10.—The Gas came to the scratch staggering, his knees almost bending beneath his weight; he, however, showed most determined fight, and contended like a hero till he was hit down.

11.—The state of the Gas was truly pitiable, and on setting-to he scarcely seemed to know where he was, and made a short pause before he attempted to put in a hit. Neat's left hand again was planted on his nob, which sent the Gas staggering from him. Neat endeavoured to repeat the dose, but he missed his opponent; it might be considered fortunate that this blow did not reach its place of destination, as, in all probability, it would have proved Hickman's quietus. The latter, after some exchanges, was again hit down. (Four to one.)

12.—It was quite clear that the Gas was not yet extinguished, for this round was a complete milling one. Hickman followed his adversary, exchanging hit for hit; but it was evident, however desperate the intention of Hickman might be, his blows were not effective; while, on the contrary, the hits of Neat were terrific, and reduced the strength of his opponent at every move. Still the confidence of the Gas was unshaken, and he returned to the charge till Neat went down. (Tremendous applause. "What an astonishing game fellow!")

13.—The Gas had scarcely attempted to make a hit, when Neat's left floored him like a shot. (The shouting from the Lansdown and the St. James's Churchyard natives was like a roar of artillery. Ten to one; but all shy, and scarcely a taker.)

14.—It was now a horse to a hen, although Hickman seemed determined to contend. He was distressed beyond measure, and his seconds were compelled to lead him to the scratch.* On putting himself in attitude, he was quite upon the see-saw, and to all appearance would only take a touch to send him down. "Give him a little one for me," said Shelton. "I will," replied Hickman; "but where is he?" Some exchanges took place, till both went down. (Any odds.)

15.—The intention of Hickman was still for fighting; or, to speak more accurately, it should be called instinct, for as to reflection it seemed quite out of the question. This round was short; and, after a blow or two, the Gas was again hit down. (Loud cries of "Take the brave fellow away, he has

no chance; it is cruel to let him remain.") As Hickman lay on the ground he appeared convulsed.

16.—Shelton and Spring, when time was called, brought the Gas to the scratch. He stared wildly for a second, when he endeavoured to fight, but was on the totter. His fine action was gone, and he now only stood up to be hit at. ("Take him away," from all parts of the ring, in which Mr. Gully loudly joined.)

17.—The game of the Gas was so out-and-out good that he preferred death to defeat. He again toddled to the scratch, but it was only to receive additional and unnecessary punishment. He was floored *sans ceremonie.* ("Take him away," was again the cry; but he would not quit the field. "He must not come again," was the general expression of the spectators.)

18 and last.—On the Gas appearing at the mark, instead of putting up his arms to fight he endeavoured to button the flap of his drawers in a confused state. Neat scorned to take advantage of his defenceless situation, and with the utmost coolness waited for him to commence the round. The Gas, as a last effort, endeavoured to show fight, but was pushed down, which put an end to the battle by his proving insensible to the call of time. The contest occupied twenty-three and a half minutes. Neat jumped and threw up his arms as a token of victory, amidst the proud and loud shouts which pronounced him conqueror. He went and shook the hand of his brave fallen opponent before he left the ring. A medical man bled Hickman on the spot without delay, and every humane attention was paid to him by his backer and his seconds. He remained for a short time in the ring in a state of stupor, was carried to a carriage, and conveyed to the Castle Inn, Speen Hill, near Newbury, and immediately put to bed.

REMARKS.—To sum up the behaviour of the fallen hero in the fight, it is only common justice to say of the Gas, that he cut up, without disparagement, gamer than any man we ever before witnessed. His greatest enemy must join in this remark; indeed, if his countenance was anything like an index of his mind, the courage of Hickman was so high that he appeared to feel ashamed, and to quarrel with nature for deserting him. It is true that he was floored, but it is equally true the Gas was not extinct. "Give him," said an old sporting man, "but a chance with anything near his weight, and the odds will be in his favour; he will again burst forth with redoubled splendour." It cannot be denied that Hickman made himself numerous enemies by his chaffing. Out of the ring he was viewed as a great talker, often asserting more than he could perform; but in his battle with Neat he de-

* This, as we have already observed, would not be allowed by modern practice, and is forbidden by the new Rules of the Ring, Arts. 7 and 9.—Ed. PUGILISTICA.

cidedly proved himself no boaster; and in
the eyes of the sporting world, although suffering defeat, he raised his character higher
than ever it stood before as a pugilist. His
fault was, he thought himself unconquerable,
and laughed at the idea of weight, length,
and strength being opposed to him. If any
apology can be offered for Hickman, it is
that he did not stand alone in this view of
his capabilities, for he was flattered by the
majority of the fancy to the very echo, who
backed him, on the match being made,
nearly two to one.

A parallel might be instituted between Hickman and the lion-hearted
Hooper; high patronage, without discretion, ruined the former, and however
good nobs for milling boxers may possess, it is too commonly seen they do
not wear heads to bear sudden elevation. As a friendly hint to all pugilists
we trust this lesson will prove useful to them, and if they will endeavour to
avoid "putting an enemy into their mouths to steal away their brains," all
will go right. The fists of pugilists are only to be exercised in the prize
ring; the tongues of boxers were never intended to excite terror in the
unoffending visitor. Hickman, however, wanted discretion and self-control:
he had no reason to be ashamed of this defeat, for it was one of the most
manly fights ever witnessed. No closing, no pulling and hauling each other
at the ropes, but fair stand-up milling from beginning to end. No pugilist strained every point further to win a battle than the Gas did, and
although thousands of pounds were lost on him, his backers had no right
to complain.

The behaviour of the subject of this memoir was the admiration of all
present: it was unassuming and manly in the extreme. In a word, Neat
proved a good fighter, and was thought, before he met with Spring, to be
superior to any boxer on the list. He retired from the ring without any
prominent marks; nevertheless, he received many heavy blows.

Bristol, in the person of Neat, now claimed the championship. Although
its hero bore his blushing honours with becoming modesty, and publicly
asserted, at the Castle Tavern, Holborn, on the Thursday after the fight, that
he took no merit to himself in having defeated Hickman. "The Gas-light
Man," said Neat, "was over-weighted; but I think he can beat all the
twelve stone men on the list. He is, I am convinced, one of the gamest men
in the kingdom; and, although I have been a great deal chaffed about as a
nobody, I will fight any man in London to-morrow morning for £100 a-side
of my own money."

The result of this mill was a pretty "cleaning out" of the Londoners,
who returned to town with "pockets to let." Nevertheless, there was little
grumbling, all uniting in the opinion that Hickman was entitled to praise,
doing all that he could to win. The news arrived in London by pigeon
about half past three o'clock in the afternoon. It is impossible to describe

the anxiety of the great crowds of persons which surrounded all the sporting houses in the metropolis to learn the event. In Bristol it was the same, and the editor of the *Gazette* of that place thus describes it:—" Such was the intense feeling excited in this city, that the streets were crowded as if an election contest was at its height, all inquiring the result, which was known here about seven o'clock." The following sentences were exhibited by a boy on a board in the road:—

" Bristol illuminated,
London in darkness,
The Gas extinguished by a ' Neat hand.'"

The Bristol hero arrived at Belcher's, the Castle Tavern, Holborn, on Wednesday evening, and made his bow to the Daffy Club. He was received with loud cheers.

The turn of that " tide" which Shakspeare has declared to exist in the " affairs of man" now occurred in the milling career of the " Pride of Bristol," as he was at this time termed. This was the great match with Tom Spring for the championship, of which full details will be found in pp. 16-22, vol. ii., *ante*. The battle was for £200 a-side, and took place near Andover, May 20, 1823. Spring's weight was stated at thirteen stone two pounds, Neat's at thirteen stone seven pounds, Spring being about four years older than his antagonist. The length to which the report of the battle extends in the pages above referred to, precludes the necessity of farther dwelling on its features here, than by relating a few anecdotes connected therewith.

There is a class of men who always couple defeat with disgrace, and insinuate or assert dishonesty whenever events do not fall in with their hopes, their prophesies, or their wishes. The editor of the *Bristol Gazette* made the following remarks on the occasion:—" Round the 9th.—Here—publish it not in Gath, tell it not among the Philistines—when time was called, Neat walked up and, instead of clenched fist, stretched out his hand to Spring; it was all U P. The Londoners shouted, the Bristolians looked glum; not the recollection of former victories by all the Pearces and Cribbs, and Gullys and Belchers, could for a moment revive them: every man stared at his neighbour with inquiring eye—' What does it all mean?' At last a report ran that Neat had broken his arm in a fall. ' Pshaw! all my eye!' Mr. Jackson, the Commander-in-Chief, went round with a hat for a collection for the loser —he confirmed the report of the broken arm. Whether this was a fact or not remains to be proved; this, however, was evident, that Neat neither fought with his accustomed courage nor skill. The battle had lasted but thirty-seven minutes : neither of the men were otherwise hurt. Neat never attempted once to get in to his man; when Spring was at the ropes, he did not follow him as he might have done; he was all on the shy, and fell once with the shadow of a blow. Spring relied chiefly, there is no doubt, upon his superior wrestling, and was always eager for the hug; but Neat either had not quickness to keep him off or wanted courage to strike. The sparring of Spring was much admired; but if Neat had had recourse to the smashing which he practised on Hickman, Spring's science might have been puzzled. It is supposed that more money was lost by the Bristol boys than at any fight on record. The Londoners went chaffing home in fine style, whilst the return of the Bristol cavalcade was like that of a long country funeral."

Mr. Jackson collected for the losing man, on the ground, £47 19s. The night previous to the battle, Spring, in company with his backer, walked from Andover to take a view of the ground on which the battle was to take place, when Spring observed, "It was so beautiful a spot that no man could grumble to be well licked upon it."

The newspaper report respecting Mr. Sant, the backer of Spring, having won £7,000 on the event is erroneous; also that Mr. Gully had realised £10,000. Mr. G. did not win more than £100. It is true that Mr. James Bland picked up a tidy stake; but it was false that Belcher lost a large sum of money upon the battle: Tom was too good a judge to risk too much of his blunt. So much for correct newspaper information.

Painter left his house at Norwich on purpose to perform the office of second to Spring, it being a particular request of the latter boxer. The wags of the fancy, at the conclusion of the battle, proposed that the town of Andover in future should have the letter H *neat*-ly added to it—to stand thus, Hand-over, in allusion to the great transfer of specie on this occasion.

It was stated in the newspapers that a fine old lady of the Society of Friends, with a couple of her daughters, came in their carriage to the Angel at Marlborough, during the time Neat was training. The two daughters remained in the carriage at the door, while the old lady made her way into the Angel. She ascended the stairs, and found Belcher in a room, sitting by himself, Neat having retired to change his clothes. Tom thought the lady had mistaken the apartment, till she addressed him. "Thy name is Belcher, is it not, friend?" "Yes, madam," was the reply. Tom was in hopes to get rid of the lady before Neat returned; but she waited till the Bristol hero made his appearance. "I understand, friend Neat, thou art about fighting a prize battle. Dost thou not know it is very sinful? Be advised, friend, and give it up." Neat urged that he was bound in honour, and that if he gave it up he should not only be a heavy loser of money, but stand disgraced for betraying his friends. "If it be the lucre of gain, friend Neat, I will recompense thee," thereon, the report went on to say, that the lady offered money to the pugilist. Other journals coupled the name of the worthy and excellent Mrs. Fry with the affair, which called forth the following epistle from her husband :—

"*To the Editor of the* MORNING CHRONICLE.

"My wife and myself will be much obliged by thy insertion in thy valuable paper of a few words, contradicting the absurd story, copied from a Bath and Cheltenham paper, of her having interfered to prevent the late battle between Spring and Neat, the whole of which is without the slightest foundation in truth or probability.
"I am respectfully, etc.
"JOSEPH FRY.

"*St. Mildred's Court*, 22*nd 5th Month*, 1823.

Notwithstanding this denial, it is certain that a well-intentioned Quaker lady did act as above described, for which, viewing the peculiar tenets of her sect, we must rather applaud than ridicule her.

In disposition, Bill Neat was not only generous and cheerful, but might be termed a "high fellow," and always ready to serve a friend. He was fond of a "bit of life," threw off a good chaunt, and was the President of the Daffy Club, held at Sam Porch's, Guildhall Tavern, Broad Street, Bristol. It was said of him that, "If he is not a good fighter, Neat is a good fellow."

From this period Neat, the small bone of whose arm was really fractured, retired from the fistic arena. He became subsequently a butcher in Bristol, where he resided until his death, which took place on the 23rd of March, 1858, in the sixty-seventh year of his age. Neat was respected for many social qualities, and his genuine kind-heartedness, under a rough exterior, gained the friendship of many. His prowess in levelling the small Welsh cattle by a blow with a gauntlet glove between the eyes has been narrated to us by eye-witnesses of this Milonian feat. Bill Neat adds another to the many instances, which this history has presented, of the esteem and good opinion which the best men of the ring have earned from all classes of society.

CHAPTER VI.

THOMAS HICKMAN ("THE GAS MAN").

A SECOND Hotspur, had the sword been his weapon—fiery, hardy, daring, impetuous, laughing to scorn all fear, and refusing to calculate odds in weight, length, or strength, "the Gas Man," for a brief period, shone rather as a dazzling comet than a fixed star or planet in the pugilistic sphere. Impetuous in the assault almost to ferocity, though not destitute of skill, Hickman, like Hooper in his earlier day, prided himself that his irresistible charge must confound, dismay, and paralyze the defence of his opponent. There was certainly something terrific in his attack, for in his earlier battles his head and body seemed insensible to blows, at least they failed to drive him from his purpose or to sensibly affect his strength, cheerfulness, or vigour.   At one period it was thought by his over-sanguine admirers that no skill could repel his clever "draw" and his rushing onslaught.   Retreat, when once in for a rally, was with him a thing not to be thought of, and he carried all before him.   Success is the test and only criterion of the many, and Hickman, despite experience, was over-rated.   Out of the ring, Hickman was fond of fun, vivacious, warm-hearted, and friendly; but, as may be supposed, headstrong, violent, and repentant where wrong.   Pugilists, more liable to insults than most men, should always control their tempers.   It is necessary in the fight, and equally valuable in private life.   Our most eminent boxers (see lives of JOHNSON, CRIBB, SPRING, etc., for corroboration) have been kind, forbearing, and of equable temper.   As a runner, Hickman was known before his ring *début*, and won several prizes at this and jumping. The early career of Hickman we take upon the credit of "Boxiana," "the historian" being his contemporary.

Thomas Hickman was born in Ken Lane, Dudley, Worcestershire, on the 28th of January, 1785.   His nurse thought that he showed something like "fight," even in his cradle; but when Tommy felt the use of his pins, and could toddle out among his play-fellows, he was considered as the most

THOMAS HICKMAN ("The Gas Man").

To face page 118.

handy little kid amongst them. His skirmishes, when a boy, are too numerous for recital; but it will suffice to state that, in the circle in which he moved, when any of them were in danger of being beaten, it was a common observation amongst them, to intimidate the refractory, that they would fetch "Tom Hickman to lick him!"

Hickman was apprenticed to a steam-engine boiler maker. His first regular combat was with one Sedgeley, in a place called Wednesbury Field.* Sedgeley was disposed of with ease and quickness by young Tom.

John Miller, a coppersmith, was his next opponent in the same field. This match was for one guinea a-side; but Miller proved so good a man that Hickman was one hour and a half before he obtained the victory. Miller was heavily punished about his nob.

Jack Hollis, a glass-blower, a hero who had seen some little service in the milling way at Dudley, was backed for £5 a-side against Hickman. This turned out a very severe battle. Hollis proved himself a good man, although he was defeated in twenty-five minutes.

Luke Walker, a collier, entertained an idea that he could beat Hickman "like winking," and matched himself against the latter for two guineas; but, in the short space of nineteen minutes, Walker lost his two yellow-boys, and got well thrashed in the bargain.

Hickman now left his native place for the metropolis, to follow his business, and took up his residence in the Borough. It was not long before a customer of the name of Bill Doughty, a blacksmith, offered himself to the notice of our hero, and was finished off cleverly in thirteen minutes, in a field near Gravel Lane.

An Irishman of the name of Hollix, the champion of "the Borough"— then, as in later years, noted for its fighting lads—fancied Hickman, and a match was made for six guineas a-side. Miller seconded Hickman upon this occasion. This was a tremendous fight, in the same field as the last battle, occupying thirty-two minutes, in the course of which Hickman was thrown heavily in nineteen rounds, owing to the superior strength of the Irishman, experiencing several severe cross-buttocks. Hickman at length got a turn, when he caught the Irishman's hand, held him fast, and planted such a stupifying blow under his listener, that poor Paddy was so much hurt and so much frightened that he requested the bystanders to take him to the hospital.

Jack Thomas, a thirteen stone man, well known in the Borough, was beaten by Hickman in a short, fierce battle. He also accommodated a fellow of the name of Jack Andrews, for £1 a-side, in the Borough, who talked of

* A town once celebrated for cooking, pronounced by the natives " Wedgebury."

what great things he had done in the boxing line, and what great things he could still perform; but in the course of seventeen minutes he was so punished as to be glad to resign the contest. Hickman had not the slightest mark upon his face in this encounter.

Seven millwrights belonging to Sir John Rennie's factory, it is said, were all beaten by Hickman, in a turn-up near the John's Head, Holland Street. The latter, on leaving the above house, was attacked by this party, and compelled to fight in his own defence. These millwrights afterwards summoned Hickman before the magistrates at Horsemonger Lane; but, on an explanation taking place, Hickman had also the best of the round again before his worship, the first assault being proved.

Hickman was a well made, compact man, by no means so heavy in appearance as he proved to be on going to scale, namely, eleven stone eleven pounds. His height was five feet nine and a half inches. His nob was a fighting one, and his eyes small, being protected by prominent orbital bones. His frame, when stripped, was firm and round, displaying great muscular strength. Hickman was not a showy, but an effective, decisive hitter; perhaps the term of a smashing boxer would be more appropriate. He was, however, a much better fighter than he appeared from his peculiar style of attack.

We believe it was owing to Tom Shelton (who first discovered this milling diamond in the rough) that Hickman exhibited in the prize ring. His out-and-out qualities were whispered to a few of the judges on the sly, and a patron was at length found for him. It was then determined that he should be tried with a promising pugilist; and a match was made between Hickman and young Peter Crawley, for £50 a-side. This came off on Tuesday, March 16, 1819, at Moulsey Hurst.

The morning was threatening, but the enlivening rays of bright Sol chased all gloom, and infused animation, interest, and spirits through the multitude. It might be termed the first turn-out of the fancy for the spring season, and the vehicles were gay and elegant. The presence of a sprinkling of Corinthians gave life to the scene. More interest was excited upon the fight than might have been expected, as both the boxers on point of trial were viewed as new ones to the ring. Hickman, although a light subject in himself, was, to the amateurs, completely a dark one. "What sort of a chap is he?" "What has he done?" "Has he ever fought anybody?" were repeatedly asked, and as repeatedly answered, "That no one knew anything about him." It was, however, generally understood that he was very strong; but it was urged, as a sort of drawback, that he had too much chaffing about him. On the other hand, though "Young Rump Steak" stood high as a glove practitioner, his strength and stamina were doubted. He was a youth of not more than nineteen years of age, nearly six feet high, twelve stone in weight, but thought to have more gristle than bone; however, the keen air of Hampstead, added to good training, had not only produced an improvement of his frame, but had reduced the odds against him, and, on the morning of fighting, it was, in a great measure, even betting, or "Young Peter" for choice. The importance of the "Man of Gas" was kept up by his trainer, Tom Shelton, who confidently asserted that if Hickman did not win he would quit the boxing ring, and take up a quiet abode in the bosom of Father Thames, Oliver also declaring that he would follow his namesake's example if their "Tom" did not win in a canter. Such was the state of affairs when the moment arrived for the appearance of the heroes on the plains of Moulsey. Hickman showed first in the ring and threw up his castor, attended by his seconds, Oliver and Shelton. Crawley soon followed, waited upon by Painter and Jones. The colours were tied to the stakes, and at one o'clock the men set-to.

THE FIGHT.

Round 1.—The Gas-light blade seemed well primed as a "four pound burner," and eager to eclipse his opponent with his superior brilliancy. He showed fight instantly, rushed upon his opponent, and gave Young Rump Steak a mugger, but it did not prove effective. Crawley endeavoured to retreat from the boring qualities of his antagonist, and tapped Hickman over his guard. The latter went in, almost laughing at the science against him, and Crawley could not resist his efforts with anything like a stopper. He also received a desperate hit upon his right ear, that not only drew the claret, but floored him. In going down he unfortunately hit his head against a stake. ("Well done, my Gassy," from the Light Company; and seven to four offered upon him.)

2.—The appearance of Crawley was completely altered. He was groggy from the effects of the last blow and the contact with the stake. The Gas Man let fly sans ceremonie, and the nob of his opponent was pinked in all directions. His nose received a heavy hit, and he went down covered with claret. (£10 to £5 upon Hickman.)

3.—It was evident that Crawley had not strength enough in the first round, but now he was quite reduced. He, however, showed good pluck, put in some hits that marked his opponent, and swelled up his left eye like a roll; but he was punished in return dreadfully, and again went down. (Three to one, but no takers.)

4.—Crawley received a terrible hit in the throat, and fell on his back, with his arms extended, quite exhausted. (Five to one.)

5.—Crawley set-to with more spirit than could have been expected. He planted some facers; but the force of his opponent operated like a torrent—the stream appeared to carry him away. He was punished up to the ropes, and then floored upon his face. (Seven to one.)

6.—The pluck of Crawley was good; he tried to make a change, but without effect; he received a nobber that sent him staggering away, quite abroad, and fell down.

7. — This was a desperate round, and Crawley gave hit for hit till the Gas-light Man's face blazed again; but Crawley was exhausted, and both went down. ("Go along, Crawley; such another round, and you can't lose it.") It was almost give and take hitting.

8. — Crawley also fought manfully this round; but he had no chance, and the Gas Man again sent him down. (All betters, but no takers.)

9.—The right hand of Hickman was tremendous. Crawley's nob completely in chancery, and he was milled out of the ring.

10.—This round was similar to the famous one between Painter and Sutton during their first fight. Crawley was so severely hit from the scratch that he never put up his hands. ("Take him away," from all parts of the ring.)

11.—This round was nearly as bad; but the game of Young Rump Steak was much praised. The Gas Man did not go without some sharp punishment,

12.—Crawley floored in a twinkling. Long, very long, before this period it was "Tom Cribb's Memorial to Congress" to a penny chant. Crawley could not resist the heavy hitting of his opponent.

13 and last.—The Gas-light Man had completely put his opponent in darkness, and he only appeared this round to receive the *coup de grace*. Thirteen minutes and a half finished the affair.

REMARKS.—The Gas Man retained all his blaze; in fact, he burnt brighter in his own opinion than before. However, he was pronounced by the cognoscenti not a good fighter. Indeed, a few words will suffice. Hickman appeared too fond of rushing to mill his opponent, regardless of the result to himself, and often hit with his left hand open. The good judges thought well of the Gas-light Man from the specimen he had displayed, yet urged that there was great room for improvement; and when possessing the advantage of science, he would doubtless prove a teaser to all of his own, and even above, his weight. Crawley had outgrown his strength.

In this battle Hickman injured one of his hands severely in the third round; indeed, he kept looking at one of his fingers, and complained of it to his second, Tom Shelton. The latter, with much bluntness, told him "to hold his chaffing; such conduct was not the way to win; he was not hurt!" The Gas-light Man took the hint, and was silent during the remainder of the battle. In a few days after the fight his hand was so painful, and had assumed such a livid appearance, that he was compelled to have the advice of a surgeon. On examination it was found one of his fingers had been broken.

The Gas-light Man was now looked upon as somebody by the fancy; and several matches were talked over for him, but they all went off except the following, which was made up in a very hasty manner, for a purse of £20, at the Tennis Court, at Cy. Davis's benefit.

In this contest Hickman entered the lists with the scientific George Cooper, at Farnham Royal, Dawney Common, near Stowe, Buckinghamshire, twenty-four miles from London, on Tuesday, March 28, 1820, after Cabbage and Martin had left the ring. This contest was previously termed fine science against downright ruffianism, and seven to four and two to one was the current betting on Cooper without the slightest hesitation. On entering the ring the latter looked pale; but when he stripped, his frame had an elegant appearance. He had for his seconds Oliver and Bill Gibbons. Hickman was under the guidance of Randall and Shelton. Hickman laughed in the most confident manner, observing, "That he was sure to win." Previously to the combatants commencing the battle, Mr. Jackson called them both to him, stating the amount of the subscriptions he had collected for the winner. "I am quite satisfied," replied Hickman; "I will fight, if it is only for a glass of gin!" This sort of braggadocio quite puzzled all the swells, and the Gas-light Man was put down as a great boaster, or an out-and-outer extraordinary. Notwithstanding all the confidence of Hickman, the well-known superior science possessed by George Cooper rendered him decidedly the favourite.

THE FIGHT.

Round 1.—On setting-to Cooper placed himself in an elegant position, and a few seconds passed in sparring and in getting room to make play. Every eye was on the watch for the superiority of Cooper; but the rapidity of attack made by the Gas Man was so overwhelming that he drove Cooper to the ropes, and the exchange of hits was terrific, till Cooper went down like a shot, out of the ropes, from a terrible blow on the tip of his nose, with his face pinked all over. (The shouting was tremendous: "Bravo, Gas! it's all up with his science.")

2.—The impetuosity of the Gas Man positively electrified the spectators. He went in to mill Cooper with complete indifference. Cooper's face was quite changed; he seemed almost choked. Nevertheless, as the Gas was coming in with downright ferocity, Cooper planted a tremendous facer, right in the middle of the head. This blow, heavy as it was, only made the Gas Man shake his head a little, as if he wished to throw something off; but in renewing the attack, Hickman slipped down from a slight hit. (Great shouting, and "The Gas-light Man is a rum one." The odds had dropped materially, and Hickman was taken for choice.)

3.—The face of Hickman now showed the talents of Cooper, and he was hit down on one knee; but the former instantly jumped up to renew the attack, when Cooper sat himself down on his second's knee, to finish the round.

4.—Gas followed Cooper all over the ring, and hit him down. (Tumultuous shouting. Two to one on Gas.)

5.—The fine science of Cooper had its advantages in this round. He planted some desperate facers with great success, and the nob of his opponent bled profusely. In struggling for the throw, both down, but Gas undermost (By way of a cordial to Cooper, some of his friends shouted, Cooper for £100.)

6.—This was a truly terrific round, and Cooper showed that he could hit tremendously as well as his opponent. Facer for facer was exchanged without fear or delay, and Cooper got away from some heavy blows. In closing, both down.

7.—The assaults of the Gas Man were so terrible that Cooper, with all his fine fighting, could not reduce his courage. Hickman would not be denied. The latter got nobbed prodigiously. In struggling for the throw, Cooper got his adversary down. ("Well done, George.")

8.—The Gas Man seemed to commence this round rather cautiously, and began to spar, as if for wind. ("If you spar," said Randall, "you'll be licked. You must go in and fight.") The hitting on both sides was severe. The Gas Man got Cooper on the ropes, and punished him so terribly that "Foul!" and "Fair!" was loudly vociferated, till Cooper went down quite weak.

9.—The Gas Man, from his impetuous mode of attack, appeared as if determined to finish Cooper off-hand. The latter had scarcely left his second's knee, when Hickman ran up to him and planted a severe facer. Cooper was quite feeble; he was hit down.

10.—In this round Cooper was hit down, exhausted, and picked up nearly senseless. ("It's all up," was the cry; in fact, numbers left their places, thinking it impossible for Cooper again to meet his antagonist.)

11.—In the anxiety of the moment several of the spectators thought the time very long before it was called, and, to their great astonishment, Cooper was again brought to the scratch. He showed fight till he was sent down. ("Bravo, Cooper! you are a game fellow indeed.")

12.—This was a complete ruffian round on both sides. The Gas Man's nob was a picture of punishment. Cooper astonished the ring from the gameness he displayed, and the manly way in which he stood up to his adversary, giving hit for hit till both went down.

13.—It was evident that Cooper had never recovered from the severity of the blow he had received on the tip of his nose in the first round. "It's all up," was the cry; but Cooper fought in the most courageous style till he went down.

14.—Cooper, although weak, was still a troublesome customer. He fought with his adversary, giving hit for hit, till he was down.

15.—This round was so well contested as to claim admiration from all parts of the ring, and "Well done on both sides," was loudly vociferated. Cooper was distressed beyond measure; he, nevertheless, opposed Hickman with blow for blow till he fell.

16 and last.—Without something like a miracle it was impossible for Cooper to win. He, however, manfully contended for victory, making exchanges, till both the combatants went down. When time was called, Hickman appeared at the scratch, but Cooper was too exhausted to leave his second's knee, and Hickman was proclaimed the conqueror, amidst the shouts of his friends. The battle was over in the short space of fourteen minutes and a half.

REMARKS.—The courage exhibited by Cooper was equal to anything ever witnessed, but he was so ill before he left the ring that some fears were entertained for his safety. After the astonishment had subsided a little, the question round the ring was, "Who on the present list can beat Hickman?" The courage and confidence of Hickman seemed so indomitable that he entered the ring certain of victory. Both combatants were terribly punished, and Cooper showed himself as game a man as ever pulled off a shirt. The Gas Man, it was observed, used his right hand only.

In consequence of Hickman being informed that Cooper wished fe another battle, he put forth the following challenge in the *Weekly Dispatch*, October 8, 1820.

"*To George Cooper, Britannia Tavern, Edinburgh.*

"SIR,—

"Having seen a letter written by you from Edinburgh to Tom Belcher, at the Castle Tavern, Holborn, stating that you wished I would give you the preference respecting another battle between us, I now publicly inform you that I am ready to fight you for any sum that may suit you; and, as a proof that I am ready to accommodate you according to your request, it is indifferent to me whether it is in London or Edinburgh. But if at the latter place, I shall expect my expenses of training to be paid, and also the expenses of the journey of my second and bottle-holder. Having proved the conqueror, I felt myself satisfied, and had no idea of another contest; but I cannot refuse a challenge.

"Yours, etc.,
"T. HICKMAN.

"*October 7, 182~.*"

This produced the desired result, and, over a sporting dinner, in October, 1820, at the Castle Tavern, Holborn, a match was made between Hickman and Cooper, for £100 a-side, to take place on the 20th of December, within twenty-four miles of London, Tom Belcher putting a deposit of £5 on the part of Cooper, the latter being at Edinburgh. A further deposit to be made on the 7th of November, of £20 a-side. The odds immediately were sixty to forty in favour of Hickman. But the £5 was forfeited, and the match off, for the reasons stated in the memoir of GEORGE COOPER, *ante*, p. 317.

A match was proposed between Hickman and Kendrick, the man of colour, for 25 guineas a-side. But in a previous trial set-to, at the Fives Court, the man of colour was so dead beat with the gloves that Kendrick's backers took the alarm, and were quite satisfied that he had not the shadow of a chance. The superiority of Hickman was so evident that no person could be found to back poor Blackey. Hickman treated the capabilities of Kendrick with the utmost contempt, milled him all over the stage, and begged of him to have another round just by way of a finish. Yet this man of colour proved a tiresome customer both to the scientific George Cooper and the game Tom Oliver.

The second match between Hickman and Cooper excited intense interest, as this new trial was regarded as a question of skill against Hickman's bull-dog rush. The day was fixed for the 11th of April, 1821, and Harpenden Common, twenty-five miles from London, and three from St. Alban's, was the fixture. So soon as the important secret was known, lots toddled off on the Tuesday evening, in order to be comfortable, blow a cloud on the road, and be near the scene of action. The inhabitants of Barnet and St. Alban's were taken by surprise, from the great influx of company which suddenly filled the above places. The sporting houses in London also experienced an overflow of the fancy; and the merits of the Gas Man and Cooper were the general theme of conversation. Six to four was the current betting; but in several instances seven to four had been sported. Early on the Wednesday morning the Edgeware and Barnet roads were covered with vehicles of every description, and the inns were completely besieged to obtain refreshment. The inhabitants of St. Alban's were out of doors, wondering what sort of people these Lunnuners must be, who spent their time and money so gaily. The place for fighting had been well chosen—the ground was dry, and the ring capacious. Pugilists were employed to beat out the outer ring, and had new whips presented to them, on which were engraved " P. C."

At one o'clock the Gas Man appeared and threw his hat into the twenty-four feet square. He applied an orange to his lips, and was laughing and nodding to his friends with the utmost confidence. He had a blue bird's eye about his neck. He was followed by Randall and Shelton. In a few minutes afterwards, Cooper, in a brown great coat, with a yellow handkerchief about his neck, attended by Belcher and Harmer, threw his hat into the ring with equal confidence. Cooper went up to the Gas Man, shook him by the hand, and asked him how he was in his health. Two umpires were immediately chosen; and, in case of dispute, a referee was named. Mr. Jackson informed the seconds and bottle-holders that, upon the men setting-to, they were all to retire to the corners of the ring, and that when time was called the men were to be immediately brought to the scratch. The greatest anxiety prevailed. A few persons betted seven to four on Hickman as the men stood up.

THE FIGHT.

Round 1.—On stripping, the appearance of Hickman was fine, and no man ever had more attention paid him, being trained in a right sporting place, where many gentlemen belonging to the Hertfordshire Hunt had an opportunity of watching him. Cooper looked pale, and his legs had not quite recovered from a severe attack of boils. It was evident Cooper was not in tip-top condition; in fact, the time was too short to get his legs well. On setting-to, little sparring occurred; Cooper, with much science, broke away from the furious attacks of the Gas-light Man. The latter, however, followed him, and planted two slight hits. when Cooper kept retreating; but on Hickman's rushing in furiously to plant a hit, Cooper, with the utmost severity, met him with a most tremendous left-handed hit on the left cheek, just under his eye, that floored him like a shot, and his knees went under him. (To describe the shouting would be impossible; and several persons roared out, "Cooper for £100!" and "The Gas must lose it." Even betting was offered, and some roared out seven to four.)

2 and last.—The Gas Man came up rather heavy: it was a stunning hit; his cheek was swelled, and the claret appeared on it. He, however, was not at all dismayed, and went to work with the utmost gaiety. Cooper broke ground in great style, but missed several hits; if any one of these had told, perhaps it might have decided the battle. Hickman followed him close to the ropes, at which Cooper, finding himself bored in upon by his opponent, endeavoured to put in a stopper, but the blow passed by the head of his adversary, when Hickman, in the most prompt and astonishing manner, put in a tremendous hit, which alighted just under Cooper's ear, that not only floored him, but

sent him out of the ropes like a shot. Belcher and Harmer could not lift him up, and when time was called he was as dead as a house, and could not come to the scratch. The sensation round the ring cannot be depicted : and the spectators were in a state of alarm. Cooper was thus disposed of in the short space of three minutes. The Gas-light Man also seemed amazed: he was quite a stranger to the state of Cooper, and asked why they did not bring him to the scratch. Belcher endeavoured to lift Cooper off Harmer's knee, when his head, in a state of stupor, immediately dropped. "Why, he is licked," cried Randall. The circumstance was so singular, that, for the instant, Randall and Shelton seemed at a loss to know what to do, till, recollecting themselves, they appealed to the umpires, and took Hickman out of the ring, put him in a post-chaise, and drove off for St. Alban's. In the course of a minute or so Cooper recovered from his trance, but was quite unable to recollect what had occurred; he said to Belcher, "What! have I been fight-

ing?" declaring that he felt as if he had just awoke out of a dream: he appeared in a state of confusion, and did not know where he had been hit. A gentleman came forward and offered to back Cooper for £50 to fight the Gas Man immediately, and Cooper, with the utmost game, appeared in the ring; but Hickman had left the ground. The Gas Man was most punished.

REMARKS.—Instead of making any remarks upon the above fight, it might be more proper to say, that the Phenomenon (Dutch Sam), the Nonpareil (Jack Randall), the Champion of England, Tom Johnson, Big Ben, Jem Belcher, the Chicken, Gully, Tom Cribb, etc.—without offering the least disparagement to their courage and abilities—never accomplished anything like the following :—Hickman won three prize battles in thirty-one minutes.

He defeated Crawley in 13½ minutes.
,,   Cooper ,, 14½   ,,
,,   Ditto ,. 5   ,.
                          —
                          31

The preliminaries of Hickman's match with Tom Oliver are given in that boxer's life, we shall therefore merely detail the doings of the day of battle.

On Tuesday, June 12, 1821, at an early hour, the road was covered with vehicles of every description, and numerous barouches and four were filled with swells of the first quality to witness the Gas again exhibit his extraordinary pugilistic powers. The Greyhound, at Croydon, was the rallying point for the swells. The fight was a good turn for the road; the lively groups in rapid motion, the blunt dropping like waste paper, and no questions asked, made all parties pleasant and happy. The fun on the road to a mill is one of the merry things of the days that are gone ; more character was to be seen there than ever assembled at a masquerade. View the swell handle his ribands and push his tits along with as much ease as he would trifle with a lady's necklace, the "bit of blood" thinking it no sin to hurl the dirt in people's eyes; the drags full of merry coves ; the puffers and blowers; the dennets; the tandems; the out-riggers; the wooden coachmen, complete dummies as to "getting out of the way;" the Corinthian fours; the Bermondsey tumblers; the high and low life—the genteel, middling, respectable, and tidy sort of chaps, all eager in one pursuit; with here and there a fancy man's pretty little toy giving the "go-by" in rare style, form altogether a rich scene—the blues are left behind, and laughter is the order of the day. Such is a print sketch of what going to a mill was in days of yore.

It was two to one all round the ring before the combatants made their appearance, and at one o'clock, almost at the same moment, Oliver and

Hickman threw their hats into the ropes. Oliver was attended by Harmer and Josh. Hudson; the Gas Man was waited upon by Spring and Shelton. This trio sported white hats. The colours, yellow for Oliver and blue for the Gas, were then tied to the stakes. On Oliver entering the ring he went up to the Gas-light Man smiling, shook hands with him, and asked him how he did, which was returned in a most friendly manner by Hickman. On tossing up for the side to avoid the rays of the sun, Hickman said, "It's a woman; I told you I should win it." He appeared in striped silk stockings; and, on stripping, patted himself with confidence, as much as to infer, "Behold my good condition." Some little difficulty occurred in selecting umpires.

THE FIGHT.

Round 1.—Considerable caution was observed; each dodged the other a little while, made offers to hit, and got away. The Gas endeavoured to plant a blow, but it fell short, from the retreating system adopted by Oliver. The Gas again endeavoured to make a hit, which alighted on Oliver's right arm; the latter, by way of derision, patted it and laughed. Oliver was now at the ropes, and some exchanges took place; but in a close Oliver broke away, and a small pause ensued. Hickman at length went to work, and his execution was so tremendous in a close that the face of Oliver was changed to a state of stupor, and both went down. Oliver was picked up instantly, but he was quite abroad; he looked wildly, his left ear bleeding; and the cry was, "It's all up, he cannot come again." Indeed it was the general opinion that Oliver would not be able again to appear at the scratch. However, the Gas did not come off without a sharp taste of the powers of the Old One.

2.—Oliver was bad; in fact, he was "shaken." His heart was as good as ever, but his energy was reduced: he got away from a hit. The Gas now put in so tremendous a facer that it was heard all over the ring, and Oliver was bleeding at the mouth. In closing, Oliver tried to fib his opponent, but it was useless; the Gas held him as tight as if he had been in a vice till they both went down. Oliver was so punished and exhausted that several persons cried out, "It's of no use, take the Old 'un away."

3.—The scene was so changed that twenty guineas to two were laid upon Hickman. The latter smiled with confidence on witnessing the execution he had done; but the game displayed by Oliver was above all praise: he appeared, after being hallooed at by his seconds, a shade better, and he fought a severe round. The Gas received a terrible body hit, and some other severe exchanges took place. The cunning of Gas was here

witnessed in an extraordinary degree; with his left hand open, which appeared in the first instance as if his fingers went into the mouth of Oliver, he put the head of Oliver a-side, and with a dreadful hit, which he made on the back part of his opponent's nob, sent him down on his face. A lump as big as a roll immediately rose upon it. The Gas in this round was very much distressed; his mouth was open, and it seemed to be the opinion of several of the amateurs that he was not in such high condition as when he fought Cooper, or he must have finished the battle. The Gas once stood still and looked at his opponent; but Oliver could not take advantage of it.

4.—Hickman endeavoured to plant his desperate right hand upon Oliver's face, but missed and fell. Oliver, in trying to make a hit in return, fell over Hickman; the Gas laughed and winked to his second. It was, perhaps, a fortunate circumstance that Hickman missed this hit, as it might have proved Oliver's *quietus*.

5.—The left eye of the Gas was rather touched; but his confidence astonished the ring. The confident look of Hickman developed his mind. Oliver broke away, and also jobbed the Gas-light Man's nob; but as to anything like bitting, it was out of him. Hickman not only bored in upon Oliver, but punished him till he went down stupid. (Hickman for any odds.)

6.—Oliver came up to the scratch heavy, but he smiled and got away from the finishing hit of his opponent. Singular to observe, in closing, Oliver, by a sort of slewing throw, sent the Gas off his legs, and he was almost out of the ring. (The applause given to Oliver was like a roar of artillery.) The Gas got up with the utmost *sang froid*.

7.—Oliver put in a facer, but it made no impression; and the Gas with his left hand again felt for his distance against Oliver's nob, and the blows he planted in Oliver's face were terrific. The strength and confidence of Hickman was like that of a giant to a boy.

8.—Oliver came up almost dozing, and began to fight as if from instinct. Hickman now made his right and left hand tell upon Oliver's head, when the latter went down like a log of wood. (It was £100 to a farthing. "Take him away; he has not a shadow of a chance.")

9 and last.—Oliver, game to the end, appeared at the scratch and put up his arms to fight, when the pepper administered by the Gas was so hot that he went down in a state of stupor. The Gas said to his second, "I have done it; he will not come again." Oliver was picked up and placed on his second's knee, but fell, and when time was called could not move. Hickman immediately jumped up and said, "I can lick another Oliver now;" and finding that this boast was in bad taste, and met no response, even from his own partisans, he, upon second thoughts, went up and shook Oliver by the hand. Medical assistance being at hand, Oliver was bled and conveyed to the nearest house. He did not come to himself rightly for nearly two hours. It was all over in twelve minutes and a half.

REMARKS.—Thus, in less than three quarters of an hour, had Hickman conquered in succession, Crawley, Cooper (twice), and Oliver. In quickness he came the nearest to the late Jem Belcher; but the Gas could not fight so well with both hands. Perhaps it might be more correct to compare him with the Game Chicken; yet the latter was a more finished and more careful fighter than Hickman. It is, however, but common justice to say of the Gas, that his confidence was unexampled. He went up to the head of his opponent to commence the fight with such certainty of success as almost enforced and asserted victory. He thought himself invulnerable before, but this conquest convinced him he was invincible, and he immediately offered as a challenge to all England, once within four or six months, to fight any man, and give a stone. It is useless to talk against stale men: Oliver fought like a hero, and it was generally said "that a man must be made on purpose to beat the Gas." The latter was so little hurt that he walked about the ring, and played two or three games at billiards at Croydon, on his way to London. Forty-five pounds were collected for the brave but unfortunate Oliver. The backer of the Gas was so much pleased with his conduct that he ordered the President of the Daffies,* who held the stakes of £200, to give Hickman the whole of them.

Oliver, on his return to London the same evening, after he had recovered a little from the effects of this battle, called in at the Greyhound, at Croydon, when Hickman presented him with a couple of guineas. The backer of Hickman also gave Oliver five guineas; and several other gentlemen who were present were not unmindful of the courage he had displayed.

The decisive conquests of Hickman had placed him so high in the estimation of the fancy, and he was upon such excellent terms with himself, that he would not hear of a question as to his ability to conquer any pugilist on the list. In conversation on the subject, he often insisted that he was certain he could lick Cribb; and also frequently wished "that Jem Belcher was alive, that he might have had an opportunity of showing the sporting world with what ease he would have conquered that renowned boxer." Hickman asserted he did not value size or strength; and the bigger his opponents were the better he liked them. In consequence of this sort of boasting at various times, and also upon the completion of the stakes between Randall and Martin, in August, 1821, at the Hole-in-the-Wall, Chancery Lane, a trifling bet was offered that no person present would make a match between Hickman and Neat. A gentleman immediately stepped forward and said Neat should fight Hickman either for £100 or £200 a-side, and he would instantly put down the money. This circumstance operated as a stopper,

* Mr. James Soares.

and the match went off. In another instance, the backers of the Bristol hero sported £100 at Tattersall's, on Thursday, September 13, 1821, to put down to make a match; but the friends of Gas would not cover. It certainly was no match as to size; but, as the friends of Neat observed, "Neat has no right to be chaffed about it, as his £200 is ready at a moment's notice."

The match at length was knocked up in a hurry over a glass of wine, a deposit made, and the following articles of agreement entered into :—

"CASTLE TAVERN, October 13, 1821.

"Thomas Belcher, on the part of W. Neat, and an amateur on the part of Hickman, have made a deposit of 25 guineas a-side, to make it 100 guineas a-side, on Monday, the 20th inst. The money is placed in the hands of the President of the Daffy Club. To be a fair stand-up fight; half-minute time. The match to take place on the 11th of December, half way between Bristol and London. An umpire to be chosen on each side, and a referee upon the ground. The battle money to be 200 guineas a-side, and to be made good, a fortnight before fighting, at Belcher's."

Immediately on the above articles being signed five to four was betted on Hickman. Neat, it was said, would be nearly two stone heavier than the Gas-light Man. It will be recollected that both Neat and Hickman defeated Oliver, but with this vast difference—Neat won it after a long fight of one hour and thirty-one minutes, and during the battle it was once so much in favour of Oliver that £100 to £3 was offered, and no takers; while, on the contrary, the Gas defeated Oliver in twelve minutes, without giving the latter boxer a shadow of chance. Neat had appeared only once in the prize ring; he was a great favourite at Bristol, and one of the finest made men in the kingdom. He was also said to be much improved in pugilistic science.

The name of the Gas, on Thursday, December 5, 1821, proved attractive to the fancy at the Tennis Court in the Haymarket. The "Gas" was loudly called for, when the Master of the Ceremonies, with a grin on his mug, said, "It shall be turned on immediately." Hickman, laughing, ascended the steps, made his bow, and put on the gloves, but did not take off his flannel jacket. Shelton followed close at his heels, when the combat commenced. The spirit and activity displayed by the Gas claimed universal attention: he was as lively as an eel, skipped about with the agility of a dancing master, and his decided mode of dealing with his opponent was so conspicuous that it seemed to say to the amateurs, "Look at me; you see I am as confident as if it was over." The hitting was not desperate on either side, except in one instance, when the Gas let fly as if he had forgotten himself. Both Shelton and Hickman were loudly applauded.

The details of the exciting contest between our hero and Neat, on Tuesday, December 11, 1821, will be found in the memoir of NEAT. It came off sixty-seven miles from London, on Hungerford Downs, and produced perhaps in its progress and results as great an excitement as any contest on record. Neat and the Gas-light Man met at Mr. Jackson's rooms on Friday, December 15, when they shook hands without animosity. Neat generously presented Hickman with £5. The latter afterwards acknowledged that Neat was too long for him, and that, in endeavouring to make his hits tell he over-reached himself, and was nearly falling on his face. Hickman also compared the severe hit he received on his right eye to a large stone thrown at his head, which stunned him. Neat was afraid to make use of his right hand often, in consequence of having broken his thumb about ten weeks before, and it was very painful and deficient in strength during the battle.

"ON THE DEFEAT OF HICKMAN.

"The flaming accounts of the Gas are gone by,
  As smoke when 't is borne by the breeze to the sky,
The ' retorts ' of brave Neat have blown up his fame,
And clouded the lustre that beamed from his name.
His ' pipes ' may be sound, and his courage still burn,
But Neat to its ' service ' has given ' the turn;'
The Fancy may long be illumed by his art,
And ' the coal ' that is sported due ardour impart;
Yet never again can his light be complete,
Now sullied and dimmed by the ' feelers ' * of Neat.'

In March, 1822, Hickman, in company with Cy. Davis, set out on a sparring expedition to Bristol, where he was flatteringly received. A Bristol paper observed:—"On Thursday morning the sport at Tailors' Hall was particularly good. In the evening upwards of four hundred persons met at the Assembly-room to witness the set-to between Hickman and the Champion (rather premature this), which enabled the amateurs to form a pretty correct notion of the manner in which the great battle was lost and won. The style of Neat exhibits the perfection of this noble science—it is the cautious, the skilful, the sublime. That of the Gas is the shifting, the showy, and the flowery style of boxing. The audience were highly gratified, and the sum received at the doors exceeded £120."

Another journal of the same city remarked that—"The puissant Neat and the lion-hearted Hickman, attended by that able tactician, Cy. Davis, with Santy Parsons and others of minor note, have, within these few days, been showing off in this city in good style. The benefits have been well attended, principally by Corinthians, for the tip was too high for other than well-blunted coves. The sums received at the doors are said to exceed £120. This is really good interest for their notes of hand."

Hickman had a bumper benefit at the Fives Court on Wednesday, May 8,

* Instruments used in gas-works.

1822, and altogether the amusement was excellent. The principal attraction of the day was the set-to between the Gas and Neat. The former was determined to have " the best of it," and he most certainly had " the best of it." It is, however, equally true that Neat has no taste for sparring, and is not seen to advantage with the gloves on. The Gas was still a terrific opponent, and it was evident " the fight" had not been taken out of him. " Let those pugilists who meddle with him," said an experienced amateur, " anything near his weight, beware of the consequences." What sporting man connected with the ring, on viewing the Gas and Neat opposed to each other, could, in point of calculation, assert it was anything like a match between them ; and Neat, with the most honourable and manly feeling on the subject, never did exult on the conquest he obtained over as brave a man as ever stripped to fight a prize battle.

Hickman appeared rather unsettled in his mind after his defeat by Neat; and, when irritated by liquor, several times boasted that he was able to conquer the Bristol hero. But, as time gets the better of most things, Hickman became more reconciled to his fate, and asserted, in the presence of numerous amateurs at the Castle Tavern, when Josh. Hudson challenged him for £100 a-side, that he had given up prize-fighting altogether. In consequence of this declaration he commenced publican at the Adam and Eve, in Jewin Street, Aldersgate Street, which house he purchased of Shelton. During the short time he was in business he was civil and obliging to his customers, and a great alteration for the better, it was thought, had taken place in his behaviour ; but, before any just decision could be pronounced on his merits as the landlord of a sporting house, the sudden and awful termination of his career banished every other consideration.

A tradesman of the name of Rawlinson, a strong made man, a native of Lancashire, but well known in the sporting circles in the metropolis for his penchant for pugilism and wrestling, being rather inebriated one evening at Randall's, would have a turn-up with Hickman. The Gas-light man was perfectly sober, and extremely averse to anything of the kind ; but the set-to was forced upon him by Rawlinson chaffing, " That Tom was nobody— he had been overrated, and he was certain that Hickman could not beat him in half an hour ; nay more, he did not think the Gas could lick him at all."

Four rounds occurred, in a very confined situation ; in the first and second little, if any, mischief was done between them ; but in the third and fourth rounds Hickman let fly without reserve, when it was deemed prudent by the friends of Rawlinson to take him away to prevent worse consequences, the latter having received a severe hit on the left eye. In a short time afterwards a hasty match was made, over a glass of liquor, between an amateur, on the part of Hickman, and Rawlinson (but completely unknown to the Gas-light Man), for £10 a-side, to be decided in Copenhagen Fields. The backer of Hickman had to forfeit for his temerity in making a match without consulting him. Hickman was ten miles from London on the day intended for him to have met Rawlinson, who showed at the scratch at the place appointed.

On the production of Tom and Jerry at the Royalty Theatre, Mr. Davidge, the acting manager, went down to Bristol to engage Neat, at £30 per week, and a benefit, in order to induce him to come to London for a mouth. Hickman was also engaged; but not upon such high terms, in consequence of his residing near the theatre. The exhibition of the Art of Self-defence answered the manager's purpose, and good houses were the result of this speculation; but it was more like fighting than setting-to. The Gas-light Man could not, or would not, play light; yet he frequently complained of the bruised state of his arms in stopping the heavy hits of his opponent. As a proof of his irritable state of mind, Hickman bolted on the night of his benefit, not thinking the house so good at an early part of the evening as it ought to be, and supposing that he should be money out of pocket. Mr. Callahan, in the absence of the Gas-light Man, set-to with Neat. It, however, appeared that the house improved afterwards, and that Hickman's share would have been nearly £20.

When perfectly sober, Hickman was a quiet, well-behaved, and really a good-natured fellow; but at times, when overcome with liquor, he was positively frightful, nay, mad. It was in one of those moments of frenzy that he struck old Joe Norton, in Belcher's coffee-room, merely for differing with him in opinion. Like Hooper, the tinman, Hickman had been spoiled by his patron, who made him his companion. That Hickman was angry about losing his fame there is not the least doubt; and he must have felt it severely after boasting at the Fives Court that "the Gas should never go out!" In his fits of intemperance and irritation, he often asserted that he had received more money for losing than Neat did by winning the battle.

We now come to his melancholy death. Hickman, accompanied by a friend, left his house early on Tuesday morning, the 10th of December, 1822, to witness the fight between Hudson and Shelton, at Harpenden Common, near St. Alban's. He was in excellent health and spirits during the battle, walking about the ground with a whip in his hand, in conversation with Mr. Rowe. At the conclusion of the battle he returned to St. Alban's, where he made but a short stay, and then proceeded on his journey to London.

On returning home in the evening Hickman drove, and endeavoured to pass a road wagon on the near side of the road instead of the off side. Whether from unskilful driving, the darkness of the night, or some other cause, in clearing the wagon the chaise was overturned, and, dreadful to relate, both were precipitated under the wheels, which went over their heads. Hickman was killed instantaneously: his brains were scattered on the road, and his head nearly crushed to atoms. Mr. Rowe seemed to have some animation, but was soon dead. Randall had parted with them at South Mimms shortly before, and stated that they were both sober.

It was in the hollow, half a mile north of the Green Man, Finchley Common, where Hickman and Mr. Rowe were killed.

It appears that the last place where the two unfortunate men, Hickman and Rowe, drank, was at the Swan, between Whetstone Turnpike and the Swan with Two Necks, and within half a mile of the spot of the catastrophe. Hickman observed upon the darkness of the night, and spoke of the fog coming on when he got into the chaise. His friend anticipated some danger, and refused to accompany him in the gig unless he drove. Hickman positively refused, and, unfortunately for Mr. Rowe, the latter occupied the place of Hickman's friend. The horse escaped unhurt, and the chaise was perfect, and in it the sufferers were conveyed, more than a quarter of a mile, to the Swan with Two Necks. This shocking accident had such an effect on the nerves of the landlord of the Swan that he was also a corpse in less than a week afterwards.

Mr. Rowe left an amiable wife and three small children to lament his loss.

Immediately after the fight between Hudson and Shelton, Hickman said that, on his own account, he was sorry Hudson had lost the battle, it being the intention of the friends of Josh., in the event of his having proved the conqueror, to have backed him against Hickman for £100 a-side; and he laughingly observed, "Blow my Dickey, if I shouldn't like it vastly." It is rather a curious coincidence that, on the same day a twelvemonth previous, a report reached London that Hickman was dead, in consequence of the blows he received in his battle with Neat.

On Wednesday, December 11, 1822, an inquest was held at the sign of the Swan with Two Necks, Finchley Common, before T. Stirling, Esq., coroner, on the bodies of Thomas Hickman and of Mr. Thomas Rowe, silversmith, of Aldersgate Street, St. Luke's.

The accident excited the greatest interest in the sporting world; and although the inquest was held at an earlier period than was expected, the jury room was crowded to excess to hear the evidence.

The jury proceeded to view the bodies of the deceased persons, which laid adjacent to the house in which the inquest was held. On their arrival an appalling spectacle presented itself: the Gas-light Man laid on his back, and had it not been known that it was to that individual the accident had happened, it would have been impossible, from the mutilated state of the head, to have recognised him. His head was literally crushed to atoms.

Mr. Rowe was also dreadfully crushed about the head, but not so sadly as Hickman.

On returning to the jury-room the following witnesses were called :—

Chancy Barber, of Finchley, bricklayer, said, Before eleven o'clock last night I was in bed at home, when the alarm came for a light; it was then starlight. I got up and went along the road to where the deceased persons were; they were put into their own chaise-cart, and were both dead. They were brought to this house. A medical gentleman, assistant to Mr. Hammond, was at the door nearly as soon as the bodies arrived, and examined them. They exhibited no symptoms of life after I saw them. There was a wagon standing by the chaise, and a cart behind the wagon, when I got up. I examined the spot where the accident took place this morning. The wheels of the chaise had been on the footpath; the chaise had nearly gone the whole width on the footpath where it was overturned. The wagon was going towards town. The chaise was going the same way; the chaise was on the near side; the wagon was nearest to the near side of the road. The track of the wagon appeared to have proceeded in a direct line, and there was no room for a chaise to have passed on the near side without going on the footpath. There was more than plenty of room for one or two carriages to have passed on the off side without injury. I think the wagoner could not be in any manner to blame, as he appeared to me to have been unconscious of the chaise being there.

James Ball, of Whetstone, servant to Mr. Sutton, said, I was coming towards Whetstone, and met the wagon and chaise. I saw the wheel of the chaise on the footpath, immediately before it overturned towards the wagon. I saw the men fall out. I think the wagon wheel did not go over them, but that the drag-cart did: the drag-cart was loaded. Hickman was run over by the wheel of the drag-cart; Rowe's head was struck against the cart wheel. The wagoner was not to blame: he was driving in a regular and steady manner. Verdict—Accidental Death.

Between the hours of eleven and twelve on Thursday, December 19, 1822, a vast concourse of people assembled in Aldersgate Street and Jewin Street to witness the funeral of Hickman. At twelve o'clock the funeral procession commenced from the Adam and Eve, in Jewin Street, the house of Hickman, previous to which the interior exhibited a most melancholy scene. The pall was supported by Josh. Hudson and Shelton, Tom Belcher and Harmer, and Randall and Turner. The father of the Gas, his brother, and some other relatives were the principal mourners. The procession was filled up by Mr. Warlters, Tom Owen, Scroggins, Parish, Oliver, Jem Burn, Purcell, Powell, Bill Davies, Baxter, and Pierce Egan. The plate on the coffin stated Hickman to be in his twenty-seventh year. He was buried in the churchyard in Little Britain. On the ground were Bitton, Bill Eales, Jack Carter, George Head, etc., who were not in time to join the procession. The crowd in the streets was immense.

The prize ring expressed its high respect to one of its bravest members; and, as Randall said over his grave, "It would be a long time before we should see his fellow!" The whole of the boxers (the mourners), on taking leave of the widow, promised her their support at her house, and that they would exert themselves to procure a good benefit for herself and two fatherless children.

The Champion of England was prevented from attending as one of the pall-bearers in consequence of a restive horse, on the preceding evening, near Stockwell, having thrown him off and fallen upon him.

Mr. Rowe, the unfortunate companion of Hickman, was interred in the same burying-ground on the preceding Sunday morning.

As a proof of the *esprit de corps* which then animated pugilists, we copy a placard circulated on this melancholy occasion.

"TO THE SPORTING WORLD.

"Remembrance of a Brave Man, and Consideration for his Wife and Children. Under the patronage of the P. C. and superintendence of Mr. Jackson. A Benefit for the Widow and Two Infant Children of the late T. Hickman, denominated in the Sporting Circles the Gas-light Man, will take place at the Fives Court, St. Martin's Street, Leicester Square, on Wednesday, February the 5th, 1823, at which every exertion will be made by all the first-rate pugilists to produce a grand display of the Art of Self-defence. The sets-to by Messrs. Cribb, Spring, Belcher, Harmer, Carter, Oliver, B. Burn, Randall, Turner, Martin, Cy. Davis, Richmond, Eales, Shelton, J. Hudson, Tom Owen, Holt, Scroggins, Curtis, A. Belasco, P. Halton, Purcell, Brown, Lenney, etc.

"In consequence of the melancholy and afflicting accident which befel the late T. Hickman, instantly depriving his Wife and Two Children of his support, he having scarcely commenced licensed victualler (not more than six weeks), but with an excellent prospect of improving his circumstances in life, the above appeal is made to the noblemen, gentlemen, and amateurs composing the sporting world, in order to assist his widow towards providing for her fatherless offspring. The well-known liberality of the sporting world, so highly distinguished upon all occasions, to give a turn to the unfortunate, renders any further comment upon the aforesaid melancholy circumstance totally unnecessary to excite their interest and attention.   Tickets 3s. each, to be had of Mr. Jackson, at his rooms, 13, Old Bond Street; of Pierce Egan, sporting bookseller, 71, Chancery Lane; Cribb, Union Arms, Panton Street, Haymarket; Belcher, Castle Tavern, Holborn; Randall, Hole in the Wall, Chancery Lane; Harmer, Plough, Smithfield; Cy. Davis, Cat Tap, Newgate Market; Holt, Golden Cross, Cross Lane, Long Acre; Eales, Prince of Mecklenburg Arms, James Street, Oxford Street; B. Burns, Rising Sun, Windmill Street, Haymarket; and of the widow (Mrs. Hickman), Adam and Eve, Jewin Street, Aldersgate Street."

The rush at the Fives Court was equal to anything ever experienced.   On the door being opened the money-taker was almost carried away from his post by the pressure of the crowd.   The attraction was great, independent of the cause; and, on the whole, it was one of the best displays of the science ever witnessed at the Fives Court.   Mr. Jackson superintended the pairing of the men, and the result was talent opposed to talent.   Oliver and Acton first made their bows to the spectators; Aby Belasco and Gyblets, Gipsey Cooper and Peter Warren, Curtis and Harris, Ward and Holt, Harmer and Shelton, Josh. Hudson and Richmond, Carter and Sampson, Spring and Eales, Belcher and Neat, and Randall and Scroggins, exerted themselves to amuse and interest the audience, and their efforts were crowned with the most loud and lively plaudits.   The set-to between Spring and Eales was much admired, from the skill displayed on both sides; and Belcher, in his combat with Neat, received a severe hit on the nose, which produced the claret, when Tom, with the utmost good humour, observed, "That friendly touch prevented the expense of cupping, as it was absolutely necessary he should be bled, and was merely a baulk to the doctor."   Thanks were returned by Pierce Egan.

Neat, unsolicited, left Bristol at his own expense to exhibit at the benefit. Eales also came twenty-five miles on the same morning; and the veteran Tom Cribb hurried from the country to assist at the door, to make " all right and pleasant;" the assistance of his "strong arm" proved valuable in the extreme to all parties.   Mr. Jackson (so well known upon all occasions to render his personal interest to the unfortunate) never exerted himself with more successful zeal than in the cause of the widow of Hickman.   The receipts were £ 136 13s. 6d.

So anxious were the pugilists to exert themselves in the cause of the widow and children of Hickman that, as soon as decency permitted them, Randall, Shelton, Spring, Josh. Hudson, Curtis, etc., took the chair for several weeks in succession at the Adam and Eve, and their efforts were crowned with success.

A benefit was also got up for the widow and children of Mr. Rowe, which was liberally supported.   The company was most respectable, including fourteen M.P.'s and other persons of "the upper ten thousand." Great credit is due to Mr. Belcher for his exertions and the attention he gave in getting up this benefit, which realised nearly £100.

We have recorded these minutiæ to show the comparative want of self-sacrifice among the pugilists of " these degenerate days."

CHAPTER VII.

DAN DONNELLY, CHAMPION OF IRELAND.

"Our worthy Regent was so delighted
With the great valour he did evince,
That Dan was cited, aye, and invited
To come be-knighted by his own Prince."

THIS renowned "knight of the knuckle," whose fistic exploits and capabilities, though indisputable, are rather matter of oral tradition than of
written record (like the glorious deeds of Charlemagne, Roland, the British
Arthur, or his own countryman, Brian Boroihme), first saw the light in
Townshend Street, Dublin, in March, 1788. He was a carpenter by trade,
and, although undoubtedly possessed of milling requisites of the first order,
by no means thirsted for fame in the ring, until circumstances drew forth his
talents and made him, for a brief period, "the observed of all observers" in
the boxing world. His first recorded appearance in the roped arena was
with Tom Hall (known as Isle of Wight Hall), who was then on a sparring
tour in Ireland. The battle was for a subscription purse of 100 guineas, and
took place on the Curragh of Kildare, on the 14th of September, 1814.
Hall, who had beaten George Cribb, and other men, stood high in the estimation of his friends, seeing that Dan was looked upon as a mere novice, or
rough, by the knowing ones.

The concourse of persons that flocked to witness this combat was greater
than was remembered upon any similar occasion. It seemed as if Dublin had
emptied itself, not less than 20,000 spectators are stated to have been present.
The vehicles on the road were beyond calculation, from the barouche,
jaunting cars, and jingles, down to the most humble description, and the
footpaths were covered with pedestrians. Donnelly first entered the ring,
and was greeted with thunders of applause. Hall was also well received.
The battle did not answer the expectations previously formed; in fact Hall
was over-matched considerably in length, and therefore compelled to act on
the defensive. It was far from a stand-up fight. Donnelly received no

DAN DONNELLY (CHAMPION OF IRELAND).

From a Miniature by GEORGE SHARPLES.

injury, except one trifling cut on his lip, which drew first blood, and he slipped down once. His superiority of strength was evident, and he was throughout the first in leading off. Hall did not acknowledge defeat, and retired from the ring by order of the umpires after the fifteenth round, exclaiming "Foul," declaring he was hit three times when down. Little betting occurred during the fight, but previously it was sixty to forty upon Hall, and on the ground twenty-five to twenty. Bonfires were made in several of the streets of Dublin by the jubilant countrymen of Donnelly, who was under the training of Captain Kelly. He was also seconded by that gentleman and Captain Barclay, brother to the celebrated pedestrian. Hall was attended by Painter and Carter. During the fight Donnelly kept his temper, closed every round, and put in some heavy blows. Hall was well known as a game man; but it was urged by the partisans of the Irish champion that Hall fell three times without a blow, and Donnelly, in his eagerness to catch him, before he could execute this manœuvre, hit Hall desperately on his ear while sitting on the ground. The most independent and candid opinion upon the subject, from the best judges of pugilism who witnessed the battle, appears to be that both combatants lost it.*

George Cooper, who was teaching the art of self-defence in Ireland with much approbation, and whose fame as a boxer in England was well known to the Irish amateurs, was selected as a competitor for Donnelly. They fought for a purse of £60.

On Monday, the 13th of December, 1815, they met on the Curragh of Kildare, at a few minutes after ten o'clock in the morning. At an early hour thousands of persons left Dublin to witness the fight, and the road to the scene of action was crowded with vehicles of every description. Donnelly, followed by Coady, received loud greetings upon making his appearance; Cooper also, on entering the ring, was loudly cheered by the spectators. The combatants shook hands, and immediately began to prepare for action. Coady seconded Donnelly; Ned Painter attended upon Cooper.

THE FIGHT.

Round 1.—The boys of the sod were all upon the alert in favour of their countryman: Donnelly must win, and nothing else, was the general cry. Every eye was fixed as the men set-to. Some little time elapsed in sparring, when Donnelly planted a sharp blow on the neck of Cooper; the latter returned in a neat manner on the body. Desperate milling then took place, when the round was finished by Donnelly, who floored

* This is the account in "Boxiana," and *faute de mieux* we must adopt it. We suspect the much vaunted Sir Daniel was simply a big clumsy "rough," despite his defeat of Old Tom Oliver, who was a game boxer, but "slow as a top," as Spring often in a friendly way described him. Cooper, too, had already been beaten by Oliver, and was in anything but good condition when he met Donnelly.

his antagonist in first rate style. It would, be impossible to describe the shout that accompanied this feat; it was not unlike a discharge of artillery, and the faces of the Paddies beamed with exultation.

2.—Considerable science was displayed before a hit was made, when Donnelly put in a sharp facer. He also drew blood from one of Cooper's ears, and his strength prevailed to the extent of driving Cooper to the ropes, where he went down.

3.—Had it not been on the Curragh of Kildare, it was presumed that the fine fighting of Cooper would have told with better effect. He evidently laboured under fear, from the prejudice of the numerous spectators in favour of his opponent. Donnelly exhibited great improvement, and completely took the lead this round. After some tremendous hitting Cooper went down. (Another uproarious burst of applause.)

4.—This was altogether a good round. Cooper convinced Donnelly that he was a troublesome customer, and, in spite of his overwhelming strength, he could not protect himself from punishment. In closing, both down, Cooper undermost. (Donnelly was now decidedly the favourite, and six to four was the general betting.)

5.—The gaiety of Donnelly was hastily stopped, after an exchange of a few blows. Cooper, with much adroitness, floored him in a scientific style, but the latter instantly got upon his legs without any help. (The odds changed, and even betting was the truth.)

6.—Cooper's mode of fighting extorted the admiration of the Hibernian amateurs, from the easy and natural manner he contended with his big opponent. Donnelly was kept to his work, and had no little difficulty in getting Cooper off his legs.

7.—In this round Donnelly was seen to much advantage, and he resolutely went in as if to beat his opponent off hand. He drove Cooper to all parts of the ring till they closed, when the strength of Donnelly almost proved decisive. Cooper received one of the most dreadful cross-buttocks ever witnessed, and by way of rendering it conclusive, Donnelly fell on Cooper with all his weight.

8.—From the severity of the last fall, Cooper appeared much distressed on setting-to. Donnelly, with some judgment, turned the weakness of his opponent to good account; and, after having the best of his adversary, Dan put in so tremendous a left-hander that Cooper was hit off his legs.

(The loud cheering from all parts of the ring beggared description, and, in the pride of the moment, a guinea to a tenpenny-bit was offered on Dan.)

9.—Cooper commenced this round in the most gallant style, and the milling was truly desperate on both sides. In making a hit, Donnelly over-reached himself and slipped down.

10.—The strength of Donnelly was too great for Cooper, notwithstanding the latter fought him upon equal terms of confidence. Cooper was, however, again floored. (High odds, but no takers.)

11 and last.—It was evident Cooper could not win; nevertheless, this round was fought with as much resolution and science as if the battle had just commenced. Donnelly at length put in two tremendous blows that put an end to the contest, particularly one on the mouth, which knocked Cooper off his feet. On victory being declared in favour of Donnelly, the applause lasted more than a minute. The battle occupied about twenty-two minutes. Donnelly appeared quite elate with victory, and shook hands with Cooper and his friends.

REMARKS.—Dan displayed improvement both in science and in temper, which, added to superior strength, enabled him to beat down the guard of Cooper with ease and effect. He was also in better condition than when he fought Hall. It was urged that Cooper was half beaten before he entered the ring, from the prejudices which existed against him. The sum originally offered to the combatants was a purse of £120, and the loser to have £20; but, on the morning of fighting, after Cooper had been kept waiting in a chaise on the ground for upwards of an hour, he was told that the funds would not admit of more than £60 being given to the winner, and nothing to the loser. Upon this statement, Cooper declared he would not fight; but the reply was, "You are on the ground, man, and must fight. The multitude must not be disappointed." Under these disadvantages Cooper met his adversary, in the bold attempt to wrest the laurel from the brow of the champion, and that, too, upon his native soil. It is not meant to be asserted that Cooper could have won the battle. An impartial opinion has been given by his own countrymen to the contrary, they admitting that Cooper, with all his superior boxing skill, could not compete with Dan, who had long ranked A 1 in the sparring and boxing circles of the Irish metropolis.

It was for some time a generally expressed opinion that the recognised Irish champion would not cross the channel and show himself in this country. However, in February, 1819, it was whispered that "The 'big' hero, the pride of Hibernia, known as the Irish Champion, had slipped across the water, and shown himself in England."

Dan left full of spirits—the Pigeon House soon lost sight of—Dublin Bay and its surrounding beauties no longer visible—the Hill o' Howth (Paddy's landmark) nearly extinct—and behold our hero "half seas over" towards Liverpool, before he had time to reflect upon the hasty step he had taken. However, there was now no retreating: a few "more glasses" made everything pleasant, reflection no longer intruded, and, after some forty winks, the light-house of the Mersey broke upon Dan's ogles, and the quay of Liverpool gave him a safe deliverance from the briny deep. It was at this sea-port that Carter crossed his path, picked him up as a brother performer, which gave birth to his adventures in England; for it seems Dan's original intention was not to visit the metropolis, but, as soon as his pecuniary affairs were settled, to return to Dublin.

Dan's fame had gone before him : there was not an out-and-outer upon the Coal Quay in Dublin (and the mere appearance of some of these rough heroes is enough to appal Old Nick), who had not repented of his temerity in attacking Donnelly. It was also asserted that he had floored with ease every opponent in Ireland.

Carter, who was sufficiently well acquainted with the stage to know the advantages of a good bill, issued the following placard, on the 19th of February, 1819, at Manchester :—"Donnelly, the Champion of Ireland, and Carter, the Champion of England (?), will exhibit together in various combats the Art of Self-defence, at the Emporium Rooms." This had the desired effect : an overflowing audience was the result ; and at Liverpool they met with great encouragement. Soon afterwards the "brother champions" took the road to the metropolis, and bets were offered that Carter fought twice during the summer and won both the events. Several wagers were also made in London respecting the identity of Donnelly ; some of the best judges asserting that the new-come personage was not that Donnelly who fought with George Cooper. Donnelly, on his arrival in London, showed himself at the Castle Tavern.

On Friday, March 18, 1819, about a hundred of the most respectable of the amateurs assembled at the Peacock, Gray's Inn Lane, in a large room selected for the purpose. The following description of Donnelly appeared in a paper of the day :—"Donnelly at length stripped, amidst thunders of applause. The Venus de Medicis never underwent a more minute scrutiny by the critical eye of the connoisseur than did the Champion of Ireland. In point of frame, he is far from that sort of 'big one' which had been previously anticipated : there is nothing loose or puffy about him ; he is strong and bony to all intents and purposes. It may be said of Donnelly that he is all muscle. His arms are long and slingy; his shoulders uncommonly fine, particularly when in action, and prominently indicative of their punishing quality; his nob is also a fighting one; his neck athletic and bold; in height nearly six feet; in weight about thirteen stone; and his *tout ensemble* that of a boxer with first rate qualifications. Thus much for his person. Now a word or two for his quality. His wind appears to be undebauched; his style is resolute, firm, and not to be denied; and he maintains his ground upon the system that Mendoza practised with so much success. Getting away he either disdains, or does not acknowledge, in his system of tactics. His attitude was not admired, and it was thought that he leant too far backward, inclining to his right shoulder. He makes tremendous use of his right hand. Eight rounds were finely and skilfully contested; and Carter, equal to anything on the list for scientific efforts, must be viewed as a formidable opponent for any man. The difference of style between the two performers attracted considerable attention, produced a great variety of remarks, and drew down peals of applause. Carter possesses the agility and confidence of an experienced dancing master, getting away with the utmost coolness, walking round and round his opponent to plant a blow, with the perfection of a professor. Donnelly is not so showy, but dangerous: he is no tapper, nor does he throw blows away; neither is he to be got at without encountering mischief. He is, however, awkward; but final judgment cannot be pronounced from his sparring, more especially as he does not profess the use of the gloves. It was an excellent trial of skill. Carter made some good hits, and Donnelly some strong points; and the end of one round in particular, had it been in the ring, must have been pronounced pepper. The good temper of Donnelly was much noticed; and, impartially speaking, it was a nice point to decide who had the best of it, even in effect. Carter, without doubt, had the show of the thing."

In consequence of but few persons having had an opportunity of witnessing Donnelly's talents, the Minor Theatre, in Catherine Street, Strand, was selected on the Thursday following. Ben Burn appeared in opposition to the Irish champion. It was a set-to of considerable merit, and the science of Burn was much applauded. Donnelly soon convinced the spectators of his peculiar forte. He showed off in good style, and finished one round in a way that must have been tremendous in the ring. It was still thought he stood rather too backward, leaning from his opponent; but that could only be decided from a practical result. At all events, Donnelly was a great attraction. Carter and Donnelly finished the performances: it was a sharp and long set-to upon the whole, and loudly applauded. But a wish was expressed that Cribb and Donnelly should have been opposed to each other, in order to give the public an opportunity of deciding upon the different sort of tactics pursued by these rival champions.

At Gregson's benefit at the same theatre, on April 1, 1819, the principal attraction was the announced combat between the two rival champions, Cribb for England and Donnelly for Old Ireland. This proved an April hoax: Cribb, of course, did not show, and Donnelly set-to with Carter amid the hisses of a crowd of disappointed dupes. Sutton, the man of colour, came forward and challenged Donnelly to fight for £50 a-side. (Great applause.) Richmond presented himself to the audience on the part of Donnelly, stating, "That the Irish champion did not come over to England with the intention of entering the prize ring." (Disapprobation.) Carter soon followed, and observed that, "As Mr. Richmond had only made half a speech, he would finish it. Mr. Donnelly meant to consult his friends about fighting Sutton." Sutton again came forward, and said that he would fight Donnelly at five minutes' notice for £50, or from £100 to £200, at any given time, in a ring.

In consequence of some aspersions having been thrown upon the courage of Donnelly, he published the following document, which was pompously designated—

"THE IRISH CHAMPION'S MANIFESTO TO THE MILLING WORLD.

"At a sparring match, for the benefit of Gregson, on Thursday, the 1st day of April, Donnelly, having met with an accident, hopes the public will pardon him if he did not amuse the gentlemen present to their satisfaction; but it was his wish to do so. After the set-to between Harmer and Sutton, the latter thought proper to come forward and challenge any man, and also Donnelly in particular, for £50 or £100. Donnelly, being somewhat a stranger, did not immediately answer the challenge, until he should first consult his friends; but he has confidence in his friends, both here and in Ireland, that they will back him. He therefore begs leave to say that he did not come over to England for the mere purpose of fighting; but, as it appears to be the wish of the gentlemen here to try his mettle, he begs to say that he will fight any man in England of his weight, from £100 to £500.

"D. DONNELLY.

"Witness, C. BRENANT."

On the 6th of April, 1819, at Randall's benefit at the Fives Court, Donnelly had scarcely mounted the stage, when "Cribb! Cribb! Cribb!" was vociferated from all parts of the Court, till Carter made his appearance on the platform ready to commence the combat. The cries of "Cribb!" were now louder, added to hisses, etc., when the Lancashire hero bowed and retired. The Champion of England, however, did not appear; then Carter was called, but he had also left the Court. In the midst of this confusion Harmer offered himself amidst thunders of applause, and appeared to have the best of it; but the set-to was by no means first rate, and

Donnelly left off under marks of pain. It ought to have been announced that Donnelly had a large tumour upon his right arm near his elbow. The usage to Donnelly might be termed ungenerous; indeed, it was very unlike the usual generosity of John Bull towards a stranger, and savoured of prejudice, says his countryman, Pierce Egan.

As all this savours of benefit "gag," we are glad to record that at Martin's benefit, on Tuesday, April 20, 1819, Oliver challenged Donnelly for 100 guineas a-side, when Randall (Donnelly not being present) mounted the stage, and said he was authorized to accept it on the part of the Irish champion, who would enter the lists with Oliver on that day six weeks for any sum that might be posted.

On May 25, 1819, Donnelly, Cooper, and Carter opened the Minor Theatre, Catherine Street, to exhibit the capabilities of the Irish champion previous to his going into training.

Spring and Donnelly were received with great applause. Donnelly stopped several of Tom's hits with skill; in fact, from his quick mode of getting away, and the sharpness with which he returned upon his opponent, it was pronounced that he had either acquired considerable science since his arrival in England, or that he now let "peep" some of his fighting requisites. The latter seems to be his real character; as a sparrer he does not show off to advantage. It was a manly bout; some smart facers were given and returned; no niceties were observed, and it afforded general satisfaction.

Articles were signed for Dan's match with Oliver at Dignam's, Red Lion, Houghton Street, Clare Market. Fifty guineas level was offered that Oliver proved the favourite during the fight or won the battle. Five hundred guineas were also offered to four hundred that Oliver did not beat Donnelly in the hour, and some large sums were laid at odds that Donnelly did not prove the conqueror in half an hour. Oliver was generally declared "slow," but a gamer man was not in existence. Upwards of £100,000 were said to be pending in the two countries on the issue of this national pugilistic contest, which came off, for 100 guineas a-side, on Wednesday, July 21, 1819, on Crawley Hurst, thirty miles from London.

The sporting world in Ireland were so warmly interested in this event that numerous parties arrived in England to witness the efforts of their avowed champion. The English boxers viewed him as a powerful opponent, and, jealous for the reputation of their "prize ring," clenched their fists in opposition whenever his growing fame was chanted. In Ireland, as might be expected, two to one was laid without hesitation, from a knowledge of his capabilities; and in England, where only hearsay evidence was the induce-neat to make him the favourite, six to four was confidently betted on his winning. The torrents of rain which fell the previous evening to the fight operated as no drawback to the warm-hearted friends of Donnelly, who desired to see a "whack for the honour of Ireland," and they tramped off in hundreds on the over-night without sigh or murmur, hoping to arrive in time to see their countryman fight and win. Early on the morning of Wednesday the weather proved equally unpropitious, but the game of the fancy was not to be disposed of by rain. A string of carriages of every description, reaching nearly a mile in length, might be seen from the top of the hill above Godstone; and deep "murmurings" occurred when it was announced that the scene of action was to be removed from Blindlow Common to Crawley Hurst, merely owing, it was said, to the caprice of one or two influential persons. The lads were not prepared for this long journey of sixty-two miles out and in, and many of the Rosinantes were unable to perform it. In consequence of this removal, it was two o'clock before the contest commenced. Oliver first threw his hat in the ring, followed by Cribb and Shelton; and Donnelly, waited upon by Tom Belcher and Randall, entering soon afterwards, repeated the token of defiance. Donnelly appeared the heavier man. Betting, seven to four. The green colour for Ireland was tied to the stakes over the blue for England, and the battle commenced.

THE FIGHT.

Round 1.—Donnelly, on stripping, exhibited as fine a picture of the human frame as can well be imagined; indeed, if a sculptor had wished a living model to display the action of the muscles, a finer subject than Donnelly could not have been found. His legs were firm and well rounded, his arms slingy and powerful, and his *ensemble* indicated prodigious strength. The idle stories of his bad training were silenced on his putting himself into attitude; and his condition was acknowledged by his friends from Ireland to be far superior than when he fought with either Hall or Cooper on the Curragh of Kildare. Smiling confidence appeared to sit on his brow, his eye was sharp and penetrating, his face clear and animated, and he commenced the combat quite satisfactorily. Oliver was equally fine; and, under the training of Clark, who had waited upon him with the greatest care and attention, displayed flesh as firm as a rock; in fact, Oliver had never been in so good condition before. Such was the state of the combatants. Upon the shaking hands, the current betting was seven to four on Donnelly. The Irish champion was cool and collected, with nothing hurried in his manner. Upwards of a minute elapsed in sparring, or rather the pugilists were dodging each other to get a favourable opportunity. Donnelly made two hits with his left, which fell short, in consequence of Oliver's getting away. Long sparring. Oliver made an offer to hit, but Donnelly, on the alert, retreated. More sparring, and dodging over the ground, till they got to the ropes in a corner of the ring, when Donnelly hit severely with his left. Several sharp exchanges occurred, and reciprocal fibbing took place, till they both went down in a desperate struggle for the throw, Oliver undermost. Five minutes had elapsed. (Loud shouting from the "boys of the sod," and "Bravo, Donnelly!")

2.—Oliver aimed a heavy blow at the body, which Donnelly stopped in good style. Some sharp work occurred again at the ropes. More fibbing, and Oliver again undermost in the throw.

3. — Oliver appeared bleeding at the scratch, and exhibited symptoms of slight distress from the recent struggle. Donnelly made a feeble hit with his right hand, when Shelton exclaimed, laughing, "That's one of Carter's hits!" Oliver took the lead; some heavy blows were exchanged, and, when at the ropes, Donnelly was for a short time seen in the struggle balancing on them,

till he extricated himself, and both went down. (Loud shouting, and "Well done, Oliver.")

4.—Donnelly exhibited a new feature in the London prize ring. Oliver again pinked at the body, after the manner he fought with Neat, which Donnelly stopped with much skill; but his right hand, which had been hitherto spoken of as "tremendous," he did not make use of, although Oliver had already given him several opportunities to have used it to advantage. Oliver made a good hit on the bread-basket, when Donnelly's left hand told on his opponent's mug, which staggered him, and he followed him to the ropes. Here some sharp work ensued, and Donnelly made use of his head instead of his fists (which were occupied in holding Oliver) in bumping his opponent's nob. (Loud shouting, and some disapprobation was expressed at this mode of butting.)*

5.—Oliver put in a sharp body blow, and some good counterhits were exchanged. The mouth of Donnelly was clareted, which was the first blood. The combatants again got in the corner of the ring, when, by way of a finish to the round, Donnelly cross-buttocked his opponent. ("Erin-go-bragh," from his warm-hearted countrymen, and "Go along, my Danny," from his John Bull backers.)

6.—Caution on both sides, till Oliver made a chopping right-handed hit on his opponent's nob. In close quarters at the ropes, after some sharp exchanges, it was urged by several persons close to the ring that Donnelly had hit Oliver down from a blow on the body. On reference to the umpires, it was not admitted as a "knock-down blow," but that Oliver had slipped and fell.

7.—Oliver planted a good facer, and laughed at his opponent. He also put in a bodier, and got away. In short, it might fairly be said, he had the best of the round, and Donnelly went down bleeding. ("Bravo, Oliver!" and great applause.)

8.—Nothing of passion appeared on the part of Donnelly, which it had been urged by his opponents he would exhibit on getting a "nobber or two;" on the contrary, he was as cool as a cucumber. In struggling, both down, Oliver bleeding profusely about the face. (We must not pass over a circumstance which occurred in this round, in consequence of some altercation between the seconds. On Donnelly's being down, it was urged that, perceiving Oliver meant to fall upon him, he lifted up his legs with intent to kick Oliver, or to divert him from his purpose. This also excited the various opinions and expressions of "Foul!" "Fair!")

9.—In this round Donnelly received great applause. The men fought into a close, from which Donnelly extricated himself in style, and returned sharply to work, till he had the best of the hitting, and Oliver went down exhausted. The spectators were perfectly convinced that Donnelly was a tremendous hitter with his right hand, when he thought proper to use it. He gave Oliver so hard a blow upon the ribs that the impression of his knuckles was strongly imprinted, and remained visible during the whole of the fight.

10.—Oliver stopped a heavy hit of Donnelly's, and laughed. But Donnelly was not irritated, and got so much the best of this round that Oliver was prevented from going heavily down by Shelton's putting out his knee to ease his fall. (Belcher warmly said, "If he acted as foul again, he would knock a hole in his head;" and Randall also observed, he would give him a "topper." Shelton declared it was an accidental entangling of his legs with Oliver's, and was not done from design.)

11.—Had Donnelly used his right hand he must have reduced the battle to a certainty in his favour. This was, however, a sharp hitting round, till both went down, Oliver again undermost.

12.—Although the fighting on either side had not been of the highest order, yet the combatants were not insensible to the weight of each other's arms; and, after fighting up to the ropes, they both stood still, till Donnelly broke away and made some hits. In again closing, both down, Oliver undermost and much exhausted. Twenty-four minutes had now elapsed.

13.—Donnelly, sans ceremonie, hit Oliver with his left on the mouth, which sent him staggering from the scratch. In the corner of the ring the struggle was severe to obtain the throw. Oliver received a heavy blow on the throat, and as he was hanging on the ropes, balancing, as it were, Donnelly lifted up his hands not to hit him. ("Very handsome," and "Bravo, Donnelly.")

14.—For "big ones," more smashing rounds might have been expected. Oliver put in a mugger that made Donnelly stagger a little; but he returned to the attack till he got Oliver down.

15.—Donnelly gave some hits that made Oliver reel from his position, and also followed him up with success. At the ropes some exchanges occurred, till Oliver went down.

16.—Oliver made a tremendous blow at the body, which Donnelly stopped well. This was altogether a sharp round, and in the close in the corner of the ring the struggle was so severe that the men became exhausted, and were nearly falling over the ropes upon some of the members of the P. C., when the cry was, "Separate them," which was done by the seconds, and the round ended. ("Bravo!" and "Well done, both.")

* By the New Rules Donnelly would here have lost the fight, as Burke did in his contest with Bendigo, on February 7, 1839.—ED. PUGILISTICA.

17.—Some heavy hitting occurred on both sides. Donnelly, on the alert, followed Oliver all over the ring. The latter bled profusely, and, in closing, Donnelly fell with his knees upon Oliver. This circumstance occasioned some loud cries of "Foul," "Fair," etc.; but the umpires did not deem it worthy of notice.

18.—Both down at the ropes. Some remarks were made that Donnelly had taken advantage of the situation over Oliver. The umpire observed, in such close quarters it was impossible to discriminate to a nicety; but, from what he saw, he thought Donnelly had behaved perfectly correct.

19.—This was rather a sharp round; in fact, Oliver received so much beating that in going down he fell upon his face. Donnelly also fell on his back.

20.—This round Donnelly faced his opponent with much dexterity; Oliver's right eye got a severe hit, but he laughed, and nodded at his opponent. The left hand of the Irish champion told severely twice on his man's mug, and both down, after a good deal of bustling action, Donnelly undermost. (Loud shouting, and "Well done, Oliver.")

21.—It was not decisive fighting on either side: now and then a sharp hit occurred, till Oliver fell, and Donnelly on him.

22.—A similar round; both down.

23.—The hitting in this round was rather singular. Both the combatants made counter hits at the mouth of each other, and the claret sprung out simultaneously. It was an electrifying shock to both, but it seemed to affect Oliver most. They still kept up the attack till both went down, Oliver undermost.

24.—This was a fighting round altogether, and the spectators began to be intensely interested. Oliver kept hitting and getting away, till he fought into a close. Donnelly broke from it, and the milling was severe, till the Irish champion went down on his knees. (Loud shouting, and "Now, Oliver, go to work, my boy, and you can't lose it!")

25.—This round was also manfully contested. Donnelly appeared bleeding at the scratch. Oliver put in a bodier and got away. Some sharp exchanges took place, till both the combatants were glad to resort to sparring for wind. In fact, for an instant they both stood still and looked at each other. Donnelly at length made a hit, and Oliver got away. Both men soon returned hard to work, when Donnelly again went down from the severity of the milling. (Thunders of applause, and Cribb vociferated, "I'll bet a guinea to half-a-crown." Three to one was offered on Oliver; but two to one was current betting.)

26.—Donnelly made a hit, but Oliver stopped it. The latter also put in two nobbers, and got away laughing. This circumstance rather irritated Donnelly, and, for the first time, he showed temper, by running furiously after Oliver. Tom warded off the fury of the attack, and ultimately again sent Donnelly down by his hitting. (Another loud shout for Oliver, and "Five to one Oliver will win," was the general cry. Long faces were to be seen; hedging-off was now the order of the day. The hitherto takers of the odds against Oliver now loudly offered the odds upon the Westminster hero with the fullest confidence.)

27.—Donnelly came up weak and out of wind, but his confidence had not left him, and he gave Oliver a slight facer with his left hand. In struggling, both down, Oliver undermost. Fifty minutes had elapsed. Donnelly had received some heavy blows about the head and neck; nevertheless, it was said by his seconds that he was not distressed by the punishment he had received, but had drank too much water. It is true that many of his backers changed their situations, and went to different parts of the ring to get their money off.

28.—Great anxiety now prevailed among the partisans of Donnelly. Some hits passed to the advantage of Oliver, when Donnelly went down. (The odds were now upon Oliver all round the ring; but Donnelly's staunchest friends, having no reason to doubt his pluck, took them in numerous instances.)

29.—The men were both upon their mettle, and this round was a good one. The combatants closed, but broke away. Oliver made a hit on Donnelly's face, laughed, and jumped back. The Irish champion, however, got a turn, and with his left hand planted a ram one on Oliver's mouth that sent him staggering away. Donnelly, however, received a teaser; sharp exchanges till Donnelly fell, with Oliver upon him.

30.—One hour had expired, and all bets upon that score were lost. Oliver again bodied his opponent, but received a staggering hit on his mug in return. Some exchanges took place till Oliver went down.

31.—The eye of Donnelly began to resume its former fire; his wind appeared improved, and he rather took the lead in this round. Donnelly hit Oliver down, but also fell from a slip; in fact from the force of his own blow.

32.—The Irish champion had evidently got second wind, and, upon Oliver's receiving a hit on the mouth that sent him some yards from his position, Randall offered to back Donnelly for a level £200. After an exchange of hits, Shelton said, "It was no more use for Donnelly to hit Oliver than a tree, for that Oliver was as hard as iron." "Nabocleish," cried a Patlander; "it's all right. Now, Dan, show your opponent some play." Some sharp hitting till both resorted to sparring. The men fought into a close, and broke away. The hitting was now so sharp that Oliver turned round to avoid the heavy punishment with which he was assailed, and fell, and Donnelly also slipped down. ("Bravo!" from all parts of the ring. "Well done, Oliver!" "Go along, Donnelly!")

83.—"Have you got a right hand?" said Tom Belcher to Donnelly; "we must win it, Dan." The Irish champion hit Oliver a terrible facer that sent him away. "It's all your own," said Randall; "do it again." Donnelly did so with great force. "That's the way, my boy," echoed Belcher; "another!" Donnelly followed the advice of these excellent tacticians, and he gave a third facer in succession without receiving a return. After some exchanges passed, Oliver was getting rather feeble, from the struggle in bringing Donnelly down, and fell upon him with his knee on his throat. ("Do you call that fair?" said Belcher. "If that circumstance had happened on our side, you would have roared 'foul' for an hour.")

84 and last.—Oliver hit Donnelly on the body. The latter set-to very spiritedly, and nobbed his man. Sharp exchanges ensued, when, in closing, Donnelly put in a dreadful hit under Oliver's ear, and also cross-buttocked him. Oliver, when picked up and put on his second's knee, was insensible, and his head hung upon his shoulders. "Time, time," was called, but the brave, the game, the unfortunate Oliver heard not the sound, and victory was declared in favour of Donnelly. Time, one hour and ten minutes. The latter walked out of the ring amidst shouts of applause, arm-in-arm with Belcher and Randall, to an adjoining farm house, where he was put to bed for a short period, and bled. Oliver did not recover his sensibility for some minutes, when he was also brought to the same house, bled, and put to bed in the next room to Donnelly. The latter expressed great feeling and uneasiness for fear anything serious should happen to Oliver; but when he was informed it was all right, he was as cheerful as if he had not been fighting at all. The Irish champion dressed himself immediately, and, strange to say, Oliver, in the course of half an hour, also recovered, and put his clothes on, lamenting that he had lost the battle under such an unfortunate circumstance, as he was then able to fight an hour. Oliver and Donnelly then shook hands, and drank each other's health, and the latter then went into a wagon to see the fight between Lashbrook and Dowd. He afterwards left the ground in a barouche and four, to sleep at Riddlesdown, the place where he trained,

and arrived at Mr. Dignam's, the Red Lion, Houghton Street, Clare Market. Oliver also arrived in town the same day.

REMARKS.—Donnelly had now shown his capabilities to the admirers of scientific pugilism in England, and the judgment pronounced upon his merits was briefly this:—The Irish champion has not turned out so good a fighter as was anticipated. To be more precise, he is not that decisive, tremendous hitter with his right which was calculated upon. In fact, he did not use his right hand at all; if he had, he might in all probability have decided the battle full half an hour sooner than it terminated. In game and coolness he is not wanting, and for obtaining "a throw or a fall," he will prove a dangerous customer for any man on the list. Donnelly might have felt that sort of embarrassment which hangs about a provincial actor who first treads the London boards; and to use his own words upon the merits of the battle, he said it was a bad fight, that he had acted like "a wooden man," and could not account for it. His next essay, he thought, might prove altogether different from his defeat of Oliver. Donnelly's right hand was frequently open when he hit. His face appeared, on leaving the ring, exempt from punishment, except some scratches upon his lips. His right ear, however, was strongly marked; but the principal punishment he sustained was upon the body. Oliver was heavily hit about the throat and ears, and also on the body. The latter by no means punished Donnelly as he did Neat; but the heavy falls that Oliver received proved him thoroughly good in nature, a game man, and one that would contend for victory while a spark of animation was left. He never did, nor never will, say "No!" It would be a violation of truth, if the above battle, under all the circumstances, was not pronounced a bad fight, as regarded scientific movements on both sides. The seconds on both sides were on the alert to bring their men through the piece; and every person was astonished to see the activity displayed by Tom Belcher in picking up so heavy a man as Donnelly, and the industry used by Randall. The conduct of the Champion of England was cool and manly in the extreme; and Shelton never lost sight of a point that could assist Oliver.

Dan was, like most of his countrymen, a bit of a humourist. On the day previous to the mill a noble lord called upon Donnelly, at Riddlesdown, about one o'clock, and rather slightingly observed, "That about that time to-morrow he might expect a pretty head from the fist of Oliver." Donnelly (at all times facetious), looking the lordling full in the face, replied, with an ironical expression, "That he was not born in a wood, to be scared by an owl!" The laugh went round against the noble amateur, and by way of softening the thing, he betted Donnelly £15 to £10 upon Oliver, which the Irish champion immediately accepted.

One trait of Donnelly is worthy of notice: on quitting his room to enter the apartment of Oliver, he would not publicly wear the coloured handkerchief of his fallen opponent, but concealed it by way of pad, in the green handkerchief which he wore round his neck.

Soon after Donnelly arrived at Riddlesdown, Shelton, by desire of an amateur, who offered to back him for £200, challenged the Irish champion, to fight at his own time.

The sporting houses were crowded at an early hour in the evening by persons anxious to know the result, and the Castle Tavern, Randall's, Welch's, and Dignam's, overflowed with the well-pleased countrymen of Donnelly. The "Irish division" won large sums by this victory.

Notwithstanding Donnelly's victory over Oliver, it appeared to be the general opinion that his talents as a pugilist had been much over-rated. Challenges, in consequence, flowed in fast, and a nobleman offered Donnelly his choice out of Cooper, Shelton, Gregson, Sutton, Spring, Carter, Neat, Richmond, and Painter, for £100 a-side. The following document also appeared in the *Weekly Dispatch*, August 15, 1819.

"A CHALLENGE TO DAN DONNELLY, THE CONQUEROR OF OLIVER.

"I, the undersigned, do hereby offer to fight you for 1,000 guineas, at any place, and at any time, which may be agreeable to you, provided it be in England.
"ENOS COPE, *Innkeeper.*
"Witnesses,　WM. BAXTER, C. PALMER, J. ALCOCK.
"*Macclesfield, July 23, 1819.*"

Donnelly was now caressed in the most flattering manner by all ranks of the fancy, but more particularly by his own countrymen; indeed, it might be said that his days, if not a great part of his nights, were completely occupied in taking his drops from one end of the Long Town to the other with his numerous acquaintances. Time rolled on very pleasantly, and it appears, by the way of "seeing a bit of life," that Dan was taken by some of his friends to view the sports of the West, not forgetting those of some of the "hells" of St. James's. Here Dan was picked-up one night, and eased of £80 out of the £100 he won by defeating Oliver. It was a "secret" at the time, and only "whispered" all over London. Dan's blunt was fast decreasing, and reduced to so low an ebb as to remind him that a supply was necessary, and something must be done; therefore, after Mr. Donnelly had shown his "better half" all the fine places in and about London, he naturally felt anxious to return once more to dear Dublin, where his presence might be turned to a good account. It was accordingly agreed that his friends George Cooper and Gregson should accompany him on a sparring tour to Donnybrook Fair. But many things happen between the cup and the lip, and just as Donnelly had taken his seat upon the stage coach, and was in the act of bidding

> " Fare thee well ; and if for ever,
>   Still for ever fare thee well,"

to his numerous friends, an acquaintance of Dan's (a swell bum-bailiff) appeared close to the vehicle, and, in the most gentlemanly manner, told Donnelly he wished to speak to him. "And is it me you mane, Jemmy?" replied Dan; "don't be after joking with me now!" "Indeed I'm not; here's the writ for £18," answered the officer. "And is it possible that you want me at the suit of Carter? I don't owe the blackguard one single farthing. By de powers, it is the other way; Jack's indebted to me." Expostulation, however, was useless. The coachman had his whip in his hand, and the two evils before Dan only allowed him to make a momentary decision. The choice left to him was, either to lose his fare to Liverpool, which had been previously paid, and the advantages to result from an exhibition of his talents at Donnybrook Fair (which admitted of no delay), or to remain in London and be screwed up in a sponging house. Donnelly, in a great rage, as the preferable alternative, instantly discharged the writ and galloped off from the metropolis. It is true Dan went off loaded with fame, but it is an equally undeniable fact that he had only a £2 note left in his pocket-book, after all his great success in London, to provide for him and Mrs. Donnelly on their route to the land of Erin.

Thousands of persons assembled on the beach to hail the arrival of the Irish champion on his native shore. Dan had scarcely shown his merry mug, when his warm-hearted countrymen gave him one of the primest fil-le-lus ever heard, and "Donnelly for ever!" resounded from one extremity of the beach to the other. A horse was in readiness to carry him, as so great a personage as "Sir Dan Donnelly" (who, it was currently reported, had been knighted by the Prince Regent for his bravery) could not be suffered to walk. The knight of the fives was attended by the populace through all the principal districts of Dublin, till he arrived at his house in Townshend Street. Dan took his leave gratefully of the multitude, and after flourishing the symbol of the above Order, for the honour of Ireland, and drinking their healths in a "noggin of whiskey," the crowd retired, highly gratified at the dignified reception which the Irish milling chief had experienced on setting his foot once more on the turf of Ould Ireland.

The sports of Donnybrook Fair, on August 27, 1819, were considerably heightened by the presence of Donnelly, Cooper, and Gregson. They were thus described in a contemporary Dublin newspaper, *Carrick's Evening Post*: —"Upon no former occasion have we witnessed more enticement to eye or palate: booths of a superior and extensive nature were erected, in which equestrian voltigeur tumbling, sleight of hand, serious and comic singing, and other performances were exhibited. Donnelly, for some reason we cannot account for, has no tent; but he has a booth, wherein Cooper, Gregson, and the Irish champion exhibited sparring, to the great amusement of an admiring audience. This booth was but hastily prepared, but the persons who obtained admittance appeared much pleased with the scientific display of these celebrated pugilists. An amateur of great eminence from Liverpool, at a late hour in the evening, ascended the platform (a ten feet enclosed ring), and encountered Gregson with the gloves. He was evidently no novice in the milling school, and was much applauded. Cooper exhibited superior science, and Gregson displayed the remnant powers of a once first-rate superior man. Dan was thought by the amateurs present to be much improved, but gave himself little trouble else than to show how things ' might be done :' he was cheerful and laughing during each 'set-to.' The whole passed off in the most regular and quiet manner. The persons present seemed anxious to accord with the expressed wish of the pugilists, that the public peace should be rigidly preserved." On Tuesday the crowds were greater than upon any previous occasion. The itinerant vocalists were not wanting to contribute their portion of harmony. A variety of songs were circulated, from which we select the following crambonian lyric:—

"DONNYBROOK FAIR.

Tune—Robin Adair.

" What made the town so dull?
          Donnybrook Fair.
What made the tents so full?
          Donnybrook Fair.
Where was the joyous ground,
Booth, tent, and merry-go-round?
Where was the festive sound?
          Donnybrook Fair.

" Beef, mutton, lamb, and veal,
          Donnybrook Fair.
Wine, cider, porter, ale,
          Donnybrook Fair.
Whiskey, both choice and pure,
Men and maids most demure,
Dancing on the ground flure,
          Donnybrook Fair.

> " Where was the modest bow ?
> > Donnybrook Fair.
> Where was the friendly row ?
> > Donnybrook Fair.
> Where was the fun and sport ?
> Where was the gay resort ?
> Where Sir Dan held his Court—
> > Donnybrook Fair."

The dispute between Carter and Donnelly, respecting the arrest of the latter (whether right or wrong), was not calculated to do Carter good, even in the eyes of the sporting world in England; but in Ireland, it was certain to prejudice the character of the Lancashire hero in the opinion of the fancy, Donnelly being their avowed hero, and so great a favourite. However, with more courage than prudence, or conscious that he had done nothing wrong, Carter* almost immediately followed Donnelly to Dublin, and lost no time in parading Donnybrook Fair, going from booth to booth.

In consequence of this, the Irish amateurs wishing not only to witness their champion again exhibit his finishing talents on the Curragh, but also to show they would not suffer him to be brow-beaten upon his own soil, a meeting took place between the friends of both parties. Owing, however, to some trifling delay in making the match, the following challenge, answer, and articles of agreement appeared in the *Dublin Journal*:—

"CHALLENGE TO DONNELLY.

" *To the Editor of the* DUBLIN JOURNAL.

"SIR,—

"I beg leave, through the medium of your paper, to intimate that I am ready and willing to fight Daniel Donnelly for £200, to be lodged in proper hands, and I am induced to give him this public challenge, in consequence of his having hitherto declined to give a decided answer on a late occasion, when I staked 10 guineas in the hands of a friend of his, who has neither covered nor returned the money, nor given me any satisfaction whether he is willing to fight me or not.

> "I am, sir, your obedient servant,
> > "JOHN CARTER.

" *September* 18, 1819."

"THE CHALLENGE RE-CHALLENGED AND REFUTED.

" DONNELLY AND CARTER.

"The committee of friends and supporters of Donnelly, the Irish champion, have observed, with much surprise and regret, an advertisement in the *Dublin Evening Post and Correspondent* of Saturday last, signed ' John Carter.' Their surprise was excited by the statement of a public challenge to Donnelly, when, in fact, a challenge had been previously exchanged and ratified. They regret that any person placing himself before the public should so pervert facts. As to the deposits and binding of the contract, the friends of Donnelly have produced, and are still anxious to lodge, £200 in his support. They have repeatedly signified this intention, and appointed places for interview, at which neither Carter nor his friends (if he has any) have attended. If the object of Carter's advertise-

---

* The writer never enters into the private quarrels of pugilists. His only anxiety is to represent every circumstance connected with the prize ring with accuracy and fidelity. He entertains no prejudices, neither has he any partialities to gratify.

ment is to retract and regain his deposit (a pretty good proof that no public challenge was necessary), although the sporting world would decide against the refunding of the 10 guineas in question, he shall cheerfully have it. The public will judge of his motives; but if Carter, previous to his projected immediate trip to Scotland, is not determined to shy the combat, Donnelly's friends are ready to lodge the £200 required, and only desire that Carter may be serious and determined. The determination of Donnelly's friends is to support him to the extent his opponents require, or to the amount of the original agreement, which was to fight for £500 in six weeks, at the Curragh.

'Let the galled jade wince, our withers are unwrung.'

" *Committee Room*, 20, *Fownes' Street, September* 20, 1819."

A match between the above pugilists was at length made, and the following were the articles :—

" *Dublin, September* 20, 1819.

"Mr. W. Dowling, on the one part, and Mr. L. Byrne, on the other part. Mr. Dowling deposits £20 sterling, on behalf of John Carter, and Mr. L. Byrne deposits, on the part of Daniel Donnelly, £20 sterling, into the hands of Mr. John Dooly; the parties to meet at No. 20, Fownes Street, Dublin, on the 5th of October next, at two o'clock on the said day precisely, to make the above sum £50 each. The combatants to meet within thirty miles of Dublin, on the 25th of November next, and then fight, at twelve o'clock in the day, the place to be hereafter tossed for and named, for the sum of £200 sterling a-side. The whole of the stakes to be made good on the 23rd of November, two days previous to fighting, when the place will be appointed, or the £50 deposit money to be forfeited. To be a fair stand-up fight, half-minute time, in a twenty-four feet ring. Also, if the parties, or money for the said parties, according to this article, do not meet on the 5th of October next, the present £20 stake must also be forfeited.

"JOHN CARTER.　　　　　　　　　W. DOWLING.
"G. D——.　　　　　　　　　　　L. BYRNE.

"Present,　　THOMAS BOYLAN, ROBERT GREGSON."

To the mortification of the fancy, this match went off upon a frivolous dispute as to the appointment of a stakeholder. Donnelly, in a discussion with Cooper's backers, said fairly, addressing himself to Cooper, "When I defeated you, George, upon the Curragh, you got more money than I did; but when I fought Oliver in England, upon proving the conqueror, the whole of the money, 100 guineas, was presented to me. If this plan is adopted in Ireland I have no objection to fight Carter." This proposition, however, from motives it is now impossible to discover, was refused by Carter's friends.

Donnelly's public-house in Pill Lane was generally crowded. Carter also took a house in Barrack Street, in opposition to the Irish champion; and Bob Gregson opened a punch-house in Moor Street, Dublin. Milling topics were, therefore, the order of the day in the "sweet city."

Dan seemed now at the apex of popularity, with a prospect, backed by common prudence, of attaining permanent prosperity. His house was overflowing nightly with company, the blunt pouring rapidly into his treasury, and his milling fame on the highest eminence; but, in the midst of this laughing scene, the ugliest customer Dan had ever met with introduced himself. Without any preliminary articles, or agreeing as to time; nay, without even shaking fists, the Universal Leveller gave the stout Sir Daniel such a body blow that all the wind was knocked out of him in a twinkling; the "scratch" disappeared from his darkened optics, and he went "to sleep" to wake only to the last call of "time!" In plain prose, this renowned knight of fistic frays took sudden leave of his friends, family, and the P. R., on the 18th of February, 1820, in consequence of taking a copious draught of cold water, while in a state of perspiration after an active game at "fives." He was in the thirty-second year of his age, and not a few of his best friends declare that whiskey-punch, by over-heating his blood, hastened the catastrophe. We shall here introduce a few random anecdotes from "Boxiana."

Soon after Dan's arrival in London, he met Cooper and Hall one evening at the Castle Tavern, when, after inquiring after their health, he facetiously asked them if they should like a little of Mr. Donnelly in England, as they had stated fair play was not allowed to them in Ireland. Silence got rid of the inquiry.

A General, well known in the sporting circles, in order to try the milling capabilities of Donnelly (his countryman), soon after his arrival in England, invited the Irish champion to his house, where he set-to with a gentleman amateur, distinguished for his superior knowledge of the art of self-defence. After some active manœuvring, Donnelly put in such a tremendous facer, that for several minutes the gentleman was in a state of stupor, whereon General B—— became a firm backer of Sir Dan.

Pierce Egan finds fun in his hero's worst failing. He tells us gleefully that the severity of training did not accord with Donnelly's disposition. It was insufferable restraint to him. In fact, he did not like going into training at all, and some difficulty occurred, nay, he was almost coaxed to leave the metropolis. During his stay at Riddlesdown, while training to fight Oliver, he was at table with some gentlemen, when green peas were among the vegetables at dinner. One of the company, distinguished for his knowledge of training, observed Donnelly helping himself to the peas, and immediately stated to him that peas were improper for a person training. Donnelly laughed heartily, exclaiming, "And sure is it a pae that will hurt me? no, nor a drop of the cratur neither," tossing off a glass of brandy. He also enjoyed himself during the afternoon in the same manner as the rest of the company, till the time arrived for his going to work, i.e., walking the distance of six miles. Donnelly on starting, said, "Now you shall soon see how I'll take the paes and liquor out of me!" and ascended with great rapidity the high, steep hill in front of Wheeler's door without apparent fatigue. He returned to the company in a short time in a violent state of perspiration, having performed the distance. Solitude, however, was far from Dan's delight: company was his passion. While his friends remained with him at Riddlesdown it was all right; but when they departed, it is said, he took a small drop of "stuff" with him to bed, to prevent his lying awake. At other times he stole out in the dark to poach for petticoats, and the preserves of Croydon, it seems, supplied even more than his wants. This circumstance will, in a great degree, account for his distressed and blown state during the battle with Oliver.

It is a well-known fact that, immediately after his battle with Oliver, it was not only discovered, but he acknowledged, that he had unfortunately contracted a disease in the promiscuousness of his amours. It is usual for pugilists during their training to have a companion to look after them. It was not so with Donnelly; but if he had had such a person, it would have been of little, if any, use, as Dan was beyond control. It was, however, truly astonishing to view Donnelly's fine appearance on entering the ring to meet Cooper. When the Irish champion fought Cooper on the Curragh of Kildare, it appears he had been trained up to the highest pitch of excellence by Captain Kelly, and was strong as a giant and active as a rope dancer. To the Captain, Donnelly yielded implicit obedience; but he would not be dictated to by his equals—indeed, he was totally unmanageable.

Donnelly was extremely fond of a joke; and upon a porter coming to him, soon after his arrival in England, late one evening, at the Castle Tavern, Holborn, informing Dan that his wife would be glad to see him at the White Horse in Fetter Lane, as soon as possible, Donnelly asked, with great eagerness, "What sort of a woman she was?" The porter, surprised at the singularity of such a question, enquired, "What, sir, don't you know your own wife?" The champion, smiling, replied, "Is she a big woman? Well, never mind; tell her I'll come and look, just to see if I know her."*

It should seem that Donnelly had a great aversion to be looked upon as a prize-fighter. In the course of two or three evenings after his battle with Oliver, Dignam's long room was crowded with his countrymen, anxious to congratulate him on his recent victory. Donnelly, who was dining with some swells above stairs, was informed of the circumstance, and solicited to

* Tom Shuffleton, speaking of a female, says, "Oh! I see; she must be the sixteenth Mrs. Shuffleton." We never ascertained whether Mr. Donnelly placed his ladies in numerical order; it is, however, certain that he was a very gallant Milesian.

go down and to walk through the room. To which Donnelly replied, "Sure, now, do they take me for a baste, to be made a show of? I'm no fighting man, and I won't make a staring stock of myself to plase anybody." This was spoken angrily, and it required the utmost persuasions of his friend Dignam to induce him to comply with so reasonable a request. Dan at length conceded, and upon entering the room he was received with the loudest cheers.

In short, poor Dan was a creature of the moment. He was most excellent company, creating mirth and laughter all around him. His sayings were droll in the extreme, and his behaviour was always decorous. Forethought was no ingredient in his composition; "to-morrow," with him, might or might not be provided for: that never created any uneasiness in his mind, and was left entirely to chance, or, as Dan would express it, "Divil may care!" Such was the character of Donnelly. He was an Irishman every inch of him—generous, good-natured, and highly grateful. As a pugilist, it is true, he did not raise himself in the estimation of the English amateurs by his battle with Oliver; nor did the Irish fancy in London think so much of his capabilities as they had anticipated; indeed, those gentlemen who came from Ireland to witness the battle expressed themselves surprised at the deficiency of boxing talent displayed by their favourite. This, however, will astonish no one who has perused the few preceding paragraphs of his heedless conduct and neglect of training. He was declared to be unlike the same man who defeated Cooper. The fact is, that our Hibernian friends either undervalue or thoughtlessly neglect those precautions, without which strength, pluck, and skill must succumb to more ordinary physical qualifications, if backed by temperance. In fact, the fight was won by Donnelly by his wrestling superiority, rather than his hitting.

We now quit the living Sir Dan to note the public and literary honours bestowed upon his decease. Foremost amongst these comes *Blackwood's Magazine*, for May, 1820, wherein twenty closely printed pages are devoted to a most amusing collection of "solemn dirges," letters of condolence, lamentations, plaintive ballads, odes and songs, an eloquent funeral oration, etc., and scraps of Hebrew, Greek, and Latin poems in honour of the heroic deceased. The scholar will be delighted, and the general reader amused, by the genuine humour and erudite pleasantry therein displayed. Our space forbids us more than a selection of a few of these serio-comic effusions of Christopher North and his coadjutors,

"Recollections of Sir Daniel Donnelly, Knt., P.C.I.[*]

"When green Erin laments for her hero, removed
  From the isle where he flourished, the isle that he loved,
Where he entered so often the twenty-foot lists,
And, twinkling like meteors, he flourished his fists,
And gave to his foes more set-downs and toss-overs,
Than ever was done by the great philosophers,
        In folio, in twelves, or in quarto.

"Majestic O'Donnelly! proud as thou art,
  Like a cedar on top of Mount Hermon,
We lament that death shamelessly made thee depart,
  With the gripes, like a blacksmith or chairman.
Oh! hadst thou been felled by Tom Cribb in the ring,
  Or by Carter been milled to a jelly,
Oh! sure that had been a more dignified thing,
  Than to "kick" for a pain in thy belly.

"A curse on the belly that robbed us of thee,
  And the bowels unfit for their office;
A curse on the potheen you swallowed so free,
For a stomach complaint, all the doctors agree,
  Far worse than a headache or cough is.
Death, who like a cruel and insolent bully, drubs
  All those he thinks fit to attack,
Cried, ' Dan, my tight lad, try a touch of my mulligrubbs,'
  Which laid him flat on his back.

"Great spirits of Broughton, Jem Belcher, and Fig,
  Of Corcoran, Pearce, and Dutch Sam;
Whether ' up stairs' or ' down,' you kick up a rig,
And at intervals pause, your blue ruin to swig,
  Or with grub your bread-basket to cram;
Or whether, for quiet, you're placed all alone,
In some charming retired little heaven of your own,
Where the turf is elastic—in short, just the thing
That Bill Gibbons would choose when he's forming a ring;
That, whenever you wander, you still may turn to,
And thrash, and be thrashed, till you're black and blue;
Where your favourite enjoyments for ever are near,
And you eat and you drink, and you fight all the year;
Ah! receive, then, to join in your milling delight,
The shade of Sir Daniel Donnelly, Knight,
        With whom a turn-up is no frolic;
        His is no white or cold liver,
        For he beat O-liver,
Challenged Carter, and—died of the colic!"

" Sorrow is Dry.

"A PLAINTIVE BALLAD.

"When to Peggy Bauldie's daughter first I told Sir Daniel's death,
Like a glass of soda-water, it took away her breath;
It took away your breath, my dear, and it sorely dimm'd your sight,
And aye ye let the salt, salt tear down fall for Erin's knight;
For he was a knight of glory bright, the spur ne'er deck'd a bolder,
Great George's blade itself was laid upon Sir Daniel's shoulder.
                Sing hey ho, the Sheddon, etc.

[*] Pugilistic Champion of Ireland, we presume.—ED.

"I took a turn along the street, to breathe the Trongate air,
　Carnegie's lass I chanced to meet, with a bag of lemons fair ;
　Says I, 'Gude Meg, ohone ! ohone ! you 've heard of Dan's disaster—
　If I 'm alive, I 'll come at five, and feed upon your master ;—
　A glass or two no harm will do to either saint or sinner.
　And a bowl with friends will make amends for a so-so sort of dinner.'

"I found Carnegie in his nook, upon the old settee,
　And dark and dismal was his look, as black as black might be,
　Then suddenly the blood did fly, and leave his face so pale,
　That scarce I knew, in altered hue, the bard of Largo's vale ;
　But Meg was winding up the Jack, so off flew all my pains,
　For, large as cocks, two fat earocks I knew were hung in chains.

"Nevertheless, he did express his joy to see me there—
　Meg laid the cloth, and, nothing loth, I soon pull'd in my chair ;
　The mutton broth and bouilli both came up in season due.
　The grace is said, when Provan's head at the door appears in view ;
　The bard at work, like any Turk, first nods an invitation,
　For who so free as all the three from priggish botheration ?

"Ere long the Towdies deck the board with a cod's head and shoulders,
　And the oyster sauce it surely was great joy to all beholders.
　To George our king a jolly can of royal port is poured—
　Our gracious king who knighted Dan with his own shining sword ;
　The next we sip with trembling lip—'t is of the claret clear—
　To the hero dead that cup we shed, and mix it with a tear.

"'T is now your servant's turn to mix the nectar of the bowl ;
　Still on the ring our thoughts we fix, while round the goblets roll,
　Great Jackson, Belcher, Scroggins, Gas, we celebrate in turns,
　Each Christian, Jew, and Pagan, with the fancy's flame that burns ;
　Carnegie's finger on the board a mimic circle draws,
　And, Egan-like, h' expounds the rounds and pugilistic laws.

"'T is thus that worth heroic is suitably lamented—
　Great Daniel's shade, I know it, dry grief had much resented.
　What signify your tear and sigh ?　A bumper is the thing
　Will gladden most the generous ghost of a champion of the king.
　The tear and sigh, from voice and eye, must quickly pass away,
　But the bumper good may be renewed until our dying day."

"A Dirge over Sir Daniel Donnelly.

"TUNE—'*Molly Astore.*'

"As down Exchequer Street* I strayed, a little time ago,
　I chanced to meet an honest blade, his face brimful of woe ;
　I asked him why he seem'd so sad, or why he sigh'd so sore ?
　'O Gramachree, ooh, Tom,' says he, 'Sir Daniel is no more !'

"With that he took me straight away, and pensively we went
　To where poor Daniel's body lay, in wooden waistcoat pent ;
　And many a yard before we reached the threshhold of his door,
　We heard the keeners, as they screeched, 'Sir Daniel is no more !'

"We entered soft, for feelings sad were stirring in our breast,
　To take our farewell of the lad who now was gone to rest ;
　We took a drop of Dan's potheen,† and joined the piteous roar ;
　Oh, where shall be his fellow seen, since Daniel is no more ?

"His was the fist, whose weighty dint did Oliver defeat,
　His was the fist that gave the hint it need not oft repeat.
　His was the fist that overthrew his rivals o'er and o'er ;
　But now we cry, in phillalu, 'Sir Daniel is no more !'

　* In Dublin.　　　　　　† Poor Dan kept a public-house—Lord rest his sowl.

"Cribb, Cooper, Carter, need not fear great Donnelly's renown,
For at his wake we 're seated here, while he is lying down;
For Death, that primest swell of all, has laid him on the floor,
And left us here, alas! to bawl, 'Sir Daniel is no more!'

"EPITAPH.

"Here lies Sir Daniel Donnelly, a pugilist of fame,
In Ireland bred and born was he, and he was genuine game;
Then if an Irishman you be, when you have read this o'er,
Go home and drink the memory of him who is no more."

"Childe Daniel—A Lament.

"In Fancy-land there is a burst of woe,
   The spirit's tribute to the fallen; see
On each scarr'd front the cloud of sorrow glow,
   Bloating its sprightly shine. But what is he
   For whom grief's mighty butt is broach'd so free?
Were his brows shadow'd by the awful crown,
   The bishop's mitre, or high plumery
Of the mail'd warrior? Won he his renown
On pulpit, throne, or field, whom Death hath now struck down?

"He won it in the field, where arms are none,
   Save those the mother gives to us. He was
A climbing star, which had not fully shone;
   Yet promised, in his glory, to surpass
   Our champion star ascendant: but, alas!
The sceptred shade that values early might,
   And pow'r, and pith, and bottom, as the grass,
Gave with his fleshless fist a buffet slight—

   *   *   *   *   *

"'Tis done. Green-mantled Erin
May weep; her hopes of milling sway past by,
And Cribb, sublime, no lowlier rival fearing,
   Before, sole Ammon of the fistic sky,
   Conceited, quaffing his blue ruin high,
Till comes the swell that come to all men must,
   By whose 'foul blow' Sir Daniel low doth lie,
Summons the champion to resign his trust,
And mingles his with kings', slaves', chieftains', beggars' dust!"

The Funeral.

On Sunday, February 27, 1820, the remains of this celebrated character were borne, with all due pomp and solemnity, from his family residence in Greek Street to the last asylum at Bully's Acre, where his ancestors lie quietly inurned. An immense concourse, some in carriages and some on horseback, moving in slow and measured pace, formed part of the procession. There was a strong muster of the fancy. The gloves were carried on a cushion in front of the hearse, from which the horses had been unyoked by the crowd, and multitudes contended for the honour of assisting in drawing it. The procession took its route through the leading streets of the city, and the numbers, as it passed, increased until the body of the champion was lodged in its last resting-place. It is for posterity to do justice to the prowess of Sir Daniel Donnelly. Not the least remarkable feature in his eventful history is, that he was the last person who received the honour of knighthood during the regency: there might have been, and probably were, worse men among those who received that honour before him. Although last, he did not deserve to be held as least, among the knights of our day.

> "What dire misfortune has our land o'erspread?
> Our Irish Champion's numbered with the dead;
> And he who never did to mortal bend,
> By Death's cut short, and Ireland's lost her friend.
> Ah! cruel Death, why were you so unkind,
> To take Sir Dan. and leave such trash behind
> As Gregson. Cooper, Carter—such a clan
> To leave behind, and take so great a man?
> Oh! Erin's daughters, come and shed your tears
> On your bold Champion's grave, whose shortened years
> Have made Erin's sons this day a day of sorrow—
> Who have we now that will defend our Curragh?"

To the Blackwood collection we again resort for the proposed inscription for an obelisk to Sir Daniel's memory :—

" The Epitaph.

> " Underneath this pillar high
> Lies Sir Daniel Donnelly:
> He was a stout and handy man,
> And people called him 'Buffing Dan;'
> Knighthood he took from George's sword,
> And well he wore it, by my word!
> He died at last, from forty-seven
> Tumblers of punch he drank one even;
> O'erthrown by punch, unharmed by fist,
> He died unbeaten pugilist!
> Such a buffer as Donnelly,
> Ireland never again will see.

> "OBIIT XIII° KAL. MARTII, MDCCCXX.   ÆTAT SUÆ XXXII."

CHAPTER VIII.

JACK CARTER, "THE LANCASHIRE HERO." 1812–1832.*

THE reputation of Jack Carter as a pugilist suffered unduly from two causes.   First, from ridiculously exaggerated press flourishes about his prowess, skill, and formidable qualities by partizan scribes; and, secondly, by a factious band of provincial supporters and adherents, who spoilt their man by their indiscriminate support and attempts, by clamour and intimidation, to carry their *protegé* to the topmost position, in despite of the interposition of better men.   Poor Carter, too, an unstable, self-conceited, and, when excited, an offensive and bullying rough, was spoilt for his calling as well as for decent society, by his injudicious "following."   Pierce Egan, who prematurely dubs him in his first volume "the Lancashire hero (?)" furnishes us with the only account of the early life of Bob Gregson's *protegé*, which, its magniloquence notwithstanding, reveals the secret that Jack Carter was a mere "Lancashire rough," and not a whit too courageous; nor, for that matter, commonly honest; though Shakespere says, "to be honest, as this world goes, is to be one man picked out of ten thousand."   In his second and third volumes (for Carter figures in each) stubborn facts reduce Carter's dimensions and character as "a champion (?);" and in the last Pierce prefaces his jeremiad over this perverted "navvy" by misusing the Miltonic motto, "How are the mighty fallen!" though when or how Carter was "mighty" is a puzzler.   This he follows with an array of gasconading advertisements, challenges, and thrasonical handbills.   Here, with some pruning of redundances, is the story of Jack's early days as detailed in "Boxiana" :—

"Carter was born at Manchester, September 13, 1789, of respectable parents, who apprenticed him to a shoemaker, but being a strong, healthy lad, and not liking the confinement of the trade, left it to give a lending

---

* Carter's ring career really closed on the 4th of May, 1819, when his pretensions were disposed of by the science of Tom Spring. See Life of SPRING, Vol. II., Chapter I.

hand towards the improvement of his country, by commencing navigator, and working upon the canals in that neighbourhood. It was among those rough-hewn, hardy sons of the creation, that Carter began to exhibit his feats of strength by milling several of the best considered men in their whole phalanx. Jack was in height about five feet ten inches and a half, and weighed about thirteen stone; and it was the following droll and singular circumstance that brought him into notice, both as a pedestrian and a pugilist. The navigators, in one of their moments of hilarity, proposed a jackass race, and entered into subscriptions for that purpose; the stakes were held by a Mr. Merryman, belonging to a mountebank, who was then gammoning the flats in that part of the country. Mr. Merryman was a good tumbler, full of fun, and could fight a bit, and had rendered himself an attractive personage to the numerous Johnny Raws by whom he was surrounded. Upon the day arriving for the race to take place, no neddy was entered to run for the stakes, except one belonging to Mr. Merryman. This circumstance created surprise; in fact, much disappointment. Jack Carter instantly entered himself as a jackass. At first, some little argument took place as to the oddness of the attempt, but at length it was logically determined that Carter was a jackass, and that he should be entered as such, upon which they started. Away went neddy with all the fleetness of a prime donkey, kicking and snorting over the ground; and the jackass set out in fine style, amidst the shouts and laughs of the multitude, who now began to bet in all manner of shapes—Christian against donkey, and neddy against jackass. The distance was four miles, producing considerable wagers and much diversion among the spectators. The jackass possessing rather more knowledge than the neddy, made the best of his way, leaving the donkey behind him, came in first and claimed the stakes. No jackass was ever so much caressed before for winning a race. But Mr. Merryman now treated it as only a joke, observing that he only let Carter run to increase the sport, and disputed his claim as a jackass. It was certain that all the words in Johnson's Dictionary would not have satisfactorily explained this knotty point; and there not being logicians enough present to place the question in a proper point of view, a nearer road was taken to settle the matter. Carter gave Mr. Merryman to understand that, if he did not instantly hand over the stakes, that it should be milled out of his carcase. Merryman received this threat with a smile of contempt, entertaining an idea that as this jackass had been running four miles, his wind could not be good for much, and agreed that the fist should decide it. A ring being formed, Merryman was soon made to laugh on the wrong side of his mouth; and he who had hitherto tumbled for the pleasure of the crowd, was now, in spite of his antics, knocked down often, and punished so severely that he was compelled, not only to give in, but to give up the money."

Carter's fame as a boxer and racer was soon spread abroad, and he entered the lists in a short time afterwards with a heavy strong man, a navigator, at Preston, who had gained some good battles in his time. It was a truly severe conflict, and occasioned considerable conversation in Lancashire. He was matched in several races, in one of which he beat the celebrated Abraham Wood, though, from Pierce Egan's own showing, in another page, this seems to have been not only after his coming to London, but subsequently to his first fight with Boone, the soldier.

It was while working at the Highgate Tunnel that Bob Gregson first met Carter. He was a Lancashire man, and that was enough to recommend him to Bob, who we have proof sufficient was neither a good fighter himself nor much of a judge of what constitutes one, like his modern double, Ben Caunt. " Upon inquiry," adds "Boxiana," " it was found that Carter had proved himself a trump !" and says, "all that he wanted was *experience, science* (!), and introduction." " He shall have that," cried Bob, and instantly, at his own expense, took care of Carter, and placed him under the "Rolands" (whose distinguished skill in fencing and as pugilistic teachers was then in its zenith). Pierce continues, " It is but justice to Carter to observe that, under such tuition, he soon made considerable progress in the art, and when it was judged a proper time to give publicity to his attempt, Bob introduced him at the Fives Court." Carter's appearance is thus flatteringly described in the *Morning Advertiser* of Wednesday, July 29, 1812 :—

"SPARRING.—The last sparring exhibition took place yesterday at the Fives Court, for the benefit of Power, a pugilist, who, as a professor of the science, is inferior to none on the boxing list, but his exhibitions have been rare. The greatest novelty on this occasion was an exhibition between a trial-man of Gregson's, named Carter, from Lancashire, a candidate of first-rate weight for fighting fame, and Fuller, a scientific pupil of Richmond's. A rufflaning match took place, and, not to give superiority to either, it was a match which afforded much diversion, and it will cause a considerable sensation in the sporting world. Gregson's man, who is under the best tuition, will prove a tremendous teazer, if he be gifted with the best of pugilistic favours—game—which remains to be tried. He is a fine weighty left-handed hitter, and, *if* game be in him, he can beat anything now on the list."

With such a character, though the " if" in respect to his " game" looks very like a misgiving, Carter was matched against Boone, the soldier, for an unknown stake. Boone (made Bone in "Boxiana") has not a single fight to his credit in "Fistiana," except that with Crockey, a wretched affair, four years after this exhibition. The battle came off on Friday, September 18, 1812, near Ealing, Middlesex, when, after twelve rounds, in seventeen minutes, Boone gave in. Egan says it was "a severe contest," and adds, "In this battle Carter's patrons thought he had made good his pretensions to milling, and looked forward anxiously to place him nearly, if not quite, at the top of the boxing list." They accordingly matched him against Jack Power. (See POWER, in Appendix.) The stake was the handsome sum of 200 guineas, subscribed by Gregson's friends, and on the 16th of November, 1812, the fight came off at Rickmansworth, Herts. The battle will be found in the Life of POWER, who, despite the recent rupture of a bloodvessel, and incapacity for severe training, thrashed Carter in thirty-nine rounds, occupying one hour and five minutes. "Boxiana" says, with edifying *naïveté*, "Carter attributed the loss of this battle to his second (Isaac Bittoon) placing a Belcher handkerchief over his mouth, which tended rather to deprive him of his wind (query, courage) than to do anything to increase that necessary *quality* in a boxer." He adds, "If Carter in his battle with Power did not exhibit those traits of finished elegance which characterise the skilful pugilist, he nevertheless pourtrayed that he was not ignorant of the principles of boxing, and his patrons were perfectly satisfied with the bottom which he manifested upon the occasion," which shows they were thankful for very small mercies, as Carter brought youth, weight, length, and strength to the losing side.

After much cavilling a match was made between Carter and Molineaux. Poor Molineaux, having been twice beaten by Cribb, was now on his downward course (see vol. i., pp. 282-285, *ante*), yet, in this contest, which took place at Remington, Gloucestershire, on Friday, the 2nd of April, 1813, Carter was disgracefully beaten by the once formidable nigger. Of this affair, on which we have commented in the life of Molineaux, a contemporary writes :—"It was the opinion of the most experienced pugilists that such a set-to was never before witnessed ; one 'was afraid, and the other dared not.' Carter was the best man after the battle began, and continued so throughout the fight. Molineaux was wretched in the extreme, and at one time positively bolted from his second. But to the great astonishment of all the spectators, when Molineaux was dead beat, Carter fainted and dropped his head as he sat on the knee of his second. All the exertions of Richmond could not arouse Carter from his lethargic state, and he thus lost the battle."

In the next paragraph we find "Boxiana" stating, "as a boxer, and even as a scientific pugilist, Carter was entitled to considerable prominency (whatever that may mean); and, if viewed as a fibber (was the historian unconsciously writing autobiography?), it would be difficult to find a better one. In point of hitting and getting away, he is little inferior, if not equal, to Richmond, and very good and active upon his legs. With his left hand he dealt out severe punishment; and although in his former contests his right hand appeared but of little service to him, yet he seemed to have rather improved in the use of it. One objection which had been warmly argued against Carter by many of the fancy was, that he was soft about the head, afraid of the coming blow, and shrank from punishment; while, on the contrary, it was roundly asserted by the other part that, if he behaved correctly, his game was unimpeachable."

After his defeat by Molineaux, Carter exhibited the art of self-defence in Ireland, Scotland, and most of the provincial towns in England, with great success; and from his continual practice in those trials of skill, aided by considerable intuitive knowledge upon the subject of boxing, he returned to the metropolis an active and improved fighter. Upon his arrival in London, Carter, without hesitation, declared himself ready to enter the lists with any man in the kingdom; and this public challenge, as might be supposed, was not suffered to remain long unanswered, and Richmond, in consequence, catered a fine, strong, healthy black, of the name of Joseph Stephenson, weighing upwards of fourteen stone, from Havre de Grace, Maryland, in America, as a likely opponent.

The Pugilistic Club gave a purse of twenty-five guineas, and the combatants put down twenty-five also a-side. On Tuesday, February 6, 1816, the above heroes (!) met at Coombe Warren. This battle excited considerable interest throughout the pugilistic circles; and, notwithstanding the torrents of rain that deluged the roads, from seven in the morning till seven at night without intermission, thousands of spectators braved the elements with the utmost *nonchalance*. The men entered the ring about one o'clock; Cribb and Shelton acting as seconds to Carter, and Richmond and Oliver for Stephenson. Two to one in many instances upon Carter.

THE FIGHT.

Round 1. — On setting-to, Carter had scarcely placed himself in a fighting position when, with much dexterity, he gave Stephenson a desperate nobber. The man of colour seemed rather surprised at this sudden attack, but he bored his way into a sharp rally. The pink first appeared on Carter's face. The latter, in closing, fibbed Stephenson, but he was undermost when down. (Seven to four against the Black.)

2. — Carter again commenced offensive operations with his left hand, and the Black's

head was completely open to him. Some blows were exchanged, and, in closing, Carter found his way to the ground.

3.—It was evident the man of colour was the strongest, and that Carter might have come into the ring better prepared for action. Stephenson endeavoured to put in some heavy blows, but the science of Carter was too much for him. The latter hit and got away in good style; but, in a sharp rally, the Black showed tolerable resolution. In struggling to obtain the throw, both went down.

4.—Carter showed bad condition, and was much in want of wind; but Stephenson did not appear to avail himself of this opportunity of turning it to account. Carter, with great dexterity, not only nobbed his opponent successfully with his left hand, without experiencing any return, but made use of his right better than usual. The Black, however, in closing, endeavoured to fib his adversary; but Carter extricated himself with much adroitness, and went down. (Two to one was now offered on Carter with great confidence.)

5.—Stephenson did not appear eager to commence the attack, and some little sparring was also necessary, that Carter might recover his wind. The Black knew more about receiving than any other part of the science, and Carter milled him on the retreat with great *sang froid*. Stephenson, rather passionate from this sort of treatment, endeavoured to bore in upon his adversary, but Carter stopped short upon him, and, measuring his distance well, the man of colour measured his length on the grass in a twinkling.

6.—The strength of the Black at times gave him rather the advantage, and, in finishing this round, Carter was thrown. (Seven to two on the latter, but no takers.)

7.—Stephenson seemed almost tired of the battle, and got down in the best manner he was able. (Any odds upon Carter.)

8.—Stephenson reached the scratch greatly distressed, and Carter sent him down from a slight touch.

9.—The left hand of Carter was again in motion, but Stephenson caught hold of it, and the word "stop," it was understood, had escaped from his lips. Carter instantly made his exit from the ring, and upon his seconds preparing to follow him, Stephenson insisted it was a mistake, and that he was determined to continue the contest. Nearly half an hour had now elapsed, and Carter immediately resumed offensive operations.

10.—Carter, somewhat angry at this disappointment, went to work in sharp style, and the Black again felt the severity of his left hand. In closing, both went down.

It would be superfluous to detail the succeeding rounds of this battle. It was perfectly ridiculous on the part of Stephenson to resume the fight, as not the slightest chance appeared to turn it to his account. At the expiration of forty-four minutes, victory was declared in favour of Carter. From the well-known science of the latter, it was expected that he would have been able to dispose of Stephenson in much less time; but Carter, it seemed, looked upon the event so certain as to be indifferent respecting his appearance in the ring in good condition. Stephenson had merely to boast of strength; in other respects he was little better than a novice.

Three months had scarcely elapsed, when a formidable man of colour, of the name of Robinson, who had acquired some celebrity from the execution he had performed among second-rate boxers, and ambitiously eager to achieve conquests of greater importance, agreed to enter the lists with Carter, at Moulsey Hurst, on Wednesday, April 24, 1816, for a stake of fifty guineas, and also a purse of twenty-five, given by the P. C., in a twenty-feet roped ring. Vehicles of all descriptions were in requisition at an early hour to reach the destined spot; and the curiosity of the fancy was so strongly excited to witness this mill that, by twelve o'clock, it might be fairly stated the Hurst contained little short of 20,000 people. Robinson was a fancied article, declared capable of performing pugilistic wonders. He had beaten Crockey in prime twig,* and Butcher he had also vanquished in decent

* Sam Robinson, the Black, was born in 1778, in New York. He was a strong and courageous nigger, and after beating Crockey, beat Butcher, on March 16, 1816, at Coombe Warren, for a purse of £10. He was then beaten by Carter (twice) as here recorded. He beat Stephenson, the Black, at Coombe Wood, the 28th of May, 1816, making his third

style; and when the match was first made between Robinson and Carter, the Black was rather the favourite with those characters who are always eager for novelty, and considerable bets were laid in his favour; and even some of the knowing ones were doubtful on the subject. It cannot be denied that Carter never stood A1 in the esteem of the fancy. They knew he did not want for science; they knew he did not want for strength and activity; and they also were acquainted that he could run and jump well, and that he was a boxer above mediocrity. Still there was an inexpressible something that seemed to pervade their opinions, which kept many from going that length upon Carter they might otherwise have done; added to which, Robinson talked confidently of his capabilities of sarving-out, which blinded the too credulous as to the real state of things. But the flash side, upon looking into the chances and comparing notes upon the subject, soon became awake as to the issue likely to ensue, and previously to the fight, six to four first came forward, five to three, and lastly seven to four upon Carter. A few minutes before one the Black showed in the ring, and tossed up his hat. Carter soon followed and did the same, and immediately came up to Robinson and shook hands with him. Soon after their seconds appeared—Paddington Jones and Dick Whale for Robinson, and Painter and Harry Harmer for Carter—when they stripped and commenced

THE FIGHT.

Round 1.—Carter had scarcely sot-to, when he gave Blacky a severe facer with his left hand, and quick as lightning put in two more tremendous hits upon the same cheek, and got away with much dexterity before the man of colour was able to return. The Black, in closing, got somewhat fibbed, and went down. (Seven to four generally was offered, but no takers appeared. Two to one in many places.)

2.—The Black's nob was completely at Carter's service, and the latter put in five tremendous facers again with his left hand. The Black, notwithstanding, bored in and got Carter against the ropes, but did no execution, when, after an awkward struggle

in a close, Carter went down. (It was now ten to two against the man of colour.)

3.—The Black, at this early stage of the fight, seemed not only damaged, but rather shy, and he sparred cautiously to recover his wind. Carter again made the same successful use of his left hand, by planting three more hits upon the old place. A short rally took place, in which Blacky endeavoured to make a change in the appearance of things, but without effect, and he ultimately went down. The superiority of Carter appeared manifest in every round. In fact, the Black was dead beat, and when on his second's knee called out for "brandy."

4.—Carter hit short, but the Black gained

battle in three months. A hasty match was again made with Carter, and Robinson was a second time defeated, June 20, 1816. Sutton, the Black (see Appendix), challenged Robinson at Doncaster Races, and beat him, September 26, 1816, for a purse, in thirty-six minutes. In December, Robinson beat a big Yorkshireman, named Taylor, at Ferrybridge, in nineteen minutes, for a purse of ten guineas. He was next defeated by George Cooper (see COOPER, vol. i., p. 365), and quickly polished off. Fangill, a Scotch boxer, and a Waterloo man, was matched against Robinson, and they fought at Shellock, in Ayrshire, June 25, 1817, when Robinson proved the victor in forty minutes, after a gallant fight. His last battle was with Dent, a north-countryman, whom he beat, December 5, 1817, near the renowned Gretna Green, famed for other ring matches. He for some time attended sparring at the Fives Court, and when we lose sight of him he had entered the service of a sporting nobleman, nothing by it. In closing, the punishment which Carter served out to his opponent was tremendous in the extreme; he held the Black up with one arm, and with the other fibbed him so severely that he went down quite exhausted. The Black's consequence as a first-rate miller was all gone. His fanciers now began to look rather blue, and found, too late, that their judgment had proved erroneous.

5.—The distressed state of the Black was conspicuous to all parties, and he left his second's knee in a tottering state. He, however, endeavoured to make the best of it, and attacked Carter rather furiously, but the latter soon spoiled his intention, and again fibbed him down. (Five pounds to five shillings.)

6.—Carter, full of gaiety, smiled at the impotent efforts of his opponent, and punished him with the utmost *sang froid.* Blacky put in a body blow, but received such a staggerer in return that he was quite abroad, and at length went down.

7.—The left hand of Carter was again busy with the mug of l is antagonist. However, the Black endeavoured to make something like a rally, but he displayed more of desperation than judgment, and paid dearly for his temerity by again going down. This was the best round in the fight.

8.—The nob of the Black, from the severe punishment he had received, now assumed a terrific aspect, and in his endeavour to plant a hit, Carter stopped it dexterously, and returned so severe a facer that Blacky's pimple appeared to go round upon his shoulders, like the movement of a harlequin; he went reeling away like a drunken man, and fell.

9.—The Black reluctantly appeared at the mark, when Carter, as fresh as a daisy, added more dreadful left-handed hits to his already disfigured nob. In closing, both down, but Blacky undermost.

10.—It was almost up with the man of colour; he made a running hit and fell. Some disapprobation now manifested itself.

11.—The game of the Black, if he ever had any, was now all exhausted, and he went down from a mere push. It was thought rather currish.

12 and last.—The Black, in a state bordering on frenzy, endeavoured to follow Carter, but the latter punished him at every step, fibbed him terribly, and, in closing, both down, but Blacky undermost. So complete a finish in seventeen minutes and a half was scarcely to be expected, from the high milling qualities the Black was said to possess; and even the most knowing upon the subject offered to bet, previous to the fight, that it continued upwards of forty minutes.

REMARKS.—Blacky, from the above display, lost ground in the opinion of the amateurs; his strength was more prominent than any other pugilistic quality. He left the ring apparently much distressed in body and mind from the punishment he had experienced. Carter was in good condition and in high spirits, and disposed of his opponent in first-rate style, and positively retired from the contest without a scratch, excepting upon his back, which, it is said, occurred either from a bite or a pinch given him by the man of colour. Carter showed himself evidently improved as a scientific pugilist: there was nothing hurried in his manner of attack; he viewed his antagonist with much fortitude, and scarcely made a hit without doing material execution. He adopted the milling on the retreat system, and hit and got away with all the celerity of Richmond. Two Blacks he has thus completely vanquished; and it is generally considered to the above might be added a third (?). It must certainly be admitted that Carter gained a step or two on the pugilistic roll of fame from the above contest, and perhaps removed many doubts that hitherto existed respecting his pretensions as a first-rate boxer. An opinion was now entertained that he had only to look well to himself, and something higher was still within his reach.

Gregson now made a rather odd and suspicious match on behalf of Carter, which "Boxiana" calls a "NOUVELLE feature in the Prize Ring, namely, A MATCH AGAINST TIME!" This was, that Carter should beat Robinson within half an hour.

Carter, who had vanquished this sombre hero in seventeen minutes, laughed at this new experiment of his capabilities, and accepted the challenge without the slightest reflection. On Wednesday, June 26, 1816, at Coombe Warren, the above boxers met to decide this match, for twenty guineas a-side; and, notwithstanding the badness of the weather, the patrons of pugilism mustered strongly. Much sporting speculation occurred, and they both entered the ring in good spirits. Six to four on Carter. The latter was attended by Cribb and Harmer; Robinson had for his seconds Oliver and Richmond.

THE FIGHT.

Round 1.—Carter, as in the last fight, immediately upon setting-to went quickly to work with his left hand and nobbed the Black in style. Robinson was not able to make any return, and he received four severe successive facers. Carter did as he pleased, hit and got away with much dexterity. Two minutes elapsed before the round was finished, when the man of colour went down.

2.—It seemed not to be the intention of Robinson to make any hits, but merely to prolong the fight. He sparred with the utmost caution, but he was not able to prevent Carter from nobbing him at almost every step. The man of colour, however, was induced to make a sort of rally, but he was at length hit down. This round lasted three minutes.

3.—Carter, with the utmost activity, put in six severe blows on the cheek of Robinson, and got cleanly away, without the least return. A close took place, when Carter got the Black's head under his arm, and fibbed him so severely that he fell out of the ring, and Carter upon him.

4.—The fighting was all on the side of Carter: he planted hits with the utmost dexterity, and, had he not been fighting against time, any odds must have been laid upon him as to proving the conqueror. He again held Robinson up, and fibbed him till he went down.

5.—Carter kept hitting and getting away, till at length they closed, when he got Robinson's head under his arm, and the man of colour, to prevent being fibbed, grasped tight hold of Carter's hand; but the round was finished by Blacky's going down.

6.—The left hand of Carter was again three times in succession in the Black's face, without any return. Robinson kept cautiously sparring and drawing himself back; and those blows he attempted to make were out of all distance and lost their effect. Robinson was again sent down.

7.—It was astonishing to see with what ease and facility Carter made use of his left hand. He now put in with the utmost rapidity nine severe facers, making Robinson's head dance again, and experiencing not the least return. In closing, they both went down, but the Black undermost.

8.—The superiority of Carter over his opponent was visible in every movement; he not only gave six more facers with the utmost dexterity, and put in a body blow, but most severely fibbed Robinson down. The Lancashire hero was much distressed.

9.—Carter again felt for the Black's nob; but from the slippery state of the grass, he got off his balance and went down from a slight hit or trip, but he was up again in an instant.

10.—Notwithstanding the numerous severe facers Robinson had received, there was no confusion about him, and he was always ready to time. It appeared now that, if Carter won the battle, he must go in and do considerable execution, as the half hour was rapidly advancing, and the Black was not to be licked by merely nobbing him. Robinson endeavoured to make a change in his favour, by attacking Carter and following him up, but at length he was sent down.

11.—This was a tolerably good round, and the Black showed himself a different man altogether from what he appeared in his late combat with Carter. His mug seemed a little changed, and Carter kept repeating upon the punished places. Robinson went down from a hit.

12.—The Black set-to with much resolution, and seemed very unlike an almost finished man. His face was again severely milled, but it was very doubtful whether Carter had the best of this round. The Black was sent down.

13 and last.—Time was growing very short, and Carter to win must almost perform wonders. He again put in two nobbers, and some other hits, when Robinson fell down from a sort of slip, tumbling forwards between Carter's legs. Carter immediately threw up both his arms, and declared the man of colour had dropped without a blow. The outer ring was instantly broken, and some confusion took place. "Foul, foul!" and "Fair, fair!" was loudly vociferated by both parties, and on all sides. Twenty-eight minutes and a half had expired. It was urged that Robinson had fell once before without a blow, which had not been noticed. Upon this termination some demur occurred; but it was decided by the umpires that Carter was entitled to the money, and it was given up to him accordingly.

REMARKS.—In the eighth round Carter was evidently distressed, and showed he was much out of condition. He had been living freely, and his milling capabilities must have experienced a drawback, by his having a very painful and inflamed leg. In fact, it was rather a surprise match, and the money hastily deposited on the part of Carter when he was not in the most temperate state of understanding. It was a ridiculous wager altogether, and such a man as Robinson appeared to be in this last fight with Carter, would require the tremendous finishing hits of a Cribb to beat the man of colour with anything like a certainty in thirty minutes. The face of Robinson, never an

Adonis, was a little spoilt as to its former character, but the fight was far from being taken out of him, and in the tenth, eleventh, and twelfth rounds he changed his mode, with an appearance of going to work in earnest. He is not to be vanquished by nobbing hits alone. Could Carter use his right hand in any manner to second his left, few men, it is urged, would be able to stand any length of time before him. He appeared not the least hurt from the conflict in which he had been so recently engaged; and Robinson also was in a wagon viewing the fight between Curtis and Lazarus, with all the indifference of a mere spectator.

The Lancashire and Carlisle friends of Carter now rallied round him, and he was at length matched with Oliver. In the metropolis Oliver was everything; and Carter, in opposition to him, only named with derision and contempt. But time, which proveth all things, thus narrates this milling event:—

This contest was decided on the estate of Sir James Maxwell, in an enclosed field of Mr. Johnson, inn-keeper (and within 150 yards of the blacksmith's shop, so celebrated in the Lovers' Cabinet for the dispatch of business), at Gretna Green, four miles from Longtown, and fourteen from Carlisle, on Friday, the 4th of October, 1816, for 100 guineas a-side, in a twenty-four feet roped ring, in the presence of 30,000 spectators. The sporting world was much interested, yet so confident as to the termination of the event, that three to one was considered as correct betting. Oliver had risen progressively into fame. Not so with his opponent: he was "anything but a good one." During the day on which the fight took place the streets and houses of Carlisle and its vicinity were drained of the male population, and a horse, chaise, cart, or any sort of vehicle whatever, was not to be procured at any price. The fanciers of the metropolis, it seems, were not so numerous as usual upon great milling occasions, and a few of the "highest flight" only were recognized upon the ground. Mr. Jackson was not at Carlisle, and it was observed that the losing man was not the better for his absence. The concourse of people was so great that it was deemed necessary to form an outer rope ring, in order to prevent unpleasant consequences from the pressure of so vast a multitude. The fight had nearly been prevented, as officers, sent by George Blamire, Esq., the Mayor of Carlisle, and the Rev. Dr. Lowry and Dr. Heysham, two other magistrates, were on the look out to bind the parties over to keep the peace.

Oliver arrived at the Bush Tavern, Carlisle, accompanied by Captain Barclay, on Wednesday morning, at eleven o'clock, and he had scarcely entered the room when the officers inquired for him. Some person, suspecting their errand, introduced them to the brother of Oliver, when Tom took the hint and quietly withdrew, not being known to them. At nineteen minutes before one the battle commenced. The umpires were the Marquis of Queensberry and Captain Barclay. Carter first entered the ring with his seconds, Painter and Harmer, and the usual defiance of the castor was exhibited by him. Oliver instantly followed with his assistants, Cribb and Cooper. On stripping, the condition of Oliver appeared equal to any one that ever entered the ring; but Carter, it was thought, might have been better. The ceremony of friendship was then performed, and ten to four was loudly vociferated upon Oliver.

THE FIGHT.

Round 1.—The odds being so decidedly against Carter, the greatest anxiety was manifested by the spectators upon their setting-to, and the combatants seemed equally alive to the importance of obtaining the first advantage, by their deliberate mode of attack. Oliver endeavoured to plant a tremendous blow with his right hand, which Carter stopped in a scientific style, and returned a severe left-handed hit on the right eye of Oliver, that produced the claret in a twinkling. A good rally took place. Carter closed upon his adversary, fibbed him terribly, and ultimately threw him. Oliver bled profusely from his temple and his nose. It is impossible to describe the shouts of the populace upon Carter's obtaining this superiority. It was like a salute of artillery. (The odds had completely vanished, and even betting was now the true feature of the ring.)

2.—This burst of applause seemed to operate much upon the feelings of Oliver, and he determined if possible to get the turn in his favour by going furiously to work. Carter, partial to the left hand mode, aimed at his opponent's nob, which Oliver prevented, and fought his way into a rally. Considerable hammering took place, and Carter got his man on the ropes. Here the truth began to be told to the sceptics: the superiority of strength most completely manifested itself upon the side of Carter, who again threw his opponent. (Great shouting. It was all up with any more offering of three to one.)

3.—Oliver gave Carter a severe blow on the head, but the latter would not be stopped, and again bored his man to the ropes, punished him dreadfully, and brought him down, Oliver bleeding copiously.

4.—Oliver was now convinced that he had formed an erroneous opinion of the boxing powers of his antagonist. Carter turned out a better man in every point of view than he had expected, and was not to be disposed of in that easy manner which he had flattered himself must be the case, and in which his friends had so fatally confirmed the error. Several heavy blows passed between them, but to the advantage of Carter. The latter received a severe facer; but, notwithstand-ing, he drove his man to the ropes, and, in closing, both went down. The head of Oliver was much punished, and his back excoriated by Carter hugging him on the ropes. (Six to four upon Carter generally, and more in many places. It was at the close of this round that Carter first showed blood.)

5.—Oliver seemed at a loss how to cope with any sort of success, against his scientific antagonist, and resorted to his game qualities of going in to smash this hitting and getting away boxer, if possible. Oliver was no stranger that Carter always preferred giving to taking punishment, and drew an inference that his opponent had some fears in this respect, and that to insure victory the fight must be taken out of him by close and determined attacks. Oliver, in consequence, felt severely in this round for Carter's body, but the latter returned desperately on his opponent's head. They were again struggling at the ropes, and both went down.

6.—Some heavy blows were exchanged in a rally, and Carter was floored at the ropes.

7.—Oliver was bleeding in all directions, and, in closing, went down.

8 to 20.—The description of these rounds would be superfluous. The gameness of Oliver, his manliness of boxing, and his determination to succeed, if possible, perfectly satisfied the most sanguine of his partisans, and at intervals he met with partial success; but, in justice to Carter it must be stated, that the advantages were decisively upon his side: he hit and got away with his usual *sang froid*; his right hand was also conspicuously effective, and, whenever it appeared expedient to finish the round, he closed at pleasure upon his adversary with the most eminent superiority. Oliver gained nothing in fighting for length; and when going in he was opposed with the most determined opposition. In truth, the spectators were convinced in the above rounds that the science, the strength, and smiling confidence of victory were on the side of Carter; and that his adversary had not only been most dreadfully punished, but quite abroad as to his usual system of tactics, throwing away a number of blows by repeatedly hitting short; while, on the con-

trary, the Lancashire hero did not exhibit any very prominent marks of severe milling, and was quite in possession of himself.

21.—In this round Oliver showed himself off in a conspicuous manner, and put in so tremendous a hit in the wind of Carter, that he measured his length on the ground instantaneously. It appeared, from its severity, a complete finisher. The friends of Oliver thought Carter would not be able to come to time, if at all; and the Lancastrians looked rather blue as to its ultimate effects. (The betting, notwithstanding, varied but little.)

22.—The expected change did not take place; although Carter appeared at the scratch very much distressed, and almost gaping for breath he contrived to get himself down in the best manner he was able. No blows passed in this round.

23.—Much the same as the preceding, but in struggling Oliver was thrown.

24.—Carter was now "himself again:" his wind had returned, and he resumed the contest in the most decisive style. Oliver, like a lion, rushed forward in the most gallant manner. The hitting, in a rally, was terrible; both the combatants seemed totally to disregard punishment. The fine game of Oliver was opposed by the bottom of Carter, and this essential quality toward victory in pugilists, so much doubted to be possessed in the latter, was now found not to be wanting in the Lancashire hero. Oliver's head was disfigured, and Carter's nob was a little altered from its originality. It was the most desperate round in the fight; the closing of it at the ropes was to the disadvantage of Oliver, and his friends were now satisfied he could not win.

25.—It was astonishing to witness the courage of Oliver; he appeared determined to conquer or perish in the attempt. One eye was completely in the dark, and the other was rapidly closing. His strength was also fast leaving him; nevertheless, he contested this round in the most manly manner. He was ultimately thrown, and Carter fell heavily upon him. (Ten to one upon Carter.)

26 to 32 and last.—The die was cast, and the brave Oliver, like heroes of old, could not control his fate. Nature had been pushed to the farthest extremity that the human frame could bear. Defeat seemed to operate so much upon his mind that he fought till his pulse was scarcely found to vibrate; and in the last six rounds, during which he had not the least shadow of a chance, he persevered till all recollection of the scene in which he had been so actively engaged had totally left him. In the thirty-second round he was taken out of the ring in a state of stupor, and completely deprived of vision. The swelled appearance of his head beggared all description; his body and back were shockingly lacerated all over from his struggling so much upon the ropes; and, in point of fact, much as fighting men may have suffered in former battles, the situation to which Oliver was reduced, it appears, exceeded them all. The battle lasted forty-six minutes. He was taken and put to bed at Longtown, four miles from the ring, and in consequence of the vast quantity of blood he had lost in the contest, added to his exhausted state, the surgeons who were called in to attend upon him deemed it dangerous that he should be bled.

REMARKS.—Oliver felt confident that he should prove the conqueror, and exerted every means in his power to insure victory. He came into the ring in high condition, weighing about twelve stone eight pounds; but the chance was completely against him, either at in or off fighting. excepting the twenty-first round. Oliver tried to beat Carter after the manner he had vanquished Painter, by determined in-fighting; but the left hand of Carter always met the head of his adversary before he got to his length, when Oliver, finding the great danger of this mode of attack, endeavoured to render it useless by throwing his head back to avoid the coming blow, at the same time it gave Carter a full opportunity of striking down with his right hand, which he never failed to do. It was always in the power of Carter to close upon his adversary, and bore him to the ropes whenever he thought proper. In short, there was no comparison between the combatants respecting scientific fighting; and the character of Oliver, as a good man, was more valued than his capabilities as a boxer considered. The high patronage, too, of Captain Barclay had dazzled the minds of the fancy—individual or cool judgment was out of the question, and three to one was betted without why or wherefore. Calculation was completely against such betting, and it was a sort of overwhelming preference. Too much prejudice had existed against Carter; and it was sneeringly observed that he was without game, at best a mere flipper with his left hand, and whenever he was placed against a good one he would soon be found out. Comment upon that head is now rendered unnecessary, as facts are stubborn things. A better or a braver man than his fallen opponent is not to be found upon the list of boxers; and, although defeated, he is entitled to the highest consideration of the sporting world. Carter weighed about thirteen stone seven pounds, smiled frequently during the fight, and treated the efforts of his adversary with the most perfect indifference. There was some cry about a foul blow, but the umpires did not notice it. Carter returned to Carlisle in the evening, and was seen walking about the streets with his friends. So much was Carter the object of pugilistic admiration at this place that, at the White Hart Inn, a subscription was proposed among several amateurs, that he should fight the Champion of England for 500 guineas. It was also observed, as Richmond was walking round the ring during the fight, that Carter had beat all the blacks. "No; all but one," was the reply; when Richmond said he would fight Carter for 200 guineas. Great praise is due to Painter for the care and attention he paid to Carter during his training.

The backers of Carter presented him with fifty guineas in addition to the battle money. Oliver and Carter, a few days after the fight, met at Hawick, and received each other in the style of true courage.

Carter's pedestrian feats may here find a place. Pierce Egan says, "As a runner, the qualifications of Carter were far above mediocrity. He could run a mile in little more than five minutes; and out of fourteen races and walking matches, he won them all excepting two.

"In the spring of 1812 Carter ran a match against time, on Sunbury Common, when, to the astonishment of every one present, he performed two miles in a few seconds over eleven minutes without any training.

"Carter, from the celebrity he had gained through the performance of the above match, was backed for a considerable sum against Abraham Wood, of Lancashire, for two miles. The latter was to give Carter 100 yards; but his friends deemed it prudent to pay forfeit. However, a new match was made off-hand, condition not being considered. Wood was now to give 150 yards out of two miles. This race was decided on Saturday, the 26th of December, 1812, on the Lea Bridge Road, near London, Gregson acting as umpire for Carter, and Captain Hinton for Wood. They started at two o'clock, Carter having taken 150 yards in advance. Both of the racers seemed to fly, they got over the ground with such speed. When at the end of the first mile, Wood had gained upon Carter sixty yards, and in the next half mile Wood had made greater progress; but when within a quarter of a mile of the winning-post, he was within twenty yards of Carter. The latter had now recovered second wind, and ran the last quarter of a mile with speed at the rate of a mile in five minutes, and won by about six yards. It was even betting at starting, but Carter for choice.

"Carter had some other pretensions to public notice, independent of prize-fighting. He was a good dancer, and could perform the clog-hornpipe with considerable talent, and, after the manner of an expert clown, stand upon his head and drink off several glasses of ale in that position."

The friends of the Lancashire hero, from the improved capabilities he had so recently displayed, were now anxious to produce a meeting between him and the champion. Much conversation in consequence took place, and even personal challenges passed between the above pugilists, but no deposit was put down to make a match. Cribb offered to fight any man in the kingdom for £1,000, and not less than £300; but Carter, it seems, could not be backed for either of those sums, therefore the match was off altogether. It ought, however, to be mentioned that the latter was ready to accommodate any man for £50; and, although no decision ever occurred respecting his claim to that enviable title, yet Carter assumed the appellation of champion from the following circumstance:—A bet of £200 a-side, £50 forfeit, was made between Sir William Maxwell and the Marquis of Queensberry, immediately after the defeat of Oliver by Carter, at Carlisle Races, October, 1816, challenging all England, the Marquis to produce a man to enter the lists against the latter at the above races in 1817. Twelve months having elapsed and no competitor making his appearance at the appointed place, the £50 was forfeited, and Carter received the same (it is said) at Dumfries.

In the newspapers our hero again publicly challenged anything alive in the shape of a man, adding that his friends were ready to back him, regardless of colour, observing "that blue, black, white, or yellow, would be equally acceptable to him." In his printed hand-bills, at the Shrewsbury Races, 1817, he thus vain-gloriously described himself:—

"BOXING.—The art of self-defence will be scientifically displayed by Mr. John Carter (the Champion of England), Mr. Gregson, and others, at the Turf Inn, Shrewsbury, every race morning, precisely at eleven o'clock, and in a spacious booth on the race ground between each heat.

"*₊* Gregson, who is Carter's trainer, is taking him down into the north of England to contend with Donnelly, the Irishman, at the ensuing Carlisle Races. Private lessons given."

For three years Carter lived upon the fame of his victory over Oliver, travelling through the provinces, after the manner of more modern quack champions, exhibiting "the art," and never ceasing to assert the falsehood that Cribb had refused to fight him, whereas Carter always limited his proposal, when pressed, to the stake of £50, a mere absurd subterfuge.

At length his career of boasting received an unexpected check. Cribb argued that his "boy," Tom Spring (although beaten by Ned Painter in August, 1818), was good enough to lower the pretensions of "the Lancashire hero." Carter's friends made the match for £50 a-side, and a purse of £50 for the winner was added by the Pugilistic Club. Two to one was offered by the north countrymen. The battle was fought on Crawley Downs, May 4, 1819. The result will be found in the Life of SPRING, where the report does scant justice to the latter. The infatuation of Carter's admirers found expression in the following letters addressed to *Bell's Weekly Dispatch* :—

"Carlisle, May 12, 1819.

"SIR,—

"You will oblige the Cumberland fancy by giving insertion to the following paragraph in your next paper.

"Your obedient servant,

"H. P.

"The gentlemen of the Cumberland fancy have held a meeting after reading an account of the battle between Spring and Carter contained in your paper, and from other sources of information, and were unanimously of opinion that Carter made a cross of the battle. They have, therefore, come to the resolution of withdrawing all support from him in future: they will not back him, even if he were matched to fight an orange boy. All bets upon the battle have been declared void in the North."

This nonsense elicited the following reply :—

"SIR,—

"In reply to a letter, signed H. P., from the Cumberland fancy, which appeared in your journal of May 16, I shall briefly observe that the gentlemen who acted as umpires at the battle between Carter and Spring are well known as men of honour and integrity, and had they detected anything like a cross, would have immediately made such a circumstance public. The battle money was paid without hesitation. The noble lord who backed Carter also discharged his bets upon demand ; and no refusal has been made in the sporting world to pay, that has come within the writer's knowledge.

"Respecting the fight, sir, it was most certainly a bad one—a pully-hauly encounter ; in fact, it was nearly the same as the battle between Carter and Oliver, at Carlisle, but with this difference—the left hand of Carter was foiled, and Spring also proved the stronger man at the ropes. The Lancashire hero having thus lost the two only points for which he was distinguished, led to his defeat. Spring behaved like a man, and did not appear to have any hugging pretensions about him, had he not been dragged to the ropes. Carter was beaten against his will.

"In giving insertion to the above letter, to prevent any improper allusions going abroad, you will much oblige

"AN OLD SPORTSMAN.

"Tattersall's, Hyde Park Corner, May 28, 1819."

There is a volume contained in this. Carter beat Oliver—despite the flowing account in "Boxiana," written up by a person *not present* at the battle—by hugging and squeezing his man, who was less in weight and stature than himself, upon the ropes, after the fashion of a recent American champion. Foiled in this by Spring's length, steadiness, and left-handed skill, he was abroad. That he was beaten against his will, no impartial spectator could doubt.

Carter made his appearance, on the Friday after his battle with Spring, at Mr. Jackson's rooms in Bond Street. His crest was lowered, his former high tone quite subdued, and he acknowledged, with some touches of grief, that he could not tell how he lost the battle. Thirty pounds were collected on the ground for him, including the donation of ten from his backer.

On losing his popularity, he left London for Ireland, in which his stay was rather short, when he returned to England accompanied by the Irish champion. A quarrel, however, took place between Carter and Donnelly, when the former followed the Irish champion to Dublin, opened a public-house, and challenged Dan. See the memoir of Donnelly in Chapter VII.

Carter, who arrived from Ireland on Tuesday, February 1, 1820, being anxious to make a match with Sutton, for 100 guineas a-side, previous to his again returning thither, called in at a sporting house in Oxenden Street, for the purpose of making his intention known, and on being admitted into a room where a private party were assembled, insulted several, and ultimately threw a glass of wine in the face of one of those present, part of which alighted on Tom Cribb. This insult was not to be borne by the champion, who, although rather the worse for the juice of the grape at the time, immediately grappled with Carter. It was an up and down contest, but the champion made such good use of his time that his opponent received a severe thrashing in the space of one minute, and begged in a piteous manner that Cribb might be taken away from him, or he should be killed.

Carter once more left London, sparring his way to Dublin, in which he was assisted by Reynolds and Sutton.

On his return a few months afterwards, being in company with Shelton at a sporting dinner at the Brown Bear, Bow Street, July 10, 1821, he spoke disparagingly of Shelton's capabilities, when, after some discussion, £20 were posted for a fight instanter, and the result was that Shelton beat him to a stand-still in three rounds only. Carter afterwards challenged Jem Ward to fight for £100 a-side, but when the time came for making the match, was unable to raise that sum. In this dilemma he proposed to back himself for £50 a-side, and trust to fortune to get the money. This was refused by Ward; but, being hard pressed by Carter, who entreated him as a favour to oblige him, at length consented, and it was agreed they should fight for £50 a-side, on May 17, 1828, within one hundred miles of London, which came off at Shepperton Range, when Carter was defeated in sixteen rounds, occupying thirty-two minutes. (See Memoir of WARD, Chapter I., Period VI.)

Carter was next matched with Deaf Burke for £100 a-side, by whom he was defeated, at the Barge House, Woolwich, on the 8th of May, 1832, in eleven rounds, occupying twenty-five minutes. (See DEAF BURKE, post.)

Although he survived this defeat twelve years, it was his last appearance in the prize ring. He died at Thames Street, Manchester, May 27, 1844.

APPENDIX TO PERIOD V.

HARRY SUTTON, THE BLACK—1816-1819.

FROM the time of Molineaux no sable champion had achieved so great a name as Sutton, and that, too, in a brief period. A native of Baltimore, he ran his slavery and worked, with an industry unusual in niggers, as a corn-runner in the Deptford granaries. Led by curiosity to see two of his own colour, Robinson and Stephenson, display their tactics in the ring, he repaired to Coombe Wood, May 28, 1816. While here as a spectator, Sutton, who was a tall athletic man, was asked by a gentleman what he thought of meeting another black who had challenged for a purse to be given on the ground. Sutton, who was as brave a fellow as ever sported a black suit of nature's livery, consented readily, and another " black job" was soon started. Richmond and Harmer seconded Sutton; Cropley and Paddington Jones taking the other black under their most especial care, who was inferior in every point of view—in height, strength, make, look, and age —to Sutton. The set-to was something new and amusing.

THE FIGHT.

Round 1.—The long arms of Sutton looked formidable, and though he began in a hurry, Cropley's black seemed equally eager to meet him. Such a term as science was not to be mentioned. It was slinging, wild hitting, dodging, and turning round, till at last they came to a violent hug, when much pummelling took place. They, however, broke away from this close embrace, and made a complete standstill of it, looking at each other and panting for breath. Cropley's black now folded his arms, nodded his head, and began to point his finger, laughing at his opponent. This so enraged Sutton that he rushed in and planted a chopping hit, which made Cropley's beauty dance again. It was now a comic scene, and new tricks were introduced at every step. Sutton, in making a blow at his opponent's nob, hit his cap off, and his bald pate appearing, the spectators were in roars of laughter; yet, notwithstanding the variety of ludicrous postures exhibited by these black Quixotes, some heavy milling took place. Four minutes and a half had passed, amid the most uproarious shouts and applause, when Sutton put an end to this singular round, grappled his opponent and brought him down.

2.—On setting-to some hornpipe steps were jigged by Cropley's black. The arms of Sutton trembled astonishingly, and his frame seemed much agitated. He made use of the chopping blow, and whenever his distance proved correct, his hits were tremendous. Some few blows passed, when Cropley's black was thrown.

3.—Cropley's man did not seem to like it; and perhaps, had it not been for the charms

of a purse, he would have bolted. In fact, he was no match for his opponent. He hopped about and hit at random. Sutton chopped at his opponent. Some few blows were exchanged, when Cropley's black fell. and refused to come again. Thus finished this caricature on milling.

On June 4, 1816, at a benefit for Eales and Johnson at the Fives Court, Sutton mounted the stage to contend with the powerful Tom Oliver. Sutton appeared rather diffident. His sparring, however, was far from contemptible, and, as a novice, he achieved more than could have been expected. Oliver had very little the best of him, and it was observed that Tom took the gloves off first. George Cooper (the late competitor of Donnelly in Ireland, and who was reported to be dead) made his appearance and also had a set-to with Sutton. Cooper put in several heavy facers, and showed considerable science; but Sutton, no way dismayed, stood well up to him, and, in a sharp rally, returned some heavy hits and exchanged blows advantageously. Upon the whole, the new man of colour received much applause. Cooper, like Oliver, it was also remarked, took off the gloves first.

The milling qualities of Sutton being now better understood, he was matched with Robinson; and these men of colour met at Doncaster Races, September 25, 1816. The fight took place in a paddock (where each spectator was charged three shillings as the price of admission), in a twenty feet roped ring, for a subscription purse. Robinson, who had twice fought with Carter, and defeated Stephenson, Butcher, etc., was seconded by Crouch and Saunders, and, in consequence of his boxing notoriety, five to four was betted upon him in the metropolis, and six to four upon his setting-to in the ring. Sutton was attended by Richmond and Harmer. At half past twelve the signal was given, and offensive operations commenced without farther ceremony. It appears in the first round that Robinson sustained so severe a hit from his opponent that it quite spoiled him as to any vigorous exertion afterwards. An appeal was made to the umpires upon this momentous point, on which the fate of the battle hung; but these rustic arbiters of milling, not ignorant of the precedents of Moulsey, or the practice at Coombe Warren, and not wishing to make a chancery suit of it, instantly ordered the fight to proceed. The long arms of Sutton not only took great liberties with the upper works of Robinson, but soon put the wind of the latter out of order, and ultimately made him measure his length upon the ground. The betting now rapidly changed, and Sutton became the favourite, with odds upon him. It was all up with Robinson, and during twenty-five rounds he had no opportunity of turning the battle in his favour; and in thirty-six minutes, after receiving a severe milling, he was compelled to acknowledge that he had had "enough!" It is but fair to state that he was out of condition, never had any training, was overturned in the coach, and entered the ring within a very few hours after his journey from London. But the knowing ones asserted Sutton could beat him at any time, and that he would soon look out for a customer much higher on the boxing list than ever Robinson stood. Sutton was scarcely hurt, and gave visible proof of the great improvement he had made. Sutton by the above battle gained little more than the honour of proving a conqueror.

From the capabilities displayed by Sutton in this fight he rose in the estimation of the patrons of scientific boxing, and was judged an able competitor for the game Ned Painter. A match was accordingly made between them, for 25 guineas a-side and a P. C. purse, and they entered the lists at Moulsey Hurst on July 23, 1817.

Painter at this time had been the victor in two battles, over Coyne, the Irishman, and Alexander, the gamekeeper; but he had two defeats, *per contra*, with Tom Oliver (then in his best day), and with the gigantic Shaw, the Life-guardsman, a defeat without disgrace. The betting on the day was six to four on Painter.

Painter showed himself near the ring sitting on a basket a considerable time before the Black appeared in sight. In fact, he was sent for by the Commander-in-chief.* Sutton at length came forward with his second and threw his hat in the ring, which was soon followed by his opponent performing the same act of defiance. During the time Painter was taking off his clothes Sutton never took his eyes off his person. Cribb and Harmer seconded Painter; Tom Oliver and Paddington Jones waited upon Sutton. The anxious moment had now arrived (ten minutes after one); the combatants and seconds shook hands, and the battle commenced. Both men appeared in good condition, but Painter looked somewhat thin. Five to four upon Sutton.

THE FIGHT.

Round 1. — Some trifling sparring occurred. Sutton's long arm stood out like a pole, and upon the whole his frame looked tremendous. Painter hit first, but not effectively, when they got to hammering each other, and arrived at the ropes. Here Ned fibbed his opponent severely, until the strength of Sutton enabled him to break away. The Black now returned to the attack impetuously, but without judgment, and got nobbed preciously for his fury. Painter went down from a slight hit or a slip.

2.—The men were now both upon their

* Mr. John Jackson.

mettle, and the tremors of a first round had subsided. Notwithstanding the Black's long arm the science of Painter prevailed to that extent upon Sutton's upper works that he seemed to possess a body without a head. It was almost a question if he knew whether he was in or out of the ring. A desperate rally occurred, and, in closing, Painter endeavoured again to fib his opponent. The Black caught hold of his hand to avoid punishment, and ultimately Painter was down.

3.—It is impossible to describe the execution which took place on both sides during this round. If one was bold, the other was fearless: it was hit for hit, in the most finished style of boxing; in fact, it was truly tremendous, and the amateurs were now convinced that the man of colour possessed "devil" enough for anything. At length Painter planted a body blow with so much severity that the Black was missing in a twinkling, and seen gasping for breath on the ground. (The uproarious applause that took place was like a fire of artillery, the confusion of tongues immense. "That's the way to win my boy!" and two to one all round the ring upon Painter.)

4.—It is true the Black was brought to the scratch, but his breath escaped from his lips like a pair of bellows in full blow. This was a trying round for both parties, and Painter seemed to have out-fought his strength. They almost tumbled against each other, so much were they exhausted, till they again got into determined milling. Here Painter gave Sutton such a tremendous pimpler that his head seemed to rotate on his shoulders with the rapid twirl of a Bologna. In closing, Painter exerted himself in fibbing his opponent; but Sutton resolutely disengaged himself and threw his adversary.

5.—Painter now appeared bleeding, and half a minute time was too short for the men to appear anything like themselves, so furiously had the battle raged in this early period of the fight. This round, however, was decidedly in favour of Painter, and he stopped the rashness of his opponent in a scientific manner. He gave Sutton three such heavy facers, that the nob of the Black did not seem to belong to him, and gallantly finished this round by sending him down. (The applause here was a tumult of joy, and in the ecstacy of the moment five to one was offered. It was now the expressed opinion that Ned would win the battle in a canter.)

6.—The fight must have been finished in this round, or at least he would have rendered it certain, had Painter possessed sufficient strength. The Black could scarcely leave his second's knee, and had it not been for the skill of Tom Oliver he would not have been in time to meet his opponent at the scratch. They both stared at each other, and appeared fit for anything but milling. However, they went at it pell mell, and Painter received so sharp a blow on his left

eye that the claret ran down. The Black also got such a nobber that he was quite abroad, and moved his hands like a puppet pulled with strings. It was all chance work, and Painter went down.

7.—Painter again "faced" the Black, and had the best of the round, but he went down.

8.—The Black endeavoured to bore in, but he was stopped in fine style. Painter milled him in every direction, planted three facers with ease, and finished the round by levelling Sutton. (Great shouting.)

9.—Both extremely distressed; and notwithstanding the many nobbers the Black had received, all Painter's work in point of appearance went for nothing. Sutton's frontispiece seemed to defy all hitting. Painter was bored to the ropes, where, in struggling, both fell.

10.—Sutton floored his opponent by a tremendous hit in the chest. The partizans of Sutton here manifested their approbation.

11.—Painter's exertions in this round were astonishing. He had it all his own way. He nobbed the Black so repeatedly that his arms were of no use to him, as he could not place himself in a position, and Sutton fell from exhaustion.

12.—Some blows were exchanged, materially to the advantage of Painter. His exertions, however, were more than his strength could support, and he ultimately went down.

13.—Sutton had been so much beaten about the head, that he seemed in a state of stupor, and "time" might have been vociferated in vain had not his attendant roused him into action. He was literally pushed forward to meet his opponent, when Painter kept paying away till he went down from weakness. Painter planted eight facers without return.

14 to 17.—In the first three rounds Painter went down; but in the last, notwithstanding his bad state of vision, he milled the Black so successfully that Sutton measured his length on the grass. (Loud shouting, and "Painter will yet win," was frequently asserted.)

18.—In this distressed state a rally occurred, and Painter was floored.

19.—This was a most singular round: it was anybody's battle. Both the men were dead beat. The Black turned away from Painter on his making a hit; and soon afterwards Painter turned from him, and went down. (Two to one on Sutton.)

20.—Painter not only made some good hits, but, in closing, he fibbed Sutton sharply, and dropped him.

21 to 23.—Painter was down in all these rounds, although he had the best of the hitting. He was distressed beyond description.

24.—Painter seemed to have revived a little, and made a desperate hit on the nose of Sutton that floored him upon his back, and his legs rebounded from the earth. It appeared a finisher, and he was got upon the knee of his second with considerable difficulty. (The odds now changed again in favour of Painter.)

25 to 31.—It was astonishing to witness the desperation with which many of these rounds were contested. Painter showed most science, but the Black's strength was more than could be reduced, and the former was down almost every time from sheer exhaustion.

32 to 40 and last.—Painter was almost blind and destitute of strength, yet he contended up to the last moment for victory. He was so far gone, in some instances, that he almost tried to lie down; and it was owing to his extreme weakness that Sutton was enabled to recover his strength, and brought him the smiles of victory. It was strength alone that won it. It is due to Sutton to state that a fairer fighter never entered the ring; but it is more pleasure to assert that no prejudice was expressed as to his colour—impartiality was the order of the day. Painter was led out of the ring, while Sutton walked from the scene of action without his clothes. The battle lasted forty-eight minutes and a half. A liberal subscription was gathered for Painter by Mr. Jackson on the ground. He returned to Belcher's in the evening, where the most considerate attention was paid to him. He experienced no body blows of consequence, but his head and arms were terribly beaten.

REMARKS. — Painter, although defeated, has not fallen in the estimation of his friends. His courage was equal to the task he had to accomplish. In point of science he was far superior to his opponent; but in strength he was materially deficient. It was a complete sporting fight, and the odds were continually changing. Two better men never had a meeting; and a more determined battle could not be witnessed. Sutton has raised himself in the opinion of the amateurs, and he is considered to have evinced as much pluck, if not more, than any man of colour that has yet exhibited. Though his exterior did not show much punishment, yet his cheeks had a "rainbow" appearance. He is not likely to remain long in a state of inactivity, and will certainly prove a desperate customer to any one who dares contend with him. His prodigious length of arm is of great advantage; and he is pronounced by the best informed upon this subject to be the hardest hitter on the present list of boxers. Sutton owed his success greatly to the management and prompt determination of his second, Tom Oliver. Painter never fought so well before. He stopped fifty blows at least with his right hand, and also punished Sutton severely about the body. Upon the whole, it was one of the evenest contended battles that had been viewed for a long time, until the last seven rounds, when, during some of these Painter strained every effort to turn the chance in his favour. What the human frame could perform towards obtaining conquest this determined boxer attempted. He actually fought till nature refused to move. So much regret was never expressed upon the defeat of any pugilist as upon this occasion, owing to Painter's inoffensive disposition and respectful behaviour in society at all times.

The sporting amateurs of Norwich desiring a fight in their vicinity, had, it seems, subscribed the sum of £100, £80 to the winner and £20 to the losing man, and Painter having challenged Sutton to a second trial, they were offered a premium to bring off the affair at Bungay Common, Suffolk, the day appointed being the 16th of December, 1817. The battle was truly tremendous, and after fifteen rounds, all fighting, in one hour and forty-two minutes, Sutton was carried from the ring. (See PAINTER, ante p. 79.)

The no-fight between Shelton and Oliver which took the fancy on a wild goose chase to Blindlow Heath and Copthorne, on the tempestuous 23rd of December, 1819, led to another black job for Massa Sutton. Kendrick, the black, had come down that day, determined, he said, to fight anybody, should there be a purse, after the "big affair," and resolved, moreover, to have "a bit of beef for his Christmas dinner." Fifteen guineas were collected, when Sutton, considering it an easy prize, offered himself for a game at "black and all black." At three o'clock the men faced each other, Randall looking after Kendrick, and Jack Martin attending upon Sutton.

THE FIGHT.

Round 1.—Kendrick hit short with his left hand, and delivered his right well home on Sutton's head, but his hand was open and it did no mischief. Sutton rushed in, closed, and threw Kendrick a heavy fall.

2.—Sutton delivered a straight and well-directed blow with his left hand in Kendrick's bread-basket, which made him cry "Hem!" and drove him back two yards. Sutton, going in to follow up his success, was met in the middle of the head, when a rally commenced. Some blows exchanged, and Kendrick was thrown. It was evident here Sutton was too strong for him.

3.—Sutton put in another left-handed doubler, and followed with his right on Kendrick's eye, which floored him as if shot. Kendrick bled freely from his nose and mouth.

Nine other rounds were fought, in which Sutton had it all his own way, and Kendrick received some heavy blows and falls. In the twelfth round Sutton hit him with the left hand in the mark, and caught him on the head with the right as he was going down, which so knocked the wind and senses out of Kendrick that he could not be moved from his second's knee. The fight lasted seventeen minutes. Sutton was scarcely marked, his condition being very superior to that of poor Kendrick, who was severely punished. A liberal subscription was made for him through the exertions of Mr. Jackson, and sympathy was expressed as it was his third defeat in succession, and he was "out of luck."

REMARKS.—Kendrick's weakness was visible early in the fight; but, without taking that into consideration, he could not in his best trim conquer Sutton. Though without a chance of winning the purse, he showed himself a game man. He received a tremendous hit on the right eye, and also complained of a severe stomacher, that puffed the wind out of his empty frame like a pair of bellows; Sutton also fell upon him heavily. A gentleman very humanely gave up an inside place, and rode outside a coach, in order that poor Kendrick might be brought to London comfortably and free of expense; he also paid other attentions to his wants. Several gentlemen proposed that Kendrick should be sent into training, and that they would back him against the Gas-light Man for 25 guineas a-side. With patronage and training, Kendrick, it was thought, might become as it were a new man.

Sutton, although he attended the Fives Court and every benefit and sparring match and prize fight, could not find a customer. His thirteen stone nine pounds, and six feet and half an inch in height, were too great odds for middle weights, and the big ones wanted larger figures than Harry could get backed for. He was, however, matched with Larkin, the guardsman, to fight on the 4th of November, 1819, and 20 guineas posted; but in this he was disappointed, for Larkin was ordered off by his colonel, and Sutton's only consolation was the twenty yellow boys. Sutton now went on a sparring tour with Jack Carter through Lancashire and to Ireland, as may be seen in Carter's life. As from this period Sutton merely appears as a sparring exhibitor, we here close his pugilistic career.

BILL ABBOT—1818-1832.

BILL ABBOT, whose victories over Hares, Dolly Smith, the renowned Tom Oliver, and Phil. Sampson, give him a claim to a niche in the Walhalla of pugilism, was a Westminster lad and a disciple of Caleb Baldwin. He stood five feet eight inches, and weighed eleven stone seven pounds. His first battle of any note was with a man of the name of Jones, at Wimbledon Common, whom he defeated in good style.

Abbot next fought Dick Hares on Wimbledon Common, on June 16, 1818, after Randall and Burke had left the ring. Hares displayed his usual good fighting and game qualities; but he was compelled to surrender to Abbot. Hares was over-weighted.

Abbot was matched against Dolly Smith for twenty guineas a-side, and this battle took place near the Barge House, in Essex, on Tuesday, February 2, 1819, on which day the amateurs, heedless of rain, left the metropolis and mustered numerously on the ground. Mr. Soares was chosen umpire. Dolly was well known to the ring, from his combats with Hares, Scroggins, and Cannon, though these were all defeats. Abbot, from defeating Hares and Jones, was considered a rising boxer. At half past one Smith threw up his hat in the ring, accompanied by his seconds, Randall and Owen; and Abbot followed by Oliver and Shelton. There was also an outer ring. The ceremony of shaking hands took place, when the men set to. Five to four on Abbot.

THE FIGHT.

Round 1.—The men appeared in good condition, Abbot the best. They were more cautious than was expected, and some long sparring occurred. If Smith had not hit first, Abbot, in all probability, would have remained on the defensive. Dolly, with his right hand, put in a sharp bodier, which, had it been a little higher, must have floored his opponent. Abbot returned short. Dolly hit and got away, when, after some exchanges, they closed. Smith went down, and the claret was seen on his right eye.

2.—The caution of Abbot astonished the amateurs. Dolly again hit and got away. Some blows were exchanged. In closing, Dolly again went down bleeding.

3.—Dolly meant to punish his opponent, and went to work with his right hand, but it was out of distance, and he was again on the ground.

4.—Dolly was too short to get at Abbot; he could not nob him, and was always compelled to hit first. They closed, and some sharp fibbing occurred, when both went down, Dolly undermost. (Six to four on Abbot; the confident betters roared out two to one.)

5.—The short arms of Dolly frequently failed in planting a blow. This was a tolerable round, and Smith received a severe hit that sent him staggering away, but he recovered himself. In closing, Dolly paid away, but went down bleeding copiously.

6.—Abbot made some feints, when, after a short round, Dolly was hit down. (Bravo, and loud shouting.)

7.—Dolly came quite fresh to the scratch, but he received a heavy body hit that floored him. ("Well done, Abbot!")

8.—A sharp round, and both down.

9.—Both hit short. Long sparring. In closing, some fibbing occurred, when Dolly broke away. More sparring. Abbot hit short. In closing at the ropes, Abbot hit Dolly down. (Shouting, and "Bravo, Abbot!")

10.—The expected smashing forte of Abbot was not seen, and he kept retreating till Dolly hit first, when he then let fly frequently to advantage. Both down.

11.—Dolly's mug was painted in every direction, while Abbot had not received a scratch. Some sharp fibbing, and Dolly the worst of it, and down.

12. Abbot never tried to take the lead, although he generally got the best of the round. He was the best at in-fighting; and Dolly now bled copiously, till both went down.

13.—Both down.

14.—Dolly gave a good bodier; and, after some hard hitting, both again down.

15.—Dolly put in a snorter that made Abbot's pimple rattle again. ("Such another pretty Dolly," roared out Tom Owen, "is not to be seen in the kingdom.") After some sharp exchanges, Dolly was hit down on the right side of his head.

16.—The punishment on Dolly's mug was conspicuous. Both down.

17.—The right eye of Dolly was nearly closed. Some sharp work in a close, but Dolly down. Thirty-three minutes.

18.—This was a good round, but the left hand of Dolly appeared of no use to him, while Abbot's right seemed tied to his shoulder. The latter waited with the greatest patience for the attacks of Dolly, which did not at all times shield him from heavy blows on the side of his neck and one of his jaws. In closing, some severe fibbing occurred, when Dolly extricated himself with some talent. Two sharp counter-hits. Dolly received a facer which put him in a dancing attitude, and he performed some new steps without the aid of music; but he at length recovered himself, returned to the charge like a Waterloo trump, and made so formidable a stand that Abbot resorted to some long sparring. Dolly, however, got the worst of it, and was floored. (Shouting on both sides of the ring. Smith shared the applause with his opponent.)

19 to 24.—In some of these rounds, when Dolly was breaking away, Abbot made several chops at him, but without doing any material execution. In the last round Smith began to fight with both his hands, and the ear and neck of Abbot exhibited marks of heavy hitting. Both down.

25.—Dolly was cleanly hit down. ("Well done, my cabbage-cutter; that's the way to finish it.")

26.—The dose was repeated by Abbot, and the claret from Dolly's mug was copious.

27 to 32.—Dolly never could effect any change. Abbot was patiently waiting every round for Smith. The head of the latter was terrific.

33.—Dolly had decidedly the best of this round. Both down.

34.—Smith was down; but the ground was in a most wretched slippery state. (A guinea to a shilling was offered, but this was thought more bravado than judgment.)

35 to 39.—Long sparring, and the partisans of Abbot roaring out for him to "go in." "No, no," says Owen; "he knows the advantage of keeping his distance better. D'ye mind me, he's what I call a distance cove. By the Lord Mayor we shall win it now. Go along, my boy, with your left mauley, and his nob will be of no service to him." In spite, however, of all the encouragement of his lively second, Dolly was ultimately floored.

40 to 69.—To detail the minutiæ of these rounds would be superfluous. Dolly at times made some sharp hits, but there was no alteration in his favour.

70 to 127.—The rain came down in torrents, but the mill went on with all the regularity of sunshine. Abbot showed nothing like a decisive fighter; and there was once or twice he did not like the nobbers he had received. Dolly, in the majority of these rounds, went down.

128 to 138 and last.—It appeared Dolly entertained an opinion that he could not lose it; and even after two hours and a quarter had passed, he nodded satisfactorily to his friends that his confidence had not deserted him. There was nothing interesting in the whole of these rounds to amateurs; and Dolly endeavoured to tire out his adversary by going down, but without effect, when he at last said he could fight no more. Two hours and fifty-five minutes had elapsed.

REMARKS.—Abbot is by no means a first-rate fighter, or he ought to have beat Dolly off-hand. He was all caution, and his strength enabled him to last the longest. He was very glad when Dolly said "No." It was a most fatiguing fight; and, owing to the pitiless, pelting shower, and the amateurs having to stand up to their knees in mud, the ring was almost deserted before the fight was ended. It was only the out-and-outers that remained. To describe the pitiful appearance of the amateurs would have required the pencil of a Hogarth—they had not a dry thread about them. Abbot had scarcely a scratch upon his face; but was much distressed towards the end, and led out of the ring. Smith was put to bed at the Barge House. Little betting occurred. Owing to the bad state of the weather, no collection was made for Smith, but he had a benefit given to him, under the patronage of some spirited amateurs.

Abbot was defeated by West Country Dick in a turn up on March 2, 1819. (See vol. i., pp. 478, 479.)

Abbot fought with a knight of the last, to make up a fourth battle, for a small purse, on Hounslow Heath, on Tuesday, June 1, 1819; it served the amateurs to laugh at. Abbot had been sacrificing too freely at the shrine of Bacchus either to stand upright or to make a hit, and the "translator of soles" seemed also to have too much respect for his hide to encounter even his reeling opponent. "Master Waxy" gave in upon his pins, after jumping about in the most ridiculous postures for twenty minutes, without having a mark to show.

The sporting world felt great disappointment on Friday, February 18, 1820, in consequence of the severe illness of Spring preventing the combat which had been fixed for the above day. The ring was formed on Epsom Downs, and at half past twelve o'clock Ben Burn threw his hat up, and loudly declared he was ready to fight Spring. (See *ante*, p. 9.) Richmond also came forward and asked if any gentleman present appeared on the part of Spring, but no answer was given. The man of colour told Burn not to be in any hurry, as a fight could be made up in the interim. A purse of twelve guineas was collected upon the ground, and Abbot entered the lists with a raw countryman from Streatham, who appeared anxious for milling honours. Abbot was seconded by the Guardsman and Hopping Ned; the "yokel" was attended by Richmond and Clark. At two o'clock the men set to.

THE FIGHT.

Round 1.—Johnny Raw, who was quite a novice in the ring (in fact it was his first appearance), went to work pell mell; but the science and experience of Abbot gave him the best of it, and after a few hard blows he put in a hit upon the throat of the countryman that floored him like a shot. For the instant Johnny was quite senseless, and upon Richmond's picking him up, he asked, "Who done that? What's that for? Where am I?" Richmond, with a smile upon his mug, observed, "Why you are in the Court of Chancery; and, let me say, you are not the first man that has been bothered by its practice."

2 to 4. — Abbot had the best of these rounds, and he explained to the countryman the term pepper.

5.—The clumsy hitting of Johnny Raw gave him a turn, and Abbot received a tremendous floorer; and, notwithstanding the chevying of the lads to daunt the countryman, it was seven to four in his favour.

6 to 30.—It was a sort of reciprocal milling during all the rounds; many hard blows passed between them. Abbot showed the first blood, and was also the worst punished.

31.—Abbot got his opponent at the ropes; but with all his endeavours to fib the poor countryman's nob, he failed.

32 to 40 and last.—It was never exactly safe to Abbot till in this round, when he again floored Johnny by a tremendous blow on the throat. Johnny was now quite senseless, and all attempts to bring him up to time were useless. Water was thrown on his face; but Abbot was pronounced the conqueror after one hour and twenty minutes had elapsed. Abbot was by far the worst punished. On Johnny's recovering his recollection, he observed, "Who done that? Dang it, have I been in the Court of Chancery again? I don't like that place; it makes a body so stupid. But I am ready to take another turn."

Abbot entered the lists with a sturdy navigator, at the close of Hampton Races, 1820, for a small subscription purse. Abbot was seconded by Purcell and Brown, and the navigator by Shelton and West Country Dick. It was a good battle, and the navigator proved himself a very troublesome, dangerous customer. He stood over Abbot, and was also very strong, game, and would not be denied; but the superior science of our hero enabled him to win it cleverly in forty-five minutes.

Abbot, in a turn up in Harper's Fields, Marylebone, on Monday, June 5,

1820, defeated a Birmingham man of the name of Bennyflood, for a small purse, in the course of a few minutes, without a scratch upon his face.

Abbot fought Pitman for £5 a-side and a small purse, on Wimbledon Common, immediately after Brown and Curtis had left the ring, on Monday, August 28, 1820. The former was seconded by Randall and Callus, and the latter by Bill Cropley and Joe Norton. This was a hammering fight for thirty minutes, occupying twenty-seven rounds. Pitman was a game man, and reminded the spectators of Pearce, denominated the Game Chicken, but it was only in appearance. Pitman was beat to a stand-still. Abbot retired from the contest with a slight scratch under his left eye, but received some ugly thumps upon his head.

We now come to Abbot's most remarkable ring exploit. A dispute with Tom Oliver led to a hasty match, in which ten guineas a-side were posted; but it was thought absurd, and a forfeit on the part of Abbot fully expected. But time rolled on and the day fixed, Tuesday, November 6, 1821, came, with both men in the same mind; and the fancy received the intimation that Moulsey was the chosen *champ clos*. At one o'clock, Oliver, attended by Ben Burn and Bill Gibbons, threw in his hat; and shortly afterwards, Abbot, attended by Scroggins and Tom Jones, answered the signal of defiance. Seven to four, two to one, and in some instances three to one on Oliver were called out, without takers. The colours—dark blue for Oliver, light blue for Abbot—were tied to the stake, and the men stood up.

THE FIGHT.

Round 1.—On shaking hands it was expected that Oliver would immediately go to work and spoil his opponent; but, instead of that, Oliver thought he had a mere plaything in opposition to him, and did nothing. Some attempts at hitting were made on both sides, but without effect, when Abbot ran in and Oliver held him in his arms and got him down. (Shouting for joy, and Oliver for any odds.)

2.—Abbot trembled very much on placing himself in attitude at the scratch. Oliver planted a slight nobber and got away. A pause. Abbot received another small taste, when he rushed in and pulled Tom down. (Shouting and laughing, "It can't last long.")

3.—Abbot still shaking, yet he tried to plant his right on Oliver's nob, but the latter got away. Oliver hit short. In closing, Abbot hung on the ropes; but Oliver seemed wanting in strength to do execution. Abbot at length broke away and showed fight, till they both went down, Oliver uppermost. (Six to one, but no takers.

"Oliver can't lose it," was the general expression round the ring.)

4.—Whether it was owing to the recollection of what Oliver had once been in the prize ring could alone be answered by Abbot himself, but his nervous trepidation was evident. Abbot, however, made a heavy right-handed hit on his opponent's mouth which produced the claret. Some slight exchanges occurred, and, in a struggle for the throw, Oliver fell on Abbot in rather an awkward manner; but not wishing his opponent should entertain a bad opinion, Oliver said, "I beg your pardon; I could not help it." "Book that," said one of the time-keepers to the writer of this article. "as it serves to show the fancy it is a gentlemanly fight."

5.—Oliver got away from a hit. A pause. "Go to work," said Paddington Jones; "What are ye both about?" Abbot planted a bodier, and not a light one. Oliver gave a facer, and followed his opponent to the ropes, where they endeavoured to hold each other's hands to prevent fibbing, when Abbot got down. Oliver seemed to smile with contempt on his adversary, as much as to say, "There was a time that such 'an opponent could not have stood before me for five minutes."

6.—A scuffle, and both down. While Oliver was sitting on the knee of his second, the Gas, with a grin upon his mug, sarcastically observed, "Why this is a lark, ain't it, Tom? Surely you don't call this fighting."

7.—Oliver got away, when Abbot, in following him, hit short and napt a facer in return. They followed each other to the ropes, when the wretched condition of Oliver was evident to all the ring, for instead of fibbing Abbot, he literally pushed him away, gasping for wind; but Tom was so much the favourite of the amateurs, that they were completely blind to his defects. Abbot went down, and the shouting was loud in Oliver's behalf.

8.—Some little milling took place. Abbot was sent out of the ring, and Oliver fell from weakness. "The Sprig of Myrtle" stepped up to Abbot and told him it was all right. "We are sure to win it," answered Scroggins.

9.—Oliver appeared to view Abbot in the light of a play-thing; still his blows did not do any mischief. Abbot threw Oliver and fell heavily on him.

10.—Oliver threw his opponent right away from him. (Thunders of applause.) In fact, at every movement that Oliver made, either good or bad, he was cheered by the surrounding spectators.

11.—This round was decidedly in favour of Oliver. Abbot turned completely round from a hit, when Oliver took advantage of this circumstance, planted a nobber, and sent Abbot down. (The costermongers were now cheering to the echo, and Ned Turner offered £10 to £1, but no person would have it.)

12.—This was also a tidy round; Oliver best, but both down.

13.—If Oliver had gone up to the nob of Abbot he might have spoiled his "mitre;" but he was more intent on getting away from the blows of his opponent than punishing him. Abbot went down from a hit. (Loud shouting.) The time-keeper stated twenty-two minutes had elapsed, which floored the bets on time, that Oliver won it in twenty minutes.

14.—Abbot went sharply to work, and made a severe body hit. A pause. Oliver planted a header, smiling, but put down his hands as if tired. The right hand of Abbot, which went home on Oliver's mouth, sent him staggering, and the claret flowed profusely. At the ropes a sharp struggle took place, when Oliver threw his opponent. ("Well done, Tom; go to work and finish it." Oliver for any odds.)

15.—The right ear of Abbot appeared slightly tinged with blood; but in other respects the blows of Oliver had scarcely left a mark. Abbot was sent out of the ring.

16.—Oliver had the best of this round; and Abbot was again under the ropes.

17.—Oliver, instead of going to work, sparred away his time; but, in an exchange of blows, Abbot went down, and Oliver fell on him. ("Go along, Tommy; it will soon be over.")

18.—The face of Oliver was the most punished, but he had the best of this round. In following his opponent he caught him at the ropes, when Abbot would have gone down, but Oliver held him up with one hand and fibbed him with the other till he was exhausted, when Tom dropped him. (A roar of artillery. Oliver for any odds.)

19.—On coming to the scratch the face of Abbot did not betray the severe punishment which might have been expected, which was a sufficient proof, as the flash term is, that Oliver could scarcely "hit a hole in a pound of butter." Abbot tried to obtain a turn in his favour, and went boldly up to Oliver, but more passionately than collected; he, however, put in some severe hits, which did Oliver no good. The latter in return, hit Abbot down. (Great applause for Oliver.)

20.—If it had been any other boxer than Oliver, that is to say, not so old a favourite as Tom, the exertions of Abbot would not have been treated so slightly. He is a strong young man, not a novice in the prize ring, with a fist as hard as iron; and whenever he planted his right-handed hit, Oliver felt it, and more than once severely; yet the feelings of the amateurs were that Tom must win. After some exchanges, Abbot rushed in. Oliver stopped his opponent skilfully, and endeavoured to fib him as he went down at the ropes. (Lots of applause for Oliver.)

21.—In point of punishment, this was the worst round in the fight for Abbot. The latter went in right and left, but Oliver stopped his efforts, milled him, and, in struggling, threw him down so violently on his back that the claret gushed from his nose. ("It's all your own now, Tom, to a certainty.")

22.—Abbot made a hit, which Oliver stopped. The pause was now so long that Tom Jones roared out, "If you mean to fight, do, or I shall leave the ring." A scuffle, and both down.

23.—Abbot planted a heavy right-handed hit on Oliver's ribs, and was going to work in a sharp manner, when he received so straight a stopper on the throat that he went down in a twinkling. This was the first clean knock-down blow. (Oliver's friends were quite elated, and the cheers were very loud.)

24.—Abbot showed that he was not destitute of science, and made some good stops.

He also gave Oliver a facer, but ultimately went down. (Disapprobation. Indeed, Abbot did not appear to have many good wishers, except the Sprig of Myrtle, who often came to the ropes to cheer him up, as did also the Sprig's father.)

25.—Oliver napt a facer, and appeared to get weak; but his friends were so sanguine that they would not have it for a moment that anything was the matter. Abbot fought well this round; but, on going down, Oliver fell severely on him.

26.—On setting-to, Randall exclaimed, "Tom, my dear fellow, don't lose your fame; never be licked by such a man as Abbot. Only go to work, and you must win it easy." Abbot seemed (if a man's thoughts can be judged) as if a doubt existed in his mind about winning it, and retreated from Oliver. The latter held him up at the ropes, and kept fibbing him till he was exhausted, and dropped him as before. No favourite actor in a theatre ever received more applause than Oliver.

27.—Abbot, on putting up his hand, laughed, and planted a body hit. A long pause, the men looking at each other. This was one of Oliver's great faults: instead of commencing fighting, Oliver was getting away from hits. Oliver went down from a slight hit, owing to the slippery state of the ring.

28.—Abbot rushed in to mill Oliver; but he got the worst of it, and napped a severe nobber that sent him down. (Tremendous shouting.) Abbot, on being placed on his second's knee, dropped his head, and it was thought all was over.

29.—Abbot wanted to make this round as short as he could by going down, but Oliver caught him at the ropes and administered some little punishment. ("Bravo, Tom, you behave handsome." Ben Burn offered twenty guineas to five, but of no avail.)

30.—This was a fine fighting round; some severe exchanges took place, and Abbot, at the close of the round, planted such a tremendous right-handed hit on Oliver's ear that he went down like a shot. It was on the spot where Painter, Neat, and "the Gas" had done so much execution. Oliver seemed stunned: he was all abroad, and was lifted from the ground like a sack of sand. Randall, Sampson, Josh. Hudson, etc., with all their vociferation, could scarcely restore him to his senses to be in readiness to the call of "time." It is impossible to describe the agitation of the ring, not on account of their losses—for there were scarce any takers—but the sorrow felt at witnessing this lamentable tie up of a brave man. (Five to one against Oliver.)

31.—Oliver was brought to the scratch, but no sailor three sheets in the wind was half so groggy. Abbot went up to him like a bull dog, milled him in all directions, and floored him like a log. Hogarth's pictures were fools to the mugs of the amateurs—the brave Oliver to be sent out of the ring by a "wooden man," as Abbot had been previously termed.

32.—The old fanciers were deeply hurt in their minds at this reverse of fortune, and not a Westminster boy, or a costermonger. but almost felt for their "wipes" to dry up their moistened "ogles;" "but who can rule the uncertain chance of war?" Oliver put up his arms to avoid the punishment, and went down once more like a log of wood. (A guinea to a shilling, but it was of no use.) Oliver was in chancery, and completely at the mercy of his opponent; he was sent down by a push.

33 and last.—Oliver was brought up, but it was useless. He would not say "No." Abbot went in and gave Oliver the *coup de grace*, and he measured his length, insensible to the call of time. The fight occupied fifty-three minutes and thirty-eight seconds.

REMARKS.—Not a man on the Hurst but lamented this sad finish of Tom Oliver, who once aspired to the championship. He was slow as a top, and nature deserted him. He was still brave in idea, but he did not possess strength or wind to second his wishes. Oliver treated Abbot too cheaply; in fact, he gave the battle away from this circumstance. The smashing of Oliver was all out of the question. He was no more like that Oliver who fought with Painter at Shepperton, "the Gas," and Spring, than "I to Hercules." It is true that the partiality of the ring towards an old favourite made them anxious that he should not lose his once high fame, and be licked by an outside boxer, and every movement that he made was construed in his favour. Oliver ought to have won: if he had gone in and fought first, he could hardly have lost. Abbot gave his head, and several opportunities occurred, but Tom played with the chance, laughed at his opponent, and held him too cheap. For the first four rounds Abbot trembled, and the name of Oliver seemed a terror to him. He, however, put in some hard hits, and had none of the worst of the fighting. Oliver was punished about the nob; while, on the contrary, his blows, although planted on the face of Abbot, did not appear to make an impression. Still the amateurs were all in favour of Oliver, as an old one, and thought he could not lose it. Abbot went down several times, and the word "cur" escaped from the lips of several of the spectators. This epithet arose more from ill-nature than the fact. Abbot, however, was frightened at first, or else he could have won it in a short time, from the bad condition of Oliver. Oliver was terribly beaten: he was some time before he recovered himself, and was able to leave the ring. Abbot then shook hands with Oliver. Sampson immediately threw up his hat in the ring, and offered to fight Abbot for £25, £50, or £100.

A winning man does not want friends, and Abbot was immediately matched with Sampson for £50 a-side. On Tuesday, December 18, 1821, Moulsey Hurst was again the scene of attraction, and the day being extremely fine, a strong muster of the fancy assembled on the above spot. When the office was given to cross the water, the pressure of the crowd was so great, and the lads so eager to get upon the Hurst, that some of the boats were nearly upset, so many persons rushed into them, in spite of all the entreaties of the watermen. The large flat-bottomed ferry-boat, which conveys the horses and carriages across, capable of holding between four and five hundred persons, was so overladen with passengers that it was ten to one this motley group did not bathe in Old Father Thames; indeed, it was only prevented by the great exertions and skill of the waterman. The wind was so high as to drive this prime cargo of the fancy a considerable way down the river before they had any chance of landing, and then it was only accomplished by the principal part of the passengers wading up to their knees in water before they could sport a toe on the Hurst. On the return of this boat to the shore at Hampton, the rush of persons to obtain a place in it was equally violent, although the danger and folly of such conduct had been so recently witnessed. A first-rate swell, who was extremely eager to get on board, lost his foot, and went head over tip into the water, to the no small amusement of the crowd.

The Birmingham Youth was the favourite, six and seven to four, an idea being entertained that his good fighting would bring him through the piece, more especially as a report had gone forth that Abbot had trained under the auspices of "Mr. Lushington." At a quarter past one Abbot appeared on the ground, with a blue bird's eye round his neck, and threw his hat into the ring. His countenance indicated perfect confidence. He was attended by Spring and Shelton. The Birmingham Youth, followed by Randall and Tom Jones, also shied his "castor" with a confident air, with Randall's colours, green, round his neck.

THE FIGHT.

Round 1.—On stripping, the appearance of Abbot altogether reminded the spectators of Tom Cribb in his early fighting days: it was evident a little punishment would not reduce his strength. The Birmingham Youth was in excellent condition; indeed, he asserted he was never so well in his life before. On placing themselves in attitude some pause occurred; but they soon after rushed into a close, and from the eagerness displayed, no mischief took place, and they were both down.

2.—Abbot held his arms high in order to protect his nob from the handy-work of his opponent. This manœuvre had the desired effect, and the Birmingham Youth did not show off in his usual style. This round was similar to the first, nothing material. Sampson went down from a slight hit.

3.—Sampson on the look out to plant, but the firm guard of Abbot was not to be broken. The latter put in a left-handed hit on the throat of Sampson that sent him staggering; he, however, returned to the charge, when a long pause ensued. Abbot rushed and administered some pepper. Sampson exchanged a hit or two, but went down. Abbot also fell from a slip. (The odds had now changed seven to four on Abbot.)

4.—This was a short round. After a struggle at the ropes, Abbot got his man down, and, in falling, his knees came heavily on the "Youth's" body. (The Westminster division again chevying, offering two to one.)

5.—Abbot commenced fighting, and planted one or two heavy hits. The Birmingham Youth showed fight, but he went down from a blow in the middle of his head. (Loud shouting, and in the ecstasy of the moment the cabbage-plant heroes offered five to one "the Birmingham ware must soon be disposed of.")

6.—Abbot went to work without delay, and the result was that Sampson received a hit on his face, and dropped on his knees. ("It's all up; he's going." Two to one current betting.)

7 to 20.—To detail these rounds would be uninteresting. It is true that the Birmingham commenced several rounds well, but Abbot always finished them in his favour.

21 to 30.—In the twenty-seventh round it was so much in favour of Abbot, that a distinguished sporting man from Newmarket offered a guinea to a bottle of beer, but no taker appeared.

31 to 33.—Sampson did all he could to reduce the strength of his opponent, but in vain. He now and then put in a good nobber, but in general he napped it in return.

34.—Sampson was much distressed; but he came to the scratch like a man, and endeavoured to take the lead. Several of his friends near the ring told him "hit and get away." Sampson was not unmindful of their advice, and evinced a knowledge of the art; but it was a matter of considerable surprise to the judges of milling that he did not administer pepper to the body of his opponent, which was left unprotected, as the principal aim of Abbot appeared to be in holding his guard very high to keep his knowledge-box safe, the nob in general of all his adversaries being the object of his attack. After some exchanges the Birmingham Youth received a blow near the temple which produced the claret profusely, and he fell on his knees. (Spring offered ten guineas to two on Abbot.)

35.—The countenance of Sampson appeared dejected; he nevertheless exerted himself to produce a change in his favour, although without effect. He was floored by a severe right-handed hit. (Loud cheering by the lads from the neighbourhood of the Abbey in favour of Abbot.)

36.—It was evident to every unbiassed spectator that Sampson could not win; and although some of his shifts were well

planned, they did not in the least reduce the strength of Abbot. The Birmingham Youth was on the totter when he came to the scratch, yet Abbot did not commence fighting. Shelton said, "What are you shilly-shallying about? go right up to his head and win it." Abbot followed his instructions without delay, and the result was, Sampson was floored. "I told you so," cried Shelton; "another or two and the blunt will be in your pocket."

37.—Sampson went down from a heavy blow on the side of his head. ("He can't come again.")

38.—The Birmingham Youth smiled on meeting his adversary, put in one or two nobbers, and made a struggle at the ropes. Sampson was again hit down. ("It's all over." Any odds.)

39.—Singular to remark, Sampson, as a last and desperate effort, made play, had the best of the round, and sent Abbot down. (Thunders of applause, and "Well done, Sampson.")

40.—The punishment Sampson now received was sharp and severe. Abbot determined to put an end to the battle, showed fight the instant Sampson appeared at the scratch, and, with a right-handed blow in the middle of the nob, floored him. (Ten to one.)

41.—The Birmingham Youth scarcely put up his hands, when a severe blow repeated on the same place floored him a twinkling.

42.—Abbot now proved himself the better man, and grassed poor Sampson with ease.

43.—One must lose. A tremendous hit in the middle of Sampson's head took all the fight out of him, and he measured his length on the ground. For a short period after time was called Sampson remained in a state of stupor; he, however, recovered, and, with the assistance of Randall, walked out of the ring. The mill lasted forty-seven minutes.

REMARKS.—If it was perceived that Abbot was only a half-bred one, yet it would take a good man and a heavy hitter to beat him. In but one round (the 39th) had Sampson the best of it, although he exerted himself to the utmost to obtain victory; indeed, after the second round it was decidedly in favour of Abbot. It is rather singular that, except with Dolly Smith, the Birmingham Youth has hitherto lost every battle; while, on the contrary, conquest has crowned the efforts of Abbot. The latter possesses a tolerable knowledge of the science, and left the ring with only a mark under his left eye. The Birmingham Youth was severely punished; but although he has proved so unfortunate, it is the general opinion of the fancy that, in all his battles, he has shown himself a game man, a lively, active fighter, and done everything in his power to win for his backers.

The battle had scarcely been over a minute, when the fancy were beat to stand-still, except a few who endeavoured to bolt, but could not get away, rom the effects of the "pitiless pelting storm." Hundreds were seen scam-ering to get under the wagons to avoid the hail-stones, and flooring each ther to obtain an inch of shelter. Lots looked like drowning rats, their lothes sticking to their bodies as if they had been pasted on; while a few of he "Corinthians" in post-chaises were laughing at the ludicrous scene, and lessing their happy stars for the comfort and advantages derived from the ossession of "blunt." At length the fancy rallied, showed game, and took heir places to witness another battle.

Abbot did not refuse to meet the "John Bull fighter" when called upon, s appears by the following letter, addressed to the editor of the *Weekly Dispatch.*

"CHALLENGE TO JOSH. HUDSON.

'SIR,—

"In consequence of your challenge to me a few months ago, and my fight with Oliver eing off, I now wish to inform you that I am ready to fight you once in eight weeks for 0 guineas a-side. If this meets your approbation, my friends will meet you at any time or lace you may appoint, and make a deposit of £10 or £20 a-side.

W. ABBOT.

"5th July, 1822."

These challenges, however, ended in smoke. At length Abbot was matched with Jem Ward, for £50 a-side, and they met, October 22, 1822. Jem had beaten Acton, and was fast rising into fame. The particulars of this cross will be found in the Memoir of WARD, opening the next Period.

Larkins, the Cambridge champion, was matched with Abbot for £35. The fight took place at Fidgett Hall, near Newmarket, on Monday, November 28, 1826. Abbot was here beaten in fourteen rounds, thirty-three minutes, with five to four betted upon him. From this time Abbot figures as a second and bottle holder, until 1832, when, a purse having been collected, he entered the ring with one Search, whom he disposed of in seven rounds, at Old Oak Common, on the 28th of June in that year. The career of Abbot has no further ring interest.

═══════════

DAVID HUDSON, BROTHER OF THE RENOWNED "JOHN BULL FIGHTER"—1818–1827.

DAVID HUDSON, a younger brother of the renowned Josh., made his appear-ance about two years after his celebrated senior, namely, in July, 1818; Josh's first battle with Jack Payne dating in 1816. He was a smart two-handed fighter, of the inconvenient middle weight and height, which is too much for the light ones, and not enough for the big 'uns, namely, ten stone ten pounds, and five feet seven inches and a half in height. He was born in Rotherhithe in 1798, and in 1817, when in his 19th year, defeated Pat. Connelly, a reputed good man. His first regular battle was with Richard West (West Country Dick), for 50 guineas a-side. It was the second fight following the defeat of Tom Oliver by Neat, of Bristol, at Rickmansworth, on Friday, July 10, 1818. Randall and Tom Jones were seconds to Dick; Painter and Hall for Hudson. Dick was the favourite, seven to four and two to one.

THE FIGHT.

Round 1.—This was a good round. The combatants soon closed, but broke away. A sharp rally succeeded, and Dick was thrown.

2.—Sharp fighting. Reciprocal nobbers. A smart rally, and both down.

3.—Dick put in two facers. Some exchanges, when, in struggling for the throw, in going down Hudson was uppermost.

4.—This was all in Dick's favour. He planted some heavy hits; and both going down, they rolled over each other.

5.—Hudson's ear was bleeding, and Dick threw him.

6.—This was an active round; and in the corner of the ring Hudson fibbed Dick till he fell out of the ropes. (Applause. "Bravo, Hudson.")

7.—Both of them went to work, and some sharp exchanges occurred, till both down.

8.—This appeared a severe round, and Dick got a hit on his ribs and went down.

9.—When time was called, Dick tried to leave the knee of his second; but on getting up seemed as if bent double, and pointed to his ribs, when Hudson was declared the conqueror. This sudden termination of the fight electrified the amateurs, and the backers of Dick were chap-fallen indeed. Great murmuring prevailed that "all was not right;" but Dick declared, that in falling against the stakes he had hurt his ribs so severely that he was not able to stand upright. The battle was over in fourteen minutes and five seconds.

David fought with Ballard for a trifling stake, on Wednesday, April 15, 1819, on Kennington Common. Purcell and West Country Dick seconded Hudson, and Ballard was waited upon by Holt and Hares. It was a most determined battle on both sides; and one hour and three quarters had elapsed before Ballard was compelled to acknowledge himself defeated. He was punished severely. Hudson also did not escape without considerable beating. The science and game he displayed on this occasion gave him a lift among the amateurs.

After the battle between Turner and Cy. Davis at Wallingham Common, on Friday, June 18, 1819, there was an interval of upwards of an hour, during which time the ring was filled with amateurs, endeavouring to get up another contest between some of the "good ones." Sutton offered to fight Carter, but the latter boxer pleaded want of "condition." Hall was also called, Martin, etc., but objections were made, when at length Harry Holt threw up his hat, which was immediately answered by David Hudson. Randall and O'Donnell seconded Holt, and Tom Owen and Josh. Hudson waited upon David. It was for a purse of 20 guineas. Holt was the favourite, five to four.

THE FIGHT.

Round 1.—The game of Holt had been ascertained upon more than one occasion, and his character stood well as a "pretty, scientific boxer." He was not very well, and had walked all the way from London down to the fight. Hudson, nothing else but a "good one," was also out of condition; in fact, he had only been discharged a week from the doctor's hands for the jaundice, and, on stripping, his frame had a yellow appearance. They set-to with much spirit, when Holt rather took the lead. It was all fighting, and Hudson was nobbed down.

2.—Reciprocal facers; sharp hitting, full of work; milling the order of the round. Both down, but Holt undermost. ("Bravo! this will be a good fight;" and the amateurs were much interested.)

3.—Holt stopped in fine style, and planted some heavy hits. Both down.

4.—Sparring. Both offering and eager to hit, but awake to each other's intention, and dodging. This round was really a treat to the lovers of science. Holt was hit down in the corner of the ring. (Even betting.)

5.—More science was displayed, when Owen began to sing "Tol de rol," and said it was all right; that Hudson, of his weight, was the best little man in the kingdom, and that he should have nothing to do but merely look on. Hudson took the lead, followed his opponent over the ring till Holt was hit down.

6 to 24.—To speak impartially, it would be almost impossible to say which had the best of the majority of these rounds. Holt repeatedly nobbed Hudson so severely that his head went back; but he still returned to the charge unconcerned. In the last round Holt got Hudson on the ropes, where the latter was hanging almost on the balance; but he threw up his arms and walked away, amidst the shouts of the ring. ("This is true courage," exclaimed a Briton.)

29 to 49.—All these rounds were contested with the utmost determined resolution and science on both sides. But Hudson was now the favourite, and Tom Owen offered ten to one. He also placed the white topper on his head; but would not let his knee-string, which was loose, be tied, for fear it should change his luck.

50 to 64.—Holt continued as game as a pebble, and nobbed Hudson desperately; but he could not take the fight out of him. (The odds were now decidedly against Holt, and cries of "Take him away.")

65 to 83.—Both of their nobs were terribly punished, particularly Holt; but he had not the slightest intention to resign, though persuaded so to do by his friends and backers. It was thought Holt had lost it, from going down without a blow. ("Never mind," said Owen, "we'll give them that in; we can't lose it.")

84 to 89 and last.—Holt continued to fight, but he could not stand up to receive the hitting of Hudson, and went down repeatedly; while, on the contrary, Hudson seemed to be getting fresher, and he often ran and jumped to get in at Holt. The latter would not give in, and he was taken out of the ring by the desire of a noble lord and other amateurs. It occupied an hour and three quarters.

REMARKS.—This was a capital fight on both sides: the men covered themselves with pugilistic glory. Holt was rather too stale for his opponent; he had also some of his teeth dislodged. Hudson promises to be conspicuous in the ring: a better bit of stuff cannot be found. A handsome subscription was made for Holt.

Hudson had now got so greatly into favour with the amateurs that he was backed against the fearless Scroggins for 50 guineas a-side. The battle took place on Monday, March 13, 1820, at Dagenham Breach, Essex, about eleven miles from London.

The road exhibited much bustle about ten o'clock in the morning, and the distance being short, the amateurs arrived at the destined spot rather earlier than usual. However, owing to neglect somewhere, to the great chagrin of the fancy, Scroggins had not been made acquainted with the scene of action, and it was two to one whether he appeared at all. The "hardy hero," somehow, at length reached the Ship and Shovel, and waived all impediments like a truly game man.

At half past one o'clock, Hudson, attended by his brother Josh. and Tom Owen, threw his hat up in the ring. Scroggins, followed by Oliver and Randall, repeated the token of defiance. The odds were both ways in the course of a few minutes; and, from the remembrance of what Scroggins had once been, the old fanciers rather took the latter for choice. Tom Owen, to give an air of importance to his *protegé*, graced the ring with his hair curled and powdered, to the no small merriment of the multitude.

THE FIGHT.

Round 1.—On stripping, the fine condition of Hudson astonished the spectators, and to give him a showy appearance, he sported silk stockings. Scroggins did not look well; but it was observed he was not so bad as had been represented. The combatants sparred for upwards of two minutes, when Scroggins let fly with his left hand, slightly touching his opponent's eye. In attempting to make another hit, Hudson got away. More sparring. Scroggins now went to work in his usual heavy style, and drove Hudson to the ropes, when, after some exchanges, Hudson went down, receiving a heavy hit on his ear. (The shouting was loud; and "Well done, my old boy, you can't lose it. The stale one for £100.")

2.—Hudson did not wish to be idle, and went up to his man and fought with him, when a rally ensued, in which Scroggins had rather the best of it. The men separated, and Hudson put in a severe facer that brought the claret. In struggling, both went down.

3.—The men were on their mettle, and fighting was the order of this round. Scroggins received a jobber in the front of his nob; but he returned to the charge with vigour, till he went down from a slight hit. ("Go along, Davy! a young one against an old one any time.")

4.—Scroggins received a sharp hit in the body; he, nevertheless, went boldly in to his opponent, and put in three nobbers. In struggling for the throw, Hudson undermost. ("Bravo, Scroggy!")

5.—The face of Scroggins was much pinked, and one of his eyes rather damaged. Some good exchanges, till Scroggins was undermost. (Shouting for Hudson.)

6.—Hudson stopped the hits of his adversary well, and went again to the nobbing system till both down.

7.—This was a terrible round. It was all fighting; and the struggle at the ropes was desperate in the extreme, till Scroggins found himself on the ground, undermost. The applause on both sides was liberally dealt out, and the combatants were pronounced good men all round the ring.

8.—Scroggins began to pipe, and symp-toms of a worn out constitution could not be concealed from his adversary. The advantages of youth were evident to every spectator, and Scroggins went down.

9.—Well contested on both sides; but although Scroggins repeatedly hit his opponent in the face, he did no damage to him. Both down.

10.—In this round a faint ray of the original quality of Scroggins was conspicuous: he put in a severe hit under Hudson's right ear, and also bored him down. (Six to four was, however, offered on the latter.)

11.—Sharp exchanges; but Scroggins went down so weak that Tom Owen offered four to one.

12 to 15.—Scroggins had rather the best of some of these rounds, but never the best of the battle. He, however, threw Hudson over the ropes.

16 to 18.—The first of these was the sharpest round in the fight. The men exchanged hits like game cocks, struggled for the throw at the ropes, broke away, fought at the ropes again, till both down.

19 to 23.—It was evident the once terrific Scroggins was gone by; his milling period was over. He took like a glutton of the first appetite, but could not give as heretofore. (Six to one was current against him.)

24 to 28.—In some of these rounds Hudson held up his opponent, and punished him down. (Owen, in the exultation of the moment, offered ten to one, and said he should go home, as his man did not want any more seconding.)

29 to 33.—In the last round Scroggins turned his head away from the severe punishment he had received, and went down.

34 and last.—Scroggins attempted to hit, but it was all up, as he was quite exhausted. Forty minutes and three seconds had elapsed. Hudson had scarcely a scratch.

REMARKS. — It is a standing proverb among good judges that youth must be served, and a clearer demonstration of the proposition was never witnessed in the P.R. The constitution of Scroggins was gone, and no training could restore it. It is, however, singular to remark, that a knock-down blow did not occur throughout the fight. Hudson, gay as a lark, confident, and a boxer that can stay a good while, is not a hard hitter. In Scroggins's day a different tale must have been told; but his once terrible mode of hitting had left him, and, as a boxer, he was a shadow of his former self. It is, however, but common justice to state that Scroggins never exerted himself upon any occasion more to win than he did in contending against the young one. His gluttony astonished all present.

Hudson and Scroggins meeting at Chelmsford Races, on Thursday, July 27, 1820, the amateurs made a subscription purse of £20. It was suggested by the seconds that Hudson and Scroggins should divide the purse; but the latter boxer refused, saying, he would win if he could. It was a sharp, good fight; but Scroggins, being very much out of condition, was again defeated in twenty-five minutes.

Hudson had risen so high in the estimation of the amateurs, that he was backed against Jack Martin; nay, more, his friends said that he must win, and nothing else. This battle came off at Moulsey Hurst, October 24, 1820. Martin had beaten David's brother Josh. the year previous. The event proved that Davy's backers were too confident; it was soon seen he was over-matched, and he was signally defeated. (See vol. i., p. 406.)

On Thursday, January 11, 1821, David Hudson and Green fought in a barn at Chelmsford, at eleven o'clock at night, for £10 a-side. This fight had been a long time "hatching up," particularly on the part of Green's* friends, and, from every appearance, he had been in training on the sly; while Hudson was never in such bad condition before.

THE FIGHT.

Round 1.—Green soon let fly with his right hand, which Hudson stopped with his left. He then went to work till Green was floored.

2.—A determined rally, in which Hudson met his adversary well, till Green was again down.

3.—Cautious sparring. Green, however, went in without ceremony and napt two muzzlers, right and left, for his temerity. The claret appeared in profusion, and Green again down.

4 to 7.—The men were now extremely weak. Hudson received a tremendous hit on his right eye, and he was blind for a few seconds, having lost the sight of his left eye since he fought with Martin. ("Go along, Green, it's all your own; you can't lose it;" and five to four offered.)

8.—Hudson's right hand made a dent on Green's side; and with his left Davy put in such a conker that not only produced the claret in profusion, but he was quite abroad, and went down. These "Pepper Alley" touches brought it to even betting, and Hudson for choice.

9 to 13.—The pepper-box was again administered by Hudson, who caught Green under his right arm, and with his left he fibbed him so severely that Green called out "Foul," and said he would not fight any longer. The umpires were appealed to, and decided Hudson's conduct to be fair, and "a bit of good truth."

14.—Green, determined to try every move on the board, went sharply to work, but Hudson stopped his efforts with the utmost ease. (Seven to four on Hudson, but no takers.)

15 to 17.—Davy came to the scratch as fresh

* This Green was an Essex man, who, having defeated one Wyke, at Barnsley, in Yorkshire, for a stake of £60 (April 2, 1819), and subsequently Harris, a *protégé* of Josh. Hudson, at Dagenham Breach, Essex, March 13, 1820 (in "Fistiana" the date is wrongly given as March 1, 1829), had crept into favour with himself. He was snuffed out by David as we here find.

as his out-and-out badger, and bit Green all to pieces. By way of finishing the round, if not the fight, he cross-buttocked his opponent so severely that it was twenty to one he did not come again. Green said he would not fight any more while sitting upon the knee of his second. Hudson then went up to Green and shook hands with him, observing at the same time, "You are not half so good a man as I expected, from the chaffing there has been about you ; nevertheless, I will give you half a guinea." The friends of Green thought he could have won the fight if it had been in a ring ; but Hudson's backers were so confident of his success, that they immediately put down £50 to £30 for Davy to fight him in a ring in any part of Essex. The partisans of Green wished it to take place in the same ring as Oliver and Spring. This money was drawn, to the great disappointment of Hudson's party. The Essex friends of the latter offered to back him at any time for £100. The battle lasted forty-five minutes.

One Jack Steadman, a big one, and a good fighter, was beat off hand by David, to the astonishment of the spectators ; Steadman standing over " little David" like another Goliah of Gath, and weighing thirteen stone.

David now became a publican at Chelmsford, where his house was well frequented by sporting men. In February, 1820, we find him exhibiting sparring, having taken the Chelmsford Theatre for the purpose.

Hudson's old antagonist, Green, seems to have by no means been convinced by his first defeat, and, after much cavilling, a second match was made for 50 guineas, which came off, by desire of the London patrons of Davy, at Old Marsh Gate, Essex, about eleven miles of turnpike from town, on Tuesday, the 27th of February, 1821. Hudson having made Chelmsford his place of residence, and a bit of a favourite in that part of the world among the sporting men, they were anxious that he should again exhibit. He was backed by Mr. Thomas Belcher, of the Castle Tavern. It was reported Hudson was upwards of twelve stone, having increased so much during his training. This operated against him in the opinion of the amateurs. At one o'clock Hudson, dressed in a white great coat, appeared, and threw his hat into the ring, attended by Oliver and his brother Josh. Green shortly afterwards entered the ropes, with Randall and Martin. The "President of the Daffies"* was appointed the time-keeper. Five to four on Hudson.

THE FIGHT.

Round 1.—On stripping, Green appeared in the highest state of condition, but it was thought that Hudson was much too fat. The combatants, on placing themselves in attitude, stood looking at each other's eyes for upwards of four minutes, without making the least offer to hit. Green made a trifling offer to put in a blow, when Hudson got away, and they dodged each other over the ring till they made another complete standstill. Green made a hit, but Hudson parried it. Both the men seemed under orders, that is to say, not to go to work too quickly. Green got away neatly ; and Hudson also stopped a severe left-handed hit of Green's. The latter then put in a body blow, when David returned. The battle had now commenced. Green put in a facer, when Davy stood to no repairs, and tried to slaughter his opponent, till they got into a struggle, when they both went down side by side. (Loud shouting from the "over-the-water boys," the Chelmsford fanciers, and the Jews, who all united in backing Davy for anything.) This round occupied nearly fifteen minutes.

* Mr. Soares.

2.—This round was altogether short. They both complimented each other upon the nob *sans cæremonie*, and "Pepper Alley" was the feature, till Green went down undermost. (Six to four on Hudson.) The mouth of Davy showed claret.

3.—Not quite so fast as before, and some little science necessary. Hudson undermost.

4.—The claret was now running from the cheek of Green. Both combatants appeared a little distressed. In struggling, Hudson was again undermost. These were two tie rounds; but some of the spectators thought Green had the best of them.

5.—Hudson took the lead gaily. Some severe exchanges took place, when Green was hit down. (Loud shouting, "Davy, repeat that, and it's all safe to you.")

6.—Hudson got away well, and nobbed Green, who followed him. Some heavy blows passed between them till both down.

7.—This round spoilt Green. The latter, with good courage, gave hit for hit with his opponent; but Davy, in finishing the round, had the best of the blows, threw Green, and fell so heavily upon him that the claret gushed from his nose, the shock was so violent. (The East-enders were now uproarious, and two and three to one were offered on Davy.)

8.—David fell on Green again.

9.—Almost the same, as well as the best of the hitting.

10.—It was really a capital fight, and Green fought like a trump. He could not, however, change the battle in his favour. Hudson undermost.

11.—Green experienced another dreadful fall. (Four to one against him current.)

12.—Hudson now endeavoured to take the fight out of Green, and planted four facers in succession that Green went staggering from the hits; he, nevertheless, made several returns, till both down. (Five to one)

13, 14.—In the first round a most determined rally; but in the second Green was hit down on his knee. ("You can't lose it, Davy.")

15.—Hudson fell heavily on Green, and nearly knocked the wind out of him. ("It's all up." Any odds.

16.—The nob of Green was now terribly punished, and the left side of his throat much swelled. He was quite abroad, hit open-handed, and went down exhausted.

("Go along, Davy; it will be over in another round.")

17.—Green repeatedly jobbed Hudson in the face; but none of the blows were to be seen—they did not leave a mark. As Green was falling from a hit, Hudson caught him in the face with a right-handed blow that almost sent him to sleep.

18.—"Look here," said Oliver, "my man has not a mark upon his face." Green came up to the scratch much distressed. He, however, fought like a man; and at the ropes Hudson again fell upon him. The claret was running down in profusion.

19.—Green still showed fight, and put in several facers. Hudson went away staggering from one of them; but the latter followed Green up so hard and fast that he could not keep his legs, and went down. (The poundage was here offered, but no takers. "Take him away; he has no chance.")

20 and last.—Green behaved like a man, and he stood up and fought in a rally till he went down quite done up. When time was called he could not come to the scratch, and Hudson was proclaimed the conqueror. It was over in forty minutes.

REMARKS.—Davy, either fat or lean, out or in condition, is not to be beaten easily. A strong novice must not attempt it; and a good commoner will be puzzled, and most likely lose in the trial. There is a great deal of gaiety about Hudson's fighting: he will always be with his man. He has a good notion of throwing, and also of finishing a round. Green was not destitute of courage, and it was not a little milling that took the fight out of him. He endeavoured to win while a chance remained; in fact, till he could fight no longer; but he is too slow for Hudson. It was an excellent battle, and the amateurs expressed themselves well satisfied. One of Hudson's eyes is defective since he fought with Martin, which operates as a great drawback to his execution, particularly in judging his distances; but nothing can abate his courage. Both the Hudsons stand so high in the opinion of the amateurs as out-and-out bottom men, that they are designated the "John Bull" boxers. They increase in flesh rather too fast; and, from being "light ones" when they first appeared in the prize ring, they are now termed "Big Chaps."

This was Dav. Hudson's last victory. We find it noted, incidentally, in the remarks on the above fight that the sight of one of David's eyes was defective. Under these circumstances, it was indeed unfortunate to match him against the "Streatham Youth," Ned Neale. It is true that Ned's wonderful fighting qualities were then comparatively unknown. He had defeated Deaf Davis (a slow man, but a hard hitter), one Bill Cribb (called "the Brighton Champion"), and Miller (the "Pea-soup Gardener");

but these, as well as Bill Hall, were looked upon as mere stale men or "roughs." The defeat of Hudson (September 23, 1823), on the appropriately named Blindlow Heath, will be found in the Memoir of NED NEALE, Period VI., Chapter V.

David's last appearance in the prize ring was with an Irishman, Mike Larkins,* who had beaten Simon Byrne in Ireland, in 1825. The battle took place at Bulphen Farm, Essex, May 8, 1827, when "One-eyed Davy" was defeated in twenty-eight fast rounds, occupying twenty minutes. David, in his latter days, assisted "brother Josh." at Leadenhall; and when the latter died, in Milton Street, Finsbury, in October, 1835, David lost his best friend. He was already in ill health, and survived his brother but six weeks, his death taking place November 27, 1835, in the London Hospital.

* There were two other boxers of the name. Sam Larkins, of Cambridge, who beat Abbot (see ABBOT), Shadbolt, and John Fuller; and Larkins, the Guardsman.

END OF PERIOD V.

PERIOD VI.—1824-1835.

FROM THE RETIREMENT OF TOM SPRING TO THE APPEARANCE OF BENDIGO.

CHAPTER I.

JEM WARD (CHAMPION).—1822-1831.

ALBEIT this period does not mark any change in the "school," or style, nor in the rules which govern the practice of public boxing, there are reasons to be found for a division, in the more copious, accurate, and systematic reports of the prize-fights of this and the following periods, due greatly to the exertions and ability of the late Vincent George Dowling, Esq., of the *Morning Chronicle*, the editor, founder, and establisher of *Bell's Life in London*, for many years afterwards "the Oracle of the Ring," a title and function now well-nigh abdicated. About this time, too, other able pens lent their aid. George Daniels, Esq. (the D— G—, whose criticisms on the drama lent large value to the series known as "Cumberland's Plays," and who was for a time editor of the *Weekly Dispatch*), was among the number. That journal also had the services of George Kent (an enthusiastic milling reporter, whose son and grandson yet wield the *stylus* of manifold writers for the daily and weekly press),* and of Mr. Smith, during the period of his editorship. "Paling its ineffectual fire" before the rising glories of *Bell's Life*, and having lost its best writers, a late Old Bailey attorney and alderman, finding

---

* In the fourth volume of Pierce Egan's "Boxiana," pp. 478-481, will be found a friendly sketch of poor George's career, as historiographer of the ring for the previous twenty years. He was a Berkshire man, born August 19, 1778, apprenticed to Varley, the celebrated seal engraver in the Strand, subsequently enlisted in the 16th Dragoons, but obtained his discharge at the period of the treaty of Amiens. Then an usher in a school at Camberwell, a newspaper writer in the *British Neptune*, and proprietor of *Kent's Dispatch*, which died. Pierce Egan, who, with Vincent Dowling and George's two sons, followed him to his grave in St. Paul's, Covent Garden, says he realised in two successive years £1700, by sporting reporting. He was a scholar and a man of talent.

the *Dispatch* had lost caste with the sporting community, turned his coat, and betook himself with the zeal and virulence of a renegade to revile and slander the sports by which his journal had grown and prospered. But this is by the way. From the period we have mentioned the chronicles of pugilism have been more accurate and minute, and therefore more worthy of preservation; hence the greater bulk and volume of this portion of our history.

On the retirement of Spring, which that boxer announced shortly after his second battle with Langan, the public attention was occupied with discussing the worthiest candidate for the vacated belt. In the first instance Langan was spoken of as the "coming man;" but though there was some correspondence, as already noticed, with Tom Shelton and Ward, the Irish champion suddenly retired without making a match, and went into business at Liverpool. The champion was now to be looked for elsewhere. Three men had at this time their respective admirers and partisans—Tom Cannon (the great gun of Windsor), Josh. Hudson (the John Bull fighter), and Jem Ward (the Black Diamond). The friends of Josh. urged his claim, on the ground that he had defeated Ward on the 11th of December, 1823; but then a fortnight after the second fight of Spring and Langan (on June 23rd, 1824), Tom Cannon had beaten Hudson in twenty minutes and seventeen rounds, and again (see Memoir of CANNON) in the November following, in sixteen rounds, twenty minutes. This led to Cannon's challenging Ward for the championship, the details and results of which we shall notice in due course. We now return to the biography of Ward.

Jem Ward, the eldest of seven children of Nat. Ward, a tradesman in the vicinity of Ratcliff Highway, was born December 26th, 1800, the day of all days of the year, known as "boxing-day." and at an early age exhibited the talents of a boxer and wrestler, which afterwards won him fame. At the age of sixteen, his father having failed in business as a butcher, Jem was put to the then lucrative, but heavily laborious calling of a coal-whipper. Jem soon became the lion of a sparring club held at Bromley New Town, where he dimmed the shine of those who were ambitious of a turn with "the Black Diamond," and was never loth to accommodate any customer, regardless of weight or strength. Ward's fame spread, and it was resolved by his admirers and friends that he should quit the narrow circle of his triumphs, and give the general public the opportunity of judging of his qualifications. Accordingly, on Tuesday, January 22nd, 1822, on the occasion of the benefit of Sutton and Gybletts, at the Fives Court, Jem was introduced to the aristocratic patrons of pugilism. His appearance is thus recorded in the "Annals of Sporting" for that month. "The principal

JEM WARD (Champion).

From a Painting by Patten, 1826.

novelty was the introduction of a new Black Diamond, and although a little bit in the rough, yet now and again his shining qualities so far peeped out that curiosity asked, 'Who is he?' 'Where does he come from?' 'Is he a novice?' The replies were 'His name is Ward; he is an East-ender; he has put the quilt on all who have tried him; he is a sharp one in a turn up, but what he may do in the ring is another matter. However, he can be backed against anything of his weight (twelve stone) barring the Gas (Tom Hickman).' Ward was pitted with Spencer. Like most newcomers, he displayed too much eagerness, and more milling than steady science. He received good encouragement from the amateurs present, and his nob was pronounced to be a fighting one."

The fancy were not slow in discussing the merits of Ward, and a purse was immediately raised for the purpose of testing his capabilities. Dick Acton,* considered a resolute boxer, was named as Ward's opponent, and on Wednesday, June 12, 1822, the battle came off on Moulsey Hurst. Josh. Hudson (soon after to meet and vanquish his principal) seconded Ward, assisted by Tom Jones. Acton was waited upon by Tom Spring and Eales. The fight is thus reported in the *Dispatch* :—

THE FIGHT.

Round 1.—Acton on the defensive, as if wishing to ascertain what novelties in the art he was likely to be that day treated to by Ward. The latter, after a little dodging about, let fly with his left, but was short. Acton likewise missed; he, however, followed Ward, who kept breaking ground and retreating. Acton tried it on, but some exchanges followed without effect. The Diamond suddenly put in a straight one on Acton's nob, and got away smiling. Acton followed him to the ropes, where he got a sharp blow on the cheek; Ward making good use of his legs and getting out of the corner; nor was he long before he planted a heavy blow on the right side of Acton's conk, which drew the claret. ("That's as good as a pinch of snuff to him," cried Josh.) A pause. Ward's left hand now took liberties with the other side of Acton's nose, and the pink followed. Ward got away. ("Mind and keep your hand closed," said Josh.) Some more blows passed, when Ward again got away. Acton already seemed tired and slow; indeed he had been following the new one to a very poor purpose. Ward put in a heavy hit under Acton's right eye that produced the claret, then closed, and after some hitting both were down, Ward undermost. This round occupied eight minutes and a half, evidently to the disadvantage of Acton. (Eleven to four on Ward offered.)

* Dick Acton, a *protégé* of the scientific sparrer, Bill Eales, was like the French general who was compared to a drum, heard of only when beaten. He was a shoemaker by trade, and a ring follower by choice. His first fight in the P. C. ropes was with one Nash, at Kilburn, August 21, 1821, whom he beat, for a purse of 20 guineas, in thirty-two rounds. The next week, the love of fight strong within him, Dick threw his hat in at Edgeware, for a purse of 20 guineas, and polished off a stalwart countryman, hight Evans, in eighteen rounds, forty minutes. His next customer was a regular boxer, known as Massa Kendrick, the black. He turned the tables on "the Snob," putting him in darkness in seventeen rounds, twenty-five minutes, at Moulsey, December 18, 1821. Dick moved for a new trial, and on the 18th of March, 1822, at Moulsey, seconded by Eales and Tom Spring, the Black by Randall and Josh. Hudson, Acton reversed the verdict, with two to one against him, punishing Massa out of time in thirty-two rattling rounds, occupying thirty-five minutes. From this time he became a sort of "trial horse," and was beaten successively by Jem Ward, Young Peter Crawley, and Jack Nicholls, all good men.

2.—Acton could not stop Ward's left. The latter put in several facers, and got away without receiving any return. In closing, Acton pummelled away, and both went down, Ward again undermost.

3.—Acton made play and put in a heavy one on Ward's mug, but on endeavouring to repeat it, Ward stopped him neatly. Acton bored his opponent to the ropes, and, after a sharp struggle to obtain the throw, Ward got Acton down. (Shouts of applause for the new man.)

4.—This round decided the fight. Acton seemed to depend more on stopping than hitting, and Ward had it comparatively all his own way. He made a good right-handed hit, and again got away laughing. Acton also got nobbed right and left; but Ward following him to force the fighting, received some heavy hits that drew the claret from his nose. A pause, the men looking at each other. Ward made play and put in so severe a body blow as to make Acton drop his arms. In the close, Ward had also the best of it, and in going down Acton was undermost. ("It's nearly over," was the cry.)

5.—Acton came to the scratch staring. Ward put in two or three nobbers, and ran Acton to the ropes; but in the fall Ward was undermost.

6 and last.—Heavy counter-hits. Ward planted a severe blow on Acton's left eye that made him wink again. The left hand of the former was repeatedly at work, and by a sharp blow on the left ear Acton was finally floored. When "Time" was called, he was deaf to it, and three or four minutes elapsed before he was able to get out of the ring. Time, fourteen minutes and a half.

REMARKS. — The science, activity, and quick hitting exhibited by Ward satisfied his backers, that, with a little more experience, he was calculated to make a noise in the milling world. Acton was too slow for his opponent.

Ward, who was now anxious to do business, challenged Jack Martin for £150; and in order to keep the game alive, after Josh. Hudson had defeated Barlow, at Harpenden Common, on the 10th of September, 1822, a subscription purse was entered into to give Ward another chance of showing off with Burke, of Woolwich, brother to the pugilist who fought with Jack Randall. After he had put on his clothes, Hudson went round the ring with his hat, and collected the needful. This fight lasted only seven minutes, it being rather a display of wrestling than milling on the part of Burke. The Woolwich hero was seconded by Tom Oliver and Abbot; Ward by Tom Shelton and Harry Holt. It was a mere gift to Jem.

Some meetings were afterwards held between the parties as to the weight of Ward, and he was eventually backed to fight Bill Abbot, for £50 a-side. And here it devolves upon us, as faithful biographers, to detail a circumstance in the life of our hero, over which we would fain draw a veil. In order that we may not identify ourselves with any party, we prefer giving the account of the matter as it was published at the time, leaving our readers to decide for themselves :—

Pugilism between Ward, the Black Diamond, and Abbot, the conqueror of Oliver, for £50 a-side, at Moulsey Hurst, on Tuesday, October 22, 1822.

An unusual degree of interest had been excited throughout the fancy, respecting the event of this battle, in consequence of the superior milling talents displayed by Ward in his fight with Acton, and also in his various exhibitions at the Fives Court, but more particularly in his set-to with Cy. Davis. At one o'clock, Abbot threw his hat into the ring, followed by

Richmond and Josh. Hudson, as his seconds; and, in a few minutes after-wards, Ward attended by Eales and Tom Jones, made his appearance.

THE FIGHT.

Round 1.—Both men appeared in fine condition; and a minute or two elapsed, when Ward hit short with his left hand; but he soon rectified this mistake, by nobbing his opponent, getting away, and laughing at him. In a close, both went down, but Ward had the throw.

2.—It was already seen that Abbot was a plaything in the hands of Ward, for he not only nobbed him with the utmost ease, but put in so severe a hit on the body that Abbot went back three yards, staggering, and must have fallen, had not the ropes prevented him. Abbot, however, returned to the charge, when the round was finished by Ward hitting him down. (Seven to four.)

3.—Ward, from his tapping, light play, was denominated the Chinaman; nevertheless, the head of his opponent was so much at his service that he kept pinking without getting any return. Abbot was severely thrown.

4.—The backers of Ward were in high glee—it was all right; and Abbot received another fall ready to burst him.

5.—Abbot received a severe hit, and fell on his knees.

6 to 8.—In all these rounds Abbot appeared perfectly stupid from the repeated conkers he received, and the severe falls he experienced. (Five and six to one.)

9 to 12.—Abbot was so much at a loss that his blows were thrown away; in fact, he had not the shadow of a chance. In the last round he received a tremendous cross-buttock.

13 to 17.—The whole of the minds of the amateurs were so much made up in consequence of the superior talents displayed by Ward, who did as he liked with his opponent, that ten to one was offered, but no takers.

18.—Abbot hit down, and the battle was considered all but over; so much so that Belcher left the ring to get his pigeon to convey the intelligence to town of the defeat of Abbot. On crossing the river at Hampton, the first party he met in a boat he asked who had won the battle. "Abbot," was the reply. "Impossible!" said Belcher. He also inquired of another party. "Abbot," was the answer. "It can't be—you certainly must be mistaken," rejoined the hero of the Castle. In the third boat he saw Abbot and his second, when he repeated his inquiries; and on being informed that Abbot was the winner, Tom replied, "I'm now satisfied," and immediately sent up the pigeon, with Abbot's name attached to it instead of Ward's.

19.—At the conclusion of this round, Eales, observing something wrong in his man, called out to Ward's backer, who immediately stepped into the ring, when Eales, with much indignation, observed, "Ward says he means to cut it this round, he shall lose it." "No," replied his backer.

20.—Ward now endeavoured to drop fighting, in order to give Abbot a chance; and actually, in an under tone, said to Abbot. "Now hit me." When Eales remonstrated with him for such conduct, he observed, "I know my orders—I must not win it." (A hundred to one on Ward.)

21.—Ward gave his opponent all the opportunity he could; but Abbot was so distressed that he could scarcely knock a fly off a leaf. Ward took care to go down.

22 and last.—Ward went down after a slight skirmish, and on being picked up and placed on his second's knee, he smiled, but recollecting "his orders," and for fear that Abbot should give in, he went off in a swoon, and when "Time" was called, he would not notice it till he thought proper to come to, and quit the ring.

REMARKS.—It is impossible to describe the consternation, as well as the indignation, expressed by the amateurs; so bare-faced a robbery was never before witnessed in the annals of pugilism. The umpire, when asked his opinion, replied, "He could not swear it was a cross; but he was quite satisfied there was wrong conduct somewhere." The most honourable part of the sporting people declared they would not pay at present; and several gentlemen who had lost heavy stakes agreed to meet next evening at the One Tun, in Jermyn Street, in order to investigate the matter. Ward, on recovering from his swoon, made his way out of the ring, and in his eagerness to get across the water to Hampton, jumped with the utmost ease over some ropes.

Thus far the ring-reporter of the day. On Wednesday evening, October 23rd, a numerous meeting of sporting men took place at the One Tun, Jermyn Street, to investigate the suspicious circumstances connected with this affair, when, after hearing evidence, all bets were declared off, and a second meeting appointed at Tattersall's, on Monday, November 4, 1822; on this occasion, after a great deal of chaffing and murmuring amongst the betters, the president of the Daffy Club, who held the stakes, offered the £50 a-side to each of the backers, but they refused the offer, and the president put the £100 into his pocket, and left the meeting. It was ultimately agreed that the matter should be laid before the Pugilistic Club and Mr. Jackson, and that their decision should be final; however, after considerable disputes upon the subject, the stakes were drawn, and the backers of Ward and Abbot agreed to receive £50 each.

We cannot help remarking here, that although it was proved beyond a doubt that Ward committed the cross above alluded to, there was also sufficient evidence to prove that it was more an error of the head than of the heart; for, on his being called upon for an explanation, at the meeting at the One Tun, in Jermyn Street, he burst into tears, hung down his head, and admitted it was a cross. He further stated that he had been instigated to commit it by his backer, who promised him £100 if he lost the fight. Eales, the second to Ward, also stated, "that towards the conclusion of the battle, he wished him to go in and win it, but was greatly surprised to hear Ward say he had his orders, and must *not* win the battle." Towards the conclusion of the meeting, Tom Cribb came forward, and in a very animated manner said, that he had never done wrong in his life; that Ward was a deluded and ignorant young man; that he believed he had been led away, and that he had told the truth; as a proof of his opinion he should make him a present of a sovereign, which he did, several gentlemen present following his example.

Ward also addressed the following letter, publicly confessing his fault:—

"*To the Editor of the* WEEKLY DISPATCH.
"SIR,
"I trust you will excuse my obtruding upon you in requesting the insertion of a letter from me, whom I hope the sporting world will consider as much sinned against as sinning. My late fight with Abbot having given rise to much, I may say much merited animadversion, I hope in extenuation some consideration may be made for my inexperience in the world, and a too great reliance on those who have seduced and deceived me. Had I taken the advice of my trainer, in lieu of lending a too ready credence to the apparent friendly promises of my backer, I should not have to deplore the commitment of an act which has caused me the most bitter regret. I should be most happy, by way of retrieving in some degree the credit I have lost, to fight Abbot again for the present stakes. If I ask for too much in this, I am willing to meet him in the same ring with Hudson and Shelton, on the 19th instant, for a purse, or even for love.
"I am, Sir, with the greatest respect,
"Your obliged servant
"JAMES WARD.
"*November* 12, 1827."

At this time Ward was considered completely defunct in the milling world; the P.C. expelled Jem from the use of their ropes, and it was the general opinion that he would never again be permitted to enter the prize ring. In fact, so strong was the feeling entertained against Ward, that, on a proposal being made shortly afterwards to back him for £100 against Barlow, the friends of the latter scouted the proposition, and said that he should not disgrace himself by contending with a man who had been expelled the P.C. ropes.

Ward now remained quiet for a short time, expressed his sorrow for his misconduct, and promised his friends to do all in his power to gain the confidence of the sporting world. It was not long before an event occurred which brought Ward again before the fancy, and which tended greatly to do away with the ill-feeling which existed against him. After the fight between Hall and Wynnes, at Wimbledon Common, on Tuesday, February 4, 1823, he entered the ring for a subscription prize of the value of £5. His opponent was Whiteheaded Bob, then unknown to the London ring, but by no means a novice. This was a good battle, Ward finishing his man in twenty rounds, nineteen minutes.

The judges now pronounced Ward the best twelve stone man in the ring; and he, in order to reinstate himself in the good opinion of the amateurs, inserted three separate challenges in the *Weekly Dispatch;* but that not having the desired effect, he determined to rusticate for a few months. He therefore started on a sparring tour with two or three of his pals. Bath races was the first object. There a match was made between Rickens, a Bath man, and Jem Ward, for £20 a-side, and a subscription purse. The battle took place at Lansdown, on Friday, July 2, 1823, Ward winning it without a scratch on his face or body.

Jem and his pals pursued their excursion, and now determined upon astonishing the natives at Portsdown Fair. A sparring-booth was soon knocked-up for the edification and instruction of the yokels, and the amusement of the younger branches of the "Green" family, who had never had an opportunity of witnessing a bout at the Fives Court, in which his companions gave their assistance. The Black Diamond (who showed himself a brilliant of the first water) did all he could to accommodate the numerous customers who wished for a taste of the mufflers. Much mirth was excited by a "Knight of the Rainbow," whose length, weight, and vanity, led him to believe he could polish the Diamond. Jem's mawley was constantly rap, tap, tapping on Johnny Trot's frontispiece, and occasionally rung the bell of his ear, until poor Trot did not know whether he had his own hair or a wig on. "Why don't you look?" says Jem; "and not wink your peepers in that way." "Because," says Sir Rainbow, "you play so sharp, and I'll have no more on't."

Ward next went to Southampton races to fight a man of the name of Johnson, *alias* Jemmy the Black. The battle took place on Shirley Common, August 24, 1823, and Johnson was beaten to a stand-still in three rounds— time, seventeen minutes.

These victories induced our hero to think that he might now venture to show with a good grace in London; accordingly, at the Fives Court, in September, he informed the amateurs that a nobleman would back him against Josh. Hudson for £100 a-side. The match was made to take place at Moulsey Hurst. Ward's peace was now considered to have been made with the fancy in general, who were anxious to witness the fine fighting of our hero, opposed to one of the highest-couraged boxers upon the list; but, unfortunately for Ward, on November 11, 1823, in the course of fifteen rounds, occupying thirty-five minutes, he was obliged to strike his colours to resolute Josh. (See Life of HUDSON).

This defeat was attributed by many to mere want of condition, and his friends readily came forward to back him for £100 a-side against Phil. Sampson, the Birmingham Youth.[*] On this occasion Sampson weighed twelve stone three pounds, height five feet ten and a-half inches; and Jem weighed but three pounds more, and was of equal stature. The match was therefore in these respects even. The battle took place on the 21st of June, at Colnbrook, in the same ring as that in which Barney Aaron and Arthur Mathewson had just decided their differences. Aby Belasco and Harry Harmer waited on Sampson: Tom Oliver and Tom Owen esquired Ward.

THE FIGHT.

Round 1.—Ward stood with the left arm extended, and Sampson ready with both hands. Five minutes passed in sparring— attitudes of both beautiful. Sampson backed to the ropes. Ward threw out for a draw. Sampson returned and hit short. Sampson dropped, from a slip. No mischief.

2.—Sparring again. Sampson evidently afraid of his man. Ward let fly—stopped; again at the body—stopped. Sampson countered, and slipped half down. Ward stood over, made up to hit as he rose; but at the moment Sampson put his hand to the ground and saved his bones.

3.—Sampson began left and right. Ward broke away in gallant style, then countered upon him, and tapped the wine-vat. Sampson followed. Ward met him again. Sampson rolled down. (Three to one on Ward.)

4.—Sampson backed to the ropes, and made up for counter-hitting. Ward showed fine science to get at him. Sampson let fly; Ward stopped it, went to work, but Sampson dropped on his knees to avoid Ward's wrestling.

5.—Ward closed on him, and played left and right on his head. He seemed to lay Sampson across his right hip, while he jobbed him with the left hand until Sampson slipped away and went down.

6.—Sampson made play, and got one hand on Ward's left eye. Ward hit, and Sampson stopped well, and tried his long shots, but he could not make them tell; he then dropped. It was easy to tell how all this was to end.

7.—Ward made play—whack on the head at both sides, then at the wind. ("Well stopped. Sampson.") Ward then hitting out plump, he knocked him down.

8.—Sampson, furious from punishment,

was kept writhing, from the rapidity of Ward's blows, up and down. Ward chopped him on the ear, under the chin, and as he pleased, the blood flowing in a broad stream. Sampson went down.

9.—Ward broke away from a desperate hit, and Sampson followed, giving the chance away. Ward met him, and closed for a fall, but Sampson again dropped. (Six to one on Ward.)

10.—Ward caught him in the wind. Sampson went away nearly doubled. A good rally. Ward unwise to stand it. Sampson made his right hand tell a trifle. A close, and open fighting again. Ward's hand, darting like a viper's tongue, scarified Sampson's face all over. Ward aimed a settler. Sampson ducked and dropped.

11.—Ward chopped him over his guard on the ear, and then bang on the nose. Sampson, all blood and bluster, followed him like a savage. Ward played with him and dropped him easy.

12.—Ward hit him left and right. Sampson down in an instant.

13.—Sampson had no chance. Ward put all his fine fighting aside.

14.—Sampson got Ward into a wild rally. ("Softly, Ward. What are you at?") A round hit sent him under, but he jumped up merrily without his second's aid.

15.—Sampson made play, but Ward met him and knocked him clean down.

16.—This round was all in favour of Ward.

17.—Ward closed Sampson's left eye, which blinked a little, and chopped his ear, while the blood flowed profusely. Sampson all abroad, looking sick and sorrowful. Down he goes again.

18.—Ward got away from some desperate body blows. Sparring a little. ("Fight, Jem!" on all sides.) Jem did fight, and threw his man like a plaything.

19.—Sampson hit out well, but Ward, all coolness, stopped him and dropped him.

20.—Sampson made play, but was at once felled by Ward.

21.—Sampson down again. Ward without a mark.

22.—Ward began—one, two, both on the head; three on the ribs. Sampson, nearly up, rushed for a chance. Ward stopped a mill from him.

For the next three rounds Sampson was brought up but to receive, and in the twenty-fifth round he gave in, after fighting fifty minutes.

REMARKS.—It was delightful to witness the fine tactics of Ward, who reminded the spectators of the renowned Jem Belcher. His winning so easily against a skilful boxer and hard hitter like Sampson was a great feather in his cap. He won his battle in a style seldom witnessed, without a scratch. Another report simply adds to its description, "Ward may be champion if he does the right thing. He is far the best big man out, as a natural fighter."

Shortly after this Cannon beat Josh. Hudson (June 23rd, 1824), and as Josh. engaged Cannon for a second trial, Jem issued a challenge to fight Langan for £300 a-side. This was not accepted, and Ward put forth another challenge for the championship, in which we read,—"Having observed in the sporting journals a great deal about who is entitled to the championship—some saying it is Langan (who has retired), others that it belongs to Shelton; while Hudson and Cannon, who are about to fight a second time, have intimated that the winner of their battle will claim it,—I beg to inform the public that I will fight any man in England, Ireland, or Scotland, for £300 a-side; and if I do not meet with a customer in a month, I shall lay claim to the title myself." This offer was not accepted; but his old antagonist, Phil. Sampson, soliciting a second meeting for £100 a-side, Ward cheerfully closed with the proposition, and a match was made to come off December 28th, 1824. In the interim Tom Cannon and Josh. Hudson had fought a second time, and Cannon had utterly crushed up his brave and broad-bottomed antagonist.

The second mill of Jem Ward and Sampson came off at Perry Lodge, on the estate of the Duke of Grafton, about four miles beyond Stony Stratford. The attendance of the London division was not large, but from the neighbouring counties the muster was numerous. The total of the whole assemblage is estimated by a contemporary chronicler at 5,000 at the least; and although heavy rain fell throughout the day, every spectator remained till the conclusion of the interesting contest. The men arrived upon the ground about half-past twelve; Paddington Jones again attended upon Ward, and had upon the same side, as his brother second, Tom Oliver, known till our own time as the Commissary of the P. R. Peter Crawley and a Birmingham Friend (not a Quaker) picked up Sampson. Both men were in excellent condition; Sampson, whose weight was nearly thirteen stone, is praised for "looking better than in their former encounter;" we suspect the lack of physiological judgment in the reporter here, and should say "there was too much of him." Ward was twelve stone seven pounds. The betting was anything but brisk—Ward, the favourite; but his partisans were lukewarm, and the "hardware lads" wanted long odds.

THE FIGHT.

Round 1.—The men were brought to the scratch at a quarter to one, and instantly threw themselves into position. Sampson's manner was firm and imposing, and his looks betokened a determination to do his best. Ward gathered himself into as narrow a compass as possible, and, throwing his head and shoulders back, worked about his terrific left hand with an evident intention to bring it into action as speedily as circumstances would admit, while with his right he kept a steady guard. Sparring for a short time. Ward let fly his left, but was stopped. Sampson countered, but was stopped also. Sampson broke ground, but was again stopped, when Ward rushed to fight, and caught Sampson on the pudding-trap, rattling his grinders in a very musical manner. Sampson returned very slightly, and in a close, Ward was thrown, Sampson on him. Ward picked himself up and laughed.

2.—On coming to the scratch, Sampson showed first paint, from the larboard corner of his muzzle, but he was still firm and cheerful. Ward came up steady, and after a short manoeuvre threw another chattering smack on Sampson's gob with his right. Sampson rushed in to fight, but was well stopped. In the close, Sampson fell, and Ward close to him.

3.—All doubts of Ward's meaning to win had now passed away, and two to one was offered freely upon him, but no takers. Sampson, anxious to go in, hit out at Ward's nob, and caught him slightly. Ward was with him, and returned with interest. Sampson, not dismayed, went at him again, and caught him on the face. Ward fell from the slippery state of the ground, and the force of the blow.

4.—Ward stood for no ceremony, but delivered right and left on Sampson's canister. Sampson rushed to a rally, but Ward got away with his customary activity. Ward then jumped in, was stopped at first, but repeating his effort, he hit Sampson on the auricular, and then dropped him by a blow on his frontispiece.

5. — Sampson came up rather openmouthed, and a little worse for the paintbrush. Ward commenced fighting, hit out with his left, rather out of distance, and slipped. Sampson, anxious to take off Ward as he rose, rushed in. Ward, however, was quickly on his pins, and met his determined antagonist with a slight tap on his victualling office. Sampson, in getting away, fell outside the ropes. Ward stood up fresh and full of spirits.

6.—Good stops on both sides. An excellent rally followed, in which nozzlers were interchanged. Sampson, in getting away, fell on his nether end.

7.—Ward came up merry, and Sampson was not a whit less disposed for mischief. Sampson bored in, but Ward got away. The men came again to close quarters, when Sampson delivered a slight compliment on Ward's smuffler. Ward fell on his knees.

8. — Ward delivered another unpleasant compliment on Sampson's mouth. Sampson returned quickly. Ward rushed to infighting, when hits were interchanged, and Ward again fell on his knees. As this latter fall was supposed to have originated in the desire of Ward to escape punishment,

there were some slight marks of disapprobation.

9.—Sampson came up game, although rather in the piping order. Ward, after a flourish, once more tapped him on the mouth, and got away. Sampson followed him up, and on going to in-fighting, Ward again slipped down.

10.—Ward busy rapping at Sampson's ivories. Sampson rushed to rally, but two well-intentioned visitations to Ward's nob were stopped, and Ward catching him round the neck, fibbed him severely. It was a ratti-tat-tat. Sampson fell, and Ward also slipped.

11.—Sampson came up blowing like Boreas. He was determined not to be idle, and went in right and left. Ward, cautious, caught the blows on his wrists as they were given, and, in retreating, Sampson dropped, through the slippery state of the ground.

12.—Ward again took the lead, and hit Sampson a terrific blow on the nose, which immediately entered into co-partnership with his mouth, in the claret line. Short sparring. A rally, in which blows were interchanged, and Ward fell, through a slip.

13.—Oliver was now in the highest spirits, and exclaimed he would lay ten to one that Ward would not get a black eye. Sampson came to work a little the worse for wear, and went in manfully to fight, but Ward stopped him with inimitable skill, and then rushing in, delivered facers left and right. Sampson fell on his back, and Ward fell on him.

14.—Sparring for a short time, when Ward again went to work with his left, and napped it slightly himself on the mouth from Sampson's right. A spirited rally followed, in which Sampson received three flush hits on the nose and lips. Sampson received with the courage of a lion, and returned on Ward's head; but Ward was with him again, and hit him down with a tremendous gobster.

15.—Sampson still preserved his game, and attempted to plant a left-handed lunge on Ward's head. Ward parried the blow, rushed in, and delivered three times in succession on Sampson's now disorganized physog. He then jumped away, followed by Sampson, who, on receiving another tap, went down.

16.—It was now manifest that, however well disposed Sampson might be to punish his man, he was unable to get at him, and his blows left but little impression, although we observed a slight tinge of claret from Ward's proboscis. This was a short round; Ward, endeavouring to put in a body blow, over-reached himself, and fell on his hands and knees.

17.—Sampson put in a slight blow on the side of Ward's head. Ward jumped back, but again returned to the charge, hit Sampson on the sore spot, threw him heavily, and fell upon him.

18.—Ward planted a severe blow on Sampson's wind, again caught him a rap on the nose, closed, and threw him, adding his own weight to the impetus of the fall.

19.—Sampson came up boldly, although more cautious than heretofore. At last, on coming in, Ward hit him a terrific right-handed whack on his face, and floored him in a twinkling.

20.—Sampson rather more on the stand-off, from a deficiency of wind, and a consciousness that he was getting the worst of the in-fighting. Ward, not disposed to let him remain long in suspense, rushed and peppered his mug with great severity; and at length catching him round the neck, fibbed him with effect on the nut-crackers, and grassed him.

21.—Ward scarcely bore marks of the effects of his engagement,

" And had everything now, as Bill Gibbons
    would say—
Like the bull in the china-shop—all his
    own way."

Two to one was offered on Ward, but no takers; and the Brummagem, though no counterfeit, was evidently fast on the wane. Still he came up manfully, and in no way inclined to cry "enough." Ward, with his customary caution, met Sampson as he came in, and fought at him with vigour; when Sampson fell, Ward on the top of him.

22.—Sampson came up groggy. Ward saw his situation, and rushed in. Sampson fell weak, Ward again on him.

23.—Sampson, although unsteady on his supporters, again went boldly up, when Ward floored him with a heavy spank on the throttle.

24.—Ward, as fresh as at the commencement, came up cool and collected. Sampson was almost stupefied. Ward tapped him on the snuff-box, and again downed him, falling upon him. It was thought it was all over, and Ward went to shake hands with his friends at the side of the ring. To the surprise of all, however, Phil. came again.

25.—Sampson tried a rush, and just reached Ward's head. The latter laughed and popped in a right-hander on the body, when down went Sampson. Two more rounds took place, but they were all one way. Sampson, although the spirit was willing, had not the strength to carry out his intention, and at length, at the end of twenty-seven rounds, and thirty-seven minutes and a half, his friends took him away.

REMARKS.—The reporter adds: Ward, by the result of this battle, and the manner in which he conducted himself throughout, entitled himself to the approbation of the fancy, and we trust he will not now find any difficulty in obtaining backers against a more worthy opponent. We believe him to be the best fighter in the ring, and we know not with whom his chance of success would not be equal to his merits. With regard to

Sampson, we should be unjust if we were not to say that he fought with a bravery and determination worthy of a better result. His confidence was certainly mistaken; but having done his best, his backers have nothing with which to charge him. He is a good man, though somewhat slow, and there are many men in the ring with whom he may be fairly matched; but with Ward, it was "Mr. Justice Burroughs' wig to a farthing rushlight" against him.

This last conquest placed Ward upon "the topmost round of Fortune's ladder." He at once proposed to try his weight of metal and accuracy of aim against the "Great Gun of Windsor," Tom Cannon, and thus he framed his—

"CHALLENGE FOR ONE THOUSAND POUNDS TO THOMAS CANNON.

"SIR,

"I am happy to inform you that my friends possess so much confidence in me that they have asked me, unsolicited on my part, to have 'a shy' for the championship of England. In consequence of this unexpected and very liberal support of my backers, I am enabled to dispute your self-elected right to the above title. My heart is in its proper place on the subject; my hands are ready to support my claim; and my legs are on the alert to perform their office, when called upon, in the hour of battle. It now only remains for you, Tom Cannon, to name your day to make a deposit; also the time when it will be most convenient for you to peel, and I to strip; and likewise the sum you will put down, to set the thing a-going. In order to show you that it is no bounce upon my part, and that the sporting world may not be baulked as to a mill between us, to obtain that pugilistic honour which Tom Cribb so nobly maintained for many years, Pierce Egan has authority from my friends to make a match on my behalf for £1,000. A letter addressed to P. E., 113, Strand, respecting your answer the blunt will be fobbed out in a twinkling.

"Now, Tom, having made myself perfectly agreeable as to the terms of your challenge, and which I am sure, must also prove agreeable to your feelings (as I am well assured you fancy me as a customer), I have only to add that I sincerely wish you in good health, and likewise success in all your undertakings, except obtaining the honour of the championship. On that head I profess myself your rival; but if the chance of war should prove you the better man, the £1,000 will be awarded to you, without any grumbling on my part, and the proud title of champion into the bargain. Till then, Tom, I remain, with a couple of hands at your service,

"JAMES WARD.

"*February 20, 1825.*"

Ward felt highly delighted when the match was made between him and Cannon for £500 a-side.

We have now arrived at the mill which decided definitively Ward's right to the championship. On the 26th of May, 1825, Tom Spring took a farewell benefit at the Fives Court, when he finally retired from the ring. After some excellent setting-to, Spring addressed the company, and took his leave of them in the character of a boxer; and in his address, he impressed upon his brother pugilists the importance of integrity. He said this was the key-stone to their success, and without it they would find it impossible to preserve the respect or support of their patrons. In the course of the evening Tom Cannon, after a set-to with Tom Oliver, came forward and said that he could be backed to fight Jem Ward, who had challenged him, and would make the match for £500 a-side. He had promised Mr. Hayne, his backer, that he would never more enter the P.R., but that gentleman finding be was extremely anxious to fight Ward, had not only absolved him from his promise, but, as on former occasions, had consented to post the coal on his behalf. This declaration on behalf of Cannon was received with acclamations, and a friend of Ward's at once intimated that he would attend at Tom Cribb's, and make the match. During the same evening, Peter Crawley also advanced to the edge of the stage, and said he had intended to challenge Ward, but as Cannon had been beforehand with him, he would only put forward his claim to fight the winner. At the meeting at Old Tom Cribb's, in Panton Street, articles were duly signed, and the men were sent into training, Cannon to Henley-on-Thames, and Ward to York. The meeting was fixed for the 19th July, 1825. As the day of battle approached, Cannon removed to Marlborough, and Ward to Stony Stratford. With regard to weight there was little difference, Cannon being twelve stone eight pounds, and Ward twelve stone three pounds.

The celebrity of the battle, combined with a second treat—between Dick Curtis and Warren—produced many competitors for the honour and profit of fixing the scene of action, and at length the inhabitants of Leamington and Warwick wrote and made a liberal offer to the men, if they would fight in their district. Freedom from interruption was guaranteed, and the combatants had the choice of the race-course, or an enclosed ground adjoining a factory, which would contain 10,000 persons, and to which no person could obtain admission without leave. The latter spot was fixed upon, and the bustle on the road and in the town was fully equal to that which was witnessed on the occasion of Cannon's last fight with Josh. Hudson. Cannon, accompanied by Mr. Hayne, and some friends, arrived at Leamington on Sunday evening, but being refused admission to the principal hotel there, they adjourned to Warwick, from whence, after dinner, they moved to Stratford-on-Avon. Ward arrived at Warwick the same evening, and took up his quarters at the Hare and Hounds. Preparations commenced early on Monday morning, but before they had proceeded far, the Mayor of Warwick intimated an intention of spoiling the sport. He said it would be too much to permit two mills during one mayoralty in his bailiwick, or he would be called the " Fighting Mayor." On enquiry it turned out he was influenced in his determination by the clamours of certain spoilers of sport who are always busy on such occasions. It was known that his worship was fond of the art pugilistic, and would not interfere of his own free will. It was represented to him that the fact of the mill coming off at Warwick would materially benefit the tradespeople of the town, and other good reasons for non-interference were also brought forward, but in vain, and at length it was determined, in order to be on the safe side, that two stages should be erected, one in the factory-yard originally selected, and one on a spot not far distant, which was beyond the jurisdiction of the mayor; and as it was still thought that his worship would not, in reality, prove "rumbunctious," it was ordered that the men should meet at first in the factory-yard, and only resort to the second stage in the event of necessity.

The bustle in Warwick on Monday night was something extraordinary; every house in the town was crammed to suffocation. Some of the fancy, who had been to Stratford, returned with the intelligence that Cannon was in the highest condition and spirits, but still they were shy of backing him. What little was done was at five to four on Ward.

On the morning of fighting both stages were complete, and around that in the meadow beyond the jurisdiction of the mayor, wagons were placed for the spectators. These vehicles were not required in the factory-yard, in which there was ample accommodation for every one to see without difficulty. At ten o'clock the mayor, accompanied by other magistrates, intimated his final resolution that no fight should take place in the borough, and consequently there was no alternative but to take advantage of the second stage. Mr. Hayne arrived in the town at twelve o'clock, and with the friends of Ward, proceeded to choose umpires and a referee. Sir John Radford and Mr. Mann officiated in the former capacity, while Mr. Osbaldeston, "the Old Squire," obligingly accepted the office of referee. After this ceremony, a little more betting occurred, at five to four on Ward, and then a general move took place to the scene of action, which was about a mile from the town, on the Birmingham road. By the time the men arrived, there were about 12,000 persons present, including an unusual number of the patrician class. The heat was intense, the thermometer standing at 91 degrees in the shade. By half-past twelve the men were on the ground; they were in first-rate condition, but both were affected by the heat. They quickly mounted the stage, which was similar in form to that on which Spring and Langan fought at Chichester. Cannon was seconded by Tom Spring and Tom Cribb, while Ward was valeted by Tom Oliver and Jack Randall. On peeling, both seemed thin, and Cannon appeared to have aged considerably since his last encounter, at least there was not that ruddy plumpness observable on former occasions. Ward was fair and sleek as a greyhound, but there was a slight rash on his body, produced, no doubt, by the heat. He smiled, and had an air of confidence, which put his friends in high spirits. The toss for corners was won by Cannon, who was, of course, placed with his back to the sun.

At the moment of setting-to, there was a general bustle, and some confusion in the crowd, but order was soon restored, and all eyes were fixed on the stage. The men were brought to the scratch at five minutes to one, and the seconds and bottle-holders retired to their corners.

THE FIGHT.

Round 1.—Cannon came up as if determined to lose no time in going to work. The position of Ward was firm; he seemed armed at all points for defence. Cannon advanced towards his man, broke ground, and hit right and left. Ward stopped him, retreated, and smiled. Cannon followed him, when Ward let fly with his right, and caught Cannon over the eye, and drew first blood. Cannon still busy, came in, but was stopped with a left-handed hit in the throat, and a ruby tinge was again visible. A sharp rally followed, Ward retreating, stopping, and nobbing his man as he came in. At length they closed and, after a short struggle, went down together. (Cheers for Ward, who decidedly had the best of the round.)

2. Cannon came up on the bustling system, and tried for an opening. Ward stopped him right and left, and, stepping backward a pace, jobbed him as he approached, with his right hand, over the left eye. Cannon, not dismayed, took this compliment kindly, and returned slightly on Jem's cheek. A sharp rally followed, in which Cannon bustled to his man, and got to a close. Ward twisted his leg between the legs of Cannon, and threw him heavily, adding his own weight to the severity of the fall.

3.—On coming to the scratch, Ward let fly with his left; it was cleverly stopped by Cannon. Cannon then bored in, and Ward retired fighting. As he retreated he succeeded in putting in two facers, but was at length bored down at the rails, and Cannon fell over him. Ward had a lucky escape from his head coming in contact with the board which skirted the stage, in this round. Had this accident happened, in all probability his fate would have been decided. The chance of such injuries forms one of the strongest objections to stage-fighting.

4.—On coming up it was seen that Ward had not received a blow which left a mark. He smiled, and stood to his guard, while Cannon, all energy, rushed to the attack. Cannon made a right-handed hit, but Ward was awake, stopped it, and drew back. Cannon immediately rushed in, and after a short struggle both fell, Ward under.

5.—Cannon again endeavoured to take the lead, but Ward was too quick, and delivered several facers. Cannon, not discouraged, continued his assault in gallant style, and finally Ward, in endeavouring to escape a right-handed blow, slipped down on his hands. This was claimed by Spring as the first knock-down blow, but we did not view it in that light.

6.—Cannon renewed the bustling system, but fought wildly, and was evidently exhausting himself by his own exertions. He missed several well-intentioned blows, and as he followed his man he was met with a nozzler. A sharp rally followed, in which Ward received a severe blow on the side of the occiput, and finally slipped down close to the posts.

7.—Both came to the scratch panting. Cannon hit out right and left with great wildness. Ward retreated to the corner of the stage, and Cannon closed in to him. Ward met him as he advanced with a facer, but was unable to break away. In this situation they both stood for a few seconds. Ward fibbed slightly; when at length Cannon threw him heavily. (Shouts for Cannon; and a bet of £15 to £10 was taken by a good judge.)

8.—Both men were the worse for their efforts in the last round. The excessive heat of the sun seemed to oppress them, and, on coming to the scratch, Cannon, for the first time, sparred cautiously, while Ward waited for him open-mouthed. At last Cannon broke ground, and hit Ward under the ear. Jem retreated, but Cannon fought to a rally. In a close Ward put in a severe mussler, threw Cannon a heavy fall, and at the same time dropped upon him.

9.—On Cannon being lifted to his second's knee, the mischievous effects of the last fall were obvious; he appeared quite groggy, and was evidently much exhausted. On time being called, however, he came up to the scratch with his accustomed game. He lost no time in rushing to his man, but Ward stopped him with a tremendous blow on the side of his nut. Ward then retreated to a corner of the ring. Cannon followed him, and as it were fell into his arms. In this state they stood for some seconds, and both were apparently exhausted. Ward smiled, and attempted to fib, but his hand fell almost powerless. At length Cannon dropped nearly senseless, and Ward, unable to stand, fell upon him. It was now clear that the game was nearly up, and five to one was offered on Ward, but not taken.

10.—Cribb and Spring both exerted themselves to restore their man to animation, but he seemed quite stupefied, and came up reeling as if tipsy. Ward saw his advantage, and instantly came up, hit him right and left, on each side of the head, and on the nose, and the poor fellow dropped to rise no more. He was immediately lifted on his second's knee, but was deaf to all encouragement. His head dropped powerless on his shoulder, and the carmine was seen trickling from his nose and mouth. Loud shouts of congratulation burst from Ward's friends, and he walked to the side of the stage and shook hands with several of them. He afterwards approached Cannon, and took him by the hand, but the latter was insensible to his kindly feeling. Ward then descended from the stage, and mounting his straw tile, he was placed on a grey pony, and was conducted out of the ring in triumph. A surgeon who was on the ground mounted the stage and attended to Cannon, but a full half hour elapsed before his senses were restored, and he was then so weak that it became necessary to lift him into the carriage of Mr. Hayne, which was drawn up at the side of the stage to receive him. The fight lasted but ten minutes, and the amount of money which changed hands upon the result was immense.

REMARKS.—This battle afforded but little scope for observation, and still less in the way of a pugilistic treat to the amateurs who were present. Cannon, from the outset, pursued his bustling system, and seemed to think that upon that alone depended his chance of success. By his exertions in this way, however, from the excessive heat of the day, he only tended to expedite his defeat; and we have no hesitation in saying that his final overthrow was more occasioned by exhaustion than by punishment. In fact, on looking at him while in a senseless state, there appeared to be no very great severity in the blows which he had received. His principal injuries were to be attributed to his falls, which were certainly very heavy. Ward fought throughout with great steadiness, presence of mind, and caution, and may be said to have won without a scratch; but, like Cannon, we do not think he could have stood up much longer, notwithstanding the excellence of his condition. He had two severe falls, but received only one blow of any importance, which was under the left ear.

The friends of Ward, in the course of the evening, sent up a message to Mr. Hayne, at the Swan Hotel, that Ward should fight any man in England for £500 a-side. Spring, being present, immediately waited on Ward's backers, at the Warwick Arms, and said Brown should fight Ward for the sum mentioned; but Brown was objected to on account of his weight. Spring then said he would fight Ward for £500 aside, and come within a stone of Ward's weight, and he would put down immediately a hundred sovereigns to make a deposit. This challenge was not accepted; when Spring observed, Langan should fight Ward for £500 a-side. However, after some conversation on the subject, the parties retired without making any match.

Harry Holt took a benefit at the Fives Court, on Friday, the 22nd of July, when Ward was introduced. Jem ascended the stage amidst loud approbation, followed by Harry Holt, who, in a neat, appropriate speech, introduced the belt, which was put round the body of Ward by Oliver. The belt consisted of the blue and crimson colours worn at the late fight, bound with the skin of a tiger. The clasp or buckle was made of highly-polished steel, encircled with emblematical designs, and in the middle of the clasp was a heart, worked with gold, on which was engraved the following inscription: —"This belt was presented to James Ward, at the Fives Court, St. Martin's Street, Leicester Fields, on the 22nd of July, in commemoration of his scientific and manly conquest of Thomas Cannon, at Stanfield Park, Warwick, on the 19th of July, 1825. This battle, at the present time, entitles

him to the high and distinguished appellation of the British Champion."
Ward had scarcely got the belt on, when he said to a friend with a smile,
"I have got it, and I mean to keep it." Ward, on meeting with Cannon,
shook hands with him, and asked him how he felt himself. "Very well,"
was the reply; "the heat licked me, Jem, and not the blows. The hits
that passed between us could neither hurt you nor me, Jem." "I feel
rather stiffish," observed Ward: "it was hot, indeed; and at one time I
had no power to strike. They all talk of fighting me now; but I shall not
enter the ring for twelve months. Let some of the big ones fight—Peter
Crawley and Brown; but, Cannon, if you wish to fight me again, I will
fight you when you like." "I am very much obliged to you, Jem, for the
preference; and if I can raise the blunt, you may depend upon it I will
make another match." Harry Holt returned thanks on the conclusion of his
set-to with Ward; and the court was cleared.

A great muster of the heavy betters took place at Tattersall's, on Monday,
July 25, to receive and pay on the above milling event. Considerable surprise was manifested throughout the circle, when the following letters were
read by the stakeholder :—

"DEAR SIR,—
  "Mr. Hayne has desired me to request you will not deliver up the stakes of the fight
between Cannon and Ward until the umpires and referee meet to decide the fairness of the
battle.
                                                          "Yours, etc.
                                                            "W. A. CARTER.
        "*Furnival's Inn, July 25, 1825.*"

                    _____

                                        "*Furnival's Inn, July 25, 1825.*
"SIR,—
  "In consequence of serious doubts expressed by Mr. Hayne of the character of the late
fight between Thomas Cannon and James Ward, and those doubts having been confirmed by
others, I feel it my duty as umpire on the part of Cannon, both for the sake of Mr. Hayne
and the sporting world, to request that you will retain in your hands the stakes until a meeting shall have taken place between the umpire of Ward, the referee (Mr. Osbaldeston), and
myself. The articles specify, 'that the stakes are to be given up according to the award of
the umpires and referee;' and no award having been made on the spot, I am perhaps justified in begging this short delay. In the interim I shall expect that any evidence which can
be produced to sustain Mr. Hayne's doubts will be brought forward. By Monday next our
decision will, no doubt, be accomplished.
                                        "I have the honour to be, etc.
                                                            "J. R."

The delay required, "as to something wrong," was objected to by almost
every amateur present; it being asserted there was no necessity for time, as
it was the general opinion that a squarer fight had never taken place in the
annals of boxing. After some little argument in the subscription room on
the subject, it was decided that, as the umpires and referee made no objection at the conclusion of the battle, Ward was entitled to the stakes, and

the stakeholder had a right to give up the £1,000 to the backers of Ward. Cannon was present, and stated that he had lost the battle against his will; and, as he went £200 in the battle-money, he desired, at all events, that sum might be given up to Ward. An indemnity was offered to the stakeholder should any legal proceedings be brought against him. The stakeholder, with much promptness, immediately gave up the stakes, to the satisfaction of all sporting men. In consequence of the decision of the stakeholder, some thousands of pounds changed masters in the course of an hour. The conduct of the stakeholder prevented shuffling in any part of the kingdom.

It was generally expected that Jem's easy conquest of Tom Cannon would at once bring forward Peter Crawley, to redeem the promise he had made in print to make a match with the winner. Peter, however, remained silent; nor did he make any response when Ward issued a challenge to fight " any man in the world" for £200 or £300 a-side. It was at one time thought that a match would be made between Ward and Tom Spring—a " tiff " having taken place between the champions,—but when the thing was proposed Spring stated that he would not re-enter the ring, and Ward said he would not fight Spring unless the latter would confine himself to thirteen stone. No other claimant at this juncture appeared to dispute Ward's title to the championship. Wishing to enjoy some retirement from milling, and, like a star belonging to another stage, to make good benefits in the provinces, he issued the following notice of his future intentions :—

" *To the Editor of* ' PIERCE EGAN'S LIFE IN LONDON.'
" SIR,—

" It is my intention to start on a sparring tour for a few months. I beg you will do me the favour, through the medium of your journal, to inform those who have a wish to meet me in the P.R., that I shall not be at leisure for seven or eight months. In the interim, the various aspirants to the championship may contend with each other, and I shall be happy, at the expiration of the time specified, to accommodate the winner of the main.

" I am, Sir, yours respectfully,
" JAMES WARD.

" *Mulberry Tree, Commercial Road, July 26*, 1825.

In *Bell's Life* of the 2nd of July, 1826, the turn-up with Sampson is stated to have been the result of a quarrel as to the division of the proceeds of some sparring exhibition given by the erewhile rivals at Norwich and elsewhere. It says: "Ten determined rounds were fought, in which as much mischief was done as in many of those fights which have cost a hundred miles trot to witness. The superiority of Ward was, however, conspicuous throughout. He met Sampson's fierce rushes with coolness and scientific precision, drew his cork, and floored him in every assault. Sampson suc-

ceeded in planting some heavy facers, and was even with Ward in the claret
way; but still he was overmatched, and although he proved himself no mean
opponent, he was constrained, as he had been before, to knock under to one
who may be fairly pronounced the most accomplished boxer of the age."

In the same paper, of the following week, a letter from Sampson appears,
denying the accuracy of the above account, and stating that it was not
caused by a quarrel, but was the result of a mutual agreement to see which
was the better man, and that it took place, with the gloves, at York.
Sampson further affirmed that he had the best of it throughout, and that he
intended again to enter the ring with Ward, when the public would have
an opportunity of judging which was entitled to pre-eminence.   This intention, luckily for the "Birmingham Youth," he never carried out, for in two
months after he made a match with Ned Neale, the Streatham Youth, an
inferior boxer to Ward, by whom he was defeated in eleven rounds, occupying sixty-six minutes.   (See Life of NED NEALE).

Seventeen months had elapsed, notwithstanding all his challenges and
industry to get a job, before Ward met a customer in the person of Peter
Crawley.   During this period Jem was viewed as champion of England.
The backers of Ward having consented that he should fight for £100 a-side,
a match was made between them; and on Tuesday, January 2, 1827, the
battle was decided upon Royston Heath, Cambridgeshire.   In twenty-six
minutes, occupying eleven rounds, the title of champion passed to Peter
Crawley, as will be found in the memoir of Peter.   The backers of Ward
were so satisfied with his brave conduct, although in defeat, that at Holt's
benefit, two days after the fight, at the Tennis Court, they offered to make
another match for £1,000.   Peter, however, refused, said he would not
fight any more, and left the championship open to those boxers who wished
to fight for it.

In the same paper with the speech of Crawley at the Tennis Court appears
a letter from Ward, in which, after regretting that Peter would not give
him another chance, and declaring that to the accidental blow in the second
round his defeat was attributable, he says, his friends will back him against
any man in England for £200 to £300 a-side.   He concludes by saying,
"I still hold the champion's belt, and certainly shall not resign it to any
man who will not fight for it."

On Tuesday, the 6th of January, 1827, Ward took a benefit at the Tennis
Court, which was crowded by his patrons, who then bore testimony to their
approbation of his manly conduct in his fight with Peter Crawley.   Ward
was anxious to get up a fight with Brown, of Bridgenorth, but as the latter

would not come to the scratch under £500, for the present the match went off, Ward's friends not being strong in the shiners to that extent. The challenge, however, was again sent by Brown, and accepted at the price by Ward, in May, but went off after much dispute on the point of fighting on a stage, Brown declining to fight on turf. To this Ward's backers would not allow him to agree. Their objection was that a stage fight with so big a man would be such a manifest disadvantage to Ward, that it would be throwing away too great a chance. Brown, they urged, would fight all fifteen stone, while Ward would be twelve stone four pounds to twelve stone seven pounds; and it must be obvious that on a stage a heavier body propelled against a lighter must increase the danger to the latter, as the chances were that the lesser man would more frequently come in contact with the rails, planks, or skirting boards, and thus suffer twofold punishment from blows and contusions. At a meeting at Tom Cribb's, in April, 1827, they said, "It was true that Ward himself had no objection to the stage, that he would as soon fight Brown there, or even in a saw-pit, and it was only to be lamented that Brown did not show a similar spirit. It was their duty to curb the natural and courageous impulses of Ward's heart, and to mix up, on his behalf, prudence with valour. The stake to be fought for was not only great in a pecuniary point of view, but great in point of glory, for the winner would be champion of England. This was a prize of too much magnitude to be treated lightly, or to be risked without due foresight, and without equality in point of advantage." Cribb, on the part of Brown, could not make the match except on the terms authorised by Brown himself, and therefore nothing was done. A long angry correspondence, not worth preserving, ensued, in the course of which Brown offered to stake £320 to Ward's £300, if Ward would fight on a stage. Ward, on the other hand, offered to fight for £100 a-side on a stage, or for £300, or even £1,000 a-side, on turf. This was declined by Brown. Finally, the question of superiority was decided in another way. Phil. Sampson (thrice defeated by Ward), challenged Brown, and beat him, April 28, 1828, after forty-two hard-fought rounds in forty-nine minutes. This, in the judgment of those who can get "a line" by the comparison of performances, set at rest the question of the respective merits of Brown and Ward.

Bell's Life remarks on this fight: "Brown turned out a blank in the wheel of fortune. His main dependence seems to be on bodily strength and a terrific hit with the right hand. These requisites may be fearful when opposed to a novice, but with a scientific professor they prove of little avail." These remarks must convince any one that the big man of Bridgenorth would have proved a chopping-block for the skilful and ready Jem Ward.

An accident happened at this period which had nearly deprived the ring of Jem's services. On the day after the battle on which Ned Neale (see Life of NEALE) a second time conquered Jem Burn (November 13, 1827), the defeated man took a benefit at the Tennis Court, Windmill Street. The principal sparring bout was between Ward and the gigantic Bob Burn. The fine science of Jem was greatly admired, and he jumped in and out, nobbing the big one with both hands till Bob was so hit to a stand-still as to hold on the rail for support. Another round was called for, when Jem drove Burn, hitting away rapidly; Burn's back came forcibly against the rail of the stage, which broke, and he fell backwards to the floor of the Court. Jem, who was in the act of delivering, pitched after him head foremost, and every spectator feared a disastrous result. Jem, who was lying partly upon Burn, was first picked up. He was partially stunned by the fall, but soon recovered, and said that, except a sprained feeling in the back of his neck, and a barking of his shins over the lower rail which added to the ugliness of his descent, he was scarcely hurt. Burn escaped with even less injury—"a surprising fact," says the reporter, "seeing he weighs sixteen stone. That neither man was killed, or had broken bones, is astonishing."

We have seen Jem engaged in all sorts of correspondence with leading pugilists, especially Simon Byrne and Big Brown, when, at the beginning of 1828, a challenge appeared from the once-renowned Jack Carter, the "Lancashire Champion," a former opponent of Tom Spring. Jem had been on a tour in Lancashire, and his Liverpool patrons testified their esteem by giving him a bumper-benefit at the Gothic Rooms, at the close of the year, and he, together with Dick Curtis, Young Dutch Sam, and Stockman, reaped a rare harvest in that metropolis of the north at the commencement of 1828. Being now in capital feather and high favour, he returned to London, and on Friday, the 28th of February, 1828, a strong muster of the fancy took place at the Castle Tavern, to witness the arrangements for the match between him and Jack Carter. Jem, who had come up from Liverpool to answer Carter's challenge in person, and who looked extremely well, was early at the scratch, and was soon after joined by Carter. Jem said he was ready to post the pony forthwith, according to Carter's proposition, to fight for a hundred; but Jack's friend having, on reflection, backed out of his original pledge, and all of a sudden discovered that he liked Ward too well to lay his money against him, poor Jack was thrown on his beam end. In this dilemma he proposed to match himself for £50, and trust to fortune to enable him to get the goldfinches. Ward objected to fight for so small a sum, on the ground of its letting him down from that station in the ring which he had hitherto maintained. When being hard pressed, however, and entreated as a particular favour to oblige his customer, his good nature would not permit him to resist, and, to the satisfaction of all present, articles were drawn up and signed, by which it was agreed that the men should fight for £50 a-side, in a twenty-four feet roped ring, half-minute time, on the 27th of May, within a hundred miles of London. Ward then offered to fight Simon Byrne, of Glasgow, who had been "chaffy," for £250 to £200, and after this took his departure for Liverpool, where he had at this period many staunch friends.

Carter had not fought since his battle with Spring, in 1819, and, at the time of his present match, was thirty-eight years of age. In this respect of course Ward had an immense advantage, his years only numbering twenty-seven. In height and weight Carter had the advantage, in the proportions of five feet eleven inches, and thirteen stone six pounds, against five feet nine inches and a half, and twelve stone seven pounds. In science Ward was known to be A1, and of course the odds in his favour were very considerable. The fight took place on Shepperton Range, on the 27th of May, 1828, in the presence of a large muster of the fancy. Ward was seconded by Phil. Sampson and Dick Curtis, and Carter by Tom Oliver and Young Dutch Sam. On stripping, Ward was in fine condition. Carter also was in robust health, but his corporation partook a little too much of civic importance.

THE FIGHT.

Round 1.—Both men looked "unutterable things," and each approached the other as if perfectly conscious he had his work to do. Ward worked his guard, and poised himself on his toes in his customary form, ready to let fly as an opportunity might offer. Carter stood erect, hands back on his breast, rather on the defensive than otherwise. Some time elapsed in mutual caution, Carter getting away, and keeping out of distance. At last, after nearly four minutes had elapsed, Carter threw out his left, but Ward was awake and stopped him. The blow was too short for effect. Twice did Carter try the same manœuvre, with as little success. Ward now crept in, and caught Carter with his right on the side of the head. Another little pause, when Ward again got in, and hit left and right. Carter now fought to a rally, but hit wildly, while Ward showed great quickness and tact in in-fighting, planting a heavy blow on Carter's mouth with his left.

Carter returned slightly on Ward's cheek with his left, and in the close was thrown.

2.—More caution on the part of Carter, while Ward worked his left for a shy. Carter hit out with his left, but it was short, and stopped, as was another trial of the same sort. Ward now got within distance, planted his one, two, and three, and catching Carter round the neck with his left, hit up with fearful precision, gave him another deep cut on the lip, and floored him. (Five to one on Ward.)

3.—Carter came up bleeding from the lip, and flushed in the face. Jem was ready, and all on the tip-toe for mischief. Carter again tried his favourite left hand, but was prettily stopped. Jem made a feint; but, although Carter left himself open, he did not go in. Carter kept away for a time, and got away from a well-intentioned smack from Ward's left, and smiled. At last Jem stood on no ceremony, but rushed in right and left, jobbing well on Carter's nob. Carter fought with him, but wildly, and received a fresh visitation to his mouth. In the close for the fall, Carter was thrown over on his head.

4.—Each stopped a left-handed compliment. Carter at length went in left and right, in rather a scrambling manner and open-handed. Jem drew back and jobbed him severely on the mug. Carter caught him round the neck, but Jem was alive to his opportunity, and his in-fighting was excellent; he hit up well, and in the close threw Carter a beautiful cross-buttock, falling heavily upon him.

5.—Carter stopped Jem's left with great quickness. Jem neatly rushed in with his one, two, and then drawing back, hit up in admirable style. Carter broke away, but Jem was with him, and counter-hits were exchanged. Jem now made himself up for execution, and having tried his right at Carter's body, got to a rally, hammering away with all his might. Carter stood manfully to him, and popped in a good left-hander on the side of the nose. This roused Jem's choler; he rattled in, delivering left and right, and hitting up. A long struggle ensued for the fall, during which Jem fibbed with great quickness. Carter got down, Ward falling easily upon him.

6.—Carter hit short at the body, and stopped Jem's right and left with excellent precision. He then planted a slight blow on Jem's nob. Jem, all alive, saw his opening, and hit away left and right with the rapidity of lightning, and the activity of a two-year old. His execution was wonderful, and Carter's left eye was puffed to a close; still Jem peppered away, until at last Carter fell on his knees somewhat groggy.

7.—Carter came up game, but Jem gave him no time for reflection. He at once rushed to work, delivering with terrific precision, left and right. Carter was wild in his returns, and on closing was dropped.

8.—(Thirty to one on Ward.) Jem jobbed severely with his right, and then with his left, drawing more crimson. Carter fought manfully with him, but without precision. Jem was busy at in-fighting, and in getting away fell on his back, while Carter remained standing.

9.—Carter stopped Ward's left and right with good science, but Ward was quick upon him, made a good left-handed job, and was ready to let fly, but Carter kept his distance. Carter made a good stop with his right, but left himself open, and Ward, alive at every point, went in to work left and right, and again hit up with wonderful rapidity. Carter fell on his knees, the claret visible from all parts of his face, his left eye completely dark.

10.—Carter came up strong on his legs, though winded, and stopped Jem's left. Jem then closed for in-fighting, and hit as he liked with telling effect, and Carter was grassed without a hope.

11.—All in favour of Ward, who had it his own way and dropped his man, after he had hung for a short time on the ropes.

12.—Carter was not to be stalled off; he hit short with his left. Ward stopped a well-intentioned delivery, but in a second attempt he was not so successful, as he caught Carter's left on the nose, and a slight effusion of blood followed. Jem now rushed in, and catching Carter round the neck, jobbed and hit up repeatedly. Carter's arm got entangled in the ropes, and he tried to grapple Jem; but Jem was too leary, and continued to pepper him in the face till he fell.

13.—There was now a general cry for Carter to be taken away; but he would not have it, and again came up strong on his legs. He bored in wildly, and Ward jobbed him left and right in every direction. The deliveries were dreadful, and at length poor Jack was hit down.

14. — Carter came up in a melancholy plight. (Cries of "Take him away.") Ward went in to finish, hitting left and right, and cutting away without leaving Carter the shadow of a shade of a chance. Carter down.

15.—(Renewed cries of "Take him away.) Carter came up, and was immediately dropped.

16.—Jem delivered right and left, and hit Carter down weak and groggy.

17.—Spring and Peter Crawley, who were time-keepers, now entered the ring, and entreated Carter to give in, but he would not, and having received additional punishment, was dropped by a flush hit in the face. It was now clear that to prolong the fight would be inexcusable, and the referee entreated Carter to desist, as there was no chance in his favour. "Oh!" said the gallant fellow, "I can foight longer yet; there's nought the matter with me." The *primâ facie* evidence of the contrary was so obvious, however, that his seconds being convinced it would be inhuman to suffer him to be further exposed to the severity of Ward's hitting, gave in for him, to the general satisfaction of the spectators, who, although they could not but admire Carter's game, felt that the seconds performed their duty in the humane course they had adopted. The fight lasted thirty-two minutes, and Ward, on shaking hands with his vanquished opponent, generously forewent a claim to a purse of £5 8s. 6d., which had been collected previous to the fight. Such was the favourable impression which Carter's conduct had made in the ring, too, that a further subscription was made, which increased the original sum to £16.

REMARKS.—Few remarks are necessary where the moves were all one way. Ward had the lead throughout, and may be said to have won without a scratch; in fact, we do not think he ever had an easier, but we must add, a gamer customer. Youth and science completely served age, and poor Jack showed that in matching himself with such a man as Ward he had suffered his imagination to get the better of his judg- ment. His punishment was entirely about the head, and he walked from the ring with great firmness, being still quite steady on his legs, a proof that he had paid every attention to his training.

Some few months after his defeat of Carter, Simon Byrne, then "Irish Champion," challenged Ward to fight upon a stage. To this Ward's friends could not consent, contending that a champion was not bound to grant any unusual terms to his challengers, and that the modern and fairest practice was to fight on turf. After some correspondence, Ward gave way, and a match was made, to come off on the 8th of September, but went off by a default of Simon's backers, who forfeited £50 to Ward. A second match was made at Tom Spring's, on the 1st of October, to fight on a stage for £150 a-side, on the first Tuesday in February, 1829. This also went off, and a third was made for £100, to be decided on March 10, 1829, Byrne consenting to Ward's terms. This event proved another shadow on Jem's career, which, were we not honest chroniclers, we would have omitted, as other biographers have done. By this *suppressio veri*, however, men's lives cease to "point a moral," however they may "adorn a tale."

The 10th of March, 1829, arrived in due course, being nearly one year from the first challenge. We will not trust our own pen on this occasion, but rather give the account fresh and fiery as it came forth at that period.* It is headed thus :—

"HOAX UPON THE FANCY.—JEM WARD AND SIMON BYRNE.—DISGRACE-FUL SCENE AT LEICESTER.

"Our readers are all aware that the fight between Jem Ward (the champion of England) and Simon Byrne (the champion of Ireland, although acting under Scotch auspices, for he was generously backed by certain liberals at Greenock) was fixed to take place on Tuesday last, at the Cricket Ground, Leicester. It would be tedious to recal to the recollection of our readers all the 'fine spun' correspondence which preceded this match, or to reiterate the terms of abuse in which each man addressed his opponent. It ought not to be forgotten that Ward, or his friends for him, assumed the title of 'Champion of England,' and that the would-be Champion of England —the most accomplished boxer of the age, and the darling of the East—was publicly charged by Irish Byrne with being a coward! To the honour of the British ring this could not be endured, and, at last, out came Ward's friends to bavk him for £150. We pass by the disinclination of the Wardites to go

_____
* It may be as well to premise that this was written by one who was far from friendly to Ward. The facts, however, speak for themselves.—Ed. PUGILISTICA.

towards Glasgow, and the spirit with which Byrne conceded, and agreed to
fight within a hundred miles of London; but we cannot forget the avidity
with which Ward's friends grasped a forfeit of £50, because Byrne's deposit
came a day too late, nor avoid contrasting the conduct of the northern fancy
with that of those of the south, by reminding our readers that the distinct
request of Byrne's friends was, that no such advantage should be taken of
Ward. Suffice it to say that, after the forfeit of £50, the match was
renewed for £100 a-side, and that Jem went into training, determined, as he
said, and his real friends anticipated, on taking ample vengeance on the
bouncing Patlander, who had dared to brand him with the epithet of coward.
Indeed, so strong was the provocation that, many of Ward's admirers looked
on nothing more certain than that, in the very first round, Byrne would have
been burst like a mealy potato.

"The morning of Monday was ushered in by much bustle at Leicester.
The Fair Play Club, Tom Oliver, the commissary of the ring and his *suite*,
the *élite* of the fancy, and the most distinguished amateurs thronged the
streets. Other matches were made, and all appeared in high spirits; 'but,'
says Mr. Vincent Dowling, 'during all these scenes, we were surprised to
observe the apathy which prevailed in the betting circles: scarcely a bet was
offered, and nothing less than five to two on Ward would be taken, while
few seemed disposed to risk such odds. There was, in truth, a mysterious
backwardness on all hands, which we could not comprehend.'

"The morning of Tuesday at last broke, and a finer day was never witnessed at this season of the year. Every hour brought fresh accessions to
the visitors in the town, and horsemen and carriages came rattling in from
every point of the compass. Among the former were most of the distinguished members of the hunts in the neighbourhood of Melton Mowbray,
whose scarlet costume and high-mettled cattle as they dashed through the
streets gave a sporting feature to the assemblage peculiarly in character.
The bustle and crowd in Leicester increased to a ferment: hundreds were
assembled in front of the sporting houses. All calculated on a glorious day's
sport, and in turn ventured an opinion on the merits of the combatants; but
still scarcely a betting man would open his mouth, either to offer or take the
odds on the event.

"The Fair Play Club's ropes and stakes were pitched by Tom Oliver, and
a capital ring formed in the cricket ground. Anxiety now prevailed for the
arrival of the men; that on the part of Ward was soon dissipated by his
entering from a gate at the lower end of the ground in a carriage drawn by
four horses. He alighted amidst the congratulations of his friends, and was

conducted to the house of a private gentleman, which opened by a back way to the cricket ground. Simon Byrne arrived at an early hour in a fly with Tom Reynolds, and was soon attended by Tom Spring, who had agreed to act as his second.

"An interference on the part of the magistrates disturbed at this time the arrangements of the ring, and Tom Oliver took up the stakes and toddled to Humberston, within ten miles of Leicester. At the same time that Oliver received his directions, the post-boys of Ward's carriage were also desired to draw up to the door, for the purpose of taking him to the ground. So far not a hint had escaped that any impediment existed to the fair decision of the fight according to the articles.

"During all these arrangements a number of gentlemen, and several persons connected with the betting circles, were congregated as a sort of council in a garden behind the house in which Ward was. In this garden was a privy, and to this privy Ward was seen to proceed, attended by Peter Crawley, who seemed to keep a steady eye on his motions. We spoke to him as he came out: he said he was very well, and again returned to the house. Shortly after this Crawley came forth by himself, and a consultation of a private nature took place between him, the gentleman who brought Ward down, and one or two other persons, which ended in Spring, the stake-holder, and the reporters of the London papers, being called into a private room. Peter Crawley now said he could no longer withhold the fact that Ward was unfit to fight, and had determined not to enter the ring that day. Had a thunder-bolt burst among the auditors it could not have produced more astonishment or dismay than this declaration. Crawley went on to say that Ward had told him he had passed a pint of blood on his last visit to the garden. To this all were disinclined to give credit, and Crawley, who saw he was on tender ground, did not persevere in this assertion, but remarked he was sure something was wrong, and that, in fact, Ward could not win the fight on the one hand, and would not lose it on the other, from a sense of duty to those gentlemen who had behaved so kindly to him. He then talked of some message which Ward had received on the previous day, the nature of which he did not know, and in fact spoke so undecidedly that no clear under-standing could be formed on the subject. Ward was then called in and interrogated, when he repeated Crawley's story of the blood, and said he was not fit to fight for twopence. He denied having received or having been promised any money to lose the fight, but said he knew some of his friends would lose thousands by the result, and he thought it was better not to put either his backers on the one hand, or those who had taken the odds on the other, in jeopardy. It was in vain to endeavour to elicit more: all he added was, that ' he could not win, and would not lose.' As the only alternative, it was then determined by his backers that he should forfeit the money down.

"Thus ended this extraordinary bubble. Ward was left to the enjoyment of his brandy and water; and those who had an interest in the remaining sports of the day set out for the ring, around which twelve or fourteen thousand persons of all degrees had already assembled, including at least two thousand horsemen, all of whom, being ignorant of Ward's conduct, were anxiously awaiting his arrival. Upon this affair observation would be superfluous, as all must agree that it admits of no apology, although Ward, having got himself into the hobble, perhaps did that which, under the circumstances, was best. It was a question with him, too, whether he would have been permitted to lose the fight, for there was a party present who were backing him, and who, their suspicions being aroused, would not have failed to manifest their feelings by acts of violence."

Thus far the leading sporting paper of the time. Heavy was the visitation on Ward for his misconduct from all quarters. His backers left him, his friends forsook him, the Fair Play Club expunged his name from their list, and the supporters of the ring, to a man, turned their backs upon him. His name was never heard until the August of the same year, when a gentleman proposed to back an anonymous person against Byrne for £500 a-side. The challenge was accepted by Byrne's friends, but they barred Ward; and as the party alluded to turned out to be Ward, the challenge went off amidst groans and hootings. Byrne, however, got "chaffy," and offered to have a turn-up with Ward wherever he met him, for love, not for money. Ward, in reply, insisted on fighting for a sum, and Byrne retorted by an historical sketch of Ward's conduct and character, not in the brightest colours, concluding with a threat to "treat him as a street ruffian" whenever he met him.

This nettled Jem so excessively that he answered in a letter from Southampton, and offered to fight guineas to pounds, and as Byrne objected to meet him in the ring, he said, in conclusion, "I will fight him in a saw-pit or on the outside of a coach." More letters of the same kind followed in their turn, Byrne still taunting Ward, but declining to meet him in the ring. Ward now found a strong advocate in a party who wrote under the signature of an "Old Patron of the Ring," and public opinion took a slight turn in his favour.

On St. Patrick's day, 1830, Simon Byrne had a benefit at the Tennis Court, and took the opportunity, being in high spirits and excellent humour, to propose a fight with Ward. The challenge was eagerly accepted, and the men met the next evening at the Castle to "post the coal" and settle the preliminaries. Ward and Byrne shook hands and took a drop together to make things right, after which it was agreed that the match should be made for £200 a-side. A previous battle between Byrne and M'Kay coming in the way, it was agreed that Jem and Simon should have their grand turn-up four months afterwards. The second deposit was made good on the Friday following, when Ward expressed great anxiety to prove, by his conduct in this contest, his wish to secure the respect and confidence of the sporting world.

The fatal fight between M'Kay and Simon Byrne came off on Wednesday, the 2nd of June, and terminated in the defeat and death of poor Sandy M'Kay, and the consequent arrest of Byrne. The following Wednesday had been appointed for making the third deposit on the match between Ward and Byrne. The friends of both parties attended with the money, but Simon's backers suggested that the stakes should be drawn, as it was not decent to carry on arrangements for another fight while one pugilist was lying dead, and the victor, a party to the present match, in prison on a charge of man-slaughter. Ward's friend, however, claimed forfeit if the cash was not put down, and Simon's party thereupon paid up the deposit, the match still standing for October the 5th. Ward, however, in the next week, despite his greedy adviser, agreed to withdraw the stakes, receiving £10 for his trouble, and the match was altogether off, thereby, as was said at the time, obtaining by his conduct the approbation of every honest man. Simon Byrne stood his trial, was acquitted, and duly feasted and dinnered by the sporting world. Ward renewed the challenge immediately for £100, but £200 was required by Byrne, and much ink-shedding, but no battle, ensued. Pugilistic protocols again passed between the parties, but still, as Byrne wanted £200, and Ward could not get it, the fight was as far off as ever, and thus ended the year 1830, Ward having now rested three years without a round.

At last, however, but not without another preliminary misunderstanding, the match which " *did* come off " was made at the Castle, Holborn, on Tuesday, March 17, 1831 (St. Patrick's Day). The tin was posted, the articles formulated and signed, and the whereabouts fixed. Ward was to fight Byrne in a twenty-four feet ring, half-minute time, for £200 a-side, on Tuesday, the 12th of July, within a hundred miles of London, on the road to Liverpool. There was a clause, that if any money should be offered for the honour of the combat it should be equally divided between the men. Such an offer was made from Warwick to the amount of £60, and accepted;

and, in consequence, the men received orders to shape their course in that direction—Ward from Liverpool, where he had taken his exercise, and Byrne from Norwood, where, under the surveillance of Ned Neale, he had taken some degree of training. That he had not done sufficient work, the following remarks, taken from *Bell's Life in London*, will sufficiently show :—

"Both men were far beyond their weight when the match was made, topping, perhaps, not less than fifteen stone each, and to the reduction of this Ward immediately applied himself, by constant exercise; while Byrne remained in Ireland till within six weeks of the day of action, without taking any steps to qualify himself for the important task he had in view, and at that time arrived in London with all his work before him. That this was imprudent no judge will deny, and the consequence was, that a week before fighting he was full a stone heavier than he ought to have been; and even on the Thursday previous to entering the ring he took a sweat, which reduced the strength he then possessed and gave a shock to his system which common prudence should have induced him to avoid. On Sunday also he got drenched to the skin in a shower of rain, and caught a cold, from the effects of which he laboured on entering the ring. Ward, on the contrary, neglected nothing which either sense or judgment could dictate, and could not have been in better trim. We state these things as matters of fact, forming some apology in the minds of Byrne's friends for his defeat; but we have no hesitation in saying, had he been as well as skill and strict training could make him, he would have had no chance against the matchless tactics of his antagonist, who fully realized the high opinion that had been formed of him."

It being known that Warwick was the fixture, an extraordinary number of patrons of milling betook themselves to that celebrated fistic locality several days before that appointed for the contest. On the Saturday, however, a meeting of "beaks" took place, at which it was resolved to stay proceedings, either in the town or county, and a polite justice called upon Tom Spring, who was in attendance on Byrne, to inform him of the determination of those in authority. It being clear that their worships were in earnest, a council of war was held, when it was determined that as the inhabitants of Warwick had given the men £60, the affair should be settled as near as possible to the town, without infringing upon the bailiwick of those who had interfered. Accordingly the neighbourhood of Stratford-on-Avon, a very few miles distant, was selected, and in a field at Willeycutt an admirable ring was formed by Tom Oliver and his then assistant, the renowned Frosty-faced Fogo. There was a good gate to the field, at which a considerable sum was collected. As it was not known in London and elsewhere that Warwick had been tabooed, that town, despite the officiousness of the "blues," reaped considerable benefit from the mill, since almost all the cognoscenti betook themselves thither on the Saturday and Monday, and sojourned there until the morning of fighting. This was exceedingly fortunate for the inhabitants, who were thus in some degree enabled to repay themselves the sum they had disbursed to induce the men to come into their district. The interest was not quite so strong as it had been on the occasion of the fights between Cannon and Hudson, and Ward and Cannon, but still the muster was very great, and on the morning there was such a demand for vehicles as far exceeded the supply; in fact so great was it that poor Simon Byrne was compelled to proceed to the ground in a mourning coach, which was looked upon by the superstitious as a most decided ill omen. The morning was anything but favourable for milling: the rain descended in torrents from an early hour until twelve o'clock, soaking many of the "toddlers" to the skin. Happily, however, at this period the clouds disappeared, and left the sky free from speck, a change which had an immediate effect in raising the spirits of the company.

At five minutes past one o'clock, Ward, attended by Harry Holt and Peter Crawley, flung his castor into the ring amidst the deafening cheers of his friends. The brave Irishman was not long after him, and on entering the arena, attended by Spring and Tom Reynolds, he also received a warm welcome. The betting at this time was £300 to £200 on Ward. On the latter being completely unshelled, he looked in admirable condition. His countenance was clear and healthful, and his eye bright and playful; his deep chest and broad shoulders gave him the appearance of prodigious strength, while the general symmetry of his person presented a fine study for the anatomist. He had evidently paid great attention to his training, for, despite the immense reduction he had undergone—from fifteen stone to twelve stone eight pounds—his vigour and muscle were unimpaired.

On turning to Byrne there was a wide contrast. He was heavier than Ward by a stone; but this bulk was more to his prejudice than in his favour, for it threw a shade of sluggishness over his form that forbad the impression of active vigour: the fat hung in loose collops over his drawers, and his full habit of body showed that he was not the thing; still he assumed an air of confidence, and prepared for action with a smiling mug.

The men and their seconds having crossed mawleys, and umpires and a referee having been selected, the heroes were left at the scratch to commence—

THE FIGHT.

Round 1.—Both men stood on their guard, eyeing each other with steadiness, and each waiting for the other to commence. Byrne made a slight dodge with his left, but Ward was prepared. Byrne held his right low, and his left ready for a counter-hit. Ward made a feint with his left; Byrne drew back alarmed. Ward now covered his man in good style, and gradually drove him back to the corner of the ring. Byrne was ready for the assault, when Ward, quickly playing with his right and left, rushed in to hit. Byrne stopped the blows and closed, when both tried the fibbing system. Byrne hit up slightly, and Ward caught him on the mouth. In the close and try for the fall both went down, and on rising Byrne showed first blood from a slight scratch under the nether lip. Shouts for Ward, who showed a slight flush on the chin and right ear.

2.—Ward came up all life and smiling. Byrne steady on his guard, his right still low, and his left ready for countering. Jem made play to try his man. Byrne again gradually retreated to the corner, when Jem made himself up for mischief, rattled in, and planted his left on Byrne's mouth. A short rally followed, in which Ward had the advantage; and in the close Byrne went down to avoid in-fighting.

3.—No great harm done on either side. The friends of Ward on the chaffing system, and exclamations of "We want no Irishman for champion." Byrne's friends called on him to be leary; he smiled, and said, "don't bother me." Ward stretched out his left and nearly reached Byrne's face, but Byrne still kept his right down. "He'll stand it," cried Dick Curtis, when counters were exchanged from the left. Ward stopped Simon's blow, but popped in his own. A short rally, in which Ward stopped beautifully, and closed. Byrne would not have it, and got down.

4.—Ward made a feint with his left. Byrne steady on his guard, but made no attempt to commence fighting. Ward again made play, left and right, and darting in, planted his left on Byrne's mug. In the counter-hitting which followed, Byrne was too short, and his right no use. He caught it again on his muzzle, and fell on his knees. Ward hit up with his right as he was going down, and Byrne showed more claret from his mouth.

5.—Cheers for Ward, who evidently out-fought his man; and Byrne gave symptoms of timidity, his legs trembling under him. Ward again made a feint with his left, and Byrne drew back. Ward smiled. Byrne tried his left, but was stopped with great precision. He then hit round with his right, but Ward caught it on his shoulder, and got away laughing. Counter-hits with the left, Ward getting home first, and drawing more blood from Simon's mouth. Byrne's left was short of its mark. Ward again planted his left and rushed to in-fighting. Byrne was confused, and went down amidst cries of "Stand up and fight like a man."

6.—Jem exhibited his generalship in fine style, and Byrne could make nothing of him. Again did Ward pop in his left on Byrne's nose, and got away. A sharp rally, in which both stopped well. In getting away, Ward fell on his knees, but was up in a moment and at it again; popped in his left twice in succession on the old spot. Byrne weak on his legs; Ward all alive. In the close, Byrne down, amidst renewed cries of "Cur!" Byrne saw he had no chance in the close, and was coming the cautious.

7.—It was clear Byrne could not hit his man, who was always so well covered as to render assault dangerous. Byrne looked bothered, and was evidently alarmed for the result. The ruby was flowing from his nose and mouth. He stopped Ward's left cleverly, and tried his right on Ward's canister, but Ward caught it on his shoulder, which he threw up so as to cover his lug. Jem jobbed twice in succession with his left. Byrne's left, in attempting to counter, fell short. Jem stopped right and left. Byrne open-mouthed. Jem again busy with his left. A rally, in which slight hits were exchanged right and left, and Jem fell on his inexpressibles. The first knock-down blow was here claimed for Byrne, but disputed. The referee, we understand, pronounced it a knock-down.

8.—At the commencement of this round a wag let go a crow from a bag, which flew across the ring. Some cried "a pigeon," others "a crow," and a Hibernian praty-dealer exclaimed, "Oh, by Jabers, you're not going to crow over us neither." Loud laughter from all parts of the ring. Ward stopped a left-handed compliment, and smiled; he then popped in a left-handed snorter; but Byrne, in return, caught him a heavy body blow with his right. Ward popped in his left twice in smashing style, and in a third visitation of the same sort hit Byrne down. This was proclaimed a decided knock-down blow.

9.—Byrne weak, and bleeding profusely. Ward jobbed him with his left several times in succession with great severity. Byrne, still game, tried to plant his left and right, but was beautifully stopped. A rally, in which Ward, busy as a bee, planted right and left, hit up with his left, and, as Byrne was going down, caught him across the throat with his right, and dropped him on his seat of honour.

10.—The fight had now lasted twenty-eight minutes, and Jem had not a mark visible, save on the chin, and a trifling effusion of blood from the gums. Byrne tried his right, but Jem up shoulder and stopped him. Jem now made play, and in went his left at the mouth and nose and no mistake. Byrne tried to return, but was stopped, and in the close Byrne went down weak.

11.—Jem walked strong from his second's knee. Byrne tried his right at the mark, but Jem caught it on his elbow, and Byrne having dropped his head, he caught him cleverly an upper-cut as he recovered himself. Byrne was broken-hearted from the scientific way in which he was stopped, but again tried a rally, in which he received pepper left and right, and in the close went down weak. (Cries of "Byrne, you're a game fellow, but you haven't a chance.") This was obvious, but still Byrne's friends looked forward to Ward becoming weak.

12.—The punishment had been heretofore all on Byrne's mouth and nose, and they continued to bleed freely. Ward caught a visitation on his mouth, amidst cries of "Well done, Byrne." A rally, in which Byrne missed his hits, but received on the nose, and went down by the ropes.

13.—Ward ready, and determined not to throw a chance away. Byrne tried a body blow, but was stopped, receiving in return a smasher on the nose—more claret. Jem's shoulder again shielded his lug from a visitation. Counter-hits : Ward's told first, and Byrne's was stopped. Byrne rushed in ; Ward hit up heavily, but missed, and Byrne went down.

14. — Thirty-three minutes had now elapsed, and Jem showed slight symptoms of fatigue. ("Take your time," cried his seconds, "the day is long, and you must win without a scratch.") Byrne appeared to have got his second wind, and went in with spirit, but was stopped right and left. Ward was busy with his left, and again stopped a right-hander with his shoulder. A short rally, in which Byrne was unable to plant a blow, but was hit down with a flush hit from the left. (Twenty to one on Ward, which Neale offered to take, but no go.)

15.—Ward made a feint with his left, and the next instant popped it in in good earnest. Counter-hitting. Byrne could not get home, and had it smartly on his mouth. Several left-handed jobs, and a dreadful upper-cut from Jem, when Byrne went down groggy.

16.—Byrne tried the left at the body, but missed, and went down without a blow.

17.—Jem jobbed twice with his left, and got away. Byrne's hits were well meant, but out of distance. Byrne received an upper-cut from the left, and went down.

18.—Ward, all confidence, had recovered his temporary weakness. Byrne tried his left, but was stopped. Jem, after his feint, popped in his left three times, and Byrne was dropped.

19.—Counter-hitting with the left. Ward's blows told, but Byrne's were short. Jem stopped right and left, and got away. Byrne was completely puzzled, and did not know

what to be at. Jem tipped him a left-hander. Byrne once more tried the right, but Jem's shoulder was in the way, and he laughed at the impotent attempt. A rally, which ended in Byrne being hit down by Ward's right.

20.—One hour had now elapsed. Ward was as fresh as a kitten, completely belying the rumour that he could not stand forty-five minutes. Poor Byrne received several severe jobbers, and went down.

21. — Things were now apparently fast drawing to a close. Ward did as he liked, hitting left and right. Byrne down.

22.—It was now admitted on all sides that Byrne showed game. He would not be taken away ; and after receiving additional jobbers, was hit down, catching the upper-cut as he fell. ("Take him away," was the general cry.)

23.—Byrne made a bold effort to get a turn in his favour, and rushed to a rally, but his opponent was too good a general, stopping him at all points, and returning with great severity ; in the end hitting him down with a sweeping blow from the left.

24.—Jem tapped his man with his left. Byrne nodded, showing that he was still in hopes. Byrne made play with unexpected vigour, but Jem out-generalled him, popped in his left-hand teaser, and dropped him.

25.—A guinea to sixpence on Ward. Byrne made a desperate effort, and left-handed counters were exchanged, Byrne catching Ward on the throat. (Cheers for Byrne, and the Wardites astonished.) Byrne fought away, and gave Ward his work to stop him. He at last fell from a left-handed nobber.

26.—Byrne rather exhausted by his exertions in the last round, but still determined to do his best. Hits were exchanged—slight on the part of Byrne, but heavy from Ward ; and in going down, poor Byrne received a heavy upper-cut.

27. — Ward's friends again up in the stirrups, twenty to one going a begging. Ward ready at all points and full of confidence. Byrne a heavy receiver, and hit down with a flush tap in the mouth.

28.—Ward, fresh and jolly, hit with his left twice. Byrne bored in, and tumbled Ward down at the ropes, falling upon him.

29.—One hour and ten minutes had now elapsed, and Ward, instead of getting weaker, gained strength, showing the excellence of his condition. Byrne got away from a left-handed finisher. In a new attempt he was caught. He popped in his left at Ward's bread-basket, but as he went down had a left-handed upper-cut.

30.—Counter-hits with the left on the mouth ; both told, and were allowed to be the best exchanges yet made, all before being on the side of Ward. Byrne went down, but Ward caught him as he fell with a left-handed muzzler.

31.—A slaughtering round for poor Byrne, who had it repeatedly on the mouth with the left, and in going down received the upper-cut from Ward, who was never astray.

82.—Byrne greatly distressed. Ward went in to finish; planted his left three times. Byrne down.

83 and last.—Byrne now came up to make his last effort, but he was too far gone to make a change, and this more from exhaustion than hard hitting, for the blows were not delivered in dangerous places; still he was constantly receiving, and now again he had pepper in abundance, without being able to make any adequate return. In going down, Ward made a desperate back-handed offer with his right, but missed. It was clear to Spring and Reynolds that their man had no chance, and they prudently acknowledged Ward to be the better man. Jem immediately gave an active bound, shook hands with his fallen foe and his friends, and quitted the ring amidst loud cheers. The fight lasted one hour and seventeen minutes.

REMARKS.—Thus ended Ward's last battle for the championship of England, to which it may now be said Byrne had not the slightest pretensions. He had the vanity to hold his antagonist too cheap, and, unfortunately, deceived his friends, who followed his example. Ward, throughout, proved himself a consummate general, and never gave his opponent a chance, nor did he himself throw a chance away. He fought skilfully and scientifically, and has fulfilled that high character of his talents which was never doubted. Byrne proved himself an easy customer: he was clearly not in tiptop-condition; but it was never in his nature to beat a man like Jem Ward. He must now look for a second-rate customer, and profit by experience. That he is a game man at receiving, no one will doubt; but he was clearly afraid of his opponent after the first few rounds. It puzzled his friends to account for his never trying to stop Ward's left, nor to rush to a ruffianing fight; but the fact was, his spirit was broken, and he had not his wits about him. He says, after the third round his arms felt as heavy as lead, and that he never was so transmogrified before. It is a singular fact that neither of the men had a black eye; neither had an external cut worth mentioning; nor was there a single good fall or cross-buttock throughout the fight. Byrne was beaten solely by exhaustion and repeated slaps on the nose and mouth, which would not have prevented his coming again had such a step been wise.

The men reached London on Wednesday night, Ward without a scratch, and Byrne only exhibiting a swollen mouth and nose, rather a surprising state of his phiz considering the repetition of Ward's left-handed jobs.

On the Thursday following the fight Jem Ward was presented with a second champion's belt by Tom Spring, at the Tennis Court, Windmill Street, on the occasion of Reuben Martin's benefit; and on the following evening, when the battle money was given up, he (Ward) offered to make a match to fight any man in the world for any sum from £100 to £500 a-side. This challenge was not accepted. Young Dutch Sam, however, offered to fight Ward if the latter would confine himself to twelve stone, and stake odds; but of course, as Ward could not so far reduce himself, the offer was not accepted. On the 25th of June, 1832, Jem wrote a letter to the editor of *Bell's Life in London*, in which he stated that he had taken the Belt public-house at Liverpool, that it was his intention to retire from the ring, and to hand over the champion's belt to the first man who proved himself worthy of it. Several challenges were subsequently issued to Ward, but none of them ever led to any meeting, and Jem adhered to his intention of not again entering the prize ring. He carried on business as a tavern keeper, first at the Star and then at the York Hotel, Williamson Square, Liverpool. In 1853, Ward removed to London, and became host of the Rose, in Jermyn Street. This speculation proving unsuccessful, his friends placed him in business at

the Three Tuns, in Oxford Street, renamed the Champion's Stores. Thence Jem
Ward removed to his native locality, the east end of London, becoming landlord of the George, in Ratcliff Highway. The generation, however, who knew
Jem as "the Black Diamond," had passed away, and Ward once again migrated
westward, this time opening the theatrical house, opposite Old Drury, known
by various signs, and then as the Sir John Falstaff, in Brydges Street, a name
now merged in Catherine Street, of which it is a continuation. We last saw
Jem at the ring-side, looking, as a daily paper observed, "like a grey-moustached
half-pay major," at the wretched burlesque of a championship-fight, performed
by Jem Mace and Joe Goss, at Farningham, Kent, on the 17th of May, 1866.

We must not omit to note that Ward possessed an inborn gift of artistic
talent. His favourite pursuit was the wielding of the painter's brush and maul-
stick. On several occasions Ward's pictures were received with credit at the
Liverpool Exhibition, and were mentioned approvingly by the public journals
as displaying a remarkable degree of natural talent; so much so that an art
critic wrote, "had Ward devoted himself to the study and practice of painting
in his earlier years he would doubtless have attained eminence." The writer,
on his visit many years ago to Williamson Square, inspected in Jem's studio,
paintings (some sea-pieces especially) which bore marks of peculiar talent and
no mean skill in manipulation. At this time too (she has retired from professional life), Miss Eleanor Ward, a pupil of Sir Julius Benedict, was fast rising
in public esteem to the first ranks of pianoforte performers in the best of our
concert-rooms. Ward's hobbies, painting and music, adopted late in life, we
fear injured his worldly calling as a sporting boniface, and, after several failures,
he retired, by the assistance and votes of his friends, into that admirable institution, the Licensed Victuallers' Asylum, in the Old Kent Road; in the parlour
of one of the snug separate dwellings of which we conversed with him, still
cheery and animated, in the month of June of this present year, 1880, in
his 80th year; Jem dating his birth, as we have already stated, from "Boxing
Day" in the last twelvemonth of the last century.

CHAPTER II.

PETER CRAWLEY, ORIGINALLY KNOWN AS "YOUNG RUMP STEAK"—1818–1827.

THE "ponderous Peter," who in the year '65, passed quietly, and with the fame of a fair, courageous, and honest man, from the scene of "the battle of life," made his first public bow to the fancy in a trial set-to with a Mr. Thomas Watson, a skilful amateur and patron of the ring, whose name continually occurs in "match-makings" of that period. This took place at George Head's sparring saloon, in East Harding Street, Gough Square, on Wednesday, February 11, 1818, Peter being then a florid youth of eighteen, six feet in height, eleven stone ten pounds in weight, and of a courage well tested in several boyish and youthful encounters. Among a collection of disjointed newspaper scraps in the second volume of "Boxiana," p. 493, is a notice of this set-to, which is there called "a glove combat of two hours and a half." Pierce Egan adds: "The above set-to was pronounced by the judges upon this occasion one of the best things of the sort ever witnessed." We learn from another source, "This severe trial proved so satisfactory to his friends, from the science, coolness, and straight-hitting displayed by Peter, that he was pronounced to be capable of having a shy in the P. R., and in the enthusiasm of the moment, the sire of Crawley exclaimed, ' My boy bids fair to be champion of England !'" Before, however, we trace his rise in the ring, we will glance backward to his "birth and parentage."

Mine host of the Duke's Head and French Horn first saw the daylight at the house of his father, a butcher, at Newington Green, on the 5th of December, 1799, and was in due time initiated in the art and mystery of "cutting up." Peter, who was an open-hearted lad, somewhat given to milling when attempted to be imposed upon by "the lads of the cleaver," was placed by his father with a butcher in Clare Market, he having an idea that a boy learnt his business best away from home. Here the "ruling passion" displayed itself. Having been called upon to act as second in "the Long Fields" to a "boy" belonging to the market, words took place between

the seconds as to the fairness of the fight, and one Hurst, a big blacksmith, of
Holles Street, at once "pitched into" Peter before he could get his hands up.
"A ring" was called, and in no more than three rounds "Young Rump
Steak" had so satisfied the blacksmith's milling appetite that he had no more
"stomach for the fray."

George Colman, a man of superior age and some milling repute, had a
short drawn battle with Peter; and the same result followed a mill with
a dog-dealer of the name of Bennett. Tom Price, a well-known " kill-bull,"
of the same region (Clare Market), had talked much about "serving out"
"the boy Peter," if he got a chance. He sought an opportunity, and promised him a sound thrashing. "Come along," said Peter, " I'm quite ready
to do it at the *price*; in fact, I'll do it for nothing." This contemptuous
mode of treating the boxing pretensions of Price so angered him that his coat
was off in an instant; and a convenient spot having been found—for in those
days "peelers" were not, and day-constables only in the form of street-
keepers in the great thoroughfares—a stable-yard saw the two heroes of the
market thoroughly peeled, with seconds and the other appliances *selon le
règle*. Price showed more impetuosity than skill, but was so steadily met
that, at the end of twenty minutes, he declared he would not fight any
longer, unless Peter would allow him time to get his wind. To this curious
request Crawley agreed, and Price immediately took a walk, as his second
termed it, to get a little air; but he never returned to finish the battle,
leaving Peter master of the ground.

Crawley changed his place of residence, and Bloomsbury Market became
the scene of his exploits. The Bloomsbury boys had quarrelled with the
lads of the Coal-yard in Drury Lane, and a strong muster on both sides of the
question met in battle array to decide the dispute. The pals of Crawley
became panic-struck, bolted, and left Peter in the lurch. Harry Buckstone,
the leader of the Coal-yard party, pitched into Peter, and had it not been for
a gentleman who was passing at the time in all probability Crawley must
have been soundly drubbed by the whole of the squad. The gentleman
offered his services as a second to Peter, to see fair play. Crawley set-
to hard and fast with Buckstone, punishing him in all directions; the
latter took to his heels and bolted, followed by his mob, the spectators laughing and Peter receiving their applause.

The next customer that came in the way of Peter was Tim M'Carthy, in
the Long Fields. The late Jack Randall witnessed this battle. The match
was regularly made for 5s. a-side, and contested with as much spirit as if it
had been for £500. In the course of twenty minutes poor Pat was done over.

PETER CRAWLEY, AT THE AGE OF 27.

From a Portrait by WYVILL.

During a visit to Bermondsey, Peter was abused by a saucy waterman of the name of Tom Tyler, who had flattered himself that, in consequence of a skirmish with Deaf Davis, he could fight a "tiny bit." He was most egregiously disappointed in standing before Crawley. One punch from Peter, perhaps not altogether unlike the kick of a horse, so alarmed and satisfied Tyler that he would not fight any more. This ludicrous circumstance took place opposite the Green Man, in the Kent Road.

Peter had scarcely passed his seventeenth year, when he had an accidental turn-up with a strong carman, weighing twelve stone and a half, and about twenty-five years of age, belonging to Messrs. Shirley, the distillers. Peter was driving his father's cart to collect skins, when he was met in Warwick Lane by the carman, who would not give way, although on the wrong side of the road. Crawley remonstrated with the carman on the impropriety of his conduct; but the "knight of the thong" threatened to horsewhip Peter for his impertinence. "Stop a bit," says Crawley, "two can play at that fun." Shirleys' carman was well known in Newgate Market as a troublesome customer; but Peter tackled him without the slightest fear or apprehension of the result. The science of Crawley soon told on the upper works of the carman; and, although a strong fellow, in the course of less than half an hour he was so severely punished by Peter as not to be able to keep his pins. He was carried into the distillery of his master, and, notwithstanding every care was taken of him, some little time elapsed before he resumed his daily occupation. So much for the decisive handywork of Peter.

Crawley accidentally went one evening to the King's Head, in Cow-heel Alley, Whitecross Street, to treat an acquaintance with something to drink, when he was rudely accosted by some Irishmen, and otherwise roughly treated. Peter begged the Grecians not to interfere with his company, when words arose between them. A row commenced, when Peter and his pal Oliver (not Tom), disposed of several of the hod-men in succession, and ultimately cleared the room of the Patlanders; but not until one of them had made use of the fire-shovel belonging to the landlord to crack Peter's sconce and let out the claret. The Charleys were brought in to take Peter and his friend to the watch-house; but the landlord behaved like a trump, and planted Crawley in his bar until the watch had left, when Peter departed in safety.

Owing to some trifling dispute between Crawley and an athletic brewer's servant in Whitecross Street, a turn-up was the result; but in the course of four rounds the big drayman was glad to acknowledge he had received too much.

One Paddy Flanagan, an Irishman, full of pluck, and not less than six feet in height, much heavier than Peter, and having also the advantage of ten years in age, had a turn-up with Crawley. Flanagan purchased a loin of pork at the shop of Peter's father during the bustle of Saturday evening, and appearing well satisfied with his bargain, went away; but in a short time he returned with the pork, after he had cut off on the sly two of the ribs of the loin, and insisted they had deceived him with short weight. Of course this insinuation produced a row and great confusion in the shop, and Peter, at the request of his father, endeavoured to turn out Flanagan. Paddy showed fight, and for a short time was a strong, troublesome customer on the stones. Peter was thrown flat on his back into the running kennel, and was completely wetted through to the skin, and almost choked by the grasp of his antagonist upon his throat. On rising, however, from this rushing hug, Peter changed the scene. He stopped Paddy Flanagan's rush and nobbed him, one, two, got the lead and kept it; indeed, he tipped it to Paddy Flanagan so completely, that at the end of half an hour he gave in. But Flanagan had recourse to the strong arm of the law. He appeared before the magistrates at Worship Street police office, complaining of the unmerciful treatment he had experienced at the hands of Crawley; indeed, "his face bespoke a heart full sore!" Armstrong, the officer, was despatched to execute the warrant, but the father of Peter made it right at the expense of £2. The senior Crawley, from the striking abilities displayed by Peter over the powerful Flanagan, formed an opinion that "his boy" would stand a good chance in due time with the best pugilists in the prize ring.

About three weeks after the above row, Peter was standing during the evening at the corner of Redcross Street, when three Patlanders of the same squad rudely assailed him, and nearly pushed him off his balance. Remonstrance was in vain, but Crawley said to them, "Do not attack me altogether; only stand in a line, and I will lick you one after the other." This speech had not the desired effect—they all pitched into Peter at once; but he soon floored two of them, and the third bolted without waiting for a taste of Crawley's quality.

We have seen, in the opening paragraph of this biography, how Peter began the year 1818 by a promising bit of gloving, and he was not slow to follow up the impression thus made. A Westminster election in those days of fierce Whig and Tory battles was a sight to see, and the newspapers of the time teem with accounts of the "scrimmages" arising out of the fierce political partizanship of the rival factions. Peter had been sworn in extraconstable at Sir Samuel Romilly's and Sir Francis Burdett's election, and in the discharge of his duties was threatened by Ben Sutliffe, also a butcher, and an understanding was come to that their personal differences should be settled when the political contest was over. This grew into a regular match, £20 a-side was deposited, the F.P.C. ropes and stakes engaged, and on Friday, August 7, 1818, after Ned Painter* had defeated Tom Spring, Crawley and Ben Sutliffe sported their colours. Sutliffe was the favourite for choice; he weighed about twelve stone ten pounds, and stood full six feet in height. Peter did not exceed eleven stone eight pounds, and was not so tall as his adversary by half an inch. There was no time for training, and the combatants fought off-hand. In the short space of nine minutes and a half, the science of Peter was so excellent, his hitting so decisive, and his generalship so complete, that Sutliffe was defeated without a shadow of a chance, being punished dreadfully.

This victory brought "Young Rump Steak" into high favour with the amateurs, which Peter's civility, respectful demeanour, straightforwardness, and good temper, strengthened and confirmed. He was now, however, matched against a desperate boxer, no less an antagonist than Tom Hickman, the formidable Gas-light Man, whose exploits will be found recorded in pages 118-137 of this volume. Peter was as yet but nineteen years old, and was declared by the ring goers to have "more gristle than bone;" and Pierce Egan observes, "Crawley had outgrown his strength," which was only partially true. It is true, in this battle Peter was not disgraced, although defeated; he fought bravely, and he convinced the tremendous Gas that he (Peter) was a dangerous customer. Crawley afterwards sent a challenge to Hickman, which was declined on the ground of other engagements.

At several benefits at the Fives and Tennis Courts the sparring of Peter with Tom Spring, and all the first-rate boxers on the list, was much admired by the amateurs.

Peter about this time sent the following reply to a challenge inserted in the *Weekly Dispatch* :—

"MR. T. SHELTON,—

"At the time of my addressing a letter to you in the *Dispatch* of the 20th ult. I was not aware but my bodily health would have admitted of my doing the thing in 'Neat' style. At the request of my friends, I was advised to have the opinion of a medical gentleman, whose certificate is below, from which, I have no doubt, the pugilistic world will see no fault arises on my part in not meeting my challenge.

"I am yours, etc.,
"PETER CRAWLEY.

"*Royal Tennis Court, February* 1, 1822."

"I do hereby certify that Mr. P. Crawley is not in a fit state to enter the ring with any one at present (labouring under a serious body calamity), neither do I think he will be able so to do for five or six months.

"THOMAS HUGHES, *Surgeon.*

"5, *Waterloo Road, February* 1, 1822."

* See Life of PAINTER, *ante*, p. 82.

Thus forbidden to take part in a ring contest, owing to an inguinal rupture, Peter went on a sparring tour, and in May, 1822, he set-to with Jack Carter at the Cock-pit at Chester, at the time of the races. During the above exhibition, a chap denominated Bully Southerns, of the above place, offered to take the gloves with Carter. Southerns weighed seventeen stone, and in height he measured six feet two inches; notwithstanding, he was light as to flesh. Southerns, full of confidence, threatened to serve out both the fellows from town, and also reduce the consequence of Carter, who at that period styled himself "The Champion of England." Carter could not get the best of Southerns, and, after two rounds, he sat down, when the bully boasted that he would mill Peter off-hand. The contest was long and severe between them, occupying fifty minutes; and numerous rounds were truly terrific. The strength of Southerns enabled him to carry on the war; but, after the first three rounds, he was so nobbed by the fine science of Peter, floored frequently, and punished in all directions, as to be laughed at by the whole of the company for his vain boasting. Crawley was not only applauded for his high courage in finishing the bully in such first-rate style, but also well rewarded for his trouble by the amateurs who viewed the contest. Peter was nearly five stone under the weight of his powerful adversary —a fine example of the advantages of science over downright ruffianism.

On Peter's return to London, Dick Acton,[*] well known in the prize ring, sent forth a challenge to our hero, who returned the following answer:—

"TO RICHARD ACTON.

"SIR,—

"As I understand you have several times expressed a particular wish to meet me in the prize ring, I hereby inform you that I am ready to fight for £50 or £100 a-side, which may be most convenient to you and your friends; and in order to give every accommodation you can reasonably require, meet me at Mr. How's, Duke's Tavern, Seven Dials, on Wednesday evening, the 26th inst., between the hours of seven and ten o'clock, when my friends will be ready to make a deposit, or before that time if you like it best.

"I remain your humble servant,

"PETER CRAWLEY.

"*March 13, 1823.*"

The friends of both the pugilists met according to appointment, and a match was made for £25 a-side. This battle was decided at Blindlow Heath, in Sussex, twenty-five miles from Westminster Bridge, on Tuesday, May 5, 1823.

For four years Peter had exhibited only in sparring exhibitions; and, labouring under hernia, it was generally understood that he would not appear again in the prize ring. Acton had at this time won a battle with Kendrick, but

---

* See Life of WARD, p. 201, *ante.*

had been defeated by Ward.   Crawley was the favourite at seven to four and two to one.   At one o'clock, Peter, attended by Ben Byrne and Harry Holt, threw up his hat in the ring; and shortly afterwards, Acton, followed by Eales and Scroggins, repeated the token of defiance.   Acton was in fine condition, and to all appearance weighed fourteen stone.   Crawley looked thin, but was well, and about twelve stone four pounds.

THE FIGHT.

Round 1.—No time was lost, and Crawley, with his left hand, marked the body of his opponent.   Acton missed in return, when an awkward sort of hugging took place. Both down, Crawley undermost.

2.—Young Rump Steak endeavoured to cut up his opponent, and his fine science gave him the lead. He nobbed Acton, and got away; he also endeavoured to repeat, but Acton stopped him with considerable skill. Crawley made himself up, and by a well-measured hit, planted under Acton's right ogle, the latter went down like a shot. A more tremendous hit was never witnessed in any battle. (In the pride of the moment ten to one was offered, and the general opinion was that Acton would not come again.)

3.—If Acton had not been a truly game man, he would not have again appeared at the scratch. Milling on both sides, till Acton and Crawley found themselves both on the ground. (Seven to four.)

4.—Acton had rather the best of this round, and Crawley went down. (Loud shouting for Acton. "You shall have plenty of wittles to-morrow," said Scroggins.)

5.—Some excellent science on both sides. Acton napped so much pepper that he turned round from the punishment he received; but, in closing, threw Peter out of the ropes. ("Well done, Acton.")

6. — Both were distressed.   Acton hit Crawley very hard, and the latter was again down. ("Go along, Acton; Crawley is getting weak." Indeed, it was no two to one at this moment.) Acton stood up to his opponent, and fought like a truly brave man.

7.—A turn took place in favour of Peter, and the skill of Crawley in this round won him the fight. Acton received at every step, but endeavoured to ruffian it with Peter. Acton, for his temerity, napped a blow in the middle of his head, and the claret flowed in torrents; he, nevertheless, bored Young Rump Steak down. (Great applause on both sides.)

8.—Acton appeared at the scratch much better than was expected. He gave Crawley a severe body blow, calculated to do mischief.   A short, but sharp rally, when Crawley fell down, and Acton on him.

9.—This was a scientific round on both sides. Acton got away well, and parried some tremendous blows. The latter received a chancery nobber, but contended every inch of ground till he went down.

10.—Acton terribly distressed, and Peter piped a little. They soon closed, and Crawley, to avoid struggling, got down in the best manner he could. ("Mind what you're after," from the friends of Acton.)

11.—This round was decidedly against Peter.   Acton put in several blows, and, in closing, fell heavily on Crawley. Peter was getting weak.

12.—Acton had the best of it; and Crawley, to avoid punishment, went down in rather a doubtful manner. ("Foul," "fair," etc., when Belcher, one of the umpires, told Crawley to recollect it was a stand-up fight. "I assure you," replied Crawley, "I went down from a slip.")

13 and last.—This was a most terrific round, and a better one was never witnessed in any battle. Crawley hit Acton all to pieces, and followed his opponent all over the ring till he was floored, and fell on his face.   When time was called, Acton was insensible to it. The battle was at an end in sixteen minutes; but before Crawley was taken out of the ring by his seconds an inquiry was made whether he had won the battle, to make all right.   The umpires answered "Certainly."

REMARKS.—It was a fine battle. Crawley won it in superior style; Acton proved himself a game man, and fought till nature deserted him.

Peter, in order to fill up his leisure time and increase his stock of blunt, opened a butcher's shop in Seven Dials.   Here he likewise taught the art of self-defence in his rooms up-stairs, and was honoured with the patronage of several swells, who became his pupils.   During the time of his residence at this place, he was employed at Westminster Hall to assist in keeping order at the coronation of George the Fourth, and also at the time the Hau was shown to the public. After having dined sumptuously at the Exchequer Coffee House, and drank the health of George the Fourth, he retired to his domus rather jolly, and fell fast asleep. Peter's rib having occasion to go a small distance on some particular business, was most rudely insulted in the street by a fellow of the name of Sullivan. The proposals made to her were of the most insulting description, accompanied by offer of money; he also laid his hands upon her. All entreaties on the part of Mrs. Crawley to desist were in vain, and he followed her home to the door. It was some time before Peter could be awakened from his sleep to come to her assistance. Sullivan, with the most unblushing effrontery, told Peter, on his expostulating with him for his improper conduct towards his wife, " Your wife, indeed; she's my wife as much as yours." " Say you so; then take that," said Peter, and immediately planted such a tremendous blow on one of his ogles as to produce a serious cut over it, and making Sullivan measure his length on the pavement. The fellow, as soon as he recovered the use of his pins, started off, leaving his hat behind him. Crawley, as a token of victory, publicly hung out the hat at his shop door; but Mr. Sullivan never had the courage to claim his topper.

Crawley, while standing at his door in Lumber Court one evening, in company with Peter Brookery, a pugilist of light weight, the latter was rudely attacked by an engineer, a rare big one. Crawley told him it was no match, when the engineer threatened to put his foot on the seat of honour of our hero. This insult so raised the choler of Peter that he pitched into the engineer *sans ceremonie*, and polished him off in the course of four rounds.

In September, 1826, Ward again put forth a challenge to the world, which was at length taken up by Peter Crawley, who affirmed that it was not from fear of Ward, but from the want of "corianders," that he had been unable to make the match before. He said he could not now get £200 a-side, but would fight Ward for £100. This did not suit Jem, who said it was beneath the dignity of the Champion to fight for so small a stake. Crawley repeated that he could not get more money, and at length Jem Ward, fearful that his pretensions to the championship would be called in question, consented to meet Peter on his own terms, and on the 17th of October, 1826, articles were drawn up at Tom Belcher's, Castle Tavern, Holborn, to fight on the 2nd of January, 1827. The men shortly went into close training, and got themselves into admirable condition.

In *Bell's Life* of the week previous to the fight between Ward and

Crawley we find the following remarks on the subject of the mill between Crawley and Acton :—"It was an excellent fight. Each man did his duty manfully ; but Crawley took seven rounds more than Ward had done to polish off the same customer, as well as a little more time. It was thought also, by good judges, that he did not do his work half so well. To this it must be answered, however, that he was labouring under hernia, and was by no means so fresh as Ward, who has not the fault of being fond of lushing. In comparing the fights, it must not be forgotten that it was Ward's first fight, and Crawley's last, and also that Crawley punished Acton more severely than Ward had done."

The mill now under notice took place on the appointed day (the 2nd of January, 1827). According to articles the fight was to come off within a hundred miles of London, and the neighbourhood of Royston was selected as most convenient, there being three counties handy in the event of any interruption. A special messenger was sent down a day or two previous, who made application to a gentleman possessing large landed estates to grant a site for the combat. The trump in question liberally granted the required permission, and a farm called Haydon Grange was selected. Here, by the day appointed, an excellent spot was prepared by Tom Oliver and Cannon in which to pitch the ring. In fistic circles even in those days, however, there was the same jealousy and wilfulness we have to deplore at the present time. The then Commissary, Bill Gibbons, in direct opposition to his instructions, thought proper to choose a place for himself, and instead of proceeding with the ropes and stakes to Haydon Grange, where Oliver and Co. had prepared a place for them, he went off to Royston Heath, and there pitched his ring, thus frustrating the comfortable arrangements that had been made, and throwing out many old patrons of the fancy, who went to the place first mentioned, and were thus prevented from witnessing the greatest treat that had been enjoyed for many years. Among others who were put to inconvenience was Mr. Jackson, the Commander-in-Chief. The throng was by no means so numerous as had been anticipated, many gentlemen absenting themselves on account of the expected death of the Duke of York, which did not take place until the following Friday. The betting in Royston on Monday, and also at Tattersall's, was two to one on Ward, which odds were taken to some amount, but still much money went " a begging ;" and the friends of Ward were so anxious to be " on," that on Tuesday (the day of battle) they advanced another point.

At ten minutes before one the heroes entered the ring, Ward attended by Josh. Hudson and Reuben Martin, and Crawley being under the auspices of

Tom Belcher and Harry Harmer. They approached each other with good humour and shook hands cordially. Some time elapsed in appointing umpires and a referee; but this done, they soon peeled for action, Tom Belcher winning the choice of corners for Peter. As soon as they were in fighting costume, their condition was eagerly scanned. Both were extremely well. Crawley weighed twelve stone twelve pounds, while Ward did not exceed twelve stone seven pounds. The odds were now eleven to five on Ward. All being in readiness, the men were conducted to the scratch, and commenced

THE FIGHT.

Round 1.—Short sparring, each man looking out for an opening, and both cautious. At last Crawley, anxious to begin, went in and hit out ineffectually with his left. Ward was awake, stopped him with his right, countered with great cleverness with his left in return, and catching him severely on the right eye, dropped him as if he had been shot, amidst the cheers of his friends. The blow produced first blood at the corner of Crawley's eye, and thus decided at once the bets on the first two events. The Wardites were in extasies. (Odds three to one.)

2.—On coming to the scratch the effects of the blow on Crawley's ogle were clear, the flesh being a good deal puffed; still he was cheerful and prepared for mischief. The men again sparred for the first hit, when Crawley threw out his right, but was stopped. Ward then went in and hit right and left at Crawley's canister, but did not make any impression. More caution. Ward again made play, but Crawley was awake, stopped his left with great precision, and smiled confidently. Crawley then commenced fighting; but Ward threw up his right and left, and got away in beautiful style. More sparring and mutual caution. At last Crawley saw a vulnerable point, pushed in, and delivering a thundering hit with his right on Ward's forehead, just above the eye, dropped him in turn. (Loud cheers, and exclamations of "Peter, it's all your own.")

3.—On Ward's being lifted on his second's knee he looked wild, and was evidently suffering from Crawley's tickler. Josh., however, shook him, and brought him to the scratch ripe for action, although a little posed. After some sparring and admirable stops on both sides, evincing the superior science of the men, Ward hit short with his right at the body. Crawley smiled, and collecting himself up for work, threw out his right and caught Ward slightly on his nob. Ward, in endeavouring to get away, fell upon his hands and knees. Crawley was about to strike him jocularly on the part that was uppermost, when Ward jumped up, and both went to their seconds.

4.—More good stops on both sides, when a tremendous rally commenced, in which the deliveries right and left excited the loudest applause. Ward retreated towards the ropes, and Crawley closed with him. In this situation there was some good exchanges, and claret was freely drawn from the conks of each. In the end Ward went staggering down, Crawley upon him. The greatest agitation was here exhibited among the spectators. The outer ring was broken in, and confusion prevailed to the conclusion of the fight, although the pugilistic corps, under the auspices of the Commander-in-Chief, did wonders in endeavouring to preserve order. Many persons got inside the roped ring, and were with difficulty ejected.

5.—Both came up bleeding and a little puffy from their late exertions. After some sparring for time, Crawley hit out with his left, but was stopped, and in turn Ward was stopped by Peter, who had all his senses about him. At last the men came to a rally, and desperate hitting ensued, each countering with great force, and making due impression by their handiwork. Ward, in getting away, repeatedly hit up with his right, but missed his blows. In the end they closed and went down, Crawley uppermost, and both bleeding at the mouth and nose. During this round Josh. repeatedly cheered his man by cries of "Fight, Jem; fight, Jem; fight, my boy!" and Jem bravely, though imprudently, followed his advice, and thereby greatly distressed himself.

6.—A good weaving round, in which Ward caught Crawley round the neck with his right, and as he pulled him across the ring hit him several times with rapidity. Crawley at length closed, and both went down in a scramble, heavily punished and distressed.

7.—The men came up piping, and as if mutually feeling the necessity of recovering their wind, sparred with caution for some seconds. At last Crawley let go his left, but

Ward got away. Another short spar, when Ward hit with his left, but was cleverly countered by Crawley's right. A terrific rally ensued, in which all science seemed to be set aside, and the weaving system went on in a style of manly indifference to the result. Each appeared bent alone on making an impression, and the appearance of their pimples showed that mischief alone was intended. The whole ring was electrified, and a more courageous attack was never witnessed. The Burgundy flowed freely from each. Crawley retreated towards the ropes, Ward still with him, till at length Ward rushed in, and seizing him with the grip of a Hercules, threw him an appalling cross-buttock, which not only shook Peter himself, but the very earth on which he fell. The fall was allowed by Crawley's seconds to have done him more harm than all his previous punishment; and a good judge who was within the ring rushed out and offered ten to one against him, but found no takers.

8. — Peter came up open-mouthed and greatly distressed. It was thought Ward would have gone immediately to finish, but to the surprise of most he kept out, and only sparred at arm's length. It was pretty clear, however, that he was himself the worse for wear, and did not consider it politic to throw a chance away. After some time Crawley tried with his left. Ward stopped this intended visitation, and returned with his right. More sparring; when the men having recovered their wind, once more got to work on the weaving system, and the interchanges were sufficient to daunt the stoutest heart; but still both gave and took without shrinking. Their cocoa-nuts echoed again with the quick following blows, till Ward, becoming weak, or desirous of avoiding further compliments, went down on his knees. Crawley went to his second's knee, and was evidently coming round.

9.—This round commenced with distant sparring. Ward attempted a blow at Peter's mark, but hit short. Peter laughed, and kept out. A few seconds were occupied in this light play, when another terrific rally took place. Both men again went to work, putting science aside, and rattling away at each other's nobs with downright good will. Hit followed hit with the rapidity of lightning; neither would give an inch, but stood to each other with as much *sang froid* as if sparring with the gloves. Nothing could exceed the fearless execution of this rally, and the shouts of the multitude bore testimony to the determined game of the men. Ward, who repeatedly hit up, was met by Crawley's left, who preserved his self-possession and never lost sight of his object. At length, as a sort of climax to terrific weaving in all parts of the ring, Crawley retreated to the ropes, where a close took place, and both fell, Crawley uppermost. Both were much distressed, and evidently

fast approaching the close; but Ward was still the favourite, and two to one was bet upon him by one who professed to be a good judge.

10.—Notwithstanding the severe exertion in the last round, Crawley came up smiling. Sparring was continued for a short time, when another most desperate rally commenced: it was clearly a most powerful effort on both sides to bring the fight to a close. Nothing could exceed the resolution which both men displayed. They followed each other from place to place, hitting with unprecedented game and courage, Ward repeatedly having recourse to his under hits. In this extraordinary way did the conflict continue, till both men, on approaching the ropes, were so exhausted as to be incapable of lifting their hands or striking another blow, and at length both went down, unable longer to stand, although supported for some time against the ropes. A more terrible encounter was never witnessed in the prize ring, and the repeated jobbing of Crawley's left produced the most fearful effects on Ward's face.

11 and last.—Such was the state of the combatants on coming up at the commencement of this round, that it was impossible to form an opinion of the probable issue. Both were piping, and in painful distress, but Crawley appeared to stand best on his legs. Very little time was lost in consideration, and Ward, open-mouthed, attempted to go in. Crawley, as if aware that this round must terminate the fight, collected all his strength, struck out lightly with his left, and then drawing back a short step, he rushed in, and catching Ward a severe job with his left on the mouth, dropped him to rise no more. He fell flat on his back, and drawing his hands up towards his stomach, became to all appearance senseless. Josh. lifted him from the ground, and placed him on Martin's knee, but he was no longer "himself:" he was deaf to the call of his friends and admirers, and, with the battle, lost his claim to the championship. Crawley stood looking at him, satisfied that his labours were at an end. He endeavoured to shake hands with his fallen foe, but poor Ward was insensible to this noble conduct, and Peter walked to his chaise. Ward was shortly after carried out of the ring, and from thence to his inn, in a state of insensibility. All was surprise and confusion. The multitude collected *en masse* in the centre of the ring, and the congratulations of some, and the complaints of others, were scarcely less astounding than the confusion of tongues in the Tower of Babel. It was too true, however, the champion was stripped of his laurels, and the bold Peter was borne off in triumph, one of his backers declaring that he had won £530 by the issue. How many followed his example we know not; but it is certain many thousands changed hands.

REMARKS.—In taking a review of the

whole of this fight, it would be impossible not to say that both men exhibited courage and game of the most unquestionable description; in fact, a better battle had not been fought for many years. Independent of patience under severe punishment, great skill and science were displayed. The stopping of both men, under trying circumstances, was admirable. Neither flinched from his duty, and, with the exception of Ward's slipping down on his knees in the early part of the battle, there was not a suspicion that he was not as game a man as ever peeled. In the second round Josh. Hudson described Ward as having been nearly blinded by the force of the blow on his head, but he very soon recovered his presence of mind; and in the last round there were not wanting some who were disposed to think that he might have come again. Judging impartially, however, from all that passed before us, we should say there was not a shadow of ground for complaining of Ward's conduct in the ring, or for doubting the sincerity of his intention to win throughout. His deliveries were severe, although their effect might not have been so decisive as we had anticipated. It was clear that he tried his utmost to gain the ascendancy, and in this endeavour he reduced himself, in the tenth round, as well as his antagonist, to a state of complete helplessness, hitting with all his force, until both fell without the power of striking another blow. Had his object been other than honest, this never would have been the case. In plain truth, however, he had been overrated, whilst the probable improvement which Crawley might have obtained in two years was altogether lost sight of. In point of length, and weight, and bodily strength, we may also say Ward was over-matched, while in science he was fully equalled; for although Crawley's style of setting-to may not be so elegant, nor his stops so frequent, still the severity and quickness of his counter-hitting, and the rapidity of his motions, added to his calm reception of punishment, gave him on this occasion equal advantage; added to which, Peter, in having Tom Belcher for his second, had at least two points in his favour, for a better second never entered the ring, nor a man whose knowledge of the art better qualifies him to give good advice. We must admit that we have seen Ward fight in better style, and make a

better use of his acquirements. We do not say this with a view of disparaging his good qualities; but had he exercised a better judgment, we think he would not have rushed into desperate rallies, intent only on administering punishment, without regard to the consequences which might follow to himself, but would rather have availed himself of his tact of hitting and getting away, and only going in when an opportunity occurred of closing for the fall—and his superiority in throwing has been repeatedly established. In the present instance he seemed to have lost his usual caution, and to have forgotten that in fighting against superior weight and strength he was completely giving a chance away by standing to be hit in close quarters. Such another fall as that he gave Crawley in the seventh round must have decided the battle, but the opportunity when offered was neglected, and having at length become weak, he was unable to keep his right hand sufficiently high, and thus lay exposed to the terrific jobbing of Crawley's left. We have no doubt his seconds acted to the best of their knowledge; but situated as Ward was towards the close of the fight, it was anything but good advice to incite him to go in to rally: he should rather have played round his opponent, and kept at a distance till his wind was restored, and fresh opportunities were afforded for bringing his scientific and wrestling powers into play. With so vigorous an opponent as Crawley, it was clear he must have the worst of in-fighting; and that this was the case the result of the conflict has shown. These are points which naturally strike an observer, but which a man in the heat of combat, and unassisted by a cool and dispassionate counsellor, may not duly appreciate. It is certain that Ward never had so good a man to deal with before, and, barring the few remarks we have felt it our duty to make, it was impossible for him to have done more to attain the ends of his backers. In falling, he has fallen nobly, and must only hope for better luck another time. We may add that he has still few equals in the ring. We cannot close these remarks without stating that, in losing Tom Oliver as a second, Ward may be said to have lost his battle; for Tom's prudence and good sense would have taught him the folly of bustling with superior weight. The fight lasted twenty-six minutes.

Ward was conveyed in a state of unconsciousness to the Red Lion, at Royston, and was immediately put to bed between warm blankets. A surgeon was then sent for, who found his pulse scarcely perceptible; he, however, took proper precautions, and by six o'clock he recognised those about him. He complained very much of his head, where he received the knock-down blow in the second round, and said that such was the effect of that hit that four rounds elapsed before he had recovered himself. Ward arrived in London on the following Wednesday, much cut up in mind, but still determined to put in a claim for another trial to recover his laurels. He declared he had lost the fight by holding Crawley's abilities as a boxer too cheap, and had resorted to an attempt to fight him down, in which he had exhausted his strength and his power of hitting. He considered, too, his chances in milling Crawley as greatly increased from the fact of the latter having hernia. This would seem without good foundation. It is a singular fact that Joe Grimaldi—than whom, in his pantomimic exertions, no man encountered more violent exercise—had been ruptured from his youth, but never experienced inconvenience in his labours.

On the 4th of January, 1827, two days after Peter's victory, the Tennis Court was crowded for the joint benefit of Harry Holt and Ned Baldwin, and to get a peep at the heroes who were admitted to "show." Ward, on mounting the stage, was loudly applauded. His nob was covered with a handkerchief, and his face exhibited marks of severe punishment. The "Cicero of the ring" (in buff) addressed his patrons for Ward. He said, "Ward had lost the battle, and, what was dearer to him, his proud position; but still it was cheering to him to think that he had not lost his honour. ('True,' and applause.) It was not in man to command success, but he had done all that a brave man could do to win the battle. One must lose, and Crawley was the conqueror. By every person who had seen the battle it was admitted that Ward had established his character as a game man, and he had no doubt, by such conduct, he would never want friends. (Approbation.) He was sorry to observe the subscription on the ground was trifling indeed (25s.); but he well knew the generosity of the fancy would be displayed to him in town. For himself, he would subscribe a sovereign; and he was perfectly satisfied other persons would subscribe their mite." ("Bravo, Harry!")

Jem's backer presented himself, and said he would back Ward, without any hesitation, against Crawley, or any other man in the kingdom, for from £100 to £1,000. (Great applause.)

The hero of the tale, Peter Crawley, now mounted the stage, and was welcomed by loud plaudits. His face was rather damaged, but not so much as his opponent's. With considerable modesty Peter stated, "He had been a winning man, but he had never been opposed to a better one than Ward; in fact, he thought him as good a man as himself. He had been lucky, and gained the fight; and he felt proud he had obtained that honour, because Ward had been considered the best man in England. It was impossible, therefore, that he could have got more honour, or gained a higher conquest. ('Well done, Peter; you are a liberal, brave fellow.') He was determined not to accept any challenge, and he had also made up his mind to give up all pretensions to prize fighting, and, to please the King of England, he would not again enter the ring. He meant no disrespect to the patrons of the art of self-defence; but if he were to fight for seven years, he could not have obtained a higher place in the fancy. Fame was his object, and not money; he therefore left the championship open for those who wished to fight for it, and gave up all pretensions to that high milling honour. He hoped Ward would be dealt with according to his merits; and, as a losing man in general stood in need of support, he should give him two sovereigns." (Cheers.) Peter made his bow amid loud applause.

Peter, acting upon the adage that "all's well that ends well," and having obtained a most brilliant conquest in the eyes of the sporting world, sensibly made up his mind to leave the P.R. for aspiring heroes to bustle in, and commenced publican. He therefore, without delay, opened the Queen's Head and French Horn, in Duke Street, West Smithfield, and the fancy in general gave Peter their support.

Crawley's "free and easy," aided by the musical talents of his father, brought overflowing houses. Mr. Crawley, senior, was a first-rate chaunter, and, as a room singer, his voice in "Tom Moody," "The Sapling Oak," etc., was the delight, again and again, of admiring audiences.

At the Queen's Head and French Horn, soon after Crawley became landlord of the house, he was visited by a blade of the name of Grays, and with that respect and civility which always marked the conduct of our hero, he invited Mr. Grays into his bar, to drink his wine and crack his walnuts. But before the bottle was finished, and during the short absence of our hero, who was waiting upon his customers in various parts of his house, Mr. Grays made free with the character of Peter to Mrs. Crawley, or, to use the vulgar phrase, he was nosing upon the inconstancy of our hero, and his amours out of doors, and boasting that he was a better man at any price than the host of the Queen's Head and French Horn. On Crawley becoming acquainted with his conduct, he told Mr. Grays that he had not conducted himself like a man or a gentleman, when Grays repeated the insult, that he was a better man in every point of view. "That shall soon be decided," said Peter, with a contemptuous sneer. An appeal to arms was the result, and, in the course of two short rounds, Mr. Grays so napped it for his impertinence that he staggered about like a man overcome with liquor, and the boaster, as he lay sprawling on the ground, gladly acknowledged, to prevent further punishment, that he had been egregiously deceived in his estimate of his own prowess, and promised Peter the next time he took wine and walnuts, not to crack jokes at his expense behind his back, and to keep his tongue within proper bounds.

Although Peter was one of the mildest and most inoffensive of men, the lion slumbered within him. We will cite a small specimen of this. When Harry Broome fought the Tipton Slasher, at Mildenhall, in September, 1851, there were strong misgivings of a wrangle, and the writer and others firmly declined the thankless office of referee. It looked as though there would be no fight, for the Tipton's friends rejected several gentlemen nominated, as being backers of Broome. Johnny Broome rode up, and proposed to fight "without a referee." This was very properly declined; but at last Peter Crawley was agreed to by both sides as an impartial arbiter. The details of the fight will be found under the Life of HARRY BROOME, in the Seventh Period. Suffice it to say, the Tipton hit Harry foul, and Peter gave it against "the Tipton." Remonstrance did not shake Peter's decision, and the Slasher, who thought himself hardly dealt by, used disparaging language to Peter. Fired at the imputation on his honesty, Peter proceeded to uncase his huge carcase, declaring he was "good for a few rounds," and nothing but the gentle violence of his friends, and those of the Slasher, who separated them, prevented the brave Peter from there and then having a turn-up with the well-trained Tipton for "love and a bellyful." We have seen other instances of Peter's readiness to resent insult, though the most placable of men if an apology was offered.

From the period he retired he held but one house, the Duke's Head and French Horn, in Duke Street, West Smithfield, a house interesting for years to "country cousins," the fancy, and those who wished a "wrinkle" upon sporting topics. As a teacher of the art of self-defence Peter acquitted himself with great credit, being perfectly master of the science. Several of his Guardsmen pupils have shown their acquaintance that they can hit, stop, and get away with the best of glove amateurs. Peter died, generally respected, on the 12th of March, 1865, in the 66th year of his age. Peace to his manes!

CHAPTER III.

TOM CANNON, "THE GREAT GUN OF WINDSOR" (CHAMPION)—1824-1827.

FOR a short time the name of the hardy Tom Cannon was a word of strength in the annals of the ring. Tom, however, came out too late in life as a public exhibitor of the art pugilistic; his first great victory being over Josh. Hudson, in June, 1824, his last a defeat by Ned Neale, in February, 1827; a career of little more than two-and-a-half years, throwing out his victory over Dolly Smith, in 1817.

Eton, renowned for its College and the classic memories which surround it, gave birth to our hero, but it does not appear that Master Tommy profited much in the *literæ humaniores* by the accident of his birth under the shadows of the pinnacles of " Henry's Sacred Fane." On the contrary, the son of a " Windsor Bargee," he grew up an athletic uncultivated young colt, distinguished for his speed as a runner, his activity as a jumper, his strength as a wrestler, and was known as " a lad who could box a bit." The only parts of Gray's " Ode " which could apply to the young Cannon being, that he could—

" Ply the oar,
And urge the flying ball.

Indeed, his rowing and cricketing qualifications endeared him to the youngsters who practised on the silver Thames and verdant Brocas; as a quoit thrower and a single-stick player, at " the Revel " in Bachelor's Acre, young Cannon distinguished himself, and was known throughout the neighbourhood as " good at any game." Tom followed alternately the calling of a fisherman and a " bargee," or rather mixed them both, *more majorum suum*, and " the Merry Wives of Windsor " often relied on Tom's net or tackle for the delicacies of speckled trout, glittering umber, or slippery eel, from " Thames'

TOM CANNON ("THE GREAT GUN OF WINDSOR").
From a Portrait by WAGEMAN.

silvery flood." Apropos of this, we find from contemporary records that Tom, acting in the spirit of Charles Dibdin's song,

> " I be a jolly fisherman, I takes all I can get,
> 　Still going on my betters' plan, all's fish that comes to net,"

forgot one night—if ever he knew them—the privileges of the corporation of Windsor. He was detected, with a companion, fishing, contrary to Act of Parliament, within the preserved waters of the corporation, whereby a fine of £5 to "our Lord the King" was incurred. Tom demurred to swelling the royal exchequer by impoverishing his own: he put in "leg-bail," and for a time migrated from ungrateful Windsor to live an exile at Newbury, whither he does not appear to have been pursued, for he was here known as the "milling bargee." This was in 1814. We will therefore "hark back."

Thus, in his early manhood, our jolly bargeman lived a life of labour, independence, and humble competency, and like

> " The jolly miller who lived on the river Dee,
> 　He work'd and sang from morn till night, no lark more blithe than he."

Tom's earlier practice with his bunch of fives appears to have been at wake, fair, race, or revel, with the military always abounding at Windsor and its vicinity, and with such "rough chawbacons" as, feeling strong in the spirit of fight, might offer themselves to his notice.

Tom's first recorded engagement was with one Tom Anslow, a grenadier belonging to the Staffordshire militia, in the year 1809. Anslow was the crack boxer of his regiment, and the audacity of young "bargee" (Tom was nineteen years of age) was laughed at by the red-coats, for Anslow was fourteen stone in weight, and all six feet in height. The battle money was three guineas a-side. Cannon, on the day, was a little under twelve stone, and stood five feet nine inches and a half. It was a desperate battle for thirty-two minutes, when the soldier gave in, and Cannon was carried off in triumph by his fellow townsmen. "Boxiana" fills some pages with notices of casual fights with nameless men, on Eton Brocas, at Maidenhead, at Egham Races, and elsewhere, embellished with the usual lively skimble-skamble of the inventive author. The first time Cannon had to do with a "professional" was in this wise. At a raffle in Peascod Street, Windsor, Dolly Smith,* of Hammersmith, was present, and threatened to chastise

---

* Bill (known as Dolly) Smith was born at Hammersmith, and was well thought of by many patrons of the art pugilistic. His principal battles were with Cannon, Abbot, Phil. Sampson, Joe Nash, and Jack Scroggins, by all of whom he was beaten, so that his name has been preserved by the fame of the antagonists who defeated him. His one successful battle was with Harce, whom he defeated after a slashing fight of fifty-eight minutes, during which forty rounds were fought, at Coombe Wood, May 3, 1814. This was for a purse of twenty-five guineas, given by the Pugilistic Club.

Cannon for interfering in a dispute. "Although I know you're a fighting man," said Tom, "I will not be frightened into submission." Dolly threw off his coat, and they adjourned to the street. After a smart turn-up, in which Cannon claimed best, they were interrupted. This led to a match for twenty guineas a-side, which came off in a field contiguous to Shirley Common, near Windsor, May 6, 1817. The battle proved a most determined one. The swell stage-coachmen—for Dolly was a horse-keeper, known on the Great Western road—sported their gold freely on their man, though there was a remarkable disparity in size and weight. Smith, who was a round-built sturdy fellow, measured only five feet five inches, and weighed eleven stone four pounds. Cannon stood five feet ten inches, and weighed thirteen stone. The men were in the ring as early as eleven o'clock, Dolly being esquired by the veteran Caleb Baldwin and Dick Whale; Cannon attended by a couple of stout countrymen. The battle was half-minute time. Six to four on Smith offered.

THE FIGHT.

Round 1.—Neither combatant seemed disposed to waste much time in sparring, and they went to work *sans cérémonie.* Cannon from his height, length, and strength, seemed completely to overshadow his opponent, but "Dolly," not in the least dismayed, planted two heavy body hits, and fought at half-arm gaily, till in closing both were down.

2.—Both on their mettle, and some sharp blows exchanged. Dolly manœuvred cleverly till he hit up through Cannon's guard, and gave him such a teaser on the side of the head, that it seemed to electrify the "bargee's" upper works. He seemed confused for a few seconds, then went in a rattler, and fought till both were down, Dolly first to earth.

3 to 17.—During the whole of these rounds the combatants were far from being idle, and much severity of milling occurred. The claret had long made its appearance upon both their nobs, and their mugs had undergone some little change, from the repeated thumps they had reciprocally and liberally bestowed upon each other. Upon the whole, Dolly as yet might be said to stand forward in the most favourable point of view, and betting continued on him.

18.—In this round Dolly gained great applause, he fought his opponent in the most gallant style, and milled him in all directions, and, by way of finishing, planted such a tremendous hit in Cannon's "middle piece," that he went off his pins in such quickness of style, resembling more the celerity of a cannon shot than being floored by the fist of a man. (Loud shouting, and seven to four on Dolly.)

19 to 60 and last.—Punishment was the order of the day in all these rounds. The gaiety of Dolly never forsook him, and he contended against an opponent every way so superior with the most determined courage and manhood. It was a good fight throughout, and both men displayed true resolution. The claret flowed profusely, and both were so equally painted that it was remarked by a spectator they both belonged to one flock of sheep, they were so regularly "ruddled." Their peepers were nearly obscured, and such a punishing mill has not been witnessed for a long time. One of Dolly's arms was so much beaten, and his wrist so terribly sprained and puffed up, that he was reluctantly compelled to relinquish the contest at the expiration of an hour and four minutes.

REMARKS. — Cannon was so much exhausted that, on his being declared the winner, he was led out of the ring, and upon being lifted into a coach by three men immediately fainted. The battle had scarcely finished one minute when a magistrate appeared to put an end to the sports; but his worship was politely informed there was no necessity for his functions then to be brought into action, as it was all over for that day. A great number of sporting men from the neighbouring counties and from London witnessed the encounter, and much money changed hands.

As this is not a record of sack-jumping, quoits, foot-racing, jumping, and cricket playing, we shall omit the contents of some pages of "Boxiana," with the remark that Tom, who was good at all these, has numerous victories for small sums placed to his account during the seven years between 1810 and the mill with Dolly Smith just reported. For several years Cannon remained a spectator of prize battles, until fired with pugilistic ambition on witnessing the fight between Josh. Hudson and Jem Ward (November 11, 1823), he publicly announced his readiness to enter the ring with either of those boxers. The "John Bull Fighter" hearing of the circumstance, on meeting Cannon, asked him if the report was true. Tom replied in the affirmative, when Josh. instantly produced a "fiver," which was covered by Cannon, to make a match for £200. At this period Mr. Hayne (known by the *sobriquet* of "Pea-green," and his breach of promise with Miss Foote, Dowager Countess of Harrington) had just returned from the "grand tour," and recollecting the numerous sporting feats of Cannon during the time he, the "Pea-green," was one of the *alumni* of Eton, he became Tom's patron and backer. Articles were drawn up at Mr. Clode's New Inn, Windsor, April 26, 1824, in which Cannon agreed to fight Josh. for £100 a-side, on Wednesday, June 23, 1824, within forty miles of London. The match was laughed at by the fancy, as "a good thing" for Hudson, and the £100 looked upon as a "sweetener" to "keep his hand in" till he should grasp the championship.

On the appointed morn the Western road displayed a thick sprinkling of swells and equipages, the place selected being Yateby, in Hampshire, thirty-three and a half miles from London, on the borders of the counties of Berks and Bucks, in a field near Everfield Churchyard. Everything being ready, at a quarter to one Cannon entered the ring, in a dark drab great coat, and threw up his hat, followed by Tom Cribb and White-headed Bob as his seconds. He walked about with the utmost composure, and was loudly cheered by the audience. His legs were decorated with white silk stockings. In a few minutes afterwards Hudson appeared, supported by the President of the Daffy Club and "the Nonpareil," threw up his "castor," and rolled himself into the ring. Oliver and Randall were his attendants. During the time the combatants were preparing for action the backers of Hudson went round the ring offering two and a half and three to one; but the friends of Cannon were shy, and no takers were to be found. The colours, pink for Cannon and chocolate for Hudson, were tied to the stakes. The office was then given, and the men set-to,

THE FIGHT.

Round 1.—On peeling, Cannon appeared so highly improved in condition as to excite the astonishment of every person present. He was cool and confident, and looked firm and "all right." The "John Bull Fighter," always "big," in spite of the most rigid rules of training, was now bigger than ever; indeed, to use the words of a wag, who laughingly observed to his companion, "My dear fellow, you are mistaken as to Josh. Hudson going to fight; it's Sir John Falstaff in buff." On placing himself in attitude, Josh. smiled at his opponent, but still was cautious. Cannon tried to go to work, and let fly at Hudson's victualling office, but the latter hero, to prevent a row in the interior, got away. The "Popper," full of bustle, again tried it on, but, in a counter-hit, received an ogler that made his pimple shake again, and put him on the winking system. Hudson was anxious to administer pepper; but in rushing in he received a slight topper, and slipped down on one knee. Cannon lost no time, convinced the amateurs by his conduct that he was not the novice he had been previously represented, and kept hitting away *sans ceremonis.* We were surprised that Hudson did not finish the round by going down; as on his getting up he received a severe facer. A short pause. Cannon aimed a tremendous blow at his opponent's nob, but he missed. ("Never mind that," said Richmond; "he means to win it, and nothing else.") Cannon showed he was not destitute of science; he got away from a slogger, but immediately commenced an exchange of blows, and had none the worst of it. Josh. stopped well, and also planted an ear-wigger, that rowed the upper works of Cannon. (A pause.) The bargeman went boldly up to his adversary to commence mischief, when Josh., in retreating, ran against the stake. Both the combatants found their way into the corner of the ring. Here a little fibbing occurred, and Josh., after a desperate struggle, succeeded in placing the Popper on the ground. (The East-enders in high spirits, cheered their hero, and offered five to two.)

2.—Hudson came piping to the scratch; his bad condition was visible to all the ring. He was no longer the smashing hero as to effective quality, and a pause was the result. He was now aware, but too late, that he had treated his adversary too lightly, and also that Cannon was not a novice as to prize milling. But, like a trump, acting upon the good maxim that "dangers retreat when boldly they're confronted," he stood up to his man with the true courage of a lion. Cannon, extremely active, endeavoured to take the lead; but Josh. made two good stops. The bargeman received a heavy topper; but he would not be denied. A desperate rally occurred, and the claret first made its appearance on Hudson's lip. Josh. tried milling on the retreat; but the bargeman rushed upon him, bored Hudson to the ropes, and, after having the best of the hitting, got Josh. down, and fell heavily on his abdomen. (The Windsor folks and Johnny Raws now gave a loud shout for joy. "Why, Cannon, you fell on a soft place, did n't you? a feather-bed, was n't it?")

3.—The last fall distressed Hudson so much that he appeared scarcely to have a puff of wind left in his body; his face was also covered with claret. The mind of Josh. was eager to administer punishment; but his energy was leaving him fast. Cannon was determined to bustle the John Bull boxer, and attacked him gaily. The bargeman saw the exhausted situation of his opponent, and would not allow Hudson to recover himself. Josh. retreated, but fighting all the time, till he was bored to the ropes, when Cannon obtained the superiority so clearly, that Josh. was fibbed severely down. The East-enders were now on the funk: hopes and fears alternately succeeded; but disinterested spectators were satisfied that Cannon must win.

4.—This was a good round. The blows of Hudson were heavy; and Cannon found out, if not stopped, they were likely to prove dangerous. The bargeman put in a sharp hit in the wind which made Josh. blow again; however, Cannon's mug showed the handiwork of Josh., and the claret was conspicuous about it. Another rally, hit for hit, but which ended to the advantage of Cannon, who again got Josh down. (The Windsor folks were full of joy, and opened their mouths as wide as barn-doors, vociferating, "You have done the job.")

5.—Hudson, game as a pebble, stuck to his man like glue, and a terrible rally was the finishing stroke of the round. Both down; by a sudden effort of Hudson he threw Cannon over him.

6.—The bargeman was piping a little, but nothing in comparison to his opponent. Some ugly thumps passed on both sides. In struggling for the throw, Cannon was undermost. ("Well done, Josh.!")

7.—Cannon found he had his work to do, although his adversary was so fat and out of condition. Josh. stopped his attempts; but Cannon bored in and nobbed Hudson. The latter in turn administered pepper; however, in closing, the strength of the bargeman gave him the best of it. He fibbed Hudson, got him across the ropes, and punished him down. ("Foul, foul!" "Fair, fair!")

8.—This was a fighting round altogether; but if Josh. put in a heavy blow Cannon planted two for it. The John Bull boxer was punished terribly till down. Twelve minutes and a half.

9.—In this early stage of the fight the backers of Hudson saw, with tears in their ogles, that the chance was against him, therefore they now had only his game to stand upon. In closing, both down.

10.—In all the previous battles of Hudson he was never so roughly handled before, without returning the compliment. Josh. now felt that his own weight was too much for his legs, and he staggered about and missed two well-intended nobbers. Cannon, in a most determined and clever style, floored the John Bull Fighter like a shot. This blow operated like the shock of an earth-quake upon the nerves of the backers of Josh.; their peepers seemed too big for their heads, and they stared like stuck pigs. (The odds were dropped, and Cannon decidedly the favourite.)

11.—Hudson had not strength enough to follow up his wishes; indeed, it was Sir John Falstaff in trouble. "Go it, my Joshy; it's all your own." "You can lick twenty countrymen yet." "When you say 'No,' it will be a fine treat for Cannon;" and a thousand other things were uttered to in-spire the John Bull Fighter with new ardour for conquest. But Josh. seemed to have lost all his chaffing—the customer before him was rather too serious for a joke, and his time was too much occupied to attempt to be funny. Hudson, full of pluck, endea-voured resolutely to take the lead, and cer-tainly was mischievous; but the bargeman was too good: he had the best of it, and threw Josh. across the ropes.

12.—This round was unimportant. Can-non slipped, and fell down while attempting to plant a hit. ("He's getting weak, Josh.; Cannon will soon cut it." "Walker," re-plied Tom Cribb. "Cut it, indeed; why, he's won it. But never mind; go on, and you'll soon find it out.")

13.—This was a bang-up round on both sides, and Cannon full of mischief. A ter-rible rally; no favours asked; hit for hit given, till Hudson was almost abroad. In this rally Josh. put in a tremendous facer, that for an instant Cannon seemed almost at a stand-still, and in a state of stupor. He, however, recovered, and got Hudson down. The Windsor folks were now all happiness, laughing at the poor Cockneys and the knowing ones. During the time Cannon was on the ground he also showed great distress; and if Hudson had possessed any-thing like his strength in former battles, he might have gone in now with a great chance of winning. But poor Josh., on leav-ing the knee of his second, was twice as much exhausted as Cannon; the chance and betting was now six to four against him.

14.—Nothing else but hammering on both sides. Hudson tried the pepper-box, but the Cayenne was wanting. Josh. retreated from wisty-castors, but Cannon would not be denied. Hudson received a tremendous nobber that made his peepers roll again, and the upper works of Master Cannon were a little disordered. In closing, Hudson got his nob through the ropes, and in this un-fortunate situation Cannon played upon it as on a drum till he was tired, and then let him down in a state of distress truly piteous.

15.—The exhausted state of Josh. at this period beggared description. A gasp of breath seemed worth "a hundred" to him, so dreadfully was he distressed. He was like a man almost suffocated with asthma. Yet, anxious for victory, in opposition to the powerful effects of nature against his mind, he came to the scratch full of pluck. Can-non determined to turn everything to good account, again put Josh. on the bustle. He closed with the John Bull Fighter, and fibbed him down till nearly all the wind in his body had deserted him. (Two to one on Cannon.)

16. — The bargeman had taken several good doses, and was a little sickish; but, nevertheless, he was the best man now—a guinea to a shilling. Hudson's bottom was good to the end of the chapter; but it might be urged he was fighting for breath as well as for glory. It was impossible he could win: he was almost choked with fat. The bargeman planted a nobber that made the John Bull boxer quite abroad; fibbed him till he was tired, and finally floored Josh. with the utmost ease. The bargemen, the yokels, and the Windsor folk united in one general shout for Cannon, and offered any odds. It was Windsor Castle, the Great Park, and all the deer in the bargain, to a potato patch against Hudson, and no chance to win.

17 and last.—The exit of the John Bull boxer from the ropes was at hand. He was brought up to the scratch with great diffi-culty. Hudson still showed fight, but it was little more than putting up his hands. Can-non, very unlike a novice, saw there was no time to lose; he rushed in and administered pepper, then, with a tremendous blow on the side of the head, he floored his opponent. Oliver and Randall picked up Josh., but he was nearly insensible, and when time was called he could not come to the scratch. Some little demur took place, and also some time elapsed in debate between the umpires on the subject; but Spring being appealed to as a referee, decided that Cannon was the conqueror. The bargeman left the ring amidst the shouts of the populace, and was driven off the ground in the barouche of his patron, with the colours flying, etc.

REMARKS.—

"Can such things be,
And overcome us like a summer's cloud,
Without our special wonder?"

The John Bull Fighter defeated by an "out-side" boxer in twenty minutes and a half.

Tell it not in the West! Hear it not in the East! How are the mighty fallen! How will the yokels triumph! and how will the Cockneys get rid of their grief? It is a severe lesson for the John Bull Fighter. Want of condition was the ruin of Broughton. We trust it will not prove the overthrow of Joshua, and hope he will be remembered for what he has done, and have another shy to recover his lost laurel. In the above battle the only thing sound in the John Bull Fighter was his heart; and with all the dilapidating powers of Messrs. Sherry, Black Strap, and Co., added to their immense partnerships and overflowing capital of eau-de-vie, daffy, ginger-beer, heavy-wet, etc., they had not subdued that invaluable article, the heart of the brave but fallen Joshua Hudson. But it should seem that his friends, instead of training the John Bull of the P.R., rather adopted the mode pursued by the members of the Agricultural Society, in fattening prize animals for the Smithfield Show. We were told Hudson had nothing to fight against—a mere novice, a muff, a yokel; in fact, anything but a milling cove. Under this mistaken notion, the heart of Josh. intimated to him it was no matter if he was as big and as full of turtle-soup as an alderman, or possessed the rotundity of abdomen of a Falstaff. He had only to peel in the ring, show his laughing, jolly face, fight a few rounds to put the polish on his adversary, and the battle was his own. Josh. trusted alone to his heart, and if that only had been wanted, his out-and-out true courage doubtless would have brought him through the piece. If the truth can be ascertained, we verily believe he weighed nearly, if not quite, fifteen stone. He is almost twice as big at the present period as at the time he commenced fighting in 1816. It is true, Josh. cannot be compared to, or called a second Daniel Lambert; but it will not be disputed that he bears a great resemblance to George Colman's "Two Single Gentlemen rolled into One." In a word, want of condition prevented him from having a chance of winning the battle; but it is the opinion of many judges of prize fighting that Cannon is too good a man for Josh. under any circumstances. This opinion, of course, remains to be decided. After the first round, it appeared to us that all his former gaiety of manner had left him; and towards the conclusion of the battle he hit completely round, scarcely knowing what he was about, and quite abroad. His fine courage never deserted him, and nature kept up the desire for glory to the last effort. In the ring Hudson did all that a man could perform. His backers have no right to find fault with him for being beaten, however they may feel disposed to quarrel with him for his neglect of training. Josh. was severely punished about the head: but all the milling he received in the battle was a trifle light as air compared to the punishment of his mind. The "Popper," in reality, proved himself a Cannon, produced a loud report, went off well, hit numbers of persons much harder than they expected, and left the field of battle with the proud title of conqueror affixed to it. No man has been more mistaken in being termed "a novice" than Cannon: his conduct in the ring rather showed him master of the ground than otherwise, and he never let a chance escape him. He will prove an ugly customer for any antagonist. Cannon hits out, and hard too, with his left hand, not inferior to Josh. Hudson. The bargeman ought rather to be praised for his courage and his ambition, as things have turned out, than sneered at for his presumption. Cannon selected Hudson as an opponent, notwithstanding the high-sounding pretensions of the latter, and the great fame he had acquired in the milling circles, as a boxer worthy of his attack. In obtaining the victory, his judgment has proved to be correct. It is worthy of remark, that during the time of the battle between Ward and Hudson, Cannon loudly observed, "If they call this fighting, I think I can lick both of them." And again, when in training at Virginia Water, he met with Langan, to whom he said, "I wish you was as sure of winning your fight as I am of beating Josh. Hudson." Cannon is much indebted to his worthy patron, Mr. Hayne, for the high condition in which he entered the ring, and also for some valuable tuition. The veteran Bill Richmond, we believe, endeavoured to put Cannon awake to the movements of the ring; and White-headed Bob, who had him under his care while training, tried to make the bargeman "fly." It is said Cannon's ambition is gratified, and that he does not intend again to appear in the P.R.

We may here note that the same week that witnessed the downfal of Josh. Hudson saw the defeat of Barney Aaron by Arthur Matthewson, of Birmingham, and of Phil. Sampson, beaten by Jem Ward, a remarkable series of miscalculations by the knowing ones.

Hudson met Cannon in the spectators' part of the Fives Court, at Richmond's benefit (June 29, 1824), when he told the Windsor hero he would fight him in three months for £200 a-side. Cannon replied, "His master had said he should not fight under £500; but for himself, he should not mind fighting Josh. for any sum." In consequence of this conversation, the following letter appeared in *Pierce Egan's Life in London.*

"SIR,—

"In answer to Mr. Hudson's letter, inserted in your valuable paper of Sunday last, I have only to observe that my patron and backer, Mr. Hayne, will not allow me to fight under £500 a-side.

"I cannot conceive how Mr. Hudson should be at a loss to make good his stakes. Surely, after the chaffing of Mr. Randall at the Fives Court, where he volunteered to come forward to the tune of £300, and the calls Mr. Hudson intends making in the northern, southern, eastern, and western parts of the kingdom, there will be little difficulty (with the fifty my backer presents to him) in his making up his money.

"Mr. Hudson expressed a wish that I should name a day and place to make a deposit for the mill; I therefore name Mr. Cribb's, in Panton Street, on Tuesday, the 17th of this month, when I shall be armed with the ready to any amount that may accommodate Mr. Hudson.

"I beg to take this opportunity of assuring the sporting world that, should I enter the lists again with Mr. Hudson (and which I heartily desire may be the case), that it will be my last turn-up in the prize ring.

"I have to apologize for taking up so much of your valuable paper, but feeling it essentially necessary that something like a decisive and perfectly understood answer should be given to Mr. Hudson and the fancy, I have trespassed thus far.

"And am, sir, your obedient humble servant,

"THOMAS CANNON.

"*August* 4, 1824."

The sporting world at the east end of the town were so confident as to the success of the "John Bull Fighter," in his second contest with Cannon, that, in addition to the liberal gift of £50 by Mr. Hayne, they made up the remaining £450 without delay, and the battle was fixed for Tuesday, November 23, 1824. It was proposed by Mr. Hayne that the men should fight on a stage, a proposal induced by the fact that in the former fight some friends of Josh. had cut the ropes when they found the fates were adverse to their pet, and had attempted to create a disturbance and wrangle. The proposition was at once acceded to by the real backers of Hudson, who had not been parties to the misconduct of his admirers; and it was stipulated in the articles that the battle should come off on a stage, similar to that on which Spring and Langan fought at Chichester. Matters having been thus amicably arranged, Josh. went into close training, determined to do all that could be done to get himself into fitting condition to justify the confidence that had been placed in him. Cannon, who, from following the calling of a bargee at Windsor, had been elevated to the dignity of gamekeeper to Mr. Hayne, also took immense pains with himself. Josh. had to reduce himself to the extent of about twenty pounds, and this task he manfully accomplished, and his weight on the day of battle was exactly thirteen stone ten pounds. His condition was such that his friends backed him in some cases at five to four, and commonly at guineas to pounds. Cannon, like his antagonist, was also in prime twig: he had not a superfluous ounce of flesh, and his weight was thirteen stone one pound.

The nomination of the place of fighting was left to Mr. Jackson, who received applications from sundry places to bring the mill to certain districts. Among other towns, Andover, Peterborough, and Warwick were liberal in their offers of reward to the men. At length the advantages appeared in favour of Warwick, and thither accordingly Mr. Jackson ordered that the men should proceed. The race-course was, as in the case of Spring and Langan at Worcester, preferred as the scene of action, and an agent was sent down from London, who, in conjunction with the clerk of the course and a committee of gentlemen, made the requisite arrangements.

As it was expected that Barney Aaron and Dick Curtis were to fight on the same stage as the big ones—although in the end this battle did not take place—of course the spectacle was doubly attractive, and the attendance proportionably great. For admission to the grand stand the charge was 10s., while to the different wagons round the outer ring the figure varied from 2s. 6d. to 5s. The proceeds of the standings in wagons were divided equally between the boxers and the ring constables. The regulations for preserving order were first-rate, as, in addition to the knights of the mawley themselves, there were twenty-five regular constables with their staves of office to assist. The men arrived on the ground about half-past twelve o'clock, and shortly afterwards mounted the stage; Josh. attended by Peter Crawley and Phil. Sampson, and Cannon waited upon by Tom Spring and Tom Cribb. Mr. Woodward was chosen umpire for Josh., and Captain Radford for Cannon, and these two gentlemen nominated "the squire," Osbaldeston, of racing and hunting renown, to be referee. These were the days when the patronage of sporting men raised the character of the assemblages at the ring-side. Mr. Jackson, to fill up the interval of expectancy, called upon Jem Ward to show his arm to the amateurs. That boxer did so, and an eminent surgeon of the vicinity pronounced its symmetry to excel any arm he had ever seen. Tom Oliver also stripped, and Mr. Jackson placed him in various attitudes to exhibit the action and beauty of the muscles of the trunk and arms. The arms of "White-headed Bob" (Ned Baldwin) and of Phil. Sampson were shown, and declared to be studies for the sculptor and modeller of the highest interest. On stripping, Cannon was obviously in the better condition. His flesh was hard as ivory, and as clear and bright. Josh. looked perfectly well, but it was evident he might have spared a few more pounds with advantage. He was, nevertheless, as we have said, the favourite at five to four. We have preferred the report of *Bell's Life* to the rhapsodical farrago of "Boxiana," as more practical, actual, and life-like.

THE FIGHT.

Round 1.—The men threw themselves into position; Josh. with a sort of rolling guard, Cannon with his fists straight before him. Each eyed the other with a determined regard, and the brows of both portended mischief.

"With daddles high uprais'd, and nob held
 back,
 With awful prescience of th' impending
 thwack,
 Both kiddies stood, and with prelusive
 spar
 And light manoeuvring, kindled up the
 war."

Cannon was clearly resolved to lose no time; he advanced towards Josh. Josh. retreated, to draw his man; but Cannon was not to be out-generalled: he was steady, and followed his enemy. He at last hit out with his right, and caught Josh. on the sneezer. Josh. countered, but did not make much impression. Cannon then fought with his left, and a bustling rally followed, in which there were some straight and forcible returns. Josh. found it was no joke, and having been followed to the rails, he turned round quickly and met his man in another direction. Cannon followed him, and caught him again on the snout, drawing first blood. Josh., nothing abashed, met his antagonist manfully, and some desperate, but not scientific hitting followed. At last Josh. went in for the close, and after a slight struggle both fell, Cannon under. It was again proved that Cannon was no *petit maitre*, and Josh.'s sconce exhibited woful marks of his meaning. Cannon, too, had a mark under his left eye.

2.—The men came up with courage, but Cannon appeared most collected. Little time was lost in sparring. Josh. broke ground with his right, tipped Cannon on the left eye and got away. Cannon followed him, and returned the compliment, when a heavy tussle again took place, smack for smack, and no attempt at stopping. It was regular took-mill hammering, and all head-fighting. Cannon was still busy with his man, and, in closing, a sharp tussle followed, in which both were down, Josh. under.

3.—Josh., on coming to the scratch, was observed to pipe, although not much distressed. He did not wait to gain breath, however, but rattled in manfully to

"Seek the bubble reputation,
 E'en in the Cannon's mouth;"

and placed a tremendous hit on the Great Gun's eye, which drew his cork and produced a general cheer from the Joshuaites. Cannon took it kindly, and rushed forward with alacrity; he hit Josh. on the potato trap, which drew forth another purple stream. This led to an unsparing rally, in which both men gave and took with astonishing fortitude. Josh., in this tussle, again received heavily on the mussle, and was about to return, when Cannon, from the slippery state of the boards, fell on his knees.

4.—Both came up in true John Bull style, Cannon preserving his original straight-forward guard, and Josh. working for an opening. He got it, and caught Cannon on the nob. Cannon took without flinching, and returned with activity. It was a fine specimen of unshrinking courage on both sides, and slashing hits succeeded each other, right and left. In the end, Cannon slipped down, while Josh. stood firmly on his legs. Some thought this was a knock-down blow, but the fall was attributable only to the wetness of the stage. Josh. was loudly cheered by his friends.

5.—Cannon was first on his legs when time was called, but in rising showed the punishing effects of the last round; still he was fresher than Josh., and commenced his handiwork, and as he scorned to stop, Josh. countered terrifically on his right ogle. Another desperate interchange took place, till the men closed. After a vigorous wrestle, Cannon threw his man close to the rails. Poor Josh. fell on his face, and the crimson spurted from his mouth.

6.—Many thought it was all up with Josh. in the last round; but his seconds were on the alert, screwed his nob to the right bearing, and he again came up with undiminished courage, although a very ugly study for an artist. He rushed to his man with true game, and in his characteristic style planted a heavy blow on Cannon's left cheek, close to the eye, on which he inflicted a cut, and nearly shut up that shop. Cannon was again active, and followed his man to the stakes, when a rally followed, and ultimately Josh. went down on his hands and knees. Both were weak.

7.—Both men on reaching the scratch were distressed, but Josh.'s bellows went the fastest. Josh. retreated, and was closely followed; he, however, hit straight from his shoulder, and made his mark; but Cannon, nothing behind, returned the compliment with a terrific sneezer. A grapple followed, and Josh. was severely hit, and fell heavily.

8.—It was now manifest to all that Cannon was the strongest man and in the best condition, and the backers of Josh. began to take an affectionate farewell of their blunt: in fact, the good judges thought Josh. had no chance. On coming to the assault, however, both men were groggy, and although they interchanged blows, the effect was not very apparent. A gentle tap on Cannon's old sore assisted in completing that part of the mark, and the eye was completely closed. Cannon now bored in with undeniable spirit, and a struggle took place for the fall. Josh. had the advantage, and threw Cannon, but afterwards rolled over him. The fall was not of an effective character.

9.—Cannon came up fresher than Josh., and mutual blows were given, neither shrinking from their weight. It was all tussle and punishment. Cannon at last slipped down, and it was still thought probable that Josh. might come round and win.

10.—Both came up dreadfully punished, Cannon's remaining ogle getting the worse for wear, and Josh. distilling the Burgundy in half a dozen directions. Again did the men show their unshaken fortitude: there was no retreating, but milling in the first style. At last they came to a stand-still, and their blows were as powerless as if they wore the gloves. In the close both went down, Cannon under.

11.—Cannon's left cheek, on coming to the scratch, was bleeding, but still he was first to the call, and again showed his superiority of condition by his active readiness. He rushed in to fight, but was met boldly by Josh., and interchanges followed. Cannon, in getting away, slipped on his crupper a third time: his shoes were without spikes or nails, which rendered this accident more frequent.

12.—Both came up steady, but Josh. was "piping all hands." A longer spar, or rather stand-still, took place in this round, before commencing, than had occurred during the fight. At last Cannon let fly with his right on Josh.'s canister, and Josh. returned heavily on his smeller. ("Well done, Josh.") Bustle followed—tap and tap—when Cannon once more slipped down.

13.—Sparring for breath. Josh. on the retreat. At length Cannon delivered an ugly compliment with his left on Josh.'s mug. Josh. returned, and they both fought to the stakes. They here showed their resolution and their disinclination to "take it easy;" and at length Cannon slipped down. Both were dreadfully punished, but Josh.'s physog. exhibited the strongest marks of seasoning—it was peppered all over.

14.—Cannon hit Josh. with his left, and Josh. countered with his right. In a rally, Cannon hit and slipped, but brought up before he reached the boards, and rushing again to his man with thorough game, evidently showed his heart to be in the right place. Good milling followed, and both went down distressed. Nothing could equal the goodness of Josh.'s nature, but he was

evidently on the wane. Both men, in fact, hit till there was not a hit left, and in this round Josh.'s head came heavily in contact with one of the side stakes. (The odds were now two and three to one on Cannon, but there was not much betting.)

15.—Josh. had clearly booked himself for a suit in chancery; but Sampson exclaimed that he was better on coming to the mark. Both were anxious for the affray, and, rushing in, they struggled to the stakes, where several hits were exchanged; but neither of the men were capable of doing execution. They embraced, not very lovingly, and struggled hard for the fall. Josh. got it, and fell on his man, but the exertion did him more harm than good, and Cannon was not much hurt.

16 and last.—The men fought to the stakes, and here they hit at each other, change for change, like smiths at an anvil, but they were both powerless in their blows. Josh., however, was evidently in the worst state, and was reduced to a complete doldrum. At last they broke from the stakes, and Cannon, grappling his man, threw him a tremendous fall, dropping on him as he fell. It was now all UP. Josh.'s head had come in contact with the boards, and his frame was shaken to a stand-still. Sampson picked him up, and did all he could to awaken him to time. It was in vain, however: his time for fighting had ceased, and he could come no more. Cannon did not seem conscious that it was all over, and advanced to the scratch. Spring, however, threw up his hat, and a general shout announced the termination of the contest, in a few seconds under twenty minutes. Cannon had some heavy bets on himself, and has cleared upwards of £1,000 by his exertions, which will tile him for the rest of his life. All the knowing ones were floored: they made certain of Josh.'s success, and backed him in large sums. The East-enders were dreadfully chop-fallen at this second disappointment of their hopes, and downfal to their pride. Little was said, but the elongation of faces and shrugging of shoulders afforded sufficient evidence of what was felt.

REMARKS.—With regard to the character of this fight little is to be said beyond an unqualified eulogium on the bravery of both the men. In the first round it was clear that Cannon was the best man, and that his confidence in himself had not been misplaced. Neither of them showed science: it was, in the true sense of the word, a John Bull affair, in which giving and taking was the only study. He who could give and take most proved to be the best man. Praise is equally due to the one and to the other; and we consider that Cannon's success is attributable solely to his superior condition. Josh. could not bear to be reduced beyond a certain point; and by his training at this late season of the year, whatever might be his appearance at first sight, he had evidently weakened his constitution. Cannon is not a showy fighter, but he holds his hands up well before him, and in a rally he is always doing a little. He was heavily punished, and was removed in the carriage of his backer to the Regent Hotel, Leaming-ton, and under the medical care of Mr. Jeffson he recovered from his injuries in a shorter time than could have been expected. Hudson was taken to the Castle Inn, Warwick, and put to bed.

On November 29, 1824, Cannon left London with £750 of his winnings, with the intention of opening a tavern at Windsor, with Mrs. Cannon.

Early in 1825 (February 15), in compliance with a desire of the amateurs, Tom Cannon gave a sparring exhibition at the Fives Court, in which Josh. and himself fought their battle of Warwick over again with the mufflers. Josh. was pronounced, despite his fat, to have the best of the "science," but the activity was with Cannon. "Bravo, Josh.!" at each hit or stop, resounded from all parts of the Court at each manœuvre of the old favourite. The bills and advertisements were headed "Tom Cannon, the Champion of England," and a challenge for £1,000 was given to any disputant of his title. The door-money was over £100, exclusive of the sale of private tickets.

Cannon now went on a tour, after winning a foot-race of 200 yards with "Squire Smith," at Shepperton, for a stake of £20 a-side, February 19, 1825, in handsome style. In the following month we find him at Brighton, with his patron, Mr. Hayne, where matches at billiards and wrestling had been made by Mr. Hayne with a well-known Irish adventurer, Mr. Carney. At billiards Mr. Hayne had chosen the celebrated Jonathan (Kentfield) as his representative. It would appear that Mr. Carney caught Mr. Hayne "upon the bustle" early one morning, and backed himself for 100 guineas, p. p., 100 up, Mr. Hayne to find a player who should give him (Carney) 70 points! and this without consulting Jonathan on the matter. At the same time Mr. Hayne backed Cannon to wrestle with Mr. Carney, "collar and elbow," for £50 a-side, "best of three falls." Jonathan, winning the toss, named his own table in Manchester Street, for the trial of skill. There was a great muster of sporting men on Thursday, March 24, 1825, and ten to one was betted that Mr. Hayne would forfeit. There was little betting on the play, as it was the general opinion that the odds were preposterously great. Cannon offered £20 to £15 that Carney won. The affair was over in eighteen minutes, Carney winning straight "off the balls," so soon as he got the cue in hand. Carney played with judgment and coolness, and won the match with credit to himself. He declined another match with forty given. With regard to the wrestling, the following placard was posted in Brighton:

"Ireland's Royal Grounds will be a scene of great attraction this day (Thursday). A wrestling match, for a heavy stake, will take place between

Cannon from Windsor (the celebrated pugilist) and a sporting gentleman amateur from Ireland, at two o'clock; the best of three falls. In addition to which, the art of self-defence will be exhibited by White-headed Bob and Gaynor, with other gymnastic sports. Price of admission, 2s. The large room will be appropriated entirely for the ladies who may honour the above manly exhibition with their presence. Every attention will be paid to render the amusements highly interesting to the visitors."

The crowd at " Ireland's Ground" was immense, and there was no end of wrangle as to the true definition of " collar and elbow," the Carney division determining to have " the pull" on their side, if possible. Then arose the question as to whether the game allowed the elegant and humane practice of kicking each other's shins. Mister Carney had come with his legs swathed in woollen list; but at last Cannon took off his boots, Carney divested himself of his bandages and heavy shoes, and it was finally settled that the umpires should place the hands of the wrestlers on each other's shoulders and elbows, and leave them. Cannon was dressed in a new jacket and breeches, without any handkerchief on his neck. Carney wore an old blue dress coat and light pantaloons; his fine figure was much admired. We remember him well about town, in his fatter and latter days, when he was a constant frequenter of " Silver Hell," near Leicester Square, and perpetually engaged in legal or personal war with the notorious Barnard Gregory and the *Satirist* newspaper; his six feet of height, and fifteen or sixteen stone of weight, still marking him as an opponent one would rather let alone than challenge.

There was little in the match to call for description. Cannon declared he did not understand the style of wrestling. After a short struggle, Carney succeeded in tripping his man, and bringing him almost sideways to the ground. Cannon denied it was a " back-fall." The umpires disagreed, but the referee gave it to Carney. £10 to £5, and then £30 to £10, were offered on Carney. After some play the men were down in a scrambling fall; Cannon was on his knees, and Carney fell over him. This was declared " No fall." The third and deciding bout was more spirited. Cannon tried to show off, but Carney, with great activity, " heeled" his man so cleverly, that down went " the Great Gun" clean on his back. Cannon jumped up, and with the utmost good humour exclaimed that he had lost the match. He repeated that " he didn't understand the game." The whole was over in eight minutes.

White-headed Bob and Gaynor next made their bows, and set-to. The talents of the " White-nobbed One" gave him the best of it, although Gaynor exerted himself to give satisfaction. It was expected Cannon would have had a turn with Baldwin; but "the Great Gun" immediately set off for the metropolis. Five-and-twenty pounds were collected at the doors, which were distributed among the candidates for fame, Mr. Ireland reserving one-fifth for the use of his grounds. Mr. Carney, however, generously made the host a present of his share.

Cannon's pretensions to the championship were not allowed to remain unchallenged. Jem Ward put in his claim, and, as already recorded,* on July 19, 1825, at Warwick, Cannon was defeated, in ten rounds, occupying ten minutes only. The heat of the weather was so intense that several persons fainted and were carried from the ground. Cannon stood £200 of his own money, and £200 in his backer's bets. During the dispute at Tattersall's about the stakes, Tom publicly said, that as £200 of the battle-money belonged to him, *that* should be given to Ward, whatever might be done with the rest. He added, that he should like another trial with Ward, but that he had lost all his spare cash.

In August, 1825, Tom Cannon and Peter Crawley "starred" it at the Coburg (now the Victoria) Theatre in a piece called "The fight at War-wick," which, we are told, was attractive and lucrative to the management.†

Cannon's next match was with Ned Neale (see Life of NEALE, *post*), the Streatham Youth, which was decided in an enclosure at Warfield, Berks, February 20, 1827. Neale proved the winner in thirty minutes, after twenty-two hard-fought rounds. The odds were at one time in Tom's favour, who attributed his defeat to a severe hurt in the shoulder from a heavy fall.

This was Cannon's last public appearance as principal within the ropes. In November, 1827, Tom seconded Jem Burn in his second fight with Ned Neale, on the same ground at Warfield. The day was wretchedly damp and wintry, and Cannon caught so severe a cold that he was laid up with lum-bago, and for several months was a cripple. Cannon still found a friend in

---

* See Life of JEM WARD, pp. 211-215, *ante*.
† The following we find in the *Weekly Dispatch* of the Sunday which announces Tom's engagement :—

> "So the nobs at the Coburg (forgive me the pun)
> Are about to let off, for six nights, a Great Gun :
> Tom Cannon, whose backer his prowess esponses,
> Is form'd to draw claret, and may draw great houses ;
> May he make a good 'hit,' for the managers' sake,
> If they're liberal in 'giving,' Tom doubtless will 'take.'
> But, jesting apart, may the town aid their plan,
> Nor the whole turn out merely a flash in the pan.
>   "TIMOTHY TRIGGER,
> "Gun Tavern,"

Mr. Hayne. Though that gentleman had retired from "the turf and ring," he placed him in the Castle, in Jermyn Street, St. James's. Here, through his civility and attention, he was well supported for a time; but Tom's friends wore off, and new ones came not. His health, too, was precarious, and he retired from business, not upon a competency, we regret to say. For nearly eighteen years Tom disappeared from an active part in ring affairs, and resided at Strand-on-the-Green, in the capacity of a swan-watcher for the Corporation. Severe attacks of the gout and rheumatism disqualifying him from all exertion, he fell into a state of hypochondria, and on Sunday, the 11th of July, 1858, terminated his existence by suicide with a pistol, in the sixty-ninth year of his age, leaving a constant and attentive widow in narrow circumstances to lament his loss. Jem Burn and some other friends of the old school kindly strove to alleviate her forlorn condition.

CHAPTER IV.

JOSH. HUDSON, "THE JOHN BULL FIGHTER."
1816--1826.

AMONG the names which a pugilistic Plutarch might find difficult to parallel for lion-hearted, fearless, and indomitable pluck, that of Josh. Hudson may be fairly cited. "The John Bull Fighter," as his friends and admirers at the East-end fondly called him, fought his way into the battle of life at Rotherhithe, on the 21st of April, 1797. Although fond of a mill from his youth upwards, the juvenile John Bull earned the character of a thorough good-natured fellow, and this he preserved through life. There was no ferocity in Josh.'s composition, though once aroused in the fight his hitting was truly terrific, and his gameness in receiving as remarkable as his readiness in refusing to take an advantage of his adversary. Josh. was by no means an uninformed man, and, barring a propensity for practical jokes—a common thing in his day—remarkably inoffensive.

Josh.'s first reported contest was with Jack Payne, the butcher, at Dartford Brim, October 22, 1816, for ten guineas a-side. Jack, when he pleased, could fight well, but he was thought, not without reason, to lose pluck whenever he had not the "lead" in his hands. He soon found he had "caught a Tartar" in young Josh., for in thirty-five minutes he cried "enough!"

Our hero now flew at higher game, and challenged Aby Belasco. After a determined battle of one hour and thirty minutes the affair ended in a wrangle; Clark and Peter Warren, who seconded Josh., taking their man away. Belasco, however, got the stakes.

Hudson's next battle was with Street, April 5, 1817, which he won in one hour and ten minutes. In "Boxiana," vol. ii., p. 477, "Street" is called "Connelly." It was David, Josh.'s brother, who fought and beat Connelly. Tom Oliver and Clark seconded Josh. in this battle.

His next match was with Charles Martin, at Sawbridgeworth, for a stake of twenty guineas, June 10, 1817. Richmond and Harry Holt seconded Josh., who won cleverly in thirty minutes.

Thompson, an Essex coachman, and rather fast with his fists, fancied Josh. for a "tenner," and challenged him within six weeks of the last-named battle. They fought at Woolwich, July 17, 1817, when, in twenty-five minutes, Thompson dropped his whip and declined any further proceedings.

Josh. having in a spree "milled the wrong person," was bound over by keep the magistrates to keep the peace for twelve months. He determined to cut of the way of mischief for that period, so engaged himself as butcher on board the Surat Castle, Indiaman. Pierce Egan embellishes this voyage with fights with nobodies, to fill up the story of Josh.'s sea life. On his return, Hudson accepted the challenge of a formidable Chatham caulker, of the name of Bowen. This rough and ready customer stood six feet two inches in his stockings, and weighed thirteen stone and a half without an ounce of superfluous flesh; while Josh. drew ten stone seven pounds at scale. The battle was truly desperate; but in seventeen minutes Josh. was knocked out of time. This occurred on March 25, 1819.

Josh. lost no time in emerging from the cold shade of defeat, and on Tuesday, April 17, 1819, a month after the last event, he entered the ropes with Williams, the waterman, for ten guineas a-side, in Essex, opposite to Woolwich Warren. There were 5,000 persons present, say the reports at the time. Hudson was the favourite at five to four. At thirteen minutes past one Tom Owen and Donnelly conducted Josh. into the ring, followed by Williams, who was seconded by Tom Oliver and Harry Holt. The first three rounds were full of manœuvring, and decidedly in favour of the water-man; but when Josh. came to force the fighting, the scene was quickly changed. The waterman, however, proved a truly game man: he was terribly punished before the sponge was thrown up; and Josh., too, had napped it heavily. It was on both sides a manly fight, and Josh. was prophesied by Tom Owen—who dubbed him "his boy"—as likely to take a top place among the boxers of England.

On the 24th of August, 1819, at the renowned battle-field of Moulsey, after Cy. Davis had beaten Boshell, a purse of 25 guineas was made up on the ground, and Jack Scroggins (JOHN PALMER, see his life in vol. i.) agreed to fight Josh. Hudson for the amount. Tom Owen and Sutton esquired Hudson, Harry Harmer and Tom Shelton picked up "Scroggy." Scroggins hesitated, saying, he had been drinking overnight, and was in bad condition: but, added the daring little sailor, "Here goes—I'll have a shy for it." The fight requires but little description; Scroggins rushed headlong at his

JOSHUA HUDSON.

From a Miniature by T. Cooper.

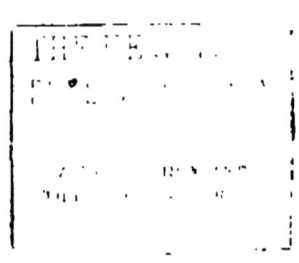

opponent, scrambling for a hit, and often losing his balance. Josh., on the contrary, was steady, and nobbed the once formidable hero with stupefying effect. When Scroggins fell at the close of round one, two to one was offered on Josh., and soon after three to one was without takers. At the end of the sixth round Tom Owen exclaimed, "It's your own, Josh., my boy; you don't want any seconding. Meet him as he comes in—one more like that, and the 'pence' you shall have." In the eleventh and last round Scroggins over-reached himself, and came down on his knees, when Josh. caught him a stinger on the side of the head. "Foul, foul!" "Fair, fair!" echoed from all sides of the ring, for the rough and ready "merry-andrew of the ring" had many friends. The umpires decided the blow to be unintentional, and ordered them to "go on." Scroggins refused, declaring he "was not used fair." The purse was then awarded to Hudson. Scroggins, during the first few rounds was as full of antics as a clown in a pantomime, but soon became convinced that he was getting the worst of it, and broke off with an attempt to "snatch a verdict." About this period Phil. Sampson, the Birmingham Youth, who had, as will be seen by his biography, a talent for quarrelling with his friends, fell out, Phil., *more suo*, talking about "serving out" Josh. at the first opportunity. Hence, after Ned Turner and Martin had left the ring (see Life of TURNER, vol. i.), on the 26th of October, 1819, at Walling-ham Common, Surrey, ten guineas a-side having been posted, and a ten guinea purse subscribed by the P. C., Sampson intimated his readiness to meet Josh., and the John Bull Fighter stepped into the ring with alacrity. Tom Owen and Purcell waited upon Hudson; Shelton and Harmer seconded the Birmingham Youth. On stripping, Owen said to Josh., "Now, my boy, remember the *multum in parvo*." "Is that a new hit?" asked Josh. laugh-ing. "No, my boy," replied Tom; "it's Latin for doing a lot of work in a little time." "I'm awake," replied Josh.; "he won't catch me napping." The men stood up, and the seconds having retired to their corners, they began—

THE FIGHT.

Round 1.—Scarcely had the combatants shaken hands than it appeared that they had no intention to protract hostilities. Sampson dashed in at Josh. and planted a tremendous teaser flush in his ivories. Josh. returned, and some rattling exchanges fol-lowed, Sampson literally nobbing Hudson till he reeled staggering away; but he re-turned to the attack like a bull-dog, and went on weaving away till he was hit down. (Tumultuous applause for Sampson, and the two to one offered on Hudson no longer heard. "I'll bet six to four, and have Sampson," cried a Corinthian amateur.)

2.—Sampson again led off, and nobbed Josh. three times on the head. Josh. re-turned, and caught Phil. heavily on the ribs and side of the head. The men got into a ding-dong rally, right and left, in which unshrinking courage was displayed on both sides. The round closed by both being down side by side covered with claret.

Twenty-five rounds ensued, occupying forty minutes, all of which were distinguished for tremendous fighting. Hudson received three or four flooring hits. In one instance, in the struggle, he fell with his knee on the private parts of Sampson, when the latter observed, "Is that the way you mean to win it, Josh. ?" "I couldn't help it—it was accident," replied Hudson. "Well, I believe it was," said Sampson. This small trait of feeling during the rage of battle is a fine proof of the generous courage of Englishmen. Such a good fight has not often been witnessed. At length victory was declared in favour of Hudson. It was a nice thing, and dearly bought, for Josh. fainted on his second's knee after he was proclaimed the conqueror.

Hudson, from the game and milling talents he had displayed, was next matched against Jack Martin, for 50 guineas a-side, which took place at Colnbrook, on Tuesday, December 14, 1819, when, in the second round, Hudson's shoulder was dislocated, and of course he lost the battle. (See the Life of MARTIN in vol. i.)

In the course of the evening after the battle, Hudson, in company with a friend, called at the house of Abrams (Little Puss), near the Royalty Theatre, to take a glass of liquor. One Guyly, a big costermonger, took up some money which was upon the tap-room table, belonging to Hudson, and refused to return it. The courage of Josh. made him forget the crippled state of his shoulder for the instant, and he let fly so severely upon the nob of Guyly that the saucy costermonger quickly gave back the cash. Owing to this circumstance a report got into circulation that it was untrue that Hudson's shoulder had ever been put out by Martin.

An off-hand match was made for Hudson against Rasher, a determined Welshman, a butcher belonging to Whitechapel Market. The latter boxer had the weight of Josh.; nevertheless, he fought Rasher ten guineas to eight. This contest took place at Plaistow, in Essex, on Tuesday, January 11, 1820. Hudson was seconded by Owen and his brother David; Rasher by Mendoza and Cy. Davis. It occupied twenty-nine minutes and a half, and fifteen rounds. After the first round, which was tremendously contested, Hudson had it all his own way. The science displayed by Josh. was much admired, and he made many clever feints with his left hand, to get the right well into play. Rasher was covered with claret, and his gameness astonished every one present, but he was too slow in his movements. He was floored in the last round; and on coming to himself wanted to renew the fight.

Hudson, still continuing to rise in the estimation of his friends, was backed against Benniworth, the Essex champion, the hero of the country for several miles round, for 50 guineas a-side. Benniworth was six feet in height, weighing thirteen stone twelve pounds; nevertheless, Hudson was the favourite. This contest took place on Tuesday, April 4, 1820, on a common near Billericay, in Essex. Hudson was seconded by Owen and Purcell; Benniworth was attended by his brother and another yokel.

THE FIGHT.

Round 1.—About a minute elapsed in sparring, Benniworth making numerous awkward feints, and dancing about, sometimes standing with his right leg first, then changing it for the left. He made three or four hits, but they proved short. At length Benniworth made a slight blow with his right hand on Hudson's body. Josh. seeing what sort of a customer he had before him, made play, and let fly right and left in the middle of Benniworth's nob, both of which told, and the claret flowed copiously. Benniworth's left eye was much damaged. He rushed in to his opponent, when, in getting away, Hudson's heel hung in the grass, and Benniworth made a slight half round hit on the neck with his left hand, flooring him. (Great rejoicings from the yokels.)

2.—Hudson, with much dexterity, in a sort of half-arm rally, placed three straight hits on Benniworth's nob. Josh. also drew backwards, and avoided all Benniworth's half round blows. Hudson now made himself well up, and planted a most tremendous right-handed blow on the nose of his opponent that floored him like a shot. (Any odds, but no takers, and the Johnny Raws all blue.)

Further description would be useless. Hudson had it thenceforth all his own way. He laughed at Benniworth, and nobbed him at pleasure. The Essex champion lost his temper, rushed in, and followed Hudson all over the ring, with his head leaning forward and both his hands open. Hudson kept retreating, and jobbing his adversary on the head with his left hand. Benniworth was a complete receiver-general; nevertheless, he succeeded in driving Hudson to the ropes; but here he had the worst of it, a guinea to a shilling. Josh. nobbed him terribly away; and in following him, floored him with a terrific right-handed hit on his nose. Benniworth, when "time" was called, was in such a state of stupor that he could not leave the knee of his second, whereon Hudson was declared the conqueror.

Thus was the vaunted rustic champion disposed of in the short space of seven minutes. As a scientific pugilist, Benniworth did not appear to possess a single point: he had no idea of fighting. From the moment he entered the ring Hudson kept laughing at him, and beat him without a scratch upon his face. It certainly was a laughable, but not an interesting contest; and it was matter of astonishment how such a boxer could have obtained so terrific a character. Upon the Essex champion coming to himself, he exclaimed, with great surprise, "Be I licked?" "You are, indeed," replied Josh., laughing; "but you may have a round or two for fun, if you like it, Benny." "Noa, noa," said the champion; "as I've lost the stakes, there be no fun in that loike." Benniworth, it seems, had made so sure of conquest, that he invited his mother and sister to be near at hand. The yokels had also booked it, and provided themselves with blue ribbons to decorate their hats the instant victory was declared in Benniworth's favour.

Josh. was suddenly called into action with Spring at Moulsey Hurst, on Tuesday, June 27, 1820, for a purse of £20; and, notwithstanding the disparity of size, weight, and science between the combatants, Hudson showed himself a good man. (See the Memoir of SPRING, vol. ii.)

Hudson, during the time he was at Norwich, had a battle with Abraham Belasco in the long room at Gurney's Bowling Green, July 19, 1820. In this contest, which might be termed for honour, Josh.'s shoulder went in and out three times.

Moulsey Hurst, on Tuesday, December 5, 1820, was again the favourite "bit of turf" for a genteel mill between a swell of the name of Williams and Josh. Hudson. Williams was unknown to the mass of sporting men; but those persons who knew him pretended to be acquainted with his prime fighting qualities, and chaffed all the old ring goers out of conceit of their own judgment, and Williams was the favourite, six and five to four. This sort of "whisper" importance was also kept up at friendly Bob Lawrence's, the Red Lion, at Hampton, where the fancy met to take a bit of a snack

before they crossed the water, and make their "books" complete. Richmond, downy as a hammer, spoke in raptures of the swell's superior science
with the gloves. Bill Eales, who had stood before Williams many times,
nay, who had given him instructions several years back, pronounced him "a
downright slaughterer." The Master of the Rolls was quite infatuated with
this pink of the gloves. Martin had tried him again and again, and not
having found Williams "wanting," was this day £50 the worse for his
opinion. Tom Shelton was also led away by the stream, and Spring was
taken in upon the same suit. Oliver, too, was out of his know, and out of
pocket in consequence. Cocker had nothing to do with the fight in question;
indeed, who could make any calculation about an unknown man? Randall
and Belcher, somehow or other, were persuaded into the good milling
qualities of their hero; in short, there was a sort of fashion attached to the
betting. The "Swell" was supported and brought forward by the swells.
Judgment was shoved, as it were, into the background, or else a novice in
the ring would never have been backed, at high odds, against a well-known
high-couraged man, one who had often been put to the test, and admitted to
be a boxer of talent. But then the shoulder of Hudson was ricketty; no
dependence could be placed upon it. Things went on in this manner till
about a few minutes before one o'clock, when Williams appeared and threw
his hat into the ring, followed by Belcher and Randall as his seconds. The
look of Williams was swellish in the extreme. He bowed in the most
graceful manner, and there was a superior air about him. He paced the
ring up and down for about eight minutes, when Josh., with his white
topper, a fancy upper Benjamin, and a blue bird's eye round his neck, came
brushing along and threw his castor into the ring. He immediately went up
to Williams and shook hands with him in the true open-hearted English
style. To witness the manly act, this characteristic trait of Britons, is
worth more in its influence upon society than the perusal of a thousand
canting essays tending to fritter down the courage of Englishmen. Williams
observed to Hudson, that he hoped there was no animosity between them.
"Not in the least," said he; "we are going to fight for a prize, and to see
which is the best man." Tom Owen and Ned Turner were the seconds for
Josh. The latter tied his colours (yellow) to the stakes, and Randall covered
them with the blue of Williams. Owen, who had never seen "the Swell"
till he entered the ring with "his boy" Josh., observed to the latter, "Why,
my chaff-cutter, if you don't go and lick this Bond Street blade in a jiffy,
the white topper shall never more be placed on your nob. My dear boy, the
East against the West End for milling."

THE FIGHT.

Round 1.—On stripping, Williams displayed a fine muscular frame, and good legs; but his face was pale, and his countenance showed him to be between forty and fifty years of age. Josh. was in high trim, and seemed confident of winning. Some time elapsed after the combatants had placed themselves in attitude before Williams let fly; but Hudson got away. Counter hits followed, when Josh.'s right eye showed blood, and the nose of the swell looked a little red. Williams made a right-handed hit, which Hudson stopped prettily, and then went to work. The exchanges were sharp and hard, but the wisty-castors of Josh. were so tremendous that he spoilt the gentility of the Swell, and positively milled him down. (Great applause from the plebeians; and Tom Owen smilingly said to Josh., " I told you so, my boy : that's the way to clear Regent Street in a brace of shakes." Seven to four.)

2.—Josh.'s eye was bleeding when he came up to the scratch. The Swell looked rather puzzled; but he touched Hudson's other peeper so severely that his nob was chanceried for an instant. Hudson made a plunge with his right hand upon his opponent's face that produced the claret, followed him up to the ropes, and punished him down. (Three to one, and " It's poundable," was the cry. Here Owen told Josh. he had " done the trick, and lots of Daffy were in store for him.")

3.—The confident appearance of Williams had left him; he had paid a visit, as Tom said, to " Pepper Alley." Williams showed game, but he had no chance to win. He, however, made some sharp hits; but the pepper-box was again administered, and Williams went down distressed. (Ten to one.)

4.—This round was the quietus; the Swell was hit out of the ring. It was Cayenne at every dose. Williams was completely done up, and his seconds dragged him up all but gone.

5.—Williams was brought up to the scratch in a most distressed state. He, however, showed fight, and with his right hand put in a heavy body blow : it was his last effort. Josh. now went in right and left, and punished the Swell so terribly that he staggered and fell against the ropes; but, on recovering himself a little, Tom Owen said

to Josh., " Don't give a chance away; a finisher only is wanting." The finisher was applied, and Williams was down all abroad. The swells looked blue, and Josh. received thunders of applause. (" Take him away ! " was the general cry.) Josh. in this round did not like to hit the Swell when he had got him at the ropes, feeling like the British sailor, so finely described by Dibdin—

" In me let the foe feel the paw of a lion ;
   But the battle once ended, the heart of a
     lamb ! "

6.—Williams came to the scratch in a deplorable state, and Hudson pushed him down sans ceremonie. When time was called he could not leave his second's knee.

REMARKS.—Thus, in the short space of nine minutes, Josh. defeated this much-vaunted opponent. After remaining a short time in a state of stupor, Williams came to his recollection, and asked if it was over. The flash side were completely floored in consequence, according to themselves, of their calculating upon Josh.'s shoulder giving way. The Swell showed great steadiness in the first round, which occupied upwards of three minutes; but afterwards had no chance, and found out the great difference between sparring and fighting. Instead of losing so much time in sparring in the first round, as he was clearly a stale man, he ought to have gone to work. He could hit hard, and most certainly did not want for knowledge of the science. But he was too old to take; his mind might be firm enough to endure punishment, but his frame could not stand it. At all events, he should have commenced pugilism (if he wished to obtain a high place in the prize ring) some seventeen or eighteen years earlier. Drummers and boxers, to acquire excellence, must begin young. There is a peculiar nimbleness of the wrist and pliancy of the shoulder required, that is only obtained by early practice. Youth and strength, however, are indispensable ingredients in a pugilist. The backers of Williams, i.e., those amateurs who made the match for him, had no right to complain of his conduct. There was nothing of the cur about him; on the contrary, he fought like a game man : he never said " No," and he tried to win the battle till he lost sight both of his opponent and friends.

Josh.'s combat with Ned Turner, when *Bacchi plenus*, and which ended in a defeat, will be found noticed in the life of that boxer, *ante*, vol. i.

A second match with his former antagonist, Phil. Sampson, was the next public appearance of Josh. This took place on Saturday, March 3, 1821, at Banstead Downs, Surrey. The torrents of rain did not deter hundreds from leaving the metropolis, and several aristocrats of the highest class were upon the ground.

At one o'clock the Birmingham Youth, followed by Spring and Randall, threw up his hat in the ring; and in a few minutes after, Hudson, attended by Oliver and Purcell, repeated the token of defiance. Spring and Oliver went up smiling together, and tied the colours of the combatants to the stakes.

THE FIGHT.

Round 1.—On stripping, Hudson looked extremely well, but rather too fat. Sampson was in excellent condition: both gay, confident, and eager. They had tasted plentifully of each other's quality in their former fight, and much difference of opinion existed among the spectators who had really won it. A short pause occurred, when Hudson made an offer to hit, and Sampson drew back. Another pause. Sampson endeavoured to put in right and left, which proved short, in consequence of Josh.'s getting away. After looking at each other for about a minute, Hudson went in; some sharp work took place, and in the struggle, Sampson was undermost. (Loud shouting, and "Josh., you have begun well.")

2.—The nose of the Birmingham Youth appeared rosy. Both now began to slash away, and the pepper-box was handed from one to the other, till Josh. either went down from a hit, or slipped on his knees. ("Go along, Sampson.")

3.—Hudson missed a tremendous hit at Sampson's head. The latter drew the claret from Josh.'s mug by a facer; but Josh. rushed in and exchanged hits to his own advantage, and sent his opponent down. (The shouting was now like thunder—the old fanciers dancing hornpipes, the Eastenders all in spirits, and the Bermondsey boys offering odds on their favourite, Hudson, six to four.)

4.—The Birmingham Youth took great liberties with the upper works of his opponent. The round was terrific. Both went down, Sampson undermost.

5.—"It's a good fight," was the cry all round the ring. Sampson was more than busy, and the face of Hudson was clareted. The latter, bull-dog like, did not care about receiving, so that he could go in and punish his opponent. He did so most effectively in this round, and Sampson was hit down. It is impossible to describe the joy of Hudson's friends. (Seven to four.)

6 to 9.—These were all busy rounds, and the partisans of each of the combatants claimed the best.

10.—Sampson meant nothing but mischief, and at out-fighting placed his hits, in most instances, with tremendous effect. In this round he went down from the force of his own blow.

11 and 12.—The Birmingham Youth always good for punishment in commencing the round; but Josh. finishing them all to his own advantage.

13.—Sampson in this round was, from the heavy blows he received, almost at a standstill, till both down.

14.—This was a terrible round on both sides. Hudson's mug was terrific. The men hit each other away staggering, then returned to the charge game as pebbles, till Sampson scarcely knew how he went down. ("Go along, my Joshy; it's as safe as the Bank.")

15.—Sampson was floored from a heavy blow under the listener. (The Hudsonites were uproarious, and offering any odds.)

16.—Sampson came up like a true Briton, and, after several severe exchanges, was again sent down.

17.—Hudson either could not, or did not attempt to, protect his head, and Sampson hit him down. ("Bravo, Sampson! do so again, and you can't lose it," from his friends; "you behave like a good one.")

18.—If Josh. had not been an out-and-out bottom man, from the repeated tremendous facers he received, he must have been beaten before this period; but the more he received the more courage he appeared to have, and after another desperate round, Sampson was sent down.

19.—It was Pepper Alley on both sides, and neither appeared anxious to stop. Josh., as usual, napt it in the first part of the round, but finished it in prime style, and hit the Birmingham Youth down. (Here some hissing occurred, as it was said by a few that Hudson touched the head of his opponent improperly as he laid on the ground; but it was evident that Hudson was moving out of the way to avoid it. "He's too high-couraged to behave unhandsomely to a brave opponent," was the general expression.)

20.—Sampson, after a few exchanges, was again hit down. (Two to one.)

21.—It was evident that Sampson was getting weak; his knees began to tremble, but his courage and anxiety to win were strong. He strained every nerve to turn the fight in his favour, and, although he did not succeed in this respect, he was still a dangerous customer. All fighting till Sampson was down. (Three to one, and the Hudsonites quite up in the stirrups.)

22.—Sampson took the lead. The face of Hudson was pinked all over, and his head went back twice. Sampson's mug was also painted. The latter could not keep Hudson out; he would always be with his man till he had the best of him. Sampson down.

23 to 25.—All milling; but, in the last round, Sampson was exhausted and dropped.

26.—Sampson came up distressed, and was soon sent down. ("It's all u-p up," says an over-the-water lad. The Hudsonites all in good humour.)

27.—No chance remained to win; but Sampson would not allow his seconds to say "No." He came unsteadily to the scratch, but it was only to be sent down. ("Take him away.")

28.—Sampson, it is true, reached the scratch; and although Hudson was in a bad state, from the punishment he had undergone, yet he still remained fresh enough to finish the exhausted Sampson, who went down without knowing where he was. The shouts of victory gave Hudson new life; he jumped up, put on his own coat, and was immediately taken to a carriage.

REMARKS.—All that a boxer could do towards victory Sampson attempted; but he had not strength enough to dispose of Hudson, who would not be denied. Sampson by no means disgraced his character in defeat. He was led out of the ring in a very distressed state. The fight was over in thirty-two minutes. Hudson received by far most punishment about the head; and, although quite abroad once or twice, his game was so out-and-out that he returned to fight with his opponent at each repulse as though nothing could daunt him.

A slight skirmish took place between Josh. and Jack Ford, the pugilist, on Thursday evening, March 29, 1821, at the east end of the town, over a pot of heavy. Ford offered to fight David Hudson, when Josh. said it was cowardly to challenge "a blind one." Ford immediately gave Josh. a snorter, which produced the claret. Josh. could not return the favour till he had put the pot and glass out of his hand, when the John Bull boxer caught hold of Ford, and put in such a shower on his nob that he roared out for help, and begged of the company to take Josh. away from him, if they did not wish to see him (Ford) murdered! Josh. offered to accommodate Ford any time in a public ring, if he liked it, but observed that he must take no more liberties in future with his head, or he should answer before "the beak" for such conduct.*

In June, 1821, Josh., by way of keeping the game alive, offered to fight Tom Oliver for £100 a-side; and in October of the same year sent the following to the editor of the *Weekly Dispatch*:—

"SIR,—

" 'The John Bull Fighter,' as he is termed, without meaning any offence, or a long preface on the subject, wishes to make it known that he can be backed for £100 a-side against Martin, if it meets with the approbation of the latter. Also, the same sum is ready to enter the lists with Garrol, the Suffolk champion; but if Garrol cannot get £100, I have no objection to accommodate him for £50. I am to be found at all times ready to make a deposit to the above effect.

"Yours, etc.,
"JOSHUA HUDSON.

"*October* 10, 1821."

The second fight which was to have taken place between Josh. Hudson

* Jack Ford, in his day, fought some of the best men. He was defeated by Tom Oliver and Harry Harmer (see Life of OLIVER, vol. ii.); but beat Harry Lancaster, George Weston, and Josh. Ebbs. His weight was twelve stone.

and the Suffolk champion on Tuesday, the 11th of December, 1821, after Neat defeated Hickman, for £50 a-side, went off, in consequence of a demur about the stakes. An appeal was made to Mr. Jackson, who advised the money to be returned. The Suffolk champion threw up his hat in the ring, but Hudson did not think it necessary, under the circumstances, to answer it. Had the fight taken place, Tom Owen was on the ground to second his boy Josh. The forfeit of £20 was given to Hudson by consent of Garrol's backers.

A match was made immediately after the above forfeit between Hudson and the Chatham Caulker for £100 a-side. Bowen, six feet two inches in height, as the reader has seen, had defeated Josh. a few years before, at Chatham, in seventeen minutes. David Hudson had likewise surrendered to his conquering arm. However, the gay boys—the East-enders, with ould Tom Owen at their head—said Josh. should have another shy for it, if he lost his stick. The odds were six and seven to four against him. "What of that?" said Tom Owen; "do you mind me, the bigger the Caulker is, the better mark my boy Josh. will have to hit at." This battle was decided on Wimbledon Common on Tuesday, February, 5, 1822.

Soon after peep of day the fancy were in motion to reach Banstead Downs, the appointed spot for the mill; but the secret had slipped out, and the beaks had got hold of the scent; yet timely notice was given to the travellers, to prevent their proceeding farther than the Cock at Sutton. Some doubts also existed upon the subject on the preceding evening at the sporting houses in town, and several swells preferred starting for Croydon to be in readiness for the result. Sutton, however, was the rallying point; and after some little consideration, Smitham Bottom was the next place determined upon, to accomplish which, two roads presented themselves (and precious ones they were), when the company brushed off in all directions, and bad was the best. To describe the ludicrous incidents which occurred across the country for nearly seven miles a small volume would scarcely suffice. In many instances several of the horsemen, mounted on good cross-country bits of horseflesh, went the pace in steeple-chasing style; and, by way of increasing the effect, at one period sly Reynard appeared in view, followed by the Surrey hounds in full cry. A few of the ring goers, who were upon horses (now reduced to hacks) which in better times were hunters, found their situations become ticklish, and one of the "Jemmy Green" fraternity, who was floored slap in the mud, observed, with a face as long as one's arm, "that the stable-keeper had not used him well by putting him on a nunter, and not tellin' of him." The puffing and blowing of the poor toddlers to keep up with the carriages: gigs shivered to pieces, upset, or their springs broken; post-chaises fast up to the naves of the fore wheels in clay, altogether formed so serio-comic a sketch that the pen cannot do justice to it. Boreas, too, took unwarrantable liberties with the head covers of the company, and many a hero's tile was not replaced on his upper story without a scampering of a quarter of a mile for it. Smitham Bottom was at length reached in a tremendous shower of rain, the turnpike was paid without murmuring, and all the preceding troubles were forgotten on the ring appearing in sight. But here another difficulty arose: the stakes had been scarcely put into the ground, when a "beak" unexpectedly appeared, attended by his clerk, and put a stop to the battle. This was a reverend gentleman, upon whom no remonstrances could prevail. A funny fellow immediately observed to the preacher, "That it would not hinder him from receiving one jot less of his tithes; but if he was determined to prevent the contest taking place, he might, in lieu thereof, be kind enough to give them a sarmon against the noble old English practice of boxing. This might have two advantages—make them disperse, if not, perhaps change their opinions upon the subject." The only answer elicited was, "That he would follow them all over the county." No time was to be lost, and the assemblage again hurried off in all directions to gain Wimbledon Common. The sudden influx of company which poured into Croydon, put all the good people of that place on the stare; the doors and windows of the houses were crowded to witness the movements of the discomfited fancy. The bipeds by this time were dead beat; in fact, they were off their legs. The horses, too, were almost baked to a stand-still; and the storm coming on thicker and faster, many preferred the comforts of a good inn and a prime dinner to a doubtful chase; indeed, numerous bets were laid that no fight would take place on that day. The champion, Tom Cribb, with several of his friends, being of this opinion, preferred toasting milling over a bottle of black strap to further adventures. But the out-and-outers, whom neither wind, weather, hail, rain, nor shine can get the best of, regardless of the pitiless pelting storm, braved its fury for many a long mile, without a dry thread upon their backs, till they again met Bill Gibbons, with the stakes, on Wimbledon Common. The ring was quickly made; but the spectators were select and few, some thousands being left behind. Neither had the beak pluck enough to encounter the storm or distance, the persevering ones having travelled nearly forty miles to witness the battle. At seventeen minutes to five o'clock, Hudson, attended by Tom Owen and Randall, threw his hat into the ring. The Caulker immediately followed him, attended by Sutton and Jackson, a butcher, from Chatham. The Caulker was decidedly the favourite, six and five to four. Hudson immediately went up to his opponent and shook hands heartily with him. The President of the Daffy Club (Mr. R. Soares) held "the ticker."

THE FIGHT.

Round 1.—The person of the Caulker was unknown to the ring-goers. True, his fame had gone before him, and he had been represented as nothing else but an out-and-outer, a terror to all milling coves in the neighbourhood of Chatham, and the best and strongest man in the dock-yard. David Hudson proved a mere chick in his hands, and Josh. had been licked against his will in seventeen minutes. The knowing ones, who do not like to remain idle, and who always endeavour to get a guinea upon a safe suit, were thus induced to lay the odds upon the Caulker, and in many instances rather heavily. It was farther said of him that he was a second Bill Neat, and that his right, whenever it told, was a sort of quietus. On the appearance of the Caulker in the ring, the general remarks were in his favour —"That he was a good nobbed one, snake-headed, had the length of his adversary, and looked a dangerous customer." However, on peeling and getting rid of the swell white upper tog (which, by-the-bye, seemed to fit him like a purser's shirt upon a handspike), he appeared a thin, lanky man, yet with good arms. On shaking hands with Hudson, he stood over the latter several inches. The round frame and ruddy face of Josh. was in singular contrast with the countenance of his opponent. It was observed on all hands that the John Bull Fighter was too fat, when a wag remarked that the contest being between roast-beef and soup-maigre, John Bull was perfectly in character. Very little sparring took place before the Caulker endeavoured to put in his right hand, but Hudson got away from its force with much dexterity. The Caulker endeavoured to repeat this mode of attack, when Hudson again retreated with success. Some hard fighting ensued, several hard blows were exchanged, and the length of the Caulker was thought to give him the superiority. Hudson planted a tremendous hit upon his opponent's ivories, that not only made them chatter, but produced a pinky appearance upon his lips. The Caulker, however, was not behind hand in returning the favour, and put in such a slap under Josh.'s right ogle as started the claret, sent him off his balance, and dropped him on one knee; he would have fallen, if he had not been caught hold of by Tom Owen, when the round finished.* (The Chathamites were up in the stirrups at the success of their hero, and loudly offered to back him at six to four.)

2.—This triumph was of short duration, and Josh. convinced the spectators that he was by far the better fighter, as well as the harder hitter. John Bull was now in his glory; laughing at all danger, he resolutely went in to his opponent. Some tremendous blows were exchanged in favour of Hudson; indeed, it was all fighting. For a rally, there was never a better boxer or a more determined one than Josh. Hudson. He finished the round in fine style, and floored his adversary by a terrific hit on his knowledge box, that gave the Caulker quite a different view of the battle. (The East-enders were now dancing with delight, and offering to sport their blunt like waste-paper. In the ecstacy of the moment, five to two and two to one was current betting. The Chathamites looked blue. "My boy," said Tom Owen, "I always knew you were good at a short cut, but I did not think you could play half so well at long bowls. Do you mind me, Josh.; another such a tickler will send all the Chathamites to Gravesend with pockets to let." "I'm awake, my Tommy," replied Josh.)

3 and last.—John Bull came up to the scratch jolly, and eager to commence offensive operations; while, on the contrary, the Caulker came up slow and shaky; however, as a last resource, he endeavoured furiously to attack Hudson, who got away laughing. The combatants now got into a desperate rally, and Josh. received the most pepper, till he put in a Gas-light Man's shot in the middle of his opponent's mug that sent him staggering some yards; he appeared as stupid as a man without a nob. Hudson lost no time, but, from the length of his opponent, two blows fell short upon his shoulder, till he finished the battle by another Gas-lighter under his opponent's ear, when the Caulker fell in a state of stupor, from which he did not recover for some time after Josh. had regained his post-chaise. When time was called, the battle had only occupied three minutes and a half and a few seconds.

Remarks.—This last hit was an electric shock to the backers of the Caulker, many of whom were naval men. Not a few of the travellers, too, were disgusted at so short a fight after such a long and weary journey. "How we have been gammoned," said those who had been persuaded to lay the odds on Bowen; "this man a terror to all the dock-yard men and milling 'salts' in the neigh-

* This would now be objected to as an improper interference on the part of a second.—Editor.

bourhood of Chatham? If so, what a prize Josh. must be!" When Josh. met the Caulker the first time he was a stripling of ten stone four pounds; he was now over twelve stone, had learnt much, and by his in-fighting set at nought the Caulker's great length of arm. Large sums of money were lost throughout Kent upon the Caulker. A bright moon and pleasant air, after the day's storm, rendered the ride home doubly pleasant to the winners.

Josh., ever anxious to be doing, addressed the following to the editor of the *Weekly Dispatch* :—

"SIR,—

"I wish, through the medium of your paper, to inform Mr. Martin that I am ready to fight him for one or two hundred pounds, either before or after his fight with Randall. Should he accept this challenge, I am ready, at any time he shall appoint, to meet him at Mr. Holt's, Golden Cross Chop House, Cross Street, Long Acre, to make a deposit; should he refuse (having been once defeated by him), I must, to use the language he so generously adopted when challenging Randall, pronounce him 'a cur.' I also wish to inform the sporting world that the challenge to Ned Turner, which appeared in your paper of last Sunday week, as coming from me, I know nothing of; and be assured the John Bull Fighter, as I am termed, possesses too much of a John Bull heart to exult over a defeated pugilist; and Messrs. Old Tom and Old Time having made great inroads upon the constitution of poor Ned, it was farthest from my thoughts to give a challenge, which I know his proud heart could not brook, nor his health admit him to accept.

"I am, sir, your obedient servant,
"JOSHUA HUDSON.

"*Golden Cross Chop House, May* 4, 1822."

A month or two subsequently, Bill Abbot having dared Josh. to the field, he inserted the following as an answer to Abbot's challenge :—

"SIR,—

"With reference to your letter of Sunday last, I shall be happy to accommodate you for fifty a-side, and any day this week you will find me or my money at the Cook and Cross, Red Cross Street, London Docks, to make the match. If your friends will back you for £100, I wish to say my money is ready, and in that case I will wait upon you to make a deposit of £20, as far West as you may appoint. I went the other evening to Mr. Belcher's, and did hope to have found you, or some friend, to have made the match; but was there informed by one of your backers it was a mistake.

"I am, sir, yours obediently,
"JOSHUA HUDSON.

"*July* 14, 1822."

The John Bull Fighter was matched, at short notice, with a countryman of the name of Barlow, called the Nottingham Youth, for £50 a-side. This battle was decided on Tuesday, September 10, 1822. Great sums of money were pending, and the road from London to St. Alban's was covered with vehicles of every description, their inmates anxious to behold the "new hero" make his *debût*. Barlow, according to report, had beaten twelve of the best men in Yorkshire, and the knowing ones were persuaded into the delusion that he would swallow Josh. at a bolt, afterwards dispose of Shelton, and ultimately put out "the Gas." So many wagons on the ground well filled with country gentlemen (particularly from Yorkshire) had not been witnessed for a long time. A few minutes before one, Josh. threw his white topper into the ring with more than usual animation, as much as to say, "I mean to win, and nothing else!" He was followed by that "special original," Tom Owen, and Randall, also in white hats. Hudson was loudly cheered by the spectators. The backer of Josh. accompanied him within the ropes, wearing the same emblem. Barlow was not forgotten by the crowd on making his appearance arm-in-arm with Belcher and Harmer. Hudson went up and shook hands with him. Josh. peeled instantly, and got ready; but the countryman was so long in preparing, George Head lacing his shoes carefully, and a number of officiating attendants crowding about him, that Tom Owen sung out, "What are you arter, Mr. Bel-s-h-a-r; you are keeping us waiting? Your man don't seem to like it much. D'ye mind me?" Hudson also observed, "Come, what are we waiting for; I'm ready —let's go to work." Five to four on Barlow.

THE FIGHT.

Round 1.—On peeling, the frame of the Nottingham hero did not appear calculated to punish, and most of the pugilists present made up their minds Hudson must win. It is true, the John Bull Fighter was rather too fleshy; nevertheless, he was in fine condition, and, united with his laughing, open, and confident countenance, setting defeat at defiance, made a considerable impression in his favour with the surrounding multitude. On setting-to, Josh. stood firm as a rock, with his left arm extended, nearly touching the fists of Barlow, for half a minute; on the contrary, the knees of the countryman shook (by-the-bye, he was a bad-legged one); he appeared puzzled, and at a loss how to commence the attack. Josh., finding his opponent in no hurry to begin, let fly, and counter-hits took place. The ivory box of John Bull received a small taste; but the nose of Barlow napped a rap which produced the claret. Josh., laughing, said to the umpires, "First blood." This decided numerous wagers. (The East-enders began to chevy it was all right, and the "special original" offered ten to one on Hudson, when Belcher replied, "I'll take it." "Stop till the round is over," said Owen, "and it will be twenty to one.") Hudson put down his hands and rubbed them on his drawers, but the countryman did not take advantage of this opening. Josh. saw that he had got him, stepped in, in the Randall and Curtis style, and, without ceremony, planted a tremendous hit under the listener of Barlow that sent him down like a shot. The countryman seemed all abroad. The shouting by the boys from the Tower was uproarious in the extreme, and five to one was offered all round the ring. Anything like description must fall short in portraying the emotions of the various countenances. The chaff-cutting countrymen, who had been so jolly before, were all struck of a heap; the few knowing ones, too—who knew everything about the feats of Barlow, and had been let

into the secret, "as how the Nottingham boy had beaten twelve men in the country, had knocked Tom Belcher about in a private set-to, and had got the best of Gully in a bout with the gloves"—began to drop down a little, and to look blue; while the sages of the East offered "little all" that John Bull would again prove victorious. "Do you mind me, Josh.," said Tom Owen, "it's as right as the day; you have only to go in and lick him off hand." "Yes," replied Josh., laughing, "I've got him safe enough now; I liked him when I first saw him."

2.—The countryman was reduced to a mere dummy: he was quite puzzled, and came up to the scratch to be floored by Josh. in a twinkling. (Ten to one offered, but no takers. Hudson as strong as a horse.)

3.—Similar to the last: Barlow again measured his length on the turf.

4.—Barlow, although without a chance to win, showed himself a game man, and came to the mark for another shy; but it was only to be hit down. (Here the president of the Daffy Club interfered, and requested he might be taken away. The long faces of "I's Yorkshire" beggared all description.)

5 and last.—Barlow came again to fight, but soon found himself in Pepper Alley. Belcher satisfied that he could not win, put up his arm to stop further punishment, and he fell down. Josh. jumped out of the ring as conqueror, only six minutes and a half having elapsed.

REMARKS.—The friends of Barlow showed great want of judgment in selecting such a well-known, often-tried, high-couraged man as Josh. Hudson for his trial opponent in the London prize ring. It was a hundred pounds to a farthing against Barlow after the first round; indeed, it was next to an impossibility that he should recover from the stupefying effects of so tremendous a hit. That he was a game man there is no doubt: his conduct in the ring decided that fact. This battle afforded no opportunity of judging accurately upon the subject of Barlow's real capabilities. Hudson had not a single mark, and said it was one of the easiest things he had ever had in his life. On recovering from his surprise, in the post-chaise, Barlow wished his friends to let him renew the combat on the ground.

Josh., anxious not to let his faculties lie idle, addressed the subjoined letter to the editor of the *Weekly Dispatch* :—

"SIR,—

"You will oblige me by inserting the following challenges in your valuable paper. I understand that the friends of the Suffolk champion have been at the other end of the town to make a match against me; in answer to which I have only to say my friends are ready to meet them any day next week, where they think proper, to make a deposit, for 100 guineas a-side, to fight once within two months. I am also informed that Mr. Abraham Belasco wishes to have another trial with me. If any gentleman will make the match for Belasco, my friends will meet them at Randall's any day next week they shall choose to appoint. I have only to add that, if either of them wish to do as they say, they must enter the ring before Christmas, as I mean to be like the rest of the pugilists, and declare off. Answers from the Suffolk champion and Belasco will oblige me, that I may know where to meet them on the subject, if they mean to come to the scratch.

"I remain, sir, your humble servant,
"JOSH. HUDSON.
"*Cock and Cross, Redcross Street, October* 4, 1822."

Tom Shelton, after some delay, was matched with Hudson for £100 a-side, the mill to take place on Tuesday, November 19, 1822; but, owing to some reports having got into circulation that it was to be a cross on the part of Shelton, Mr. Jackson refused the use of the P. C. ropes. The friends of Shelton, nevertheless, were so satisfied with his integrity that they immediately made the following match :—

"*Golden Cross, Cross Lane, Long Acre.*

"Thomas Shelton agrees to fight Josh. Hudson on Tuesday, the 10th of December, in a twenty-four feet ring, for £100 a-side, half minute time; to be a fair stand-up fight. Mr. Jackson to name the place, and to hold the stakes of £200. £6 a-side are now deposited in the hands of the P. of the D. C., and the remainder of the stakes, £94 a-side, to be made good at Mr. Holt's, on Saturday, the 23rd of November, between the hours of eight and ten o'clock in the evening, or the deposit money to be forfeited. An umpire to be chosen on each side, and Mr. Jackson to name the referee.

"*November* 22, 1822."

This remarkable contest came to issue on Harpenden Common, near St. Alban's. Josh. was defeated in less than fifteen minutes, and fourteen rounds. He was hit out of time, and Shelton was so dead beat that it was with difficulty he appeared at the scratch to answer the call of "time."

On the 17th of December, 1822, Josh. (full of Christmas before it began) had a turn-up in a room with Tom Gaynor, the carpenter, a strong, wiry chap, then little known, and said to be a bit of a plant. Hudson's hands were quite gone, and altogether he was not in a fit state to fight, and if he had any friends present when the row took place, they ought to have prevented the battle. The high courage of Josh. brought him through the piece; but he was severely milled, and met with a very troublesome customer for thirty-five minutes, before Gaynor could be choked off. To mend the matter, it was for love.

Josh.'s defeat weighed on his mind, and he thus proposed a renewal of hostilities in a letter :—

"SIR,—

"My late defeat by Shelton having occurred through accident, has induced me to wish to meet him once more in the ring, for the satisfaction of myself and friends and the sporting world, for which purpose I have seen Tom personally; but, for reasons best known to himself, he declines fighting any more, at least with me. I am therefore disengaged; and as my friends are ready to back me for £100 against any one (that fact coupled with the idea I entertain of myself), I wish, through the means of your valuable paper, to say, should either Bill Neat or Tom Spring have a leisure hour, once within three months, to display in real combat the scientific art of self-defence, I am ready, at any time and place either of these gents may appoint, to make a deposit to fight for the above sum.

"I am, with respect to Neat and Spring, yours obediently,
                                             "JOSHUA HUDSON.

" Cock and Cross, Redcross Street, London Docks, January 25, 1823."

The second match was made between Hudson and Shelton for £100 a-side, but on Thursday evening, May 23, 1823, Josh. and his friends attended at Shelton's house to make his money good for the fight on the ensuing 10th of June. The money of Hudson, fifty sovereigns, lay on the table for ten minutes. Shelton in reply, said he was under recognizances, and should not fight nor would he forfeit. Thus the battle went off, and Hudson received £30.

Hudson was anxious to make a match with Neat, but the friends of the latter never appeared at the scratch. Hudson attended at Randall's house for the purpose on May 30, 1823.

The John Bull Fighter never let a chance go by him, and the following epistle clearly decides his anxiety at all times to accommodate a customer :—

" To the Editor of the WEEKLY DISPATCH.

"SIR,—

"On perusing the daily papers, I understand that Ward challenged me at the Fives Court on Tuesday last; you will therefore have the kindness, through your sporting journal, to inform him that the John Bull Fighter, whether abroad or at home, is always ready to accommodate any of his friends, to afford a 'bit of sport.' If Mr. Ward, or his backers, will call at Mr. Randall's, the Hole-in-the-Wall, Chancery Lane, on Thursday evening next, Hudson will make a match either for £100 or £200 a-side, as may suit his opponent.

"I remain, sir, yours, etc.,
                                             "JOSH. HUDSON.

" Birmingham, August 28, 1823."

On the arrival of Hudson in London, the following articles were agreed to :

" Hole-in-the-Wall, Chancery Lane.

"Josh. Hudson agrees to fight James Ward for £100 a-side. To be a fair stand-up fight, in a twenty-four feet ring. Half minute time. Mr. Jackson to name the place of fighting. The battle to take place on Tuesday, November 11, 1823. The men to be in the ring, and ready to fight, between the hours of twelve and one o'clock. An umpire to be chosen on each side, and a referee to be appointed on the ground. £10 a-side are now deposited in the hands of a person well known in the prize ring; £40 a-side more to be made good at Mr. Shelton's, Hole-in-the-Wall, Gate Street, Lincoln's Inn Fields, on Tuesday, October 7, 1823, between the hours of eight and ten o'clock in the evening, or the £10 a-side to be forfeited. The remainder of the stakes, £50 a-side, to be made good a fortnight before fighting, on Tuesday, October 28, 1823, at Mr. Randall's, Hole-in-the-Wall, Chancery Lane, between the hours of eight and ten o'clock in the evening, or the money deposited to be forfeited.

" Signed,   For JOSH. HUDSON, G. H.
" Witness. B. BENNETT.   "JAMES WARD.
" September 4, 1823."

Upon the above articles being signed, six to four was offered to be taken by the friends of Ward, and several bets were proposed that Ward's money would be made good.

The following remarks were made respecting the milling capabilities of the combatants previous to the match :—

"The friends of the Black Diamond in the rough (Jem Ward) flatter themselves he is so much polished by his recent experiments on the nobs of the provincials, as to be able to take a high number among the metropolitan boxers. Ward, in point of frame, is a second Hen. Pearce, so say the ould ones; and his chest is thought to be equal in point of anatomical beauty and immense strength to any boxer on the P. L. Ward is likewise a most scientific fighter, active on his legs, and mills on the retreat in first-rate style. The principal drawback is said to be, that he is more of a tapper than a heavy punishing hitter; and it is also a question at present, which time can only answer (in order to make his resemblance to the Chicken complete), whether the little but important word 'game' is to be added to his character. Ward, on account of his youth, is much fancied by a great part of the betting world at the west end of the metropolis, who assert, and back their opinion, he will win it easily. On the contrary, something like grief has escaped the lips of the coveys near the Mint; and the Sage of the East has also been caught on the sly wiping his ogles, that necessity should compel the 'two Stars of the East' to be opposed to each other. Josh. and Ward being positively in want of a job, and sooner than remain idle, or stand still, are anxious to take each other by the hand, no opponents from any part of the kingdom offering to enter the lists with them. Their match seems made upon the same principle as that of the late Tom Johnson and Big Ben. 'Tammy,' said the latter, 'you and I never fell out, and that is the reason why I think we ought to fight.' This is exactly the opinion of the John Bull Boxer, who delights in fighting, but detests quarrelling, laughing heartily at the incidents of a mill, and weeping over any real distress. Great sums of money are already betted upon the battle between Hudson and Ward. The former hero is thought to be too fleshy; but his lion-hearted courage, among his staunch admirers, overbalances all defects; and numbers take Josh. for choice, while others are so fond of him as to bet the odds."

The fight took place on the 11th of November, 1823, on Moulsey Hurst. Hudson was the favourite at six to four some days before the battle; but by a dodge on the evening when the final stakes were to be made good, he reduced the betting to evens, and finally six to four on Ward. He stuffed himself into a great coat, a dress coat, and seven or eight under waistcoats, which gave him such a puffy appearance that many even of his own friends imagined him out of condition. Hudson was always an attractive feature in the prize ring; and Ward, by anticipation, was expected to turn out a hero of the first milling class. From the time Dutch Sam fought Nosworthy, so many vehicles were not seen upon Moulsey Hurst. A sprinkling of Corinthians ornamented the ring, numerous swells, a great variety of heavy-betting sporting men, thousands of independent respectable spectators, lots of commoners, and plenty of persons a shade below the last mentioned, and, lastly, a multitude of chaps still a shade lower. The whole was conducted in the most respectable and orderly manner, under the direction of the Commander-in-Chief, seconded by the efforts of the Commissary-General. The exertions of Oliver, Scroggins, Harmer, Sampson, Turner, Carter, etc., also tended in a great degree to give every individual an opportunity of viewing the fight. Five and seven shillings each person was demanded for a standing place in the wagons; and the watermen who ferried the crowds across the Thames were well paid for their exertions. The Red Lion at Hampton was head quarters, and every room in the house overflowed with company. Between twelve and one o'clock Josh., in a drab white coat, with a blue bird's eye round his neck, attended by his seconds, Randall and Peter Crawley, followed by Jem Burn, threw his hat into the ring. Hudson was received with loud shouts. He looked cheerful, nodded to several friends, and appeared quite at his ease. After walking about the ring for the space of ten minutes, "Ward, Ward," was the cry. "He ought to have been here before," said Josh.; "half past twelve o'clock was the agreement." The Black Diamond was seen, arm-in-arm with his backer and trainer, making his way through the crowd, followed by his seconds, Spring and Aby Belasco. He was cheered as he passed along, and threw his hat spiritedly into the ring. Ward looked extremely pale on entering the ropes; and the contrast between the mugs of the combatants was decidedly in favour of Hudson. While the Black Diamond was sitting on the knee of his second, preparing for action, he turned round and surveyed his opponent from head to foot. Randall tied the colours of Josh., "true blue," to the stakes, and Spring placed Ward's, green, alongside of them. "Go to work," was now the order of the day.

THE FIGHT.

Round 1.—Hudson, on throwing off his togs, amused the spectators by a dramatic touch—a new feature in the prize ring—something like the comic business in Hamlet. On getting rid of his linen, which had been nicely got up by his laundress for the occasion, a flannel camesa was discovered, and the eager peepers of the amateurs were disappointed in not beholding Josh.'s canvas, a second layer of Welsh obscuring it. "Hallo!" said the Nonpareil, "how many more of them have you got on?" "Why, you are made of flannel," rejoined Peter. "Leave it all to the cook," replied Josh., smiling; "and

Ward about that by-and-bye." To the great astonishment of the crowd Randall divested a third from his frame before Josh.'s rotundity of abdomen, broad jolly shoulders, and round arms were exposed for action. At length the John Bull Fighter appeared all in his glory: "His soul in arms, and eager for the fray." "Let no person assert that Josh. has not been careful of himself," observed a young sprig of aristocracy. "Careful, indeed!" replied an old sporting man; "do not say a word about being careful: he is in no condition at all; he is not fit to fight. For myself, I never make any calculations upon his training; no, no, system and Hudson are not pals; and the old Sage of the East, Tom Owen, has deplored this defect in his darling boy times and often with watery ogles. It is his invincible bottom that never flinches while nature holds her empire over his frame that renders Hudson a safe man to back at all times. Recollect Ben Burn's character of Tom Cribb, 'I wouldn't mind fighting Cribb,' said Ben, 'but Tom has not sense enough to leave off; he never knows when he has got enough.'" The John Bull was now only waiting to shake the hand of his opponent to show the spectators that animosity had no place in the contest, fame and glory being his only object in view. Ward was in tip-top condition; in fact, he could not have been better: he was nearly, if not quite, as heavy, without the grossness of his opponent, and thus possessed the advantages of training. The bust of the Black Diamond was pronounced "beautiful" by the admirers of anatomy; indeed, the whole figure of Ward was of so manly an appearance, that a sculptor might have long looked for such a model of a pugilist. The combatants placed themselves in attitude. Hudson stood firmly with his left arm extended, looking steadfastly at his opponent, ready for any chance that might offer, well knowing that he had an active and scientific boxer before him. The forte of Ward immediately showed itself: hitting and getting away seemed to be the object he had in view. After a short pause, and both moving a few paces on the ground, Josh. let fly with his left, but the Black Diamond got away with activity. Ward endeavoured to make a hit, but his distance from Josh. was too respectful to do any mischief. Hudson looked cheerful and Ward smiled. Hudson aimed a heavy blow with his right hand, but the Black Diamond was not to be had, and retreated. Josh., perceiving that long bowls were of no service, determined to try if a broadside would not bring his adversary into action; he went to work sans ceremonie, and an exchange of heavy blows was the result. The Black Diamond napped a blow on the side of the neck, which, if it had been planted a little higher, might have been mischievous. In closing at the ropes Ward commenced the weaving system actively, but the situation of Josh. gave him the oppor-

tunity of beating the back part of Ward's neck and head. In struggling for the throw, Ward obtained it cleverly, Hudson being undermost. (Shouting, and "Well done, Jem! that's the way, my lad; you can win it by throwing only." "Walker!" said an old sailor from the Cock and Cross; "lick my old messmate by a throw indeed! You don't know him.")

2.—Josh.'s forehead was a little rouged, and the right ear of the Black Diamond vermilioned from the effects of the last round. Ward would not make play, and Hudson found his man very difficult to be got at. A short time was occupied in dodging, when Hudson again resolutely commenced the attack. Several blows of no tender nature were exchanged between them till they fought their way into close quarters. Ward, with great spirit and activity, fibbed his opponent à la Randall, but not without return. After severe struggling they separated, and both went down.

3.—Josh. stopped well, and also got away from a heavy hit. Ward smiled. A smart rally took place, in which Hudson received a rum one that caused him to stagger, stagger, and stagger till he went down on his rump. It is true it was from the effects of the hit; but perhaps it would be too much to term it a knock-down blow. In the above rally Ward also received a teaser on the tip of his nose which produced the claret, and he dropped, a little exhausted, on one knee at the conclusion of the round. ("Ward will win it," from his partizans; "he'll be able to make a fool of the fat one in ten minutes." The odds decidedly on the Black Diamond.)

4.—This round was short, but very sweet to the backers of Hudson. The latter, on setting-to, floored Ward like a shot. (The joy was so great on this event that the Bullites roared like bulls, the Black Diamond's friends looking a little blue at this momentous triumph.)

5.—This was an out-and-out round on both sides. Ward was on his mettle, and nothing else but milling followed. Josh. made play, and Ward turned to with equal gaiety. Some heavy blows passed between them, and Josh. turned round in breaking away from his adversary. A short pause, when Hudson kept creeping after Ward, who was retreating, till another rally was the result, in which the Black Diamond had the best of it, till Josh. again broke away. Hudson was terribly distressed, and Ward committed the error of letting the John Bull Fighter make a pause till he recovered his wind; in fact, Ward would not fight first. The high-couraged ould one, puffing and blowing like a grampus, again commenced play, but received three facers for his temerity. Another pause. Hudson was now at a stand-still, and his bad condition was visible to every one, but he would attempt to mill undismayed, till he received a tremendous blow on his left cheek bone, which sent him down in a twinkling. This was a clean knock-down blow. (The Black Diamonders were now in turn brilliant. "That's the way, my Jem's eye; it's all your own. We'll back you now two to one, nay, three to one. You can't lose it.")

6.—The heart of Hudson was as sound as ever, and his eye still possessed its wonted fire, but his distressed state was evident. Two severe counter-hits separated the combatants from each other, and both of them felt the severity of the blows. Ward retreated fast from Josh.; but the latter kept creeping and creeping after him till the Black Diamond was near the ropes, and compelled to fight. Here the John Bull Fighter found himself at home, that is to say, at close quarters, a sort of yard-arm and yard-arm fighting, where all his blows told. Josh. not only stopped skilfully, but he put in two such tremendous hits on Ward's body, that the face of the Black Diamond exhibited excruciating grimaces. Hudson also finished the round by throwing Ward. (Another uproarious shout. The spectators all alive, and the John Bull Fighter, if not the favourite among the betting men, seemed to have the interest of the unbiassed part of the audience.)

7.—Hudson, while sitting on Crawley's knee, appeared exhausted, but not in pluck, and laughed at Randall's telling him to recollect his invitation of dining with the Lord Chancellor to-morrow. On time being called, Josh., with much judgment, kept sparring at the scratch to recover his wind. Hudson cleverly stopped a heavy blow. In closing at the ropes the activity displayed by Ward in fibbing his opponent was the admiration of the ring, but it was more showy than effective. Hudson, though awkwardly held, nevertheless administered most punishment. Ward again threw his opponent cleverly.

8.—Some pausing occurred, Ward waiting for his opponent to make play. "You must come to me, Jem," said Josh.; "I shall not go after you; I shall stand here all day." "So can I," replied Ward. Hudson soon broke through his resolution, and went to work, Ward fighting and retreating till he was against the ropes. Here the combatants closed, and the Black Diamond endeavoured to fib his adversary, until Josh., in rather a singular manner, extricated himself from the gripe of his adversary, and found himself outside of the ring, when he put in a blow across the ropes which floored the Black Diamond. (Loud shouting in favour of Hudson; but in betting generally Ward was the hero of the tale.)

9.—The face of Hudson was red and puffy, and it was astonishing to witness a man fight so well who laboured under such an evident state of distress. The skill of Ward, added to his goodness on his legs, should have given him confidence to have fought immediately with Josh. on his appearing at the scratch. Owing to the want of this confidence, he gave a chance away. "The John Bull" again commenced play, but Ward would not be hit. Hudson, on the creeping system, gently followed Ward all over the ring, until the latter was in a situation that he was compelled to fight. A slaughtering rally took place, hit for hit, till both the men went down. (Spring, on picking up his man and looking at Hudson, observed, "I should like to have a calf's head as fat as Josh.'s face." "Softly," said Crawley, "you don't know how soon your own mug may be in a worse condition.")

10.—This was a fine fighting round altogether, exhibiting skill, bottom, and bravery. Josh., after a short pause, endeavoured to feel for his adversary's nob, but Ward retreated. The Black Diamond, however, returned upon Hudson quickly, and missed a tremendous blow aimed at Josh.'s head; it alighted upon his shoulder. A severe but short rally occurred, till the combatants separated from distress. Hudson was determined to put his opponent to the test, and the exchange of blows was severe, till they were compelled to make a pause. "To lick or be licked," says Josh., "here goes!" and hit for hit occurred till both the men went down.

11.—This round led to the decision of the battle. Ward was pinking Josh.'s nob and retreating, as the John Bull kept creeping after him, till a severe rally was the result. Josh. put in a tremendous blow under Ward's left eye, which closed it. The Black Diamond was wild and quite abroad from its severity, hitting at random. It was now blow for blow till Ward was floored.

12.—It was evident that Ward could not measure his distance accurately, and his blows were given like a man feeling for his way in the dark; nevertheless, this was a complete milling round. Hudson's mug was red in the extreme, and he did not appear to have wind enough to puff out a farthing rushlight. Ward was also distressed; indeed, it was the expressed opinion of some of the old fanciers that "it was anybody's battle." When time was called, a minute, if it could have been allowed, would have proved very acceptable to both parties. After a short pause at the scratch Ward got away from a heavy body-blow. At the ropes a smart exchange of blows occurred, when they separated. Hudson stopped a heavy lunge in great style. At the ropes another sharp encounter took place, till both of the men were at a stand-still. Ward endeavoured to put in a nobber, which Josh. stopped so skilfully as to extort applause from all parts of the crowd. In a struggle at the corner of the ring Ward was sent out of the ropes, and Hudson fell on one of his knees. (The backers of both parties were on the funk. There seemed no decided certainty about it: hope and fear were depicted on the faces of the friends of both men at this juncture. It was an awful moment for the cash account—the transfer of some thousands was at hand.)

13.—Hudson's little smiling eyes, although nearly obscured by the bumps and thumps above and below them, had not lost their fire, and he said to Randall, on coming to the scratch, "I am satisfied, Jack, I have got him." The face of the Black Diamond was completely metamorphosed, and his peepers nearly darkened. On setting-to Hudson planted a nobber, which sent Ward staggering two or three yards, and he was nearly going down. Hudson followed his opponent, and some blows were exchanged; when, in closing, Josh. fell on Ward with all his weight. ("John Bull for £100; five to one," and higher odds. Victory was now in sight. "Hudson can't lose it," was the general cry.)

14.—Badly distressed as Josh. appeared to be, on coming to the scratch he was by far the better man of the two. Ward did what he could to obtain a turn, and, in closing at the ropes, endeavoured to fib his adversary; but Hudson pummelled Ward so severely behind his nob, that in a confused manner he let go his hold. A few blows were then exchanged, when the John Bull gave Ward a *coup de grace* that sent him down flat on his back. ("Ward will not come again; it's all over!")

15 and last.—When time was called, Spring brought his man to the scratch, but Ward was in so tottering a state that he was balancing on one leg. ("Take him away!" "Don't hit him, Josh.") The John Bull Fighter, with that generosity of mind which distinguishes his character, merely pushed his opponent down, when the battle was at an end. Josh. took hold of Randall's hat and threw it up in the air, and at the same time he tried to make a jump. If not quite so light, graceful, nor so high as the pirouette of an Oscar Byrne, yet, it was that sort

of indication that he did jump for joy. Hudson immediately left the ring amidst the shouts of the populace, crossed the water, and prudently went to bed at the Bell, at Hampton. The battle was over in thirty-six minutes.

REMARKS.—Ward must be pronounced a fine fighter: he completely understands scientific movements, and, perhaps it is not too much to assert, he is master of the art of self-defence. His most conspicuous fault in this battle appeared to be in not fighting first, and evincing too great anxiety to avoid the blows of his opponent. The Black Diamond is excellent upon his legs—few, if any, boxers better; but, in his fondness for retreating, his blows, however, numerous, did not reduce the courage of the John Bull Fighter. It has been urged that Ward was shy of his adversary. The name and character of Josh. Hudson, as one of the gamest of the game boxers on the list, no doubt has some terrors attached to it, and we think it had a little effect upon the feelings of Ward. Hudson was now in his twenty-seventh year, and victory had crowned his efforts sixteen times. In the battle with Ward the extraordinary courage he displayed was the theme of every one present. To courage, and courage alone, he may attribute his success; but at the same time we are sure that he might have been in much better condition, if he had paid more attention to his training. Hudson, we must assert, relied too much upon his courage; in fact, he was so completely exhausted two or three times in the fight, that his most sanguine friends were doubtful of the result. Ward proved himself a troublesome customer, and difficult to be got at. Josh. won the battle out of the fire. Ward was considerably punished about the head, and put to bed immediately after the battle, at Hampton. Upon the whole it was a fine manly fight.

On the fight being over, "Home, sweet home," was the object in view, and the night fast approaching, the proverb of the "devil take the hindmost," seemed to be uppermost. The toddlers brushed off by thousands to the water's edge, and, in spite of the entreaties of the ferrymen, the first rush jumped into the boats in such numbers as nearly to endanger their own lives. However, the watermen soon got the "best of it," by demanding a bob or more to carry over in safety select companies. Yet so great was the pressure of the crowd, and so eager to cross the water to Hampton, that several embraced Old Father Thames against their will, amidst the jeers and shouts of their more fortunate companions. A nice treat, by way of a cooler, in an afternoon in November, sixteen miles distant from home. The other side of the Hurst produced as much fun and laughter, from the barouches, rattlers, gigs, heavy drags, etc., gallopping off towards Kingston Bridge through fields covered with water, to save time. Several were seen sticking fast in the mud, the proprietors begging assistance from those persons whose horses were strong enough for the purpose; but "a friend in need" was here out of the question. Two or three drags that were overloaded with "live stock" broke down in similar situations, which a wag observing, sung out, by way of consolation to the Jacks in the water, "that they were going home swimmingly." One block up of this kind operated on a string of carriages upwards of half a mile in length. Upon the whole, it was a lively and amusing picture. The vehicles were so numerous, that two hours had elapsed before the whole of them had passed over Kingston Bridge, to the great joy and profit of the proprietors of the gates. For miles round Moulsey Hurst it proved a profitable day for the inns; and money that otherwise might have remained idle in the pockets of persons who could afford to spend it, was set to work in the consumption of articles tending to benefit hundreds of tradesmen, who otherwise (like Dennis Brulgruddery) might have been long on the look-out for "a customer."

Josh. purchased several pieces of blue silk handkerchiefs, and as a convincing proof to his friends that he meant nothing else but winning the battle, he presented one to each of them on the condition that if he, Hudson, won the battle, he was to receive a guinea; but if defeated, not a farthing was to be paid to him. Hudson cleared £100 by the above speculation several of his backers presenting him with £5 a-piece for the blue flag.

Hudson, on meeting with Ward in London the morning after the battle, enquired after his health, shook hands with him, and presented him with a £5 note.

At a meeting of the Partiality Club, held at Mr. Tuff's, the Blue Anchor, East Smithfield, on Thursday evening, November 13, 1823, it was proposed by Pierce Egan, seconded by Tom Owen, and carried unanimously, that a silver cup, of the value of 100 guineas, be presented to the John Bull Fighter for the true courage displayed by him at all times in the prize ring. The room was small, the company but few in number, yet in less than five minutes, so glorious was the East-end upon this occasion, that the subscriptions amounted to £20. The money was immediately put down, and Mrs. Tuff (wife of the landlord), as an admirer of true courage, begged the favour of being permitted to add her guinea.

At Crawley's benefit at the Fives Court, Wednesday, November 12, 1823, on Hudson showing himself on the stage, he was warmly congratulated by his friends. "Gentlemen," said Hudson, "I have been informed by Mr.

Egan that Shelton has made an assertion that Ward received £100 to lose the battle with me. I will bet any person five to one that he does not prove it. (Bravo!) I will also fight Tom Shelton for from £25 to £200 a-side when the time he is bound over for expires. If Ward is in the Court let him come forward and meet this charge made against him." (Applause.) Shelton appeared upon the stage and said, "I have been told by Ben Burn that Ward received £100. I merely repeated it, and give up the author." "That's right, Tom; you've cleared yourself." Burn then appeared and said, he had heard in casual conversation what he had repeated to Shelton. Here Ward rushed up the steps and said, as he stood between Shelton and Burn, "The whole is a direct falsehood;" and added indignantly, "I will fight either of them, gentlemen, for £100, and cast back the slander. (Applause.) I now publicly assert that no individual whatever ever offered me one single farthing to lose the battle. I felt confident I could win." (Great applause.) Josh. Hudson: "And I will fight Ben Burn any day he likes to appoint, my £100 against his £60." Vehement cheering, during which Uncle Ben tried a reply. He had no more chance than an unpopular candidate on the hustings. All that could be heard was a declaration that he had not had fair play, and they did not act towards him like Englishmen. The suspicions, if any had legitimately existed, as to the fairness of the fight between Hudson and Ward, were utterly dissipated.

Hudson and Sampson were matched on the bustle for £100 aside, owing, it would appear, to a word and a blow, Sampson—always very fast—entertaining an opinion he had improved, not only as a boxer, but was a better man in every point of view than heretofore, while the John Bull Fighter always thought he could polish off Sampson at any period in a twenty-four foot ring.* Articles were entered into; but Josh., in order to gain three

* As a sample of what our fathers thought smart writing, we give a contemporary specimen or two of *les impromptus fait à loisir* which appeared in the leading papers of the day:

"IMPROMPTU ON SAMPSON AND HUDSON'S MATCH.

"If what the ancients say be true,
That Samson many thousands slew,
And with a single bone;
How can Josh. Hudson's skill in fight,
Avail 'gainst modern Sampson's might,
Who carries two 'tis known?"

Another, alluding to a rife topic of the day—the treatment of Napoleon the Great by the Governor of St. Helena, Sir Hudson Lowe, whom Byron has damned to everlasting fame in the lines—

"Or to some lonely isle of gaolers go,
With turncoat Hudson for my turnkey Lowe,"

runs thus; the plagiarism in idea is manifest.

"Josh. Hudson now is *high* in fame;
Should this against him go,
His glory passes like a dream,
He'll then be—Hudson Low-e."

weeks in training, forfeited £10 to Sampson, at Mr. King's, the Cock and Cross, East Smithfield, on March 8, 1824, and a new match was made the same evening, for £100 a-side, to come off on Tuesday, May 11, 1824.

PRESENTATION OF A SILVER CUP TO JOSH. HUDSON.—On Thursday, May 6, 1824, previous to this trophy being deposited in the hands of the John Bull Boxer, the Partiality Club dinner took place at Mr. Tuff's, Blue Anchor, East Smithfield. The festive board was truly inviting; the wines excellent; and a silver cup which had been given to a gentleman of the name of Docker, for his spirited conduct in behalf of the oppressed poor in the parish—as one of the links connected with "true courage"—was also placed in view of the visitors. On the cloth being removed, the John Bull Fighter's cup, filled with five bottles of port, was placed in the front of the Chairman, and Hudson took his seat on the right hand side of the President. Pierce Egan occupied the chair, and accordingly fills six pages of "Boxiana" with a newspaper report *apropos* of—nothing. The health of Hudson having been drunk, he received the cup with great emotion. "Gentlemen," said Josh., "I cannot make a speech, but, believe me, my gratitude and thanks are sincere, and as you have honoured me with this cup in the name of true courage, why I will endeavour to support my character for true courage to the end of my life." The cup then passed round. The healths of Mr. Jackson, Tom Cribb, and the leading supporters of the prize ring, were drunk, and Josh. departed to the country to finish his training for his fight with Sampson.

The cup bears the following inscription :—

"THIS CUP
Was presented to the
JOHN BULL FIGHTER,
ON THURSDAY, THE 6TH OF MAY, 1824,
As a Reward for the
TRUE COURAGE
which
JOSHUA HUDSON
Displayed throughout all his Contests in the
PRIZE RING.
John Bull in the ring has so oft play'd his part,
The form let it be in the shape of a heart—
A true British one! at its shrine take a sup:
Can a more noble model be found for a cup?—P. E.

This Piece of Plate was raised by Subscription;
The Contributors were
Several Members of the PARTIALITY CLUB,
a few frequenters of the WIDOW MELSOM;
(and in confirmation that ' *None but the Brave deserve the Fair!*'
The HOSTESSES of the above houses);
And by those Amateurs who are supporters of the Noble
ART OF SELF-DEFENCE."

The cup, as indicated in the doggrel to which P. E. is engraved, is heart-shaped. On the cover is the figure of a sailor, with an anchor and foul cable. The report goes on:—"In front of the cup a small heart appears over four divisions, intended for the boxers' coat of arms. The first division represents the pugilists in attitude. The second portrays one of the combatants down on his knees, his opponent with his arms held up walking away, in order to show that he will not take any unfair advantage. The third division exhibits the battle at an end, the defeated man sitting upon the knee of his second in the act of shaking hands with the victor, to evince that no malice exists between them. The fourth depicts the honours of conquest—the conqueror carried out of the ring upon the shoulders of his seconds, with the purse in his hands. Several other appropriate embellishments appear on the different parts of the cup, on the bottom of which the lion is seen with the lamb reposing at his feet; and at no great distance from the lion is the English bull-dog, as a second to the king of the forest."

The affair of Hudson and Sampson was fixed for Tuesday, May 11, 1824, at Haydon Grange Farm, forty miles from the metropolis. Hudson was originally the favourite, at five and six to four, and heavy sums were laid out on him at Tattersall's at these figures. But on the day before the fight there was a rush to get on to Sampson, and the odds went about at six to four on the Birmingham Youth. This sudden change terrified the East-enders, and many tried to get off.

At one o'clock the ring was formed in a most delightful situation, and, punctual to time, Josh. threw his white topper into the ring. Just before, however, the backers of Sampson declared that they preferred forfeiting the £100 stakes to the risk of losing more than £1,000, as numbers of sporting men had declared off, and that they would not pay if Hudson lost the battle. Hereupon Hudson's backers offered to cancel the old articles, and post £100 for a new match to come off there at two o'clock. This was refused, and the altercation became violent, but Sampson's backers said he should not fight that day. The wrangle having subsided, two Cambridge men, Samuel Larkins* and William Shadbolt, of local fame, and both styled "champions," threw their hats into the ring. The Cantabs, who were in force, took great interest in the result. Paddington Jones and Jem Ward seconded Larkins, and Tom Oliver and Ned Stockman picked up Shadbolt. Larkins, in nineteen rounds, polished off Shadbolt completely.

* Larkins afterwards beat John Fuller, Abbott, and Kelly, and was beaten by Keene and Tubbs. He came to London, and his name occurs in the Fives and Tennis Courts glove bouts.

Hudson walked round the ring, conversing with his friends during the battle. The John Bull Fighter was never in such excellent condition in any previous battle, and loudly expressed himself dissatisfied at receiving the battle money without a fight. "The sporting world," said Josh. "are my best friends; to them I owe everything, and I am sorry they should have come so many miles on my account to be disappointed. It is not my fault, and I hope they will not blame me for circumstances I have nothing to do with." On leaving the ground, and passing the Grange Farm House, Hudson met with Sampson, when they shook hands together. The ground was soon cleared, and the company was off. Hudson returned to London in a post-chaise and four, and arrived about two o'clock in the morning. Sampson also moved for the metropolis with the utmost speed. The sporting houses were filled with company, and every one out of humour at having travelled nearly a hundred miles to be laughed at for his pains.

By the advice of his best friends, and in consequence of his constitutional tendency to corpulency, which resisted the effects of ordinary training, Josh. now took leave of the P.R. in an address at the Tennis Court. His next step was to "commit the crime the clergy call matrimony," with the complicity of a very amiable and respectable young woman, who quickly developed into the agreeable hostess of the Half Moon Tap, in Leadenhall Market, where "Jolly Josh.," brimful of fun and facetiousness, held his opening dinner on the 23rd of January, 1825. Josh., though he retired from activity as a principal, kept up his ring connection, and was foremost not only in backing and matchmaking on behalf of the Eastenders as in rivalry with the Corinthians of the West, but never spared himself in the anxious and often laborious duties of seconding any man worthy of his care and patronage, or of setting-to for his benefit, as may be seen in these pages on many occasions. A paragraph which we find in a newspaper of this period may show that Josh.'s "right hand" had not "lost its cunning" by reason of bar-practice, and also throws a side-light on our hero's manly readiness to champion the defenceless.

"GALLANTRY.—As Hudson, the well-known pugilist, was passing along Ratcliff Highway, a clumsy coalheaver elbowed a pregnant woman off the pavement into the road. The feelings of Josh. were roused at this unmanly conduct, and he remonstrated pretty forcibly with Coaly for his bad behaviour. The reply he got was a cut from a trouncing whip. This was too much. Without further ceremony Josh. judged his distance and gave Coaly such a pile-driver that he went down on the stones as if he had been shot. It was a minute or two before he recovered, and then, declining to get up for 'another round,' Josh.'s name being upon every one's tongue, the humbled bully sneaked into a public-house to talk the matter over with his brethren of the sack."—*Sunday Monitor*, July, 1825.

Among Josh.'s generous qualities were his grateful remembrance of past services and favours and his firm adherence to a friend in adversity. Of this there is extant an instance so creditable to both parties concerned, that we cannot forbear its repetition.

An old friend of Josh.'s early days having, by reverse of fortune, by no means unfrequent among sporting men, fallen into a difficulty which called upon him for the immediate payment of some £50, applied, in his extremity, to mine host of "the Half Moon." Josh., who had not the cash by him, was sadly annoyed at the idea of being compelled to refuse such an application from one from whom he had received favours. A sudden thought struck him. There was his "Cup," lying snug in its case in his iron safe. On that he could raise a temporary loan, and nobody the wiser. Desiring his friend to make himself at home while he went for "the mopusses," Josh. possessed himself of the piece of plate, hurried out at the side-door, and after a sharp toddle presented himself, blowing like a grampus, in one of the small boxes of a neighbouring "Uncle" in Bishopsgate Street. Josh. was not only a well-known public character, but it so happened that "mine Uncle" was an admirer of the "noble art." Josh. unlocked his box, and drew forth his well-earned trophy. The assistant eyed him with some curiosity.

"How much?"

"Forty pounds!" gasped Jolly Josh. not yet recovered from his run.

The assistant stepped into his employer's sanctum, who instantly returned with the shining pledge in his hands.

A brief colloquy explained the position of affairs. Josh. wanted forty pounds.

"Mine Uncle" proceeded to his desk, but not to make out the "ticket" required by law. He merely wrote an acknowledgment, to be signed by Josh., that he had received a loan of forty pounds. This "mine Uncle" presented to him for signature. Josh. was overwhelmed.

"No, no," said mine Uncle! "Take back your Cup, Josh., you must not be without it. Pay me, as I know you will, as soon as you are able. I'll not have *that* piece of *wedge* go to sale anyhow."

Josh returned to the Half Moon with both money and cup; discharged the duty of friendship, and the pawnbroker lost nothing by his confidence.

We must preserve the name of the generous pawnbroker (strange coupling of epithets!), it was Folkard, and the assistant was the youth who, in after years, was the well-known Renton Nicholson, of newspaper and "Town" celebrity, from whose lips we have often heard this little episode of "John Bull and his Uncle."

> "Mine host in the market, a prime jolly fellow,
>   As rough and as ready as here and there one;
> In his lush-crib when seated, good-humoured and mellow,
>   Looks very like Bacchus astride of his tun.
> But more to advantage, with Davy beside him,
>   This John Bull, the picture of frolic appears,
> Discoursing on battles, which those who have tried him
>   Confess to have rung a full peal in their ears."

In 1827, Mrs. Hudson presented, as a second offering, a son and heir, which occasion the friends and admirers of the father celebrated by a festival on Christmas Day, whereat a silver cup was presented to the young "John Bull," inscribed: "The gift of a few friends to Josh. Hudson, junior, born February 28th, 1827, within the sound of Bow Bells."

The free life of a publican, with one who certainly had no inclination to check free living, was not long in telling its tale. Josh. was now visited with increasing frequency by gout and its too common sequel, dropsy, and died at the age of thirty-eight, on the 8th of October, 1835, at the Flying Horse, in Milton Street, Finsbury.

CHAPTER V.

NED NEALE ("THE STREATHAM YOUTH")— 1822—1831.

IN the memoir of the redoubtable Tom Sayers, in our third volume, will be found a few remarks on the persistency with which Hibernian reporters and newspaper scribes, old and new, claim an Irish origin for fighting heroes, naval, military, and pugilistic. Ned Neale furnishes another instance of this assuming proclivity. Indeed, at the time of Neale's appearance, the talented editor of *Bell's Life in London*, Vincent George Dowling (himself of Irish descent), and Pierce Egan, were the recognised reporters of every important ring encounter—the clever but eccentric George Kent, who for twenty years had been its most active chronicler, having previously gone to his rest in the churchyard of Saint Paul's, Covent Garden. The *Bell's Life* and *Dispatch* accordingly prefixed a "big O" to the name of our hero, and plentifully larded their reports of Neale's doings with Hibernian humour, misspelling his name "O'Neil," until, in a letter to *Bell's Life*, signing himself "Ned Neale, the Streatham Youth," the young aspirant disclosed his parentage and place of birth, depriving "ould" Pierce's rhodomontade of its applicability and point.

Ned Neale first saw the light in the pleasant village of Streatham, in Surrey, on the 22nd of March, 1805, of humble but respectable parents. His youth, it may be remarked, was passed in a period when the ring had for its patrons noblemen, gentlemen, and sportsmen, and among its professors Gully, the Belchers, Randall, Cribb, and Spring. At an early age he was in the employ of Mr. Sant, an eminent brewer near Wandsworth, and a staunch patron of the ring. Neale often stated that the first battle he witnessed was the second fight between Martin and Turner, at Crawley, on the 5th of June, 1821, and from that moment felt convinced that he "could do something in that way" himself. That he was not mistaken, his career, as here recorded, will bear witness.

Neale now placed himself under Harry Holt, and by glove practice with that accomplished tactician soon became a proficient in the use of both hands.

His patron, Mr. Sant, gratified his desire to figure in the " 24-foot " by backing him for £20 a side against Deaf Davis, a well-known veteran, a game man, and a hard hitter. The battle came off at the Barge House, Essex, opposite Woolwich Warren, on the 21st of May, 1822, Neale being then in his eighteenth year. The odds were seven to four against " the youth," as he was booked to lose the battle by the knowing ones. Neale was seconded by Harry Holt and Paddington Jones, while Davis had the skilful seconding of Ned Turner and Dick Curtis. The contemporary report, which is brief, remarks of this battle, that it was " a rattling mill for the first forty minutes," prolonged for another hour by Davis's " manœuvring and going down," without even getting a turn in his favour. In the " remarks " we are told " Neale proved himself a good hitter, a steady boxer, and one who can take without flinching ; we shall no doubt hear more of him by-and-by. His youth and good condition carried him through triumphantly." We may here note that in " Fistiana," by a typographical error, the battle is set down as for " £100 " and lasting " 20 minutes." It should read " 100 minutes and £20 a side."

The ordeal passed, Ned did not long stand idle. After Brighton Races, on the 21st July, 1822, a purse was subscribed, and the announcement being made to the London pugilists, some of whom were exhibiting their skill in the booths on Lewes Downs, Peter Crawley proposed that Neale should offer himself to " any countryman on the ground." One Bill Cribb, a brick-maker, who held among his companions the title of the Brighton champion, and known as an exhibitor at the Fives Court, accepted the challenge. Neale was seconded by Peter Crawley and Peter Warren, Cribb by Belasco and Massa Kendrick (the man of colour). No time was lost, and the men at once began.

THE FIGHT.

Round 1.—The Brighton man looked hard and muscular. He at once went to work right and left, but was short, from his opponent's activity. Neale nobbed his man prettily, but Cribb returned in a rally, with a sounding body blow. " Well done, Brighton." Neale stopped prettily, and in closing sent his man to grass.

2.—Neale, after a feint or two, stopped a right-hander and sent in one, two, cleverly, got away, and repeated the pepper. Cribb stood it gamely, like his namesake, but he could not get home well. In the close Cribb got Neale under.

3.—Cribb's dial much battered, but he took it cheerfully and tried to lead off. Neale again gave him a postman's double knock on the middle of the head that sent him back into his corner. He, however, fought his way out, but slipped down.

4, 5, 6, 7.—Similar to the third round, except that in the last Neale hit Cribb clean off his legs. Two to one offered.

8.—Cribb could not keep Neale's fist from his face, yet he fought game till his strength failed, and he got down anyhow.

9.—Neale set aside the efforts of his opponent with ease and coolness. Cribb could not keep him out, and was again down.

10.—The Brighton man, still game, was up determinedly, and showed fight, getting in a slovenly crack or two in a rally until punished down.

11, and last.—Cribb, without a shadow of a chance, bored in; Neale caught his head under his left arm and fibbed him severely, until he broke away quite groggy. Neale sent him down, and he was deaf to "time." Over in fifteen minutes.

REMARKS.—Neale out-fought his man at all points. It is clear no yokel must meddle with the Streatham youth. Hickman, the Gasman, held the watch, the ring was well kept, and the subscribers declared themselves well pleased with the short but sharp battle. Neale was without a mark on the face.

Three days after, on the 3rd of August, 1822, Neale being at Lewes Races, and a purse being declared, Miller, a London pugilist, known by the odd sobriquet of "The Pea-soup Gardener," offered himself. Young Ned, "to keep his hand in," accepted the challenge. Neale on this occasion was waited on by his late opponent, the Brighton champion, and Peter Warren — Miller by young Belasco and a friend. The fight was a fiasco. Pierce Egan says, "The *pea-soup* cove was made *broth* of in the first round." The affair went on for six more rounds, when Miller gave up the battle, saying "he would fight any man of his weight." Over in seven minutes.

This little provincial practice brought Neale forward, and his next appearance was on the London stage, with Hall, of Birmingham, as his opponent. Hall had just distinguished himself by defeating the once-famous Phil Sampson, of whom more anon. The affair came off at Wimbledon, on Tuesday, November 26th, 1822, Hall being the favourite at six to four, and much money was laid out by backers of Hall from the "Hardware Village."

The road exhibited a good sprinkling of the fancy, particularly the milling coves. Martin, Randall, Shelton, Spring, Oliver, Abbot, Lenney, Brown, Hickman, Stockman, Carter, A. Belasco, Ned Turner, Scroggins, Barlow, Dolly Smith, Spencer, &c., assisted in keeping a good ring. This fight was announced to be on the square, and "lots of blunt dropped on it."

At one o'clock Hall, accompanied by Josh Hudson and Jack Carter, attempted to throw his nob-cover into the ring, but the wind prevented it reaching the ropes. Neale soon followed, attended by Harry Holt and Paddington Jones. Hall was favourite, at six to four.

THE FIGHT.

Round 1.—Hall displayed a fine frame, and his features reminded some spectators of Tom Reynolds, while others declared his figure to resemble the formidable "Gasman" (Tom Hickman). Neale also looked well, but was by no means in as good condition. Hall began, breaking ground and working round, but by no means cleverly. Neale faced him, armed at all points. Hall went in with a half-arm hit, and Neale, stepping back, caught him a flush left-hander on the nose. Hall staggered, and as Neale went in, slipped down. The Streathamites uproarious. "Take him back to Brummagem! he can't stop, except with his head!"

2.—Hall tried to shake off the last facer. He sparred, shifted ground, and stopped one or two blows neatly. Neale forced the fighting and the men closed. Hall got hold of Neale to fib, but the Streatham Youth extricated himself, not, however, before Hall had damaged his nose and mouth by a round hit or two. Neale went down.

3.—Neale planted a heavy blow on Hall's ear. Hall bored in and got hold of Neale, hugging him on the ropes, and trying to fib, but not effectively. Neale got down. Hall was evidently the stronger man, but the worse fighter.

4.—Hall rushed in, got a nobber, but closed and threw Neale heavily. Cheers from the hardware lads.

5.—The Streatham Youth met his man boldly and coolly, hit him twice on the head, avoiding the return, and after a sharp rally sent Hall down. The odds changed, Neale for choice, 5 to 4.

6.—Hall fought rather wild—Neale steady, and active in defence. Again Neale visited Hall's right eye heavily, raising a large mouse. A severe struggle. Hall fell through the ropes. 6 to 4 on Neale.

7.—Hall was piping. He did not like to commence milling, for fear of consequences. "You have been a soldier," said Josh. "Fighting is their business; why don't you fight?" A good round was the result, and Neale was thrown.

8.—It was "bellows to mend" with Hall; and Neale was none the better for the throws. A long pause, both combatants sparring for breath. "How is your wind?" said Josh. "Like a horse," was the reply from Hall. "Then go to work, instead of standing as independent as a gemman," Hudson said. Neale thrown in a struggle.

9, 10, 11, 12.—More struggling at the ropes

than effective blows, although lots of fibbing took place.

13.—Neale took the lead in this round, nobbed Hall over the ring, till he went down. A Babel shout of applause.

14.—Neale showed weakness; in closing he went down.

15.—The Streatham Youth went to work in this round, put in three facers without any return, and got Hall down.

16, 17, 18.—Hall showed plenty of game, but he could not fight; in close quarters he had generally the best of it.

19.—Neale, on setting to, floored Hall; but the latter instantly jumped up, put up his hands, and said, "Oh, that's nothing at all."

20.—Hall came to the scratch in a shaky state, when Neale planted some sharp hits, till he went down.

21.—Hall ran Neale off his legs furiously.

22, 23.—Struggling at the ropes, till both down.

24.—Hall was so distressed that on setting-to he caught hold of Neale's hands, when both went down in a struggle; not a blow passed between them.

25.—It was evident a round or two more must finish the fight. Much execution had been done on both sides; Neale was severely peppered about the body; he slipped down.

26, and last.—The Birmingham man getting bad in struggling at the ropes to obtain the throw he received so severe a fall on his head, that his seconds had great difficulty in lifting him from the ground. When time was called, Hall was insensible, and remained in a state of stupor for more than five minutes.

REMARKS.—It was a manly fight, and the heavy hits of Neale did considerable execution. Had he been well, it was thought that Neale could have won the battle in twenty instead of thirty minutes. Hall knows little about scientific fighting; he is a random hitter, a strong wrestler, can pull and haul a man about, and does not want for game. Opposed to science and straight hitting he is lost.

Ned was now the conqueror in four succeeding battles, when Dav Hudson * (brother to the John Bull fighter) was matched against him for £40 a side. The fight took place on Tuesday, September 23rd, 1823, on Blindlow Heath, in Sussex, twenty-four miles from London. Early in the morning the fancy were in motion, the amateurs grumbling at the long distance they were compelled to go to witness a minor fight, when Wimbledon Common would have answered the purpose. Hudson came on the ground in first-rate style—a barouche and four—accompanied by a mob of

* See Appendix to Period V., pp. 191-198.

East Enders. At one o'clock Dav threw his hat into the ring, followed by his seconds, Tom Owen and Josh Hudson. Neale, a few minutes afterwards, waited upon by Harry Holt and Jem Ward, repeated the token of defiance. Six to four on Neale.

THE FIGHT.

Round 1.—Hudson appeared too fat, while Neale looked as fine as a star. David hit short; Neale also got away from a second blow. In fact, it was a long scientific round, displaying considerable boxing skill on both sides, but no work; ultimately a few blows were exchanged, yet no mischief done. In struggling for the throw, Hudson was undermost.

2.—This was a similar round. Neale would not fight first, and showed great agility in getting away. It was evident in this early stage of the fight that Hudson was too short for his opponent; the loss of his eye was also a great drawback. Hudson often missed his adversary, hitting at random, owing to the above defect. In closing, both down.

3, 4, 5, 6.—Neale received two severe cross-buttocks, but he did not appear to be injured by them.

7, 8, 9, 10.—Tedious to the spectator and of no interest to the reader.

11.—This round reminded the amateurs what Davy was in his prime. He went to work boldly, when a sharp rally commenced, but the length of Neale gave him the best of it. Hudson received a tremendous hit on the left ear; the claret flowed profusely.

12.—This was a similar round, but Neale went down. Great shouting from the East Enders. "Go it, my little Davy!"

13.—Neale received another cross-buttock. David was the better wrestler.

14, 15, 16.—Hudson was terribly distressed. He was too puffy. Neale was piping a little. Neale was thrown by Hudson, alighting, like a tumbler, on his hands. Seven to four on the Streatham Youth.

17, 18, 19, 20.—The truth must be told. Stale cocks must give way to younger birds.

Davy had been a publican, and the ill effects of the waste-butt here began to peep. Davy thought himself now as good a man as when he beat Harry Holt, disposed of West-Country Dick, and defeated Scroggins. That his courage was equally good cannot be denied. But nature will not be played tricks with; and training cannot make a young man, though it may help an old one. In all the above rounds Hudson could not reduce the strength of his adversary.

21, 22.—Hudson's face had received pepper, and Neale's mug was rather flushed. Each seemed to be anxious to throw the other, and closed quickly.

23.—Neale received a severe hit between his eyes, that made him wink again. He, however, recovered, and made the best of a rally, till, in closing, both went down. Two to one on Neale.

24.—Hudson fought like a Hudson. For high, if not the highest, courage in the Prize Ring, no boxers stand better than Dav and Josh. But a man cannot have his cake who has eaten it. This was another sharp rally, but terribly to the disadvantage of Hudson, who was nearly finished.

25, and last.—Neale, as the term goes, had "got" David, and by a very severe hit on the latter's throat, floored him. On Josh picking up his brother he said he should not fight any more—a proper and humane decision. It was over in fifty-three minutes. Josh carried David in his arms out of the ring. A collection to the amount of six pounds was made for Hudson.

REMARKS. — It was by no means the smashing fight which had been previously anticipated. If Neale had gone to work, instead of being over-cautious, he must have won it offhand.

Neale, by his repeated conquests, now became an interesting object to the fancy, and was matched by his friends against the scientific Aby Belasco for £50 a side.

To render the battle more interesting to the sporting world, the day was fixed by mutual consent for the 7th of January, 1824, to fight in the same ring with Langan and Spring. Both the combatants were in attendance on the ground ready to fight at Worcester; but owing to the lateness of the hour when the championship battle was decided, the fight unavoidably was postponed. This untoward circumstance was a great mortification both to Belasco and Neale.

A short time after this disappointment Ned accepted a challenge from Tom Gaynor, at the Fives Court, at the benefit of Tom Reynolds, for £50 a side. This battle was decided at Shepperton Range, on Thursday, the 24th of May, 1824.

The ring was soon made, and at one o'clock Gaynor appeared, and attempted to throw his hat into the ring, but the wind prevented its arrival ; one of his seconds, Callas, picked it up and threw it into the ropes, Gaynor's other second being Ben Burn. Neale soon followed, and dropped his castor gently into the ring, under the protection of Josh Hudson and Harry Holt. The colours were tied to the stakes—dark blue for Neale, and blue mixed with yellow for Tom Gaynor. Two to one on Neale, but numerous bets that the latter did not win in an hour.

THE FIGHT.

Round 1.—Neale was quite up to the mark in point of condition and confidence, and really looked a formidable man. Gaynor was well enough, but by comparison the greatest novice must have taken Neale for choice. Gaynor, who was a carpenter by trade, had been represented as a tremendous hitter, which accounts for the caution observed by Neale. Five minutes passed without a blow being struck, Neale being prepared at all points. Neale made several good stops, and at length put in a rum one on the body of his opponent. ("That's the way, Ned!") Feints, offers, retreating, occurred till nine minutes were past, when Neale gave Gaynor a sharp left-hander on the side of his nob. An exchange took place, and in closing, both down, Gaynor undermost.

2.—Gaynor's left eye was touched a little, and after a number of movements, similar to the first round, Gaynor rushed in and threw Neale.

3.—Twenty minutes had elapsed and no claret seen, so great was the caution on both sides. This round was concluded by Neale putting in two or three clumsy thumps, Gaynor falling forward and Neale upon him.

4-10.—Neale had not a mark about him, but Gaynor had napped punishment, and went down tired.

11.—Gaynor, it was said, went down without a blow ; but the umpire was appealed to, when he gave it as his opinion that blows having been struck in the round it was not foul.

12-17.—Neale had got his man to a certainty, and Gaynor was all the worse for the fighting. The nob of the carpenter was damaged, and his upper lip cut through. In one of the above rounds a singular circumstance occurred. The men struggled at the ropes, got through them, and fought a good round outside in the open. One hour and three minutes.

18-21 and last.—Gaynor had not a shadow of chance in any of these rounds, and at the conclusion of the last, in which Gaynor was thrown heavily, Cribb stepped into the middle of the ring and said, "I will give in for Gaynor."

REMARKS.—It is impossible to please all parties—in fact, a man cannot at all times please himself. Many persons called the above battle a bad fight, others said it was not half a good one, while, on the contrary, several excellent judges insisted that Neale had won it "cleverly." It is true Neale obtained the victory without a scratch, and that alone is saying something for a man. after fighting one hour and ten minutes with a boxer who had been called "a tremendous hitter." Neale was determined not to give a chance away—he meant winning and nothing else; his backers we are sure will not find fault with him on that account. We never saw the Streatham Youth so cautious before. At all events Neale has won all his battles, and it will take a good man indeed to make him say, "No;" indeed, the Streatham Youth asserts the word "no" is not to be found in his spelling-book. *

* In a reprint in *Bell's Life* (May 15th, 1879) this fight is reported throughout as "O'Neale and Gaynor," without a word of allusion to Neale's previous battles.

Neale had now risen so high in the estimation of the patrons of boxing that he was backed without hesitation by his friends for £100 a side against Edward Baldwin (White-headed Bob). The battle was fixed for Monday, July 26th, 1824. The bill of fare at Shepperton [three fights] was rather inviting to the fancy, or, as the professionals belonging to another stage phrase it, "a good draw." There was accordingly an immense attendance of all classes at Shepperton. At the appointed hour Neale was there, and threw his hat into the ring. Baldwin soon after arrived in the carriage of his backer (Mr. Hayne). But, alas! it was but the shadow of the stalwart White-headed Bob of a few months previous. His complexion, as old Caleb Baldwin facetiously remarked, might have earned him the name of "White-faced Bob." Imprudent indulgence, late hours, loose associates, women, and wine had prostrated him; and his "Pea-green" backer, alighting from his drag, said, "Bob's health is such he can't fight with anything like a chance; so, as I don't want to creep out, or to expose a brave fellow to defeat, I now declare Neale entitled to the stakes as a forfeit." And thus ended round the first, by the transference of a cool hundred to the pocket of the Streatham Youth, without even holding up his hands.

In a few weeks, the medicos having doctored the White-headed one sound in wind and limb, a new match was made for £100 a side; the day fixed was the 19th of October, 1824, and a field contiguous to Virginia Water selected as the *champ clos*. A goodly muster of the Corinthian order, as "the Upper Ten" were then designated, surrounded the lists. Baldwin endeavoured to throw his hat into the ring, but the wind prevented its falling within the ropes. He was seconded by no meaner men than the champions, Tom Cribb and Tom Spring. The castor of Neale arrived at its proper destination, and both men were loudly greeted. Harry Holt and Jem Ward attended upon the Streatham Youth. The colours were tied to the stakes—blue bird's-eye for Neale, and crimson for Baldwin. Five to four had been previously betted upon Neale; even betting, however, was about the thing—the Streatham Youth for choice.

THE FIGHT.

Round 1.—So eager were the men to begin that they were both in attitude before the umpires were chosen. This deficiency was soon remedied, and both on the look-out for an opening. The frame of Baldwin was muscular and fine: Neale also had a robust appearance. Both shy, cautious, and nothing like work. Feints on both sides, shifts, stops, and no go. "Are you afraid, Bob?" from a voice in the crowd. Baldwin made a good stop with his left. Counter-hitting; a slight shade of the claret appeared on the right side of Neale's nose.   A long pause ; both ready, but no opening ; at length an exchange of blows took place, Baldwin retreating to the ropes ; Neale in the struggle for the throw showed most strength, and the White-headed one was thrown. This round occupied nearly seven minutes.

2.—The ear of Neale looked red ; Bob attempted to do "summat," but missed. Neale planted a clean facer, but he napped one in turn. Both were now busy, but Baldwin was again undermost.

3.—Neale took the lead in this round in gay style ; he gave a facer so hard and sharp that Bob's pimple shook again ; indeed, he was upon the stagger from its severity. Ned repeated the dose twice with success ; and over Bob's left eye appeared a cut. Neale ran in to do execution, but Bob put up his left hand, and bobbed his head away to avoid punishment.   In the struggle both down, Neale undermost. (A shout for Baldwin.

4.—This was a gallant round. Baldwin planted a severe hit on the middle of the Streatham lad's face; the claret ran down in streams.   Counter-hits and good work. Neale was thrown.

5.—Bob was now advised to fight first, but he did not take the hint.   Caution again the order of the day. (Here Cribb mimicked the attitudes of Harry Holt, who was eloquently advising his man.) Bob retreated, and Neale hit him on the back as he was going down.

6.—Nothing ; of no use to either side.

7, 8.—Not effective ; Bob was a difficult man to be got at. Both down.

9-12.—Bob napped a rum one on his body which made him twist.   In the eleventh cries of " foul" occurred ; Neale was in the act of hitting as his opponent was going down.   It was not intentional. Bob went down in a close at the last round covered with claret.

13.—The superiority of Neale was evident; he nobbed Bob successfully ; and at the ropes the White-nobbed one went down exhausted.

14.—The left peeper of the Streathamite was considerably damaged; and his friends were alarmed lest it should soon be dark. Neale obtained a point towards victory in this round ; he threw Baldwin heavily, and fell upon him.

15.—This was a hotly contested round, and both men did their best. Bob proved himself a much better man than Neale had anticipated ; giving and taking were prominent, but the round finished in favour of Neale, who threw Bob on his head.

16.—A good rally, but Bob appeared to be at a loss in sharp attacks; outfighting should have been his game. The faces of the combatants exhibited severe punishment. Both down. Serious faces all round the ring and great doubts who had the best of it. The truth was, at this period of the fight, it

was almost anybody's battle, though Neale hit swiftest and straightest.

17, 18, 19, 20, 21.—All these rounds were fought manfully ; and Neale satisfied all his backers that he was nothing else but a game man.   He was severely punished, but his courage was so high that he never flinched. The friends of Bob still thought he might win it.   The Streatham Youth gave Bob such a severe cross-buttock that the latter showed visible symptoms of bellows to mend ; yet a tolerably good judge cried out, " Bob will win this battle !"

22.— Six to four was offered freely at the conclusion of this round. The nob of Bob was at the service of his opponent, and in getting him down Neale rolled over his man.

23.—Severe counterhitting, Neale undermost in the fall. The Streatham lad appeared rather weak, yet his eye was full of fire.

24.—"It is a capital fight," was the general cry ; and the hard hitting and gaiety displayed by Neale gave his friends confidence that he would last too long for Bob. Neale went down on his opponent.

25.—This was a severe round, and considerable execution was done on both sides. More than an hour had elapsed, yet bettors were shy as to the event. Neale went down rather exhausted.

26.—Spring whispered to Baldwin to fight first—to lead off with his left hand, and it would be "all right." Bob tried it, but Neale got away, hit him in retreating ; in closing Bob was thrown.

27.—Counter-hits effective, but nothing to anybody but the combatants ; " lookers on" will find fault at times. Neale slipped down by the force of his blow, which missed the object intended.

28.—In this round Bob seemed to be recovering his wind a little, and endeavoured to take the lead. A rally ; but Bob did not appear to advantage in close fighting. Neale down, and Bob with him.

29.—The right hand of the Streatham Youth felt for the face of his antagonist three times in succession.   Bob went down weak.

30.—Neale napped a smart one on his nose, which produced the claret ; he was anxious to return the compliment, and in attacking Bob, the latter attempted to retreat, but fell.

31.—Ward, who was the bottle-holder, thought it prudent to give Neale a small taste of brandy, which had the desired effect. This was a milling round on both sides, until both measured their lengths upon the turf.

32.—Neale put in a sharp body blow, which almost doubled up poor Bob. The latter, at times, appeared a little abroad, and Neale took advantage of every opening that offered itself. The Streathamite had the worst of the throw, and Bob fell upon him.

33.—Neale now proved himself to be the more effective boxer ; he hit and followed Bob till he went down at the ropes. Neale could not stop himself in the act of delivering, and cries of "foul" were repeated.

34.—Bob was getting very weak, and went down from a slight hit.

85.—The story was nearly told; without an accident, it was almost a certainty Bob must lose it. The latter fell on his face.

86.—Neale planted three successive facers, and by way of a climax, threw White-headed Bob. Three to one.

87.—Baldwin was so weak that he almost laid down. "Take him away!"

88.—Short but sweet to Neale; the stakes nearly in his hands; he hit Baldwin down cleverly.

89.—It was almost useless to show at the scratch, but Baldwin did not like to resign the contest. Bob down.

40, and last.—Bob was no sooner up than he was down. Cribb said he should not fight any more. Neale jumped several times off the ground, so much was he elated by his conquest. It was over in one hour and thirteen minutes.

REMARKS.—Some would-be critics declared that Neale did not fight well; we think he won the battle with great credit to himself. He has clearly manifested to the sporting world that he possesses two good points towards victory—Neale can take as well as give. It should be remembered Neale had not yet numbered twenty years, yet he had attained, step by step, the high situation he held upon the milling list. Bob asserts he was not well. He might have been ill, but still he might have made use of his left with more effect, and not bobbed his head back so often. At all events, it was a capital mill.

Neale, gaining higher ground in the fancy, was matched against Jem Burn, for £200 a side. On Tuesday, December 19th, 1824, this battle was decided at Moulsey Hurst. Neale was decidedly the favourite.

At one o'clock Jem Burn, attended by his uncle Ben, and Tom Oliver, threw his hat into the ring; and almost at the same instant Neale, waited upon by Harry Holt and Sam Tibbutt, repeated the token of defiance. The colours, blue for Neale and a dark grey for Burn, were tied to the stakes; hands were shaken in token of friendship, and the fight commenced.

THE FIGHT.

Round 1.—Jem, on peeling, obtained the approbation of all the spectators, and "He is a fine young man," was the general opinion round the ring. Neale was cool and steady, and seemed quite aware of the height and length of his opponent. Jem, in a hurry, went to work, and with his right hand touched an old place, damaged in the fight with White-headed Bob. Neale got away from two or three more attempts of Jem; but the young one, at length, succeeded in planting another sharp blow over Neale's eye, which produced the claret. ("First blood!" exclaimed Uncle Ben.) Neale still on the defensive, till they got close together at the ropes, when Ned put in one or two good ones. In closing, Neale got his man down, and fell upon him.

2.—Burn, full of spirit, made play on witnessing the claret trickling from the forehead of his opponent, and obscuring his eye. ("Go it, Jem! it's all right!") The length of Burn enabled him to plant a facer; but Neale returned sharply. This round also finished by Burn being undermost in the fall.

3.—Jem showed himself more troublesome than Neale expected, but it was evident he wanted stamina. Small symptoms of piping betrayed themselves; Burn had been getting on beyond his strength. Neale planted two sharp hits with his right; some good fighting took place, and Burn, by his stops, convinced the spectators he was not destitute of science. Counter-hitting; but the blows of Burn, from his length, were the most effective, and the claret flowed freely from Neale's damaged peeper. A rally, when they separated. A pause; a little wind necessary for Jem. In closing, Uncle Ben's "nevvy" met with a heavy fall.

4.—The Streatham Youth cleared away the blood from his eye. This round was decidedly in favour of Burn; and, after an exchange of blows, Neale was knocked clean down by a blow on his chest. This event decided two bets in favour of Burn—first blood and first knock-down blow. ("We shall win it, for a thousand!" cried Uncle Ben. Loud shouting for the young 'un, and his friends, quite nutty upon him, took the odds.)

5.—In point of punishment, the appearance of Neale was the worse, but his confidence never forsook him, and he stood firm as a rock. The men closed, but after an attempt at fibbing, separated. The right hand of Neale did a little now and then, and Burn did not make such good use of his left as he might have done. Burn again lost the throw, and Neale went down heavily on him.

6.—In this round Neale gave his opponent pepper, met him right and left, and threw him at the ropes. ("Well done, Ned!")

7.—Jem showed weakness, when the Streatham Youth drove him to the ropes, and in closing, Jem, with great activity, planted a facer; but Neale laid hold of his adversary so tightly as to throw him over the ropes.

8.—This round was "a chalk" for Neale; he took the lead, kept it, and milled his opponent down. ("That's the way, Ned—never leave him!" Two to one on Neale.)

9.—Burn commenced the rounds in general well, but Neale finished them. Jem again thrown.

10.—Jem got away well, but Neale was after him, and planted a body blow with his right hand that nearly made an 8 of Burn; his game, however, was so good that he shook it off. Neale met with a stopper on his head, but nevertheless he threw Jem.

11.—The weakness of Jem could not be disguised, and he hit short. Neale began a rally, and Jem was determined not to be behindhand with him. In closing, Neale, with the utmost ease, gave his opponent a complete cross-buttock.

12.—Nothing; Burn slipped down.

13.—Jem got away from several blows, and Neale did not do so much execution as heretofore—in fact, the length of Burn rendered him extremely difficult to be got at. In closing, Neale slipped on his hands, but napped it on his ribs.

14.—Nothing the matter, and Jack as good as his master. Burn was thrown.

15.—If the fight had not been taken out of Burn, it was clear to the unbiassed spectators that he wanted stamina. Jem put up his hands to defend himself, but he did not show any disposition to go to work. Neale waited for him, when he went to mill, and poor Jem was not only fibbed, but Neale fell upon him so hard as almost to force the breath out of his body. ("It's all your own, Ned!")—three to one on the Streatham Youth, by some desperate bettors.

16.—The fight was nearly over in this round, and if Jem had not proved himself a game man, it would have been to a certainty. A sharp rally took place, when Neale put in a slogger with his right on Jem's nob, that dropped him like a shot. ("He will not come again!—Take him away!—He's done for, poor fellow!") However, a little brandy revived him, and, when time was called, Jem appeared at the scratch.

17.—This was short, and to add to the distress of Burn, Neale fell upon him.

18.—Burn was down almost as soon as he appeared at the mark.

19.—After some futile attempts on the part of Burn to stop his opponent, he was hit down.

20.—"It will soon be over," said the friends of Neale. "Not for three hours," answered Uncle Ben. Jem was again sent down.

21.—Burn napped a facer, and was soon down, owing to weakness.

22.—Jem a little better; he appeared to be getting second wind. to the great joy of his backers; he also made play, and planted a couple of hits; but at the end of the round the finishing was on the side of Neale, who got Jem down.

23.—This was a singular round. Neale bored his opponent to the ropes; and in closing Jem struggled himself out of the ring. Burn showed fight outside, but as Neale could not reach him, he returned to the scratch, and sat himself down on his second's knee. Burn then entered the ropes, and followed his example, and so the round ended.

24-26.—In the last round, Jem dropped weak.

27.—The battle might now be said to be at an end; the event was almost reduced to a certainty. Fighting, as to execution, was out of the question on the side of Burn, and Neale was determined not to give the slightest chance away. Burn went down.

28.—Jem now bobbed his head aside to avoid the coming blow, and was hit down distressed.

29.—A severe cross-buttock nearly shook out the little wind left in Jem's body.

30.—After a trifling exchange of blows Jem went down.

31-54.—It would be a waste of time to detail these rounds; suffice it to say that Burn fought like a brave man in all of them, and never resigned the contest till Nature completely deserted him. We repeat he is a brave young man, and ought to have been taken away half-an-hour before the battle was over, which occupied one hour and thirty-eight minutes.

REMARKS.—Neale was opposed to superior length, height, and an active, aspiring young man, and moreover was in nothing like such good condition as when he fought White-headed Bob; his hands also went a little, and he had too much flesh upon his frame; yet he never had the slightest chance of losing; his firmness never forsook him, and he always kept the lead. He left off nearly as strong as when he commenced. Neale is not a showy fighter, but the truth is, winning eight battles speaks a volume as to his milling character; and any boxer who enters the P. R. with Ned will find a good deal of work cut out before he says "No." Ned is an honest man, and deserving of support; he is a civil, quiet, inoffensive fellow, which entitles him to the attention of the fancy, and a great enemy to "Lushington," which renders the Streatham Youth a safe man at all times to back. Jem was put to bed at the "Red Lion," Hampton, and Neale started for London at the conclusion of the battle.

By the advice of his friends, Neale inserted the following letters in the sporting journals as to his future conduct in the P. R. :—

" *To the Editor of* 'PIERCE EGAN'S LIFE IN LONDON.'

'SIR,—In order that Baldwin's (better known as White-headed Bob) journey may not be delayed an hour on my account, I take the earliest opportunity of acquainting him that it is not my intention to appear again in the Prize Ring at present. As he has declared he will fight no one but a winning man, he must excuse me if I am a little particular upon that point, as I have never been beaten.

"My determination is adopted in deference to the wishes of those of my friends by whom I consider it an honour to be guided, and who possess the strongest claims to my grateful respect. When it is recollected that I have fought and won three battles, besides receiving forfeit, within seven months, I trust the liberal portion of the sporting world will consider me entitled to a cessation from labour for the present.

"I am, Sir, yours respectfully,

"*Streatham, Jan.* 15, 1825."   "EDWARD NEALE.

" *To the Editor of* 'PIERCE EGAN'S LIFE IN LONDON.'

"SIR,—It was with much surprise I saw a paragraph in the *Dispatch* of last Sunday stating that Cannon had declared, at Harry Holt's, his readiness to fight me for five hundred pounds. He probably was not aware that in your paper of the 16th ult. I declared my intention not to appear in the Prize Ring *at present;* he may, therefore, save himself the trouble of again challenging me in my absence. I believe I may with safety claim the merit of being cool and steady in the ring, and I trust I shall always be firm and consistent out of it ; and if I could be induced to change my mind, my late brave and manly antagonist, Baldwin, certainly claims the preference.

"If, however, Cannon is particularly anxious to fight me, *and is not in a hurry,* I am ready and willing to make a match with him for three hundred pounds, to be decided the first week in the next year, and shall be happy to meet him at any time or place, and put down a deposit of fifty pounds. If I hesitate to meet his terms, it is because I think five hundred pounds too great a sum to call upon my backers for, to contend against a man so much my superior in weight and height, and particularly one who aspires to the Championship of England—a title which, I believe, is a considerable distance from both of us. If, however, the chance of war should place the laurel upon his brow this year, I will endeavour the next to remove it to that of

"Your obedient, humble Servant,

"*Streatham, Feb.* 12, 1825."   "EDWARD NEALE.

Neale, in consequence of the above declaration, having plenty of time upon his hands, was induced to visit Ireland—not only as a tour of pleasure, but as a profitable spec., under the wing and mentorship of Pierce Egan. The *Dublin Morning Post* thus notices him :—

"THE FANCY.—On Monday night there was a grand muster of the fancy at the Raquet Court, Winetavern Street, for the benefit of Neale and Larkin. They were patronised by an immense number of swells and tip-top Corinthians of this city. O'Neal, the big Irishman, displayed a 'pretty considerable' deal of science in a set-to with his trainer, Pat Halton. Larkin next put on the gloves, and gave a newly-arrived Corkonian a dose that may probably induce him to relinquish any relish he might have had for the pugilistic profession. Minor candidates then mounted the stage ; they forgot, in their ardour for punishing, that a good boxer, like a good reader, always minds his stops. Just as the meeting was about dissolving, a sprig named Jackson, anxious to gather some ' Olympic dust,' challenged any man in the ring to a turn-up for fun. Neale, the Streatham Youth, who was standing near him, offered his services, merely for the pleasure of accommodating the young customer, whom he soon convinced of having been under a mistake with respect to his prowess. Five times did Ned treat the ' aspiring youth ' to a smashing facer, and five times did the boasting would-be pugilist (Jackson) fall to his mother earth—

> "'————— Like a full ear of corn,
> Whose *blossom* 'scaped, but wither'd in the *rip'ning*.' "

"TO THE SPORTING WORLD.—Ned Neale, the Streatham Youth, will have the honour, on Monday night (for the first time in this kingdom), of soliciting the patronage of his countrymen, at Fishamble Street Theatre. He begs leave to state—and he trusts it will not be considered egotism in him to mention it—that he has already contested the palm in eight battles, with eight different candidates belonging to the Prize Ring of London, and as yet he has not been the cause of a stigma on his country. On this occasion a correct representation of that famed spot Moulsey Hurst, with a view of a wood. In the foreground the ring, with umpires, secords, bottle-holders, fighting men, &c., &c. He begs to state that Pat Halton, who is backed to fight the Chicken on the 4th of August, has, assisted by all the first-rates of this city, offered his services for this night only. A youth from Cork, named Donovan, will appear, who wishes it known that he will peel with any man in the world of his own weight. Ned begs leave to add that no exertion on his part shall be wanting to show as much and as good sport as possible to those friends who may honour him on Monday evening with their company. Boxes, 3s. 3d. ; Pit, 2s. 2d. ; Gallery, 1s. 1d. Doors open at seven, and sparring commences at half-past seven o'clock."

Neale, on his return to England, made the happiest match of his life, in which the " Ring " was also concerned, and, singular to remark, the name of Baldwin was attached to the register as a witness. It was thus announced in the journals of the day : " Fancy Marriage.—Married, on Wednesday, June 29th, 1825, at St. Luke's, Old Street Road, Mr. Edward Neale to Miss Mary Weston. The happy pair, after a sumptuous breakfast at Bob Watson's, the ' Castle,' Finsbury, started for Margate to spend the honeymoon."

Neale was now installed Boniface of the "Black Bull," Cow Lane, Smithfield, one of the many old inns swept away by the modern Farringdon Road and Smithfield improvements,

Sampson, who was always a restless and quarrelsome fellow, was continually taunting Neale upon his "judicious retirement," &c., and at length, after some quires of correspondence, Neale declared his readiness to accommodate him, to finally set at rest the question of "best man." Articles were signed to meet in June, 1826, and at the signature Neale backed himself for an even £50.

The next week brought an afflicting event. In March, 1826, Mrs. Neale died in childbed, and on the night of the second deposit at Holt's, Sampson, in a handsome and feeling manner, declared he should not claim forfeit, and that the third deposit should be made as the second, on that day month. The friends of Neale, however, declined the postponement, and forfeited the money down. Thus matters rested until the month of August, when Neale declared himself ready to meet Sampson for not less than £200 a side. The articles, now before us, run literally thus:—

"*Articles of Agreement entered into this* 11th *of September,* 1826, *between Edward Neale and Philip Sampson.*

"The said Edward Neale agrees to fight the said Philip Sampson a fair stand-up fight in a four-and-twenty foot ring, half-minute time, for £200 a side, on Tuesday, the 12th day of December, 1826. In furtherance of this agreement £10 a side are now deposited in the hands of Mr. Pierce Egan. A further deposit of £40 a side to be made good on Wednesday, the 4th October, at Harry Holt's, the 'Cross,' in Cross Lane, Long Acre. A third deposit of £50 a side to be made good on Tuesday, the 7th of November, at Edward Neale's, the 'Black Bull,' Cow Lane, Smithfield. And the fourth and last deposit, of £100 a side, to be made good on Tuesday, the 5th of December, at Josh. Hudson's, the Half Moon Tap, Leadenhall Market. The fight to take place within thirty miles of London, Mr. Egan to name the place of fighting. The men to be in the ring between twelve and one o'clock; and in the event of failure on either side to comply with the terms of these articles, the party failing to forfeit the money down. Two umpires and a referee to be chosen on the ground, and if any dispute shall arise, the decision of the referee to be conclusive, and the battle-money to be given up accordingly.

"EDW. NEALE.
"P. SAMPSON.

" Witness—JOHN ROOKE."

On Tuesday, December 12th, 1826, at South Mimms Wash, Middlesex, fifteen miles from London, this interesting contest was decided. Sampson was thought by his friends to have improved considerably in frame and science since his second contest with Jem Ward—nay, so much so that he was placed as the "second best" on the list of pugilists; indeed, to make use of Sampson's own words, he acknowledged Jem Ward as his master, but styled himself "foreman to the champion." In calculating the advantages he possessed over the Streatham Youth, three points were considered in his favour—length, height, and weight; and another point was added by some—the best fighter. Sampson's immediate friends therefore booked his winning as a certainty, urging, as a proof of their good opinion, that Neale had never beaten or stood before so capital a boxer as Sampson. The latter pugilist also supported this opinion by offering to take long odds that he won the fight in fifteen minutes, and without a black eye. Equally confident were the friends of Neale. They urged that Ned had always proved himself a conqueror, and acted upon the general rule adopted by sporting men—always to back a winning horse and a winning man to the end of the chapter. Five and six to four were betted in numerous instances upon the Streatham Youth.

As the time of fighting drew near the interest upon the battle increased, and large sums of money were sported on the event. At the John Bull Fighter's dinner, when the whole of the four hundred sovereigns were made good, Sampson and Neale met, but not upon the most friendly terms. Sampson informed the company that he had heard Neale had spoken of him in a disrespectful manner, and he now gave him the opportunity of offering a contradiction to the aspersions he had made upon his character. Neale, with considerable warmth, replied : " You behaved unmanly to me in my own house, Sampson, while I was in a bad state of health, and I will never forgive you till you and I have decided our fight in the ring. Give me five pounds and I will bet you one hundred that I lick you." To prevent an open row it was judged necessary by the backers of both of the men that they should separate as soon as possible.

Every precaution was used to select a secure place for fighting ; and after an assurance that it was likely no interruption would take place, Dunstable Downs was the spot appointed. Sampson left the " Crown " at Holloway, his residence during the time of his training, on the Wednesday previous to the battle, and took up his quarters at the "Posting House," in Market Street. Neale did not leave the house of his backer at Norwood until Monday morning, when he was placed, on his arrival in London, under the care of Mr. William Giles. Neale, in company with the gay little Boniface of the first market in the world, and Harry Holt, in a post-chaise, reached the Crown Inn at Dunstable about eight in the evening of the Monday.

It might have been anticipated that in consequence of Sampson having pitched his tent in the neighbourhood of the scene of action, a buzz would be created that a prize-fighter was on the spot, and the magistrates would become acquainted with the circumstance. It proved so, for on the Monday morning a notice was sent that he must not fight in the counties of Bedford and Buckingham. This information got wind early on the

Monday afternoon, and the town of ˋDunstable, which otherwise would have been filled to an overflow, was completely spoilt, as the amateurs preferred halting at Redburn and Market Street to proceeding forward on a matter of doubt.

During the whole of the night carriages filled with persons were on the road. An hour before daylight another magistrate arrived in Dunstable, in his gig, declaring himself a magistrate for three counties, and that no mill should take place in Bedfordshire, Buckinghamshire, or Hertford-shire. On his meeting with Sampson, Phil promised the gent he would not exhibit in either of the proscribed counties. It therefore became necessary to hold a council of war. Sampson wished to proceed to Stony Stratford, as a spot where no interruption was likely to take place, but Pierce Egan, on whom the selection of the ground had devolved, decided for Middlesex, acting upon the articles agreed to, which stated the fight was to be within thirty miles of London. The office being given " towards home," con-fusion began, and " The devil take the hindmost," was the word. The northern stage coaches were all filled inside and out, for the sudden turn round had nearly thrown most of the passengers bound for the fight out of distance. All the post-chaises and horses had been previously hired, so nothing else was left to numerous persons, with plenty of cash in their purses, but to toddle for miles through mud, slush, and heavy showers, to the scene of action. It was truly laughable to see lots of heavy swells, with their thick upper toggery tucked up under their arms, trudging along as if pursued by an enemy, their brows covered with perspiration, and their hinder parts splashed with dirt. The muster of the motley group was immense, and the turn-out of Corinthians more numerous than had been seen for months past at a fight. A crowd of fours-in-hand, tandems, curricles, post-chaises and fours, cabriolets, gigs, drags, &c., were all trying to get the best of each other to be early on the ground, and so obtain a good place. At length Mimms Wash appeared in view, a large sheet of water, when Bill Gibbons dashed through the stream with as much *sang froid* as if he had been crossing a kennel in the streets of London. " We are not going to be outdone by the Ould One ! " exclaimed some coster-mongers, following Bill, and suffering for their temerity by going head over heels in the muddy water mixture, to the no small chaffing and laughter of the crowd. Several pedestrians, regardless of cold or con-sequences, waded the Wash with as much indifference as if it had been a summer's day. A swell, who had plunged in up to his middle, invited his fellow-travellers to accompany him through the flood, exclaiming: " I'm a philosopher! Come along! Follow me. I'm not wet at all. You only *fancy* it is water!" But even this logic had not the desired effect, and his companions preferred being conveyed across the Wash in a coach. The ring was soon made, upon a rising spot of ground in a field hard by, and at a quarter past two o'clock Sampson threw his hat into the ring, amidst loud cheers, followed by his second and bottle-holder, Jem Ward and Jem Burn. Neale soon afterwards repeated the token of defiance, attended by Josh Hudson and Harry Holt. Sampson deliberately tied his colours (pink) upon the stakes; and Holt placed the dark blue bird's eye for Neale upon those of his opponent. The men were not long in peeling, and at twenty-five minutes after two they shook hands, and the battle commenced.

THE FIGHT.

Round 1.—Both men appeared in excellent condition. Sampson was quite tiptop, but Neale, it was thought, was not exactly weight—that is to say, what he ought to have been—and the judges hinted he was rather thin. The attitudes of the combatants claimed attention; in fact, the contrast was singular. Neale held his left hand firmly above his nob, operating as a kind of office that he was perfectly aware of the danger of the Strong Man's right mauley. Sampson's guard was low, but his ogles were on the alert, and he kept a good look-out to do mischief. In most fights, the first round, if not tedious, is generally expected to show superiority of science in one of the men. as the first blow is considered of consequence; but in this instance it was extreme caution against extreme caution. Sampson, however, had previously asserted that only let him have the chance of getting Neale before him in the ring, and he would cut his nob to pieces. Such is the difference between theory and practice; Sampson soon found out the difficulty of going to work off-hand with his clever opponent; and Neale, like that great master in the art of war, the Duke of Wellington, was determined not to give away a chance, and preferred the retreating system. Several minutes were occupied in making offers, retreating, dodging, and pacing all over the ring without any effect, Neale jumping back from every attempt of Sampson. The goodness of Ned upon his pins attracted the attention of all spectators. After numerous attempts to do " summat," Neale having retreated to a corner of the ring, Sampson went in and planted a slight facer. Ned, having no opportunity to make a hit, closed with his adversary. In struggling for the throw, Sampson down and undermost. (The Streathamites opened their chaffing-boxes, and gave him the benefit of their red rags, by repeated shouts of approbation.)

2.—The left arm of Neale was again raised, and Sampson could not make him out. The latter boxer did not at all seem prepared for the mode of defence resorted to by his adversary. Neale, it should seem, had made up his mind to a certain mode of fighting, and was not, by any stratagem of Sampson, to be led away from it. Neale kept walking round his adversary, anxious to obtain an opening, and retreating when anything like danger showed itself. It was remarked by a spectator that " if the one was afraid, the other dared not commence fighting." Several minutes passed away in looking at each other, and in making feints. Phil at length went to work, but missed a slashing hit, which was calculated to have done mischief. Neale returned, but it was not effective. In closing, Neale threw Sampson heavily. (" Bravo, Neale!" from his partisans.)

3.—Sampson eyed his opponent from head to foot. Both combatants were tired of holding up their arms, or appeared to be so, and Sampson, finding nothing was to be done, dropped his guard, and stood still. Neale also crossed his arms, and viewed his opponent. In fact, it was a complete suspension of hostilities—the spectators at length became impatient, and expressed their disapprobation. Each man several times made himself up to do mischief, and every peeper was upon the stretch to witness some hits, instead of which retreating was again the order of the day. Sampson, in following Neale, got the latter boxer again in the corner of the ring, when he hit out right and left, and caught Neale on the mug, but Ned returned the compliment. In closing,

Sampson went down on his knees, and brought down Neale with him. Odds were betted on Neale.

4.—"He'll go to work soon," said Ward, pointing to Sampson, "and give Neale a slogger." "I should like to see it," said an old ring-goer; "I never saw such a mill before!" "I call it anything but fighting," replied a third. The men looked at each other, and Sampson, with all his cleverness and experience, could not put Neale off his mode of fighting. An exchange of blows, but no mischief. Sampson made a good stop, or his wind-market must have been disturbed. Neale, however, got another turn, and planted a rum one on Sampson's canister. (Loud shouting from Neale's friends.) Sampson missed one of his wistycasters at the nob of his opponent, or Ned's upper works might have been in chancery. In closing, Sampson endeavoured to fib his adversary. Ned was thrown, Sampson uppermost.

5.—This was a short round. Neale rushed in and got Sampson down.

6.—A little bit of fighting this bout. Sampson tried all he knew, but Neale would not be had, and got away from all his opponent's feints. After some manœuvring Sampson again had Neale in the corner of the ring, and planted one of his heavy right-handed hits on his temple. Ned for an instant appeared stunned, and fell on his knees, but jumped up directly to renew the fight. Hudson, however, pulled him down on his knee, and the round was finished.

7.—After some little dodging about the ring, each crossed his arms and stood still. Barney Aaron begged the fight might be put off, and begun again the next day with day-break. "No, no," exclaimed an Old One, "recollect there's moonlight." "I am happy," exclaimed Josh, "that I am a patient man." These, and a thousand such remarks, occurred all round the ring, but still the combatants were not roused into action. ("Come," said Sampson to Neale, "why don't you fight?"—"When I like," answered Ned; "you begin, I'll soon be with you.") This round was tediously long. Counter-hitting, Neale planted a sharp blow on Sampson's nob, and the latter returned with his right. ("He can't make a dent in a pound of butter, Sampson. Go to work, and hit him as you did me," said Jem Burn. —"Be quiet," said Harry Holt; "look to your man. It's as safe as if it was over." This latter remark seemed to make Sampson angry, and with a sneer he observed, "What signifies what a fellow like you says?"—"I'll give you one presently for that," answered Neale; "he is my second, so you don't like him.") Neale napped a heavy one to all appearance on his head; but Sampson received a smart body blow. A variety of feints—great preparation—retreating, but no blows. In closing, Sampson fibbed his antagonist slightly. Both

down, Neale undermost. The friends of Sampson here gave him a chevy for luck. During the short space of time Neale sat upon Josh's knee, he said to him, "Sampson is but a light hitter."—"Well, then," replied the John Bull Fighter, "there can be no mistake about your winning!"

8.—Sampson said "First blood!" pointing to a slight scratch near Neale's mouth. "Don't be foolish," replied Hudson; "it is only a touch of the scurvy on his cheek—a pimple irritated." Neale stopped in style a tremendous right-handed hit. A pause. Sampson made a stunning hit on the head of his opponent, which nearly turned Ned round. ("What, you've caught it at last," said Jem Ward, rubbing his hands. "Another blow like that, and good night to you, Master Neale."—"Walker," replied Josh. "Why, Jemmy, you are all abroad, to talk so!") In closing, Sampson obtained the throw.

9.—This was an excellent fighting round After the numerous standstills which had occurred—feints, getting away, &c.—Neale seemed quite ripe for execution. Sampson received a rum one on his listener, but returned cleverly on Neale's index. Some good stopping occurred upon both sides, and it appeared to the spectators that the fight had just commenced. Neale stopped one of Sampson's tremendous right-handed hits so well that several persons exclaimed, "Beautiful!" Sampson missed one or two blows. A short rally occurred, when Sampson went down from a slight hit. Ned, as yet, had scarcely the slightest mark of punishment. His friends were satisfied he was so good upon his pins that he would wear out his opponent if it came to staying.

10.—Neale saw an opening, and without hesitation turned it to his advantage. He commenced milling with severity, and planted two good hits. He also repeated the dose by a heavy right-handed hit on the jaw of his opponent, which took Sampson off his legs as if shot. He was picked up by his second like a log of wood. His eyes were closed, and his nob was swinging on his shoulder as if it did not belong to his body. "It is all U P," was the cry—"the Strong Man is done over." Any odds in favour of Neale. Ward endeavoured to keep Sampson's head steady, and led him to the scratch.

11, and last.—Sampson appeared incapable of keeping his legs, neither did he attempt to put up his arms. He was of no use. Neale, by way of finisher, planted a light blow, and Sampson again measured his length upon the grass. When time was called, Sampson did not leave the knee of his second. Holt threw up the hat, and victory was declared in favour of Neale; Sampson observing he would "fight no more," when asked by Ward, and requesting his second to take him out of the ring. Neale jumped about the ground for joy, and soon left the ring for London, neither fatigued nor hurt. Sampson was taken by some of his Birmingham friends to Market Street. The fight lasted one hour and six minutes.

REMARKS.—That this fight was not a good one was certainly not the fault of Neale. He expected, from the boast of Sampson, that he would go in and win offhand, or fall in the attempt. Hence Ned's over-caution, as it proved. Neale never was a showy pugilist;

on the contrary, he was steady, cautious, and safe. Sampson, when he found he could not confuse his man by impetuosity, fell off sadly. and the affair, which it was anticipated would be a rattling fight, became a tedious succession of bouts of sparring, with short intervals of hitting, in which Neale was slowly but surely establishing his superiority, and Sampson was beaten against his will.

Many of the friends of Cannon, the "Great Gun of Windsor," were of opinion that their man was just the sort of pugilist to "make Ned fight." Accordingly a proposal was made for a meeting for a stake of £200 a side, and accepted by Neale. On Tuesday, February 20th, 1827, the men met at Warfield, in Berkshire. The morning was intensely cold, and both men appeared at the ring-side with their nobs covered with Welsh wigs, Neale having slept overnight at the "Crown," in Windsor, and Cannon driven over from his training quarters, the New Inn, at Staines. The men shook hands with smiling cordiality, each assuring the other he "felt quite well." The colours were then tied to the stakes, a blue bird's-eye for Neale, and crimson with a white spot for Cannon. Peter Crawley and Harry Harmer waited upon Cannon, Harry Holt and Josh Hudson on Neale.

THE FIGHT.

Round 1.—The Great Gun, on stripping, showed excellent condition; but in spite of good skin training, age cannot be concealed; and Cannon, according to the exclamation of "The Gas," was "an old man." The fact is that Neale was not yet twenty-three years of age, while Cannon had passed his *thirty-sixth!* Cannon appeared cheerful, smiling, and confident. The body of Neale was covered with spots, like a leopard—his condition was anything but good; he had a slight cold, and his flesh was soft; yet the grand points in his favour were youth, and a "heart in the right place." On setting to, Cannon did not display that bulldog sort of eagerness which characterised his efforts in his second battle with the John Bull Fighter, but he was upon the alert, ready to punish, and anxious to obtain an opening. Cannon commenced offensive operations, but his wary opponent "would not have it," and got away. Cannon tried it again, but it would not do; Ned endeavoured to plant a hit, but the Great Gun was not to be had, and retreated from mischief. Sparring on both sides, but no hitting. Neale at length went to work, and with his left mauley slightly touched his opponent's canister;

Cannon returned sharply. A short struggle occurred, and Cannon went down.

2.—The milling qualities of the Great Gun were prominent, and he was upon the bustle to do business; but Ned was "up and dressed," and his left hand again told upon his opponent's mug. Cannon was not behindhand, and some sharp blows were exchanged. Milling on the retreat (after Tom Cribb's successful mode) was now adopted by Neale; he planted a tremendous blow under the listener of his adversary, and the claret followed profusely. If this heavy blow had been a little lower, it might have been "Good night to the Great Gun!" Cannon, rather confused and wild, rushed in to work—he obtained the throw, Neale went down, and Cannon also; in falling, his nob came in contact with the stakes. Neale was the hero of the tale.

3.—Cannon, like nothing but a game man, appeared at the scratch smiling. This was a short round. The Great Gun tried to fire a heavy shot, and boldly went up to his man; but the Youth hooked him round his neck, and endeavoured to fib. Cannon proved himself the stronger man, got Neale down, and fell on him.

4.—The Streatham Youth got away from

mischief, and made good use of his pins. Some blows were exchanged, when they closed. A desperate struggle occurred for the throw; both down, Neale undermost.

5.—The Great Gun, as gay as a lark, went to work, but napped a conker; yet he would not be denied, and a sharp rally was the result. Some heavy hits were exchanged: the fire proving too hot, Ned turned round from mischief; the Great Gun pursued him, when Neale turned and rushed to the attack; some clumsy thumps passed. In closing, Ned had the best of it, but fell on his head. Neale was much shaken by the fall.

6.—The Great Gun was all for fighting, and kept to his work. Neale was ready, but nevertheless kept a good look-out. In a rally, both their faces napped punishment, but Ned retreated in style. In struggling for the throw, both down, Neale undermost.

7.—The weakness of the Streatham Youth was visible to his friends, but they still felt satisfied he must win. A good rally, and Cannon up to the mark, giving hit for hit. In closing, they both stood still, trying to hold the hands of each other. Ned broke away, and tipped it to Cannon in his victualling office; he ultimately obtained the throw, and the Great Gun came down on his nob, a shaker. ("Neale for a thousand!")

8.—The Great Gun showed distress on appearing at the scratch. Ned tried to be with him, but Cannon closed in by catching Neale round the neck. The fibbing system was adopted by Ned, and upon Cannon getting the worst of it he dropped upon his knees. The coolness of Neale was here seen to great advantage; he was in the act of hitting, when he stopped himself and held up his arms, amidst loud cheers from all parts of the ring. ("Bravo, Ned! well done, it's manly!")

9.—The Great Gun was rather unsteady; but his pluck was as good as gold. The science of Neale gave him great advantages, although he was out of condition; he watched the movements of Cannon with the keen eye of a general till it answered his purpose to commence fighting. Ned planted a facer, but Cannon countered. In closing, holding of hands to prevent punishment was again the feature; and Neale was so weak that he could not get the best of his opponent in his usual workman-like style. The struggle became long and desperate, when the Great Gun went down undermost.

10.—This round was all in favour of Ned. He planted a rum one on the muzzle of the Great Gun, repeated the dose with his left, then brought in his right to great advantage. In closing Cannon did his best to grasp his opponent firmly; but Neale broke away cleverly, and planted a heavy body blow with his right hand. Cannon fought his way into another close; in struggling both down, the Streatham Youth undermost.

11.—The Great Gun wanted breath, and sparred for time, but anxious not to be idle, went to work. Ned was ready for him, and some blows were exchanged. Cannon rushed in determined, as it were, to have the fall. In struggling he threw his opponent, although he went down himself. Neale's nob came in sharp contact with the ground, his face underwent a momentary change, and he appeared hurt by the fall. He rested his head upon the back of his bottle-holder, and his friends became alarmed for the consequences. But when time was called, he was ready.

12.—Neale seemed anxious to recover the accident, and put in with the utmost ease two teasers on Cannon's nob, right and left, that made his pimple shake again. A sharp rally followed, and "Jack was as good as his master." It was Millers' Place, Cannon Row, and Pepper Alley, all brought down from town. Neale had the worst of the punishment; he, however, stuck close to his man. Cannon was sent out of the ropes, and Ned also went down.

13.—Good on both sides; Cannon always ready, and no flincher. In fact, he appeared as cheerful as if he was at work on the river. Neale got away from mischief, but Cannon would follow him, till a rally was the result. In closing Cannon received a cross-buttock that shook him seriously.

14.—Neale was much distressed, and the Great Gun tried to have the best of him by bustling. In closing he got Neale's nob under his arm; and the latter, for a short time, could not release himself from his perilous situation. ("Bravo, Cannon, now's your time! you have got him—don't let him go!") Cannon at length let Neale down. The backers of the Great Gun flattered themselves the chance was in their favour, and actually took him at evens.

15.—Neale, aware of his weakness, acted upon the defensive; and Cannon went to work, as the best means to turn the tide. The Great Gun, in closing, again caught hold of Neale, the latter trying to hold the hands of his opponent. In this unpleasant situation, both to themselves and the spectators, they continued for a minute, until quite exhausted they both went down, Neale undermost; Cannon for choice, and some were jolly enough to offer 5 to 4.

16.—The Great Gun, acting under the advice of his seconds, endeavoured to have his opponent upon the bustling system, and went to work. He bored Neale to the ropes, and here another disagreeable struggle took place, both for a short time hanging upon the ropes, till they fell outside of the ring. The Great Gun was undermost. ("Cannon for ever!" was the cry. "He can't lose it! The battle is changed! 6 to 4 on the Great Gun!")

17.—At the scratch Cannon appeared the fresher man of the two. Ned was out of wind, and sparring was necessary for both. Neale tried his right hand, but without effect. A cessation of arms for a short period, and both on the look-out. Cannon at length rushed upon Neale with an intent of punishment, but Ned, wide awake, retreated, followed by his opponent. At the ropes Cannon went to work, but Ned put on the stop capitally. The Streatham Youth broke ground, when Cannon would not be denied, but he napped a facer. In closing Ned threw Cannon, and fell upon him severely.

18.—The Great Gun, rather unsteady, bored in to punish his adversary; but Neale, who was now getting better, made use of his pins to great advantage, and got away with ease. One severe facer Cannon napped, a second followed without any return, and a third finished the round, the claret running from Cannon's nose, when he fell exhausted. (Loud shouting for Neale, and 6 to 4 on him.)

19.—Cannon was game to the backbone, and appeared at the scratch like a trump. Neale, with great judgment, made himself up to do something good; he viewed his adversary well, then let fly a tremendous nobber, which sent Cannon staggering back to the ropes; Ned followed him and threw him heavily.

20.—Neale was on his mettle; he commenced play with his right with good effect, and Cannon's nob met punishment. The Great Gun was now reduced to a little gun, nevertheless he showed fight like a brave man, by returning hits. Ned put in another severe facer, and in closing Cannon went down on his back, Neale upon him. (2 to 1, and no takers.)

21.—Cannon came up quite groggy, but the fight was not out of him. The courage and game he displayed were admirable, and he earned the praise of all spectators. But in boxing term he was of "no use." Ned put in a nobber that almost stunned him, and Cannon staggered about like a drunken man. In closing, Ned again obtained the throw, and the fall was indeed severe. Cannon lay on the ground, declining to be lifted up till the call of "time."

22, and last.—The Great Gun came up like nothing but an out-and-outer, but his shot was not point-blank, and he swerved and reeled unsteadily. Neale put in a left-handed push, when the Great Gun rolled through the ropes and fell outside. He was in a state of stupor. His seconds brought him into his corner, but while they were busy the umpire declared he had not answered the call of "time." The referee agreed, and the victory was declared to Neale. The battle lasted only thirty minutes. Neale cut several capers at the announcement, and returned to his carriage, while the defeated man was taken to his quarters at Staines.

REMARKS.—The report here given leaves little room for comment. Cannon, whose courage had "moulted no feather," was beaten by freshness, activity, and a better style of boxing than his own. This was his last fight, and thus, after his defeat by Jem Ward, the once formidable bargeman, like many another champion who has "trusted to the energy of a waning age," furnished one more instance of the truism that "youth will be served."

At Sam Tebbutt's opening dinner on the occasion of his taking the "Bull's Head," Saffron Hill (another of the demolished purlieus of Old Smithfield), Uncle Ben expressed his "Nevvy's" desire to meet Neale once more in the lists, provided Ned would deposit £250 against £200 of "mine uncle's" money. Neale closed with the proposal, and posted £10, but Neale's principal backer considering the conditions imprudent, he wrote from Brighton, whither he had gone, forfeiting the £10 down.

A few weeks afterwards, however, articles were signed at the "Castle," Holborn, for Neale to fight Jem Burn, £120 to £100, and the day fixed for Tuesday, Nov. 13th, 1827. So confident was Neale of the result that he named Monday, Nov. 12th (the day before the fight), for his benefit at the Tennis Court. After the sparring, Neale, accompanied by Harry Holt, started for Bagshot, to be near the proposed field of action.

Early on Tuesday morning the road to Staines was covered with all sorts of vehicles from London, and Shirley's, the New Inn was overflowing with first-rate company. Winkfield Plain, in Berkshire, was the spot in view, and the fancy lost no time in surrounding the ring. Near the appointed hour Jem Burn threw his hat into the ropes, accompanied by Tom Belcher and Tom Cannon as his seconds. Neale was close at his heels, and delivered his tile with the utmost confidence, attended by Josh Hudson and Harry Holt. The colours—blue, with a white spot, for Ned, and a Belcher handkerchief for Burn, were tied to the stakes. The men shook hands smilingly, and at eight minutes past one commenced

THE FIGHT.

Round 1.—On peeling, Jem looked the picture of health. He weighed thirteen stone, and was three inches taller than his adversary. Neale did not exactly answer the expectations of his friends; he looked pale, and his back and bosom were covered with a scorbutic eruption. Ned did not exceed twelve stone. He held his left hand remarkably high in defence, and in every other point seemed prepared for attack. Burn kept manœuvring to obtain an opening, but Neale was too wary to give a chance away. Jem at length let fly at the body, but Neale was away. Jem then tried left and right, but Neale, as before, got out of mischief. Burn, puzzled, made another attempt with his left hand, which alighted slightly on Ned's left ogle. Neale, in return, endeavoured to plant a heavy right-handed hit on the nob, but it fell short on the shoulder. Burn, anxious to do some execution, again let fly right and left, but out of distance. Ned took advantage of the mistake, went in to his man, and by a heavy right-handed blow on the side of his head, floored Burn like a shot. First event for the Streatham Youth.

2.—Jem came well up to the scratch, and commenced offensive operations right and left, but Ned, laughing, said it was "no go," and got out of the way of mischief like a skilful tactician, yet instantly returned to the attack, when Jem napped another floorer, to the great joy of the Streathamites. The Yorkites began to look blue.

3.—Jem could not measure his distance, and again threw his blows away, when Neale went in to punish sans cérémonie. ("Hit with him," says Tom Belcher. "Yes," replied Josh, "he will get much the best of that.") Burn stopped some hits, and returned on Neale's nob. The latter, however, soon resumed the lead. Jem was once more sent down with comparative ease, and Neale rested himself on his second's knee.

4.—Short but sweet to the Streatham Youth; Jem could not plant his blows, when Neale put in a throttler which sent Burn down in a twinkling. It is impossible to describe the exultation of the friends of Neale. Two to one offered.

5.—This was more a wrestling than a fighting round; both combatants were down side by side.

6.—Neale seemed perfectly awake to every move of his adversary, and got out of trouble with the utmost sang froid. In closing, Jem struggled hard, and both down.

7.—Jem endeavoured to plant two well-meant hits, but the science of Neale rendered them harmless. After a little manœuvring, Ned went to work, when Jem was soon sent down on his latter end.

8.—Jem had a small slice of luck at the opening of this round, by planting a left-handed hit on the right peeper of Neale, which produced a slight tinge of the claret. ("First blood," was claimed by the friends of Jem, but the Streatham Youth laughed, and said, "I shall soon make that even.") A sharp rally concluded the round, in which Jem threw many blows away, while Ned administered pepper until Jem went down staggering.

9.—Burn endeavoured to do something, but his blows generally fell short. Ned was always with his adversary upon the slightest mistake, and Jem was ultimately down.

10.—This was a well-fought round on both sides. Jem's right hand told on the side of Ned's head, and several other blows of Burn were also planted with effect, when Ned fell on the ropes and went down. ("Go along, Jem! that's the way to win! Keep it up, my lad," from his backers.)

11.—Burn put on the stopper well; and in closing Burn got down cleverly from the fibbing system attempted by his adversary.

12.—The nob of Jem looked rather the worse for wear; but he planted some slight facers. Neale fought his way into a rally, had the best of it, and in closing Burn was down.

13.—Jem went to work rather wild, but planted a hit or two. Ned, however, was with him, and dropped Burn by a blow in the mouth, like a shot.

14.—This round proved extremely serious to the Burnites. The combatants soon got into a rally, in which the blows of Neale operated like cannon-shot, till Jem was quite abroad, and went down of no use. (This severe punishment operated so severely upon the feelings of Uncle Ben that he fell on his back on the ground dreadfully convulsed. Several men who immediately ran to render Uncle Ben assistance could scarcely hold him during the time he was bled by a surgeon. On his recovery, he was immediately conveyed to Staines, and put to bed in a very exhausted state of body and mind.)

15.—Jem appeared at the scratch quite in a groggy state. The pepper-box was again administered in the most effectual manner by Neale; resistance seemed almost out of Jem's power, until he once more measured his length on the grass.

16.—Burn could not measure his distances, and fought wildly. Ned had it all his own way, punishing right and left, until Jem was down.

17, 18, 19.—In all these rounds Jem not only napped it in all manner of directions, but was sent down.

20. — Burn missed a well-aimed left-handed blow at the head of his opponent, when Neale, in return, planted a tremendous hit on his sensitive box, which not only produced the claret freely, but floored him. (Any odds, but no takers.)

21.—The quality of game could not be denied to Jem; he stood and took the milling like a receiver-general. He was knocked off his pins without any ceremony.

22.—The left hand of Neale met Jem bang in the middle of the head, which produced the claret in torrents, as he measured his length on the grass.

23.—Jem hit down before he had scarcely got up his arms.

24.—Jem slipped down by accident.

25.—Burn was piping, and almost abroad; but Belcher was on the alert to keep Jem at his work. ("Be ready, my dear boy," cried Tom; "hit with him, he's coming." "Yes," replied the John Bull Fighter, "Ned is coming, and your man will soon be going—or rather, like the auctioneer, gone!") Neale received a facer which produced the claret; but he returned the favour with interest, and Jem was again sent down.

26.—Jem now tried desperate fighting, hitting away in all directions; but Ned was too leary. The latter boxer got a stopper on the nob; but Jem was again down. ("You must admit, gents," observed the elegant Holt, "that Jem is a down-y one; he has been down almost to the end of the chapter. The finish is also near at hand. I'll bet any odds.")

27, 28, 29, 30.—In all of these rounds the lead and punishment were decidedly in favour of Neale, and Jem was sent down in every one of them.

31. — Jem showed fight, and planted a facer; but it was too slight to do anything like damage to Neale. The latter followed Jem all over the ring, until he sent him down. (Tom Cannon, by way of raising the spirits of Burn, said, "He can never lick

you, Jem." "Yes," replied Ned, "and you afterwards, and no mistake; and I'll try it, if you like.")

32, 33, 34, 35, 36.—It is true that in some of these rounds Jem planted facers which produced the claret, but he could not turn a single round in his favour. Ned was continually administering punishment, and Jem was down in all of these rounds. ("Take him away!")

37.—Jem was cruelly distressed, but he would not say "no," and showed fight at the scratch. He napped lots of milling in a rally, and went down as heavy as lead. ("Take him away! he's of no use!")

38.—Down, and no return; so much did Neale show his superiority over Jem.

39.—Of the same class; he appeared at the scratch only to be milled down. ("It's a shame to bring him up! Take him home, Belcher!")

40.—Burn, almost as a forlorn hope, went to work with more spirit than could have been expected from his exhausted state, and planted several hits in better style than in most of the preceding rounds; but this exertion was now too late, and he was milled down flat on his face. (The cries were extremely loud: "Take him away; you'll be lagged else." "Why don't you listen to the advice of your friends," said Josh, "if you wish to prevent serious consequences to yourselves?")

41.—It was all the cash in the Bank to a ninepence that Jem must lose it; in fact, his backers and seconds ought to have had him taken out of the ring. Jem down, with his face on the earth.

42.—Nearly U P; Burn was down as soon as he appeared at the scratch.

43, and last.—Jem could scarcely show at the scratch, he was so completely exhausted. He staggered about like a drunken man, when Neale did little more than push him down. It was all over; and when picked up by Tom Belcher, his head fell on his shoulder, and he was insensible. The fight continued forty-six minutes. Jem was bled in the ground; nevertheless, he remained in a state of stupor for several minutes. He was severely punished about the head, while Neale was scarcely the worse for the fight. In truth, so little did he care for the punishment he had received that he offered to fight Tom Cannon off-hand, for £100 a side, and it was a matter of difficulty that Neale's friends made him quit the ring. £7 10s. only were collected on the ground for Jem Burn.

REMARKS.—The perusal of the rounds of the above battle are so decisive in themselves as scarcely to require any observation. Ned had it all his own way, from the beginning of the fight to the end of the contest. His superior confidence, united with the science which was conspicuous in every round, pronounced him a master of the art of self-defence. Coolness is a winning faculty on the part of Neale, who possesses it in an eminent degree. Jem fought bravely, no one can deny; but contending in long bowls instead of close quarters rendered his blows non-effective, and he was completely beaten at out-fighting. It is, however, due to Jem Burn to state that he contested every inch of ground like a man of the highest courage. He would not say no, and refused to be taken away, which he might have done without compromising his character as a pugilist. He never left the scratch until nature had deserted him; and the best man in the world must, like Jem, submit to the fortune of war. Neale, in this conquest, obtained in such a superior style, placed himself high in the ranks of pugilism; and his backers entertained so high an opinion, not only of his talents, but of his integrity and thorough trustworthiness, that it was resolved to match him against the accomplished Jem Ward.

The very next day, at Burn's benefit at the Tennis Court, Neale, whose face was but slightly disfigured, mounted the stage after the principal bout, between Jem Ward and big Bob Burn, in which Jem sent the burly one off the platform with surprisingly little damage to his sixteen-stone carcass, and presented himself to the amateurs. He offered, such was the readiness of good men in those days, to meet Baldwin for £250 to £200 or £500 to £400, that day week, or that day month, or two months, at his option; or he would fight Tom Cannon, Reuben Martin, or any twelve-stone man in England, for any sum they pleased; or he would fight the three men named within three months, with a month's interval. This sweeping challenge brought up Ned Baldwin, who said he was not at that moment prepared to make a match, but would appoint an evening for the purpose, and give Neale notice to attend. Tom Cannon next showed. "Gentlemen," said the Windsor Gun, "I am out of condition, and both my shoulders are bad. I have now plaisters on my chest. But I hope to be well by April, when Neale shall not want a customer."

At a sporting dinner on Thursday, Nov. 22nd, 1827, at Sam Tebbutt's, the "Bull's Head," Peter Street, to celebrate Neale's victory, Ned was surrounded by backers and friends. The chairman (Pierce Egan) reviewed the victorious career of Neale, stating his battles, and that his name had never yet been associated with defeat—that he had proved himself as honest as he was brave, a dutiful son, an affectionate brother, a kind-hearted husband, and a sincere friend—in short, a true man in all the relations of life. He therefore proposed a subscription to present him with a silver cup of the value of one hundred guineas, as a testimony to his upright and brave conduct. The proposition was agreed to, and twenty-one guineas subscribed in the room.

The subject of a match between Jem Ward and Ned Neale was on the carpet at the Castle Tavern, Holborn, on Tuesday, Nov. 20th, 1827, when two gentlemen posted £5 a side, to be made £100—£15 a side to be posted the next evening. On the Wednesday Neale's backer announced that he had not been able to see Neale, and wished a postponement; but Ward's friend claimed forfeit, and it was paid over accordingly. £20 was then deposited by a friend of Neale's, to be made £200 if Neale consented to fight Ward in two months—the money to be returned (less half-a-dozen of wine) in the event of Neale's non-compliance. On Friday, Nov. 23rd, an immense assemblage of the fancy took place at the "Castle," when, Jem Ward not being present (he did not appear during the whole evening), forfeit was claimed. The gentleman who backed Ward demurred, stating he knew Jem was ready to go on with the match, and he was ready with a further deposit. Neale, who was in attendance, said, as the deposit had been made to fight for £200 within two months, he must decline complying with those terms. He did not think he could get into sufficient condition to meet such a man as Jem Ward, and he was resolved never to peril his own reputation, and the interest of his friends, by entering the ring unfit. The deposits were hereupon drawn.

Ned Baldwin now offered himself once again to Neale's notice for £150 a side. To this Neale replied, offering to fight Baldwin, as once beaten, for £250 to £200. Articles were formulated and signed, and Tuesday, March 11th, 1828, fixed as the day. Baldwin left town for Leicestershire to train. Here a trivial occurrence had well-nigh wrecked Baldwin's chance and money, as will be seen by the subjoined letter to the editor of the *Weekly Dispatch* :—

London, *Feb.* 2nd, 1828.

"SIR,—On my return from Melton Mowbray I was sorry to find my character had been assailed by a Leicester paper, in which my conduct has been entirely misrepresented. I refer to the account of a dispute which took place between two respectable coach proprietors, who, I hope, have settled their differences amicably. It is stated I took an active part in the 'disturbance.' Now, sir, the truth is that I was merely a passive spectator of the quarrel, and never interfered by word or act—in fact, I was equally a friend to both parties. Like others, I laughed, but knew my situation too well to interfere. I knew that I was backed against Ned Neale, and that by joining in such a dispute I should be 'throwing a chance away'—conduct of which even my enemies would scarcely accuse me. For being present, however, I was taken before a magistrate, and held to bail till the sessions, which will be held at the beginning of April; but even this fact did not justify the false statement to my prejudice made in the *Leicester Herald*. However, as my recognisances only stand good till the sessions, I shall continue to make my deposits with Ned Neale good; and I have too much reliance on his honourable feeling not to believe, even if I am obliged to put our meeting off for a month, that he will willingly grant me that time. He has said that he means fighting, and so do I; and as the articles express that the stakes shall remain till we have fairly decided who is the best man, upon that understanding I mean to act. I shall attend with my backers at Tom Cribb's, on Tuesday next, with the needful, and hope to meet my antagonist on friendly terms. With regard to the worthy magistrate who held me to bail, I have no doubt he felt he was justified; but when my trial takes place, I shall be able to prove my entire innocence of any illegal act whatever. By my profession, if fighting a few battles can be so called, I have been taught to love 'fair play.' I know enough of the sporting gentlemen of Leicestershire to believe that they are equal admirers of that truly British characteristic; and I rest perfectly satisfied that I shall not be sacrificed to any unjust prejudice which may have been excited against me from my being a member of the P. R.

"Yours respectfully,
"EDWARD BALDWIN."

On Tuesday evening, the 5th of February, the time appointed for making the fifth deposit, the "Union Arms," in Panton Street, was overflowing at an early hour. Neale and Baldwin were both present, and on "time" being called, both said their money was ready. Baldwin, alluding to the late unfortunate affair at Leicester, although perfectly innocent of any act of disorder whatever, said he had been held to bail to appear at the sessions, and also during the intervening period to keep the peace towards all His Majesty's subjects. This was an event which he had not foreseen, and he hoped Neale would liberally assent to the match being postponed for such a time as would allow him to appear at the sessions, when he should be enabled to show that he had been the victim of prejudice. Neale had said he meant fighting; so did he, and he hoped the stakes would be permitted to remain till the event came fairly off.

Neale said he was willing to give his antagonist every indulgence, and to meet his wishes to the fullest extent.

The articles were then altered according to the new arrangement, the men to fight for an even £250 a side, and the match fixed for the 22nd of April. If Baldwin should be bound in recognisances at that time, he would pay Neale's expenses to go to France; and if imprisoned, he would agree to forfeit £200 of the stakes down. With this all parties were satisfied, and Baldwin was applauded for the spirit he had displayed.

On Tuesday evening, March 4th, 1828, a meeting was held at Harry Holt's for the purpose of making good the last deposit towards the £250 a side. Neale's money was ready, but Baldwin had been disappointed in the expected arrival of a friend, who was to have posted a portion of the needful on his behalf. Neale said that he would not claim the forfeit. The word of a gentleman being therefore given that the required sum should be placed in the hands of the stakeholder in the course of a week, it was considered as understood that the whole of the money was made good. Another alteration was then made in the time of fighting. Baldwin remarked that the 22nd of April (the day then fixed) was in the week appointed for the Newmarket meeting, and this might prevent many of the turf men from being present. Baldwin therefore proposed an adjournment of the fight for a week. Neale said a week would make no difference to him; but if he acceded to Baldwin's wishes, he ought to have the right to name the place of meeting. To this Baldwin at once agreed, and it was therefore arranged that the fight should stand over to the 29th of April, and that Neale should have the right to say "where." Ill luck, however, pursued the fixture; and on Thursday, April 29th, 1828, many hundreds left London, and returned, few of them until the next day, after a weary journey to Liphook, in Hampshire, thence to Guildford and Godalming, to find that warrants against Neale and Baldwin were out in Surrey, Sussex, and Hampshire. A move into Berks was decided on, and Bagshot made the rendezvous. Here, at Hatchard's Lane, in the parish of Wingfield, the ring was pitched, and shortly after Neale arrived in the carriage of his patron, Mr. Sant. Ned quietly alighted, and threw his hat into the ring, attended by his seconds, Josh Hudson and Harry Holt. Bob was equally on the alert, and repeated the token of defiance, followed by Peter Crawley and Dick Curtis. Bob won the toss, when the colours were tied to the stakes, a bright purple for Baldwin and a dark blue bird's-eye for the Streatham Youth. The betting was seven to four on Neale. At half-past one o'clock the fight commenced :—

THE FIGHT.

Round 1.—The condition of Neale appeared good on stripping, but a few of his friends thought he was rather too fat, and blotches on his body were, as usual, prominent; Bob was also well, but he looked pale. Ned was confident, and after a little manœuvring for the first advantage, Bob hit out with his right, but Ned was leary, and it fell short; Bob then commenced the bustling system, when a few blows were exchanged. In closing Bob napped one on his cheek as he was going down. Neale fell on him. "Well done, Neale!"

2.—Bob, still on the bustle, hurried to his work, but again hit out of distance and fell on his hands. Ned missed a heavy upper cut with the right, that might otherwise have done mischief.

3.—Both hit short. Baldwin missed in a second attempt; but Ned planted a nobber, then went to work in right earnest, and not only put in a teaser on the side of Bob's head, but closed and gave the white-headed one a cross-buttock.

4.—Bob planted a slight facer, but received a severe return. In closing, Ned fibbed his opponent, and then threw him like a first-rate wrestler.

5.—On Neale's coming to the scratch, Curtis claimed "first blood" from Ned's nose, but the umpires could not perceive it. This was a short round, facers on both sides, the White-headed one again thrown.

6.—Ned planted two severe facers; Baldwin, in return, hit out wildly, and lost his distance. Neale repeated the dose on the left ear of Bob, which produced the claret, and the event of first blood was decided in favour of Neale. In closing Baldwin got down skilfully to prevent being thrown.

7.—The right hand of Neale again told, but in struggling for the fall Ned was undermost. "Bravo, Bob!"

8.—Nothing. Both men hit out of distance, when Bob ran in wildly after his adversary, missed him, and fell.

9.—Bob fond of bustling, but in rushing in he napped a snorter, the claret following the blow. In going down Neale was successful in planting two hits.

10.—This round looked like fighting; both men were on their mettle, and anxious to do mischief. Ned's right hand told—ditto, ditto, and ditto; yet Bob was not idle, and returned well; nevertheless, Baldwin was hit down. ("It's as right as the day," said the John Bull Fighter; "Ned's turned auctioneer; he knocked down the last lot cleverly, and Mr. Baldwin bought it.")

11.—The right hand of Bob would have been mischievous if he could have timed his blows; but he appeared so much in a hurry that they fell short. Baldwin put in a heavy body blow, but was thrown.

12.—Ned took the lead, and nobbed his adversary; Bob, endeavouring to return, missed. In closing, Baldwin slipped on his knees. Ned threw up his hands and walked away, amidst thunders of applause.

13.—Neale again had it all his own way; he threw Baldwin. Four to one and no takers, so satisfied were the spectators that Neale would prove the conqueror.

14.—Baldwin's left hand told on Neale's cheek, but the latter countered with effect. Bob received another severe cross-buttock.

15.—Bob could not change a single round in his favour, hitting wildly, and quite out of distance. He received a heavy blow on the nose. In closing Bob was thrown on the ropes.

16.—Bob did not heed scientific movements; he endeavoured to overwhelm Neale by bustling in helter-skelter, missed his aim, and fell.

17.—Of no importance. Bob piping. Ned planted his right hand. In closing, both down.

18.—A straight facer, and ditto by Neale, Bob returning as wild as a novice. Baldwin thrown.

19.—Bob had a small turn in this round. He planted a heavy hit on the left peeper of Neale, and another blow, which produced the claret on Neale's cheek. In going down Neale was undermost. ("That's the way to win," said Dick Curtis; "wait for him and make your right tell.")

20.—Both milling, counter-hits. Bob tried the bustling system again, and bored Neale down. ("Well done, Bob!")

21.—Bob stopped Ned's left hand cleverly, and gave Neale a teaser on his left eye. In struggling for the throw, both went down.

22.—This was a milling round. Bob seemed steadier, and returned hit for hit; but Neale planted a tremendous blow on his opponent's left eye, and threw him cleverly.

23.—Ned got out of mischief like an able tactician. He, however, soon returned to the charge, and with his right floored the White-headed one. This was the first knock-down blow.

24.—Bob came to the scratch rather abroad; he ran in wildly, slipped, caught hold of Ned, and fell on his knees. Neale again walked away, receiving lots of applause for his forbearance. In fact, he actually helped him up, which kindness Baldwin returned by a shake of the hand.

25.—Bob, full of pluck, fought his way into a spirited rally, and give and take was the feature for a short period, until Ned finished the round by giving Bob a severe cross-buttock.

26.—Bob commenced fighting as wild as ever. Ned endeavoured to stop his rush, when Bob slipped down with his hands up. Neale, though in the act of hitting, restrained himself, to prevent anything foul.

27.—Ned planted his right and left with success, Bob hitting out of all distance, as heretofore. In closing both down.

28.—Baldwin retreated to the ropes, followed by Ned. In closing at the ropes Neale tried fibbing, and also threw Bob.

29.—Had Baldwin steadied himself, and measured his distance, he could not have thrown so many right-handed hits away. Ned planted some slight taps, when both went down.

30.—The blows of Ned did not appear to do so much execution as heretofore; his friends thought he hit with his left hand open; Baldwin was met in his rush by a flush hit on his nob. In closing, Ned went down.

31.—Baldwin, by a sort of scrambling hit, felt for the left peeper of Neale, but the latter made good his right and left. In closing, both down.

32.—Neale again triumphant. He went up, sans cérémonie, to Baldwin's nob, and floored him. (A tremendous shout of applause from all parts of the ring.)

33.—Decidedly in favour of Neale; the right hand of the latter told with severity on Baldwin's already damaged listener; another desperate cross-buttock closed the round against Baldwin.

34.—The game exhibited by Bob was loudly praised; both men were fighting at points in this round. The advantage, however, was on the side of Neale, and Bob was ultimately thrown out of the ropes.

35.—Counter-hits. In closing, both went down; Neale struck his nob rather in an awkward manner.

36.—In spite of all the advice given by Dick Curtis to Bob he would still rush forward to attack his adversary. Ned, like a skilful general, got out of the way of danger, rendering the attempts of Baldwin abortive. Bob was thrown.

37.—The rounds now were short. Ned hit right and left, but not severely. Both down.

38.—Neale took the lead, and planted several hits; both again went down.

39.—Baldwin almost ran in to punish his adversary, which Neale perceiving stepped aside nimbly, and Bob fell.

40.—Up to this period of the battle Neale was the favourite. The latter got away from Bob's fury, and in closing Baldwin was thrown.

41.—Bob got a small turn in his favour in this round. It is true he was the most punished, but he did not appear reduced much in strength. Bob again missed with his right; but in closing he made a desperate effort, and threw Neale a severe cross-buttock. (The friends of Bob gave him thunders of applause, and the disinterested spectators were not backward in crying out, "Bravo!")

42.—Both men countered well; and after a long struggle, in closing, both down.

43.—("Hit with your right hand," said Dick, "and the battle must be your own. Don't run at your man like a mad bull.") But all advice was thrown away—Bob acted as heretofore, when Ned got neatly out of trouble. Baldwin received a heavy right-hander on the side of his head, which he endeavoured to return with his left; in so doing he fell on his knees, but instantly jumped up to renew the fight, when Ned obtained the throw.

44.—Ned made play with his right hand, but Bob was again on the bustle, and in struggling for the throw got Neale down.

45.—This was a short but busy round. Both on the alert—counter-hits—a rally, and in closing for the fall, Ned was thrown.

46.—Ned, as if determined to finish off his man, went to fight, *sans cérémonie.* He caught Baldwin on the right side of his nob, threw him a heavy cross-buttock, and fell over him.

47.—Neale's right and left told; Bob bored in, caught hold of his adversary, and fell on his knees. Ned, instead of punishing him, patted Baldwin on the back, and once more walked to the knee of his second, amidst uproarious applause.

48.—Neale took the lead right and left. Bob, wild at such treatment, closed, and got Neale down.

49.—A fighting round; capital counter-hits. Bob received so severe a facer that he went down like a spinning-top.

50.—The game displayed by Baldwin was the admiration of the spectators; his mug was punished, and his eyebrow badly damaged. Ned took the lead; and Bob, anxious to return, fell in the attempt.

51.—Bob was piping, and rather abroad; nevertheless his right hand was always dangerous; he was again unlucky in his distance. Ned planted his right hand, and Bob found his way to grass.

52.—Bob without delay fought into a rally, when Ned got out of trouble by turning round, but immediately resumed milling. In closing, Bob obtained the throw, and Neale came heavily down on his neck.

53.—Bob was no sooner at the scratch than he rushed in without any system, and succeeded in getting Neale down.

54.—The execution of Neale was not so severe as in the early part of the battle; and his left hand was open. In closing, Baldwin obtained the fall.

55.—Each trying for the best; stopping and hitting until both down.

56.—Neale appeared angry, and did not deliver his blows so steadily as heretofore. In closing, Baldwin found himself on the turf.

57.—The left hand of Neale was a little puffed, but he planted his right severely. Both down.

58.—Bob now stood higher in the opinions of the spectators; his strength was not so much reduced as might have been expected; but high odds were still offered on Neale. In closing, both down, and both weak.

59.—Baldwin certainly appeared better, and did not pipe so much as he had done in several of the preceding rounds. Neale went to work right and left, Bob endeavouring to be with him, but Ned obtained the throw.

60.—Bob left all system out of the case, and hit in all directions. Exchanges, when Bob, in closing, almost pinned Ned to the ground by superior strength.

61.—Counter-hits, Baldwin soon down.

62.—The right of Neale told; but with his left he could not do any execution. Bob went down from a slight hit.

63.—Baldwin crept into favour with the spectators this round, by the game he displayed, and his determined mode of fighting. Ned made play, but Bob was with him; and some smart exchanges took place. In closing, after a severe struggle, Bob got his opponent down.

64.—Bob, revived by a nip of *eau-de-vie*, planted his right well; but Ned countered, and mischief was done on both sides. Bob pushed on his luck, and boring in, laid hold of Neale by the neck, and in a severe struggle for the fall the Streatham hero received a dangerous twist, and fell in a singular manner. Ned was quite abroad for a few seconds. Dick Curtis exclaimed, "We have won it!" The anxiety of the spectators was intense; but Ned revived, and was ready at the scratch when time was called.

65.—Neale was distressed by the late fall, but he began his work well. Some sharp counter-hits. In closing, Bob again tried for the throw, but he was not so successful. Neale punished Baldwin as he was going down.

66.—The White-headed One was kept on the alert by his admirable little second, Curtis, and slashed away like a good one. Had his distances been anything like correct at this juncture, he had yet a chance of winning. In closing, Neale was again thrown, and he told Harry Holt "to take care of his neck" as he was picking him up.

67.—Baldwin was quite alive to the position, and neglected no opportunity to turn it to account. He again kept Neale on the bustle, caught the latter round the tender place on his neck, and obtained the throw. ("Bravo, Bob! you'll win it now, if you mind what you are at!")

68.—Neale still distressed; Bob to all appearance the stronger man. The White-headed Blade now thought the bustling mode to be successful, and tried it on at once. Neale fearlessly met him. In closing, Baldwin squeezed his opponent, got him down, and fell on him. ("Why, Bobby," said Curtis, "you have found out the way at last. You are doing the trick.")

69.—Neale commenced milling. In closing, Bob's strength enabled him again to get the fall. At this moment a great bustle was heard on one side of the ring, and a cry of, "The beak! the beak!" An elderly, pale-faced gentleman in black was observed making his way for the ring. He proclaimed himself a magistrate, and called upon all parties to desist. The smooth-tongued blades of the Fancy tried all their eloquence to appease the wrath of the beak, by stating to him what a pity it would be, at such an interesting period, to put a stop to the event, which, as a matter of course, an hour having elapsed, would end of itself in the course of a few minutes.

70.—During the argument time was called, and the men appeared at the scratch. Neale was ready, and Bob equally so—no flinching, until Baldwin was floored.

71.—Neale rallied himself, and went to work with considerable spirit; Baldwin attacked his adversary wildly. Both down.

72.—The beak endeavoured to break through the crowd to get at the combatants, but he could not. Hitting away on both sides, but Neale now and then jobbing the nob of his adversary. In closing, both down.

73.—("Now's the time," said the Pet to Rob; "go to work, hit steady with your right hand, and you can't lose it." "What nonsense!" replied Hudson; "how can you mislead the poor fellow so!") Both on their mettle, and several blows were exchanged. In closing, Baldwin obtained the throw.

74.—The rounds were now very short. Baldwin bustling, while Neale was endeavouring to catch him as he was coming in. Both down, Neale undermost.

75.—Exerting themselves like brave men, regardless of danger, until both of them fell out of the ropes.

76.—Neale successively planted three jobbing hits; nevertheless, Bob returned to the attack undismayed. In closing, Baldwin pulled down his adversary.

77.—Counter-hits, and a good round altogether, until both went down, Baldwin uppermost.

78.—The fight had materially changed. Bob, who, in the early part of the battle, in the opinion of nearly all the spectators, had

no chance of success, was viewed with a different eye. Neale's left hand was of little use to him. Both down.

79.—Neale took the lead, and planted his right and left. Baldwin fell on his knees.

80.—Counter-hits, but not heavy enough to put a finish to the battle. In closing, both down, Neale undermost.

81.—(The disinterested part of the ring—those persons who had not a copper on the event seemed to think that it was anybody's battle.) Neale, always ready, went to work; Bob, on the bustle, endeavoured to be with him. In closing, both down, Neale undermost.

82.—Neale hit with his left hand half open, then planted a facer with his right. Baldwin, still wild, but determined, endeavoured to return. His distance as heretofore proved incorrect. He rushed into a close, when both fell.

83.—Neale had not lost his gaiety, and tried to administer punishment. In closing, the struggle was desperate for the throw; after a severe encounter, Bob was uppermost. Both men much distressed.

84, and last.—Baldwin at the scratch, and Neale also ready to the call of "time." Both combatants went to work without hesitation. Some sharp hits were exchanged, when both men went down in the corner of the ring, close to the magistrate. One hour and a quarter had elapsed.

His worship now waxed angry at the want of attention paid to his authority, exclaiming, in a peremptory tone of voice, "I'll endure this no longer!" Laying hold of the arm of Josh Hudson, he told Harry Holt of the consequences which must result to the whole of them, if they did not put an end to the battle. Hudson, obedient to the law, resigned his situation as second, when an amateur rushed into the ring and gave his knee to Neale. The magistrate then spoke to Neale and Baldwin, and observed that he had been sent for by a gentleman in the neighbourhood, to interfere and put a stop to the fight: that he entertained no hostility against any person present, and if they immediately quitted the ring peaceably, he should take no further notice of what had occurred. "If the battle is continued," said he, raising his voice, "the combatants, seconds, and every individual present aiding and assisting must take the consequences." The magistrate, however, good-naturedly acknowledged that he had met with more civility and attention than he could have expected from such a multitude. His worship then retired from the scene of action, amidst loud cheers from the spectators.

Further opposition was voted imprudent, and hostilities ceased. Bob and Ned shook hands together, left the ring, and walked to their vehicles.

The reporter asked Baldwin how he felt, when he emphatically replied, "What should be the matter with me?" It was thought advisable by the friends of both parties that the combatants should return to Bagshot, and be put to bed.

It was not to be supposed that the question of superiority would remain thus undecided between two such courageous and well-matched men; so, after some little debate upon the "draw," consequent on magisterial interference, they agreed to add £50 a side to the stakes, and to meet once more —the time the 28th of May, 1828, the place No Man's Land, in Hertfordshire. How gallantly Neale fell, after a desperate battle of sixty-six rounds in seventy-one minutes, may be read in Chapter VII. of this volume.

Neale's friends and admirers did not desert him in defeat. At Neale's benefit at the Tennis Court, on the 21st of July, 1828, at which Tom Spring, Peter Crawley, Holt, Curtis, and the leading men appeared, a silver cup of the value of 100 guineas was presented by Pierce Egan as a testimonial of his "bravery, honour, and incorruptible integrity." This trophy for many years formed one of the treasures of the "Rose and Crown."

Reuben Marten now proposed to back John Nicholls for £100 a side against Neale, and the cartel being accepted, the match was made offhand, at Marten's house, the "City of London," Berwick Street, Soho. The deposits were duly made until £60 was down, when Nicholls's backers were absent, but Neale waived the forfeit, and generously agreed to take £25 when the fight should come off; £50 being promised by a gentleman, a backer of Nicholls, for the fight to take place on his estate. We note this, as on another occasion, with Baldwin, Neale waived his claim to forfeit when £170 was down.

The day was fixed for the 23rd September, 1828, the place Fisher Street, in Sussex. Nicholls—a fine, powerful young man, whose recent victory over Dick Acton, a pugilist thought good enough to be matched against Jem Ward and Peter Crawley, had raised him by a jump to the pinnacle of fame—had good friends. The sporting men of London, however, did not believe in a comparative novice being pitted against the victor of a dozen battles, and seven to four was laid at the "Castle," "Queen's Head," and "King's Arms," on the Streatham champion.

On Tuesday morning Guildford, Godalming, and the villages near the scene of action were all alive, the amateurs having left London overnight.

An immense cavalcade was soon on the move towards Fisher Street, where, at the Royal Cylinder Works, the property of Mr. Stovell, preparations had been made from an early hour. Banners were displayed, two military bands, and six small pieces of cannon in a turf battery were discharged occasionally, and a general rustic merry-making, more like a fair than the preliminaries of a fight, was going on. Tables and forms, with eatables and drinkables, were provided gratuitously for certain visitors within the houses and factory of Mr. Stovell. In an enclosed piece of ground a twenty-four feet ring of turf, laid and levelled, was roped in, with seats for the umpires and referee. At a distance of twelve feet a roped circle kept back the spectators, while round all was a double line of wagons, the inner ones sunk in the ground by holes dug as deep as their axletrees, the outer line being on the level of the field. The ground was kept by 150 stout countrymen with staves, in white smocks, with blue ribands in their hats, marshalled by the indefatigable Mr. Stovell.

At eleven o'clock a curious procession approached. Reuben Marten and Nicholls, in a light two-wheeler, followed by some friends, were succeeded by Neale in a barouche, in which were seated Tom Spring and Harry Holt, the "ribands" handled by Will Scarlett, the renowned "dragsman." The men were accommodated with separate apartments in Mr. Stovell's house till the hour of battle arrived.

At ten minutes past one Nicholls dropped his hat within the ropes, and Neale immediately followed his example. Neale was attended by Tom Spring and Harry Holt, Nicholls by Jem Ward and Reuben Marten. Nicholls won the toss for corners, and both men sported true blue for their colours.

THE FIGHT.

Round 1.—Nicholls justified the report of his superior personal requisites. He stood nearly two inches over Neale, and his weight, thirteen stone four pounds, was well and evenly distributed. He was indeed the model of an athlete. Neale, whose weight was twelve stone four pounds, looked hard, brown, and muscular, and well capable of a long day's work. Great caution on both sides. The men stepped round and round each other, making feints, for full five minutes—the seconds of Nicholls advising him to use caution and let his man "come to him," which Neale did not seem inclined to do. At last Nicholls sent out his right at Neale's throat. It was short, for Neale jumped away. More tedious sparring and manœuvring, until both men seemed weary of holding up their hands, the young one most so. Neale, seeing a favourable opening, sprang forward, delivering a straight right-hander on his adversary's collar bone. It was intended doubtless for the side of his head, but fell lower from the superior height of his opponent. It was a terrific blow, and sounded like the crack of a pistol-shot, leaving a broad red mark, that soon after swelled, as a token of its force. A rally followed, in which Neale planted a heavy body blow with the right, and his left on Nicholls's mouth, who returned on Neale's head. Neale finished the round prettily by getting hold of his huge adversary and throwing him neatly from the hip. Immense applause from the Londoners.

2 to 12.—All similar in character. Neale drew his man and punished him for coming in, Neale now and then getting down to end the round.

13.—Nicholls, finding himself out-manœuvred, rushed in ding-dong. Neale met him coolly, and actually sent him off his legs. ("It's all U P," cried Ned Stockman. "Who'll take two to one?")

14 to 17.—In every round Neale made his right and left tell with effect, getting away or stopping the return, until poor Nicholls was a pitiful spectacle. In the sixteenth and seventeenth rounds Neale sent Nicholls down with a straight left-hander. Cries of "Take him away."

18, and last.—Nicholls tried to get in at his man, but was literally hit out right and left. Neale closed and threw his man heavily. Jem Ward stepped forward and said his man should fight no more, and Neale, stepping up to the umpires and referee, was told he was the conqueror.

REMARKS.—This one-sided affair hardly calls for comment. It merely adds one more instance to the innumerable proofs that mere strength and courage are more than balanced by the skill, readiness, and precision of the practised master of the science of defence.

Roche, a publican of Exeter, whose provincial reputation as a wrestler was higher than his boxing capabilities, was matched by his overweening friends against Neale. The preliminaries duly arranged; the stakes, £100 a side, made good; and the day fixed for the 2nd December, 1828; the men met on the North Chapel Cricket Ground, Sussex, forty-four miles from London by road. Neale trained at Milford, in Surrey, and there, it afterwards came out, he was "interviewed," as modern reporters would style it, by an envoy from Roche's party, who offered to secure to him £500 to lose the fight, and a further sum of two hundred if he would give in under fifty minutes. All this Neale communicated to his backers; and so well was the secret kept that a double defeat awaited the " Knights of the × ," in the disgrace of their champion and the depletion of their pockets. Had the countermine been discovered, the defeated Devonian declared, " all the King's horses " should not have drawn him into the ring. In order yet further to keep up the "fool's paradise" into which these bucolic knaves delivered themselves, the emissary presented Neale with a new suit of clothes and £18 " earnest money," keeping £2 for commission; and on the very morning of the battle he added £8 out of £10 entrusted to him for the same nefarious purpose. The " cross coves," assured that all was right, freely backed their man, and were not aware of the mine until it burst beneath their feet, scattering to the wind their hopes and calculations. Roche, who had come up to London, finished his training at the renowned Johnny Gilpin's house, the " Bell," at Edmonton, then a charming rural retreat, with its flower and tea gardens; now a well-accustomed modern ginshop, resplendent in gilding, gas, and plate glass, and belted in with brick, mortar, and shops.

Roche, who reached Godalming overnight, set out a little before twelve in a barouche; while Neale, in a four-horse drag, started from Milford, and soon overtook him on the road. Tom Spring, the " Portsmouth Dragsman," Harry Holt, and other friends, were on the roof of Neale's coach, and were first on the ground. Roche soon after alighted, under the care of Ben Burn and young Dutch Sam, who were engaged as his seconds. His colours were a light blue, Neale's a dark blue bird's-eye. The toss for corners was won by Harry Holt for Neale, who was also waited on by Tom Spring. As the men stood up, the contrast was striking. Roche, who stood nearly six feet, weighed, it was reported, fourteen stone. His advantages in weight and length, however, were fully counterbalanced by his apparent age and staleness. His superfluous meat hung in collops over the belt of his drawers, and he was altogether soft and flabby. The Streatham man, *au contraire*, looked bright, sinewy, fresh, and active, though he had trained rather lighter than on some former occasions, weighing twelve stone two pounds. The umpires and referee having been chosen, the men stood up, at ten minutes to one, for

THE FIGHT.

Round 1.—As Roche held up his arms and moved half round to face the movements of Neale, he betrayed the yokel in every move. The Streatham hero eyed him with satisfaction, and walked round him with his hands well up. Roche flourished his long arms awkwardly, with no particular object but defence, and as soon as Neale saw an opening in he dashed, delivered with his left a half-arm hit on Roche's eye, following it by such a tremendous bodier with the right that down went the mighty wrestler on the broad of his back, amid the shouts of the Londoners, the long faces of the provincials, and the consternation of the "ready-made luck" division, who were utterly dumbfounded at such a commencement. As Roche was picked up and taken to his corner he looked towards Neale with a mixture of surprise and reproach, as if to say, "Is this the way I am to be served?"

2.—A repetition of Round 1. Roche made play awkwardly; Neale retreated and shifted, stopping him cleverly. At length he in turn stepped in, delivered his one, two, cuttingly, and down went the Devonian. Roche was evidently remonstrating with his seconds in his corner, while his friends of the + division were running about frantically, hedging their bets if they could.

3.—This round only differed from the two preceding in the fact that, after some exchanges, in which the balance was all in favour of Neale, the latter suddenly closed, and giving Roche his leg, clearly threw the wrestler, amid the shouts of the Londoners and the astonished silence of the men from the "West Countrie."

4, 5, and 6.—Ditto, ditto, ditto. Roche tried, however, a little up-hill fighting, and hit Neale twice or thrice, but with little effect, while Ned's left-handers operated like kicks of a horse. (£100 to £10 on Neale offered.)

7.—In a bustling exchange Ned sent his left obliquely over Roche's shoulder, who instantly clutched him, and endeavoured to bear him down. To the surprise of all Ned fairly lifted his ponderous adversary, and sent him down heavily by the back-heel, falling on him. (Utter dismay among the Devonians, and uproarious joy among the regular ring-goers. Ten to one going begging.)

It would be a mere waste of space to detail further the ensuing rounds, which went on up to the 30th. Roche, however, cut up game, and manfully did his best when he found how he was "sold" by his friends, who were themselves deservedly "sold" in turn. In Round 29, Ned being called upon by Spring to "put on the final polish," went and delivered a left jobbing hit; Roche shifted, and in returning got Ned by the neck, under his arm, and fairly lifted him off the ground. Neale was for a few seconds in a critical position, but Roche, as he hung his weight on him, did not know what to do with him, and instead of being severely fibbed Ned got down cleverly, to the great relief of his anxious friends.

30, and last.—Neale broke ground cautiously, but confidently, making play with both hands, first delivering on the head and following it with a body blow, in the coolest and most workmanlike manner, Roche "standing it like a lamb," as one of his backers bitterly remarked. Neale after following him round the ring, at length caught him a straight one on the nose, then a flush hit on the mouth, and Roche went down on his back, Neale falling over him. When Roche was in his corner there seemed to be a sort of conference, when Ned walked across and assured Roche that he "meant to win and no mistake, so he might go on if he liked." This plain hint was duly appreciated, and Roche declared he would "fight no more." Time, thirty minutes.

REMARKS.—A less accomplished fighter than Roche never stripped to contend with so tried a boxer as Ned Neale. Independent of heavy slowness, his ideas of defence and stopping were of the clumsiest and most puerile description. Though no doubt superior to Ned as a mere wrestler, even in this he was taken by surprise and signally overthrown. Great pains were taken to circulate stories of the strength and prowess of Roche, to cover the arranged defeat of Neale, as the vanquished man afterwards confessed. There is no doubt that Roche first issued his challenge inconsiderately, and, from an undue estimate of his own boxing capabilities; but that his confidence was based upon the information that he was to have an easy victory, all matters being made smooth for the result. Poor Roche, in truth, was a mere tool in the affair, and paid the penalty of his presumption and credulity.

Neale returned to the Swan Inn to dress, and after his ablutions met a party of friends from Portsmouth at dinner, his features being without a scratch. In the afternoon his " caravan " set out, decorated with blue and white favours, and accompanied a pair of Kentish-keyed bugles—the predecessors of our modern cornets-à-piston—on a drive through the villages, amid the cheers of the multitude, to Milford, where, on reaching his training quarters, he found the house ornamented with blue and white bunting, and bannerets of blue and white ribbons, with mine host Mandeville at the door, his old wrinkled face cracking like a mealy potato as he announced dinner number two, which was prepared in his spacious and convenient club-room. A score of smiling friends welcomed the victor, and Ned's health was drunk with enthusiasm. Neale declared, in returning thanks, that " he was never happier, and hoped he had convinced his friends that he would not deceive them, as honour was dearer to him than money. He had punished those who would have had him rob those to whom he owed his fame and good name, and to deceive those who meant wrong he considered both fair and honest."

Far different was the case with poor Roche. After being taken back to his inn and bled—for which one of his chapfallen backers tendered the operator a shilling—he was deserted, and but for one friend might have been almost penniless. That the downfall of the " clever ones " was signal was manifest, and those country friends whom they " let into the secret " were loud in their protestations of the whole affair being a " a fluke." Two or three London houses used by the conspirators, which had prepared illuminations in honour of the " certainty," were conspicuous for their total eclipse when the real news arrived.

Neale and Roche showed on the following Thursday, at Harry Holt's benefit, Roche exhibiting heavy marks of head punishment, while Neale had not a scratch.

With the close of 1828 came our hero's retirement from the P. R., and it is to be regretted that mine host of the " Rose and Crown "—for he had now settled down as Boniface in the pleasant village of Norwood, then celebrated for its rurality and gipsy encampments—did not adhere to this resolution ; but it was not to be. Some taunting words of a very " fast " young boxer, Young Dutch Sam, led to Neale's acceptance of his challenge for £100 a side. The fight came off at Ludlow, April 7th, 1829, and after a gallant struggle of seventy-one rounds, in one hour and forty-one minutes, Neale succumbed to his youthful and scientific opponent. Dissatisfied with the issue, Neale lost no time in challenging Young Sam to a second encounter, which, after an arrest of Neale and a postponement, came off near Bumstead, in Essex, on the 18th of January, 1831. Here the result was again defeat, this time in fifty-two minutes and fourteen rounds. It was clear that Neale's best days had gone by.

Prompted by courage rather than prudence, he made yet one more appearance in the P. R. It was with an early opponent, Tom Gaynor (See LIFE OF GAYNOR, Chap. IX., *post*), and here again he had miscalculated his energies, succumbing after a gallant battle of 111 minutes, during which forty-five rounds were contested.

The fistic career of Ned Neale thus closed, as with so many other athletes, in defeat. Yet he retired with his laurels unsullied, his character for courage and honesty unsmirched ; and respected by all who knew him, he shuffled off " this mortal coil " at the " Rose and Crown," Norwood, near the place of his birth, on the 15th of November, 1846.

CHAPTER VI.

JEM BURN ("MY NEVVY"). 1824—1827.

THE sobriquet " My Nevvy " with old ring-goers long survived the sponsor (Uncle Ben), who first bestowed it upon his *protégé* on introducing Jem Burn to the P. R., an event which took place in 1824.

Jem first saw the light at Darlington, in the county of Durham, twenty years previous—namely, on the 15th March, 1804—and was in due time apprenticed to a skinman (*vulgo*, a " skiver ") at Newcastle-on-Tyne. We need not say that Jem came of a fighting stock—both his uncles, " Big Bob " and " Ben " being well known within and without the twenty-four-foot roped square miscalled the " ring ; " the latter at this period being the popular host of the " Rising Sun," in Windmill Street, Piccadilly, in after years the domicile of " Jolly Jem " himself.

Now the fame of his muscular relatives had reached the remote northern residence of Jem, and, like Norval, " he had read of battles, and he longed to follow to the field some warlike chief ; " so, having tried " his 'prentice han' " on a north-country bruiser of some local fame, hight Gibson, he, like other aspiring spirits, looked towards the great Metropolis for a wider field for the exercise of his talents.

It is recorded that Jem's battle with Gibson was a severe one, occupying one hour and twenty minutes ; and that in another bout with a boxer named Jackson, a resolute fellow, Jem, in a two hours' encounter, displayed such quickness and ability as to spread his fame throughout the district.

Brown, a twelve-stone wrestler, with some fistic pretensions, challenged " Young Skiver," as his comrades then called him. In twenty-five minutes he found out his mistake, retiring from the ring with second honours, while Jem was comparatively without a mark.

As a matter of course, on his arrival in London Jem made his way to Uncle Ben's, where he was received with a hearty welcome, had the run of a well-stocked larder, and was soon hailed as a " morning star " of the first magnitude, and fit herald of new glories to the " Rising Sun."

Uncle Ben lost no time in presenting "My Nevvy" to the Corinthian patrons of his "crib;" and as Jem was certainly clever with the mufflers, stood five feet ten in his shoes, with good arms, no lack of confidence, and great youthful activity and dash, he was looked upon as a likely aspirant, at no distant day, for the championship of England, recently vacated by the accomplished Tom Spring, after his two fights with Langan.

The friends of Uncle Ben, however, were too prudent to risk Jem's opening prospects by matching him with a first-class professional. At this period there was an immense immigration of heavy "Patlanders," chiefly *viâ* Liverpool, of whom Pierce Egan was the literary Mæcenas, and Jack Langan the M.C. Among them was one styled "Big O'Neal," who must not be confounded with the "Streatham Youth," Ned, whose name, for some time, Pierce insisted on printing with the national prefix "O'," though he expunged it from the fifth volume of "Boxiana," and on his presentation cup.

Articles were drawn for the modest figure of £25 a side, witnessed by Langan and Uncle Ben, and the day and place fixed for the 26th of July, 1824, within fifty miles of London. At the appointed time the men met at Chertsey Bridge, near Staines. O'Neal, attended by Langan and Peter Crawley, first threw his hat into the ring, and "My Nevvy" soon followed suit, esquired by Tom Owen and Uncle Ben—so that all six, principals and seconds, were emphatically "big 'uns." The Irishman was the favourite, at six to four, his fame having "gone before him." The colours, a green bandanna for O'Neal, and a chocolate with light blue spot for Burn, having been tied to the stakes, the men lost no time in peeling, and stood up at a few minutes past one for

THE FIGHT.

Round 1.—On stripping, it was any odds in favour of O'Neal; it was a horse to a hen by comparison; indeed, some said that it was a shame for Ben Burn to have matched his nephew against a man of such superior weight. "The young one can foight a bit, I know, and we'll soon tell'ee all aboot it," replied Ben. Burn went to work with considerable judgment, held up his hands well, shifting round cleverly, and milling on the retreat, Cribb's favourite mode. Burn put in two nobbers, and got well away; when O'Neal, like novices in general, kept following his opponent all over the ring, napping punishment at every step, till the Young One was bored upon the corner of the ropes, when he dropped. (Loud shouting for Burn; and "My Uncle quite proud of his nephew.")

2.—O'Neal wiped his peeper; in fact, he had received a nasty one between his ogles, that had placed them on the winking establishment. Burn was a little too fast. He stepped in to draw his man, when Pat met him with a smart jobber on his nose, which convinced the North Country Sprig that he must avoid O'Neal's clumsy fist as much as possible, or his fine science might be of little service to him. O'Neal made a hit, but Burn returned the blow with interest. The Sprig kept the ring well, and Pat was compelled to run all over the ground to make a blow. Burn went down from a slight hit.

3.—The mug of O'Neal was altered a little; the claret was streaming down from his temple, and his right eye was damaged. Burn fought in great style; he made a number of good hits without any return. The Irishman was bothered: he got a lick every now and then, and he looked about him, as much as to say, "Where the devil did that polt come from?" Burn finished the round by going down.

4-10.—In all these rounds, except the last, Burn had the "best of it;" and it was evident, if his strength stayed with him, he could not lose the battle, but he was getting weak. Burn was hit cleanly down. ("That's the way," said Langan. "Do that again, and I can make money by you, if it is only to floor oxen for the butchers.")

11-15.—The nob of O'Neal was sadly disfigured, and he was almost a blinker. He gave every chance away, instead of fighting his opponent. ("Long Bowls," said the Sage of the East, who was close to the ring, "will never do for a novice, especially when he has got weight on his side. O'Neal ought to be placed close to his man, and told to hit out, and never leave off till he has put the gilt on his antagonist.") Burn, after bestowing all the pepper he was able to on O'Neal's face, went down weak.

16-20.—The gameness of O'Neal could not be questioned; and although so bad a fighter, he was backed as a favourite on account of his strength. He got Burn down, and fell heavily upon him.

21-25.—The last round was the best contested during the battle; the Irishman, though nearly blind, administered some heavy hits, and finally knocked Burn down.

26.—It was anybody's battle at this period. Burn was getting extremely weak, and O'Neal in such a dizzy state that he threw most of his blows away. The fighting of Burn was highly praised; he planted three or four nobbers on the old places; but the Yorkshire Youth was hit down.

27-30.—O'Neal was nearly in the dark, and Burn nobbed him as he thought proper; in fact, the Irishman was completely at the mercy of the fists of his opponent. O'Neal went down in a state of stupor, and Langan could scarcely get him up. ("Take the game fellow away!")

31.—O'Neal was quite abroad—he could not see his opponent, and, in making a hit at the air, stumbled forward on the ground.

32, and last.—On time being called, O'Neal left his second's knee, and turned away from the scratch. He was completely blind. Over in fifty minutes. Langan gave in for him.

REMARKS.—Great credit is due to young Burn, not only for the pluck he manifested throughout the battle, but the science he displayed, and the mode he persevered in to win the battle. We never saw better judgment displayed upon any occasion. It may be urged, we are well aware, that he had nothing to fight against but weight: yet, if that weight had been brought up to him on setting to every round, there was a great probability that that weight would have so reduced his exertions as to have prevented young Jem from proving the conqueror. He ought not to be over-matched again. O'Neal did all that a brave man could do. He proved himself an excellent taker, and there is some merit even in that quality belonging to a man who enters the P. R. We have seen several fine fighters who do not possess the taking part of milling, but who have been most liberal in giving handfuls of punishment to their opponents; but to give and not receive is one of the secrets of prize-fighting. We never saw a man more interested in the success of another, or exert himself more, than Langan on the part of O'Neal; but O'Neal is not of the stuff of which clever pugilists are made.

Sir Bellingham Graham, who viewed the contest, was so pleased with the exertions and courage of Jem Burn that he made the young pugilist a present of five sovereigns.

Jem was matched by Uncle Ben against Martin (the well-known "Master of the Rolls") for £300 a side. This match was to have been decided on Thursday, October 26th, 1824, and was looked for with anxiety, as the goodness and skill of Martin were well established.

On the day appointed the cavalcade had reached Staines, when part of the secret was let out, that "it would be no fight between Martin and Jem Burn." Upwards of an hour having elapsed in consultation, the mob started off to Laleham, to take a peep at the ring. It was ascertained at Laleham that Martin would not show; but in the midst of the doubts a magistrate appeared. Luckily for the backers of the Master of the Rolls, this circumstance saved their blunt, otherwise the stakes must have been forfeited to Jem Burn. Something wrong evidently had been intended ; but that wrong could not be performed so as to deceive the amateurs of pugilism, and therefore the fight did not take place. Jem Burn threw his hat into the ring, declared he meant to fight a fair battle, and demanded the battle money. This, however, was contrary to agreement, as the magistrate remained, and declared he would not allow a breach of the peace.

Jem was backed against Aby Belasco, to fight on the 18th of November, 1824, but the stakes were drawn by the consent of both parties. This was in consequence of a meeting at which Ned Neale offered himself to " My Uncle's " notice, who thought this a better match. Articles were drawn and signed for Jem to do battle with Neale for £100 a side ; to come off on Tuesday, December 19th, 1824, on Moulsey Hurst. After an obstinate contest of thirty-one rounds, occupying one hour and thirty-eight minutes, Jem was defeated, as related in our last chapter.

Our hero was next matched with Phil Sampson for £50 a side. This battle took place at Shere Mere, in Bedfordshire, on Tuesday, June 14th, 1825. Jem did all that a brave man could to win the battle, and his backers were perfectly satisfied with his conduct ; but, after twenty-three rounds, occupying one hour and ten minutes, Burn again sustained defeat.

Jem stood so well in the opinion of his friends, notwithstanding he had lost his two last battles, that he was matched against Pat Magee for £100 a side. Magee, in Liverpool, was patronised by the fancy of that place, but he was only known by name in milling circles in the Metropolis. He had beaten a rough commoner of the name of Boscoe, a fine young man of amazing strength, and a tremendous hard hitter with his right hand ; but, in a second contest, Magee had surrendered his laurels in turn to Boscoe. Such was the history of the Irish hero, Magee. It was asserted, however, that he had recently made great improvement as a boxer, and as he was determined to have a shy with a London pugilist, he was backed against Jem Burn.

It was agreed the mill should take place between London and Liverpool ; but the backers of Magee having won the toss, it gave them the advantage of twenty miles in their favour, and Lichfield racecourse was selected as the place for the trial of skill. A more delightful situation could not have been chosen ; from the windows of the Race Stand the prospect was truly picturesque and interesting.

On Tuesday morning, July 25th, 1826, the road from Birmingham to Lichfield exhibited some stir of the provincial fancy; and although the races at Derby and Knutsford and the Nottingham Cricket Match might have operated as drawbacks to the spectators at the fight, not less than six thousand persons were present.

On Monday evening, Burn and his uncle took up their abode at the Swan Inn, in the city of Lichfield; Magee and his friends patronised the " Three Crowns." The ring was well made, and everything conducted throughout with the most perfect order. Randall, Oliver, Sampson, Dick Curtis, Ned Neale, Fuller, Barney Aaron, Young Gas, Fogo, Harry Holt, Tom Gaynor, and Arthur Mathewson, appeared on the ground to render their assistance to the combatants. The swells in the Grand Stand were admitted at the low figure of six shillings per head. Previous to the combatants appearing in the ring, it was whispered that two men, " dressed in a little brief authority," were in attendance to stop the fight; but this matter was soon disposed of, and made " all right," when Jem Burn threw his castor into the ring, attended by Tom Belcher and Phil. Sampson. In a few minutes afterwards, Magee, arm-in-arm with Donovan and Boscoe, also repeated the token of defiance, by planting his pimple-coverer in the ropes. The colours were yellow for Burn and green for Magee, which were tied to the stakes. The odds were six to four on Jem. Burn weighed twelve stone one pound, and Magee thirteen stone five pounds. Donovan won the toss for the latter boxer, when hands were shaken in friendship, and the battle commenced.

THE FIGHT.

Round 1.—On stripping, Magee reminded us of Ned Painter. Magee was in excellent condition; but some friends thought him rather too fat. The comparison between the combatants was obvious to every one present. Burn looked thin and boyish before his opponent; but, nevertheless, he had been well trained, and no fault was found with him by his backers. Magee, at the scratch, planted himself in a fighting attitude, kept up his hands well, and was not the novice that had been anticipated by the Londoners. He had been for some time under the tuition of Jack Randall in Ireland; and by the advice and practice with such a master Magee must have profited a good deal as to an acquirement of science and hitting. Pat made play, after a little dodging about with his right and left hands, but he was out of distance from the leariness of Burn, and nothing was the matter. Jem was extremely cautious, looked upon his opponent as a dangerous customer, and the hit he made alighted slightly on Magee's canister; but the latter countered without any effect. A tiny pause, and both on the look-out for squalls. Pat, quite alive to the thing, planted a blow under the left eye of Burn, which produced a small drop of claret. Donovan quite elated, exclaimed, "First blood!" Both now went to work, and Magee bored Jem to the ropes; here a blow or two was exchanged, when Burn went down. Pat viewed the circumstance for a second, and then fell upon his opponent.— Disapprobation was expressed by the spectators, but Donovan said, "Magee could not help it."

2.—Burn with much dexterity planted a body blow, and got away. Some sparring, when Jem returned the compliment for Pat's favour in the last round, and drew the claret from Magee. Both of the men were on their mettle; but it appeared that Magee was the stronger man. A sharp rally occurred, and Pat's left ogle napped it. Magee, however, bored Burn to the ropes, where he went down, and Magee fell upon him with his knees upon the abdomen, which operated so severely that he uttered a loud groan.—Loud expressions of disapprobation —"foul fighter," &c.

3.—Jem appeared at the scratch in pain, and extremely weak; Magee, too, exhibited symptoms of "bellows to mend." Sharp work for a short time, the blows telling on both sides, when Jem was compelled to retreat to the ropes, where he fell with his back upon the ropes. In this situation, Magee with all his weight lay upon him; and the struggle was so great for the advantage that Randall exclaimed, "Burn's eye is out." The claret was pouring from his peeper. (Cries of "shame"—hisses—and a tremendous uproar in all parts of the ring.) Jem, after extreme difficulty, extricated himself from his perilous situation, and with much skill planted a conker on his adversary. In closing, both down; Magee uppermost.

4.—A pause. An exchange of hits and another pause. Well done on both sides. The science of Jem gave him the advantage; but his extreme caution in several instances operated as a drawback. Magee went in with much spirit, and Burn went down with a slight hit. ("That's the way, my boy; try it again, Magee, and you can't lose it," from his Irish friends.)

5.—Pat fought this round with much ability. He stopped well, and was successful in planting his blows. A sharp rally; and at the ropes Magee had the best of it, punishing Burn till he went down. ("It is all your own," cried Donovan.)

6.—This round was soon over. Magee stopped very neatly a left-handed blow, and obtained the praise of Randall. Burn in planting a facer appeared weak, and slipped down.

7.—Magee was in full force, and bored Burn to the ropes. In close quarters, some sharp fighting occurred, till the nob of Jem was under the cords, and he was screwed up tight by his opponent. Burn ultimately succeeded in getting away, and with much quickness put in two facers. Magee was almost wild, and he ran at his opponent like a bull, forcing him again to the ropes till "My Nevvy" went down.

8.—Magee stopped the left hand of his adversary extremely well, but Jem at length had the best of it. As Magee bored in he gave him a tremendous teaser on his ivories, which operated as a stopper for a short period. Magee, full of game, was not to be deterred, and pursued his opponent to the ropes, till Burn went down.

9.—In the minds of several of the spectators the battle did not appear so safe to Jem as had been anticipated. Magee, in this round, fought with skill and spirit, and stopped and countered his man well. Jem

nobbed Magee right and left; a sharp rally took place, when Jem went down rather weak.

10.—Burn was out of wind, and endeavoured to get a little time by sparring. Pat made play with his adversary, and Jem retreated to the ropes, when he fell on his knees. Pat lifted up his hands, and was loudly applauded for his conduct.

11.—Jem was extremely cautious, in fact, rather too cautious, as in retreating from his adversary several of his blows were ineffectual. The right ogle of Magee received so severe a hit that he was again on the wild system, and pushed Jem to the ropes. As the latter was balancing, Magee fell on him, and with his knees hurt Burn severely. (A tremendous roar of disapprobation; "shame! shame! cowardly!" &c. &c.) Jem ultimately fell on the grass, and Magee upon him, and his face appeared full of anguish. Belcher complained to the umpires of the conduct of Magee.

12.—Burn was in great distress, from the conduct he had experienced in the last round, nevertheless he endeavoured to do some mischief. The nob of Magee was again peppered, although he made several good stops. In a rally, both of the men were bang up to the mark, till Jem went down.

13.—Burn appeared to be rather better, and went to work without delay, but Magee stopped his left hand. Burn pinked his opponent with dexterity, and retreated. Magee always forced Jem to the extremity of the ring, as if to obtain the superiority. Burn was now in a dangerous situation; his neck was on the ropes, and Magee, with all his weight, upon his frame. (Loud cries of "foul! foul!" and hissing from every part of the ring. Several of the fighting men were round the combatants, but none dared to interfere, as Burn was in a balancing situation on the ropes.) Jem, quite exhausted, fell to the ground, and he was placed on his second's knee almost in a state of stupor.

14.—The friends of Burn were now in a state of alarm, lest the repeated pulling and hauling he received at the ropes should take the fight out of him, as Jem came up to the scratch in a tottering state. Magee, by the advice of Donovan, went to work without delay, but Jem met him in the middle of the head like a shot. Magee, however, was not to be deterred, and rushed upon his opponent in a furious state, and drove him to the ropes, at which Jem got out of his difficulties and went down like an experienced milling cove.

15.—In this round the fighting of Jem was seen to great advantage. He put in three facers without any return, till the strength of Magee compelled him to retreat. Magee again fell upon Burn, and more disapprobation was expressed by the spectators.

16.—The blows Jem had received were "trifles light as air," compared with the injuries he had sustained upon the ropes,

"My nevvy" was recovering a little, and Magee soon found it out by the pepper-box being administered upon his nob. Some good fighting occurred on both sides, until Magee endeavoured, as usual, to finish the round at the ropes. Once more Jem was at the mercy of his adversary, by hanging across the ropes; but unlike the days of the "Game Chicken," who exclaimed, when he found Belcher in a defenceless state, "Jem, I will not hurt thee!" and walked away, Magee threw the whole weight of his person on him, and was also not nice as to the use of his knee. (Disapprobation, and "the foulest fighter that ever was seen.")

17.—This was a short round, and although Burn was the weaker of the two, yet he pinked his adversary to advantage. Magee's nob exhibited considerable punishment, but it is right to say of him that he never flinched from any blows; he also stopped the left hand of Burn with good science. Jem had the best of the round, and was fast improving in the opinion of his friends.

18.—Burn was now decidedly the hero of the tale—"He'll win it now," was the general cry. It was ditto, ditto, ditto, and ditto, as to facers upon Magee's pimple, and then Jem got away without return. Magee seemed abroad, and in a wild manner ran after Burn to the ropes, but Jem got safely down.

19.—"My Nevvy" went gaily to work, and "my uncle" said, "Jem Burn for £100." Magee napped a severe body blow, but he returned a rum one for it. Magee also hit Jem down in style—the only knock-down blow in the battle. (Donovan observed, "Pat, see what you have done—you have almost finished him: another round and it is all your own.")

20.—Jem had now reduced the "big one" to his own weight, and had also placed him upon the stand-still system. Magee, on setting to, stopped the left hand of Burn, but, on endeavouring to rush in and bore his opponent to the ropes, he received such a stopper on the mouth that he almost felt whether his head was left upon his shoulders. Pat wildly again attempted the boring system, and in retreating from his adversary Jem fell down: Magee also went down with his knees upon his opponent, amidst one of the most tremendous bursts of disapprobation that ever occurred in the P. R.

21.—The case was now altered: Jem Burn the stronger man. "Bellows to mend" was upon the other leg, and Pat in trouble. Burn peppered away right and left, until Magee was as wild as a colt. He pursued Burn to the ropes, when he again hung upon him. ("Shame!" hisses, &c.)

22.—The finish was clearly in view, and Pat was nobbed against his will. Magee was distressed and piping, when Jem, on the alert, punished him right and left. Magee again bored his adversary to the ropes, and also fell upon him.

23, and last.—Magee was quite abroad, when Belcher said, "Go to work and put the finish to it." Jem took the hint, and slashed away right and left a good one. Every step Pat moved he got into some trouble, and Jem continually meeting him on the head, as he was boring forward. Pat became quite furious, and rushed in scarcely knowing what he was about, and having got Jem upon the ropes, he caught hold of him in a foul manner. It is impossible to describe the row and indignation which burst forth from all parts of the ring at the unmanly conduct of Magee. An appeal was immediately made to the umpires by the seconds: the umpires disagreeing on the subject, the matter in dispute was left for the referee, who decided the conduct of Magee to be foul, and contrary to the established rules of fighting. The seconds of Magee insisted upon renewing the fight, and declared they should claim their money if Burn left the ring; but Belcher took Jem out of the ring, observing at the same time his man had won the battle, yet he would instantly back him if they would commence another fight.

REMARKS.—Had not this wrangle taken place, we have not the least doubt that Burn would have been proclaimed the victor in less than half-a-dozen more rounds: as Jem had "got" his man, who only wanted polishing off, which "My Nevvy" would have done in an artist-like manner. Magee is a game man, and better acquainted with the science of milling, as far as stopping and hitting goes, than the cockneys had anticipated; but as a boxer he is one of the foulest fighters we ever saw in the P. R. If any apology can be offered for his conduct in this, we hope it will be imputed to his ignorance of the rules of boxing as established by Broughton, rather than to intention. The referee not only acted with promptness, but his decision ought to have a good effect, by making boxers more careful in future.

The victorious Jem partook of a hearty dinner at the "Swan" at Lichfield, in the evening. He declared himself none the worse for Mr. Magee's fistic visitations, but sore from the pulling and hauling he got while being hugged at the ropes.

Burn now rested upon his laurels for a few months, and during this interval, in the autumn of 1826, he took unto himself a spouse, in the person of Miss Caroline Watson, daughter of Bob Watson, of Bristol, of milling fame, who was brother-in-law to Tom Belcher.

The honeymoon had scarcely waned when the friends of Ned Baldwin (" White-headed Bob ") made another sort of " proposal " to jolly Jem. It was that he should box their man for £100 at his own convenience. Jem placed the matter in the hands of Uncle Ben, and April 24th, 1827, was set down in the articles, for Jem to meet another sort of " best man " than that of a bridegroom.

During the three months from signing Baldwin was decidedly the favourite, at six to four, as Jem had taken a public (the " Red Horse," in Bond Street), besides (though he was never a heavy drinker) being a sought-for chairman and companion at Uncle Ben's and elsewhere. Tom Belcher, however, took Jem in hand as mentor and trainer, and this was a great point—while on the night before the battle a gent at Tattersall's took Burn for a " cool thousand " at evens.

The road to St. Albans on Tuesday, the 24th April, 1827, was thronged with vehicles, No Man's Land, Herts, on the borders of three counties, being the rendezvous. Baldwin, with his mentor, Tom Cribb, took the road from his training quarters at Hurley Bottom, and reached St. Alban's overnight; while Jem remained at Kitte's End, near Barnet, where he had taken his breathings for some weeks previous. Jem's weight was twelve stone eight pounds; Baldwin's, twelve stone ten pounds.

The morning was cheerless and stormy, but this did not damp the spirits either of spectators or combatants; and shortly before one o'clock the veteran Commissary, Ould Caleb, having completed his arrangements, Jem Burn, attended by Tom Belcher and Harry Harmer, threw his white castor inside the ropes. He looked the picture of health, youth (his age twenty-three), and smiling good-humour, and was warmly cheered. Baldwin quickly followed, Tom Cribb and Ned Neale (his late antagonist) being his seconds. The operation of peeling soon took place, and the active condition of the men attracted all eyes. Bob looked full of muscular power, but was thin in proportion to Jem. His countenance did not exhibit that florid glow which characterised Jem's, nor did we recognise that confidence which his previous declarations betokened. Jem had the advantage in height and length, and on shaking hands it was clear that he had screwed his courage to the sticking-place. It was all or nothing with him, and he advanced like a man about to play for his last stake,

The seconds and bottle-holders all agreed to stake colours against colours, which were all tied to the stakes, and at the moment of setting-to, Ned Neale bet, and Tom Belcher took, six to four on Bob.

THE FIGHT.

Round 1.—Baldwin placed himself with great coolness in front of his antagonist, as if prepared more for defence than attack, while Jem seemed all anxiety to begin. A very few seconds were occupied in sparring, when Jem went to work upon the hay-sack* system; he hit out with quickness with his left, and caught Bob slightly, a sort of half-hit; his right then went out with great activity and force, and alighting on Bob's cranium, dropped him cleverly, amidst loud cheers.

2.—Ned came up smiling, but Jem left him no time for reflection, for he again went to work left and right. The former was stopped, but the latter came in contact with Baldwin's muzzle, and again floored him, while it loosened his grinders and drew first blood. More acclamations in favour of Jem. Bob looked both surprised and alarmed. The odds were now five to four on Jem.

3.—Ned, on coming up, was bleeding from the mouth, and his phiz was a good deal flushed. He again assumed a posture of defence, but Jem had no intention to spar. Mischief was his maxim, and to it he went left and right, putting Baldwin's guard aside, and catching him with terrific force on the left ogle. The visitation was awful; Baldwin was hit off his legs in the most finished style. Nothing could exceed the consternation of Bob's friends. "He is licked," was the cry; and the White-headed one, on getting to his second's knee, seemed anxious to ascertain whether his eye was yet in its proper position, and if possible to stop the swelling, which was rapidly advancing. During these rounds Bob had not made a single return, and Jem was as gay as one of his uncle Belcher's larks.

4.—Neale now urged Bob to go in, as he evidently saw that he had no chance at out-fighting. "Yes," said Bob, but he kept still *à la distance*, when Jem again burst upon him, and delivered right and left with great force, while Bob was getting away, and trying to stop. Jem followed him up, and was well stopped in some of his straight ones, but he succeeded in planting another floorer, and away went Bob for the fourth time off his pins.

5.—On coming up it was seen that Baldwin's left eye was completely closed. Jem saw his advantage, put aside Bob's science, tipped two facers, right and left, and then catching him on the sneezer, tapped the claret in a new quarter; and in the close, Bob was down again.

6.—Bob, though dreadfully punished, came up game. Neale shouted to him to go in, and Bob replied, "he knew what he was about." A good rally followed, in which Bob went boldly to his man. Some good exchanges followed, right and left, in which Jem received a heavy blow on his left cheek, which was cut, and bled freely. He returned as good as he got, and Bob fell on his knees. ("Bob is not beat yet," said his friends; and hopes were entertained that Jem would fall off. Bob was still strong on his legs.)

7.—Jem pursued his old game, hitting left and right with great severity. Baldwin made some good returns, but in a rally which followed had the worst of it. In a close by the ropes, Jem was pushed down.

8.—Bob stopped Jem's left with neatness. Short sparring, when Jem again went in with his left, his right hand being a good deal puffed. Bob stopped him, and was rushing to hit, when Jem slipped down.

9.—Jem again went to work with energy. Bob stopped him cleverly at first, but Jem would be with him, and planted a rattler on his nose with his left, drawing more of the carmine. Bob shook it off, and went to fight, when a good rally followed, in which Bob was almost hit stupid. Again did Neale call upon him to fight. He rushed in and bored Jem to the ropes, when Jem went down to avoid harm, and Bob fell on him with his knees.

10.—Bob stopped a well-intended visitation from Jem's left, but Jem succeeded in jobbing him several times. A close at the ropes, in which each tried for the advantage. At last Jem broke away, and in a rally Bob hit him down with a random blow. Jem now showed weakness, and piped, although his spirit seemed unbroken, and Bob showed most fearful marks of punishment.

11.—Bob now thought there was a chance in his favour, and rushed at once to his man to increase his distress. Jem, however, was ready, though puffing, and met him with a couple of facers. Bob fell on his knees.

12.—Bob again made a desperate effort to increase Jem's exhaustion, but Jem broke away, hitting him with his left as he approached, in the middle of the head. Bob

* This is an allusion to a system of exercise adopted by Jem in training, and recommended by many, of practising right and left upon a sack stuffed with hay, to teach straight delivery.

planted a slasher on Jem's mouth, but Jem countered in good style. Jem then bored him to the ropes, and both went down piping.

13.—Jem threw in a nobber. Bob nodded, and put in a good body blow. Jem returned a facer with his right. A long and desperate rally followed, in which good hits were exchanged. In the end, Bob went down. Both were much distressed, but Bob decidedly the worse.

14.—Bob came up as if determined to strain every nerve to make a turn in his favour, but it was in vain. Jem, after sparring for wind, repeatedly jobbed him right and left on the old spots, and both eyes were nearly on a par in point of darkness. Bob retreated, stopping Jem's slashing hits, but Jem never left him, and he fell heavily at the ropes.

15.—Jem pursued the jobbing system, and Bob, though he stopped some blows, received too many to be agreeable. He stood for some time almost stupefied. Jem peppered away, until he fell in a dreadful condition as to punishment. Any odds on Jem, and Bob's friends wished him to give in, begging that he would not fight a second beyond his own inclination. He would not, however, be persuaded to stop, but again got up with a resolution to do his best.

16.—Jem rushed to his man, and after a severe struggle both fell out of the ring.

17.—Bob only came up to be hit down.

18.—Jem seemed to get fresher with the consciousness of victory, and caught Bob a nasty one on the body. He then followed him up, jobbing as he went. In the close, both went down.

19.—Jem jobbed his man right and left, and he went down at the ropes.

20, and last.—Jem popped in a body blow. Bob, still disposed to make a desperate struggle, after a short rally, seized Jem by the ropes, and held him fast for a considerable time, in the exertion getting his finger in Jem's mouth. Jem at last got a little free, and then forcing Bob with his back over the upper rope, poised him equally, and delivered three finishers with astounding force in the middle of the head. Bob tumbled over, and was senseless. Jem was, of course, pronounced the conqueror, amidst the shouts of his friends. He walked with great firmness to his drag, while Bob was carried to a post-chaise, and driven off the ground to St. Albans.

REMARKS.—The result of this fight excited no small surprise in the minds of many who profess to be good judges. Bob, it was said, never fought worse. He never seemed to be firm on his legs, but kept hopping back as if sparring. It was also obvious that he did not go in to his man with that determination which could alone give him a chance of victory until too late. When jobbed in the head, he kept nodding as if he considered all he was getting was nothing compared with what he was about to give; but the giving time never came, and with the exception of the blows on the cheek and mouth, and a tolerably good body blow, he never made any impression. On the other hand, Jem's blows all told with tremendous effect, and the game and resolution with which My Nevvy conducted himself throughout was highly creditable. He set out with a determination to hit out left and right at Bob's nob, and he stuck to this system till the close of the battle, winning in very gallant style. Towards the middle of the fight he certainly was distressed, and Bob did all he could to take advantage of his piping, but was himself too far gone, and Jem by keeping away gained his second wind and made all safe. Jem's right hand was a good deal puffed, and the skin was knocked off most of his knuckles, from coming in contact with Bob's masticators. In other respects he was not damaged, and in fact, when he arrived at Wildbore's, at St. Albans, he sat down to dinner with a large party, and ate as heartily as if he had been merely taking a morning walk. After dinner he paid a friendly visit to Bob, who was in bed, and completely blind. Poor Bob said he didn't know how it was; he felt he had not fought as he was wont to do, and attributed his misfortune to the severe hitting in the first three rounds, which he said completely took away his senses. The fight lasted thirty-three minutes. Jem, after offering his fallen opponent some pecuniary consolation, returned to town in a swell drag and four.

On the Thursday after the fight, Jem Burn took a benefit at the Tennis Court, at which Baldwin showed, and expressed his regret at having been beaten, more, as he said, for his friends' than his own sake, and announced his readiness to make a fresh match, to come off as soon as possible. Burn was by no means disinclined to consent to a new trial, and on the very next evening, at a meeting at Belcher's, the Castle Tavern, Holborn, articles were duly signed for a meeting on the 3rd of July. Betting was begun by " Uncle Ben " laying seven to four on " My Nevvy," and so the wagering went, especially at Tattersall's, where seven to four in hundreds was taken by one of the best judges of the day. The sequel proved the soundness of Mr. John Gully's opinion. Baldwin defeated our hero, after a desperate contest of eighty-five rounds, occupying ninety minutes, as may be seen in the life of BALDWIN, Chapter VII. of this volume.

On the 13th of November in the same year (1827) Jem a second time met Ned Neale, but after a hard battle of forty-three rounds, occupying forty-six minutes, had again to succumb to the conquering arm of the Streatham Youth. (See Life of NEALE, *ante*, Chapter V., p. 310.)

This was Jem's last appearance as a principal within the ropes of the P. R. As a second, a backer, and a demonstrator of the art, the Press and the sporting public never lost sight of him. His house, the " Queen's Head," Windmill Street, Haymarket, which he kept for some years, was the resort of all lovers of jolly companionship, and those who wished to keep themselves *au courant* to all sports of the ring.

Jem's Master of the Ceremonies at his sparring *soirées* was for some time the accomplished light-weight Owen Swift; and many an M.P. slipped away from St. Stephen's, and many a smart guardsman from a Belgravian dinner-party, to give a look in at Jolly Jem's snuggery; an inner sanctum, communicating with the sparring-room, and set apart for " those *I* call gentlemen," as Jem emphatically phrased it. The inscription over the mantelpiece of this room, from the pen of " Chief Baron Nicholson," was appropriate :—

> " Scorning all treacherous feud and deadly strife,
> The dark stiletto and the murderous knife,
> We boast a science sprung from manly pride,
> Linked with true courage and to health allied—
> A noble pastime, void of vain pretence—
> The fine old English art of self-defence."

In vain did mere playmen, or " calico swells," attempt to gain a footing in Jem's " private room." Jem instinctively detected the pretender. " There's just as much difference in the breed of men as there is in the breed of horses," he would say. " I read that fellow in a minute; the club-room's his place."

In his later days Jem shifted his domicile to the " Rising Sun," in Air Street, Piccadilly (previously kept by Johnny Broome), where many a night burly Jem was to be found, enjoying his pipe and glass, surrounded by the few surviving members of the old school, and visited during the season by many youthful saplings of the Corinthian tree, to whom Jem

would mirthfully and cheerily impart the adventures and sporting experi
ences of his earlier days.

> " A merrier man,
> Within the limit of becoming mirth,
> I never spent an hour's talk withal.
> His eye begat occasion for his wit,
> For every object that the one did catch
> The other turned to a mirth-moving jest."

For several years, as Jem grew in years and in portliness, and, though not
a hard drinker, fully enjoyed the good things of this life, he was subject
to intermittent attacks of gout, which, towards 1862, assailed him with
increasing frequency, yet failing, when they gave him even a short truce,
to subdue his natural fun and frolic. It was during one of unusual
severity that we looked in to inquire after Jem's health, and his pleasant
daughter (Mrs. Doyle) having taken up our name, the bedridden boxer
desired us to be " shown up." We expressed our sympathy, regarding at
the same time with some curiosity a contrivance suspended from the
curtain-rods of the four-poster in which Jem was recumbent.

"Ha! old fellow," said the merry Yorkshireman, "you're wanting to spell
out the meaning of that. I'll tell you, if this blessed crab that's just now got
me in *toe* don't give his claw an extra squeeze. If he does, why, I'll strike,
and he shall *tow* me into port at once."

"No, Jem, it's not come to that yet."

"But it very soon must, if it don't stalk. See here," said he, pointing to
a strong cord stretched from the top rail across the bed, from which another
cord was suspended midway, and made fast to the handle of an old-fashioned
corkscrew. " If it warn't for this tackle I'd get no sleep night nor day. Inside
the bedclothes I've got a bung—good idea for a licensed victualler—into
that I screws the corkscrew through the bedclothes, which I then raise
tent-fashion by this hal'yard, and that I make fast down here to the bed-
post. There's a wrinkle for you, Miles's Boy; but I hope you'll never
want it for yourself." Poor Jem we never saw again. His arch-enemy
ascended to his portly stomach, and on the morning of the 29th of May
Jem slept with his forefathers.

> " ——Men must endure
> Their going hence, even as their coming hither.
> Ripeness is all."

CHAPTER VII.

EDWARD BALDWIN ("WHITEHEADED BOB")
1823—1828.

NED BALDWIN, whose sobriquet was suggested from the profusion of his pale flaxen hair, was born at Munslow, near Ludlow, in Herefordshire, on the 6th May, 1803. His youth was spent in his native county, in which, and in Shropshire and Worcestershire, several unimportant battles are placed to his credit by "Boxiana." After a gallant contest on Worcester Race-course with a local boxer named Souther, whom he defeated in an hour and a quarter, a gentleman well known in the London Ring, finding him an active, civil, and intelligent fellow, engaged him as his groom, and brought him to London. A trial battle in Harper's Fields, Marylebone, with a big Irishman named O'Connor, in which the youngster displayed more pluck than science, led to his master putting him under the tuition of the scientific Bill Eales, who then superintended a boxery at his house in James Street, Oxford Street. Here he rapidly improved his style, and gained the reputation of a quick and fearless hitter, with some skill in defensive tactics. In February, 1823, he went down to Wimbledon, and there, after Hall and Wynes had settled their differences, Bob, as he was now called, threw up his hat to accommodate any man who had not yet fought in the Prize Ring, for £10 of his master's money. Here he was made the victim of a not very creditable "plant." The afterwards renowned Jem Ward, who had already defeated Dick Acton and Burke (brother to "Warrior" Burke), and fought a draw with Bill Abbott, habited in a countryman's smock frock, was introduced as a "yokel" aspirant. The men set to, but the *ruse de guerre* was soon seen through, and after nineteen minutes Bob's friends took him away, though Bob was game enough to have fought it out with defeat staring him in the face.

After a disappointment with Harry Lancaster, Baldwin was matched with Maurice Delay, for £50 a side, and the battle came off at the classic

EDWARD BALDWIN ("Whiteheaded Bob").

ground of Moulsey, on the 11th of February, 1824. Bob was brought upon the ground in a carriage, in a smart Witney upper, and threw his hat into the ropes, esquired by Bill Richmond and Paddington Jones; Delay, accompanied by Josh Hudson and Ned Neale, quickly followed. Tom Owen fastened a green bandanna to the stakes for the East Ender, and Richmond tied a blue bird's-eye over it for Bob. The seconds and principals shook hands, and the men threw themselves in attitude. Five to four on Maurice Delay.

THE FIGHT.

Round 1.—Delay on peeling looked an effective man; and the White-headed One also appeared well as to condition. Bob did not weigh more than 11st. 7lb. Delay was heavier by several pounds. The latter made himself up for mischief, although he wore a cheerful smile, and Bob had also a grin upon his countenance. Very little time was lost in scientific movements, when Bob made a feint, but it would not do. Delay hit out, and Bob got away. Delay stopped well the right hand of his opponent. ("Stopping is very well," said the John Bull Fighter, "but hitting is better; be with him, he's coming, Maurice.") Delay put in a heavy body blow, but Bob prevented a repetition. A tiny bit of sharp work occurred, in which Delay's lip showed a slight tinge of claret, when the man of colour called out, "First blood for a hundred!" The lads tipped it each other heavily. In a sharp rally Delay was rather too much for his opponent; Bob went down, and Delay hit him as he was going down. (A tremendous shout from the East Enders; Tom Oliver offered 2 to 1 on Delay.)

2.—The left side of Delay's temple, also his eye, exhibited specimens of the handi-work of Bob. This was a short but a good round, and Bob again went down. (The East Enders were "all happiness;" and Maurice gave them the office it was as right as the day.)

3.—Maurice, full of spirits, gave Bob's chest an ugly touch; ditto, and ditto. ("What are you arter?" said Tom Jones to his man. "Go to work, he can't hurt you.") Bob countered in good style, also caught Delay's nob under his arm, and fibbed him down. ("Well done, Bob!")

4.—Bob was piping a little. The White-headed One took the lead, fibbed Maurice severely, and hit him twice as he was going down. ("Where's the umpires?" from the John Bull. "We must look after this man. We will have nothing foul.")

5.—Short and sweet to Bobby; a sharp rally; Delay went down distressed.

6.—This was nothing else but a good fighting round; it was give and take like a couple of good ones. Maurice satisfied the ring that he was a game man; but Bob convinced the amateurs he was the best fighter. After a sharp rally in which some ugly counter-hits occurred, Maurice went down on his knees.

7.—Delay bored Bobby all over the ring, till he went down distressed.

8.—Nothing. At the ropes a struggle took place for the throw; Maurice was undermost.

9.—The counter-hits of Bob did precious mischief to the phrenology box of Delay. He bothered Maurice's order of caution. Bob also got into his wine-cellar without a key, and tapped his claret without the aid of a corkscrew. "Only look," said Paddington Jones, "here's a bit of good truth," while Bob kept fibbing his opponent till they both went down, Maurice undermost.

10.—Wind was necessary on both sides, and both found that a little pause was agreeable to their feelings. Delay's hand told on Bob's body. After an exchange of blows, Bob again got Delay's nob under his arm, and tipped it to him à la Randall, till he went down.

11.—Both had quite milling enough in this round. It was hit for hit when they separated, and both fell.

12.—When time was called, Maurice came up as gay as a lark, and endeavoured to mill his adversary all over the ring. Bob stopped two heavy hits skilfully, and in closing got Delay's head under his arm, and punished him so severely that Delay fell down stupid. ("Go along, Bob, it's all your own!")

13.—This might be called a Big Ben and Tom Johnson round. Maurice's face was completely changed, his left eye nearly closed. He made one or two good stops, and also planted a stomacher, but game was more prominent than science. They stuck to each other blow for blow, till they were both distressed to a standstill. At the conclusion of the round they merely pushed each other down.

14.—The strength, however, appeared on the side of Delay, and he bored in to mill his adversary. Some severe blows were exchanged, when Bob went down from a left-handed blow.

15.—The White-headed One had the best of the fighting; and at the commencement of this round Delay bored his antagonist to the ropes, when Bob put in two tremendous nobbers, and in turn drove Delay across the ring, and sent him down on his knees.

16.—Bob was piping, and it was the opinion of several of the amateurs that the strength of Delay would ultimately bring him through. Maurice again drove Bob before him to the ropes, and got him nearly down, when the White-headed Cove, full of pluck, recovered himself on his pins, and milled away, till both went down.

17.—Very short. Delay napped several nobbers, and went down terribly distressed.

18.—Hudson, with all his industry and attention towards his man, could not keep him clean. Still he would bore in upon Bob—this conduct brought him terrific punishment. The White-headed One planted one, two, and three blows in succession, right in the middle of his already damaged face. He was positively hit to a standstill; but on recovering himself, he went resolutely in to mill, and got Bob down. ("His game will win for him!" was the cry.)

19.—Both as good as gold; true courage displayed at every step, with conduct and fortitude, adding honour to the character of Britons. (Our eye at this instant observed the French Hercules in a wagon, in company with another Frenchman, expressing their admiration, and applauding the manly and honourable mode of settling a quarrel in old England.) Delay commenced this round with the pluck of a gamecock; and the gluttony he displayed astonished the ring. At every step he received a jobber, sending him back; nevertheless he would not be denied, and absolutely bored in, fighting hand over head till he sent Bob down. "It's as right as the day," said Maurice to his second.

20.—The counter-hits of Bob told unmercifully upon Delay's nob. This was a manly-fought round, good on both sides, when Delay dropped, Bob also very much exhausted.

21.—This was a terrific round. Bob, although extremely weak, had decidedly the best of the milling; he planted his hits effectually, and in several instances he broke ground well. Delay, who was met at every movement on the nob, would not retreat, but contended for victory like the best out-and-outer upon the list. The determination of Maurice enabled him to send Bob down.

22.—This round decided the battle. It appeared to us that Delay wanted elasticity about his shoulders—his blows were not effective. Yet with as fine game as any man ever exhibited in the Prize Ring, he persevered

without dread or fear. Delay appeared at the scratch undismayed, and after receiving three severe hits, pressed upon his antagonist, and, strange to relate, he sent Bob down.

23.—Of a similar description. Delay went down exhausted. "Bob for any odds!"

24.—This was short but effective against Delay; he had the worst of the hitting, and in going down Bob fell upon him. ("Three to one—take him away!")

25.—This was a sharp round. Delay would not give up an inch of ground; but he stood up only to receive additional punishment. He however got Bob down.

26 and last.—Nature had done her utmost, but Delay, game to the end of the chapter, appeared at the scratch, and fought "while a shot remained in him." Bob did not like to punish his opponent any more, and Delay went down quite exhausted, falling forward upon his hands and knees. Here the John Bull Fighter showed his true character to the spectators. Josh loves winning; but he was satisfied that Maurice had done all that a brave man could perform; so, with consideration and humanity, he loudly exclaimed, "My man shall not fight any more!" The battle was over in forty-two minutes. The first words uttered by Delay to Josh, after his recollection returned, were, "Have I won it?"

REMARKS.—Bob did not win the battle without receiving a sharp taste of Delay's quality. The White-headed One was not in such good condition as his backers wished him to be; in fact, he was sick and ill from a cold four days before fighting. It was countering with his opponent that gave him the victory. In the middle of the fight it was by no means safe to him; nay, it appeared to us that he was so weak as almost to leave off fighting. But he recovered himself, and turned the tide in his favour till the 22nd and 23rd rounds, when some of the best judges declared it "anybody's battle." In the 11th round Bob turned round to avoid the punishment of Delay; but the sun was so powerful at that period as to deprive him almost of viewing his antagonist; he therefore shifted his ground with dexterity. In the 3rd round Bob hurt one of his hands considerably against his adversary's nob; and Baldwin has since asserted that the latter circumstance, and also having the sun continually shining in his face, prevented him from winning the battle so soon as he might otherwise have accomplished. Baldwin's back was cut by the ropes. Delay was put to bed at the "Bell," at Hampton, and every attention paid to him that humanity could suggest, backed by the advice and assistance of a medical man. A collection was made on the ground for one of the bravest pugilists that ever took off a shirt in the Prize Ring.

This manly battle placed the milling talents of White-headed Bob in a favourable point of view with the amateurs. He aspired to riding inside a carriage instead of holding the horses; and thus, unfortunately for himself, the injudicious patronage and loose companionship of swells were brought within his reach.

Bob might now be said to have obtained a footing in the sporting world, and he was determined to push his fortune without delay. Notoriety in the Metropolis is a taking feature, and Bob was determined not to remain in obscurity; he visited most of the places of amusement, and manifested indications of his fondness for a "bit of high life." He soon recommended himself to the notice of Mr. Hayne, then and afterwards known as "Pea-green Hayne," and for his affair with Miss Foote and Colonel Berkeley; and Bob had the art to induce this liberal-hearted gentleman to become his patron and backer. Baldwin was fond of dress, and knew its advantages; he was frequently seen in the company of swells of the first water, at the "Royal Saloon," and other resorts of "fast life" where the "Corinthians" of George the Fourth's time "most did congregate." As a proof that Bob possessed some knowledge of "character," he appeared at one of the masquerades at the Argyll Rooms,* habited "as a fine gentleman" of the modern time!

Bob took his first benefit at the Fives Court on Tuesday, May 14th, 1824, when he was well supported.

Soon after his benefit Baldwin was matched against the Streatham Youth, for £100 a side. The parties met on Monday, July 26th, 1824, at Chertsey. Bob appeared on the ground in the drag of his patron, and would have entered the ring, but Mr. Hayne, on account of his bad state of health, preferred forfeiting £100 rather than risking his reputation. So much for dissipation.

A second match for £100 a side was immediately made between Bob and Neale at Harry Holt's, and three months were allowed to Bob to get himself right. This battle was decided at Virginia Water, on Tuesday, the 19th of October, 1824. The fight continued for one hour and thirteen minutes, occupying forty rounds, when Cribb said Bob should not fight any more. Fast living is fatal to athletes.

Bob, anxious to recover his lost laurels, inserted the following letter in the sporting journals, to the editors :—

"SIR,—Having recovered from my recent illness, to which alone I attribute the loss of my fight with Neale, I feel anxious for another job; and as Neale is matched with Jem

* The original Assembly Rooms in Regent Street, by Argyll Place, not the Windmill Street "Argyll," recently "disestablished" by the Middlesex magistrates.

Burn, and Jack Langan does not appear to fancy Shelton for a customer, I am ready to accommodate Langan for £200 a side, as soon as he pleases. If Langan does not accept this challenge I shall offer myself to the notice of the winner of the next fight between Neale and Jem Burn.

"*November 26th, 1824.*"

"Yours, &c.,
"EDWARD BALDWIN.

Baldwin did not wish to leave London for Scotland (January 9th, 1825) without announcing his intention to Neale, that his friends were ready to back him for £200 a side; but if the time was too soon for Neale to enter the ring, he was open to any twelve-stone-and-a-half man in England.

To the surprise of the admirers of scientific pugilism, Bob was matched against George Cooper, distinguished in the annals of boxing as a fighter of superior pretensions, for £200 a side. This battle was decided at Knowle's Hill, thirty miles from London, on Tuesday, July 5th, 1825. It was completely a foregone conclusion in the minds of the "judges" that George Cooper must win in first-rate style; nevertheless, the ring was surrounded by amateurs of the highest distinction. At ten minutes before one Bob threw his hat into the ring, attended by Holt and Oliver. He was applauded by a few backers, but his countenance was angry, and he complained of having been neglected by his friends, and said that if it had not been for the kindness of one gentleman (Mr. Hines) he might have arrived completely unattended at the ring. George Cooper was seconded by Hudson and Shelton.

THE FIGHT.

Round 1.—Condition was not wanting on either side, and every spectator was perfectly satisfied that both men had paid the necessary attention to training. The frame of Cooper was fine and manly, but it did not exhibit that muscle and strength which characterised the body of the White-headed One. The knowing ones, the old ring-goers, booked it as a certainty that Bob would be little more than a mere chopping-block for the display of Cooper's great milling talents, and the John Bull Fighter, the Nonpareil, Tom Belcher, and Tom Shelton, looked upon the event as a certainty. Under such flattering circumstances, and backed liberally at odds, George Cooper entered the ring, equally confident in his own mind that victory was within his grasp. Bob, on the contrary, had but few friends, excepting his late opponent Ned Neale, who observed, "Bob will turn out a better man than is expected, and I have no doubt he will win the fight." However, this opinion had no weight, as it was thought Ned was paying himself a compliment. The attitude of Cooper was elegant, and Bob seemed perfectly aware that he was opposed to no commoner, by the caution he displayed. The White-headed One hopped away from a feint of Cooper's, but at length he tried the bustling system, and planted a single hit on his opponent's cheek. (Applause, and "Well done, Bob!") Cooper, however, returned a swinging right-handed hit on Bob's ribs. Bob did not seem to mind it, but rushed in, and gave Cooper a facer; the latter returned on the body. Exchange of blows, and Bob as good as George; the former also made a good stop. ("Bravo, Bob!") Cooper napped another facer. George, on the alert, put in a severe ribber, and also produced the claret from Bob's right eye. ("Mind, Pierce," cried Josh, "this decides first blood.") The White-nobbed One displayed more science than was anticipated against such a skilful fighter as Cooper. He took the lead gaily, bored Cooper to the ropes, who acted on the defensive till he napped a rum one on the side of his head, when George went down. (Uproarious applause for Bob, symptoms of uneasiness among the friends of Cooper, and the majority of the spectators exclaiming, "Why, Bob will win!")

2.—This slice of luck put Bob on terms with himself, when he observed George's nose displayed some of his handiwork. Cooper planted a ribber with his right, but Bob said it was "no go" with his left. The fighting was excellent on both sides; Cooper found out he had indeed a troublesome customer, one not to be disposed of as a matter of course. Bob had sense enough to see that out-fighting was dangerous to him, therefore he resolutely went in, hit George's sensitive plant, and in struggling for the throw Cooper went down and was undermost. ("Hallo, where's the six to four now?")

3.—This round was decidedly in favour of Bob. He found out that the bustle of a young one is very tiresome and dangerous to an "old cock," and he went in sans cérémonie. Bob took the lead, planting blows right and left, and also by a well-planted hit on the nose of George the claret flowed freely, and he was also sent down completely out of the ropes.

4.—Bob's rush was stopped by a facer, but he was not dismayed, and in endeavouring to get in at his opponent he fell.

5.—The spectators were now satisfied that the capabilities of Bob had been treated too lightly, and that more danger was in him than had been anticipated. Cooper again planted his favourite hit on the ribs of his opponent, but injured the knuckles of his right hand. The science of Cooper was delightful, and although bored by Bob, he stopped several blows. The White-headed One, however, would not be denied, and the result was Cooper went down weak. Bob was now the favourite, and five and six to four was offered on him.

6.—George had the best of this round. He administered the pepper-box in style, and Bob put up his hand. Counter-hits, and severe ones; Bob, in closing, had the advantage, and Cooper went down.

7.—Short. Bob rushed in, caught hold of Cooper, and both went down.

8.—The White-headed One had made up his mind to adopt the bustling system, and rushed in to work, but he met with a precious stopper, very near his middle piece. Bob recovered himself, and was resolved to "try it on" once more; but Cooper, on the alert, put in a cracker on the jaws, and Bob went down on his hands and knees. The friends of Cooper recovered their spirits, and George was once more the favourite.

9.—This round amounted to nothing; it was almost over before it began; a struggle at the ropes, and both down.

10.—Fighting on both sides, till Cooper took the lead, punishing his opponent with his left hand, until Bob went down across the ropes, and fell out of the ring.

11.—George appeared anxious to go to work, and although Bob stopped his left with great skill, Cooper fought his way into a sharp rally. Harry Holt, who was behind Bob, was forced against the stakes, and the bottle broken which held the water. Both combatants were on their mettle, and some hard hits were exchanged, till, in closing, Bob was thrown.

12.—Cooper had not done enough to make it satisfactory to all his friends that he must win, although his backers flattered themselves that his fine skill, united with his game qualities, would ultimately bring him through. On appearing at the scratch, both went to work like good ones, particularly Bob, who stood to no repairs, and rushed at his opponent, determined to do mischief. In struggling at the ropes, both down.

13.—The White-headed One was determined to tire George, if possible, and to reduce his skill and strength Bob's scheme did not succeed, and George stopped his efforts with science. Bob likewise showed science. Some rum ones passed between them; in closing, both down, Bob undermost.

14.—Youth must be served; and Bob, in this respect, had the best of it. Cooper appeared weak, and in struggling for the throw, went down, and rolled over his opponent. Bob astonished the spectators by his good fighting.

15.—The science of Cooper told to advantage, and Bob's nob napped it in two instances; but the latter was now confident that to bustle his man was the way to win it; he therefore fought his way in, but in closing Bob went down, Cooper on him. The friends of George flattered themselves he would win it by his skill; and some even betting, for small sums, occurred at the close of this round.

16.—Bob received punishment on going in, but would not be denied. Cooper was now compelled to fight on the defensive, and in retreating went down at the ropes.

17.—Although Bob was almost sure to receive it in the bustle, he preferred that mode; he got two stoppers, and by way of a finish George threw him. The friends of Cooper cheered.

18.—The right hand of George was puffed, and was nearly, if not quite, gone. In point of strength, it was now two to one in favour of Bob. A severe struggle took place for the fall, and by a desperate effort on the part of Cooper, he succeeded in giving Bob a tremendous back fall.

19.—Bob had completely proved himself a game man, and also a good fighter. He was now decidedly the favourite, and two to one offered on him. Bob went to work uncommonly sharp, and planted a heavy facer. In struggling for the throw, Cooper got his leg twisted in going down. During the short space of the half-minute, he communicated to Hudson that he had hurt his leg, but before it could be examined 'time" was called.

20.—Cooper stood up at the scratch, but his leg gave way, and he fell without a blow, as Bob was making himself up for a hit. (Loud murmurs, "Foul!" "Foul!") "His leg is broken," said Josh. "We've won it," observed Holt—"do not leave the ring, Bob"—when time was called.

21, and last.—Cooper, although in great pain, endeavoured to meet his man in the highest style of game, when Bob dropped him by a straight hit. It was ascertained (by a surgeon) that one of the small bones of Cooper's ankle was fractured, when Hudson gave up the contest in favour of Bob. It was over in twenty-six minutes and a half.

REMARKS.—Cooper's accident leaves the event of the battle in some doubt; but in canvassing the matter fairly the opinion of the majority was in favour of Bob. The courage he showed was excellent; he was not deficient in science, and his judgment was equally good in the mode he adopted in fighting an older man, by keeping him at work. Scarcely an amateur would allow Bob a shadow of chance against such an accomplished boxer as George Cooper. The front piece of Bob was rather the worse for the engagement, but in other respects his strength was undiminished; and as a proof he put on his clothes, and walked about the ring, to witness the battle between Young Dutch Sam and Stockman. Bob also observed he was extremely sorry for the accident, and had much rather the battle should have been terminated by fighting, as he felt confident of winning. Upon recapitulation of the whole affair, Bob had the advantage of fourteen years in age, but proved a much better and cleverer man than was calculated upon by the *cognoscenti*.

Bob, still soaring into swelldom, in imitation, *longo intervallo*, of John Jackson, opened what he called "The Subscription Rooms," in Pickering Place, St. James's Street, for the purpose of "giving private lessons in the art of self-defence," having previously, as a contemporary wit said, "studied Chesterfield in the stable," to qualify himself for the professorial chair. Like other "stars" Bob now took a provincial tour with Jem Burn, Neale, and others, and was well received at Liverpool and in the north. A severe illness, said to be "the measles," laid Bob up during the summer of 1826; a retirement from London life restored him, and in January, 1827, at the "Castle," Holborn, Baldwin was matched with Jem Burn for £100 a side, to meet on Tuesday, April 24th, 1827.

At No Man's Land, on the day appointed, in nineteen rounds, occupying thirty-three minutes, Baldwin was knocked out of time and the stakes by the fresh and vigorous arm of "My Nevvy." (See life of JEM BURN, in preceding chapter.)

Baldwin took a benefit at the Tennis Court on Wednesday, May 9th, 1827.

The difference between winning and losing a battle, Bob asserts, was clearly proved to him on that day. However, a respectable muster of the amateurs assembled to witness the sports. The sets-to were effective, particularly the bout between Tom Belcher and Jem Burn, which proved a high treat of the art of self-defence. Scroggins, as Clown to the Ring, afforded much fun in his set-to with Deaf Davis.

It was not to be supposed that Baldwin, whose stamina certainly improved, thanks to youth and a good constitution, whenever he was under a cloud, and compelled, by what he called "the neglect of his patrons," to practise self-denial, would long lie idle. Hence, on the day of trial, July 3rd, 1827, when Bob peeled at Ruscombe Lake, he was "himself again."

The second trial for £100 a side took place on a fine piece of common about a mile from Twyford, Berks, called Ruscombe Lake, from its being covered with water in winter time. From the facility with which Bob was beaten by Burn in their previous encounter, and the rumours, of course exaggerated, of Bob's "saloon" exploits in "the wee hours ayont the twal," Jem was the favourite at six and seven to four; Uncle Ben having actually booked two to one "rather," as he said, "than not do business." There were those, however, who thought, with us, that there was nothing in the comparative qualities of the men to justify odds, and it was impossible with those who witnessed the former battle not to see that Bob was not only not "all thar," as the Yankees have it, but so utterly surprised by Burn's mode of attack in the first three rounds that he never recovered his fighting tactics. Nevertheless, there was a period, in the middle of the fight, when Jem became so distressed that had Baldwin a vestige of strength left, he might have snatched the victory. The long odds were therefore freely taken by many, and especially at Tattersall's. The sequel proved that the opinions thus founded were fully borne out, and that a solitary instance of defeat under peculiar circumstances ought not to deprive a man of the chance of redeeming his credit. Both men quitted their training-grounds on Monday, and proceeded to Twyford, Burn taking up his quarters at the "Bell," and Baldwin at the "King's Arms Inn." They were accompanied by their friends, and professed themselves to be equally confident. In point of condition, too, they appeared to be pretty much on a par. Bob's weight was twelve stone and a half. Jem Burn never lost a day during his training, and could not have been better. His weight was twelve stone, six pounds.

On the morning of action Twyford exhibited the usual lively scene; vehicles of every denomination were seen pouring in from the surrounding country, and among them were many carriages and four; in fact, few had witnessed a more slap-up turn-out of the Fancy. An excellent ring was formed at an early hour in the morning by Tom Oliver, Fogo, and Jack Clarke, in the centre of an immense number of wagons, within which there was an inner roped circle, so as to confine the spectators to a proper distance from the stakes. The veteran Bill Gibbons arrived just in time to perform his part of the duty, and all was in readiness soon after twelve o'clock—the weather delightful, the crowd numerous, but orderly, and not the most distant apprehensions of an unfriendly beak. Orders having been issued from headquarters, the men left their respective inns for the place of rendezvous, Bob dressed in a smock frock, sporting his blue fogle, and Jem in a post-chaise, wearing a yellow squeeze with black stars. Both were cheerful, and on their departure scarcely an inhabitant was left in the village.

Shortly before one they entered the ring; Bob attended by his backers, and his second and bottle-holder, Jem Ward and Dick Curtis, and Jem Burn by Tom Belcher and Harry Harmer. The ceremony of peeling was soon performed, and the excellent condition of both men became visible. Bob showed most muscular strength and sturdiness of frame, but Burn was the longer and taller man. Jem was still a marked favourite, and just before setting to was backed at two to one, but there was little money laid out on the ground. At last the interesting moment arrived, and the men were placed at the scratch, Baldwin having won the toss for choice of position

THE FIGHT.

Round 1.—Jem did not now, as on the former occasion, let fly the moment his man was placed before him, but having the sun in his face, veered a little round, to get rid of that disadvantage. Bob soon showed that he had not come on a waiting job. He at once rushed to work, and hit out right and left at Jem's nob. Jem stopped him, and got away, but immediately returned, and caught Bob with his right on the left ogle. Bob pursued his quick system, and hit away with rapidity, but did not succeed in planting any important blow. Jem fought with him, and again jobbed him with his left, while he caught him on the body with his right. Bob stopped some well-intended compliments, and after a bustling rally, was forced against the ropes, where a long and severe struggle took place, equally exhausting to both, which ended in their going down, Jem uppermost. ("That's the way," cried Bob's friends, "wear him out; he can't stand bustling.")

2.—Bob, true to his orders, lost not a moment in going to work, but commenced hitting right and left. Jem stopped him cleverly; some slight wild returns followed, and, in the close, Bob was thrown, scratching Jem's face with his nails as he went down, to the dissatisfaction of the spectators, who cried out against such practice.

3.—The moment the men were at their posts counter-hits were exchanged on their canisters, and Bob proceeded to pepper away as quickly as his power would permit. Jem was all alive, and hit with him, but science was laid aside, and nothing but downright rattling followed. In the end, Jem bored Bob to the ropes, and threw him. It was obvious, however, that these rapid movements set his bellows to work, and the judges exclaimed, "If Bob keeps to that, he'll win it."

4.—Jem came up flushed, and Bob was at him. Jem was ready, and hit away, straight, but wild. Some hits were exchanged, when Jem, in hitting, went down.

5.—Bob pursued the bustling game, and threw in a blow with his right on Jem's ribs. Jem returned on his face. A desperate rally followed, to the advantage of Jem in hitting, but the pace seemed too fast for him. At last, after a severe assault, both fell in different directions from the force of their own blows, and on rising Bob showed first blood from the eye.

6.—Bob again took the start, and hit Jem on the body. Jem returned on his canister, and both closed at the ropes, when another severe struggle took place; both down, Bob under. In this round Jem made a right-handed up-hit, as Bob was following him, with great success.

7.—Bob came up piping. Bob stopped Jem's right and left, but did not return. Jem was more successful in the next attempt, and touched him heavily on the ogle, drawing more blood. A spirited and rapid rally followed, hits trod on the heels of hits, and both received heavily. A close and violent struggle at the ropes followed. Both down, blowing.

8.—Bob came up black in the peeper, but game. He hit out with his right, but the blow went over Jem's shoulder. He received a right-handed job in return, and Jem forced him back on the ropes, himself falling over him on his head, out of the ring.

9.—Bob came up rather more cautious. Jem jobbed him right and left in the face. Bob fought wildly, and missed several blows. He fought round, and did not hit at points. Jem was more steady, and had him repeatedly. Bob, in boring in, was thrown.

10.—Bob took the lead, but his right hand again went over Jem's shoulder. Jem closed, threw him, and fell heavily on him.

11.—Jem put in two of his favourite nobbers, but received in return slightly on the head and body. The weaving system now commenced, and both men fought wildly, but interchanged several blows. A close at the ropes, and a struggle in which both went down, Jem under.

12.—Bob made some good stops, and again held off on the defensive. Jem rattled at him and caught him for the fall, but Bob slipped through his arms and went down.

13.—Bob made a good stop, but had a jobber in the next trial. Wild weaving followed, Bob planting a few blows on Jem's ribs, which Jem returned on his head. In the bustle Jem went down on his knees.

14.—Bob again stopped Jem's right and left, and then hit away, Jem retreating and jobbing. A close at the ropes, and Bob pulled Jem down.

15.—Jem delivered right and left. Bob instantly closed, and both went down.

16.—Jem popped in a good body blow with his left, and then retreated. Bob followed him wildly, and was hit up in good style on the mouth, from which more claret was drawn. In the close Bob was thrown, Jem on him.

17.—Bob rushed in on the bustling system, but Jem met him right and left on the canister. Jem then retreated, and Bob, in following, fell on his face.

18.—Bob received a right-handed facer, and in attempting to close for the throw, fell on his knees.

19.—Bob kept his hands well up, and stopped Jem's jobbers. He still preserved his strength, and went in to mill. Jem got away, hitting as he retreated. At last Bob, in a wild effort to punish, fell forward, scrambling down by Jem's legs.

20.—Bob came up abroad, and rushed in to fight open-handed. Jem caught him right and left. Bob, urged on by Dick Curtis, bored in with his right, but the blow passed over Jem's shoulder. In the close Bob was thrown, Jem standing over him.

21.—Jem, elated, went to work. Bob fell on his knees, and immediately jumped up to renew the round, but his seconds prevented this unnecessary display of game.

22.—A scrambling round, hitting away without judgment on either side. Jem went down by the ropes, but no mischief done.

23.—Bob came up as lively as a lark, although his left eye was completely closed, and he bore other marks of severe punishment. He delivered a right-hander on Jem's body. Jem countered on his nob. A spirited rally followed; both worked might and main, and at last Bob was thrown across the ropes, Jem upon him.

24.—Jem became a greater favourite, and the moment Bob came up he rushed at him. Bob retreated, and they reached the corner of the ring. A violent struggle followed, Bob hanging on Jem, and attempting to fib. He did, in fact, catch Jem on the paunch, below the waistband. We thought the blow a foul one, but it was not seen by the umpires. Bob was at last thrown, and was weak. The fight had now lasted thirty minutes, and some bets were decided on Bob's being licked in half-an-hour.

25.—Bob stopped well Jem's jobbing manœuvres. He then went to work. Jem was ready, stopped Bob's rush, and caught him right and left. In the close both down.

26.—Bob, still holding his hands well up, again stopped Jem's right, but did not return. Jem caught him on the nozzle. Bob bored in; both down, Bob uppermost.

27.—Bob, on the bustling system, but fought open-handed. Jem nobbed him and closed. Bob showed great strength. He threw Jem over the ropes and fell on him.

28.—Bob, desperate, fought away without reflection. Jem was ready, and after a short rally, in the close both went down.

29.—Bob showed most physical strength. He rattled to Jem and put in a blow on the ribs. Jem let fly right and left, but Bob stopped the favours and bored in to a close. A long struggle followed at the ropes. Bob at last got the fall, and was loudly cheered. Jem piped woefully, and another change took place in the betting; Bob, from his lasting qualities, reducing the odds to even betting.

30.—Jem distressed, and Bob not much better. Jem delivered right and left, and Bob fought wildly, missing his blows. In the close both down.

31.—Bob's face was now much punished; one eye shut, divers gashes on his phiz, his conk distilling the ruby, and lips pouting. Jem also showed his marks, but nothing like so severe; his body was red and scarred from the ropes, his right hand puffed, and his bellows in full play, while his right eye was a little swollen. Jem occasionally popped his fives into Harry Harmer's jacket pocket, in which there was a supply of powdered resin, to assist him in keeping his hands tight. Jem made his left good on Bob's right ogle and closed, when both went down heavily. Bob very weak.

32.—Jem came up as bold as brass, and made up his mind for quick work. He rushed at Bob, caught him right and left, and Bob fell on his knees distressed. Another change for Jem, who was the favourite at five to four.

33.—Bob bored in wildly; Jem met him in the canister with his left, and Bob fell.

34.—Jem now had recourse to the brandy bottle. Bob came up wild as a colt, and went sprawling down.

35.—Jem missed a tremendous jobber with his right. Bob fought to a scrambling rally, and, in the close, was thrown on the ropes,

36.—Bob, cheered on by Dick, bored in to bustle, and forced Jem down on the ropes.

37.—Jem met Bob, as he rushed in, on the conk with his left, and in the close Bob was thrown.

38.—Again was Bob hurried in, fighting open-handed, and was thrown.

39.—Bob, game, followed Dick's orders and rushed in, but Jem was ready, hit away, and in the end floored him.

40.—Jem put in a jobber between Bob's guard with his left, and got away. Bob pursued him, and Jem fell in the retreat.

41.—Good counter-hits for Bob was still determined, though groggy. Jem jobbed him right and left, but as his left hand had now gone as well as his right, his blows wanted force. In the close Bob was thrown across the ropes, Jem upon him. The latter fell out of the ring.

42.—Bob was first to go to work, but Jem was awake, and after a short and fruitless rally, threw him.

43.—Bob, urged on, hit away, but Jem retreated, and met him as he advanced, right and left. Bob at last closed in and Jem fell, Bob getting weaker.

44.—Jem now seemed to make certain of his work, and nobbed away in good style to finish. Bob went down from a clink on his noddle, all abroad.

45.—Bob, still alive, was cheered on by Curtis. Counter-hits. Bob went in to weave, but made no impression, Jem getting away in good style. Bob, in pursuing, fell on his marrow-bones.

46.—Bob rushed in wildly, closed upon Jem, and pulled him down. Fifty-four minutes had now elapsed, and it was thought it could not last much longer.

47.—Jem set to work to polish off his customer. Bob, almost blind, was hit right and left, and then turned his back to his man. Jem tipped him two luggers. right and left, and dropped him. Both men remained on their seconds' knees a minute after time was called.

48.—Bob stupid. Curtis roared in his ear. He then bored in, and hit Jem on the body, and fell over the ropes.

49.—Bob, still a stickler, rushed in to mill, hit wildly, was jobbed, and thrown.

50.—Bob's stubborn gameness surprised the ring. He went in to bustle, and received Jem's right and left, but, as we before remarked, the force was deadened by the state of Jem's hands. Weaving on both sides. Bob down weak, and almost dark of both ogles.

51.—Jem made another attempt to finish, rushed to Bob hit him right and left, and threw him at the corner of the ring.

52.—Jem again took the lead, but Bob was with him, wild, though weak, and grappling with Jem, at last threw him, and fell heavily upon him.

53.—Jem had another sup of brandy. The fight had now lasted an hour. Both men got to work on coming to the scratch, and were both greatly distressed, but Jem succeeded in throwing Bob from him.

54.—Jem, on the cautious system, to repair his bellows, kept off. Bob was halloed on by Dick, and in he went, neck or nothing. Both fell, side by side.

55.—Jem very weak. Bob rushed to him, and was the first to fight. Jem rattled away, right and left, and as Bob was falling on his knees, caught him on the ear.

56.—Bob made a body hit, but not in the right place. A close at the ropes. After a struggle, Jem went down, Bob on him.

57.—Both groggy, but Bob the first to begin. Wild fighting ; no discretion. Bob. in getting away, fell heavily on his back, Jem upon him.

58.—It was now considered that Bob had every chance of winning, as Jem was unable to steady himself with sufficient precision to finish his work, and both, on "time" being called, seemed much disinclined to quit their second's knees. Still Jem was the favourite, and "My Uncle," seeing his distress, called upon him not to hurry himself. In this way, to the 65th round, Bob bored in to bustle, and was loudly cheered by his friends, who assured him that he had every chance of victory. In the closes, Jem went down, evidently to gain time, and the turn was again in Bob's favour. In the 70th round. Jem produced another change, delivering heavily right and left. Bob, almost blind, never attempted to return, and dropped.

71.—Bob was lifted up, was hit right and left, and fell. Curtis again rang a peal in his ear. "It's all up," cried the Burnites, and a good deal of excitement followed, several persons calling out time who had no right to do so, and Bob was actually taken from his second's knee before the proper time had arrived.

72.—Bob, dreadfully weak, rushed in to close, hung round Jem's neck, and both went down.

73.—An hour and twenty minutes had now elapsed. Bob made a desperate effort, and cheered on by his seconds, bored in to Jem, who caught him on the nose, and both fell. The water was now exhausted, and Bob had not a drop to wash his mouth with. Still he bore up, and looked round as if still fit for battle. Tom Belcher, with great kindness, gave him a swig from his bottle.

74. Bob came up all abroad. Jem peppered away, and dropped him.

75 to 77.—All in favour of Jem, who hit away, and dropped his man in good style, although he was greatly exhausted.

78.—It was any odds on Jem, and "Take him away !" was the cry, but "No," said Dick, "we'll win it yet." Bob had a drop of brandy, and was again driven in with desperation. He grappled Jem by the ropes, and, after a short struggle, threw him heavily.

79.—Jem, after this, came up very weak; his head sank on his second's back, and he seemed much exhausted. The backers of Bob ran to the time-keepers, and loudly called on them to watch the time, while they cheered Bob with the cry, "It's all your own." Bob, like an old hound, pricked up his ears, and, on going to the scratch, darted at Jem, bored him back over the ropes, and fell on him. Here was another extraordinary change.

80.—Bob got new life, rushed in, and again threw Jem heavily, with his loins on the ropes, and fell on him. The ring was in an uproar, and Bob's friends in extasies.

81.—Bob got up from his second's knee before time was called, as if sure of winning. He rushed in, but fell from his own attempt.

82.—Jem, at the last gasp, stood up to fight, but Bob bored in hit him with the right on the body, closed, and threw him.

83.—Jem came up hardly able to stand. Dick shouted, Bob rushed in, and both went down.

84.—Bob again bored in, hit with his right, and floored Jem. Bob fell with him.

85, and last.—Jem, all but gone, collected his remaining strength, and jobbed slightly with his left. Bob returned, catching him on the front of the head, and Jem fell at the stake, completely doubled up from exhaustion. Belcher tried to bring his man to the scratch, but he could not stand, and "time" being called, Bob was proclaimed the conqueror, in exactly one hour and a half, amidst the warm congratulations of his friends. Jem remained for some time unconscious, while Bob stood up shaking hands with his admirers, and was carried off in triumph. Belcher was, of course, dreadfully mortified. He accused Jem of laziness, for not going in to finish before; and charged the time-keeper with calling time too quickly at last, when Jem was distressed, while he gave additional time to Bob when he most wanted it. This was denied; and, in fact, the irregularities in time-calling, as we have already stated, were not attributable to the time-keeper, but to those who assumed his prerogative, and thereby created much confusion. Some time elapsed before Jem could be removed from the ring, but on comparing punishment, the odds were fearfully against Bob, who, we think, was more punished than in his last battle. His wiry frame, however, added to the uncommon pains taken by Curtis and Ward, brought him through, and, in fact, as it were, be performed a miracle.

REMARKS.—Never was there a fight in which so many extraordinary changes took place. Nor ever was there an event won so completely out of the fire, except the fight between Cooper and Shelton. In speaking critically of the affair, without disparaging the bravery of the men we must pronounce our opinion to be unfavourable to the character of the contest. Bob fought badly. It is true, profiting by experience, he kept his left hand well up, to save his nob from Jem's right-handed jobs, but in his returns he was irregular and wild, fought round, and with his hands open. He did not hit at points, and, in fact, as far as punishment went, made but little impression; bustle was his motto, and bustle alone gave him the day. Jem Burn fought infinitely better; he hit straight both left and right, but his in-fighting was bad, and he did not make as much of his man as he might in the closes. At the time when Bob was brought to a stand-still, too, he was unable to make an effectual finish. This may be attributed to the disordered state of his hands; but from the distress of his opponent, if he could not hit, he ought to have rushed in and got him down any way, for Bob, at one time, had no notion of protection left. Perhaps his seconds were to blame in not giving him this hint, instead of permitting him, after time was called, to sit upon the knee until Bob made a move. At one time it was a hundred to one in his favour, and yet Bob was suffered to recover, and thus gain those laurels which appeared at an immeasurable distance from his grasp. Looking at the quickness of the fighting, and recollecting that at least 50 minutes were devoted to time, some judgment may be formed of the men's condition, for it will be seen that 85 rounds were fought in 40 minutes, during which the exertion on both sides was immense. This proves that training had not been neglected, for nothing but the finest physical powers could have stood such a test. There was no standing still, no idle sparring, but all slap-up work. Jem lost the fight solely from exhaustion. Nature left him. His frame is not anatomically so well calculated to endure continual work as Bob's, and thus Nature, and not the want of good milling qualities, lost him the victory. He was weak when he most wanted vigour, for if he could have steadied himself to put in two or three good hits in the middle of the battle, his labours must have been brought to a conclusion. Whatever may have been said of Bob's game, he, on this occasion, proved himself entitled to every praise. Large sums were dropped by Jem's friends on the event.

Baldwin, by his defeat of Jem Burn, having turned the tables on one of his adversaries, appeared to think the time had arrived for effecting a similar operation upon another. Accordingly he issued a challenge to Ned

Neale for a second trial of skill. The Streatham Youth, ever willing, accepted the proposal, and articles were signed to meet on the 29th of April, 1828, for £200 a side. The details of this undecided battle, which was interrupted by a magistrate, will be found in Chapter V., under " NEALE," p. 316.

On the Thursday after the fight Baldwin took a benefit at the Tennis Court. He took the money at the door, was as gay as a lark, and bore but little marks of face punishment. He jestingly remarked that he had " just got half through his job of beating Neale when the beak popped in." As neither man was satisfied with this unsettled question of superiority, a third match was made, the stakes being increased by £50. Wednesday, the 28th of May, 1828, was agreed upon ; as the fight between Jem Ward and Carter was fixed for the Tuesday, both men's friends, thinking them too good to play second fiddle in a second fight on the same day, shifted the tourney a day forward.

St. Albans was, accordingly, all alive on the Wednesday morning, and before one the gathering round the ring at No Man's Land amounted to over four figures, including a goodly muster of the Corinthian *élite* of ring-patrons. Neale first put in an appearance, accompanied by Harry Holt and Dick Curtis as his seconds, Baldwin soon after following suit, attended by Young Dutch Sam and Tom Olion. Betting seven to four on Neale. All being in readiness the men were led to the scratch, shook hands smilingly, and their seconds having retired to their corners, threw up their hands for

THE FIGHT.

Round 1.—An opportunity of judging the condition of the men, about which there had been so many rumours, was now given. Neale was a trifle lighter than we have seen him, but looked bright and well, his weight, in all his clothes, being under 12st. 4lbs. Bob was as fine as a star, every muscle in his splendid frame fully developed, his skin fair, his eyes clear, and in every point in first-rate trim. His weight was said to be 12st. 4lbs.; we believe it was a few pounds more. For the first five minutes the men manœuvred steadily, each watching for an opening, and each endeavouring by mutual feints to throw his antagonist off his guard. Both, however, were extremely cautious ; and Neale more than once, in jumping back from a threatened attack, displayed great activity. At last Neale, as if impatient of fencing, stepped in, and delivering right and left rapidly, caught Baldwin on the side of his head and on the

mouth, drawing first blood from the latter. Bob hit out rather wildly, and closed. In the effort for the fall both were down.

2.—Bob came up smiling, and Ned made himself up for quicker operations. After a short pause he again planted his right and left on his adversary's nob. Baldwin returned with the left lightly, and closed. Ned grappled for the throw, and chopped him on the back of his head with the right ; he then put out his leg for the lock, and threw Baldwin over on his head, falling with him. Five to two on Neale.

3.—On coming up, Neale said, "Fight fair, Bob; don't push your finger in my eye." Baldwin nodded, then dropped in his right on Ned's left side. Ned hit out heavily with his right, but it went over Bob's shoulder, and some half-arm hitting followed. In the close Baldwin got down easy.

4.—Both began at a quick pace. Slight

hits were exchanged, when Bob tried for the fall, but got thrown himself, amid cheers from the Streathamites.

5.—Bob came up laughing, and kept his guard well up. Ned, determined on work, went in left and right. Bob slashed away in the weaving style, but without much effect; in the close Baldwin was thrown, Neale upon him.

6.—No serious marks of punishment as yet. Ned planted a right-handed jobber on Baldwin's frontispiece, and jumped away. Bob stopped the repetition of the compliment with the left, and then hit short with his left. Ned drew back, but coming again quickly, popped in left and right. He then closed, and some in-fighting followed, in which Ned caught it on the ivories, showing blood on the lips. In the close, both down, Bob falling awkwardly.

7.—Ned lost not a moment in going in, delivering right and left. Bob countered with his left, and in a rally which followed, Ned hit up cleverly, and then threw Bob from him. Bob fought wildly, and not at points, and Neale continued the decided favourite.

8.—Bob hit out resolutely, but Neale jumped away. At length Bob planted slightly on Neale's smeller, and stopped his return neatly. The latter, after parrying a vicious right-hander, stepped in to mill, and got on heavily with his right. Baldwin fell backward, rather from a slip than a blow.

9.—Ned reached Baldwin's ear with his right; Bob instantly closed, and catching him round the neck, both were down in a scramble, Neale laughing.

10.—Bob tried right and left on the weaving system, but Neale retreated nimbly. Exchanges, but little done. Baldwin was down in the close.

11.—Neale rushed in and hit Bob on the *os frontis* with little effect, except on his own knuckles. Bob hit out right and left, and closed. Ned pegged him on the back of the head with the left, and both went down.

12.—Bob stopped Neale's left, and put in his right once more on Ned's ribs; Ned returned on his nob, and a wild rally followed, in which heavy blows were exchanged, Bob catching it on the leg. Both down.

13.—Ned put in his left with cutting precision on Bob's cheek, then popped in his right above the eye, cutting his adversary's eyebrow, which bled profusely. In the close, he threw Bob a cross-buttock. Offers of ten to one on Neale.

14.—Bob came up game, though evidently shaken by the last fall. Ned was ready, and went in, but Baldwin cleverly stopped his left, and was in turn stopped in his return. Ned went in for in-fighting, and tried to screw up Bob for another cross-buttock, but he was foiled, and both were down together.

15.—Bob stopped Neale's left neatly, and

went in turn for close quarters. Exchanges, in which Bob was cut on the cheek and Neale on the brow. Bob got hold of Neale round the neck and threw him. (Shouts for Baldwin. " It's all right as yet.")

16.—Bob short with the left. Ned again missed with both hands, and his man shifted. Bob, in trying for the return, missed, and fell forward.

17.—Ned jobbed with his left, but Baldwin was on the alert, and caught him on the cheek with a counter. Bob then kept out, but Ned would be with him, hit right and left, and forced a rally. Bob fought bravely, though rather wild, and Ned fell.

18.—Ned tried three times unsuccessfully to lead off with the left, Baldwin sparring neatly. At last Neale closed, and gave Baldwin another heavy cross-buttock. (Shouting for Neale.)

19.—Bob, awake, though blowing slightly, stopped Neale's left. Many blows thrown away on both sides. In the close Baldwin was thrown.

20.—The fight had now lasted thirty minutes. Bob rattled in left and right, but was neatly stopped. Ned pursued the same game, but was more successful. Bob fought with him, but rather wildly; in the close Baldwin was down.

21.—Ned received a sharp hit on the right eye, and retreated. Bob rushed to a rally, and the men fought in the corner of the ring. Neale planted a nobber, and Baldwin went down. A claim was made for Baldwin that Neale hit him with his right when on his knees. The referee said he did not see the blow given, and the men were ordered to " go on."

22, 23.—Wild fighting on both sides, and both down.

24 to 34.—Similar in character. Each man with slight alternative advantage, and each in turn distressed, and fighting on the defensive to recover.

35.—Bob rushed in hand over hand, and was met by Neale with a flush hit, and fell. Ned's hand was uplifted, but he withheld the blow, and walked to his corner. (Applause.)

36.—Science seemed to be disregarded on both sides. The men went in weaving right and left, each determined to make a turn. At length Baldwin was down, Neale on him.

37.—Forty-five minutes had now elapsed, and Neale was favourite at two to one. The latter hit down Bob with his right.

38, 39, 40.—In all these rounds Neale led off, and Baldwin fell from a blow. In the last-named round there were cries of " Take him away !" from the opponents of Baldwin. Indeed, the proportion of punishment at this time was largely on the side of the White-headed One.

41 to 48.—Much of the same character, but Neale's blows seemed to lack steam, especially those from his right hand, which

was visibly swelled. Bob's friends saw this, and he went in desperately. In the 47th round Neale fell from his own blow, apparently rather weak. In the 48th Baldwin got in heavily with his left on Neale's head, who went down.

49 to 54.—Anybody's battle. Baldwin now the stronger man, though Neale yet fought best at points. In the 54th round Neale was hit on the nose, but returned the blow with interest, Bob slipping on his knees. In this position Neale hit him on the side of the head. There were cries of "Foul!" and an appeal, but as Baldwin had his hands up it was not allowed.

55.—Great confusion round the ring, and loud shouting for Baldwin. Ned planted his puffy right hand without much effect, and continued to weave away. Both down.

56.—Neale rushed in, but was evidently unsteady. He missed both hands; both went down.

57.—Neale groggy, Bob regaining strength. Ned went in as before, and a rally ended by both rolling over.

58-63.—Wild but courageous fighting. In the 61st round Bob rushed in like a lion. Neale met him cleverly with an up-hit, but went down from his own blow, greatly distressed. In the 63rd Ned fell from a heavy body-blow, Baldwin on him. ("It's all over!" from Bob's friends.)

64.—Neale guarded his ribs and head steadily, making some good stops, but Baldwin bored in; Ned could not keep him out, and was hit in the body and thrown, Baldwin falling over him. (Shouts for Baldwin.)

65.—Neale planted his left, but Bob hit with him, gave him a rib-bender with the right, and finally hit him down. ("It's all over, Neale's beaten!" was the cry.)

66, and last.—Neale came to time greatly distressed; Bob was loudly called on, and as he came in met him with a right-hander in the mark, and poor Ned fell heavily. This was the *coup de grace*. On Neale being lifted on his second's knee his head dropped, and he became perfectly insensible. On "time" being called Baldwin was saluted as victor of the hard-fought field. Both men were reconducted to St. Albans, where they were carefully attended to. Neale, whose condition was certainly the worst, complaining chiefly of pain from the body blows he received, and the disablement of his right hand. The fight lasted one hour and eleven minutes.

REMARKS.—By this victory Baldwin placed himself on the topmost round of the ladder as a game, enduring, and resolute boxer, while Neale's superior art, activity, and precision all but balanced Baldwin's advantages in weight, strength, and stamina. It was an heroic battle, and either of the men at different changes of the well-fought fight might have resigned the prize without discredit to his courage or his honour. Indeed, more than once a scrupulously strict timekeeper might have called on one or other of the men with fatal result to his chance of success. A fairer or better ring, and more fair-play principle in those surrounding it, have seldom been seen of late.

Baldwin and Neale both showed on the following Tuesday, when Whiteheaded Bob took a benefit at the Tennis Court. Considering the severity of the contest, both men looked well—a satisfactory proof of their excellent condition, and of the effects of careful training.

This was Baldwin's last encounter in the P.R. By the assistance of his aristocratic patrons he became host of the "Coach and Horses," St. Martin's Lane, afterwards kept by Ben Caunt. Baldwin was a free liver, and his position one of temptation, which he was by constitution and temperament by no means inclined to resist. He died at his house in October, 1831, aged twenty-eight years, from an inflammatory attack, after a short illness.

CHAPTER VIII.

SAMUEL EVANS ("YOUNG DUTCH SAM")—
1825—1834.

AMONG the town celebrities of the second quarter of the nineteenth century the subject of this memoir held a prominent place. His immediate and personal intimacy as boon companion or "pal" of a certain notorious marquis, and an earl whose career, while "sowing their wild oats," savoured rather of the early days of the Regency than those of Queen Victoria, brought him too often before the public. Indeed, the nature of the associations into which he was thus unfortunately thrown, acting upon a volatile and reckless disposition, led him into excesses which destroyed a fine constitution, prevented his availing himself of more than one opportunity of achieving competence and a fair social position, and finally consigned him to a premature grave. In the ensuing pages, however, we shall chiefly deal with Young Dutch Sam as a public demonstrator of the art of self-defence, and as one whose biography furnishes an illustrative chapter in the history of the Ring.

Samuel Evans, deservedly distinguished as "the Phenomenon," was born in Wells Street, Ratcliff Highway, on the 30th of January, 1808. He was descended from a sire whose fame as a professional boxer the son did no discredit. The battles of Samuel Elias, in his day also dubbed "the Phenomenon," will be found in our first volume. Sam's earlier years, from all that we have gathered from his own lips and his intimates, were spent in the same "university" which another famous "Samuel" (not Johnson, but Weller) declares to be the "best for sharpening the intellect" of the youth who may chance to be subjected to its rough discipline. The traditions of Rosemary Lane, now itself swept into what Thomas Carlyle calls "the dustbin of the past," were once rife with reminiscences of the intuitive fistic skill and the marvellous mastery of milling manœuvres displayed by "Young Sam," in many an encounter with the pugnacious progeny of the "peoplesh," who once populated that inodorous but sweetly named thoroughfare, renowned for the "ancient and (fried) fish-like smell" of its edibles, and the yet more fusty emanations of its clobbered and thrice-renovated garments.

Thus Sam fought his way upwards in the rude "battle of life" until his sire "shuffled off this mortal coil" in the month of July, 1816, when Sam appears to have been thrown upon his own resources. Sam was evidently a precocious youth, for in his fifteenth year, if we take Pierce Egan's account, he was following the employment of a baker, when his associate in dough, one Bill Dean, a chap with some milling pretensions, threatened to serve out Young Sam for some trifling fault. This brought forth the father's blood in his veins, and in emulation of his warlike sire, he challenged Dean out to fight early the next morning; but old Burntcrust, his master, locked Sam up in his bedroom to prevent the mill. Sam, however, in defiance of bolts and bars, got out of the garret window, scrambled over the tiles of several houses, found his way into a strange house, ran down the stairs, ultimately into the street, and met Bill Dean at the appointed place, Kennington Common, when the battle commenced without delay. In the course of four rounds Young Sam played his part so well that Dean would not fight any longer, gammoning it, as was supposed, that his thumb was out of joint.

Dean was not exactly satisfied with this first battle, and, after several quarrels, a second match was agreed upon, Sam fighting Dean for three half-crowns to two. This mill was also decided upon Kennington Common, Tom Cooper and Spencer acting as seconds for Young Sam, a fact which shows that "the Young Dutchman" was already an associate, if not a member, of the P.R. Dean "screwed his courage to the sticking-place," and fought well for three-quarters of an hour; but finding the chance was against him, he declared his knee was injured, and he would fight no more. Sam was loudly applauded by the spectators for the pluck and science he had displayed throughout the battle.

Soon after this affair our hero migrated westward, leaving the "dead men" of the east, and becoming an apprentice at case in the office of Mr. Charles Baldwin, in the Crescent, Blackfriars, on the very spot now occupied by the Ludgate Terminus of the London, Chatham, and Dover Railway. Sam had scarcely taken his initiatory lessons in the mystery of a typo when he got into a fracas with the peripatetic potman of the neigh-

SAMUEL EVANS ("Young Dutch Sam").

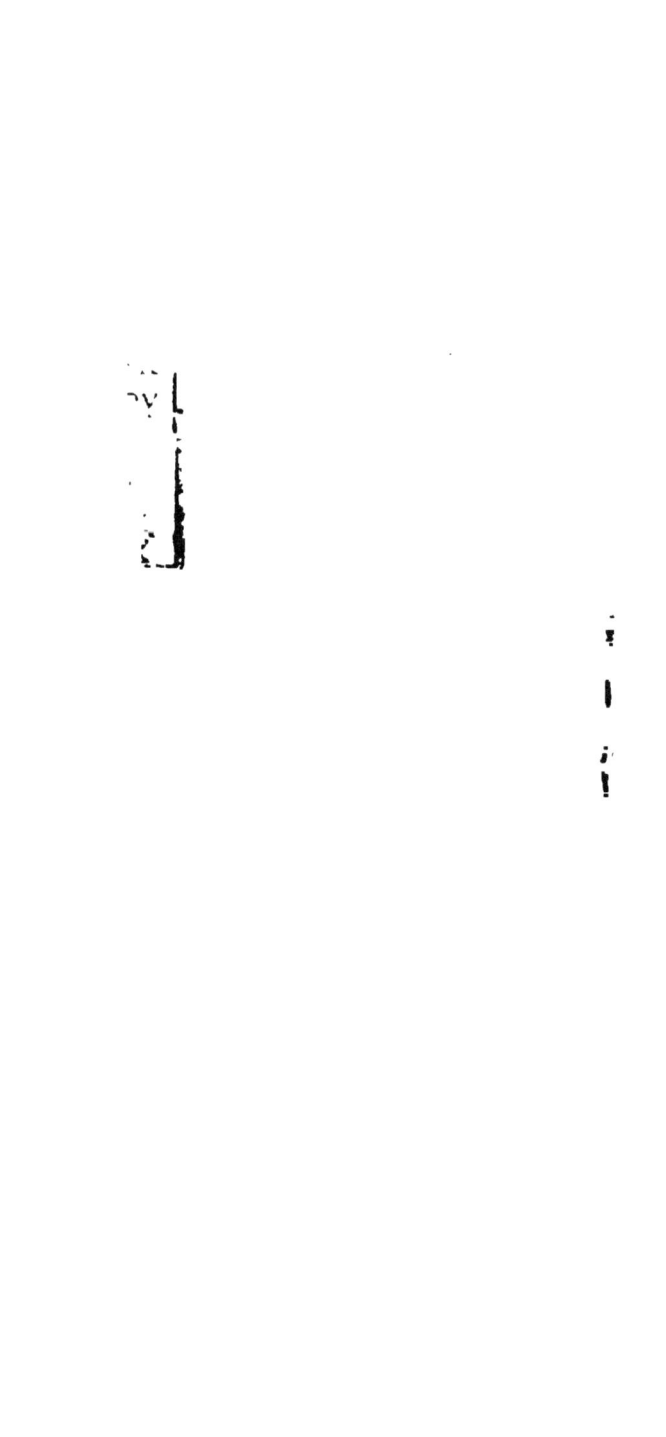

bouring public, which supplied the printing-office with beer and other
alcoholic stimulants. The purveyor of heavy wet had with him a pair of
gloves, and he and the youthful Sam (we had this from his own lips) at
first began to spar " in fun," for the entertainment of such of the compositors
as were taking their midday meal beneath their " frames " and on the
" stone " from pressure of business. The publican and sinner was short-
tempered as well as conceited, and Sam having " pinked him " more than
once on his prominent proboscis, the ginspinner's deputy threw off the
mufflers, let go right and left viciously, and " went in " in earnest. He was
a strong fellow, a stone, or perhaps two, heavier than the youthful Sam, but
the Young 'Un retreated milling, and popping in " teazers" all along the
passage and out into the short street, when, after half-an-hour's fighting,
from Apothecaries Hall to Bridewell, Mr. Gin-and-Bitters cried, " Hold,
enough !" In the opinion of Mr. Charles Baldwin's overseer, however, Sam's
skill in " setting to" did not seem to compensate for his deficiencies in skill
in " setting up," and our hero was soon after a " gentleman at large."

Released from the confinement of a printing-office, Sam turned his
attention to selling newspapers instead of setting them up. In this vocation he
became known to Pierce Egan, and with his natural predilection for sporting, Sam took up the supply of his sporting paper to sporting houses. It
must be remembered that newspapers were then costly articles—the
Dispatch, *Bell's Life*, and *Pierce Egan's Life in London* being 7d. to 8½d.
per copy, and the trade profit proportionate.

About this time, also, Young Sam obtained an introduction to Mr. John
Jackson, Captain Dudley, and other amateurs of distinction, whose
judgment of the pretensions of the young aspirant for fistic fame was
decidedly favourable. London then teemed with " professors " of the noble
art, and among them one known as Jack Poulton, of the Mint, opened a
school in that classic locality " to teach the young idea how to shoot"
straight from the shoulder. Sam was " planted " on the-rough-and-
ready Southwark bruiser as a lad who wanted improving. The result was
comical to all but the " professor." Sam stopped him, got away, nobbed
him as he came in, and so completely bothered the *soi-disant* " professor "
that he threw down the gloves, and never again showed as the principal
of an academy. At this period, Pierce Egan says of him : " On comparing
likenesses, it is the general opinion that the Young 'Un's countenance
does not possess the fine-spirited animation of the late renowned Dutch
Sam's face, yet the resemblance was admitted to be genuine, allowing for

the difference between youth and age, and the want of large whiskers. The sparklers of the Young 'Un, if not partaking (? possessing) the penetrating look of the once Phenomenon of the P.R., nevertheless gave Young Sam's nob a lively appearance throughout the battle. Our hero is in height five feet eight inches and three-quarters, weighing ten stone and a half, and generally considered a fine-grown young man."

Soon after Sam's introduction to the sporting world, his friends were so satisfied with his abilities as a sparrer that they matched him, as a trial, against Jack Lenney (the Cowboy), a boxer who had won three ring fights, but had surrendered to the " Pet of the Fancy," Dick Curtis. Monday, the 28th of March, 1825, was named as the day, and the Old Barge House, opposite Woolwich, as the battle-field. Young Sam showed at the scratch, his "soul in arms, and eager for the fray," but no Cowboy came in sight. It was reported he was locked up in town, so the Young 'Un claimed and pocketed the stakes (£25), without a struggle for the prize. About this time Sam, while in training at Tom Shelton's house at Walton, in Surrey, made the acquaintance of the scientific Dick Curtis, an acquaintance that soon ripened into a warm friendship. Dick's report to Hughes Ball, Esq. of Sam's capabilities led to a glove exhibition before that gentleman and his friends at Combe Park (when Dick gave his opinion that the " novice" *must* beat Lenney), and the subsequent patronage of "The Golden Ball," one of the notabilities of the Fourth George's reign.

Sam declared himself much disappointed, and possessing the utmost confidence in his powers, he soon found an opening for a public *début.*

On Tuesday, July 5th, 1825, after White-headed Bob (see Life of BALDWIN, *ante,* p. 342) had defeated the game George Cooper at Knowle Hill, Berks, Young Sam made his first bow in the Prize Ring, as the opponent of Ned Stockman, for a purse of twenty pounds. Stockman was well known to the Fancy as " the Lively Kid," and, in addition to several victories, had beaten Harry Jones (the Sailor Boy, 10st.) three times, and lately defeated Raines. The general idea was that Sam was too much of a novice and too boyish to defeat so experienced and crafty a boxer as Stockman, who was therefore backed freely at six to four, and at setting to at two to one. On this occasion Sam was waited upon by two East End friends, Dick Curtis and Josh Hudson, the John Bull Fighter. Stockman had the attentions of Harry Holt and Dick Acton. The colours, a canary-yellow for Sam and a blue bird's-eye for Stockman, being tied to the stakes, the men shook hands and stood up for

THE FIGHT

Round 1.—Sam was not only in excellent condition, but appeared the better man of the two, as he had length and weight over his opponent. Stockman soon perceived he had reach against him, and did all he could to get between the guard of Sam, but in vain. Stockman, determined on mischief, let fly, but Sam stopped him with perfect ease, and returned with advantage. In a sharp rally Sam hit his opponent so neatly as to call forth the admiration of the ring; he also adopted Cribb's favourite mode of milling on the retreat, and jobbed Stockman's nose repeatedly, till he went down. (Immense applause. "This," said Josh, patting Sam on his back, "is not a chip of the old block, it's Old Sam himself. He'll win, for £100.")

2.—Stockman, full of gaiety, came to the scratch, and in a resolute manner tried to find out a soft place on Sam's head, but it was "no go." Sam sent down his opponent by a rattling hit with the left in the neck. (Thunders of approbation; and "Here's a Shiloh for Duke's Place! Here's the pink of Petticoat Lane!")

3.—This round, at this early stage of the battle, decided victory in favour of Young Sam. He jobbed Stockman all over the ring; in fact, the nob of Stockman was a mere drum to the hands of Sam. The latter finally floored his opponent. (The Sheenies, who always claimed the Dutchman, were uproarious in the praise of Sam. "Vat a nishe boy! Vat a shweet hitter! Isn't he like iah fader!")

4—Stockman positively had not a shadow of chance, and if he planted one blow he got five in return. The jobbing system was resorted to by Sam, and in closing at the ropes he held Stockman in his left arm, and with his right hand he nobbed him in the Randall style, ditto, ditto, ditto, ditto, and ditto, till Stockman went down quite bothered, amidst the loudest applause ever heard in the Prize Ring.

5.—The length of Sam, his steady guard, and his confidence, prevented Stockman from placing any hits with effect. Stockman, after the receipt of several blows, went down on his knees; but Sam held up his hands, smiled, and walked away. "That's right Sam; he only wants a foul blow."

6.—We never saw Stockman so much at a loss before; he was nobbed with the utmost ease by his opponent, and fibbed tremendously till he went down.

7.—Sam stopped the rush of Stockman, hit him as he liked, till Stockman dropped. Two to one, but no takers.

8.—Stockman might have resigned the contest—every round was against him. The left hand of Sam was continually in his face, when with a heavy blow Stockman was floored. Three to one.

9.—Stockman countered well, but Sam got out of the way of punishment with the skill of an old general. Stockman received a staggering hit, and a repeated blow sent him down.

10.—This was a good round. Fine science was exhibited on both sides, till Sam sent Stockman down on his knees. Sam raised his hand. ("Be careful," said Josh, "we won't have it that way at all, Sam; mind, don't be caught for a foul blow!")

11.—"Move your feet in and out," said Curtis; "but it is all your own." Stockman made a good stop, and also put in a heavy blow on Sam's throat. In closing both down. Any odds against Stockman, but shy of taking.

12.—Stockman went down on his knees from a hit, but Sam held up his hands, and walked away. Applause.

13.—Stockman put down his hands, and appeared to wish the battle was at an end. Sam planted a tremendous blow bang in the middle of his opponent's head; Stockman's eyes flashed fire, he was quite abroad, and went down completely exhausted. Ten to one laid and taken.

14.—The battle nearly over; by way of a finish, Sam caught hold of Stockman and fibbed him down. The Jews in rapture on beholding the talents of Dutch Sam the second.

15.—It was all U P.; Stockman, groggy as a Jack Tar three sheets in the wind, was sent down before he was scarcely at the scratch.

16.—Stockman still showed fight, but he was met by Sam on going in, when he fell on his knees, but he instantly got up, and with much fury rushed in to mill Sam. The latter, however, floored him like a shot.

17, and last.—Sam had it completely his own way, till Stockman went down. While sitting on his second's knee he hinted that he had enough—if not too much. Sam was hailed the winner in thirty-six minutes and a half.

REMARKS.—The "Downy Ones" were completely thrown out, as the non-favourite proved victorious. Stockman did all he knew to win; but he could not get at his opponent. Sam was completely his master in every point of view; in fact, he felt so surprised on being declared the conqueror that he exclaimed: "Is it all over? Why, I'm not hurt in the least; I could fight an hour longer." Stockman, on being taken out of the ring, was quite exhausted, and insensible for a short period. Young Sam was positively without a visible scratch.

Young Sam was now welcomed as the true son of the Phenomenon of the Prize Ring, entering eagerly on a life of gaiety which must impair the stamina of an athlete. Dick Curtis, too, selected him as his partner in public sparring exhibitions. At this period it was the fashion to illustrate the art of self-defence at the theatres, and more especially upon the stages of the transpontine houses. Dick Curtis and Young Dutch Sam figure frequently in the playbills of this period, and he showed off his graceful and effective style with much *éclat* behind the footlights of the Surrey, Coburg (now Victoria), and Royalty Theatres, and at the Sanspareil, in Catherine Street, Strand.

Sam was not long allowed to be idle. Harry Jones, the Sailor Boy, offered himself to his notice, and a match was made for £25 a side.

This battle was decided at Shere Mere, on the borders of Bedfordshire, on Tuesday, the 18th of October, 1825. Jones was backed for this event in consequence of his being said to have had the best of Sam in a sparring match at the Jacob's Well, Barbican. The odds, nevertheless, were against Jones, six to four, and in several instances two to one, and some persons even ventured to lay three to one on the ground. Sam was attended by Dick and George Curtis, and Jones by Goodman and Reid. The Young One had the length of his opponent, but Jones showed most muscle and strength, and also the best condition. Two to one on setting to in favour of Sam.

THE FIGHT.

Round 1.—Caution was the order of the day on both sides—Sam on the look-out, and the Sailor Boy equally leary to guard against squalls. Sam tried all the manœuvres he was master of to do summat, but Jones, who had a good knowledge of milling, was not to be had. Some minutes elapsed and nothing was done, until the Sailor Boy rushed in to work. He made a hit with his left hand on Sam's cheek, and closed. The weaving system was now adopted; Sam was thrown; and the Sailor Boy fell on the young Israelite. ("Well done, Jones!")

2.—Jones cleverly stopped Sam's left hand; sparring for advantages; and Sam hit short. The Sailor Boy, eager for work, went boldly up to his adversary, and planted a right-handed hit on Sam's nob. A sharp rally of give and take occurred. In closing, the Young One received a cross-buttock, and Jones fell heavily on his opponent.— ("Bravo, Jones! that's the way to win.")

3.—Jones hit short, being too eager to make play; however, he soon made up for it, by planting a heavy blow on Sam's cheek. In closing, the pepper-box was handed from one to the other, the Sailor Boy fighting at the nob, while his opponent was hammering at the body. The round was finished by Jones getting down as well as he could, Sam keeping on his pins.

4.—The Young One did not show anything like the superiority he exhibited in the fight with Stockman. The claret was running down from Sam's mouth, while, on the contrary, the Sailor Boy looked none the worse for his engagement. Sam's mouth was open, rather piping. Jones, with excellent skill, stopped a heavy left-handed blow of Sam's. In fact, considerable science was displayed by both combatants, till Jones rushed in to mill; sharp counter-hitting; in closing, the pepper-box was in full use until they separated. Another sharp rally took place, when the Sailor Boy went down.

5.—This was a prime round; and the fighting was excellent on both sides. Sam's peeper napped a rum one from Jones—the Sailor Boy repeated the dose. (Great applause; and "He'll win it!") Sam was also bored down at one corner of the ring.

6.—The Sailor Boy appeared as fresh as when he commenced the battle. Sam's condition was not satisfactory. He sparred, and looked anxious. The Sailor Boy appeared quite up to the movements of Sam, and would not be decoyed from his mode of fighting by the stratagems of the young Israelite. Severe counter-hits, which told on both sides. Jones, however, received a heavy one on his listener as he was going down.

7.—A long fighting round, and Harry as good as Sam. A sharp rally, and mischief in it. The Sailor Boy broke ground, but soon returned to his adversary, laid hold of him by the body, and sent him down in an ugly manner. ("Well done, Jones—you can't lose it!")

8.—Sam's left hand was stopped by Jones; still the former persevered till he made a good hit. Sharp counter-hitting; rather too hot for Jones, so he retreated; nevertheless he returned to the charge in a passion, and planted a flush hit on the young Israelite's face. Jones ultimately went down.

9.—The upper works of Sam napped a little one; and Jones got away laughing. A severe rally; give and take without flinching. Sam tried milling on the retreat, was successful, and the Sailor Boy slipped down.

10.—This round was decidedly in favour of the Sailor Boy. The latter began his work without delay; and Sam slipped down by accident, receiving a heavy hit on his conk; but, like a trump, he jumped up and slashed away without ceremony. The Sailor Boy drove him to the ropes. Sam adopted the weaving system, but not with effect; the Sailor Boy hung upon his neck, till both went down.

11.—The Sailor Boy was a dangerous customer. He planted a heavy blow with his left hand—then boldly went up to his opponent, and caught him round his neck—it was then blow for hit, till Sam was thrown. (Lots of applause for the Sailor Boy.)

12.—The chaffing-box of Sam received rather an ugly thump from Jones; but Sam was determined to be with him, cutting the skin of his eyebrow like a knife, the claret following. Good milling, till Jones seemed a little abroad, and pulled Sam down.

13.—Jones parried well; and in a sharp rally the Sailor Boy was extremely active. Sam was cautious, but kept milling with his opponent. Ultimately Jones went down.

14.—The young Israelite appeared distressed, and also exhibited marks of punishment. The blows of Sam, at this period,

seemed to have but little effect on Jones. The Sailor Boy again parried the hitting of his opponent with much skill; but he bored in, and caught hold of his adversary round his neck. Sam, in order to extricate himself, fibbed his opponent, and at length got away. Jones went down.

15.—Severe counter-hitting, after which, Jones bored Sam to the ropes. It was expected the Sailor Boy would have done some mischief, but after a little struggling he went down.

16.—Jones planted a sharp facer with his left, but the young Israelite, in return, jobbed him with his right. A rally, of no long duration; and in closing Sam was thrown.

17.—The Sailor Boy planted several hits, after which he bored in with his head down, in order to escape milling. A struggle for the throw, when Jones got down anyhow. ("I don't like that," observed an Old Ringgoer; "he's going to cut it.")

18, and last.—Sam came up to the scratch quite gay; and the Sailor Boy was lively to all appearance. After some sparring, Sam planted a blow on the right side of his opponent's nob, and he fell on his back. It did not appear by any means a finishing blow, and the amateurs did not like it. When time was called, the Sailor Boy was deaf to it; and Young Sam was declared the conqueror. The battle was over in fifty-three minutes.

REMARKS.—There is nothing new in the Sailor Boy's cutting it: in several of his battles he has done the same thing, when the amateurs have been perfectly satisfied that he had the best of it. It was exactly the same sort of thing in his last battle with Stockman. He showed himself decidedly the best fighter, and was also the strongest man. In truth, when he had got his clothes on, he was very little the worse for milling! The blows of Sam were more showy than effective, and his hits were trifling on the nob of Jones, compared to the style with which he finished off Stockman. To sum up the matter, it was the opinion of the majority of persons present that Jones, although a good fighter, a strong chap, and capable of doing severe execution, by the manner of his giving in, showed the "white feather" most unmistakably.

Sam's defeat of Harry Jones did not add much to his reputation; but he was soon matched with Tom Cooper, the Gipsy, for £30 a side. This battle was decided on Tuesday, the 25th of April, 1826, at Grays, in Essex, nearly opposite Gravesend, twenty miles from London by road.

It would be wrong to state that the road was covered with amateurs on the appointed Tuesday; nevertheless, the "Old Ring-goers" were in motion at an early hour, and a good muster of the Fancy, in gigs and other vehicles, were trotting over the ground, to arrive in time at the scene of action. Tom Cooper, by his manly behaviour in a turn-up with Bishop Sharpe, which continued for twenty minutes and upwards, was viewed as an opponent likely to test the "staying capabilities" of the Young 'Un. Nevertheless, the betting was decidedly in favour of Sam, six and seven to four. The ring was formed in a field near the Thames, in a most delightful spot; the ships in the river added to the picturesque effect. The ride from London was truly charming. At one o'clock the combatants entered the ring, Dutch Sam attended by Dick Curtis and Harry Holt, and Cooper waited upon by Jem Ward and his brother Jack Cooper. After the hands were crossed together in friendship, the men made their toilets, and in a few minutes set to.

THE FIGHT.

Round 1.—Sam looked well, and the advantages of careful training were perceived in the improvement of his frame. The "Hero of the Bush" was also in good trim; in fact, Cooper is naturally a hardy, wiry sort of chap. Both on the alert, but cautious; and a short time occurred in manœuvring to obtain an opening. At length the Gipsy let fly, and touched Sam's canister slightly, but the son of the Phenomenon returned a sounder on the body of his opponent with his right. In a rally, counter-hits took place. Sam, however, got away in style; but the Gipsy, anxious to do mischief, again made use of his right hand, when Young Dutchy, with great celerity, planted a second body blow. Sam also, by his skill, bored the Gipsy into a corner, and exhibited his superiority, to the delight of his backers, by using his left and right hands on the index of Cooper, producing the claret, until he went down. (Uproarious shouts of applause for Sam, and two to one offered without the slightest hesitation. "Sam will win in a canter.")

2.—The blows of the Gipsy were seen on the frame of Sam, but did not appear mischievous. Caution again on both sides; but the Gipsy, always fond of slashing, used his left hand with success on Sam's head. Dutchy, like a good one, and master of his art, took the lead, went in, and punished the nob of his opponent like fun. The Gipsy did not like it, but kept fighting as he was retreating from danger. A sharp rally, and milling on both sides. Sam, perceiving that he could go in without much danger, again drove his antagonist to the ropes, where the Gipsy, rather tired, went down. ("It's as right as the day!" said the Pet of the Fancy; "we shall win without any trouble." "Sam for a hundred.")

3.—The mug of the "Hero of the Bush" was now the worse for fighting, but his pluck was as good as ever, and mischief seemed his object, by his slashing away at his adversary. Random shots seldom tell, and so it turned out for the Gipsy. Sam took advantage of this sort of wildness, and put in a conker so sharp that Cooper was quite mad, rushed in to work, helter-skelter, and planted a severe blow under Sam's right ogle, which produced the claret. ("Capital!" from the friends of Cooper; "another like that, and summat will soon be the matter!") Young Dutchy, as gay as a lark, returned the compliment by two severe hits, and as a sort of tie-up to the round, sent his opponent headlong on the turf. ("Dat's de vay!" from the Sheenies; "Vat a peautiful hitter! Dat's vat he ish. my dears! He's an article not to be shold for his vally!"

4.—The coolness displayed by Sam, as well as his superiority as a boxer, satisfied the judges he must win it, although he had nobbed a severe one under his left eye, which bled rather copiously. His left mauly was also a tiny bit damaged, and the friends of the Gipsy announced the circumstance with delight and hopes that it was a good chance for their man, who, they said, could last a long time. Sam got away cleverly from a desperate blow, but went in to his opponent, and by a flush hit on his mouth set Cooper's ivories dancing. The Gipsy, not dismayed, returned on the body. A sharp rally followed, in which Cooper was floored; and Sam, rather weak, reeled against the stake. (Five-and-twenty pounds to ten, but the backers of the Gipsy did not fancy it.)

5.—This was a prime round; and the friends of the Gipsy observed, if he had but commenced the battle as he now fought, the chance might have been in his favour. The

Gipsy wildly fought at the body, while Sam (adopting the traits of his master, Curtis, who was at his elbow) kept milling at the head, and doing considerable execution at every hit. Sam also got away from numerous blows; and such was the fine science he exhibited, uniting tremendous punishment, that he nobbed the Gipsy five times, one after the other, and then, by way of a quietus, floored him. (The Sheenies were now roaring in ecstasy, offering any odds on their "beautiful Young Dutch Sam!")

6.—The courage and resolution of the Gipsy were admired by every one present, but his mode of fighting was wildness instead of science. He trusted much to desperation, and slashed out without looking at his opponent; in a word, he was no marksman. In the hands of a scientific boxer like Young Dutchy he stood no chance. When once kept out with a few nobbers such a fighter becomes an easy prey, and is licked offhand at the leisure of the cool miller. Thus was the Gipsy disposed of in this round. He napped "divers blows in sundry places," and was ultimately floored. (Five to one, but no takers.)

7.—The appearance of the Gipsy was considerably altered, but his friends insisted he was now fighting better, and thought they perceived a small turn in his favour. Anxiety and friendship for a man, in addition to backing, too often punishes the pocket of the amateur—he does not view the contest in a proper light. The Gipsy was still mischievous, and a chance blow might win the battle. ("Be on your guard," said the Pet. "Give nothing away. Be ready for him; he's coming, wild as an ox.") Sam waited for his adversary, met him in the head, and in the struggle for the throw both went down.

8.—In this early stage of the battle it was a guinea to a dump as to the best fighter. Sam did as he pleased, as a superior tactician, and finished this round in great style by a flooring hit. Any odds.

9.—The Gipsy was piping, all abroad, and of little use, with his index out of shape. He was also fatigued, yet he went to work desperately, in order to obtain something like a chance in his favour. It, however, was "no go." The wildness of the Gipsy was fast leaving him; and the jobbers he received at every turn rendered him nearly stupid. He was hit down distressed.

10.—It was "bellows to mend" with Cooper—in addition to which, Sam's fists were never out of his face until he was floored. (Thirty to ten. "Take him away; he can't win it.")

11.—The Gipsy in this round endeavoured to hit up, which, if it had told upon Sam's nose, might have been dangerous. But he was punished severely, and in endeavouring to make a return Cooper fell exhausted.

12.—The Gipsy was nearly done over, but he was gay, fought like a man, and contended till he went down. ("Take him away.")

13.—Wildness and mischief was still the tactics of Cooper, but it was all up with him as to victory. Sam planted his hits as safely as if he had been attacking a dead mark. The Gipsy down.

14.—Cooper was now so distressed that all the champagne in Charley Wright's extensive cellars—successful as it is in most cases towards recruiting drooping spirits—would have proved of no use towards renovating the strength of the defeated Gipsy. He was severely punished till he went down like a log of wood. ("Pray take the brave fellow away!")

15, and last.—All things have an end, and the Gipsy was compelled to submit to defeat. Like a drowning man that catches at a straw, Cooper made a desperate rush as his last effort. But Sam finished his opponent by a tremendous blow on the nose as he was falling forward, which deprived him of his senses. When time was called the Gipsy was deaf to it, and Sam was declared the winner. The Young 'Un left the ring little the worse for the combat, excepting his hands, which were much swelled. The Gipsy did not open his eyes for several minutes, when he was not only carried out of the ring, but also to the nearest public-house. In fact, Cooper could not stand. The battle was over in thirty-eight minutes.

REMARKS.—Sam not only proved himself worthy the confidence of his backers, but he raised himself a step higher in the sporting world by his victory over Tom Cooper. He won the battle like a master of his art. His coolness was admirable. He was perfectly prepared at all points, and he met his man with all the skill of an experienced warrior. Cooper did not disgrace himself by this defeat, but he ought to have paid more attention to science. His mode of fighting may suddenly dispose of ugly commoners in a street row, but with a skilful pugilist, when desperation is stopped, the chance is gone, and it is a heart-broken attempt to retrieve the day.

At Ascot Races, on Thursday, June 8th, 1826, after His Majesty (Geo. IV.) had left the ground, a subscription purse of £50 was subscribed for a fight. Sam, determined not to let a chance pass him, entered the lists.

This mill was patronised by some swells of the first order, £50 being collected in the Royal Stand with little difficulty, and great interest was manifested by the spectators when Young Sam was announced as prepared to contend for the prize-money. It will be observed that only six weeks had elapsed since his last fight, and Sam's hands were said to be somewhat damaged. His opponent, Bill Carroll, was a good man. He was seconded by M'Kenzie and Lenney; and Sam was handled by Dick Curtis and Barney Aaron. Sam took the lead, at two to one, till the tenth round, when he received a severe cross-buttock. This circumstance rather alarmed his friends; but he soon recovered from its effects, and finished off his man in a canter, in sixteen rounds, occupying thirty minutes. The Duke of Wellington was present during the fight, and subscribed £30 towards the stakes, and to a purse for the losing man.

From the great improvement exhibited by Sam, not only in his person, but his knowledge of milling, he was matched, without hesitation, against Jack Cooper, known as the Slashing Gipsy, for £50. This contest was decided upon a stage, on Tuesday, February 27th, 1827, at Andover, after Dick Curtis had defeated Barney Aaron. The Gipsy, attended by Jem Ward and Mr. Nathan, ascended the stage, and Dutch Sam was waited upon by his faithful friends Josh Hudson and Dick Curtis. The appearance of the latter hero as Sam's second excited general surprise. Curtis said, " Gentlemen, a bet was laid me, ten pounds to one, that I did not win the fight and second Young Dutch Sam. I believe," said he, laughing, " I shall win both events." The combatants appeared in excellent condition ; Sam seemed lively as a dancing-master, and full of confidence. The Gipsy's mahogany mug bore a smile of triumph as, after shaking hands, the men set to.

THE FIGHT.

Round 1.—Sam did not exhibit the determined character of his late sire, who was considered the hardest hitter of his time. Young Sam stepped in and out exactly after the lively manner of Curtis, and he also held up his hands like that great master of the art of self-defence. The Pet is a model for all boxers ; and Uncle Ben (Burn) publicly expressed his regret that his Nevvy Jem was not at Andover, to have taken a lesson from the battle between Curtis and Aaron. Sam endeavoured to make a hit, after long sparring ; but the Gipsy got away from mischief. A precious long pause, and both upon the watching system ; at length the Gipsy went in hand over head, and planted a heavy blow on the left arm of Sam, which left its mark. (" I say, governor," observed an old ring-goer, " if that there hit had knocked at the door of Sam's victualling office, summat would have been the matter.") Sam, on the alert, got away from another random shot. The Gipsy followed Sam all over the stage, but gained nothing by his bustling system. The Young One planted a facer ; an exchange of blows was made, but Sam had the best of it. In closing, the strength of the Gipsy prevailed, and Sam went down upon his knees.

2.—This was a long round, Sam taking his time to punish his opponent. After several pauses, feints, and other manœuvres, Sam gave a facer which produced "first blood." The Gipsy, rather wild, rushed in and planted a body blow ; but it was a chance hit. Sam, upon the whole, was too leary for his opponent, and having Curtis at his elbow might be considered three points in his favour. He nobbed the Gipsy frequently, without any return. The long space of twenty-five minutes elapsed before this round was finished. In struggling for the throw, both down, the Gipsy undermost. Sam for £100.

3.—The Gipsy, at times, stopped well; but in general he had little discretion about his hitting; he, however, planted a body blow. Sam kept out of mischief with considerable skill, every now and then planting facers, which put the Gipsy out of temper—nay, made him so wild that he rushed in like a bull, and by a sort of scrambling pull, he got the Young One down; five and six to four on Sam.

4.—Had Sam been a punishing hitter, the numerous blows which the Gipsy had received upon his mug must have reduced the fight at this period to a complete certainty, and also short in its duration. Cooper is always a dangerous customer, and his scrambling hits may win a fight. Sam, aware of this feature belonging to the Gipsy, kept out of harm's way with considerable talent, nobbing the Bush Cove at his leisure. The Gipsy's mug was bleeding profusely, and in rushing in to do mischief, he ran himself down weak.

5.—This was a long round, but the Gipsy, although desperate at times, could not turn the fight in his favour. The face of Sam did not exhibit punishment. It is but right to observe that Cooper stopped several well-meant blows; but he fought open-handed, and missed numerous hits. If he had measured his distance properly, another account might, perhaps, have been given of the battle. The face of the Gipsy was bleeding in every direction, and he did his utmost to win. In struggling for the throw Sam undermost.

6.—"You need not be in a hurry, Sam," said Dick, "you are sure to win it; he's about cutting it now. It is £100 to a kick of the rump." Sam planted a facer that sent the Gipsy staggering, but he returned to the charge, and fought desperately. In closing Sam fibbed Cooper down. Six to one upon Sam, and "Take him away! He's of no use!"

7.—The Gipsy, quite abroad, ran at his opponent like a madman, receiving facers at every step; nevertheless, he bustled Sam about, who appeared a little distressed. In closing the Gipsy again napped it severely, and went down, covered with claret. ("Take him away!")

8.—Strange to say, the Gipsy answered the call of time with alacrity. He also made two good stops. ("Bravo, Gipsy! you behave like a brave fellow!") Sam now had nothing to do but wait for the rush of his opponent and nob him with ease and certainty. The Gipsy was again punished severely till he went down. ("It is all up now! ten pounds to a crown he does not toe the scratch again! Take him away!")

9, and last.—The Gipsy, however, showed fight, and proved himself a much gamer man than his friends had anticipated. But he only stood up to receive. Sam milled him down without ceremony. The Gipsy would again have answered the call of time. He was game enough to have had another round, but his backer humanely interfered, and said "he should fight no more." The battle continued for one hour three minutes and a half. It is impossible to describe the joy felt by Sam; he performed some regular dancing steps in the ring on being declared the winner.

REMARKS.—Sam is an improving fighter; and if he can but add force to his blows, bids fairly for the highest honours of the P.R. He left the ring without a mark upon his face, and no casual observer could have told that he had been engaged in a battle. The face of the Gipsy exhibited severe punishment. Jack Cooper never took anything like such a licking before. He did his best to win, and the bravest could not have done more. Sam is anxious to get higher on the pugilistic list; and if he can find friends to back him, expresses no hesitation to fight Bishop Sharpe. We should say, upon this point, to him, "Be bold, but not too bold!" But the Young One, perhaps, knows best what he is about. He asserts that he fancies "the Bishop" as a customer in preference to any other boxer in the Ring.

In the days of old "the road to the fight" was one of the features of sporting life, nor was the "return from the fight" made without its vicissitudes. On this occasion the sudden alteration in the weather, and the overwhelming showers of rain, rendered the roads almost impassable between Andover and Basingstoke, and the men and horses were beaten to a standstill. But "it is an ill wind that blows no one any good," and the "Wheatsheaf Inn," at Virginia Water, was not neglected either in the journey from or return to London. A good larder, excellent tipple, prime beds, and moderate charges are sure recommendations to the sporting world; and here many of the

London division rested for the night. Curtis and Sam arrived in town on Wednesday night, with full pockets, and amidst hearty greetings. Before he left Andover for London, Sam called upon the Gipsy, and made him a present of two sovereigns.

On Thursday, March 1st, 1827, Young Dutch Sam took his benefit at the Tennis Court, and was well supported. The sets-to generally were good, the wind-up by Young Sam and Ned Stockman. Sam was as gay as a lark, fresh as a four-year-old, and quite ready for another mill. Stockman stood up well against his clever adversary; but Sam had decidedly the best of the bout. Curtis also appeared at the Court, and was congratulated by his numerous friends upon his recent conquest over Aaron. His face was considerably swollen, and the handiwork of Barney evident. The Star of the East also showed himself. Barney's peepers were completely in mourning; his mouth also damaged, and he complained of soreness of his throat. He was quite cheerful, consoling himself that he had done his duty like a brave and honest man.

The Gipsy did not exhibit much punishment—his head was rather out of shape—a proof that Sam was not so hard a hitter as the Pet. Sam himself had no visible signs of recent fighting about his nob; his face was entirely free from marks. He returned thanks for the support he had received, and hoped he had given his friends satisfaction.

Dick Davis, the " Pet of Manchester," stood so high in the provincial Fancy, from his repeated conquests, that the patrons of boxing in Manchester were determined Davis should have a shy in the London Ring. He was accordingly matched with Young Sam for £100 a side. This battle was decided on Tuesday, June 19th, 1827, near Stony Stratford. The journey was rather too long for the cockneys, being nearly sixty miles from the sound of Bow bells; as it is also one hundred and twenty-nine miles from Manchester, it was also above a joke for the Manchester lads to leave their homes. Therefore the muster of the Fancy was but thin at Stony Stratford, although the battle between Sam and Davis excited considerable interest among the lovers of boxing, both in town and country. Davis was a native of Lancashire, and twenty-eight years of age. He was employed in Mr. Peel's iron foundry, at Manchester, as a moulder—in height about five feet six inches and a quarter, weighing ten stone twelve pounds. Davis, by his numerous victories, stood high as a milling cove; and his friends at Manchester flattered themselves that he was invincible, as with his country opponents he was never particular as to weight and size. Davis defeated twice Jack Wilson, also Witman twice; with Tom Reynolds he made a capital battle, which was brought to a wrangle; and he likewise defeated Fidler Hall. Davis entertained an opinion that he could conquer any pugilist of his own weight with the greatest certainty. Sam had now proved victorious in five battles; Ned Stockman, Jack and Tom Cooper (Gipsy), Carroll, and Harry Jones (the Sailor Boy), all in succession had surrendered to his conquering arm.

Davis, with two of his backers, and Phil. Sampson, arrived at Stony Stratford on Saturday, making the "Cross Keys" their headquarters. Davis wore his working dress, consisting of a fustian jacket and wide thick trousers; he also wore a check shirt, and he looked as rough a customer as might be met with in a day's walk, offering in these respects a striking contrast to the smart and natty London boxer, who was a decided swell in dress and deportment.

Sam arrived with Curtis during Monday, and made his headquarters at the "George." In walking through the streets of Stratford, the men met each other for the first time, and shook hands like brave fellows. After this *rencontre*, Davis appeared yet more confident he should prove the winner, the opinion of the countryman being that "such a fine gentleman couldn't stand to be spoilt."

On Tuesday morning the knowing ones laid their nobs together as to a spot of ground, and a field at Haversham, about five miles from Stony Stratford, was named as the scene of action. Thither the travellers repaired, and a few minutes past twelve o'clock Sam, attended by Curtis and Oliver, threw in his tile. Sam sported silk stockings. Davis appeared immediately afterwards, followed by Sampson, and Johnny Cheetham, of Manchester. The colours, yellow for each of the combatants, were tied to the stakes. Sam was the favourite for choice; but his friends were not inclined to give above five to four. Sam won the toss.

THE FIGHT.

Round 1.—Davis reminded us of Bishop Sharpe, but was even more formidable in appearance. He had been well trained; in fact, he was up to the mark, and his heart also in the right place. To win, and nothing else but to win, he said, he left Manchester. Sam was gay as a lark, but his friends did not think him so well as he might have been, and one of his knuckles on the left hand was tender and swelled. Sam had the advantage in height and length, but the superiority in weight was with Davis,

The latter hero looked every inch a milling cove. On appearing at the scratch Davis was still cautious, and watching the movements of Sam from his eyes down to his toe. Sam also measured his opponent at all points, and felt assured that he had a rum customer before him. Offers on both sides, but no blows; at length Davis rushed in, and slightly planted a hit on Sam's arm. Sam, with great skill, crept, as it were, by degrees, up to his adversary, and let fly on Davis's sensitive plant. Davis's ogles winked again.

("Sam for £100!") A trifling exchange occurred, when Sam cried out, "First blood!" the claret slightly appearing on the mouth of Davis. Sam was not long before he planted another snouter, but Davis received it very coolly. Davis put in a body hit. Exchange of blows; when they separated, Sam waiting for another turn. A long pause. Davis would not make play. Sam planted another successful noser. Several minutes had elapsed; so much caution was observed on both sides that it was certain that a long fight would be the result. Sam retreated from some heavy work to a corner of the ring, where he received a bodier; but he returned a heavy nobber, which sent Davis staggering until he went down. This was considered a knock-down blow; and the two events had been obtained upon the part of Sam, as to first blood and the first knock-down blow. (The Samites opened their mouths like good ones, saying, it was as right as the day, and offering any money on the son of the Phenomenon.)

2.—Davis hit Sam on the ribs. Sam returned right and left. Davis missed two heavy blows. A long pause. Sam again felt for the nose of his opponent. Davis gave two body hits, but they were short, and not effective. Counter-hits; but the length of Sam gave him the "best of it." Another tedious pause. Sam walked round his opponent to get an opening. ("As you are a fine fighter," said Sampson, "why don't you go to work?" Curtis observed to Sampson, "Do you recollect Ned Neale?") Davis stopped a left-handed blow cleverly; he also got away from another. The men now went to work, and several blows were exchanged. In closing Sam endeavoured to fib his adversary; but the strength of Davis was too much for him, and in struggling for the throw Sam got down well. "Well done, Sam!" from the London boys.

3.—The claret was now visible upon the mug of Davis, and the nose-enders he had received put him on the winking system. This round was a truly tedious one—five minutes at a time and no blows passed. Sam was determined, like a skilful general, not to lose an inch of ground, and only to hit when it was a certainty to get home. Sam let fly, and the face of his adversary napped it. Some sharp fighting occurred, Davis endeavouring to do mischief, and he ultimately succeeded in planting a desperate left-handed hit on the side of Sam's head, which floored the Young One. The Lancashire lads began to open their mouths—"That's right, Dick!" —while the Samites not only looked blue, but were silent as fish.

4.—Sam looked rather stupid; he was labouring under the effects of the last blow. Davis did not follow up his success, but waited for Sam to make play. The latter with great ease put in a rum one, and Davis put up his hand to feel if his nose was in the right place. Sam stopped a well-meant body blow. A short rally, but Sam broke away. In closing some expressions of disapprobation saluted Davis for his mode of throwing. But as it did not appear to be done intentionally, the umpires did not notice it, and Sam was under.

5.—This was a short round, but the milling in it was better than in any of the preceding rounds. The exchanges were at par. Davis thrown.

6.—Several of the London Fancy began rather to be alarmed, and got their money off by backing Davis. Excepting his nob he was none the worse for the battle, although one hour and more had passed away. The science displayed by Sam was the delight of the amateurs; he jobbed Davis repeatedly; but the game of the latter was not to be reduced by the left-handed blows of Sam. The right eye of Davis was cut in the corner, and the claret was streaming from his nose. He made some counter-hits, but had the worst of the round until he went down.

7-9.—The fighting of Davis in all these rounds was the same; he would not go in; and stood out to be nosed at the will of Sam. The latter was thrown heavily in the last round.

10.—This was a long round. Sam was more than cautious; and under the circumstance of his bad hand his fighting was entitled to praise. The lip of Davis was cut severely. He received lots of smashers in the face, and the claret running down his throat annoyed the Lancashire man much. In closing Davis was under.

11-16.—The superiority of the style of Sam's fighting in all these rounds gave him the lead; yet the goodness and game of Davis rendered him a troublesome customer. The latter could not get at Sam with anything like certainty, and therefore his favourite hits were at the body. Sam was thrown, and also received some heavy blows. In the last round he received a severe cross-buttock.

17-21.—("Pray take him away," said Tom Oliver to his backer; "he is one of the gamest fellows I ever saw, but he cannot win; you will get yourself into trouble—nay, all of us. It is a shame to let such a brave fellow fight any longer." "Well done, Tommy," replied a Manchester covey; "he is not half licked yet; Davis will soon begin; he can't lose it. Sam has not strength to lick a baby.") The head of Davis, by the repeated jobbers he had received, was quite out of shape; both his peepers were damaged, his cheeks puffed up, and his nose cut and bleeding. But his backers relied upon his gameness, and several of them calculated upon his winning. The last round was well fought, and rather in favour of Davis, who went in to fight. Sam was down.

22, 23, 24.—Nose and mouth. Although it might be termed quite safe to Sam, and three to one offered upon him, yet the son of the Phenomenon treated Davis as a dangerous rival, and kept out of mischief. He jobbed Davis at his leisure, reducing his strength every round. ("Take him away!" from all parts of the ring.)

25-27.—Davis would not listen to anything like "giving in," and although his nose was hit two or three times in every round, he fought in the most manly style. He was down in every round. ("Take him away!")

28.—The gameness of Davis never deserted him; and it did appear to the spectators that he would sooner part with his life than lose the battle. (Ten pounds to a crown—any odds—but no takers.) Davis sent down.

29, 30, and last.—Davis again appeared at the scratch and showed fight. Sam now did as he liked with his brave opponent, punishing him in all directions, until he hit him down in the corner of the ring. His backers said Davis should not fight any more. In fact, Davis could not have appeared again at the scratch. The fight occupied *three hours and thirty-five minutes.*

REMARKS.—Against a fine fighter like Dutch Sam something more than gameness is required. Davis may defeat a mob of yokels, but it is quite a different thing to tackle London prize-fighters. Davis is a good man, a scientific hard hitter, and stands up like a chopping-block; but the above requisites, although essential to a boxer, will not ensure victory unless he can fight more than a little. He must learn to give as well as to take; a receiver-general is but a foolish character. Davis was severely punished about the head. Had he gone in according to the direction of Sampson a different account might have been given of the fight; yet it is but common justice to say of Davis that he exerted himself all in his power to win the battle. Sam, notwithstanding it took him upwards of three hours to defeat his opponent, won the fight like a first-rate tactician. If the left hand of Sam had not been injured he would probably have won the battle in half the time. He left the ring quite fresh, and could have fought another hour without difficulty.

The backers of Sam, without hesitation, now pitted him against the " all-conquering Bishop Sharpe " for £100 a side. This match excited an unusual degree of interest. Sharpe had the majority in his favour, particularly the old ring-goers; nevertheless, Young Sam stood well with the Corinthians and the lovers of fine fighting. The following remarks as to the different capabilities of the combatants were published a few days previous to the day appointed for the battle to take place: " First on the list stands Bishop Sharpe, the Bold Smuggler, who has proved himself successful in upwards of twenty battles, both in and out of the Prize Ring. The Smuggler never picked his customers, but took them as they came, and always got through the piece with victory. As a fighter, Bishop Sharpe is not generally admired; but as a hitter he is tremendous, and one blow well planted has often rendered it ' no go ' to his opponents. The Sage of the East pronounces him to be ' prodigious;' and the John Bull Fighter asserts, ' He hits them as I like, and so hard as his opponents do not like!' But Sharpe will be opposed by a ' leary ' fighter in Sam, cautious in a high degree, and who has a very great aversion to be hit at all. This renders Sam a very difficult cove to be ' got at.' He is also a very dangerous adversary for those customers who like to ' go in,' as he nobs and gets away, frequently without any return; his blows are considered light, and of the sparring school; but the Manchester Pet tells another tale. We are inclined to think—nay, almost certain—that Young Sam cannot punish anything like his late papa, nor hit as hard; but he has a knack of hitting a man twice in a place which nearly amounts to the same thing. Sam is confidence personified, and the Bishop thinks victory is as safe to him as if the battle were at an end. Sharpe is at present the favourite, five to four."

Tuesday, October 23rd, 1827, was the day set apart for the battle to take place, and great anxiety was manifested upon the event. Many of the Londoners started overnight for the scene of action; and in consequence the Bonifaces on the road to No Man's Land came in for a turn, more especially at St. Albans, the "Blue Boar" being the grand rallying point.

Before peep of day on Tuesday morning, the North London road was covered with vehicles of every description, filled with the lads of the Fancy, picturing to themselves a prime day's play between Sam and the Bishop, and the complete fill-up of the scene by Barney Aaron and Redmond. The "Crown," at Holloway, kept by Joe Emms, was attractive; Young on Highgate Hill was not forgotten; Pepper, at the "King's Arms" at Barnet, came in for a good slice, and "Little Tim's Crib," near to the twelfth milestone, was overflowing with company.

Sharpe, on the Monday evening, made his quarters at St. Albans, and Sam took up his residence for the night at "Little Tim's."

As the day wore on, it was ascertained that a screw was loose, and five to one offered that no fight would take place. Such was the state of things for two or three hours at St. Albans; at length it was announced that Sam was upon the road, and he shortly afterwards made his appearance in a post-chaise.

Time was on the wing; and Sharpe and his seconds, Peter Crawley and Ward, made the best of their way to No Man's Land, where the ring had been previously made by Joe Fishwick. At one o'clock Bishop Sharpe threw his hat into the ring, according to custom, in order to claim the stakes should Sam not make his appearance, but Sam, attended by Curtis and Harry Holt, showed himself within the ropes. All was happiness amongst the crowd for a few minutes, and nothing but a scientific battle expected to take place; but the mishap was soon developed; Sam took off his fogle, but the remainder of his toggery remained untouched. The traps now appeared, and said they had a warrant against Sam; but on no occasion whatever did officers ever conduct themselves more gently, or act " according to their instructions" to behave in a gentlemanly manner to the offender against the law, than these did. This compliment is most certainly due to them. The warrant was demanded, and was soon brought to light,

It purported to be from Marylebone Office, signed by Mr. Rawlinson, directing all constables, &c., " to apprehend Samuel Evans and bring him before the said magistrate of the county of Middlesex, on suspicion of his being about to commit a breach of the peace with one Bishop Sharpe." During the conference with the traps, the Bishop addressed himself to several gentlemen in the ring, observing, " It is too bad—it is rascally conduct to rob me of the battle-money," and taking off his clothes, went up to his opponent, and said to him, " Sam, do you mean to fight? I am ready for you." Sam replied, " What am I to do?—I can't fight in the face of the officers." His seconds, Holt and Curtis, declared they would not give a chance away by seconding Sam in defiance of the law. The traps, to prevent any further misunderstanding on the subject, and to make " their visit pleasant," in the most gentle manner gave Sam a hint that his services in the ring would be dispensed with, so, like " a good boy," he retired from within the ropes without giving them any further trouble. Bishop Sharpe put on his clothes; but before he left the ring he said he had no doubt the lovers of fair play would not let him be deprived of the stakes," and thus the affair ended.

On Thursday, October 25th, 1827, the Pet of the Fancy took his benefit at the Tennis Court; and, considering the unfavourable state of the weather, it was a good one. Several bouts proved attractive; but the great feature of the day was the set-to between Harry Holt and Young Dutch Sam. This gave the amateurs an opportunity of judging of Sam's condition; and, in the general opinion of the audience, he appeared nothing wanting; on the contrary, he was considered up to the mark. Young Sam was pitted against one of the best sparrers on the list, and one who has had great experience, not only in fighting with Jack Randall, but continually setting to with the Nonpareil in his best days. Holt has been opposed to all the first-rate men on the list, and always proved himself a distinguished scientific artist. The attack and defence were a masterpiece on both sides. Harry was perfectly aware that he had a troublesome customer before him, and Sam had not to learn that the eyes of all the Court were on him. We do not know a better opponent than Holt for Sam to produce a trial scene for the Fancy in order that they may draw their own conclusions. Harry was capital, and Sam proved himself excellent. The " best of it " was of a doubtful nature, and a feather in the scales of candour and justice might have been the award on either side; but it should be recollected that Sam was in condition, and Harry quite out of it. This, however, was not the point in view; but the most remarkable and valuable feature in the above set-to was this—Sam, it was seen, could change his mode of fighting as circumstances presented themselves—no hopping about, no standing still, but stopping and hitting his opponent with the utmost ease, rallying like the most determined boxer, and getting out of trouble with ease, style, and decision. Indeed, such was the display of Sam and Harry Holt that the greatest admirers of Bishop Sharpe on witnessing the set-to, must have pronounced the " Young One " a formidable and dangerous customer to the Bold Smuggler. Tumultuous applause crowned their exertions and exits from the stage. It was pronounced by the whole of the visitors one of the best sets-to ever witnessed at the Tennis Court.

Several persons of rank who were present wished that Sam would give some explanation on the subject of his not fighting with Sharpe. He replied " that he had no explanation to give ; he had been used very ill, and it was not his fault !"

DECISION OF THE STAKEHOLDER.—The " Castle Tavern " was over-flowing on Wednesday, October 24th, 1827 ; Bishop Sharpe and his backers were present. The stakes of £200 were demanded by the Bishop, on the score that he was in the ring, and ready to fight, according to the articles of agreement. He said that Sam had declined to fight through the collusion of parties, under the idea they would lose their blunt if he fought, and not on account of any fair magisterial interruption. One of the backers of the " Young One " resisted the stakes being given up until the whole of Sam's backers were present, as they had nothing to do with the matter in dispute. The stakeholder, Tom Belcher, considered, in point of right and fairness, the Bishop was entitled to the battle-money, and accordingly gave Sharpe one hundred pounds, holding the other hundred as an indemnity against any legal proceedings which might be instituted against the stakeholder.

Sam, full of pluck, and anxious to obtain a job, offered to fight Peace Inglis, but no match was made.

In April, 1827, Dan M'Kenzie was matched against Young Sam for £50 a side, but the backers of M'Kenzie ultimately preferred a forfeiture to running the risk of a battle.

In a set-to with " the Young Gas " at the Tennis Court, Sam distinguished himself, proving a most troublesome customer. Jonathan had " all his work to do" to prevent his being placed in the background by the superior tactics of Young Sam.

The set-to between Young Sam and Harry Holt had given so much satisfaction to the amateurs that a second bout was called for by the admirers of the art of self-defence. At the benefit of Jem Burn at the Tennis Court on Tuesday, December 11th, 1827, the above pugilists again met. Sam, as a rising performer, appeared anxious to obtain the superiority, and Holt was equally on the alert to prevent losing his laurels obtained as an accomplished sparrer. The latter defended himself with considerable skill; but the length and activity of Sam ultimately gave him the advantage. Upon quitting the stage they received thunders of applause from a delighted audience.

The following statement, addressed to the sporting world, appeared in the newspapers in vindication of Young Sam's character:—

"November 1st, 1827.

"GENTLEMEN,—I have been much surprised to perceive that almost all the blame of the disappointment experienced by the fancy owing to the fight not taking place between Bishop Sharpe and myself has been laid upon my shoulders, and yet I have been unquestionably the greatest sufferer; for I am confident that had no interruption taken place the battle-money would be now in my possession. An inference is drawn to my prejudice that as the warrant from the Mary-la-bonne Office was granted on the information of my mother, I had employed her to give such information, or, at least, that she acted with my knowledge and consent; but I declare most solemnly that this was not the case. I had no previous knowledge whatever that any one intended to adopt such a course, nor did I know that such a warrant was issued, till informed of it on the morning of fighting. Whether or not this warrant was obtained at the instance of persons who had taken a strange alarm and were afraid to risk their money on me, I shall not pretend to say; but of this the Fancy may be assured, that I meant *to do my best to win*, and felt fully confident of success. With respect to the assertion that the officers had no authority to take me, as their warrant was issued from Middlesex, and was not backed by a Hertfordshire magistrate, I can safely plead that they told me they certainly had full powers to act, and I did not feel sufficiently acquainted with legal niceties to resist their authority. I could not venture to fight in defiance of a couple of experienced officers, who I reasonably concluded must be much better judges of the extent of their powers than I could be. As to the alleged error of a *misnomer* in the warrant, *my real name is Samuel Evans*, so that the document was correctly drawn in that respect at least. The whole affair has ended most unfortunately for me; I am bound over to 'keep the peace towards all his Majesty's liege subjects for twelve months,' and am thus prevented from exercising my profession in the Ring during that period—a consequence of most serious import to a young man who, vanity apart, was rising into notice, and had been hitherto invariably successful. Of course, it is useless for me to talk of making any match at present; but, when the above period has expired, I shall be prepared to fight any man in England, of my weight, for from £100 to £500. And now a word or two to Bishop Sharpe: If he has one spark of English feeling belonging to him, he will not fail to give me the preference as soon as I am free from the fetters of the law and able to meet him. I have a prior claim upon his notice, and shall never rest satisfied till I have a fair opportunity of proving which is the best man. Good luck, and the unfair precipitation of the stakeholder, have placed the battle-money for our late match in the Bishop's possession (to which, under all the circumstances, he was not entitled); let him add to the windfall as much more as he pleases up to £500; and, at the end of one year from the date of this letter, I will fight him for the whole.

"Yours, &c.,   SAMUEL EVANS
" (Commonly called Young Dutch Sam)."

During the twelve months of enforced exclusion from the ring as a principal, Sam figured in a turn-up in February, 1828, with a big carman who insulted his friend, Dick Curtis, near London Bridge, polishing off the wagon-driving Hercules in five rounds. The affair will be found in the memoir of Dick Curtis, *post.*

In the autumn of 1828, in consequence of some personal unpleasantness, the veteran Jack Martin (the once-renowned conqueror of Scroggins, Josh Hudson, Phil. Sampson, and Ned Turner) challenged Young Sam to the battlefield, and a match was made for £100 a side. For some months this affair was the talk of sporting circles; Sam's conduct being the subject of much censure. At length, all preliminaries being arranged, the men met on the 4th of November, 1828, at Knowle Hill, Berks, thirty-four miles from London, a spot celebrated from its having been the scene of similar exhibitions on a former occasion—we allude to the fights between George Cooper and Baldwin, Young Dutch Sam and Ned Stockman, and Goodman and Reidie, all of which were decided on the same excellent arena without interruption. In fact, a more suitable spot could not have been selected; first, from its being at a distance from any populous neighbourhood; and next, from one side of the grounds being bounded by a gradual elevation, from which the spectators could look down upon the sports as from a sort of amphitheatre. The distance from London, too, four-and-thirty miles, brought the journey within the scope of a day, and enabled the amateurs to go and return without any serious sacrifice of time or labour.

Both men had been attentive to their training; Martin at Milford, in Surrey, and Sam first at Hartley Row, and then at the " New Inn," Staines. In the early part of his training, Martin, from having but just recovered from a severe fit of illness, as well as from the deep wound which his feelings had sustained, was in anything but promising condition. At last he came out with every appearance of renovated health. At his benefit, on the previous Tuesday, he seemed to have reached his pristine vigour, and, as he said himself, was quite as well as an " old 'un " could expect to be. Of the result of the battle he always spoke with perfect confidence, and led his friends to believe that victory was certain. So persuaded was he himself of this issue that he advised all whom he knew to back him without hesitation, and actually gave them money to lay out on his account. In the end this confidence proved to be misplaced, and the milling maxim that " old stale ones are of no use to young fresh ones," was fully exemplified; Martin, who had been for some years a licensed victualler, being in his thirty-third year, while Sam's summers numbered but twenty-one. It was stipulated in the articles that Martin should not weigh more than 11st. 7lbs. on the morning of fighting—a superfluous condition, seeing that his weight, in his prime, was under 11st., and his recent illness had reduced him some pounds. Sam stated his weight at 10st. 12lbs.; to us he looked more than half a stone heavier. The toss for choice of place was won by Sam, and he very naturally named the scene of his former good fortune. On Monday afternoon Martin reached the "Castle Inn," on the further side of Maidenhead; and Sam, accompanied by Dick Curtis and other friends, shifted his quarters from Old Shirley's at Staines, to the same neighbourhood. It was soon ascertained that the magistracy would not interfere, and the anticipation of the approaching contest was thus unalloyed by those fears which were but too common even in those days in meetings of a like character.

The road from London during Monday afternoon was crowded by drags of every description. A great number pushed on to Maidenhead, while others pulled up at Cranford Bridge, Colnbrook, or Slough.

The dawn of day produced a new cavalcade from all quarters. Carriages, post-chaises, and gigs kept pouring through the town all the morning in an almost uninterrupted line, reminding men of the days when Crawley Downs was the favourite resort of the Fancy. Many persons of distinction were among the motley assemblage, whose patronage, under the encouragement afforded by the Fair Play Club, was hourly increasing. The weather was as propitious as the most fastidious could desire; the sun shone with brilliancy, and every countenance seemed gladdened by the cheering prospect of a good day's sport.

The Commissary was early on the ground, and formed the ring with his usual judgment. The whole was surrounded by wagons and other vehicles, which were drawn up three and four deep, and the most perfect regularity was preserved. As the hour of combat approached the throng came rattling in from every point of the compass, and the "yellowman" of Sam and the "blue bird's-eye fogle" of Martin were everywhere sported. Tom Cribb and most of the old members of the P. R. were present, and we were glad to recognise in the circle many of those old Fancy mugs whose countenance in former days lent life to the scene.

At half-past twelve there were not less than ten thousand persons assembled. At this time the F.P.C. whips were put into the hands of twelve of the "Order of Regulators," and the ring was immediately cleared of interlopers, all of whom, with a few exceptions, retired behind an outer ring of ropes, in which situation they remained throughout the contest.

At a quarter before one o'clock it was announced that both men were on the ground, and in a few minutes afterwards Sam entered the ring, attended by Dick Curtis and Jem Ward. He looked serious, and was a little pale, but still appeared well and confident.

In a few minutes afterwards Martin entered from the opposite side of the circle, attended by Tom Spring and Peter Crawley. He was received with loud cheers, and appeared in high spirits. He came forward with a smile on his countenance, as if, to use the words of an old toast, " the present moment was the most happy of his life."

Martin paid but little attention to his antagonist, while Sam eyed him with a searching look, and, turning towards his friends, said, " It will be seen to-day whether fear forms any part of my composition." On peeling, Martin showed a fine muscular pair of understandings, and had some good points upwards ; but it was obvious that his frame was not in its prime. His breast showed marks of recent blisters as well as the bites of leeches, and the flesh about his collar-bone and ribs wanted that fulness and fresh-ness which betoken good health. Sam was " all over right," and was evidently in slap-up condition. Though not so well pinned as Martin, his upper works were symmetry itself, and the fine muscle of his shoulders and arms was visible at every move. At length, both men being ready, the toss for choice of position took place, and was won by Curtis. The men then went to the scratch, and shook hands slightly, and immediately threw themselves into position. Breathless silence prevailed, and the seconds retired to their corners. At this time the betting was twenty-five to twenty on Martin.

THE FIGHT.

Round 1.—The men set to across the sun, with their sides to it, and each got close to the side of the ring. Sam had the higher ground, and made one or two dips or half plunges with his left, as if going to let fly ; but Martin was steady, and held his arms well up to guard his nob. In this way they stood opposite each other for some seconds, when Sam again made a feint with his left. Martin immediately broke away, and veering round, got the upper ground, so that they, in fact, changed positions. Three minutes had now elapsed, when Sam hit out slightly with his right, but was stopped. He tried it again, and popped in his left and right with great force on Martin's right eye and left cheek. Martin then rushed in to a rally, but was cleverly met by Sam with his left, and both hit away, Sam well in, and quick with his right and left. Martin slipped on his knees from the moist state of the ground, or from a hit in the neck, but was up in a moment. Sam, ready at all points, instantly plunged in to a close in the corner of the ring, and a desperate struggle ensued, each trying for the advantage, Sam hitting right and left at the body and head, while Martin grasped him round the neck. Sam cleverly disentangled his left hand, and delivered a slashing hit on his right eye ; he then hit him with the right, and both still continued to struggle with all their force, Martin receiving some severe hits, but making no return ; at last Sam threw out his leg, and catching Martin on his thigh, flung him over, and fell heavily on him. The ring was in an uproar, and all Martin's friends in dismay. It was a fearful but decisive struggle in favour of Sam, for on Martin rising to his second's knee his right eye was closed and dreadfully swollen, while his face exhibited other marks of Sam's handiwork. Sam himself had not a mark. " It's all over," was the general cry—"Sam must win;" and, indeed, it was evident that Martin was quite abroad, as well as obviously distressed. The round lasted five minutes, and six and seven to four were freely offered on Sam, but no takers, for all were too much astonished to think of hedging.

2.—Both men came to the scratch with deliberation, and each seemed desirous of recruiting his wind, which was in full play from the violence of the previous struggle. Sam again poised himself on his left leg, keeping his head well up, and his fists ready for delivery. At length Martin, as if he considered something desperate was necessary, hit out with his right, but the blow fell short; he then rushed in, but was met cleverly by Sam with his left. Martin, quite wild, bored him to the ropes, but Sam, cool and steady, broke away and jobbed him with his right. Martin, rather abroad, now tried at the body, and rushed in with his head down—Sam again met him with his right, and closed, when he caught poor Jack's nob under his right arm, and hit up with his left ultimately flooring him, and falling on his head. Three to one on Sam, and no takers.

3.—Sam cautious, and in no hurry to begin. Martin stood with his back close to the ropes, and many thought Sam ought to have gone in to finish. He seemed to think, however, he had the game in his own hands, and was evidently collecting his wind. At last he put in a fearful job with his right on Martin's left eye, and again with his left on the nose, drawing claret in abundance. Martin broke away and took up fresh ground (Approbation). Both got to the corner of the ring, and again waited for Captain Wind-'em. Martin hit out with his left, but was neatly stopped, and Sam smiled; Martin then tried his right, but was short, and this was followed by another desperate rally, in which Sam's deliveries, right and left, were precise and severe. His hitting was admirable, and style of attack beautiful. Quick as lightning Martin had it in the chops, without being able to make a successful return, and again in the throat. At last Martin closed for the fall, running in with his head down, and succeeded in getting Sam down, and falling upon him. (Ten minutes had now expired, and it was pretty evident the first round had taken the fight out of Martin).

4.—Martin all abroad; but still kept his hands well up. At length he rushed in with his head down, and attempted to deliver a body hit, which fell on Sam's breast. Sam stepped back and met him as he came in, and then closing hit up with great force, and delivered a tremendous body-blow with his right. In the struggle for the fall both went down, Martin under.

5.—Spring now called for a lancet, if possible, to let the blood from Martin's right eye, but could not obtain one; he endeavoured to scarify the shin with a pen-knife, but without effect, and poor Jack was again brought to the scratch, when Sam lost little time in jobbing left and right on the sore spots. This dose he repeated and broke away. Martin rushed in wild, hitting right and left, but short and without effect. Sam again closed, fibbed, and threw him. (Fourteen minutes had elapsed.)

6.—Martin came up quite abroad, when Sam, after a feint, threw in a tremendous smack with his right on the left jaw, and dropped him, thus winning the first knock-down blow as well as the first blood.

7th, and last.—It was now Bushey Park to a lark sod. On Martin being brought to the scratch Sam jobbed him right and left on the head and ear, and repeated this discipline till his man went down completely abroad and woefully punished. He tried to make a rally, but it was all in vain, and on being lifted up by Spring, he said it was no use, he was too stale, and had not a chance. Spring tried to persuade him to get up for a few more rounds, but he would not "have it," and on his rising on his legs Spring gave in for him. He then walked a few paces, and Spring gave him his knee. when he complained of his being sick at stomach. Sam was declared the victor in sixteen minutes.

REMARKS.—In the history of Martin's pugilistic feats—with the exception, perhaps, of his quick despatch by Jack Randall in his second fight, upon which so much was said at the time—we never witnessed greater disappointment or astonishment than was manifested on the present occasion. Hundreds of individuals, many of the highest respectability, who had long since abandoned the sports of the Ring, were induced to come from distant parts of the country in full confidence that they would be gratified by seeing something worth looking at, but what was their surprise to find that their anticipations were groundless, and that the man on whose talent and game they had relied proved to be below mediocrity, indeed, we have never seen even the most unpretending commoner so easily and so quickly disposed of. After the first round, in fact, he had not the ghost of a chance. It is said that he was taken by surprise by the quick assault of Sam, who from being a cautious out-fighter suddenly changed his style and became the assailant. This may have been the case; and we know that Sam, under the advice of Dick Curtis, adopted this mode as the most likely to puzzle a man of Martin's bustling manner. Sam's first feints were evidently dictated by a desire to try what Martin meant, and whether he would stand to be jobbed if an opening offered. The experiment told. Curtis saw the advantage, and exclaiming to Sam, "Go it!" the latter at once made play. This quickness immediately drew Martin to a rally, in which he clearly lost his presence of mind, and left himself open to the severe punishment, which he received without making anything like a return. Feeling the sting of Sam's hits he had recourse rather to hugging and endeavouring to get his man down than to the more prudent course of dropping or breaking away. This effort in his state of constitution was decidedly the worst he could have made, as it could only lead to exhaustion on his part much more easily than with his more vigorous and youthful assailant. It also gave Sam an opportunity of hanging upon him, and fibbing him in a way which, of all things ought to have been evaded. Sam was alive to all his advantages and availed himself of them in the most decisive manner, and in so short a time we have seldom witnessed more decided execution. If anything were wanting to prove the "patched up" state of Martin's frame, it was the rapidity with which his eye puffed up from the effect of Sam's left-handed hit, and the distress which he exhibited when he was placed on his second's knee. It has been observed that after this he lost his temper, but to this we do not subscribe, as he came up with great coolness and courage. He had, however, sufficient reason to lose his confidence, which combined with the punishment he had received, led him to the wild efforts he subsequently made, and exposed him to the excellent generalship which Sam displayed—not only in averting his antagonist's injudicious rushes, but in making the best of the openings which were offered. It is true that after the first round Sam's work might be considered as done, but still he preserved his caution, did not throw his chance away, and finished his man in a very masterly manner. After the first round Martin was sick at stomach, and when all was over this was his principal complaint, for, though severely hit, we have seen him take five times the hitting with not one tithe of the effect. A good deal of regret was expressed that Martin should have had so signal a defeat added to his other mortification. We have only to look to the character of the men in the ring; and, in this view, to give Sam every credit for his milling talent, which we unhesitatingly pronounce of the first order. From the ring Martin was led to an adjoining cottage, where he was put to bed, and received every necessary attention. Previous to Martin quitting the ring Sam went up to him and begged him to shake hands. This Martin for a long time refused, but at last put up his hand coldly, and Sam promised to give him £10 of the battle-money. Sam dressed on the ground, and appeared as if nothing had happened. He returned to dinner at Shirley's, and arrived in town the same night. Martin, on recovering went to the "Castle Inn," and set off the same evening for Godalming, where he arrived alone at twelve o'clock at night and remained there. He was much depressed, and refused to see any person who called.

The battle-money was given up to Young Dutch Sam on the following Thursday evening at Tom Cribb's, in Panton Street, in the presence of a full muster of the Fancy, and all bets were of course paid.

In the September following the defeat of Ned Neale by Baldwin (Whiteheaded Bob), Neale fought and defeated Nicholls, who had defeated Acton, an opponent of Jem Ward. This match was for £100 a side, and was won by Neale in eighteen rounds and seventy-eight minutes. On the 2nd of December, 1828, he beat Roche for £100 a side, in thirty rounds, occupying exactly half-an-hour, and was now without a competitor. At this time Young Dutch Sam, who was in the zenith of his fame, was naturally anxious still further to increase his reputation, and, although he knew that Neale was a much heavier man than himself, he, with a different feeling to that which is now but too prevalent, issued a challenge to fight Ned, provided he would confine himself to 11st. 10lbs., he (Sam) undertaking not to exceed 11st. His fighting-weight was declared to be under 10st. 10lbs., so that, in fact, he gave away at least a stone. Neale, although his milling-weight was 12st. 4lbs., agreed to reduce himself to the stipulated 11st. 10lbs., the match was made, and everything went forward satisfactorily, the battle exciting intense interest.

FIRST FIGHT BETWEEN YOUNG DUTCH SAM AND NEALE,

FOR £100 A SIDE.

The battle took place on the 7th of April, 1829, at Ludlow, in Shropshire, but, owing to the distance from the Metropolis, and the difficulty of getting thence to the scene of action, did not attract that crowd of London Particulars which the known capabilities of the men would have undoubtedly attracted had it come off nearer home. The inducement to the men to go so far afield seems to have been a sum of £100 subscribed for them by the inhabitants of Ludlow.

Neale, it may be remembered, had but once found his master, and that in the never-flinching Baldwin (Whiteheaded Bob); and Sam, although not quite so old a member of the pugilistic corps, had at this time never been beaten.

Strong apprehensions were entertained that Neale, by reducing himself so much below his fighting-weight, would weaken his frame, and give his more youthful antagonist an advantage over him (apprehensions which were fully justified by the result). Neale, however, did not participate in this feeling, and, after a sparring tour, he set out for his training quarters, at Milford, where, by constant labour, he gradually got off his superfluous flesh, and, a few days before fighting, was five pounds under the stipulated weight. This was certainly carrying the point too far, and although Ned himself said he never was in better health, he was forced to confess he did not feel so strong as when his weight was greater. In point of spirits and confidence, it was impossible that he could have been in better form, and he booked winning as a certainty. He left Milford on Saturday, and proceeded direct by mail to Ludlow, where he arrived on Sunday afternoon, under the convoy of a gallant Captain, and the Portsmouth Dragsman, the well-known Will Scarlett. It is needless to observe that such a journey so near upon the approaching struggle was not consistent with strict prudence, but such was Neale's estimate of his opponent, and such his reliance on his own physical powers, that he treated the remarks on this subject with levity, and fancied the laurels of victory already entwining his brow. Young Sam, who trained first at Staines, was not less attentive to his duties. He was known to be in tip-top condition, and as sleek and active as a deer; showing at the same time a confidence in his carriage not less obvious than that of Neale. He said his game had been doubted, but the approaching combat would show whether these doubts were well or ill founded. He, more wisely than Neale, left London with his backers and friends on Friday, slept at Worcester, and reached Bromfield, near Ludlow, on Saturday, and there remained till the morning of fighting. He was attended by Dick Curtis and some of his favourite pals, who lost no opportunity of reminding him of those qualifications which he had so often shown to advantage, and which, in fact, had obtained for him the character of one of the prettiest fighters of the day. In point of age there was but little difference, Sam being twenty-two, and Neale twenty-five. In the course of Monday the town of Ludlow was all bustle and gaiety, and the certainty that no apprehensions were to be entertained from the officiousness of the beaks gave universal satisfaction.

The ground chosen for the lists was admirably suited for the purpose, and was situated upon the top of a hill, in Ludford Park, within a hundred yards of the adjoining county of Hereford. The ring was formed under the direction of Tom Oliver and his secretary, Frosty-faced Fogo, in their very best style, and was encompassed by an extensive circle of wagons, which were liberally contributed by the farmers in the neighbourhood, who behaved like trumps on this occasion, and were heart and hand in favour of the game.

On Tuesday morning the men were "up with the lark," and having taken their customary walks, laid in a few strata of mutton chops, and other belly furniture, after which they submitted to the titivation of their respective barbers, who turned them out as blooming as a couple of primroses, and looking as well as the most sanguine hopes of their friends could have desired. As the day advanced, the crowd thickened, and all betook themselves to the ring-side. By twelve o'clock upwards of 5,000 persons were assembled. The weather partook of the varied character of April—alternate showers and sunshine—but, on the whole, was favourable.

At half-past eleven o'clock the men went to scale, and were both found within their weight, Sam about 2lbs., and Neale full 4lbs., but neither was weighed to a nicety. Neale, when stripped, looked extremely thin, and excited the surprise of many who had seen him in the same town a few weeks before in the full proportion of thirteen stone, and it was evident that his admirers became less sweet upon his chances, for the odds of two to one, which had been freely offered on the night before, received a sudden check, and few were found to offer them.

Immediately after the weighing had taken place, the £100 promised to

he men was placed in the hands of a gentleman chosen by both, and thus
he good folks of Ludlow honourably performed their part of the contract.

Soon after twelve o'clock Neale and his friends set out for the ground in
a barouche and four, all sporting the blue bird's-eye; while Sam, also in a
carriage and four, displaying a bright yellowman, with a scarlet border, and
a garter in the centre, surrounding the letters D.S., and bearing the Latin
inscription, "*Nil desperandum*," was close at his heels.

At ten minutes before one Sam entered the lists, attended by his
backer and Phil. Simpson and Dick Curtis, who was very lame, as his
second and bottle-holder. He was as gay as a lambkin, and remarked, as
he paced backwards and forwards, "It has been said that I am not game,
but the issue of this battle will prove whether this imputation is well or ill-
founded. I have made up my mind to take a bellyful, and let him who
first says 'hold!' be written down a coward." There was nothing of
foolish bravado in his manner, but his demeanour was such as betokened a
man who felt the importance of the stake he had to play for, and the consciousness that he should have his work to do. His friends immediately
offered to take £100 to £50, but there was no "done" in the case. Sam
was loudly cheered on his arrival, and a similar compliment was paid to
Neale, who soon approached, attended by Tom Spring and Harry Holt.
He was the picture of health and good humour, and it was pretty clear
that the last thought which found place in his breast was the apprehension
of defeat. He shook hands with Sam, and offered to bet £5 each on first
blood, first knock-down, and the battle, but this was no go. All was now
fixed attention. The ring was admirably kept throughout under the superintendence of the Fair-play Club Whipsters. The toss for choice of position
was won by Curtis for Sam.

THE FIGHT.

Round 1.—On coming to the scratch, the
frames of the men were open to general
criticism. Sam was admirably proportioned
and had a decided advantage in height and
length of arm over his opponent. His
muscles, too, were well developed, and we
must say that a finer looking young fellow
of his weight, age, and inches, has never
entered the ring. Neale also looked well,
and his broad shoulders and muscular arms
betokened strength and vigour; but, taking
him downwards from the waist, he was
much thinner than he appeared in his former
battles. Each threw his arms up, ready for
attack or defence. Mutual feints were
made for an opening, but both were on the
alert. Sam poised himself on his left foot
ready for a shoot, and kept working for
mischief, but Ned stood well to his guard.
At last Sam broke ground and planted his
left slightly. Ned was with him, right and
left, and rushed to a close. Sam stepped a
little back, and jobbed him right and left as
he came in. Ned grappled for the throw,
when Sam caught him round the neck, and
fibbed with great quickness. Ned stopped
this game by seizing his arm, and endeavoured to get his favourite look, and
give him a cross-buttock, but Sam was too
much on the *qui vive*, kept his legs well
away, and at last both went down at the
ropes, Ned under.

2.—Again did each manœuvre for an opening, and show his readiness for defence by throwing up his guard when assault was offered. At length Ned rushed in, and planted his right on Sam's head. Sam returned as quick as lightning, when Ned rushed to the close, and another trial for the fall took place, during which Sam fibbed slightly, and at last got Ned down.

3.—Sam, elated, dodged on his left leg three or four times, and tried to pop in his left, but was prettily stopped. Ned broke away. Both sparred cautiously. Good stopping, right and left, by both men. Ned now finding that nothing was to be done at long bowls, rushed in, planted one of his right-handed slashers on Sam's left cheek, and then, boring Sam to the ropes, shoved him across them, chopping with his fists as he lay, and this he continued till Sam fell on the ground, amidst cries of "foul," and "fair," but no exception was taken.

4.—Sam came up rather flushed in the physog, and looked serious. Sam, steady, tried again for his favourite plunge with the left, but Ned stopped him in good style, and then rushing in, hit Sam down with a left-hander on his bird-call. (First knockdown blow for Ned; and a cry of first blood, but none was forthcoming from Sam's dominoes, although pointed at.)

5.—Ned again bored, and planted a blow on Sam's mouth, but had it beautifully, right and left, in return. Ned now closed, and tried once more for the fall. Sam, ready, fibbed prettily, and in the end, Ned, finding it would not do, slipped down.

6.—Both their mugs flushed from hitting, and both looked serious. Ned stopped Sam's left, when Sam tried left and right in succession, both hitting away in a beautiful rally, and each receiving pepper, but the balance against Ned. Sam delivered a stinging upper-cut as Ned got away. After a pause, both again fought to a rally, in which the nobbing was heavy. In the close, Sam hit up, and Ned got down.

7.—Little time was lost in going to work, and a beautiful rally was fought, in which hit followed hit in rapid succession. Sam's blows were delivered with most precision, and Ned's right ogle began to swell, while first blood was visible on his nose. Sam looked wild, and a swelling on his temple showed that Ned's operations had not been without effect. Sam's upper-cuts in this round were excellent, and Ned went down weak; he had clearly reduced his ordinary strength, and was altogether out in his wrestling calculations, as Sam was too quick, and, when seized, too firm on his pins for a clear throw.

8.—Ned's face much altered and swollen, and Sam's jowl puffy. Sam dodged for his left, and planted it neatly on Ned's smeller. Ned rushed in, and forced back Sam to the ropes. Sam caught him round the neck, and hit up. Ned slipped down.

9.—Ned distilling claret from his snuffler, and rather abroad. Sam, ready, jumped in and jobbed him right and left, and Ned was down, bleeding at all points. Sam decidedly the best out-fighter, and betting even.

10.—Sam steady to his guard. Ned finding no chance at out-fighting, rushed in, his right hand passing over Sam's shoulder. Sam grasped him round the neck, and hit up with great severity. Ned went down.

11.—Ned rushed in, planted left and right-hand round hits, and, in getting back, fell.

12.—Ned rattled in with his left, but received a heavy counter-hit on the nose. In the trial for the fall, both went down, Ned on his back, Sam on him.

13.—Ned again rushed in, and planted his left on Sam's throat, but in return, Sam jobbed him right and left, with dreadful effect and precision, and in the end Ned fell.

14.—Sam put in a left-handed snorter. Ned fought wildly, and, in coming in, received the upper-cut, and fell.

15.—The odds were now in favour of Sam and the fight had lasted half-an-hour. Ned hit short with his left, when good counter-hits with the right were exchanged; both had it heavily, and Ned got down.

16.—Sam tried to plant his left, but was stopped; the blow was not well home. Ned retreated, Sam following him rapidly, and Ned stopping right and left. Ned at last fell, weak.

17.—Ned came up a little fresher, and well on his legs, but Sam was too quick for him, and popped in his left and right. He then retreated, Ned following him up, when Sam gave him a severe upper-cut. Ned seized his arm to prevent repetition, and after a struggle at the ropes, both went down, Sam uppermost.

18.—Ned stopped Sam's left very scientifically, and planted his right in exchange. Sam, not dismayed, drew back a step, and then plunging in, caught Ned left and right as he approached, and hitting up very heavily, Ned got down.

19.—Good stops on both sides. Ned closed for the fall, and after a struggle, both went down.

20.—Good counter-hits, right and left. Ned rushed in, when Sam seized him round the neck, and gave him a couple of heavy upper-cuts. In the trial for the fall, both down, Ned under.

21.—Ned stopped Sam's right and left, and after a short spar, Sam rushed in to work. Ned retreated, and actually turned round and bolted, to get away from his impetuosity. Sam still persevering. Ned went down, amidst some grumbling, and cries of "Sam, it's all your own."

22.—Good stopping by both, when Ned planted his right, and, in retreating, fell.

23.—Ned popped in his right at the body, but had a nobber in return. Good scientific stopping on both sides, when Ned popped in his right on Sam's muzzle. Sam rushed in to deliver tit for tat, but Ned got down.

24.—Ned made his left on Sam's mouth, but received a severe return on the right eye. Hits were then exchanged, rather in favour of Sam, who hit Ned down with a right-hander. Ned lay at full length on his back till picked up by his seconds, and his face exhibited severe marks of punishment, both eyes black, and his right all but closed.

25.—Ned stopped Sam's left, and fought on the retreat. Sam followed him up, jobbing him right and left, and Ned soon went down at the ropes any how.

26.—Sam stopped Ned's right and left, and, retreating, met Ned with the upper-cut as he followed with his head inclined. Sam's style of fighting was the admiration of the ring ; he was ready at all points. Ned went down.

27.—Sam jobbed with his left. In a second effort his left was stopped, but he planted his right on Ned's jaw. Ned, in getting away, fell, amidst cries of "foul," but again the umpires saw nothing to grumble at ; indeed, there never was less disposition to take frivolous advantage.

28.—Ned stopped Sam's first attack, but in a weaving bout which followed he had the worst of it, and went down.

29.—Ned showed his scientific powers of defence, stopping as he retreated. Sam, however, pursued his assault, planted his right and left, and hit Ned out of the ring. Two to one on Sam.

30.—Sam rushed in to punish, when Ned slipped on his knees.

31.—Heavy hits exchanged, right and left. In the close, both down.

32.—Right-handed hits exchanged. Sam retreated, but met Ned with the upper-cut as he came in, and, in the close, Ned pulled him down.

33.—Ned rushed in rather wild. Sam again gave him the upper-cut, and Ned went down.

34.—Ned rushed in wildly. Sam retreated, and met him with the upper-cut right and left. Ned, still game, would not be denied, and hit out desperately with his right, but it went over Sam's shoulder. His hits were not straight, and consequently, did not tell with half the effect of Sam's. In the close, he went down.

35.—Ned, still game as a pebble, though wofully punished, rushed in to fight, and caught Sam a nasty one with his left on the mouth. Sam, ready, returned left and right, and hit Ned down with his left.

36.—It was now evident that nothing but an accident could deprive Sam of victory ; but still Ned was not beaten in spirit. In this round counter-hits with the right were exchanged, and Ned went down, thereby avoiding a severe slap from Sam's right.

37.—Ned, still resolved to do his best, jobbed prettily with his left on Sam's mouth. Counter-hitting. Sam had it again on the whistler, which began to pout most un-couthly, while the left side of his face was considerably swollen. He was not idle, planted his left, and Ned went down.

38.—Sam came up rather stupefied from the hits on his mouth in the last round, and was bleeding freely from his grinder-case. Ned went to work right and left, but was well stopped. He would not be denied, but rushed in, when Sam gave him his favourite upper-cut, and Ned went down bleeding and dark in the right ogle, the left greatly swollen.

39.—Sam kept a respectful distance, and hit short. Ned rattled in, but hit open-handed. Sam planted a couple of good nobbers. Ned down.

40.—A good peppering rally, both had it, but Ned went down.

41.—Ned, still trying his utmost, made an admirable delivery on Sam's left eye, with a cross-hit from his left. Sam winked and blinked unutterable things, and Ned's friends were again shouting for victory. A reprieve to a trembling culprit could not have been more welcome. Ned followed up this with a right-handed smack on the mouth, receiving the left in return, and going down.

42.—A good rally, Ned stopped uncom-monly well, though dreadfully punished, and was still good on his pins. Spirited fighting on both sides, which ended in Ned going down. The fight had now lasted one hour, and the hopes of Ned's friends were kept alive that he would ultimately wear Sam out, which was clearly the game he was playing, although Sam had the best of the fighting.

43.—Ned's right hand was much puffed, but his left was still sound, as he proved to Sam by planting another cross-hit on his mouth. Sam returned the compliment by a terrific job with his right, and another with his left. He then gave the uppercut with his right, then with his left, as Ned was going down. Sam's style of fighting was still the admiration of the throng, while Neale's determined game was equally the theme of praise.

44.—Counter-hitting, and a rally, in which Ned got more pepper, and went down weak.

45.—Ned popped in two excellent jobs with his left on Sam's mouth, and went down.

46.—Sam was awake to the renewed energies of Ned's left, and stopped it neatly. Ned rattled away. Sam retired, tried the upper-hit, but missed, most fortunately for Ned, who fell.

47.—Sam caught another poser from Ned's left on the conversational, and looked more than surprised. Sam again missed his upper-hit, being out of distance, and Ned went down.

48.—Sam rather abroad, though still steady on his pins. He bled considerably at the mouth. Ned cautious, when Sam, after a short pause, rushed in and delivered his one two heavily on Ned's canister, who dropped almost stupefied, and many thought it was all up; but not so, Sam had yet much to do.

49.—Ned went in to hit with his left, and that was stopped, and he went down.

50.—Ned planted his left, while Sam missed his upper-cut, and Ned dropped.

51.—Sam jobbed with his left, and, rushing in, hit up. In the close, both down, Sam uppermost.

52.—Ned popped in his left once more. In retreating, Sam rushed to punish, and Ned got down.

53 and 54.—Counter-hitting in both rounds. Ned down.

55.—From this to the 62nd round, Ned always commenced fighting, but Sam was quick in his returns, and Ned invariably went down. Nothing but a miracle, it was thought, could save Ned, and, indeed, the severity of his punishment, and the fast closing of his left eye, seemed to forbid even the shadow of a hope; still his heart was good, and he continued to come up.

63.—Sam jobbed right and left. Ned did not shrink, but, boring in, delivered another heavy smack on Sam's mouth, and drew more crimson. Renewed shouts for Ned. Sam rushed in, and Ned went down.

64.—The long exposure to the cold air, as well as the profuse use of cold water, seemed now considerably to affect Sam, and he trembled violently. Ned seeing this, rushed in and delivered right and left. Sam was quick in his return, but Ned fell, and Sam tumbled over him.

65.—Ned popped in his right, but got a severe upper-cut in return, and went down.

66.—Sam, ready, though cold, met Ned as he came in, caught his head in chancery, and fibbed till he got down. From this to the 71st round, although Ned tried every manœuvre in his power, Sam had the best of the hitting, and Ned always got down. Still these exertions seemed to be exhausting Sam, and although every care was taken of him by his seconds, he got rather groggy at this point. It was remarked that chance might yet turn the scale in Ned's favour. Sam, however, rallied himself, and, though apparently weak when on his second's knee, on being placed at the scratch, resumed his self-command, met his man bravely, and planted several severe hits. To the last Ned stopped well, but in the 78th round received a finishing jobbing hit with the right on his left eye, and fell in a state of stupefaction. Every effort was made to restore him, but in vain, and when time was called, Sam was pronounced the victor, amidst the most triumphant shouts. Ned

was totally blind, while Sam was enabled to walk to his carriage, but his punishment was severe on the left side of his head. There were scarcely any body blows during the fight, which lasted one hour and forty-one minutes.

REMARKS.—We have been thus minute in detailing the rounds of this fight as it excited an extraordinary degree of interest among the betting circles. Neale was such a favourite on Monday and Tuesday evening that he was actually backed at three and four to one; a degree of confidence in his merits to be ascribed, we think, rather to a supposed want of pluck in Sam, than to any superior fighting points on the part of Ned, who, although a game man, and known to possess a good deal of ready resource in the ring, has no pretensions to be what is called a fine fighter. Whatever might have been the grounds for want of confidence in Sam, however, they seemed to have been strangely out of character, for he not only showed himself a quicker and more scientific fighter than Ned, but proved that he was equally possessed of courageous qualities; in fact, he never showed the slightest inclination to say "Nay." When before his man he was ready at all points, and, by the quickness with which he took advantage of every opening, showed that he was perfectly cool and collected, and even when most punished would not throw a chance away. Of his weight there is not a man in the country who can cope with him, and, by his victory over Neale he has ranked himself deservedly high in the list of pugilists of the age, while he proved himself to be a true "chip of the old block." Of Neale too much cannot be said in favour of his bravery and perseverance. It was clear, from the very first round, that the reduction of his weight, and especially so much below the necessary standard, had also brought down his strength, and that those closes, which with Cannon, Baldwin, Jem Burn, and Nicholls, were so effective, with Sam were of no avail. In fact, in Sam he found a man as strong as, and certainly more active, than himself, and the only chance which was left him to save his honour, and his friends' money, was by endeavouring to take advantage of that chapter of accidents, which, in the course of a protracted fight, are often found to produce a fatal change where victory seems most inclined to rest. Neale was blamed for going down so often, but it was his only game, and we need not say he fought to win. It was admitted on all hands that a better fight has not been witnessed for many years.

Neale did not appear at all satisfied with this first defeat by Sam, and therefore issued a challenge for a fresh trial. A good deal of disputing took place as to terms, but after many angry meetings a match was at length made, which it was determined should come off on the 1st of December, 1829, Sam staking £220 to £200. Previous to the eventful day, however, Sam was grabbed and bound over to keep the peace. There was an immense deal of fending and proving, recrimination and abuse, on both sides. A postponement was, however, inevitable, and it was at length agreed that the fight should take place on the 18th of January, 1831, on which day, accordingly, the gallant battle, of which the following is an account, came off at Bumpstead, in Essex.

Sam's victory in the first battle was by Neale's friends attributed to the fact of Neale being reduced twelve pounds below his natural weight, while Sam's friends, on the contrary, claimed all the credit of superior science and generalship, persuaded as they were that on the day of battle Sam was by no means up to the mark in point of condition. In order to set these doubts at rest, there were no restrictions on either side in making the second match, and thus the respective qualifications of the men were fairly brought to the test, the extra weight of Neale being placed in the scale against the superior science of Sam. Thus balanced, the general opinion of the sporting world was that a more equal match could not have been made, and of this feeling the betting throughout was characteristic, for with slight fluctuations, in which Sam was the favourite at guineas to pounds, the betting was even. It was thought, from the friends of Sam being members of high Society, and his following including several noble and aristocratic backers, that the odds on him would have advanced to five and six to four ; but they were steady to their point, and rather than advance beyond the nice limits of their calculation they remained stationary. In point of stakes Neale had a decided advantage, for what between forfeits from Sam's apprehension and *laches*, and a hundred guineas given on one occasion by Sam for a postponement, he had received back £165 of the original stakes of £220 put down, so that in point of fact Sam was fighting £365 to £55.

Sam won the toss which entitled him to choose the place of fighting ; he named Newmarket as "headquarters," and proceeded thither himself on the Wednesday before the mill, taking up his residence at the "White Hart." Neale, who had been training at the Isle of Wight, on the Monday before fighting proceeded to the "Swan," at Balsham, within six miles of head-quarters, where he pitched his tent till the next day.

The road down to Newmarket, both on Sunday and Monday, exhibited considerable bustle, but the Londoners were by no means so numerous as might have been expected; still the town was crowded, and all the inns had a fair proportion of visitors. The "White Hart" especially was thronged to overflow, the friends of Sam being decidedly more numerous than those of Neale, and the display of his colours (the bright yellowman) gave a lively finish to the scene.

On Monday evening it was arranged that the ring should be formed in a field a short distance beyond Burrough Green, about seven miles from Newmarket, whither the Commissary and his assistants proceeded to make the necessary arrangements.

On Tuesday morning the rapid arrivals of swells and commoners from all parts of the surrounding country gave additional life to Newmarket; many had travelled 100 miles, and the towns of Birmingham, Nottingham, Norwich, and even Liverpool and Manchester, had numerous representatives. All the post-horses were in requisition, and the turn-out of drags was highly respectable, but the equestrians were by far the most numerous. At an early hour Sam, accompanied by Holt and Curtis, set out for a farmhouse close to the ring, where they met with the most hospitable reception. Thither they were followed by the toddlers in great force, and as the day advanced a general move took place in the same direction. Neale and his friends·were seen in the cavalcade, and by 12 o'clock the approaches to Burrough Green were occupied by a dense mass of spectators, the distant view of the ring, surrounded as it was by thousands, filling them with happy anticipations of the sport. A sudden stop, however, of the advanced guard produced a general feeling of alarm, which was confirmed by the report that a beak was abroad; and in truth it was soon announced that Mr. Eaton, a magistrate of the Quorum, had appeared, and declared his fixed determination to prevent hostilities, either in Cambridgeshire or in the adjoining county of Suffolk. This was, indeed, a damper, and the cry of "no fight" became general. Every effort was made to soften the heart of his worship, but in vain; he had determined to do his duty. At length, finding resistance to such a mandate would be not only absurd but dangerous, it was resolved that a move should take place into the county of Essex, a farmer at Bumpstead having kindly offered a field for the accommodation of the belligerents. This resolution was soon communicated to the multitude, and a simultaneous advance of horse and foot was commenced amidst a general feeling of mortification, which was increased by a change in the weather for the worse, the bright rays of the sun having given way to the gloomy influence of murky and dark clouds. The vicissitudes attending the march were numerous and characteristic, many of the toddlers were bowled out, and some of the cattle which had come from long distances were completely knocked up, so that the throng, on reaching the given goal, although still immense, was stripped of much of its original proportions.

The Commissary lost no time in fixing the lists afresh, which were soon surrounded by a larger circle of horsemen than we ever remember on former occasions, behind which were ranged the carriages and gigs, the wagon train being, of course, completely thrown out. The men arrived by the time everything was ready, Sam attended by Dick Curtis and Harry Holt, and Ned waited on by Tom Spring and Tom Oliver. Sam first entered the mystic quadrangle miscalled "the ring," and was quickly followed by Ned.

At half-past three both were stripped. Neale looked uncommonly well, his skin clear and healthful, his eye brilliant, and his weight 12st. 4lbs. Take him for all in all, we think it impossible a man could have been in better trim. With respect to Sam, he looked as fine as a racehorse; every muscle showed to advantage, and the symmetry of his frame and fine proportions of his bust were particularly conspicuous. In height and length of arm he had an evident advantage over Neale, although his weight was but 11st. 2lb. The important moment for commencing operations at length arrived; the ring had been beaten out, and was in excellent order, and at thirty-two minutes after three business commenced.

THE FIGHT.

Round 1.—On coming to the scratch both looked serious; there was nothing of idle bravado on either side. The position of each was the defensive—the hands well up, and the manner confident. Each seemed desirous for his antagonist to commence, and a long pause followed. Sam made one or two of his dodging feints, but Ned simply threw up his guard. Absolute silence prevailed round the ring. Sam at last hit slightly at Ned's body, and Neale sprang back. Sam tried his left short, but Neale again threw up his right, and was well on his guard. At last Sam let fly his left, catching Ned slightly on his nob. Ned countered with his right, and this brought them to a rally, in which facers were exchanged right and left. Neale bored in; Sam retreated, fighting, to the ropes, against which he was forced. Neale then closed, and a struggle took place for the fall, which Neale obtained, falling heavily on Sam in a cross-buttock. Neale's friends were loud in their cheers, but on rising the marks of Sam's right on Ned's left eye were obvious from a slight swelling, while Sam showed a blushing tinge also on each cheek. In the hitting Sam had the best, and while in fibbed prettily.

2.—Both men again assumed the defensive, Ned waiting for Sam, and Sam trying to get an opening, but for some time in vain. At last Sam let fly with his left, and Neale countered, but not effectually. A smart rally followed, in which Neale was hit heavily left and right. Good fighting on both sides. Sam fought to the ropes, but got well out, and again went to the attack with quickness and precision. Ned hit with him, but not so much at points. All head-work. At last Sam planted his left well on Neale's mug as he was on the move, and dropped him prettily on his nether end, amidst loud shouts of applause, thus winning the first knock-down. Neale, on coming up showed a flushed phiz, and Sam exhibited trifling marks of additional hitting on the face.

3.—Again both cautious. Neale stopped Sam's left with neatness, but had it in a second effort. He returned with his right. Neale popped in his left cleverly on Sam's mouth. Good counter-hitting followed, left and right. Sam had it on the left ear, and Neale on the left eye, which increased in swelling. A spirited and determined rally, in which Sam swung round on his leg, and then renewed the attack. Neale rushed to the charge. Sam endeavoured to get from his grasp, and fibbed at his nob. Neale, however, seized him round the waist, lifted him from the ground, and threw him heavily. The exertion on both sides was great. Neale, though most punished, was loudly cheered by his friends, and was now the favourite from his superior strength ; he however, showed first blood, giving Sam the second point.

4.—Sam on coming up began to blow a little. and was clearly on the pipe, from the exertion in the last round ; he was steady, however, and both kept on the defensive. Neale tried his left, but was short, catching Sam under the right eye. Sam, ready returned with his left, but Neale jumped away. Each tried to plant his left, but without success. The stopping was excellent. Long sparring. Sam popped in his left, and Neale countered. A rally, in which Sam shook the pepper-box in good style. Both were rather wild, and in the end fell from their own exertions on their hands and knees. Ned in this round tried his right-handed chopper, but hitting round it went over Sam's shoulder.

5.—Sam having caught it on the nose in the last round, came up with his eye watering and blinking. Neale tried to pop in his right but was beautifully stopped. Ned put in a left-handed nobber, but had it in return on the neck. Ned stopped the left of Sam with the effect of a brick wall, and caught him on the shoulder with his left. Both awake, and the slaps and returns excellent. A pause. Sam put in his left on Ned's body and made him curtsey. The blow was rather short. Ned stopped right and left and made a chopping return with his right, which caught Sam on the right side of his mouth. Had he been an inch nearer, the effect would have been severe, and as it was it made Sam look serious. Both again on their guard, and each waiting for the attack. Ned again stopped the left and tried his return, but his blow shot over Sam's shoulder, and his arm caught him on the neck. Sam put in his right, and a spirited rally followed. Neale bored him to the ropes, but Sam hit as he retreated, and broke away. Ned, after him, closed, and tried for the fall. He could not succeed in getting the lock. Sam kept his

pins wide apart, and each grasped the other's neck. Holt cried to Sam to go down, and Sam at last fell on his knees, Neale falling over him.

6.—Neale again on the waiting system stopped Sam's left-handed lunge with great precision. Ned hit out with his left, and in a rally heavy blows were exchanged. Neale again missed his right-handed lugger, which went over Sam's shoulder. He then rushed to the close, but Sam began to fib. Neale pinioned his arms, and at last, finding he was wasting his strength, went down himself, Sam upon him. On getting up Neale exclaimed, "You may punch me as much as you like, but don't put your finger in my eye ; " alluding to Sam's touching his eye when on the ground.

7.—Neale again kept his hands well up, and waited for the attack. He stopped a slashing hit from Sam's left. Sam tried his left again, but did not get home. Neale dashed in right and left, and a terrific rally followed. Severe counter-hitting took place, Sam catching it on the nose, from which blood was drawn, and the side of the head and neck, and Neale on the nose, mouth, and both eyes. Sam retreated to the ropes, but still hit with vigour, and ultimately shifted his ground and got away. Neale rushed after him, and the flush-hitting was repeated. Both men strained every nerve. At last Neale jumped in to catch Sam for the fall; Sam received him in his arms and fibbed. Neale pinioned him, and finding he could not gain the throw, fell. On getting up both showed additional marks of punishment as well as distress. The fighting had been extremely fast, and the wind of both was touched. Sam, especially, piped ; but was still steady and collected. Neale's left eye was nearly closed, a slight glimmer only being open.

8.—Ned pursued his system of waiting, and again stopped Sam's left-handed lunge beautifully, and almost immediately caught Sam a left-handed chop on the mouth, which he repeated. Sam looked serious, but shortly after put in his left on Ned's body. A severe rally followed. The hitting on both sides was quick and effective. Sam caught a desperate hit on the neck from Ned's arm, which almost put it awry. Nevertheless, he fought fearlessly, gave Ned a smasher on the mouth, and closed. After a struggle, both went down, and Sam, being raised on his second's knee, was faint and sick ; his colour changed, and he was clearly in a ticklish state. Ned's friends called out he was going, and urged Ned, in the next round, to go in and finish. Ned was himself, however, piping, and distressed from punishment.

9.—On being brought to the scratch, Sam was weak and groggy on his legs. "Go in," cried Ned's friends, but he did not obey the call. He was himself in such a state as to be incapable of making this effort with safety. At last Ned rushed in, hitting with his right, which went over Sam's shoulder, and caught him on the back of the head. Sam retreated to the ropes, Ned after him, but here Sam showed his quickness, even in distress. He hit away with precision, right and left, catching Ned flush in the mug. At last both got from the ropes, and after a sharp rally and close, Neale went down.

10.—Ned made himself up for mischief, and after stopping Sam's left, got into a desperate rally. The hitting was severe on both sides, but Sam's muzzlers told most. The men got on the ropes, where a hard struggle took place, Ned leaning heavily on Sam, and Sam hitting away, while Neale was not idle. At last both went down, Ned uppermost. Sam was now more distressed than ever, and all hands were very busy in fanning him with their hats.

11.—Sam came up evidently weak. Ned pushed in, and hit right and left. Sam was bored to the ropes, and Ned kept hitting away, but wild. Sam, though distressed, jobbed with vigour, left and right. Ned got away, and Sam was after him. A spirited rally, and both fought boldly, but Sam had the best of the hitting. In the close, Sam fibbed, and Ned, finding he could do no good, got down, heavily punished, his left eye quite gone, and his right fast closing, while the claret trickled from a tap on the top of his head.

12.—Ned came up steady, but cautious; and Sam, though somewhat groggy, was well on his guard. Ned put in his right on Sam's body, and succeeded in jobbing him twice on the mouth with his left. A rally, in which both caught nobblers, but Ned the worst of it, from Sam's strength. At last Ned caught a flush hit on the mouth and, falling on the ground, rolled over, weak.

13.—Sam came up more collected, and commenced the attack with his left, which Ned stopped. Sam, after trying a feint to bring Ned out, gave him a tremendous hit on the swollen eye, drawing more of the ruby, and the light was again partially restored. After a slight rally, Ned closed for the fall, but could not get his lock. He at last pulled Sam down, and fell himself.

14, and last.—Both weak, but steady. Ned tried his right, but his hand opened, and no damage was done. Sam countered beautifully with his left, and put in his right at the body. Good fighting on both sides. Ned again put in his right at the body. A pause; both on their guard. Neale distilling claret from many points. Another short rally, and both away; Sam getting more steady and collected, but still disinclined to throw a chance away by trying too much. He hit short at the body to see whether Ned could return, and Ned returned weak with his right, and his hand open. Another pause, in which neither seemed capable of doing much. Ned kept his hands well up for some time, but appeared too cautious for a rush. At last Sam hit out left and right, catching Ned on the phiz. This was the finisher. Ned dropped, and, on being again picked up, his head fell, and he slipped from his second's knee. He was stupefied by the repeated hits on his head, and could not be again brought to the scratch. Sam was now well on his legs, and the welcome sound of victory restored all his vigour. The shouts of his friends were deafening. He was borne off in triumph, after shaking hands with his vanquished but gallant antagonist, whose tie-up was quicker than had been anticipated, but it was clear that he had received enough to satisfy an ordinary glutton, even before the last round, and he had not strength enough to make a turn in his favour. The ring was instantly broken and it was some minutes before Ned could be brought to his carriage. The fight concluded at 24 minutes after 4 o'clock, thus making its duration 52 minutes.

REMARKS.—This was decidedly one of the best styles of fights for science and good generalship. It was admitted that Neale never fought so well before, but the superior length and tact of Sam gave him every advantage. It was remarked in counter-hitting, that Sam always caught Neale first, so that the force of Neale's blows was diminished; added to this, all Neale's heavy lunging hits at Sam's ear passed over his shoulder, and this saved him from certain destruction. Had the return in the fifth round been an inch nearer, it was thought Sam's jaw would have been broken. In the 9th round, too, could Neale have summoned strength to make an impression, his chances would have been certain, but what Sam had lost by exertions, Neale wanted in hitting. The precision and straightness of Sam's blows told with unerring certainty; even when piping, and in distress, his presence of mind never left him. He was always ready for opportunities, and invariably seized them with success. Throughout, the battle was fair and honourable. There was no wrangling or dispute, with the exception of Holt once having thrown himself in the way of Sam to prevent his falling; and even those who lost their blunt could not but confess that Neale did all that his natural powers permitted. Neale was himself dreadfully mortified by the result of this battle. Sam fully confirmed his claim to the title of the Young Phenomenon, and, of his weight, was considered without a rival.

Two years now elapsed, during which Sam was chiefly heard of as a "man about town," and the boon companion of a clique of young swells noted for

their exploits in the night-houses of the Haymarket and the saloons of Piccadilly, then in all their rank riot and disorder.   He was then pitted against
Harry Preston, but owing to magisterial interference, was apprehended and
bound over to keep the peace for six months, and Preston's friends being
unwilling to wait so long, a draw took place.

In the interim, Ned Neale, his last opponent, had been defeated by Tom
Gaynor (*See* life of NEALE, *ante*, p. 325), and that boxer, immediately on
the expiry of Sam's recognisances, challenged him for £100 a side.   This
Sam's friends declared insufficient, but proposed that Sam should fight the
Bond Street carpenter for £300 to £200. The offer was closed with, and the
mill came off, after several attempts made by the authorities to put a stop
to it, on the 24th of June, 1834, near Andover, Wilts.   It appeared that a
warrant was obtained from Sir John Gibbon, to apprehend both men. This
came to their ears, and they each had to make several moves, the persevering constable who held the warrant contriving on several occasions to
find them out, and get his warrant backed by the magistrates in the neighbourhood of their places of retirement.   The men, however, on the day
before fighting, cautiously approached the trysting-place (Hurstbourne
Green, near Andover).   Here they were pursued by the constable with his
warrant, which he again got backed; but by some "unfortunate accident" (?)
he fell into bad company, got drunk, and lost his warrant, a fact he did
not discover until he became sober the following morning, when he went
off to obtain a fresh warrant.   This he succeeded in doing, but owing to
the secrecy which had been observed as to the place of fighting, he did not
discover it until the men had been fighting some time; and then, after
making a vain effort to interfere, he judged discretion the better part of
valour, and having done his duty so far as he was able, he retired from the
ring-side, and did not again endeavour to spoil sport.

The men and their friends set off from Andover at an early hour for the
scene of action, but owing to the caution it was found necessary to exert
to keep things dark, the heroes of the day did not reach their tilting ground
till 12 o'clock, when Sam entered the ring attended by Dick Curtis and
Frank Redmond, Gaynor being seconded by Jem Ward and Deaf Burke.
The ring was preserved admirably throughout the day, and nothing was
left to be desired by the men or their friends.

On stripping, Sam looked uncommonly well, although his friends said
he might have been better had not his presence in town for a few days
when at his best, become necessary, in consequence of an action-at-law

in which he was engaged. To the casual observer this was not visible, and his fine muscular and symmetrical form never appeared to better advantage, while his countenance displayed the utmost self-possession and personal confidence. His weight was about 11st. Gaynor also appeared in admirable trim, and was not less confident than Sam, although there was more solidity in his manner. His round shoulders offered a striking contrast to the elegant proportions of Sam, and gave him the appearance of a natural stoop, but in all other respects his shape was faultless, and his condition of the first character. He did not seem to have a superfluous ounce of flesh on his body, and weighed as nearly as possible 12st. In length of arm, Sam had the advantage, and the discrepancy in years (Gaynor having the disadvantage of ten years) was sufficiently obvious. So " nutty " were Sam's friends on their man at this moment, that the odds rose from two to one to five to two, and at this price much business was done.

THE FIGHT.

Round 1.—Precisely at 7 minutes to 1 the men commenced business. Both put up their hands in a defensive position, and eyed each other with scrutinising looks. Each was ready, and appeared to wait for his antagonist to commence. Sam made two or three slight dodges, and Gaynor drew back. Each moved to the right and to the left, but still no opening was offered. The movements on a chess-board could not have been more scientific. At last Gaynor hit out at the body with his left, and got away. Sam stopped the compliment, and smiled. After a long pause, they both made themselves up for mischief, and at last ended suspense by slashing out their counter-hits with the left, Gaynor planting on Sam's jaw, and Sam on Gaynor's mouth, which showed a prominent mark. The blows were heavy, and while first blood was drawn from Gaynor, Sam licked his lips, but certainly not with the *gôut* of a cat over a pat of butter. Another pause, when counter-hits with the right were exchanged. Sam stopped Gaynor's left with great neatness, but in a second effort with the same hands, in the counter-hitting, Sam caught it over the mouth, while Gaynor had it on the left cheek. "How do you like that?" cried Gaynor, laughing. Sam looked serious. Gaynor dodged, but found Sam ready for a fly, and drew back. Gaynor stopped Sam's left, and tried his right at the body, but was short. Sam hit out with his left, but was short. A long spar, in which each seemed determined not to throw a chance away. Gaynor hit short with his right, open-handed. Sam smiled. Tom again stopped a nasty one from the left, and popped in his right slightly at the body. Sam played a steady game, and drew on his man. Gaynor on the look-out, retired to the side of the ring. Both extremely cautious. At last Sam saw his opportunity, and with great quickness sent in his left, with plenty of elbow grease, on Gaynor's nob, and dropped him as if shot, thus giving first knock-down, amidst the shouts of his friends. This round, which was admirable, from the exquisite science of the men, lasted ten minutes.

2.—On being called to the scratch, Gaynor came up bleeding at the mouth, and Sam showing symptoms of receiving on his lips and cheek. After long and cautious sparring, neither giving a chance, Gaynor suddenly planted his right on the side of Sam's head. Cheers for Gaynor, who thus stole a successful march. Sam was not behind in returning the compliment, and after a short time for reflection, popped in a tremendous slap on Gaynor's mouth with his left. Gaynor's blow, in countering, passed over Sam's shoulder. Another cautious spar, when Gaynor hit short with his left. Heavy counter-hits, Sam on the mouth, Gaynor on the left eye. Sam dropped his left on Gaynor's ribs, and got away. Sam in left and right, but rather out of distance. Gaynor stopped his left in another shy, as well as a hit at his body. Another pause, each on the look-out, when terrific counter-hits with the left were exchanged. Gaynor pointed at Sam's mouth, which had tasted his knuckles, but he had it heavily himself on the cheek. Excellent stops on both sides, Gaynor planted a round blow on the side of Sam's head, but it was with the front of his knuckles, and seemed to make no impression. Counter-hitting with the left, Sam's blow falling heaviest. A pretty rally, in which some wicked blows were exchanged. Both broke away, and sparred for a fresh opening, Gaynor showing most punishment. Sam planted his left three times in succession, hitting first, and Gaynor's counters non-effective. Gaynor hit short with his left, and fought on the retreat. Counter-hits with the left. Gaynor had now got in the corner, and was so covered by Sam that he could not escape. He waited for the assault, when Sam jumped in with his left, and caught him on the eye. Gaynor returned, and in the close, after some in-fighting, Sam got the fall, and fell heavily on Gaynor, who fell out of the ropes. This round lasted twelve minutes and a half, and it was admitted that Sam had not the easy customer that his admirers anticipated.

3.—Gaynor looking the worse for wear, but strong as a horse, and gay as a lark. Sparring for an opening, when Gaynor caught Sam slightly with his left on the mouth. Sam tried a lunge with his left, but was beautifully stopped. In a second attempt he was more successful, for he planted left and right, cutting Gaynor's left cheek with the latter. Gaynor countered, and the men closed for the fall, which Gaynor obtained, giving Sam a cross-buttock, and falling heavily upon him. Sam's right shoulder came heavily against the ground. Cheers for Gaynor. The round lasted four minutes.

4.—Both cautious, and sparring for an opening. Gaynor hit short with his left. Another pause. Counter-hits with the left. Sam caught his man first and hit him heavily. Gaynor's blow was not so effective. Sam popped in a tremendous muzzler with his left, and Gaynor bled profusely; his old wounds were opened, and his mouth became much swollen. Gaynor again planted his right on Sam's head heavily. Shouts for Gaynor, and Sam seemed puzzled, but preserved his steadiness. A pause, during which Sam recovered himself. Counter-hits with the left, and a brisk rally, in which heavy hits were exchanged. The men broke away. Long sparring; both ready, and no opening offered. Good stopping on both sides, and the game played with matchless skill. Mutual dodging, but no chance. Sam tried his feint, but it would not do. At last Sam crept well in, and delivered a heavy left-handed jobber. Gaynor countered, and in the close, after a severe struggle, Sam threw Gaynor a beautiful cross-buttock. Cheers for Sam; his friends up in the stirrups. The fight had now lasted forty-five minutes.

5.—Gaynor, on coming up, showed a little distress, and heavy marks of punishment on the mouth and left eye. Sam dodged, but Gaynor was well on his guard. Both stopped by consent, put their hands down, and looked at each other. At it again. Gaynor hit short with his left, and got away. Sam again dropped his left on Gaynor's eye, and followed this up by a hit with the same hand on the body. Gaynor went in with his one two, catching Sam with his left on the cheek, and his right on the side of the head. Sam returned with his left, and after a short rally, the men closed, and went down. Sam had the best of the round.

6.—Gaynor's left eye shutting up shop, and he was otherwise much damaged in the frontispiece. "Sam will win it without a black eye," cried Curtis. Sam made himself up for mischief, and kept stealing on his man, but Gaynor got away. A rally, and exchange of hits. Gaynor's leg tripped Sam, and he fell upon him. Fifty minutes had now elapsed.

7.—Curtis chaffed on time, and said, as the hour was nearly up, on which he had been betting, Sam might go in to finish. Gaynor, distressed, tried his left, but was out of distance. Sam rushed in to hit with his left, but was cleverly stopped. Gaynor rushed to in-fighting; Sam hit up cleverly with his left, but in the close was thrown a cross-buttock, which gave him a serious shake.

8.—The men had now fought fifty-four minutes, and both were distressed, while it did not seem so safe to Sam as had been booked. Both steady on their guard, and waiting for an opening. Sam's left well stopped. Gaynor away. Heavy counter-hits with the left; both received stingers, but Sam hit hardest. In the close, both down.

9.—Gaynor's left eye quite closed, but he was still strong on his legs, and resolute. He again stole a march on Sam, popped in his left, and got away. Both fatigued, but a fine breeze blew over the common, and gave them fresh vigour. Gaynor's left stopped, and he napped it severely on the nose in return. Gaynor made some admirable stops, and popped his right heavily on Sam's ear. Gaynor on the defensive, and retreating to the ropes. Sam thought he had him, but Gaynor broke away. Sam followed him, dodged, and popped in with his left. Gaynor closed, caught him round the neck with his left, and hit up with his right. In the souffle, both fell.

10.—"Not so safe as if it was over," cried Gaynor's friends; and it was clear Sam had yet his work to do, as Gaynor got up strong and confident. On going to the scratch, after a short spar, both again put their hands down for a short time. Beautiful fighting followed, and the stopping on both sides was first-rate. The fight had now lasted one hour and five minutes. "Tom can fight another hour," cried Ward. Mutual dodging. Gaynor planted his left slightly, but there was not sufficient pepper in his blows. A rally, close to the ropes, with hard hitting, when Sam in getting away fell. Shouts for Gaynor.

11.—Both came up steady and serious. Gaynor gave Sam a heavy slap on the mug with his left. Sam was full of self-possession, and looked out for an opening. Gaynor was steady on his guard. Sam popped in a left-handed teaser, and hit at the body with his right. Gaynor made his one two on Sam's face. Counter-hitting with the left. A body hit with the right from Gaynor. Hard counter-hits with the left; heaviest from Sam. Sam now delivered his right on Gaynor's ribs; the latter hit short with the left. Some excellent generalship on both sides. Sam dropped his arms as if fatigued. Sam now popped in a slight left-hander, but had it heavily in return on the phiz. Gaynor, whose conk was bleeding, now put both hands down, and beckoned Sam to come to him. Sam approached him, and, after a sharp spar, received a touch on the bread-basket. Gaynor stopped a tremendous left-hander, intended for his good eye. Sam also stopped, and got away. Gaynor tried at the body with his right, but was stopped. Sam got away from a heavy lunge from Gaynor's left. Sam in with the left; Gaynor returned. Sam dodging, and Gaynor, in getting away, fell.

12.—Gaynor came up steady. Sam waited for him. Gaynor tried his left, but was stopped, and got away. Sam then, throwing his head back, saved himself from a heavy delivery from Tom's right. Gaynor stopped a left-hander, and popped in his right at the back of Sam's head, but was heavily hit with the left in return. Both covering themselves well. Sam in with his left on the body. Tom got back, and put his hands down. Counter-hits with the left, and Gaynor short at the body with his right. Both men with their hands down. On again getting into position, Gaynor seized one of Sam's hands with his left, intending to give him a swinger with his right, but Sam pulled his mauly away, and smiled. Gaynor stopped a left-handed job with the utmost precision. Heavy counter-hits with the left; Sam first in. Gaynor hit out with his left, but his hand was open; he, however, planted a right-hander on Sam's nob. Sam gave him a tremendous smasher on the gob. Gaynor looked a painful spectacle, though still full of pluck. Some heavy exchanges with the left. In the close, Sam, at in-fighting, gave his antagonist some severe punishment on the ropes, and Gaynor, in pulling himself away, fell over Sam.

13.—Gaynor showed weakness, and Sam seemed now to think he had got him safe. Gaynor hit short with his left. Sam tried his left, but was stopped. A close, and severe struggle for the fall, at the ropes. Sam gave an upper-cut with great force, while Gaynor was not idle. Both down.

14.—Gaynor made play, but was short with his left. Sam steady, and jumping in, delivered his left heavily on Tom's altered maxxard. A close, and some good in-fighting.

A tough struggle for the fall; both down. This effort was exhausting to both. In the close, Sam hit up well.

15.—Gaynor piping, and Sam not fresh. Gaynor in with his left; tried his right, but was stopped. Heavy counter-hits. Both again paused by mutual consent, and put their hands down. Again to work. Good exchanges; Sam at the head, Gaynor at the body. Both cautious. Gaynor on the retreat. Sam got close to him, and hit out viciously, but Gaynor ducked his head, got away, and fell.

16.—Gaynor's friends were still very confident, as he seemed strong, and Sam appeared fatigued. Counter-hitting with the left, but Sam hitting out first, got home the heaviest. He put in a tremendous left-hander on Tom's left ogle. Again did both take breath, and drop their arms. Sam steady, and both well on their guard. Mutual stopping. Gaynor short at the body with his right. Counter-hits with the left, terrific from Sam. Two hours were now completed, and the men walked about for wind. Gaynor hit out of distance with his left, but Sam measured him with more precision, and dropped in one of his left-handed chops with full force. Gaynor, after a short pause, seized Sam's right, while Sam seized his left, each holding the other down. Sam looked at his man for a moment, and then dashed his head into his face with great force. (This, as our readers are aware, is now foul.) Gaynor staggered back, while Sam rushed after him, and jobbed him severely on the nose with the left, and, repeating the dose in the same spot, hit him down as clean as a whistle, being the second knock-down blow in the fight.

17. and last.—Gaynor came up groggy, when Sam popped in his terrific left, and downed him. This was the finisher. The butt, followed by such polishing hits, reduced poor Gaynor to a state of insensibility, and on being raised on his second's knee it was at once seen that it was all U. P. "Time" was called, and Sam was proclaimed the conqueror with triumphant shouts. The fight lasted two hours and five minutes. Sam was immediately taken to his carriage, much exhausted, but soon became himself again. Gaynor was in a complete state of stupor, and was carried away in a helpless condition.

REMARKS.—This was decidedly one of the finest displays of courage and science combined which had been witnessed for many years, and was acknowledged to be so by the oldest patrons of the Ring who were present. The courage exhibited by both men was unquestionable, and considering the disadvantages under which Gaynor fought, he earned for himself a reputation that placed him in the first class of game men. There is no doubt that the butt in the last round but one proved his *coup-de-grace*, or he would have prolonged the contest for many more rounds—with what chance of success we cannot say. The reader should be informed

that this manœuvre, though seldom practised, was not at this time against the rules
of the Ring, and the position, Gaynor holding both Sam's hands with an iron grip,
was peculiar. The "chapter of accidents"
might have produced alterations, and as
it was Sam, during the fight, showed great
weakness, which was not surprising, as it
was afterwards ascertained that in the cross-
buttock in the third round his right shoulder
was so much injured as to deprive him
of the use of his right hand, so far as hitting was concerned, for the remainder of
the battle. During the fight, many expressed surprise that he should have kept
that hand so idle, and that Gaynor was so
repeatedly enabled to job him with his left.
Sam could not, in truth, lift it above his
head, and but for throwing his head back
when the blows were coming in, his punishment would have been much more
severe. Although Gaynor had clearly
the gift of hitting with equal force, it is considered that but for this accident Sam's
labours would have been considerably cur-
tailed. At one time it was thought to be
anybody's fight, and Sam's friends were by
no means jolly as to the result. His fine
generalship, however, enabled him to overcome every difficulty, and the quickness with
which he took advantage of Gaynor's ill-
judged seizure of his hand, in the last round
but one, while it showed his self-possession,
proved him to be a thorough master of the
art as then practised. The account of the
rounds will show that in point of science
Gaynor was little behind Sam, but it must
be confessed his powers of punishment were
very inferior, while the force of his blows
was greatly diminished by Sam's generally
hitting first in the counters. From first to
last the combat was conducted with the utmost fairness and good humour; and while
all sympathised in the fall of a brave man,
they could not but admit that he had honourably sunk before the superior power of his
younger and more expert opponent. Such
was the impression made in Gaynor's favour
that £17 7s. was collected round the ring,
and other sums afterwards contributed. This
was the last appearance of either Sam or
Gaynor in the P.R.

Sam's last match in the Ring was with Reuben Martin, for £100,
subsequently made into £180 a side; it was fixed to come off in June,
1838, but an unfortunate occurrence occasioned a forfeit of £80 on
the part of Sam. He had volunteered to second his friend Owen Swift
in his battle with Phelps (Brighton Bill), and officiated in that capacity on
the fatal 13th of March, 1838, at Royston. The details of this unlucky
encounter will be found in our memoir of OWEN SWIFT, in Vol. III.

The coroner's jury having found a verdict of manslaughter against Owen
Swift, as principal, and Samuel Evans, Richard Curtis, Frank Redmond,
and Edward Brown, as seconds aiding and abetting the same, Sam, Curtis,
and Swift at once gave "leg-bail" to the law and departed for the Con-
tinent, where they remained until the time for surrendering to take their
trial at the Hertford Assizes. Frank Redmond,* whose business as a

_____

* Frank Redmond, although his Ring career was not marked by success, was a skilful
sparrer and an excellent teacher of the art of self-defence. He was born on the 26th of
February, 1803, and as a young aspirant was so highly thought of that he was matched (at
the age of twenty) against the renowned "Star of the East," Barney Aaron, whose recent
victories over Samuel Belasco, Collins, Ned Stockman, and Lenney (twice) had raised him
to a proud position among the middle weights. Young Frank was soundly beaten in thirty-
two minutes, after a game and manly battle with an opponent by whom it was no disgrace
to be defeated.
  Four years afterwards Frank again challenged Aaron, and a match was made for £50
a side. to fight on the 21st August, 1827, but Frank was arrested on the day on the road to
the appointed place. Strange to say, although this was proved, the stakes were given up
to the Israelite, which so angered Redmond that he threw up his hat in the room at the
"Castle" and offered to fight for £20 on the spot. A third match was then made for £50
a side. After a high-couraged battle (which will be found in the Life of BARNEY AARON, in
the Appendix to this Period) Redmond was again defeated. Redmond's other battles were
a game but unsuccessful combat with Harry Jones (the Sailor Boy), and a single victory

licensed victualler at the "George and Dragon," in Greek Street, Soho, was suffering ruinously from his enforced absence, alone surrendered. He was defended by Mr. Dowling (who was also a barrister), and acquitted on the 10th July, at the summer assizes. Thereupon Curtis and Brown, who were awaiting the result, surrendered themselves and took their trial. They were not so fortunate as their predecessor in trouble, for the jury convicted them of manslaughter in the second degree, as "present, aiding, and abetting," when the judge passed the lenient sentence of three months' imprisonment.

Young Sam and Swift, alarmed at this result, did not return at once. Besides, they found their stay in the French capital, where some of Sam's aristocratic patrons were also residing, both pleasant and profitable, of which further details will be found in our Life of OWEN SWIFT. Some violent newspaper attacks upon the Ring, and denunciations of prize-fighters and their backers, in the now defunct *Morning Herald* (a renegade sporting paper) and other publications, made it advisable to await the blowing over of the storm.

Sam's residence in France, however, found in its result the adage of " out of the frying-pan into the fire."

Jack Adams was in Paris teaching the art of boxing. Adams, a ten-stone man, was twice matched with Swift, and on the second occasion the

over Tom Davis, near Leominster, on the 14th of November, 1833. Frank soon after married, and went into business as a licensed victualler at the "George and Dragon," Greek Street, Soho, which, from Frank's abilities as a professor of the fistic art, and his thorough knowledge of the points of a dog, became a popular resort. At an after period, for many years, Frank Redmond was known and respected as the proprietor of the " Swiss Cottage," St. John's Wood. We extract the following from "Walks round London," published in 1846 :—

"The 'Swiss Cottage,' at the intersection of the London and Finchley Roads and Belsize Lane, is a pleasant summer retreat; and it would be hard to name a more competent authority on sporting subjects than the worthy host, than whom
      'A merrier nor a wiser man
      To spend a pleasant hour withal'
is not to be found within the bills of mortality. Well versed in all sporting matters is Frank Redmond; and behind a yard of clay, and over a glass of the best Cognac, the proprietor of this hostelrie will discuss with you the merits of a Derby nag; the pluck, game, bravery, and stamina of the aspirant for fistic fame; the construction and merits of a prize wherry; the skill of a batsman and cricket-bowler; or detail to you the speed and breeding of a crack greyhound. On this last theme Frank will become a monopolist; you have touched the chord that will vibrate, for on the subject of the canine species he will become as learned as England's ermined Chief Justice on a knotty point of law, or as eloquent as Demosthenes himself. A better judge of the merits, breeding, and qualities of the dog does not exist. Frank is reputed to be the best dog-fancier in the kingdom, and on that point is generally consulted by the aristocracy and Corinthians of the first water.

"Such are a few of the many inducements, and we own they are no small ones, which prompt us to notice 'the Cottage.' We say nothing about the accommodation offered to the guests; for it were a libel on Frank's administration to assert that they are not of the first-rate order, and he must be an epicure, indeed, who could find fault with the *cuisine* of the establishment. Had the 'Swiss Cottage' existed in Shakspere's days, we should have been inclined to assert that it was from some such a house as this that the 'fat-ribbed knight' first acquired his idea of the comfort a man feels in taking 'mine ease at mine inn.'"

Frank Redmond retired from this life and its business in 1863.

French law, which deals so leniently with murderous duels and homicide in general, was scandalised and outraged by a duel with fists; so Young Sam and Swift were tried (in their absence), convicted, *par contumace*, and sentenced to *thirteen months of imprisonment and a fine!*

Soon after his return to England Sam was arrested and conveyed to Hertford Gaol, and on February 28th, 1839, at the spring assizes, Swift took his place beside his friend Sam, and the trial proceeded. From a failure of evidence a verdict of "Not Guilty" was recorded, and the friends quitted the dock amid the congratulations of the crowd.

Owen Swift arrived in London the same night, but not so his companion in misfortune; Sam's exit was stopped by a detainer from London, for a forfeiture of bail, incurred in this wise.

A short time previous to the battle of Swift and Phelps, Sam, in company with a "noble earl" and some aristocratic friends, had been engaged in a fracas at a public-house in Piccadilly. This was the disgraceful period when, fired by a vulgar emulation of the worst characteristics of Pierce Egan's vulgar, vicious, and silly caricatures of two town and country sporting gentlemen, whom he named "Tom and Jerry;" and whom he made the heroes of his wretched, grammarless galimatia called "Life in London," clerks, apprentices, prigs, pugilists, and peers played the blackguard and ruffian on the stage of real life. The great and beneficial changes which have taken place in our police and street Acts, as well as in the hours and regulations of refreshment rooms and all licensed houses in the Metropolis, make it almost impossible for the present generation to realise the scenes of disorder, profligacy, and ruffianism with which "the West or worst End of the city" nightly abounded. From Temple Bar westward, through Drury Lane, Covent Garden, St. Martin's Lane, Leicester Square, and its surroundings, to the Haymarket and Piccadilly, "night-houses" admitted the drunkard (when not too drunk), the night prowler, the debauchee, the gambler, the thief, and the prostitute of every grade—the only distinction being the higher or lower tariff. From the swell supper-room, saloon, elysium, or "finish," of "Goody Levy," "Goodered," "Rowbotham," "Mother H.," or the "Brunswick," through the musical and more respectable chop-and-kidney-grilling "Evans's," the "Garrick," the "Cider Cellars," "Coal Hole," or "Shades," down to the common dramshop kept open on the plea of the neighbouring cab-stand or theatre until the small hours of the morning grew large, all appealed to those who sought "recreation and refreshment *after the theatres.*"

In one of these houses, the "Royal Standard," in Piccadilly, on the morning of the 17th of February, 1838, there appear to have been assembled after a night's debauch a number of loose characters. Among them were the Earl of Waldegrave and several "Corinthians." According to the evidence of Mr. Mackenzie, the prosecutor, he, after leaving duty, entered the house in question, where " he saw the prisoner (Young Dutch Sam) and several gentlemen, some of whom he certainly had interfered with in their nocturnal sprees ; indeed, he had been instrumental in introducing them to the magistrate at Marlborough Street." We think nowadays this policeman's conduct would be strictly canvassed. " Whilst he was standing before the bar," we copy the report, " the prisoner whispered to Lord Waldegrave, and immediately afterwards, addressing the company, he said, ' Gentlemen, do you care to see a policeman laid on his back ? ' He then seized him (the prosecutor) and threw him on his back, falling upon him with all his weight. He was so much injured as to be under the doctor's hands for some time, and unfit for duty. The prisoner was held to bail by the magistrates at Marlborough Street, and had forfeited his recognisances."

Mr. Ballantine addressed the Court on the part of the prisoner in mitigation of punishment. The prisoner had been made the tool of certain parties with whom he had been drinking on the night before the assault was committed, and although they had urged him to the commission of the offence which led to his present position, not one of them had been to visit him, or render him the least assistance during his incarceration.—Mr. Doane, having addressed the Court for the prosecution, described the defendant as a pugilist, but added " that he did not say this to create a prejudice against him on that account, for he felt convinced that the unmanly and terrible crime of stabbing was increasing in this country, in consequence of the absurd and mischievous interference of the county magistracy with the sports of the Ring. Those sports (the learned gentleman observed) had some disadvantages, but they were amply counterbalanced by the habit they engendered of fighting in a fair and manly manner, and by the universal indignation with which anything unfair was regarded in a pugilistic contest." The Court sentenced the prisoner to three months' imprisonment.

A motion was subsequently made that the estreat on the recognisances might be taken off, but was refused, on the ground that the Court had no power to interfere.

We have been the more particular in the narration of this case as the facts were known to the writer, and as a most false and exaggerated report of the affair was subsequently published in the *Morning Herald*, in an attack upon the Prize Ring, penned by an Irish sporting reporter who had been discharged by the editor of *Bell's Life*. The conduct of the policeman, to our thinking, more resembled that of a French *agent provocateur* than a guardian of the peace ; and, without defending the assailant, we may remark that the fact that Young Sam so carefully avoided using his unquestionable pugilistic skill, although under the excitement of champagne and provocation, is a sufficient answer to the charge of "ruffianism" and "ferocity" cast upon him for this foolish escapade.

Shortly after this fracas a new police Act, and increased vigilance in the stipendiary magistrates, checked effectually these disgraceful excesses, by substituting imprisonment for fine, at the discretion of the justices, whereupon we find, in a contemporary "daily," the ironical "Lament" of which the subjoined are a few of the leading stanzas :—

LAMENT OF THE "DISORDERLY GENTLEMEN."

A plague on the new law ! bad luck to the beaks,
Opposed as they are to "disorderly" freaks ;
Ye pinks of high rank, let your sorrows have vent,
And join with your pals in a doleful lament.

No longer at midnight, when coming it strong,
Ripe for riot and row, shall we stagger along ;
No more of brave acts shall we "gentlemen" chaff,
Nor floor a raw lobster and fracture his staff.

Till lately, when liquor got up in the nob,
A fine of five shillings would settle the job ;
And none will deny who has starr'd on the town,
A frolic or spree wasn't cheap at a crown.

But now we're informed by the beak, *Mr. Grove*
(Whoever could seat on the Bench such a cove ?),
That if with strong liquors our tempers get hot,
He'll send us at once on the treadmill to trot—

That the pastime of wrenching off knockers and bells
Must no longer be practis'd by high-minded swells ;
Or he'll send us, to settle each paltry dispute,
For a month to the treadmill our health to recruit.

O haste, brother pinks, such disgrace to prevent,
Before this vile Bill has the Royal Assent ;
For herself it is certain Her Majesty thinks,
And I'm sure she'll attend to a prayer from the "pinks."

What, never again be permitted at dark
To insult modest females by way of a lark !
Gone for ever our joys, and our gay occupation ?
Must we now like vile felons be marched to the station ?

Forbid, ye proud nobs, any steps so degrading—
The swells' charter'd rights they are basely invading ;
Let us stand up for sprees and our leisure amuse,
And still act as blackguards whenever we choose.

Young Sam, though occasionally exhibiting his skill with the gloves at the sets-to of the "Pugilistic Association" established about this period at the Westminster (now the Lambeth) Swimming Baths, by Tom Spring, Cribb, Crawley, the editor of *Bell's Life*, and other leading friends of the P.R., was not popular with his brethren of the Ring, and did not care to associate with them.   He became a publican first in Castle Street, Leicester Square, and then at the "Coach and Horses," St. Martin's Lane; but in both he was unsuccessful—it was said from inattention to business, which we can well believe.   At length, in 1840, Sam wedded the daughter of a respected publican, and with her as a helpmeet he became landlord of the "Black Lion," in Vinegar Yard, Drury Lane.   From this house he migrated to the Old Drury Tavern, in Brydges Street, Covent Garden, and here his wife's experience and management, together with her influence over his erratic disposition, seemed to be fast maturing the " Young 'Un " into a respectable and steady Boniface.   For some time, however, the effects of early dissipation were visible in recurrences of inflammation of the lungs at the approach of winter or exposure to cold.   In 1842 a severe relapse, accompanied by spitting of blood, reduced him almost to a shadow, and on the 4th of November, 1843, he died of decline, at the early age of thirty-six.   The following appeared in an obituary notice in the leading sporting journal of the day :—

" In the sparring schools Sam was a master of his art to an extent but seldom seen and rarely equalled by professors.   He often showed, and remarkably so when in conversation with his ' betters (?),' that his acquaintance with ' letters ' was not merely of a mechanical description. He spoke well, and when he chose could ' do the agreeable ' with a suavity highly creditable to his class, securing to himself throughout his career the patronage of many noblemen and gentlemen of the highest distinction. His temper was cheerful, and he possessed a flow of natural humour which rendered him an agreeable companion in social circles.   A reckless disregard to his own interests, and an unhappy disposition to mix in those scenes which constitute what is called ' Life in London,' and in which he was often the companion of sprigs of nobility, to whose wild vagaries he was but too much inclined to pander, led him into scrapes from which he had some difficulty in escaping.   It is not our wish, however, to speak ill of the dead; and knowing as we do that there are those of a higher grade whose example he was but too prone to follow, equally deserving of censure, we shall throw a veil over the past, and let the recollection of his faults lie hidden in the grave. As a pugilist he was always successful, for he never lost a fight, and as a skilful sparrer he has left no equal of his years. It was not till he married a woman who was his faithful and attached companion till the moment of his death that the foundation of prosperity was laid. She, luckily, was a woman of good sense, and considerable experience in the public line, which enabled her to 'carry on the war' with success. Throughout his last illness he was attended with exemplary kindness by his wife, who spared neither pains nor expense to alleviate his disease. He died calm and collected, surrounded by several of his friends, who while they pitied could not but condemn the headlong folly which had distinguished his passage through his short but eventful existence. Many of his faults and follies may be fairly ascribed to the nature of the associations into which the deceased, from his earliest outset in life, was accidently thrown. He was 'a spoilt child' of the Fancy, and like all spoilt children was wayward."

Sam lies buried in the vault of his wife's family in Kensal Green Cemetery.

MONODY ON THE DEATH OF YOUNG DUTCH SAM.

SCARCE the illustrious Pet * his eyes had clos'd,
When in Death's cold embrace Dutch Sam repos'd;
As brave a fellow from life's scenes dismiss'd
As ever faced a foe or clench'd a fist;
Brave without bounce, and resolute as bold,
And ever first fair fighting to uphold;
Dauntless as honest, with unequalled game
He dar'd defeat, and fought his way to fame;
And burning still with pugilistic fire,
Prov'd Young Dutch Sam was worthy of his sire,

Made of the same unyielding sort of stuff,
Ready at all times for the scratch and rough,
Delighting in the Ring at contest tough,
And proudly scorning to sing out, "Enough!"

Ah! what avails it that in many a mill,
With pluck unflinching he was conqueror still;
With first-rate science dealt the unerring blow
Which from the sneezer made the claret flow;
Perplex'd the box of knowledge with a crack,
And cloth'd the ogles with a suit of black;
Forward his foeman fiercely to assail,
And shower his body-blows as thick as hail?
Ah! what avails it? Dire disease at length
Blighted his laurels and subdued his strength,
Marking his features pale with Death's cold stamp,
While faint and feeble burnt life's flickering lamp,
'Till wasted, wan, and worn the pulses stopp'd.
The last sad scene was o'er, the curtain dropp'd.
But thou hast mark'd a course correct as clear,
By which the aspiring pugilist may steer.

* Dick Curtis died September 16th, 1848, aged 41.

Though fate decreed thou first shouldst breathe the air
Within the classic precincts of Rag Fair—
That region fam'd, as chronicles unfold,
Sacred to Sheenies and to garments old,
Owld coats, owld vests, to tempt the gazer's view,
And tiles dresht up to look as goot as new ;
But though in scenes like these Young Sam was nurs'd,
The bonds that cramp'd his youth he proudly burst,
And with ambition fired, and milling glow,
From rolls retreated, and discarded dough ;
Out Rosemary Lane, its sorrows and its joys,
And left dead men to other bakers' boys !

What though awhile he ran a printing-race
At Charley Baldwin's crib in Chatham Place ?
For though to duty never disinclined,
'Twas *Caleb* Baldwin's deeds engrossed his mind ;
The star of Westminster as tough, as bold,
Who cried *peccavi* to Dutch Sam the old.

What though awhile, the public to amuse,
Through London streets he circulated news,
Doom'd for a time from East to West to trip,
And barter broadsheets for the ready tip ?
" By heaven !" he cried, " to fighting fame I'll soar,"
And sporting journals I will vend no more,
Of adverse fate I'll overleap the bar,
And follow to the Ring some milling star ;
Consign all braggart pugilists to shame,
And show the Fancy Sam is thorough game !"

Thy spirit warmed by the exciting theme,
Nobly Dutch Sam thy pledge thou didst redeem,
And soon beneath Dick Curtis' fostering wing.
Blaz'd like a meteor in the battle-ring.
Fortune upon thy hardy efforts smil'd,
And Victory hail'd thee as her favourite child.

Beneath thy prowess prime, which nought could quell,
The liveliest of the kids, Ned Stockman, fell ;
Then 'twas thy luck, scarce injur'd, to destroy
The shine of Harry Jones, the Sailor Boy ;
'Twas thine from Carroll Pat to strip the bays,
And serve out Cooper Tom in style at Grays,
Floor the swart Gipsy in time double-quick,
And settle the proud hash of Davis Dick ;
The veteran Martin soon his colours struck,
And twice Ned Neale was down upon his luck ;
And all his senses sent upon a cruise,
It was the luck of *Gaynor* Tom to *lose !*

But vain are science, gluttony, and strength,
And Young Dutch Sam has met his match at length—
One whose sharp hits can ne'er be put aside,
And at the scratch will never be denied.
Brave man ! we only mourn that thou art gone,
Well worthy to be dubb'd " Phenomenon."
Sound be thy slumber in thy narrow cell,
While with a heavy heart we sigh farewell !

CHAPTER IX.

TOM GAYNOR ("THE-BATH CARPENTER").
1824—1834.

IT was said of Marshal Clairfait that, like a drum, he was only heard of when he was beaten. Tom Gaynor, in somewhat like fashion, takes his place among the celebrities of the Ring from the high fame of the men against whom he had the ill luck to be opposed. Beginning rather late in the London Ring, Gaynor's first antagonist was Ned Neale (who had just polished off in succession Deaf Davis, Bill Cribb, Miller, Hall, and David Hudson), while his last (and too late) appearance in the Ring was in combat with the Phenomenon, Young Dutch Sam, before whom he stood for two hours and five minutes, at Andover, in the year 1834. This was proof sufficient that Gaynor's heart was in the right place, and that his fistic skill was far above the mere "give and take" of second-rate boxers.

The sobriquet of Gaynor assigns Bath for his birthplace, and there, on the 22nd of April, 1799, the young Tom opened his eyes, as the son of a respectable carpenter in that fashionable city. Tom used to tell his friends, over a pipe at the "Red Horse," Bond Street, of a wonderful uncle of his, hight Tom Marshall, who was champion boxer of "Zummerzetzhire," and was never defeated. This uncle, who stood six feet one and a half in his stockings, seems to have been the idol of his nephew's hero-worship, as another Tom [Carlyle] would phrase it. With this uncle young Gaynor was placed at Taunton, and there, at thirteen years old, was apprenticed. Here Tom's skill with his "fives" was acknowledged, and at about seventeen years of age he was what modern times would call a "certificated pupil-teacher" in an "academy" of which a local boxer was the chief professor of "the noble art." One Turle, a fiddler, had the reputation of being a dangerous opponent, but in a turn-up with the young

TOM GAYNOR ("The Bath Carpenter").

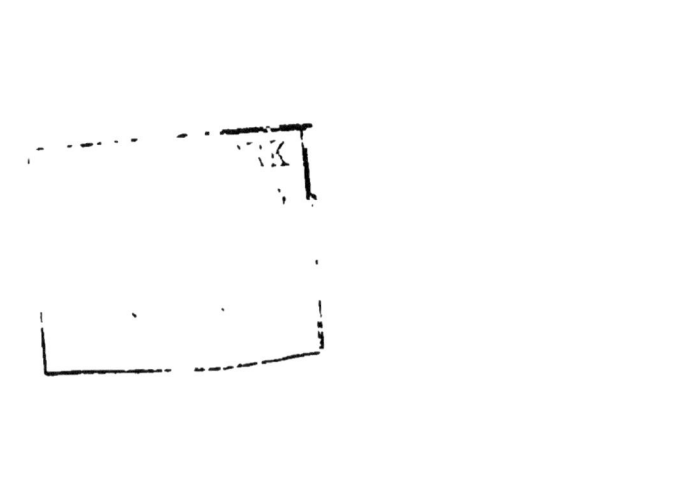

Carpenter he received such a taste of his quality that he declined any further favours, and tacitly resigned his assumed title of "champion of Taunton" to the "'prentice-han'" of Gaynor.

These were the times of election saturnalia, and though (*testé* Sir Henry James) Taunton, in these days of ballot and household suffrage, is no purer than it ought to be, in the times of borough-mongering it was much worse. A little episode in young Tom's history may illustrate this. During a contested election for that riotous, thirsty, and by no means immaculate borough, the true blue champion, whose colours young Tom wore, had set abroach a hogshead of "raal Zummerzet soyder," and to ensure the just distribution of the same had entrusted it to the care of a big rural rough, who churlishly denied young Gaynor a drop of the cheering home-made. This unfair treatment considerably riled our hero; but when the big bully threatened to add "a good hoidin'" to his refusal, "unless young Chips made hisself skeerce," the joke was carried too far. The stripling stripped, and the countryman, consigning his charge to a friend, desired him to "zee to the zwill, whoiles oi polish off this yoong jackandapes." But the battle was not to the strong, and in three sharp rounds, occupying about fifteen minutes, the "rush" of the yokel was so completely taken out of him by the cutting "props" and the straight "nobbers" of the young 'un that the countryman cried, "Enoo!" and went back to his tap, from which Tom and his friends drank success to themselves and their candidate without further hindrance or molestation.

Soon after Tom returned to his native city of Bath. Here he fought a pitched battle with a recruiting sergeant of some boxing fame in military circles. The soldier's tactics, however, were of no avail against the superior strategics of young Gaynor.

Gaynor's eyes, although he followed his calling industriously, were always cast towards the Metropolis with a longing gaze, and at the age of twenty-four he made his way to town, and having already met that professor in the provinces, he took up his quarters at the house of his "brother chip," the scientific Harry Holt, the "Cicero of the Ring," who then kept the "Golden Cross," in Cross Lane, Long Acre. Here an accident brought him into notice.

Josh Hudson being at Holt's at a jollification, the conversation, of course, was of "battles lost and won," and in the course of "chaff" Tom Gaynor was introduced with an eulogistic flourish from his Ciceronian friend and brother-craftsman. This led to Josh, who was certainly not in his " coolest state of collectedness," expressing his willingness to put on the mittens with the "young man from the country." The result was unfortunate. Josh lost his temper, and for some twenty-five minutes it was very like a little glove-fight, in which "Tom was as good as his master." Of course, Holt's friends put a stop to this; but it raised Gaynor's reputation.

Soon after, in a set-to with Ben Burn, Gaynor displayed such science and resolution that he was highly applauded by the amateurs at the Fives Court, and was hailed a clever " newcomer."

Friends now came forward, and Tom was matched with Ned Neale, at whose hands he experienced an honourable defeat, on the 25th May, 1824, in one hour and six minutes. (See NEALE, Chapter V., *ante*.)

Gaynor, about this time, frequently appeared at public sparring benefits, and was much esteemed, notwithstanding his defeat by so practised and resolute a boxer as the Streatham Youth. At Epsom Races, on the 20th of May, 1825, Gaynor was in attendance, with many of the Fancy, when a subscription purse of fifty guineas was offered by the amateurs. For this Gaynor presented himself as a candidate, and was met by Jonathan Bissel (Young Gas). Gaynor was admitted to be sadly out of condition, while Young Gas was in first-rate fettle. Gaynor was compelled to give in, after a game battle of one hour and twenty-five minutes.

In the early months of 1825 Gaynor advertised for a customer, offering to fight any man of his weight—eleven stone and a half—in three months, for £100 a side. Nearly one year passed away in sparring, when Gaynor, anxious for a job, challenged Reuben Martin for £50 a side, in January, 1826. This, however, ended without an engagement.

Tom was at length matched for £50 a side with Alec Reid (the Chelsea Snob), and the men met on Tuesday, May 16th, 1826, at No Man's Land, three miles and a half to the right of St. Albans.

The Eton Montem, Greenwich, and Wandsworth Fairs, and other places of attraction near the Metropolis, rendered the road to the scene of action remarkably thin; indeed, so scarce were drags of every description that the turnpike men declared it a holiday for their apron pockets, while the roadside houses looked out in vain for a four-horse drag, or even a Hampton van. Yet such a scientific display, with manliness united, as the battle between Gaynor and Alec Reid, on the beautiful bit of turf belonging to the ladies, on that Tuesday in May, has seldom rewarded a journey of a hundred miles.

Whiteheaded Bob was Gaynor's principal patron, and like a good judge sent out his boy to a prime training walk. Baldwin also backed Gaynor to the amount of a £50 note—so high an opinion did the Whitenobbed One entertain of his quality. The Chelsea Champion was under the protection of a Corinthian, and Richmond also looked after him. Both men did their duty while training, and their appearance, on stripping, satisfied the amateurs that they entered the ring in good condition. At one o'clock Gaynor threw his hat into the ropes, attended by Jem Ward and White-headed Bob, and a few minutes afterwards Reid repeated the token of defiance, followed by Cannon and Richmond. Gaynor was the favourite, at six and five to four; but the odds had previously been laid both ways. In fact, Reid was viewed as decidedly the best fighter, and in most instances was taken for choice. The colours, yellow for Gaynor, were tied to the stakes by Bob, and crimson for Reid were fastened by Richmond.

THE FIGHT.

Round 1.—Gaynor was the bigger man on appearing at the scratch, and having length and weight on his side were no trifling advantages in his favour. Reid looked well; he was up to the mark, and confident in the extreme. Some little caution was observed on both sides, both of them ready to let fly upon the first opening. Gaynor endeavoured to feel for the nob of his opponent, but the arms of Reid rendered repeated attempts of no avail. Reid at length got a turn, and quick as lightning he tapped the sensitive plant of Gaynor so roughly that both his ogles were winking. (The Reidites gave a rare chevy, thinking it a good omen.) The science of Reid was much admired; he stopped two left-handed hits with the utmost ease; but in counter-hitting he received a tremendous blow on his mouth, which not only produced the claret, but almost displaced his ivories. ("First blood!" cried Curtis and Josh Hudson.) Reid, with much good nature, said to Gaynor, "That was a good hit." The left hand of Gaynor again told; nevertheless, Reid was busy, and in turn felt for the upper works of Gaynor. The left peeper of the latter was damaged. Some excellent stops on both sides, until a rally ensued, when Gaynor fought resolutely until they were entangled — both down, Gaynor undermost. (It was clearly seen that the length of Gaynor made him a dangerous opponent, and he was decidedly the favourite at six to four.)

2.—Reid, like an experienced boxer, now stopped Gaynor well, but the latter would not be denied. He planted a heavy blow in Reid's face, and in closing sent him out of the ropes. ("You are sure to win it, Gaynor," observed his friends; and two to one was offered and taken.)

3.—Reid found out that he had a much more troublesome customer than he had anticipated. Gaynor got away from a heavy blow; a pause, and both on the look-out for squalls. Some sharp blows exchanged. The left hand of Gaynor told twice severely on Reid's mug. A rally ensued, and Tom went down rather weak.

4.—This was a capital round; and the mode of fighting adopted by Reid delighted his backers. He went to work with much determination, and Gaynor napped considerable punishment. In closing, Reid fibbed his opponent severely, until a severe struggle put an end to the round, and both down. ("What a capital fight—both good ones; it is worth coming 100 miles to see! We have not had such a fight for these two years past!" were the general observations all round the ring.)

5.—The face of Gaynor was materially altered, and his right ogle in "Queer Street." The mug of Reid was likewise damaged—his nose had increased in size; he had also received some heavy body blows. Good stopping on both sides; and Reid, in the estimation of his backers, put in some beautiful facers. In closing, Reid went down.

6.—A small change had taken place in favour of the "man of wax;" and he had now made his opponent a piper. The seconds of Reid and all his friends called to him to go to work; but Gaynor was not to be beaten off his guard—he sparred for wind till he recovered from his distress. Reid, how-ever, got the lead, and milled away, till in closing at the ropes he was thrown, and had a bad fall. Reid was now backed as favourite.

7.—Gaynor was much distressed; and Reid, like a skilful general, never lost sight of the advantage. In closing at the ropes, Gaynor went down exhausted. ("Reid for £100!" and uproarious shouts of applause.)

8.—Reid, most certainly, at this period of the fight, was the hero of the tale; he tipped it to Gaynor at every turn, till the latter boxer went down. (Rounds of applause for Reid.)

9.—A more manly round was never witnessed in any battle whatever—it was hit for hit, the claret following almost every blow. Both men stood up to each other like bricks, and appeared regardless of the punishment they received. Both down. ("Here's a fight—this battle will bring the Ring round! Reid's a fine fellow, but he is over-matched.")

10.—This was also a capital round; but whenever Reid made a hit Gaynor returned upon him. The length of the latter boxer enabled him to do this; and also in several instances his left hand did much execution, without being stopped by the Snob. Both down, and summat the matter on each side.

11.—Reid had the worst of it in this round; he received three jobbers, which made his nob dance again; but his courage never forsook him. In closing, the head of the Snob, in going down, went against the stakes, enough to have taken the fight out of most men, but he was too game to notice it.

12.—The changes were frequent, and at times it was anybody's battle. Reid was never at a loss, and he fought at every point to obtain victory. In struggling Reid was thrown, and Gaynor fell on him.

13.—The left hand of Gaynor committed desperate havoc on Reid's face; nevertheless, the former napped sharp ones in turn. In struggling, Reid went down.

14.—The appearance of Gaynor was now against him; and strangers to the Ring might fairly have entertained an opinion that he could not have stood up for a couple more rounds. Reid took the lead for a short time, but the round was finished by Reid being thrown.

15.—Nothing of consequence. Short, and both on the turf.

16.—This round was a fine display of science in favour of Reid. He punished Gaynor all over the ground, and floored him by a heavy facer. The Reidites were now uproarious, and applauded their man to the echo.

17.—Both men exhibited symptoms of distress. After an exchange of hits they staggered against each other, and went down. ("What a brave fight! Jack is as good as his master!")

18.—Gaynor, although in distress, made some good hits; he also nobbed Reid, and fell heavily upon his opponent.

19.—This was a short round. Reid was exceedingly weak, and went down—Gaynor quite as bad, staggering over his man.

20.—Reid came to the scratch full of pluck, but he received two jobbers. Both down, Reid undermost.

21.—The falls were decidedly against Reid; and in this round he received shaking enough to have put an end to the battle. Reid went down, and Gaynor fell on his head.

22.—The oldest and best judges of the Ring still stuck to Reid, and made him the favourite. He commenced the rounds well, but in general, as in this instance, he was thrown.

23.—Gaynor now appeared getting rather better; but his mouth was open, and so were his hands. (The friends of Reid advised Gaynor to leave off, as he was a married man, and had a family; "It don't suit me," said Gaynor. "Hold your tongue," said Ward; "it is six to one—sixty to one, I meant, in your favour—ain't it, Bob?" "Yes," replied the Whiteheaded One; "it is a horse to a hen.") Reid fell weak.

24.—Reid, like a good one, showed fight, and put in a nobber, but his strength could not second his science, and he was heavily thrown. Still Reid was offered as the favourite for five pounds, but no taker.

25.—It really was astonishing to view the high courage displayed on both sides, and the firmness and spirit with which they opposed each other's efforts. In finishing this round, Reid went down, and Gaynor fell on him.

26.—This was a very good round, and the determined spirit displayed by Reid astonished every spectator. Counter-hits. Gaynor tried to escape punishment, and in retreating fell down. ("He's going; you have won it, Reid.")

27.—Gaynor's face was badly battered, and the index of Reid was little better; but no complaints were made, and when time was called both appeared at the scratch with alacrity. Reid was busy and troublesome, till he was thrown. Another bad fall against him—worse than ten hits.

28.—Reid down; but he contended every inch of ground like a Wellington—a better little man is not to be met with, and the courage and good fighting he displayed this day delighted his backers.

29.—Gaynor was evidently the stronger man, although "bad was the best." Reid was getting very weak, missed his blows, and went down on his knees.

30.—The change was now decidedly in favour of Gaynor; and in closing he gave Reid a severe cross-buttock. ("It's all up," was the cry. "I'll give you," said Josh, "a chest of tools if you win it." "I have promised him," said Tom Oliver, "Somerset House—but he can't lose it.")

31.—Reid got away from a heavy nobber, with much more activity than could have been expected by a man in his truly distressed state. Reid down.

32.—Gaynor pursued Reid to the ropes, where the latter fought with fine spirit and resolution, till he was sent out of them by Gaynor.

33.—Several persons were yet of opinion that Reid would win; in truth, the battle was never safe to either until it was over. Reid went down distressed.

34, and last.—Reid still showed fight, and an exchange of blows took place; but in closing, Gaynor in obtaining the throw fell heavily upon him. Reid's head came violently against the ground, and when picked up by his second he was insensible. Gaynor was declared the conqueror. The battle occupied one hour and ten minutes.

REMARKS.—It was a near thing after all; and Reid, although in defeat, raised himself in the estimation of the Fancy. He fought up-hill against weight and length, and was likewise opposed to a man of science and a game boxer. Reid, it is said, weighed ten stone four pounds, and Gaynor eleven stone six pounds—but Gaynor declared, at the Tennis Court, on the Wednesday following, that he was under eleven stone. A better fight, in every point of view, has not been seen for many years. Gaynor received most punishment; but his conduct throughout the whole of the battle was cool and praiseworthy.

Gaynor was matched for a second battle with Young Gas, for £100 a side, to take place on the 5th of September. The stakes were made good, but owing to a misunderstanding the match went off.

In consequence of Gaynor having proved the conqueror with Reid, he was considered an excellent opponent for Bishop Sharpe, and his friends backed him against Sharpe for £50 a side. This battle was decided also at No Man's Land, on Tuesday, December 5th, 1826. Sharpe won the fight, after a very hard battle of one hour and ten minutes, Gaynor showing fight to the last. (See BISHOP SHARPE, Chapter XI., *post.*)

Gaynor's defeat by the Bold Smuggler did not diminish the number of friends made by his general good conduct and excellent demeanour to his patrons and backers. But despite his readiness for a match, it was more than a year before one could be satisfactorily arranged. His challenge was then accepted by Charles Gybletts, whose reputation as a slashing hitter and well-scienced boxer was established by his defeats of Rasher, Phil Sampson (see *post*, Chapter XIII.), Robin Rough, and Harry Jones, and who had lately fought a draw with Reuben Martin.

Gybletts was the favourite, at six to four, and the stakes (£100) being made good, the men met on the 13th of May, 1828, at Shere Mere, Bedfordshire, on the borders of Herts. At this fight, Tom Oliver, who had received the true-blue ropes and stakes of the Pugilistic Club, by order of Mr. John Jackson, its president, first appeared as Commissary-General of the P.R., and displayed that tact in the formation of an inner square and an outer circle which we so well remember, and so oft commended in long after years. Gaynor, who trained at Shirley's, at Staines, came over on Monday to the " Blue Boar," at St. Albans, Gybletts at the same time reaching the " Cross Keys," Oldaker's, at Harpenden. Both men were in the highest spirits, and in first-rate condition. Gaynor, joined by some Corinthian patrons, came on the ground in a well-appointed four-in-hand, decorated with his colours, a bright orange, and accompanied by a Kent bugle player, to the enlivenment of the road and scene.   Gybletts was driven to the ring in a less ostentatious conveyance, a high, red-wheeled, yellow, one-horse "shay," of the then "commercial" pattern, but was none the ess heartily greeted by his admirers.

The day was brilliantly fine, and the attendance of the right sort, who are always orderly.   Gybletts, waited on by Dick Curtis and Josh Hudson, first threw his castor into the ring.   Gaynor, esquired by Harry Holt and Tom Oliver, quickly answered the challenge, and Oliver won for him the choice of corners.   Gaynor's weight was stated at twelve stone, Gybletts's at eleven stone seven pounds.   The odds were, however, still on Gybletts, and no takers.

THE FIGHT.

Round 1.—On throwing themselves into attitude, each man showed his judgment in keeping the vulnerable points well covered. Gaynor manœuvred with his hands well up, and Gybletts played in and out, seeking an opening for a left-hand delivery.   After some cautious movements, Gaynor broke ground, trying his right at Gybletts's body, but he was cleverly stopped, and Gybletts jumped away nimbly.   His left at the nob was also stopped, but in a second trial with the right Gaynor got home on his adversary's cheek.   Gybletts now went in to fight, and caught Gaynor a smack on the mouth with the right, Gaynor striking the centre stake with his heel in retreating.   He recovered himself, however, and rushed to a rally, delivering right and left on his opponent's frontispiece.   Gybletts fought with him until they closed, when, after a sharp struggle, Gaynor threw him a heavy back fall, and tumbled on him.   On getting up a tinge of blood was visible on the face of each, and the first event was undecided.

2.—Gaynor, first to fight, delivered his right on Gybletts's body, who got away actively, and propped Gaynor as he came in.   Gaynor again tried his right at Gybletts's ribs, but was stopped.   He got on, however, one, two, on Gybletts's head, cutting his left cheek.   In the close Gybletts struggled hard for the fall, but Gaynor, dexterously shifting his leg, got the inner lock, and threw Gybletts head over heels, amidst the cheers of his friends.   Odds still six to four on Gybletts.

3.—A good scientific round ; hitting, stopping, getting away, in pretty stand-up style. Each got it on the body and pimple in turn, but the out-fighting was certainly in favour of Gaynor, who had the reach of his opponent.   In the close, Gybletts got the fall, and the cheering of the last round was returned.

4.—Good stopping by both. Charley missed his right at the body, and received a heavy smack on the left cheek from Gaynor's right, which sounded all over the ring, and imprinted a blood-mark on the spot. Charley was puzzled, but good counter-hits were exchanged.   Gybletts stepped back, wiped his hands, and did not seem to know how to get at his long-armed, round-shouldered opponent.   Caution the order of the day, and some excellent stops on both sides.   Gybletts swung in his right on the body, but got it on the jaw.   The men closed, Gybletts pegging away at Gaynor's ribs, Gaynor at Gybletts's head-piece ; Gaynor threw his man heavily. (Even on Gaynor.)

5.—Charley got in his left on Gaynor's neck, and followed it by a body blow.   Exchanges, in which Gaynor's length of arm told, Gaynor getting home on Gybletts's forehead and mouth, Gybletts on his opponent's ribs and ear.   A close for the fall.   After a short struggle Gaynor threw his man cleverly.

6.—Gaynor again caught a blow on the neck from Charley's left, but the latter missed his body blow.   Stopping in good style ; at length Gybletts went in, delivering his right heavily.   Gaynor turned round, and in getting away fell on his hands and knees by a slip.   Loud cheers for Gybletts, and two to one offered by his friends, though both out and in fighting were in Gaynor's favour.

7.—Gybletts got another sharp one on his wounded cheek.   He retreated, but Gaynor followed, forced the fighting, and threw him.

8.—On coming to the scratch Gybletts's shoe was down at heel.   Dick Curtis came forward and busied himself in getting it up, Gaynor quietly looking at him.   Tom Oliver made an appeal of "Foul," but the umpires said they had nothing to remark, except that Gaynor was at liberty to get to work, as "time" had been called. During the discussion the heel was put to rights, and the men stood up. Gaynor got his right on to Gybletts's body, Gybletts returned short, when Gaynor jobbed him twice on the head, and in the close both were down.

9.—Gaynor, first to fight, put in one, two, and closed; both down at the ropes.

10.—Good counter-hitting; both men stood bravely to the scratch. In the close, after a struggle, both fell, Gybletts on his head.

11.—Both men rushed to a close, and after a violent effort for the fall Gaynor grassed his man, falling on him.

12.—Good science on both sides. Alternate hits and stops. Gybletts had discovered that closing was not to his advantage, and kept out. In the exchanges he caught a heavy foreheader from Gaynor's left, and was finally thrown.

13.—Gybletts cautious, but Gaynor would not wait his convenience; he went in right and left, and Gybletts dropped.

14.—Mutual exchanges and good stops. Gybletts again visited on his olfactory organ. Both down harmlessly in a scramble.

15.—Gaynor delivered a right-handed chop, and Charley, in return, caught him in the ribs with the right. A close at the ropes, and both down.

16.—A slashing round; hit away on both sides until Gybletts was floored.

17.—Gybletts came up remarkably cheerful, considering the last bout. He got a good hit in on Gaynor's mouth, which bled freely. Gaynor returned, and went down in the exchanges.

18.—Both cautious. Gybletts sent in a teaser with his left on Gaynor's mouth. Gaynor, a little surprised, rushed to a close. Charley got Gaynor cleverly in his arms, lifted him from the ground, and backheeled him, falling on him heavily. (Shouts of "That's the way, Charley!")

19.—Wild fighting on both sides. Gaynor rattled away, hit or miss. Gybletts returned at random; in the exchanges Gybletts slipped, and was on his knees, when Gaynor knocked him over.

20.—Forty-five minutes had now elapsed. The knuckles of Gybletts's right hand were much puffed by repeated contact with the point of Gaynor's elbow, which he dropped to protect his ribs from the unpleasant visitations of his adversary. Yet Charley was still the favourite, from his known gameness, and his friends maintained he must wear Gaynor out. Gybletts delivered his right at the body, and Gaynor closed for in-fighting. In the close, Gybletts got Gaynor down.

21.—Gybletts crept in, got in a blow on Gaynor's proboscis, and was uppermost in the close.

22.—A good weaving round. Gybletts had it left and right, and was thrown unmistakably.

23.—Gaynor made a right-handed job, closed, and threw his man.

24.—Gybletts applied to the brandy-bottle. He went up, sparred a little, tried at the body, missed, and was thrown.

25, 26, 27.—Gybletts fighting an uphill game, but contending manfully, hit for hit. In the 26th round Gaynor caught his man on the nose, cutting the cartilage, the wound bleeding profusely. In the last round both were down.

28, 29.—Gaynor first to fight. Gybletts down.

30.—Gybletts got home sharply with his left in Gaynor's left eye. Gaynor cautious. At length he let fly, but Gybletts ducked his head, thus saving it from a smasher. He then caught Gaynor heavily on the mouth, and drew the claret from that organ as well as the nose. Gaynor returned, but slipped down on his knees.

31.—One hour and five minutes had passed. Charley succeeded in planting a "snorter," but Gaynor gave him a *quid pro quo*. Gybletts once again visited his adversary's masticators, when Gaynor went in hand over hand, drove him to the ropes, hit up, and threw him.

32.—Gaynor took the lead in fighting. Charley drew back, putting in slightly on the nose. He got it in return on the mouth, and went down, Gaynor also falling back on the ropes, but quickly recovering his perpendicular.

33.—Gybletts came up cheerful, and after a few feints and parries went in for close quarters. After a stiff struggle Gybletts was thrown completely over the ropes out of the ring; Gaynor went over the ropes with him, with his heels in the air and his head on his man's body.

34.—Gybletts, though piping, seemed strong on his legs. He stood well to his man, and it was hit for hit with no decided advantage, till, in the close, both were on the grass.

35.—Gaynor went in, and Charley jobbed him on the nose. Tom shook his head, and went at Gybletts with the right. Exchanges, a rally, and a heavy cross-counter; both men were on the ropes. Gaynor in an awkward position, when he got down. (Cheering for Gybletts.)

36.—One hour and a quarter had elapsed, and the odds were still on Gybletts, notwithstanding Gaynor's out-fighting and wrestling were superior. Tom, first to fight, got in a mugger, and received a rib-roaster in return. Merry milling for a turn. In the close Gaynor got the fall.

37.—Gybletts stopped Gaynor's left neatly, and got away; Gaynor followed. Both missed in the exchanges, closed, and Gybletts gained the throw.

38.—Gybletts, amazingly active on his pins, missed a right-hander; exchanges with the left, and a cross-counter. Gybletts went in wildly, but was heavily thrown.

39.—From this to the 45th round the men fought spiritedly; Gaynor, getting better, generally had Gybletts down at the ropes. In the 46th round Gybletts's right hand was seen to have given way, and he had his left only to depend on as a weapon of offence. In the 48th and 49th Gaynor fought Gybletts down, and in the 50th threw him heavily.

51, and last.—When Gybletts showed at the scratch, Harry Holt called upon Gaynor to "finish the fight," but Tom was so "bothered" he could do nothing with precision. He missed with the right, got hold of his man and turned him round, when both fell together, Gybletts pegging away at Gaynor's back. Time, one hour and fifty-three minutes. An attempt was made to bring Gybletts to "time," but in vain. The game fellow had swooned, and Gaynor was hailed the victor. Gybletts was bled by a medical man on the ground, and quickly came to. Gaynor, after a few minutes, walked to his carriage, saluted by "See, the Conquering Hero Comes," from the keyed bugle.

REMARKS.—Gybletts's friends had no reason to complain of their reliance on the gameness of their man, although their underestimate of his adversary's powers led to his defeat. Gaynor's superior length, and his wrestling capabilities, in which he has few superiors in the Ring, turned the scale in his favour—added to which, his endurance in receiving punishment, and skill in hitting and stopping, proved also to be superior to those of his brave adversary. The battle, as a whole, did honour to both victor and vanquished.

Gaynor took a benefit at the Tennis Court on the ensuing Thursday, when Tom Oliver and Ben Burn, Young Dutch Sam and Ned Brown (Sprig of Myrtle), were the leading couples. Gaynor returned thanks to his friends, and in reply to an expressed wish of Gybletts for another trial, said he hoped to be shortly in a position to retire from the Ring altogether; if not his friend Charley should be accommodated. The stakes were given up to Gaynor on the same evening, after a dinner at Harry Holt's, when his backers presented him not only with the stakes he had won, but the sums they had put down for him.

So high did this victory place Gaynor in his own and his admirers' estimation that it was considered a new trial with his old opponent of six years previously might lead to a reversal of the verdict then given. Accordingly Ned Neale was sounded; but that now eminent boxer having his hands full, the matter was perforce postponed, and it was only in the latter part of 1830 that a match could be made with Neale and Gaynor, to come off after the former boxer's contest with Young Dutch Sam, as already narrated in this volume.

The terms were that Neale should fight Gaynor, £300 to £200, on the 15th of March, 1831, eight weeks subsequent to Neale's fight with Sam.

Notwithstanding Neale's defeat by "the Young Phenomenon," he was the favourite at five to four, and these odds increased when information from Neale's training quarters in the Isle of Wight asserted that the Streatham man was "never better in his life." Gaynor was declared "stale." He had for more than two years led the life of a publican, and was said to be "gone by." His more intimate acquaintance did not share this opinion, as Tom was always steady, regular, and never a hard drinker.

Gaynor took his exercise at his old friend Shirley's, at Staines, as on former occasions, and having won the toss for choice of place, Warfield, in Berkshire, was named by his party as the field of arms.

Soon after twelve on the appointed day Neale, who had arrived at Ripley the day before, came on the ground in a barouche and four, with numerous equestrian and pedestrian followers. Gaynor, in a similar turnout, soon after put in an appearance. He had for his seconds Harry Holt and Ned Stockman—Neale, Tom Spring and his late opponent, Young Dutch Sam. The men shook hands good-humouredly, and commenced " peeling," six to four being eagerly offered on Neale. Both men looked serious, and Gaynor's skin was sallow. As for Neale, he looked bright and clear, and was generally fancied by the spectators. Gaynor's weight was declared to be 11st. 2lb., while Neale's was 12st. 3lb., Gaynor's age being thirty-two and Neale's twenty-seven. The advantage, therefore, seemed greatly on the side of Tom's former conqueror, and so thought most persons, except Gaynor himself. All preliminaries having been adjusted the men were delivered at the scratch, the seconds retired to their corners, and at twelve minutes after one began

THE FIGHT.

Round 1.—Each man held up his hands as if waiting the other's attack, and this determination being mutual they stood eyeing each other steadily for two or three minutes, doing nothing. Gaynor at length made a little dodge with his left, but Neale was wary, shifted a little, and would not be drawn out. More waiting, more dodging, when, at the expiry of nine minutes, Gaynor sent out his right at Ned's body, who contented himself by stopping it with his elbow. Gaynor stepped back and wiped his hands on his drawers. Mutual feints, both cautious—the spectators becoming impatient. ("Wake him up," said Stockman, "he's taking a nap.") After twenty minutes of manœuvring Gaynor planted his right on Neale's mazzard. (Cheers, and cries of, "Now go to work.") Neale would not break ground, and Gaynor could not get at him. More tedious manœuvring. Forty minutes had now elapsed (the same time as in Neale's first round with Nicholls), when Neale went in, Gaynor retreating to the corner of the ring. ("Now's your time," cried Young Sam.) Ned went in with the right, Gaynor countered, and a scrambling rally followed. A few ill-directed blows were exchanged, a close, and some fibbing; then a struggle at the ropes, when Gaynor was uppermost. The round lasted forty-five minutes.

2.—On coming to the scratch Neale showed a small swelling over the left eye, and his face was somewhat flushed. ("Now," cried Stockman, "you have broken the ice; out away.") Neale crept in on his man, who retreated, and shifted with a good defence. Neale let go his right at Gaynor's listener, but missed, and at it the men went in a rattling rally. Gaynor hit up with his right, catching Neale on the jaw; while Ned gave Gaynor a heavy one on the cheek-bone, raising a very visible "mouse." In the close fibbing was again the order of the day; at length Gaynor got his man down.

3.—Great shouting. "The "Queen's Head" for choice. Neale's face was flushed, and he panted a little. Gaynor was as pale as a parsnip, barring the black mouse on his cheek. Gaynor made pretty play with the right, but was neatly stopped, and Neale did the same for his opponent. Gaynor tried his left, but Neale merely threw up his guard, and Gaynor desisted. Neale let fly and got home on Gaynor's ivories, but had a sharp return on his left eye. Gaynor planted his right on Ned's ribs, and got away. Caution on both sides. Neale crept nearer to his work, and Gaynor retreated to his corner; at last Neale went in, and a slight bungling rally followed. A sharp struggle for the throw, which Gaynor got, and rolled over his man. (Loud cheers for Gaynor. On the men getting to their seconds' knees, Spring claimed "first blood" for Neale, from Gaynor's mouth, which was allowed.)

4.—A new dodge was here discernible. Stockman, to prevent Neale holding his man, had greased Gaynor's neck, the grease being very visible at the roots of his hair. Neale broke ground and began the fighting; Gaynor was ready, and fought with him. Neale was hit in the body and on the nose and brow, Gaynor on the jaw and cheek. In a loose rally Ned went down in the hitting. (Cannon claimed this as "first knock-down" for Gaynor. It was allowed; but there was not a clear knock-down in the fight.)

5.—On rising Neale showed marks of hitting on the left eye and nose. After a little cautious sparring Ned rushed in wild, and the men wrestled together. Both down, Gaynor uppermost.

6.—Neale steady. No great harm done on either side. Gaynor hit short with his left, then threw in his right with the rapidity of lightning. Both attempts were beautifully stopped. Gaynor laughed, but Neale put a stop to his hilarity by a sharp lunging right-hander on the mouth, which Gaynor returned with a smart smack on Ned's proboscis. Another wrestling-match, and Neale thrown. (On rising Neale showed blood over the right eye, and Holt renewed the disputed point by claiming it for Gaynor.)

7.—Neale stole a march, and popped in his left cleverly on Gaynor's nose. Gaynor returned with the right; Ned rattled in, caught Gaynor so tightly round the waist that he could not extricate himself, then, with the back-heel, threw him on his back on the ground, adding his weight to the force of the fall. This was a smasher, and Gaynor's nose sent forth a crimson stream.

8.—Gaynor on the piping order, and cautious. Ned again visited his snuff-box with his left. Neale fought into a close, and again threw Gaynor a burster. (Ned was now a strong favourite, at six and seven to four.)

9.—Gaynor was cheerful, and there was some good counter-hitting with the right. Neale napped it on his already swollen eye, which began to bleed, as did an old wound on Gaynor's cheek-bone. In the close, Gaynor was thrown for the third time. He got up slowly, and seemed the worse for wear.

10.—Neale, still cautious, stopped a right-hander, but missed his return. Gaynor went in for the throw, and after a sharp struggle got his man down.

11.—Gaynor much distressed and groggy. Nevertheless, he planted his right on Neale's damaged eye, which was fast putting up the shutter. Ned missed a vicious lunge at Gaynor's ear, and Gaynor returned nastily on Ned's nose, who rushed in, and seizing Tom, lifted him from terra firma, flung him heavily on his shoulder, and fell on him.

12.—Gaynor came up astonishingly steady, though bleeding from mouth, nose, and cheek. He hit short at the body with his right, then tried his left at the nob, but Ned frustrated his intentions. Gaynor swung out his right viciously, but Neale jumped back and escaped. Neale then went in for the throw, and a severe struggle followed, Ned chopping and fibbing; but at last Gaynor got the lock, and over went poor Ned, with Gaynor on top of him, a most audible thud.

13.—Gaynor piping. Ned planted his right hand on the body; he then closed. A long struggle for the throw, and both down.

14.—Gaynor, game as a pebble, went in to fight, but Ned got away, and Gaynor went down in the attempt to close.

15.—Ned made play, but was open-handed. Gaynor retreated to the ropes, where a struggle took place. Gaynor got Ned under, and hung on him on the ropes, until Ned fell outside them, Gaynor inside.

16.—The fight had now lasted one hour and thirteen minutes. A wild and scrambling round. Both down.

17-20.—Gaynor, game and ready, always came to the scratch; though much distressed, he never shirked his work. In the 20th round he seemed "abroad," and fell, Neale falling over him on his head.

21.—Gaynor on the totter. Ned ran in at him, bored him to the ropes, caught him in his arms, and sent him a "Catherine wheel" in the air. (Ned's friends all alive. Three to one on Ned, and no takers.)

22 and 23.—In both these rounds Gaynor was down, and Neale supposed to be winning in a canter—any odds.

24.—Ned the fresher and stronger man, apparently. Exchanges, when Gaynor rushed in and threw him. ("Not safe yet," cried the knowing ones.)

25.—Gaynor went to in-fighting, closed, and threw Neale.

26.—Neale went in first, but Gaynor fought for a few seconds on the defensive, then closed, put on the crook, and threw Neale. ("Pro-di-gi-ous!" exclaimed Frosty-faced Fogo, after the manner of Liston's Dominie Sampson.)

27.—Gaynor, though sorely punished, smiled confidently. Neale tried his left; Gaynor missed his right over Ned's shoulder. Ned closed for the fall, but Gaynor again got it. (The odds at a standstill. "Neale has to win it yet.")

28.—Ned made another effort and won the fall, throwing Gaynor heavily.

29-31.—Neale cautious. Half-arm hitting and scrambling rallies. Both men tired, and little execution done.

32.—A wild round in the corner; Neale fell outside the ropes, and Gaynor inside.

33.—Neale walked firmly to the scratch; Gaynor was led up by his seconds. Neale fought in to a close, and heavy hits were exchanged. Gaynor fell on his knees, but was up in a second. Ned caught hold of the ropes, Gaynor closed, and Neale canted him completely over his head.

34.—Neale forced a rally. Gaynor waited for him and hit up. Neale closed, but seeing he was likely to get the worst of it, slipped down, amid cries of disapprobation, and "Take him away!"

35.—Curtis called out to Young Sam, "Six to four on Gaynor. Ned has cut it!" Neale in reply walked to the scratch. Gaynor ran in, seized Neale, and threw him with a swing. Shouts for Gaynor.

36.—Gaynor seemed getting second wind, and became steadier on his pins. Hits exchanged. Neale got the throw.

37.—Gaynor short at the body with his right. Neale nailed him with the left on the ribs. A rally in the corner, when Neale slipped to avoid. (Disapprobation.)

38-43.—Nothing remarkable except the men's perseverance. Each round began with some mutual stops and misses, resolved itself into a rally, and ended by one or both down alternately.

44.—Gaynor seemed to rally all his energies, and forced the fighting; hits were exchanged, and Gaynor tried for the close, but Neale went down. Gaynor pointed at him as he lay on the ground. (Cheers from Gaynor's friends. "We'll illuminate the 'Queen's Head' to-night!")

45, and last.—Gaynor seemed to begin with new vigour. His spirits were roused by the cheers of his friends, and he went manfully to the scratch. Neale faced him with apparent alacrity, but was clearly down on his luck, and showed heavy marks of punishment. Gaynor went at him with the right, and planted a blow. Neale fought with him to a close, when Gaynor threw him and fell across him. There was nothing to indicate that all was over, but when "time" was called, Neale's head fell back, and though Young Sam shook it and shouted, Ned was "deaf" to the call. Gaynor was accordingly proclaimed the victor amidst vociferous acclamations. The supporters of Neale were amazed and dumbfounded. Gaynor threw up his arms and cut a very feeble caper before walking off to his carriage, which displayed the orange flag of victory, and where he quickly dressed himself. Neale was some time before he recovered, and was then conveyed to Staines, and put to bed.

REMARKS.—It is difficult to account for Neale's falling-off, as ten rounds before the close he was evidently the stronger and fresher man. We can only attribute it to the repetition of prolonged exertion and of punishment at an interval too short for the entire recuperation of his bodily and mental powers after such a defeat as that he experienced at the hands of Young Sam only eight weeks before. Indeed, we cannot but think the match was ill advised and imprudent, and the odds of £300 to £200 in the battle-money presumptuous. It was, however, brave and honourable in Neale to try the "wager of battle," in which his too partial backers had engaged him. As to Gaynor, but one opinion can be formed of his courage, game, endurance, and fortitude, all of which were conspicuous in this contest with his superior in weight, youth, and the character of the boxers he had met and conquered.

On the following Thursday Gaynor took a benefit at the Hanover Assembly Rooms, Long Acre.* Here he was greeted with all the honours that wait upon success, and the best men of the Ring—Tom Spring, Oliver, Young Sam, Reuben Martin, Stockman, Reidie, &c.—put on the mittens. On Friday the stakes were given up at Tom's own crib, the "Queen's Head," Duke's Court, Bow Street, after a sporting "spread."

Tom's defeat of the redoubtable Streatham Youth led to a challenge from Young Dutch Sam. The circumstances of this defeat may be read in Chapter VIII., in the Life of that skilful boxer.

This was the last appearance in the twenty-four foot of either Sam or Gaynor. The latter, who was a civil, unassuming, and obliging man, attended to his calling, and died in the month of November, 1834, in Grosvenor Street, Bond Street, at the early age of thirty-five, of a chronic complaint of several years' standing.

---

* This was occasioned by that ancient boxing arena passing into new hands, and being leased for a circus, under the title of "Cooke's Gymnasium."

CHAPTER X.

ALEC REID ("THE CHELSEA SNOB").
1821—1830.

THE pedigree of Alec Reid showed that he came of a "fighting family."
His father was a Chelsea veteran, for many years in a snug berth on Nell
Gwynne's glorious foundation, and in receipt, as we have seen in the books
of that institution, of a "good service allowance of two shillings and
fivepence-halfpenny a day." Let not the reader smile superciliously.
Alec, the son of a humble but heroic Alexander, once demonstrated the
facts to the writer with honest filial pride, and moreover laid stress upon the
fact that while his papa was in garrison at Guernsey, awaiting orders to
sail with his regiment for the West Indies, his mamma, on the 30th of
October, 1802, presented him with a thumping boy, the seventh pledge of
her affection, who was in due time baptized Alexander, and was the subject
of this memoir. At the age of fourteen, Alec's father being then invalided,
and "the big wars over," the young 'un was apprenticed to his father's
trade, that of a shoemaker, and hence his pugilistic patronymic of "the
Chelsea Snob."

His first recorded display was with one Finch, a local celebrity who,
to the advantages of height and a stone in weight, added three or four
years in age. Mr. Finch, in two rounds, occupying ten minutes, was so
satisfied of the young Snob's superiority that he "caved in," and quitted
the "Five Fields" (now covered by the mansions of Belgravia), never again
to show in combat with the "Young Soldier," as Alec was then nicknamed
by his companions.

Reid now purchased two pairs of gloves, expensive articles in those days,
and started a series of sparring *soirées* at the "Turk's Head," in Jews' Row,
near the Military Hospital. His fame spread, and finding himself on
Wimbledon Common, attracted thereto by a mill between Fleming and

ALEC REID.

Curwen, two London boxers, and a purse being subscribed for a second battle, young Alec boldly threw his nob-cover within the ropes. His challenge was answered by Sam Abbott, a cousin of the once-renowned Bill, who beat Phil Sampson, and made a draw with Jem Ward. Young Abbott proved himself game and resolute, but notwithstanding the advice and nursing of his clever namesake, Alec punished his nob so severely that in twenty-five minutes his cousin threw up the hat, Abbott being quite blind. Alec raised himself immensely by this victory; and when, after the battle between Ward and Abbott, on Moulsey Hurst, October 22nd, 1822, a big fellow named Hearn claimed a purse of twenty-five guineas subscribed for a second fight, Alec disputed his claim. Hearn was disposed of in fifteen minutes, the big 'un being so outfought that he put on his coat, declaring "it wasn't worth a fellow's while to go on without getting a crack in now and then."

Alec now frequently showed at the Tennis Court, in the Haymarket, and Bob Yandell, a clever sparrer, who had defeated Crayfer and Dudley Downs, having expressed a disparaging opinion of Alec's talents, a challenge resulted, and the men met on the 14th of January, 1823, in Battersea Fields. After a battle of one hour and a half Yandell was carried from the ground thoroughly beaten, while Alec showed in Chelsea the same evening but slightly the worse for wear.

On the 20th of March, 1823, after the fight between Gipsy Cooper and Cabbage, the Gardener, Alec joined fists with Paddy O'Rafferty, an Irish candidate for fistic honours, but in thirty-one rounds, occupying sixty-three minutes, the Chelsea hero polished off Misther O'Rafferty so completely that he made no further appearance in the Ring.

Dick Defoe having declared himself anxious to meet any eleven stone man, a gentleman who had a high opinion of Alec's abilities offered to match Reid against him. Alec consented, and the men met on Tuesday, June 17th, 1823, in Epping Forest. After thirteen rounds, Reid's backer, considering him to be overmatched, humanely interposed, and ordered Reid to be taken away. Many were of opinion that Reid would have pulled through had he been allowed to continue. Reid lost no reputation by this defeat.

Reid's next opponent was Harris, the Waterman, who had beaten Bill Gould, Youna de Costa, and with the exception of this defeat at the hands of Alec, never lost a fight. They met at Moulsey Hurst, on the 12th of August, 1823, entering the ring after Peace Inglis had defeated George

Curtis. On the ropes being cleared Alec, in high spirits and fine condition, threw in his castor, a white one, and waited on by his late opponent Dick Defoe and Tom Callas, proceeded to make his toilet; Harris, from the opposite side, answered his token of defiance, and esquired by Josh Hudson and Harry Holt, advanced to make friendly greeting. The ceremony over, the men stood up, Harris the favourite, at five and six to four.

THE FIGHT.

Round 1.—Reid, with the advantage of youth, looked fresh and full of activity, Harris, though a few pounds the heavier man, looking leaner and more angular. Reid, after a few feints, bustled in to work, and planted a sharp right-hander on Harris's ribs. The Waterman found he must lose no time, so he rattled in for exchanges, and Reid went on his knees from a slip. ("Bravo! here will be another good battle!") Even betting.

2.—Reid came up gay as a lark, and made play like a good one. The claret was now visible on both sides, and hit for hit till Reid was again down.

3.—Harris met Reid well on his going in; but the Translator would not be kept out, and poor Harris went against the stake from a severe blow. Nothing else but fighting, till both were down. Reid for choice.

4.—Sparring was out of the question, yet good science was witnessed on both sides. Harris napped pepper, but not without returning the compliment. Both down.

5.—Reid took the lead so decisively in this round that he became the favourite, two to one. Harris went down piping.

6.—Reid got punished severely. Harris held him with his right hand, and whopped him with the other all over the ring. The Chelsea man at length rescued himself from his perilous situation, and by way of changing the scene fibbed the Waterman down. Anybody's battle.

7.—Harris commenced this round with some fine fighting, and had the best of it for a short period, till Reid put in a straight nobber, when Harris found himself on his latter end, looking about with surprise, as much as to say, "How came I here?"

8.—Nothing else but milling. Harris repeatedly nobbed his opponent, but he would not be denied. A heavy rally occurred, and Harris, being near the stakes, struck his hand against the post. Harris down like a shot.

9.—Youth must be served. Harris fought like a brave man, but the punishment he received was too heavy for him. Down in this round.

10.—Harris could not reduce the strength of Reid. The Waterman possessed the best science, but the blows of Reid were most effective. It was a manly fight. Both down.

11-12. — Equally good as the former rounds. Two to one on Reid.

13.—Harris jobbed his opponent frequently, but Reid always finished the round to his own advantage. In the last round he fell on Harris in the close. ("Take him away; he's a good old 'un, but too stale for the Snob!") Any odds.

14, and last.—Reid went up to his man and hit him one, two; Harris did not return. He seemed all abroad. Reid bustled him down, and Josh threw up the sponge in token of defeat. The fight lasted only fifteen minutes.

REMARKS.—A better fight, while it lasted, has not been lately seen. Harris was not only stale, but was stated to be a little "off" in condition and health. Harris was not disgraced, though defeated by youth, backed by resolution and strength.

Only two months after this victory Alec was at Chatham, teaching "the art of self-defence," when a rough and ready fisherman named Joe Underhill found local friends to subscribe a purse of £25, and £5 for the loser. For this, then, "the Chatham champion" proposed to meet the "London professor." Underhill's friends had miscalculated both their man's skill and Alec's science, for in the short space of nineteen minutes the fisherman's chance was more than "fishy," and at the end of the eighth and last round the Snob had so completely sewn him up and welted him that he cried, "Enough!" and refused to face his man. This battle took place on Chatham Lines, October 21st, 1823.

At the farewell benefit of the game Bob Purcell, at the Fives Court, February 15th, 1824, Reid set to with Gipsy Cooper, and gave the rushing Bohemian such a glove-punishing as led to a match. Cooper, however, forfeited a small deposit. A second match was made on Tuesday, April 13th, 1824; this, however, was prevented by magisterial interference, and the stakes were drawn.

An opportunity, however, soon offered itself, proving the truth of the adage that "where there's a will there's a way." On the very next Tuesday, April 20th, 1824, both men found themselves (of course by accident) at Colnbrook, when and where Peace Inglis defeated Ned Turner. Twenty pounds were quickly subscribed for a second battle, and Alec having tossed his beaver into the ropes was answered by the Gipsy. Both men were in first-rate condition, and both equally confident. Josh Hudson and Dick Curtis, two of the ablest of seconds, looked after Cooper; the accomplished Harry Holt and the veteran Tom Jones, of Paddington, seconded Reid.

THE FIGHT.

Round 1.—Cooper commenced the mill furiously, and his blows told heavily. Flattered with success, he went to work hand over head, throwing aside a number of blows. Reid could scarcely be quick enough for his opponent; but he stopped and shifted cleverly. A short pause, when the Gipsy again plunged in and drew first blood. In closing, both down. No harm done.

2.—The lip of the Gipsy was bleeding when he appeared at the scratch. He lashed out, neck or nothing. Reid put in two nobbing hits and threw Cooper.

3.—The Gipsy was furious indeed; he did not look at his man, to take any sort of aim, yet Reid was bustled about, and received a random shot or two on the body. In a rally he clinched the Gipsy and gave him a cross-buttock.

4.—This was a fine fighting round; the Gipsy appeared as if he meant to win and nothing else. The hitting was sharp on both sides. Reid was floored. ("The Gipsy will win!" and several now took him for choice.)

5.—The Gipsy was so desperate that he bored Reid down. Nothing.

6.—Cooper was amazingly active; he hit in all directions; nevertheless he retreated from Reid when the latter stepped in to exchange. In closing the Gipsy put in a heavy blow as they were both going down.

7.—The Gipsy had it his own way this round. Reid napped terribly, and was also milled down. ("Cooper will win in a canter. If he had fought like this with Bishop Sharpe we must have won our money," from several losers on that mill.)

8.—The hitting of the Gipsy was tremendous; and if he had not thrown so many blows away, he might have been able to have given a better account of the battle. Reid went down heavily hit. (The cry was, "The Gipsy is sure to win it!")

9.—Reid nobbed his adversary twice neatly, and kept him out, but the Gipsy bored in and both were down.

10.—The Gipsy had been so very busy that Reid had had scarcely time for a moment's tactics. He, however, now showed the Gipsy that a dangerous customer stood before him—a boxer that would make him fight, and not let him get out of his reach at pleasure. The Gipsy napped two nobbers that made him reel; he returned and tripped up Reid.

11.—Severe counter-hitting, and Reid received such a swingeing hit that he reeled about and went down. ("Come, no tumble-down tricks," cried Josh.)

12.—This was the best round in the fight. The men fought into a rally, and broke away. A pause necessary on both sides. The Gipsy slashing out hand over head, both were down, Cooper undermost. The

Gipsy, quite frantic, struck Holt, who, he said, had acted "foul" towards him; but Harry very prudently did not return it, or the fight must have been spoilt.

13.—Reid was positively run down, without harm done.

14.—The Gipsy was so fast that the spectators had scarcely an opportunity of appreciating the clever defence displayed by Reid. Cooper violent as before, and Reid down smiling.

15.—Reid got hold of Cooper; fibbing at the ropes till both down.

16.—Reid would make the Gipsy fight, although the latter retreated from him. Reid was thrown in the close.

17.—In this round Cooper was not quite so fast, and Reid put in a stopper or two on his nob, that produced the claret. Reid also put in a clean back-handed hit on the Gipsy's proboscis. Both down; Reid fell out of the ropes.

18.—Reid reminded the amateurs of Randall's neatness of style. The Gipsy could not get away from his returns. The latter, however, fought desperately, and Reid went down.

19, and last.—The spectators did not apprehend the fight was so nearly over. Reid took the lead in great style, and by a heavy blow hit the Gipsy clean through the ropes. Cooper's head rebounded as he rolled over, and when time was called the Gipsy had not awoke from his trance. Reid of course was declared the winner. Twenty-nine minutes.

REMARKS.—Reid to all appearance was little the worse for his battle, except a swelled cheek. The Gipsy is always dangerous from his lunging hits; but he trusts so much to chance that he is almost a "gift" to a steady and bold boxer. He does not look his man full in the face. Reid fought like a winning man, and showed excellent points.

What is the use of going out for a spree without making "a day of it?" say the jolly ones. Here is a case in point. It occurred, somehow or other, no matter, that a turn-up took place between Maurice Delay and Alec Reid, on the road home from the fight, after Stockman had defeated the Sailor Boy, on Tuesday, September 21st, 1824, near the "Coach and Horses," at Ilford. Notwithstanding the disparity between the men as to size and weight, it was stated in the papers of the day that Reid had none the worst of it with his ponderous antagonist during two rounds, after which they were parted. Half-an-hour after Bill Savage offered himself to Reid's notice for a £5 note which an amateur had offered for "a wind-up" to the day. A ring was formed near the Temple Mills, Essex, Harry Holt and Jem Burn waiting on Reid, and Savage seconded by his brother and George Weston. Darkness coming on a "draw" was declared after thirty-seven minutes, and the money divided. Reid, although out of condition, was said to have had the best of it.

Alec was now matched for £50 a side against the renowned Bishop Sharpe, and a gallant fight was anticipated. Bishop Sharpe was well known as nothing else but a good man; he had beaten all his opponents, the tremendous Gipsy Cooper three times. Nevertheless, in the opinion of the judges of boxing, the Bishop did not rank as a scientific fighter; he, however, was the favourite, five and six to four. Reid stood well in the sporting world; nay, so much so that it was expected that Alec would prove a second Jack Randall.

On Thursday, December 11th, 1824, a long procession of London travellers crossed the ferry at Hampton, and the ring was formed on the classic Hurst of Moulsey. The Commissary-General, with the ropes and stakes, made a pretty twenty-four feet inner square, and a spacious circular enclosure marked the outer ring. The combatants peeled, the colours were tied to the stakes, a bird's eye on a red ground for Reid, a yellowman for Sharpe. Oliver and Ben Burn attended upon Reid, Josh Hudson and Dick Curtis on Sharpe. The men shook hands, and then came

THE FIGHT.

Round 1.—Reid was in fine condition, and Sharpe looked hardy and well. Scarcely, however, had the men held up their hands, than surprise was expressed at the careless style of Reid. He stood so slovenly and with so open a guard that Sharpe at once went in and hit him slightly, when Reid stepped back and went down suspiciously. Opinions that "Mr. Barney" was not far off were freely expressed, Reid's style was so unlike his former displays.

2.—Oliver said to his man as he went up, "If you don't mean to fight, say so, and I'll leave the ring." Reid laughed and man-œuvred about. Sharpe again forced the fighting. A few exchanges took place, to the advantage of Sharpe, and Reid was again on the grass. While sitting on his second's knee Reid complained of sickness. "He's coming it," said Curtis. "No," said Reid, "no such thing." Ben Burn angrily said "he would not be second in a cross," and left the ring.

3.—"Why don't you fight?" asked Oliver. Reid could not or would not. He received a flush hit in the mouth, and first blood was claimed. Reid down, and the ring broken in. Oliver left the roped enclosure.

4, and last.—Reid came up at the call of "time," amidst great confusion. There were a few exchanges, and again Reid went down in his own corner. "You have won," cried Sharpe's backers. "Don't leave the ring yet," said Josh Hudson to Sharpe.

REMARKS.—A curious conclusion was come to. Reid declared he was ready to go on, but his seconds had deserted him. At Hampton he maintained that he had no idea of fighting "a cross," and that no one had even dared to propose such a thing to him. Our opinion is, in the absence of all direct evidence, that Reid was "hocussed," by whom was never ascertained (he himself always asserted this to be the case), and that his temporary stupefaction went off before his arrival at Hampton. The referee not having been appealed to on the ground there was no decision. Accordingly, Tom Cribb, who was stakeholder, returned the money to the backers of each man, and all bets were drawn. Pierce Egan has half-a-dozen pages of incoherent persiflage upon this mysterious affair, cut from his own paper, from which little definite can be gathered.

Reid was now certainly under a cloud of dark suspicion. Yet a few friends were found who matched him for £100 against Jubb (the Cheltenham Champion), a boxer who had recently beaten Price (the Oxford Champion) in offhand style, and whose friends were anxious to measure him with a London pugilist. The men met accordingly in Worcestershire, near Stow-on-the-Wold, on the 4th of June, 1825.

Benford, in Oxfordshire, seventy-one miles from London, was the place named, but on the morning bills were posted in the town signed by the magistrates of three counties, Oxford, Berks, and Gloucester, warning all persons against attending any fight within those counties, and ordering all constables, &c., to take the principals and seconds into custody as contemplating a breach of the peace. Worcestershire now seemed the only open point, and off went all hands to Icombe, a village on the borders, two miles from Stow-on-the-Wold, and ten or so from Benford.   At half-past two in the afternoon Reid skied his beaver, Jack Randall and the Laureate Fogo acting as his esquires.   Jubb soon followed, attended by Bill Eales, the scientific, and a provincial friend named Collier.   On stripping both men looked well.   Jubb had the advantage in weight, length of reach, and height, yet the London division laid odds on Reid at five to four when the countrymen would not take evens.

THE FIGHT.

Round 1.—Jubb stood somewhat over Reid, with his hands well out, but somewhat awkward in position. He made play at Reid's head, but was stopped neatly. Reid smiled and nodded, and broke ground actively. Jubb tried it again, but was again parried, and the Chelsea cobbler popped in such a cutting right-hander in return just over the left eye that Jubb's optic flashed fire and he seemed all abroad, winking like an owl in the sunshine. The London division delighted. Reid bustled Jubb down.

2.—Reid treated Jubb's attempts lightly. He followed him all over the ring, and after a heavy hit on his left eye, closed and threw him, amidst general cheering.

3.—Jubb, who somewhat fancied himself as a wrestler, seemed all abroad; he tried to catch Reid in his arms, but Alec hit up, caught him under the chin a rattler, and fell on his knees from the force of his own blow. Reid complained that he had no nails in his shoes.

4.—All the hitting came from Reid's side. Jubb could only stop with his ribs or head. Reid down, the Cheltenham lads grumbling, "He dropped without a blow." It was not so ; many blows were exchanged.

5-7.—Similar in character. Jubb wild,

Reid steady, and always ready as his man came in.

8.—In a rally Jubb caught Reid a swinging hit in the throat, which almost turned him round. The Jubbites cheered, but Reid returned to the rally, and the Cheltenham champion was floored.

Ten more rounds, in which Jubb was, with unimportant exceptions, receiver-general.

18, and last.—Jubb came up in the doldrums. He was hit in all directions, but was too game to go down. His backers humanely interfered, and desired his seconds to take him away. It was all over in twenty-three minutes and a half, and when Reid put on his clothes there was scarcely a mark perceptible on his face.

REMARKS.—Jubb did not avail himself of his height. On the contrary, he stooped to a level with the eye of Reid. Jubb is a game man, and would beat any countryman who merely relied on strength and going in. Reid fought with him whenever he attempted to force the fighting, and got on to him almost how and where he pleased, stopping his attack and turning it to his own advantage. Reid won first blood, first knock-down blow, and the battle, his backers drawing upon all three events.

Reid, on his return to town, addressed letters to the sporting papers challenging Bishop Sharpe, West Country Dick, or Aaron, for £100, and undertaking to weigh no more than 10st. 4lbs. on the day of fighting.

As there were difficulties in the way with Bishop Sharpe Reid's friends matched him against Tom Gaynor, a man certainly his overmatch by a stone in weight and three inches in height.   The fight, which took place May 16th, 1826, and in which Alec suffered defeat after a game contest of one hour and ten minutes, will be found in Chapter IX., *ante*, page 403 of this volume.

At length preliminaries were settled between Alec and his former opponent

Bishop Sharpe, for £50 a side.   The battle took place on the 6th of September, 1826, at No Man's Land, in Hertfordshire.   It was anybody's fight
for the first twenty-five minutes, when Alec received what might be termed
a chance blow in the pit of the stomach, from which he never recovered,
and victory was declared for the Bold Smuggler.

   Shortly after this (October 27th, 1826) Reid got into trouble for having
acted in the capacity of second to a man of the name of Crow, in a pugilistic
contest at Old Oak Common, with one Samuel Beard.   The jury found
Beard, Reid, and Michael Curtis guilty, and sentenced them, Beard to seven
days' imprisonment in Newgate, and the seconds to fourteen days, and to be
held in recognisances " to keep the peace for twelve months towards all His
Majesty's subjects."

   Poor Alec, having done his term in " the donjon's dreary keep,'
and lived out his recognisances to keep the peace, was once again matched
with his old opponent Bishop Sharpe for £100.   Little preface is necessary
to the detail of the battle between these men, which was one of the best
that had been witnessed for many years, even when downright milling and
upstanding rallies were far more common than they became in the succeeding years, which marked the decline and fall of the P.R.   They had
fought twice before, in both of which instances Reid was unsuccessful.

   As soon as the match was made they went into training, and thus all
gradually ripened for sport.   On Sunday Sharpe took his departure for
St. Albans, and took up his quarters at the " Blue Boar," and on the nex
evening, after a benefit at the Tennis Court, Reid followed his example,
pitching his tent at the " Red Lion."   Tuesday morning (July 15th, 1828)
was unfavourable, nevertheless the roads were thronged at an early hour.
Both men were visited in the town ; both spoke well of their condition,
and with modest confidence of success; Reid saying " he had everything at
stake, for if he lost he was bowled out for ever, whereas if he won
he was made a man of."   Sharpe soberly said he was " to win to-day," and
his shoemaker had already booked the event as certain by inscribing on the
the soles of his high-lows, " These are the shoes that are to win; " a
prophecy which was unfortunately trodden under foot in more ways than
one, for he was for the first time in his life forced to confess he was fairly
conquered, after a long career previously unchequered by defeat.   The
odds during the morning were five and six to four on Sharpe.

   As the hour for business approached the crowd increased, till the word
was given to march, and all toddled to the scene of action, where Tom

Oliver had previously pitched the ropes and stakes, and collected an outer ring of wagons.

Shortly before one o'clock the Smuggler bore down for the ring attended by Josh Hudson and Dick Curtis, and having thrown in his castor, entered himself. The Snob was soon with him, under the auspices of Tom Spring and the Lively Kid (Ned Stockman). After shaking hands, the Snob said he had four sovereigns, to which he was desirous of taking odds of six to four. This was at once laid him by Dick Curtis, and staked, and the operation of peeling commenced. On stripping, weight and muscle were evidently in favour of the Bishop. He looked fresher in the mug, too, although it was said he had been imprudently attending as the host of a canvas tavern at Woolwich Races and Fairlop Fair, where he dispensed the " real thing" in large quantities. Reid looked light and thin, but was in good spirits, and seemed confident.

THE FIGHT.

Round 1.—Sharpe, as usual, came forward right foot foremost, measuring his man with a keen and searching eye. Alec was on the alert, both hands well up, and his right ready for a drop to save his bread-basket from the Smuggler's favourite lunge. At last Sharpe broke ground, and planted his left slightly on Reid's ribs. Reid instantly hit with him, right and left, at the nob, and Sharpe returned with his left in similar style. Both were rather wild, but, in the close, the Bishop was thrown. On rising to his second's knee, there was a cry of "first blood" from Sharpe's mouth, but at the same moment a similar tinge was seen from the Snob's muzzle, so that on this point there was no advantage, and a tie was acknowledged.

2.—Alec ready, and the Smuggler looking for a run upon his starboard quarter. At last Alec planted his right in Sharpe's mouth a second time. The Bishop instantly fought to a rally, and jobbing hits were exchanged with great rapidity, Sharpe again napping it in the mouth, and the Snob on the dexter ogle. Both showed more claret. In the close, the Snob was thrown, the Smuggler upon him .

3.—Sharpe now popped in his favourite left, but not in the right place, being on the ribs instead of the mark. Alec hit with him, right and left, in pretty style, and floored him with a right-hand muzzler. First knockdown blow for Reid.

4.—The Bishop's mouth showed two incisions, which bled profusely. He, however, came up smiling, and delivered with his left on Alec's jaw. Alec returned in good style, The Bishop then bored in wildly, and, in the close, both went down, Alec fibbing as he resisted Sharpe's effort for the fall.

5.—Sharpe's nose now began to show the weight of Alec's fibbing, and claret streamed profusely. He, however, rushed in wildly, trying for the Snob's body. The Snob got away, and, in a second trial of the same sort, he met the Bishop with a flush hit on the forehead, and, on repeating the dose, the Bishop bored in. The Snob again met him right and left, and floored him, hitting him severely as he was falling.

6.—Sharpe again hit short at the body with his left, and Alec, always ready, met him right and left, and, repeating the experiment, hit him down with a flush smack on the ivories.

7.—Alec waited with great judgment, and, as the Bishop came in, stopped his left, and returned heavily with his right. The Bishop would not be denied, but caught Alec a nasty one on the temple. Both broke away, but on Sharpe again rushing in, Alec met him right and left on the head, and then hit him heavily with the right on the ribs, and dropped him. (Shouts of " It's all your own, Reid!")

8.—The Bishop's head the worse for bad usage, his left eye puffed, and a cut on each cheek. He, however, went in as game as a pebble to hit with his left. Alec was again away. Sharpe followed him up, but Alec, stepping back, met him twice on the frontispiece. He had then reached the ropes, and the Bishop became desperate. Alec went down to avoid, showing the tact of a good general.

9.—The Bishop rattled in, and planted his

left on Alec's eye, but received severely right and left in return, and in the end went down.

10.—The Bishop bored in open-handed. Alec retreated a little before him, but then jumped in and met him with two flush hits, right and left, on the head. The Bishop closed for a rally, and desperate hits were exchanged. In the close, both down.

11.—The Bishop capsized with a straight visitation on the smeller from Alec's left.

12.—2 to 1 on Reid. Sharpe bored in wildly, and Alec went down.

13.—The Bishop again bored in. Alec retreated, and tried his right and left, but missed. The Bishop, in returning, fell on his knees.

14.—Sharpe came in manfully, but Alec was ready, stopped his left, returned right and left on his canister, and then hit him down beautifully with a right-handed smack on his ribs.

15.—Counter-hits. The Bishop planted his left well on the Snob's conk, and again had him on the body. Alec stepped back, and on the Bishop again coming in to make play, met him with a snorter with his right, and dropped him.

16.—Counter-hits with the left, and Sharpe hit away left and right with great spirit. Alec was not idle, but returned the compliments with quickness. Bishop closed for the fall, when Alec fibbed actively, though not effectively. Both down, Bishop under.

17.—The Bishop came up as bold as brass. Alec ready, waited for him and, on rushing in, he met him right and left on the face. Bishop retreated, but, on again rushing in, Alec dropped him with another touch on the nob.

18.—Bishop, first to fight, planted his left. Alec was with him, but Sharpe would not be denied, and closing, he threw the Snob a heavy fall, and dropped on him.

19.—Bishop rushed in open-handed, in wild style. Alec drew back, poising himself on his hind leg. Sharpe followed, and as usual, napped it left and right, and was floored.

20.—Bishop again pressed in (he saw he had no chance at out-fighting), when he was met as before, with great precision, right and left. A spirited rally followed. Good hits were exchanged, and in the close, Bishop was thrown heavily.

21.—The Bishop, in rushing in, was hit down by a right-handed job.

22.—A good manly rally, with equal advantage, hit for hit. Alec down.

23.—Counter-hitting with the left. Sharpe dropped his right on Alec's smeller, and drew his cork. Alec at him again, and, after a severe rally, hit him down.

24.—Bishop bored in. Alec withdrew for the jobbing hit, but the Bishop fell on his face.

25.—On Sharpe coming in, Alec again met him with a facer, and followed this up with a tremendous body hit with his right, and dropped him.

26.—Bishop bored in wildly. Alec, as before, on the retreating system, met him with a facer, as he came in. Sharpe closed, and had the fall. Not much harm done on either side.

27.—A severe punishing round for Bishop. Alec jobbed right and left several times, and, in the close, floored him with great force, rolling him over from the impetus of the fall.

28.—Alec on the waiting system. Bishop rushed in with unshaken game, but, on delivering his left on Alec's nob, he received a terrific hit on the ribs from the Snob's right, close under his left arm, which again dropped him.

29.—Bishop again bored in, and was met, with great judgment, by another delivery from Alec's right. Both away, and some good out-fighting. Alec jobbed well. A close, and both down, the Bishop under.

30.—Alec waiting steadily. Bishop the first to go to work. Alec stepped back, and Bishop fell forward on his hands and knees.

31.—Alec popped in his favourite hit on the side, but received in return on the head. Alec then retired, Sharpe after him, hitting wildly and short. Alec watched his points, and, after stopping with his right, hit Bishop down with a blow on the throat with his left.

32.—Good out-fighting. Bishop still strong; at last he rushed in, according to his old system, when Reid had him in the side with his right. Bishop rushed to a close, and pulled Alec down.

33.—Alec delivered his right and left as Sharpe came in, and got away. The Bishop, after him, would not flinch, and was again floored with a stupefying hit on the temple.

34.—Bishop again at work, delivered with his left, but in return was hit down by a straight facer.

35.—Bishop rushed in wildly, but Alec was on his guard. Good counter-hitting, and a manly rally. In the close, Alec was thrown. Shouts for Bishop, and his friends still in spirits.

36.—Sharpe came in wildly, but Alec was steady and cautious. His right was again familiar with Bishop's ribs, and his right and left were once more in contact with his phiz. In the end, Sharpe was floored heavily.

37.—Alec had it in the right eye, but returned with interest, catching the Bishop twice on the mug, and Sharpe went down weak.

38.—Bishop on the boring system; Alec away. Sharpe caught him on the body slightly, and received on the head in return. A merry rally, hit for hit. Both down.

39.—The Bishop made his run, Alec met him with a job. Both away, and at it again. Alec pursued the same system of jobbing, but had a nasty one on the right eye, and went down.

40.—Again did Alec meet Bishop right and left. Sharpe caught him on the nozzle, and drew claret in a stream. Alec, merry, at him again, and down went the Smuggler.

41.—Alec met Sharpe right and left on the head, but received a heavy blow on the nob in return. In the close, both down, Bishop under.

42.—Alec met Bishop with a flush hit on the throat, and floored him.

43.—Sharpe caught Alec a terrific blow on the side of the knowledge-box, but had three for one in return, and Alec fell.

44.—Alec ready, but his physog. strangely out of shape, and as tender as a chicken ; he could scarcely bear to wash his mouth. Bishop rushed in, but was hit down by a right-hander.

45.—Sharpe's left ogle closed for the day ; still he came up game, but Alec, ready, met him in the face. Bishop missed his left-handed lunge at the body and fell.

46.—Sharpe wild, was jobbed on the head, and fell.

47.—Bishop, still staunch, the first to mill. Alec waited, jobbed, and got away. Bishop followed him up, hit with his left at the body, closed, and threw Alec a burster, falling heavily on him.

48.—Alec, still awake, met Bishop right and left, and dropped him.

49.—Bishop again hit down with a heavy blow on the left ribs.

50.—Sharpe hit down from a left-hander on the nob.

51.—Again was Bishop hit down.

52.—Bishop charged. Alec retreated, but meeting Sharpe, dropped a heavy one on the body with his right. In closing, Alec hit the Bishop up terrifically with his right, on the smeller, and grassed him.

53.—Bishop hit down right and left.

54 to 60.—All in favour of Alec, who hit his man down every round, either from blows on the head or body.

61.—The Bishop went down without a blow. Cries of "foul," but no decision.

62.—Bishop gathered all his strength, and came up in good force. He hit Alec with the left, but was jobbed down right and left.

63.—Bishop again hit down.

64.—Counter-hits. Sharpe went boldly to his man, but was dropped.

65.—Curtis now began to use all his tact to encourage his man, chaffed the Snob, and doffed his own shirt to be more at ease. Alec hit Bishop right and left, and he went down.

66.—Alec drank out of the bottle himself, and winked to his friends, as much as to say, "It's all right." Alec stopped his man with his left, and hit him down as he came in.

67 to 71.—All in favour of Alec, and Bishop went down every round.

72.—Bishop gathered himself for mischief, and tried his favourite left-handed body hit, but it fell short, and he caught it right and left and went down.

73.—Bishop attempted to hit, but went down without a blow.

74.—Alec jobbed with his left, and caught

Bishop on the dexter ogle, which began to swell, and he went down.

75.—Sharpe hit down.

76.—The Bishop hit with his left at Alec's mark, but it was without effect. Alec rushed at him to hit, but Bishop dropped, on the saving system.

77.—Again did Bishop try his left, and his friends still hoped he would pop it in the right place, but no go, he was jobbed down.

78.—The Bishop, in going in, went down without a blow. (Hisses, and cries of "foul.")

79.—The Bishop went in wild, and fell. Cries of "Take him away."

80.—Bishop again bored in, neck or nothing. Alec got away, and Sharpe fell.

81.—Similar to the last. Alec missed a tremendous up-hit, or all would have been over.

82.—Bishop jobbed down with the left, but both distressed, and severely punished in the head.

83.—Bishop hit down.

84 to 87.—The Bishop, dreadfully jobbed and hit in the body with the right, down every round. The crisis was now approaching. Alec had it all his own way, and nothing but a lucky lunge could change the aspect of affairs, and for this Bishop's friends still anxiously sought.

88.—Sharpe came up wild, and was hit down.

89.—Bishop hit down again with a body blow.

90.—Alec saw the sore point. The Bishop winced, and he gave him another appalling body blow, which resounded through the ring, and felled him.

91, and last.—Poor Bishop got up to receive the finisher, and was floored by a tremendous hit with the left. All was now over ; Sharpe was insensible, and, on time being called, his seconds gave in. The hat of victory was instantly thrown up, and the shouts of the crimson heroes proclaimed the success of their favourite, in one hour and twenty-seven minutes. Alec made a slight bound, and, after a short pause, was conducted to his carriage. He was so exhausted that some time elapsed before he could be dressed, after which he was borne off to St. Albans, with flying colours. Poor Sharpe remained for some time insensible to his fate.

REMARKS.—This was decidedly as game and determined a battle as was ever witnessed. Each man seemed deeply to feel the stake at issue. Fame and fortune were alike involved, and the contest was proportionally severe. The scientific style in which Reid fought was the admiration of the ring. His attack and defence were alike judicious. Aware of the dangerous left-handed lunge of the Bishop, by which he had before been robbed of victory when within his grasp, he took especial care not only to cover his vulnerable point, but to counteract Sharpe's plan by a move of the same sort himself. Thus we find him constantly pinking Bishop's body with his right, and so simultaneous were these efforts on both sides, that Alec's right hand often met Bishop's half-way. Alec's caution, his waiting for Bishop's rush, his judicious retreat, and rapid execution, right and left, when Bishop left his body unguarded, were beautiful; and our only surprise was, that, after such apparent mischief, Bishop was enabled to come up so steady and strong. Sharpe fought as brave as a lion, but his judgment was inferior when compared with Reid's. He fought wildly, and without discretion, although in the end, when he found the chances were against him, he had recourse to every manoeuvre to regain strength, and plant his favourite hit. His deliveries on Alec's nose with his left were very heavy, as was sufficiently visible, and Alec no doubt felt their weight, for his head presented a dreadful spectacle on that side where the blows told, and his mouth and eye were much swollen; indeed, so distressed did he appear towards the end of the fight, that Sharpe's friends to the last considered he had a chance, and the odds of three to one were offered with singular caution. It was not till Nature had deserted Bishop altogether that he struck, and his backers, though mortified, candidly confessed he could not have done more.

The conquest of the gallant but stale Dick Curtis by Perkins, the Oxford Pet, had rankled long in the minds of the London Fancy, although poor King Dick had fallen, not ingloriously, before superior weight, length, strength, and youth. It was thought that Alec would be a better match for him, and accordingly articles were signed for £100 a side, and the day fixed for the 25th May, 1830.

As a short notice of Perkins, and a detailed report of his victory over Curtis, will appear in the appendix of this Period, we shall not further dwell on his Ring career. Perkins had trained at Chipping Norton, and Reid paid every attention to getting himself fit at Burford, in Surrey; and so favourable were the accounts of his condition that he was freely backed at six to four by his old friends.

On the Monday before the battle the 'Varsity city was full of bustle and activity. The " Red Lion " and the " Anchor " were crowded by visitors anxious to get the " tip " as to the whereabouts. This was found to be the " Four-shire Stone," seven miles from Chipping Norton, at a point where the counties of Oxford, Warwick, Worcester, and Berks are conterminous. We may here note that on this occasion Reid fought under the *alias* of " Jack O'Brien," owing to his being held to bail for a period then unexpired, for being present at a mill in the neighbourhood of London. The battle is reported in *Bell's Life* as between " Perkins and Jack O'Brien."

By eleven o'clock Commissary Oliver and his lieutenant, " Fogo of the Frosty Face," had pitched the ring at the appointed rendezvous—it being surrounded by numerous undergrads, who had given the slip to " bulldogs " and "proctors " to attend the demonstration of craniology and the practical essay on " bumps " which Messrs. Reid and Perkins had prepared for their edification. At a little before twelve the Chelsea hero showed, waited on by Young Dutch Sam and Dick Curtis, the Oxonian quickly following, esquired by Harry Jones and Ned Stockman. Each man was heartily cheered. The colours, green with a crimson spot for Reid, and a fancy pink silk fogle for the Oxford Pet, were tied to the stakes. The whip-bearers of the "Fair Play Club" preserved an unbroken ring, and everything was arranged with regularity and order. The toss for choice of position was won for Perkins. The men shook hands, the seconds and bottle-holders retired to their respective corners, and the men, toeing the scratch, threw up their daddles and began

THE FIGHT.

Round 1.—Both appeared in excellent condition, but Reid had the advantage in weight, being 10st. 7lb., while Perkins was 10st. 3lb. This difference was not so obvious as they stood opposed to each other, although it might tell in the end; indeed, a more equal match as to size could scarce be imagined. A manly firmness sat on the brow of each, and everything like personal animosity seemed banished from their minds. No sooner had the seconds and bottle-holders retired than the Snob showed his determination to lose not a moment in bringing the enemy to action. Covering his points well, he advanced, and made slight play left and right; the Pet, awake, stopped these efforts with great neatness. The Snob tried the same manœuvre a second time; but the Pet again stopped and got away. He had not much time to deliberate, however, before Reid popped in his left on the "mark;" he tried his right at the nob at the same time, but it was "no go." A bustling, active rally followed, good stopping was observable on both sides, and slight exchanges took place. In the end the Snob caught the Pet on the jowl with his left, and dropped him, although the blow was not delivered with decisive force; still, this was booked as the first knockdown, and Reid was loudly cheered.

2.—The Chelsea hero again all activity, the Pet cautious. The Snob's first one two stopped, but his left was once more at the victualling office. In return, the Pet caught his opponent a nasty one on the muzzle, swelling his lips, and leading to a cry of "first blood;" but it was so slight, if at all to be seen, that he contrived to hide it from observation. A slashing rally followed, and the left-handed counters were beautiful—both "napping it" with considerable force. Reid had rather the advantage in the onslaught, but in following up his man the Pet went down, amidst cheers from his friends.

3.—The Snob first to fight, and all bustle in his operations; the Pet, cautious, stopped his one two. Perkins received a clinker on

the left ear, and first blood was visible beneath, while the ear was puffed; this was declared as unequivocal of the second event for the Snob. The Oxonian, all alive, met the Snob's attack, stopping his right, but catching his left slap in the muzzle, the Snob had it in return with equal force. The Snob put in a left-hand body hit, and got away. Returning again to the charge, he found the Pet armed at all points. The Pet retreated, stopping Reid's right and left with admirable precision, and ultimately going down without a blow, upon the cautious system.

4.—Reid, first to fight, popped in a left-handed job on the potato trap, ditto on the ogle. The Pet saw the defensive would not do, and fought a spirited rally; the exchanges were quick and effectual—hit followed hit with electric rapidity, and each dropped claret—the Pet from the mouth, Reid from the conk. The scientific stopping on both sides during this rally was first-rate. The Snob tried his body hit with the left, but was short; the Pet smiled and got away. Reid would not be denied, but went merrily to his man; there was no getting away, and to it they went "ding-dong." The counter-hits were numerous, and the stops equally so. The Pet put in a body hit with his right —but with both men most punishment was given with the left, and neither spared his opponent. In the end Perkins went down hitting, Reid smiling defiance.

5.—Good stopping right and left by both; the Snob stuck to his work, and countering was the order of the day. Perkins retreated, followed closely by Reid, who kept hitting away, when Perkins dropped on one knee, and put up his hand; Reid withheld a falling blow, though entitled to hit, and retired amidst the cheers of his friends.

6.—The Chelsea champion put in his left on the Oxford man's nozzle, which was uncorked. He then went in boldly to punish, but the Pet dropped and smiled. (Cries of "Stand up!" and "Foul!")

7.—The Snob, all alive, went to work, and

put in a left-handed muzzler. The Pet returned the compliment. Heavy hits exchanged, but the Pet had the worst of it, and again went down amidst the grumbling of the Snob's friends. (Ten pounds to five on Reid.)

8.—The Snob made play right and left—the first stopped, the second successful. Perkins returned heavily with his left; good counter-hitting, the science of both exciting general admiration. Perkins rather cautious, but Reid would be at work, and rattled in; more fine counter-hitting, and a spirited rally—the hitting was slashing. The Pet was hit down with a slinging hit over the right eye, which exhibited a gaping wound, but the Snob had it almost as heavily on the smeller, and fell on his hands and knees; both bleeding.

9.—Good fighting on both sides, but Reid had the advantage of strength. The Pet retreated before him, stopping, but caught it again on the right eye and on the cheek beneath, where an old wound was opened. Reid put in his favourite left-handed bodier, but caught a nose-ender in return. Perkins retreated, but was all alive, and popped in a jobbing hit with his left, and threw in his right on the Snob's neck. The Chelsea man returned fiercely, hitting right and left, when the Pet fell on his hands and knees.

10.—Reid, all alive, planted his left on the body; counter-hits on the mazzard, and neat stopping. Perkins went down on his knees. (More grumbling from Reid's friends.)

11.—Both showed strong marks of punishment. The Snob went to work, and cut away in good style; Perkins popped in his right at the body, but had it in return on the nob. Spirited rally. Reid again tapped at the victualling office of the Pet, and after good counter-hitting Perkins, on the retreat, went down.

12.—Perkins put in a right-hander on the throat of Reid, and stopped a counter-hit with his left; left-hand exchanges; the Pet went down. (Cries of "Shame!" from the friends of Reid.)

13.—The Pet cautious, and on the defensive; Reid went to him; good scientific stops right and left; excellent counter-hitting; the Londoner had it heavy on the grinders. (Shouts for Oxford.) A pretty active rally, hits pro and con., and Perkins slipped down.

14.—Perkins made play; Reid, ready at all points, tried to bring his man to a rally, but the Pet, after stopping some severe hits, went down on one hand and knee.

15.—Sharp jobbing right and left on both sides; heavy deliveries right and left from the Snob; claret in abundance; hit and hit; Perkins down; but the Snob, though vexed at his man dropping, stepped away, and smiled.

16.—A fine, manly rally; blows followed blows in quick succession, and both received

pepper. In the end Perkins down, Reid, for the first time, upon him.

17.—The Pet still strong and confident. Reid delivered his left at the carcass, and got away. A rally; Perkins went down stopping.

18.—Fine fighting; Perkins on the retreat, Alec with him in good style. Severe exchanges, Perkins down—both distilling the purple fluid.

19.—Severe deliveries from Reid, and some neat returns. The Snob had the best of the fighting; the Pet down.

20.—Stopping at starting, but Reid would not be denied—fought with quickness. The Pet, retreating, was down, after some pretty returns, but he had the worst of the game, and was somewhat on the piping order.

21.—The Chelsea hero hit his man down with the left in good style, and became more jolly.

22.—Reid, all activity, planted his left on the body and broke away. Perkins went to work, and the fighting was beautiful while it lasted; but Perkins went down on both knees. His opponent withheld his falling blow, and looked mortified at this cautious system.

23.—Heavy jobbing; both received and returned, and were the worse for their work; Perkins floored.

24.—Merry milling, good countering; Perkins retreated. Reid bored him to the ropes, hit away, and fell upon him.

25.—The Pet's left cheek cut with a slashing hit—claret in a stream. Perkins did not flinch, fought to a rally, but was dropped.

26.—Reid showed symptoms of fatigue, but still merry. Hit left and right, the Pet down.

27, 28, 29.—Good fighting rounds, heavy exchanges, but Perkins down in every round.

30.—Reid planted his left and right with great force; Perkins made a neat return with his left on Alec's muzzle, but was hit down with a left-handed teazer. Reid smiled, and clapped him on the back as he was on his knees.

31.—Perkins was again hit down. (A heavy shower of rain now came on, during which there was a little confusion from a supposition that certain constables were breaking into the ring to save the Pet from defeat, but this proved to be a false alarm. The men in the interim fought with great spirit, and the hitting and stopping was kept up with great vigour, with pretty equal advantage. The Pet, however, was always down.)

37.—Tremendous rally. The deliveries on both sides perfect shakers, and the Pet rather the best of the hitting. (Shouts from the Gownsmen, and betting rather in favour among Perkins's friends, but little done.)

38.—Reid again took the lead, but was courageously met. After a sharp rally, the Pet was hit down with a left-handed smack in the throttle. (Loud applause from the Londoners, and the odds again firm in Reid's favour.)

39.—Both distressed, but game as lions. Hit away right and left, no mistake as to intention. Perkins floored with a left-handed job.

40.—Reid all life and confidence, the Pet "nothing loth." Hit for hit left and right at the nobs. Perkins rushed to in-fighting, napped it as he came in, but gave the uppercut. Reid down. (Renewed cheers from the "Gownsmen," and Perkins's friends still confident.)

41.—Science well exhibited by both. The stopping excellent. Counter-hitting. The Pet down. (The referee cautioned Perkins to make "a stand-up fight," when he exclaimed "the grass was so slippery he could not help going down." At this time, from the heavy rain, which had now subsided, there was some cause for the excuse.)

42.—Reid was again busy with the Pet's bread-basket with his left. A slashing rally; good exchanges. In a close Perkins down, Reid on top of him.

43.—Reid, all gaiety, though wofully disfigured in the mug, went to his man, popped in left and right, and in the end Perkins, after a few exchanges, went down.

44.—No time wasted—good stand-up fighting, but the Pet getting weak. ("Take him away!" said the "Gownsmen." "No," said Sam, "he does not often dine at an ordinary; let him have a skinful.") The Pet down.

45 and 46.—The mischief pretty equal, and the fighting excellent. Perkins down in both rounds.

47.—A desperate rally; both did their best; the Pet hit down, but Reid also fell on his hands and knees, rather weak.

48.—Perkins's right eye was now completely closed, and his left looked queer. Reid went in to finish, but was manfully met; still Perkins had the worst of the fighting, and was hit down.

49.—Reid all gaiety, and again fresh; the Pet steady, but dreadfully punished in the phiz. The Londoner made play, and hit away right and left, the latter on the body. Perkins met him on the nose with his left, but in the return was hit down with a left-handed job.

50.—Reid was now the favourite at long odds, but the Pet's game did not desert him; his heart was still in the right place, and he made a desperate effort to redeem his falling fortune. Reid, however, was too strong, and dropped him with a left-handed touch in the physog. The Pet fell forward on his face weak.

51, 52, and 53.—All in favour of Reid, though Perkins did wonders, and fought with unshrinking courage. In the last round he fell on his knees, resting on his adversary's shoulder. Reid smiled, patted him on the shoulder, and walked away. (Cries of "Take him away!")

54, and last.—The Oxford man came up to make a last effort, but it was evidently all over. Still he did his best—made some weak returns to slashing hits, and at last received the *coup-de-grace*; he fell, but gloriously, and his seconds, thinking he had had enough, gave in for him, the fight having lasted exactly an hour. Both men were heavily punished. Reid walked to his carriage amidst the cheers of his "pals," and Perkins, having recovered from his temporary doze, rose soon after and followed his example, terribly mortified in spirit as well as altered in frontispiece.

REMARKS.—This was one of the best and fairest mills on record, and was throughout full of bustle and spirit. Reid, though not quite up to the mark of former times, was all his friends had a right to anticipate. He was active, vigorous, and quick, and never threw a chance away, save on one or two occasions, when Perkins slipped down intentionally, and when he might have been hit, but his opponent generously withheld his blows. This added to his credit; but it is due to say he suffered severely for his victory, and was heavily punished in the counter-hitting. The Oxford man fully maintained his fame, and although beaten fell gloriously before his superior in strength and weight, if not much so in science. Such was the equality of mischief in some of the latest struggles in the fight that there was no certainty till the fiftieth round; and on two or three occasions Perkins was the favourite with his friends, and backed at odds. With the exception of going down too often on the cautious system there was no fault to be found with the Oxford hero; and even this, though not consistent with the idea of "stand-up fighting," was justifiable in point of good generalship. In fact, it was impossible for a beaten man to have done more to deserve the respect and approval of his backers.

About a week before the fight, Reid, in a foolhardy experiment to show how he would muzzle his antagonist, struck his knuckles against a door, and swelled up his hand; but from this piece of folly he sufficiently recovered not to show its effects. On the night after the fight both men showed at their respective headquarters at Oxford, and exhibited heavy marks of the conflict of the morning. The University city was all bustle and commotion, and both pleased and displeased had enough to say on the subject

Tom Spring, Gully, Phil Sampson, Tom Gaynor, and several of the old school of boxers were on the ground, and resolutely assisted in preserving order.

This was Alec Reid's last occasion of exhibiting as a principal in the Ring. For some years he was a well-known exhibitor and teacher of the art in the London schools. In his latter days, being afflicted with paralysis in the left arm and side, he sunk into a sort of master of the ceremonies at boxing benefits, his civility of manner and respectful courtesy enabling him to earn a humble crust. For some years he was a room manager at Nat Langham's, old friends, who remembered his game conduct and honest manliness, often lending him support in occasional benefits. Reid died in comparative poverty and obscurity in 1875, in his seventy-third year.

CHAPTER XI.

BISHOP SHARPE ("THE BOLD SMUGGLER").
1818—1826.

BISHOP SHARPE, once a seaman in His Majesty's navy, and subsequently known as a "long-shore man" in the neighbourhood of Woolwich, was as tough a specimen of the material of which our "old salts" were made as even Jack Scroggins himself.

Of the early career of Bishop Sharpe we have but little reliable account. He beat two unknowns, named Lester and the "Deptford Carrier," and in his first recorded battle, on the 24th September, 1818, conquered Bob Hall in forty-five rounds, occupying fifty-five minutes, at Woolwich, after a determined contest. Battles with minor pugilists, in all of which he was successful, spread his fame. These we shall pass with a mere enumeration. On March 24th, 1819. he met. and defeated. on Woolwich Marshes, Dick Prior in twenty-five rounds, thirty-five minutes, for £25. In December, 1819, he beat John Street (an opponent of Josh Hudson), in one hundred rounds, 105 minutes, near Charlton, Kent. In February, 1820, John King surrendered to the Bishop in twenty-five minutes, during which twenty-five sharp rounds were fought, for £25 a side, at Plumstead.

The contest between the "Bold Smuggler" and the "Slashing Gipsy," as Jack Cooper was called, took place for £50 a side, at the Old Maypole, in Epping Forest, on Tuesday, June 17th, 1823. The patricians of the West in the days of the Fourth George, as a general rule, were greatly averse to a ride over the London stones to witness any fight in North Kent or Essex. But the fame of the Gipsy, who had conquered every boxer opposed to him—West Country Dick, O'Leary, Dent, Scroggins, and Cabbage had succumbed—and the character for determination and lasting which had run before the Bishop, had travelled westward, and proved such an attraction that quite an aristocratic surrounding witnessed the merry mill.

The Old Maypole, as we have already said, was the rallying point, and the situation chosen to make the ring was delightfully picturesque. At a few minutes past one Sharpe, in a white wrapper and a yellowman, arm-in-arm with the John Bull Fighter, threw his beaver into the ring, followed by Phil Sampson. The Gipsy shortly afterwards appeared, in a blue coat, with a blue handkerchief round his neck, and repeated the token of defiance. Spring and Richmond were seconds for Cooper, and Hudson and Sampson officiated for Sharpe. Spring and Hudson tied the colours to the stakes, and betting was five to four on the Gipsy. The latter boxer, according to report, had the advantage in weight of eight pounds.

THE FIGHT.

Round 1.—Sharpe, immediately on shaking hands, appeared in a hurry to go to work, and made play with his opponent. The left hand of Sharpe told slightly. The Gipsy retreated. Some blows were exchanged, when, in closing, a severe struggle took place; Sharpe had the best of the throw, and the Gipsy was undermost. (Great shouting for Sharpe.)

2.—The right eye of Cooper was winking from a slight hit. Sharpe was confident, and the Gipsy retreated from him; the latter, at length, made himself up, and with a right-handed lunging hit he made Sharpe stagger, and he also went down on one knee, but jumped up again immediately. ("Well done, Cooper!")

3.—Both ready—both offering—the Gipsy retreating, and Sharpe following. In closing, the Gipsy got the throw

4 to 7.—A very small tinge of the claret appeared on the Gipsy's lips. Sharpe rushed in, bored the Gipsy to the ropes, and threw him.

8 to 13.—Their blows did no execution—at least, they did not appear effective. It was bloodless up to the close of this round.

14.—Cooper showed off a little in his usual style in this round; he nobbed Sharpe, and also gave him a severe cross-buttock. ("It is of no use," cried Joah. "I have seconded Bishop seven times, and none of the coves could ever make a mark upon him.")

15 and 16.—Sharpe received a heavy blow under his listener, and went down.

17 to 26.—In the 25th round, Sharpe napped pepper, and the claret trickled down his face. ("I have fetched it at last," said Cooper to Sharpe, laughing; "and plenty more will soon follow." "Don't be too fast," replied Sharpe, putting in at the same time a severe blow on the Gipsy's throat. The latter, however, bored Sharpe down.)

27 to 37.—The friends of the Gipsy felt quite at ease that he would win the battle; and the partisans of Sharpe were equally confident, asserting that "he could not lose it." Yet the Gipsy did not make use of his severe right-handed hit, and kept always retreating from his opponent. The superiority of Sharpe in this round was so decisive, and his conduct so generous and manly, as to receive thunders of applause from every spectator round the ring. Sharpe hit the Gipsy so severely that the latter in retreating got between the ropes. Sharpe disdained to take advantage of this opportunty (what Randall would have termed giving a chance away), and walked back into the middle of the ring, beckoning with his hand for Cooper to follow him. Some exchanges took place, and the Gipsy received a heavy fall.

38 to 44.—Sometimes Sharpe had the best of it; at other times Cooper kept his friends in good humour; but nothing decisive appeared on either side as to victory; and several of the old ring-goers murmured that so little execution had been done, either by the tremendous hitting Gipsy or the heavy punishing Sharpe.

45, 46, 47.—In these rounds certain symptoms appeared that the Gipsy was going off, or, in plain terms, that he had had the worst of it; five to two, by way of chaffing, was offered against Cooper. Martin came up to the Gipsy while sitting on his second's knee, and told him, if he won it, he should have £50, at the same time offering to back Cooper for £50.

48, 49, 50.—In the last round the Gipsy was bored to the ropes by the hitting of Sharpe, and also thrown heavily. ("It is all your own way, Sharpe; go in and finish him.")

51.—A severe struggle at the ropes, and Sharpe went down.

52.—The Gipsy was hit down. The Sharpites outrageous in their applause and gestures. ("It is as safe as the day.")

53.—The hitting of the Gipsy was gone, and his right hand appeared of no use to him.

Here Spring whispered to Cooper "to use his right hand, and he must win it." "I cannot use it," replied the Gipsy; "I have hurt my shoulder." The Gipsy fibbed down at the ropes. Another tremendous shout for Sharpe.

54.—The nob of the Gipsy appeared punished severely, and his right eye was out. Both down.

55.—Sharpe now took great liberties with the head of his opponent, and fell upon him so heavily as nearly to shake the wind out of him.

56, and last.—This was short and sweet to Sharpe; he hit Cooper down, and when time was called victory was declared in favour of Bishop Sharpe. The battle occupied one hour twenty-five minutes.

REMARKS.—The judges called the above mill a bad fight—a long innings, and but little to show for it. The face of Sharpe had scarcely a mark upon it; and the Gipsy said "he was not hurt." A medical man on the ground examined the shoulder of the Gipsy, and he pronounced "the clavicle to be fractured." (Of course, this sounded more learned than to say "the collar-bone was broken.") This fracture prevented the Gipsy from lifting his arm without experiencing a grinding of the bones, producing great pain. If the Gipsy had taken the lead instead of retreating from his adversary, it was thought he must have won it. Cooper missed several blows, and at various times did not follow up his success. This was observable in the tenth round, the ninth being a guinea to a shilling in his favour.

A second match with Jack Cooper was fought by Sharpe at Harpenden Common, on the 5th of August, 1823, with the like result, Sharpe proving conqueror in thirty-nine minutes, during which Cooper fought thirty rushing rounds. The two battles were so similar that a reprint would be mere repetition. At Blackheath Sharpe and Cooper met a third time, on November 14th, in the same year, for £100, and fought a draw, daylight closing in on the undecided contest.

On the 10th of May, 1825, Sharpe, after an absence of some twelve months in his seafaring occupation, got on a match for £25 a side with an aspirant, one Ben Warwick, whom the Bold Smuggler polished off after a one-sided battle of considerable obstinacy in twenty-five minutes, being, as many said, at the rate of a sov. per minute. As Mr. Warwick, to whose credit some previous conquests of outsiders are placed, never again sported canvas in the P.R., we shall not report the battle.

Sharpe, by his victories over Cooper and his drawn battle with Alec Reid, already noticed, encouraged his friends to seek what was expected to be a decisive match with his scientific adversary the Chelsea Snob, more especially as the latter had in the interval beaten Jack Cooper, Jubb, and Savage. The stakes of £100 were made good, and on the 6th of September, 1826, the men met at the renowned battlefield of No Man's Land, in Hertfordshire.

The "Bishop" set up his training quarters at the "Castle," Highgate, while Reid took his breathings on Putney Heath, patronising the "Green Man." In point of age Reid had the advantage, being twenty-four, while Sharpe numbered thirty summers. In the former fight the odds were quoted at six to four on Reid, but on this occasion five to four were laid on the Smuggler. On the Tuesday morning the lads of "the long village" were astir as early as five o'clock, and a lively succession of vehicles bowled along the great North Road.

When Reid met Sharpe in their first battle he complained, and not without reason, of the neglect of his backers. In the present case he had cause to be grateful for their attention. Every possible care was taken of him during his training, and preparations were made for taking him into the ring in "bang-up style." His crimson favours were distributed liberally among his friends, and a dashing barouche and four, the post-boys wearing crimson satin jackets, and the horses' heads decorated with crimson cockades, was prepared to carry him to the ground. Nothing was omitted which could add to his confidence, or give importance to the contest. A favourite candidate for a popular election could not have entered the field under more dashing auspices.

Shortly before one the men arrived on the ground, and soon after appeared within the stakes. Reid took the lead, accompanied by his backers, and Tom Cribb and Ben Burn as his second and bottle-holder. He was soon afterwards followed by Sharpe, who was waited upon by Josh Hudson and Peter Crawley. A trifling shower threw a slight gloom over the assembled multitude, but this soon ceased, and the remainder of the afternoon was favourable.

The men immediately peeled for action. They both seemed well; but it was thought the Bishop might have been better. The confidence of his backers, nevertheless, was unshaken, and in a very short time the odds were decidedly five to four in his favour. These odds were freely taken by some, but not so freely by many of the professed friends of Reid as might have been anticipated.

THE FIGHT.

Round 1.—On taking their positions, the Bishop, as usual, stood with his right leg foremost, presenting rather an awkward appearance. He did not deal long in postures, however, for he lost not a moment in going to work. He let fly right and left at Reid's head, but was prettily stopped. Both now set to with activity, and a spirited rally followed, in which the Bishop planted his left on Reid's frontispiece with great success. The Snob was awake, and countered slightly, but Sharpe was too sharp for him, and following up his bustling system, after a few interchanges, put in a tremendous left-handed clink on Reid's proboscis, drawing first blood. In the close Bishop was hit down, and on being placed on his second's knee, showed a trifling mark on his left eye. (Shouts from the East Enders.)

2.—Reid came up merry, but he was not allowed much time for reflection; the Bishop again went to work as if he meant mischief. Also was ready, and successfully stopped his desperate left-handed hits. Another rally followed, in which facers were interchanged, but Reid had the worst of the hitting, and was again thrown, receiving before he went down two severe hits on the nose, from which a fresh flow of claret was extracted, and a trifling wound inflicted on its bridge. The confidence of the Bishop's friends was increased, and their joy loudly expressed, while the Chelsea lads looked blue,

3.—Reid came up like the gory ghost of Banquo, but he was still jolly. The Bishop renewed his active system, and tried a left-handed lunge at Reid's body. He was well stopped, and Reid delivered on his mouth and nose. The Bishop rushed to in-fighting, but Reid was awake, and hit him heavily on the body. The Bishop staggered, but instantly returned to his man, and a desperate rally followed, to the advantage of the Bishop, who hit his antagonist right and left, and dropped him heavily. (Six to four on the Bishop.)

4.—Reid came up nothing abashed, but the Bishop was soon with him, and attempted his favourite left-handed job. Reid stopped him, but he would not be kept off, and hit right and left, while the Snob countered with great severity, and gave him a gash under his right eye. At last the Bishop rushed to a close, and Reid was thrown. (Two to one offered from all parts of the ring on the Bishop.)

5.—On coming to the scratch the Bishop showed the effects of Reid's last visitation to his phiz. Reid seemed to derive fresh spirit from this proof of his talent, and a desperate and courageous rally followed. The Bishop's fearful attempts with his left were well stopped, and Reid put in two severe jobbing hits, right and left, which made a cutting impression. The Bishop was astounded, and Reid, seeing his advantage, lost no time in following up his handiwork; he pursued the Bishop, who retreated on the defensive, and repeated his blows; a fierce rally followed, in which there was some sharp counter-hitting, but at last the Bishop was hit down in admirable style. (An instant change took place in the betting, and from the distress exhibited by the Bishop, Reid was loudly cheered, and two to one offered in his favour. Many of the backers of the Bishop, in fact, forthwith commenced hedging.)

6.—Both came up steady, but Reid was the more confident. The Bishop was rather abroad, and his right eye began to close. Reid now took the lead in fighting, but he found the Bishop ready, and after a short rally Reid retreated. This ruse had the desired effect. The Bishop followed him, and as he came in Reid met him severely with the right and left. The Bishop bored him towards the ropes with wildness, while Reid, with great quickness, repeated his *primâ facie* compliments. In the close both went down, Reid under.

7.—Reid still a decided favourite, and two to one freely offered. He came up with apparent confidence, and planted a left-handed jobber on Sharpe's nob. Sharpe attempted in return to hit with his left, but was well stopped. A short rally followed, in which the Bishop napped it right and left; but in the close he threw Reid, and fell upon him.

8.—Sharpe came up looking serious, and the worse for wear; Reid was ready and active, and on Sharpe's rushing to in-fighting, got away, stopping as he retreated; but at last put in a severe left-handed slap on Sharpe's face. A close followed, and after a short struggle for the fall, both went down, Reid under.

9.—Sharpe came up a little on the piping order, but forthwith went to work. Reid stopped him as he advanced, and in getting away slipped down.

10.—Reid put in a teazer on Sharpe's body, and jumped away; Sharpe followed him up, but Reid pursued his retreating system, and in the close both went down.

11.—Both came up distressed, but Reid was the fresher, and taking prompt advantage of Sharpe's situation, he put in five or six tremendous blows on his nob, till at length the Bishop went down weak from want of breath. This was an excellent round as far as Reid was concerned, and showed his marked superiority in science. (Two to one on Reid. Josh thought his man was in Queer Street, and gave the office to an old pal, who offered his two to one in all directions in favour of Reid.)

12.—Sharpe came up groggy, and rushed at Reid for the close. Both went down by the ropes, and as Reid got up he patted Sharpe goodhumouredly on the shoulder. (Four to one on Reid, and but few takers.)

13.—Sharpe was brought to the scratch somewhat more steady. He made several attempts to deliver his left on Reid's body, but Reid got away. Sharpe at last delivered right and left handed facers, and received a poser in return from Reid's left. He then rushed to a close, and a scrambling scuffle took place at the ropes, when both went down; and Reid again patted Sharpe on the shoulder, as if in compassionate consideration of his approaching defeat.

14.—Reid came up fresh, and on the alert. Sharpe seemed to have become more cautious. Reid fought first, and caught him a jobbing hit with his left on the dexter ogle. Sharpe hit short at Reid's body with his left. Reid jumped away. Blows interchanged with mutual advantage. Sharpe succeeded in putting in a slight body blow; and on closing both went down, Reid under.

15.—Reid still the fresher man. Sharpe came up with boldness, and commenced by hitting short at Reid's body; Reid got away; but returning to the assault, caught Sharpe heavily with his left on the nob. Sharpe again tried his body blow, but failed; and on Reid rushing to close fighting, he went down on the safe system. This was looked upon as an indication of cutting it, and the odds were again freely offered on Reid.

16.—Both men came up determined on mischief. Sharpe tried his left and right at Reid's head, but found him at home; but at last, watching his opportunity, he succeeded in effecting that which he had so often attempted—namely, in catching Reid a tremendous blow in the wind. The effect was alarming; Reid was doubled up in an instant, and fell. Cribb, with great quickness, placed him on Ben Burn's knee, and pushing his head in his stomach to stop his bellows, succeeded in bringing him to the scratch when time was called. He was, however, very groggy, and his friends began to anticipate that their hopes were at an end, and the betting became even.

17.—Sharpe, seeing the powerful effects of his last blow, instantly prepared to take advantage of his good fortune, while Tom Owen loudly called upon him to repeat the dose in the same place. Reid, however, to the astonishment of the ring, stopped the intended finisher, and countered well with his left. After a short rally Sharpe went down, while Reid had nearly recovered the effects of the previous round.

18.—Sharpe again attempted to throw in his right and left at Reid's body, but Reid got away cleverly. Reid, who was now "himself again," pursued Sharpe with an apparent determination to make a decisive impression, when Sharpe went down without a blow, thereby exciting a strong expression of displeasure on the part of Reid's friends.

19.—Both men came up steady. Reid lost no time in going to work, and after some good counter-hitting Sharpe closed, and threw Reid cleverly. Even betting was the order of the day—Reid for choice.

20.—Sharpe hit short at Reid's body. Reid attempted to place a left-handed job on Sharpe's head, when the latter, having crept close, let fly with his left at a well-judged distance, caught him under the ribs, and he dropped as if he had been shot, drawing up his legs apparently in agony. The veteran Tom was again at his elbow, lifted him, as before, on Ben Burn's knee, but he was not equally successful. Reid continued to writhe, as in great pain, and on "time" being called, being unable to go to the scratch, Sharpe, to the surprise of some, the joy of others, and the mortification of many, was declared the victor. Sharpe was immediately conducted out of the ring, and Reid was conveyed to his carriage, where he soon after recovered, and was subsequently enabled to walk about the heath but little the worse for his defeat; his punishment, in fact, was not so great as that of Sharpe. The fight lasted twenty-four minutes.

REMARKS.—By this fight it may be supposed that the comparative merits of Reid and Sharpe have been fairly decided, but this is by no means a general opinion, for it was openly stated, and boldly asserted by Reid himself, that but for the accidental blow which prevented his coming to time, he would certainly have won the battle; and when the game which he displayed in his late fight with Gaynor is considered it is only a matter of surprise that he should have been so soon and suddenly brought to a standstill. He declared that for some time the effects of the blow rendered him utterly incapable of exertion. Having thus experienced the nature of the Bishop's tactics, however, he says he feels satisfied that he could in future guard against them, and render victory certain. In the present instance, it is the opinion of the best judges that Reid has shown himself the better fighter; but he is blamed for not taking more advantage of the opportunities which Sharpe afforded him, by leaving his head unguarded while aiming at his body. Indeed, it is thought that if he had been awake to this, and met him as he came in, there could have been no doubt of the issue of the contest. It is pretty clear that Sharpe, in all his battles, never met with such an adversary before, and that he had the worst of it is obvious from his own friends' betting two to one against him. It is said, however, that it is difficult to tell when he is beaten, and that at all times he is a dangerous customer. This character he has maintained on the present occasion, and he has also shown that his reputation for courage is well founded. The backers of Reid immediately declared their readiness to match him again against Sharpe, if the Smuggler should be disposed for another shy, a proof of their implicit belief in his honesty.

This victory placed Sharpe in the foremost rank among the middle-weight boxers of the day, and as Tom Gaynor had recently engaged with and beaten the same man, the Chelsea Snob, with great difficulty, while the Bishop had polished him off (so said his friends) with much more ease, a line was taken by which the Bishop's superiority over Gaynor was assumed. Not so thought the admirers of the Bath Carpenter. They considered the match "a good thing" for Tom, so they closed at once with the proposal, and posted their half-hundred readily, fixing the day for the 5th of December, 1826, and the trysting-place at No Man's Land, Herts. There, however, a move was necessary, owing to a magisterial interference, and a move was accordingly made into Bedfordshire. At Shere Mere, on the ground where Sampson and Jem Burn settled their difference, at two o'clock, the men met in battle array. Sharpe was attended by Josh Hudson and the veteran Tom Owen, while Gaynor had the services of Harry Holt and Tom Oliver. The colours being tied to the stakes, the men shook hands smilingly, the seconds retired to their corners, and the combatants held up their daddles for

THE FIGHT.

Round 1.—On standing up the contrast in condition was evident, and alarmed the layers of the odds of five to four on Gaynor, so that they went round to six to four on the Bishop, who looked hard, ruddy, and confident, while Gaynor was sallow, and bore the traces of a recent indisposition. After a few seconds spent in sparring, Sharpe let fly his left at Gaynor's ribs, but missed, and swung round. Gaynor immediately closed, and threw him on his back, missing a good chance of punishing his man.

2.—Sharpe short with the right, Gaynor shifting quickly. Gaynor missed his counter-hit, and got it on the cheek. Sharpe closed, and there was a struggle for the fall; Gaynor was thrown. (Shouting for the Bishop.)

3.—Gaynor put in a slight nobber with his left; Sharpe, all alive, let go his favourite body hit, catching Gaynor a sounder on the mark; Gaynor returned on the chin, but could not keep his man out, who gave him another heavy bodier and closed, but failed in getting the fall; Sharpe undermost.

4.—A scrambling round; wild hitting on both sides; Sharpe under.

5.—Sharpe, quick and ready, got in right and left on Gaynor's head, but with little visible effect; both down in the close.

6.—Sharpe bustled in: Gaynor shifted; Sharpe put in a left-hander, which Gaynor countered with the right on the Bishop's mouth. Sharpe bored in, and sent a pile-driver on Gaynor's ribs with such effect as to floor him instantly. (First knock-down for Sharpe.)

7.—The Bishop, brisk as a bee, forced the fighting, then closed, and had Tom down in a scramble.

8.—The Bishop fought rather wildly; Gaynor twice stopped his left, when Sharpe closed, and threw him, falling himself through the ropes.

9.—The marks of the body blows received by Gaynor were very visible, and his countenance showed they troubled him much in the freedom of his action. Still he was cheerful and ready. Sharpe missed a left-hander at the body, and Gaynor retorted with a sharp cutting hit over the Bishop's right eye, which brought forth the claret instantly. (Cheers, and "first blood" for Gaynor.)

10.—Gaynor in the exchanges got in two more hits on the cheek, drawing more of the crimson; a short rally; both down.

11.—Both men slipped from the moist state of the ground. The Bishop rushed to a close, and threw Gaynor cleverly.

12.—Sharpe a little piping, but gay, lost no time in getting to work; after an exchange he got his man firmly, and threw him a heavy back fall.

13.—Gaynor came up laughing, delivered a slight facer, closed, and threw the Bishop cleverly. ("Bravo!" from Tom's friends.)

14.—The Bishop tried twice for Gaynor's body, and after some sparring, sent in a straight one at the mark. The blow told with terrific effect, doubling up Gaynor, who fell.

15.—Gaynor came up pale and serious, but game and steady. The Bishop, stopped twice, rushed in, closed, and threw his man.

16.—Sharpe put in a light body blow, but napped it sharply on the canister; Gaynor caught the Bishop twice in the head, but his blows did not seem to tell; he also got Sharpe down in the close.

17.—A wrestling round; both down from the slippery state of the ground.

18.—Gaynor, busy, put in two or three toppers on the Bishop's nob, who at last got in a straight one on Gaynor's throat, flooring him instantly. (Shouts for the Bishop.)

19.—A good rally and exchanges. Sharpe twice on Gaynor's jaw and neck; Tom on the Bishop's eyes and mouth, which were considerably painted. Both down.

20.—Sharpe still trying for the body, Tom feeling for the head; in the rally Sharpe gave Gaynor a severe hit in the mouth, and Tom went backward through the ropes.

21-38.—In all these rounds a similar style of fighting was pursued, each man gallantly coming to the scratch, the hitting being nearly equal, and most of the rounds ending by Sharpe gaining the throw.

39.—A busy round of rather longer duration. Gaynor tried his best for a turn. He fought with both hands at the head, disregarding the Bishop's 'unges, and finally threw him heavily. (Tom's friends cheered, but it was clear that the Bishop was the fresher man.)

40.—Gaynor came up shaky. A wrestling round. Both down, Gaynor undermost.

41-53.—Gaynor, though contesting every round, did not seem to hit effectively, while Sharpe's frequent misses and short blows at the body were equally indecisive. Each round ended in a scramble, but the slippery mud, for such it was, foiled their efforts. In the 53rd round Sharpe, by the advice of old Tom Owen, changed his tactics, and commenced fighting at Gaynor's upper works with his left. He soon after succeeded in putting in a chattering hit on Tom's ivories, closed, and threw him out of the ropes.

54.—Gaynor came slowly from his second's knee at the call of "time." In a rally the Bishop got him down. (A pigeon was here let off for town, announcing the winning of the fight by Sharpe, in 54 rounds. To the general surprise, Gaynor jumped up briskly at the call of "time.")

55.—Gaynor rallied all his energies. He let go his left, catching Sharpe lightly on the nose; a good rally followed; Sharpe slipped in delivering a blow, and fell. (Cries of "Gaynor's not beaten yet!")

56.—Another good fighting round on the part of Gaynor; some good exchanges; Gaynor got Sharpe down and fell on him.

57.—Gaynor made several lunges at Sharpe's nob, but missed; in the close Sharpe's superior strength was shown in the style in which he lifted and threw Gaynor.

58-72.—Gaynor, willing but weak, came up in all these rounds with less and less chance of pulling through. In the 68th round Sharpe again hit Gaynor down by a blow on the throat. (In the 72nd round a quarrel took place between Harry Holt and Tom Owen, in consequence of some over-zeal of Harry towards his principal. Owen pushed Harry, who in return sportively knocked off Owen's stupendous Jolliffe hat. This indignity to the "Sage of the East" was "most intolerable, and not to be endured," so he administered a back-hander to the irreverent Orator, whereupon a merry skirmish followed. Josh Hudson, however, interposed, stopped the bye-battle, and the belligerents went back to their men, who had fought out the round during this supplementary set-to.)

73-78.—In all these rounds poor Gaynor received the larger share of the punishment, but would not say "no," though advised to give in by his seconds. In the 78th round Sharpe caught Gaynor a flush hit in the mouth, and he dropped. This was the finisher, and poor Tom was alike deaf to the call of "time" and the cheering of the victorious Bishop's partisans. Sharpe walked firmly across the ring and possessed himself of the colours, placing them round his neck with evident satisfaction. Gaynor remained for a short time in a sort of stupor, but soon recovered himself, and returned to town the same night.

REMARKS.—That the fighting was fast, may be told from the fact that seventy-eight rounds were got through in one hour and ten minutes. They were, however, in almost every instance terminated by a close. Indeed, there was as much wrestling as fighting. The men were both undoubtedly game and unflinching; but Gaynor did not seem to take advantage of his opportunities, and threw away his superior length by allowing his shorter-reached and sturdier adversary to get in on his body, and then accepting the struggle, in which, as the battle went on, he got the worst. It is true Sharpe's peculiar method of setting to with his right foot foremost puzzled Gaynor a little, but this does not account for Tom's bad tactics throughout. As to Bishop Sharpe, he deserved every praise. His daring mode of going in, and changing consequences, combined with his powers of hitting, made him exceedingly dangerous to any but a first-rate boxer of the Spring, Ward, or Young Dutch Sam school. Gaynor could not defend his body against his rushes, nor keep him at a distance for outfighting, and hence the Bold Smuggler's yard-arm to yard-arm tactics were triumphant.

Both men showed at Gaynor's benefit at the Tennis Court on the Thursday. Sharpe displayed few marks of heavy punishment, and Gaynor's chief injuries were from body blows and the failure of his left hand. The battle-money was paid over to Sharpe at Josh Hudson's on the Friday.

Early in 1827, after a failure in making a renewed match with his old opponent Alec Reid, at a sporting dinner which took place at jolly Josh's, "Half Moon," Leadenhall Market, on the 1st of August, 1827, a proposal was made for a meeting for a cool hundred between Young Dutch Sam, then rising into fame, and Bishop Sharpe. Ten pounds were deposited, and the day named the 2nd of October, to meet in the same ring as Ned Neale and Jem Burn. The matter, however, ended in a withdrawal of stakes and a forfeit by Sam. A month afterwards a new match was made for £100 a side, and the 25th of October appointed. As the successive deposits were made good, the odds in betting on the Bishop rose from five to six to four; but at the final deposit at the "Sol's Arms," Wych Street, Sam, who showed up in excellent condition, despite sinister rumours as to his health, brought the betting down to even. Of the farce which followed on the Tuesday, and Sam's mysterious arrest, we have already written. Tom Belcher, who held the stakes, after some indignant comments, resolved to give them up to Sharpe, leaving "Sam's backers, who had served him with legal notice, to take such steps as they might think proper for their recovery." Sharpe was complimented for his prompt and ready appearance in the ring, and pocketed the hundred pounds amidst the congratulations of his friends. Sam's match with our hero having thus fallen through, Tom Gaynor again offered himself to the Bishop's notice, for £100 a side, money ready at Harry Holt's. This, however, came to nothing, owing to Gaynor's match with Gybletts. (See Life of GAYNOR, *ante*.)

Sharpe's old antagonist Alec Reid, having set up a sparring-booth at Epsom Downs, as was the custom of those days, and a difference of opinion having occurred on a bout with the mufflers, the Bishop proposed a match, in which he said he could get backers for £50, and would "bet a hundred." To this the bold Alec replied by doubting the latter, but offering to meet the Smuggler in the roped lists for "a hundred, if he could get the money." The parties met on the following Monday at Josh Hudson's, and there and then signed articles for a mill on the 15th of July next ensuing. How the Bishop fell before the arm of the conquering Alec, after ninety-one rounds of "the most game and determined fighting we ever witnessed" (we quote *Bell's Life*, of July 20th, 1827), may be read in the memoir of the victor.

From this time the Bishop, after an unsuccessful attempt to get backed once more for £100 against Reid, who declined to fight for a less sum, fell into obscurity, his name only appearing in sparring benefits, or as a second in minor battles. Bishop Sharpe died in 1861, aged sixty-two years.

CHAPTER XII.

TOM BROWN ("BIG BROWN") OF BRIDGNORTH.
1825—1831.

BIG BROWN OF BRIDGNORTH, as he was appropriately styled, for a short period attracted the attention of the pugilistic world by his bold claim to the title of "Champion of England," pretentiously put forward by his friends upon the resignation of that honourable distinction by Tom Spring. Indeed, it would appear that Big Brown, who had for some time held a local supremacy in wrestling and boxing on the banks of the Severn, was first fired with the ambition of earning a name and fame in the P.R. by a visit, in the year 1824, of the ex-Champion, " with all his blushing honours thick upon him," to that part of Salop in which Bridgnorth Castle " frowns proudly down o'er sedgy Severn's flood." Brown was at this time thirty-one years of age, being born in 1793—certainly too late in the day to reverse and make an exception to the axiom of antiquity, " Ars longa, vita brevis," so far as the art pugilistic is concerned. Nevertheless, his introduction to Spring so favourably impressed the Herefordshire hero that he declared Brown " fit to fight anything that ever trod upon shoe-leather." On this dictum Brown left his friends in Shropshire and repaired to the " mart for all talent," the great Metropolis.

Brown's trial match, for £100 a side, with old Tom Shelton (see *ante*, CHAPTER VIII., PERIOD V.), was made in a very quiet manner, without any parade of newspaper letter-writing, or the sporting-crib " chaff" too prevalent in those days. Articles were entered into at the " Ship," in Great Turn-stile, Lincoln's Inn Fields, and the day fixed for July 12th, 1825. Now, as the " Ship " was not a " sporting-crib," and Mr. Pierce Egan was not duly advertised of the proceedings—indeed, was told nothing about what was going on—Tom Brown's battle ran a very good chance of not being reported at all—so far as Pierce Egan was concerned. Had this occurred, poor Brown, like " the brave men who lived before Agamemnon," might have gone down to oblivion ; " Carent quia vates sacro." But there was another reason.   Pierce Egan and all the amateurs were " full " of the fight for the following Tuesday (the 19th July, 1825), between Jem Ward and Tom Cannon ; which accounts for " the historian " nodding, like another Homer, and leaving to a rival paper the only report that week of the battle, which took place at Plumbe Park, six miles from Stony Stratford, and about sixty miles from London, on the 12th of July, 1825.

The attendance was not numerous, nor was it desired by Brown's backers ; but the Londoners who were there backed Shelton, as against " a country-man," five to four, on the ground of the old 'un's tried game and capa-bilities.   Brown, beyond his Shropshire and Worcestershire conquests over stalwart yokels, was unknown to public fame.   True, he had been heard of in a forfeit of £20 to Phil Sampson, of Birmingham.   Brown, however, had a high character from those who knew him for activity as a jumper and runner, unusual with men of his weight and inches ; and above all Tom Spring, the native of an adjoining county, had reported his quality to the swells in the terse and graphic style already cited.

Shelton, who trained anywhere and anyhow, had arrived at Stony Strat-ford on the previous day, putting up at the " Cock."   Late on Monday night Spring and Brown arrived, and took quarters at the same well-known hostelrie.   The men here met each other, and in true English style ex-changed greetings and shook hands.   Peter Crawley and Josh Hudson also arrived from London as the appointed seconds of Shelton.

Brown, a good-looking, gentleman-farmer sort of man, was a general object of interest as he walked about the town in the early morning ; his stature, six feet one inch, and his weight, a solid fifteen stone of bone and muscle, seemed big enough and heavy enough for anything.   The friends of the countryman became yet more confident when they saw Shelton, who certainly was not above twelve stone, and whose height wanted quite four inches of that of his opponent.   Among the rurals Brown was now at the odds of five and six to four.   At twelve o'clock the men and their seconds and friends started in four post-chaises for Plumbe Park, the general public making their way in the best style they could.   Brown, attended by Tom Cribb and Tom Spring, was first to throw his hat within the ropes ; Josh and Peter followed quickly.   " Come, Spring, get ready," cried Josh ; " my man is dressed and waiting in the chaise."   Shelton now made his appearance, but threw his hat so far that it went over on the farther side of the ring, where it was picked up by Young Gas (Jonathan Bissell), who dropped it within the ropes. "That's a bad omen," said a bystander. The colours were now tied to the stakes—blue for Shelton, by Hudson, and crimson and white for the Bridgnorth giant, by Tom Spring. "Never mind how you tie them, Josh," said Shelton, "I shall want you to take them down for me." "Of course," replied the John Bull Fighter, "so I have fastened them with a reef-knot." The men now stood up for

THE FIGHT.

Round 1.—On getting rid of their togs Brown looked like Hercules without his club. Shelton had trained off; his face was thin—his neck did not appear to possess that strength which characterises a fighting man; his frame was not so robust as heretofore; and his calves, in the phrase of the Ring, had "gone to grass." Nevertheless, Tom's heart was in the right place; and like a good "ould one," he thought of nothing but winning, in spite of the ravages which Master Time had made. "A countryman lick me, indeed!" exclaimed Tom, early in the morning; "I'll be carried out of the ring first—I will never live to see that day!" On preparing for the attack, Brown stood over Shelton, and the latter, aware that he had a good deal of work to perform, set about it with pluck. Tom's right hand was stopped by the novice; and in return Brown put a "little one in" on Shelton's mug, which dropped him. (The milling coves looked blue, while the Chawbacons were outrageous in their manifestations of joy at the success of the countryman. Spring said, "First blood!" but Josh said, "No!" Six to four on Brown; but no fanciers of the odds.)

2.—In this early stage of the fight, the sporting men were satisfied that Shelton had his master before him. Tom measured his opponent, and tried all he knew to plant a heavy topper; but the countryman was too cautious, and parried steadily. Shelton, not dismayed, again went to work; but Brown was up to his manœuvres, and put in a severe blow on his head. A rally occurred, which was brisk for a short time, but Tom had the worst of it, and got away. Brown took the lead in a determined manner, planting two blows on Shelton's head. Shelton, with the courage of a lion, boldly stood up to his man, till a body blow sent him down. (The friends of Brown shouted for joy, offered two to one, and declared it was "as safe as the Bank.")

3.—The position of Shelton was awkward—his legs were too wide apart; but his anxiety to punish his adversary was visible, and he left no manœuvre untried to obtain an opening. "Be ready," said Josh, "he's coming!" Brown smiled, and with the utmost ease not only stopped Shelton, but in return,

gave him a hit on his canister weighty enough to put his upper works in confusion. Tom countered his adversary on his sensitive plant so sharply that the claret was plentiful. ("Well done, Tom," said Josh; "you have made the young one a member of the Vintners' Company; go and draw his cork again.") The countryman felt a little warm—rushed in to his work—caught Shelton in his arms like a baby, and spite of the struggling of poor Tom, he went down. ("The countryman for £100!" all round the ring.)

4.—Tom was piping a little, and it was evident he was overmatched. Shelton hit his adversary on the cheek; but he could not stop the overwhelming power of Brown, who went in and caught Shelton at the ropes. After a little toppering on both sides, the strength of the countryman enabled him to hold up his adversary, as he was dangling on the ropes, but, in the most generous and humane manner, he let Tom down, and walked away. ("Bravo! handsome! Englishman-like!" were the expressions all over the ring.)

5.—Short. It was now clear that the countryman was nothing like a novice, and also that he had been under good tuition. He stopped Shelton with ease, and aimed a terrific right-handed blow at Tom's head, which, had it told, might have proved Shelton's quietus. Tom, in bobbing his nob aside, slipped down.

6.—This was a fighting round; but Shelton could not reduce Brown's pluck or strength, although he made several good hits. "His right hand is gone," said Josh. "It is, by gosh!" echoed Oliver, whose face was full of anxiety for the fate of poor Shelton, and who had also backed the Ould One at five to four previous to the battle. Shelton planted a body blow; but Brown returned the favour on the head of his adversary. Tom retreated, and endeavoured to mill; but Brown followed him, and sent him completely out of the ropes. ("A countryman, do you call him? He stands a good chance to be Champion!" said Spring.)

7.—Brown's ivory box received a rattler, but the countryman shook it off with a smile. A little pricked, he followed Shelton, with a quick step, who turned round to avoid a flush hit. Tom slipped down in getting away. Shelton made play, and Brown missed in return.

8.—After some heavy exchanges at the ropes, Shelton put in a back-handed hit so sharply that Brown napped it on his mouth, and went down. (This event put the fighting men and backers of Shelton into spirits—it was a ray of hope. "The Ould One will win it! He has changed it a little!" and "Master Brown does not like it!" with lots of chaffing, till "time" was called.)

9.—This was a round within a round, or two fights for the same stake. The age of Shelton told against him; and it was clear that he could not win. Tom came to the scratch much distressed, but nevertheless commenced milling. Brown followed him resolutely over the ring, when Shelton retreated to the ropes; but the nob of Tom got entangled, and the fibbing system was adopted by both combatants. It was rather against Shelton, when the John Bull Fighter tried to remove the rope from his man's nob, which Spring said was not fair, and shoved Josh off. Hudson persisted, and shoved Spring roughly; Spring then struck him. "I will not take a blow from any one," said Josh, and let fly at the late Champion's head, catching him under the left eye. A scramble ensued; Spring and Josh were both down, and only Cribb waiting upon his man. Brown in the interim had floored Shelton by a heavy body blow. The time-keepers had also a trifling dispute; and Tom Oliver and Young Gas placed themselves in fighting attitudes. At length the row sub-sided, order was restored, and when time was called for round

10.—Both men appeared at the scratch. Shelton exerted himself to do mischief, but he was stopped, received several hits, and was sent down by a ribber that was heard all over the ring. Shouting by the friends of Brown.

11.—Shelton with considerable dexterity put in a sharp facer; the men afterwards had a severe rally. Brown endeavoured (but we think unintentionally) to lay hold of Shelton's thigh, in order to obtain the throw; but on "foul" being vociferated, he

let go his hold. Shelton went down by a heavy body blow.

12.—Tom did everything in his power to win; but his blows were nothing like finishing ones, and Brown had the best of it. Shelton received an ugly visitation to his victualling office, and went down exhausted. Any odds, but no takers.

13.—The fight was drawing to a close, Brown taking the lead in every round. Shelton put in a nobber, but Brown seemed to say, "If you cannot hit me harder, it is no go." Tom received such a tremendous one in his mouth that he went down as if shot. Five to one; in fact, it was a hundred to one that Brown must now win offhand.

14.—The old story, so often told, but so little heeded by fighting men, was evident. Shelton was full of pluck, as to mind and heart, but his legs trembled, and he staggered like a drunken man; he made play with his right, planted a facer, and got away. The danger was out of Shelton, and Brown, in order to put an end to the battle, went to work. Tom opposed him like a trump, till he napped a shutter-up-shop on his throat, which floored him. The head of Shelton reached the ground so violently that it bounded like a ball. ("It's all over," was the cry; the brandy was administered, but it was of no use.)

15, and last.—Shelton answered the call of "time." On toeing the mark, Brown let fly on the side of Tom's head, and he measured his length on the ground. Shelton was "hit out of time," and Josh gave in for him. Tom, on recovering himself a little, said, "No, I will fight!" He, however, was so weak and exhausted that nature would not second his efforts. Time, fifteen minutes.

REMARKS.—Shelton, on coming to himself, said "he was ashamed of having been licked in so short a time"—fifteen minutes. Shelton was not disgraced by the defeat. He showed himself a brave man, and never flinched from his opponent; but overmatched by strength and youth, he found it out too late. Brown fought better than was expected. His confidence increased. Spring offered to back him against any one for £500 a side. Brown, for a big one, was extremely active on his legs, stopped well, hit hard, and did not want for courage or science.

Brown lost no time in claiming the belt, as may be seen by the subjoined:—

"BROWN'S CHALLENGE AND CLAIM TO THE CHAMPIONSHIP.
"To the Editor of the 'WEEKLY DISPATCH.'

"SIR,—Permit me to announce, through the medium of your paper, that my benefit will take place on Tuesday, the 28th of March, when I shall be prepared to make a match with any man in England for from three to five hundred pounds a side, or as much more as may be desired. Jem Ward, or his friends, will probably avail themselves of this opportunity to prove their sincerity when they did me the favour of soliciting my attendance in London; but should their courage have been cooled I shall be glad to make a match with Peter Crawley or Tom Cannon. Should the London Ring decline the challenge, I beg leave to say that I shall lay claim to the title of Champion, which has so long remained in doubt.

"I am, Sir, yours respectfully,

"Bridgnorth, March 1st, 1826." "THOS. BROWN.

On Tuesday, March 28th, 1826, the Tennis Court overflowed, as at the period when Jem Belcher was the pride of the Ring, and Tom Cribb the hero of the tale. The produce of the Court, after deducting expenses, amounted to £127 10s. One thousand persons were present.

After the first set-to between Raines and Wallace, Sampson appeared on the stage, and said that he had been matched against Brown five years since, and had received a forfeit of £20. A second match had been proposed, but Brown had not come forward. He would now fight him for £100, and put down a deposit. If that did not suit Mr. Brown he would set to with him there and then for a " bellyful." (Laughter and applause.)

Jem Ward showed, and came to the point at once. "I am ready," said Jem, " to fight Brown for £300, and no chaffing. I will put down a deposit immediately." " Well done, Jem ! "

Tom Spring mounted the stage, and was flatteringly received. He said Brown was under his protection, and it was not worth his while to fight for £100. He was in business, and would require at least a month's training under his (Spring's) care, and then if he won the battle the expenses would be greater than the gain. As to putting on the gloves with Sampson it was quite out of the question ; Brown was under his management, and he would not let him do wrong to his friends and backers. Sampson had come forward in an angry manner to challenge. Here the oratory of the ex-Champion was lost in a roar of applause and disapprobation, and calls for " Sampson and Brown."

Sampson said, " The thing spoke for itself—it was too plain ; Spring did not like to let the cat out of the bag. He would not let Brown set to with him because it would tell tales. It would show Brown's talents, and Spring was determined to keep Brown all to himself. He (Sampson) thought that the company present ought to witness the set-to between him and Brown, as in that case the Fancy would form a judgment as to the laying out their money. (Great applause ; and " He ought to set to," from some ; while others, " Spring is not such a flat as to show off Brown ; it would betray a want of judgment, and not the caution of a sporting man.")

Jem Ward rushed on the stage, and flashing a £50 note stated " he would post it immediately towards making a match for £300 with any man in England." (" Go it, Jem ! You can beat any chawbacon, let him be as big as Goliah ! ")

Spring, in reply, said he would make a match that night, at Cribb's, for Brown to fight Ward the first week in August. (Applause.)

Sampson also observed for £100 a side he would fight any man in England, and would make the match immediately.

As a wind-up to the sports Brown and Spring appeared on the stage, followed by Sampson, who stripped himself, seized hold of a pair of gloves, and appeared determined to set to with Brown. To describe the row which ensued would be impossible. Spring would not let Brown spar with Sampson. The latter asked Brown personally, but he declined, as he said he must be guided by his friends. Sampson then left the stage, observing "it was of no use." Here another uproar occurred, and Spring and Brown left the stage. After some time had passed in glorious confusion Spring again made his appearance on the stage, and solicited a hearing. Silence being procured Spring observed, that Brown had been placed under his protection, and he was determined that he should receive no foul play. In the bills of the day it had been expressed that he and Brown would put on the gloves together, but he would not let Brown set to with Sampson. "Yet do not mistake me, gentlemen," said he, "not from any fear respecting Sampson, but it would be wrong, as Brown was about being matched, and more especially on account of the anger displayed by Sampson." A mixture of applause and hisses, and cries for Sampson. "Brown, gentlemen, is here, ready to set to if you wish it." "Bravo!" Brown ascended the stage, but the mixed reception must have proved unpleasant to his feelings. "Hats off!" was the cry, and Brown and Spring were opposed to each other.

It was curious to hear the different opinions respecting the abilities of Brown. "He is of no use," said a retired boxer, one of the first heroes in the P.R. of his day. "He can beat any one in the list," observed another milling cove. "What an impostor!" "The £500 would be a gift to Ward!" "He would be nothing in the hands of Peter Crawley!" "He is a rare punisher with his right hand, one of his blows would floor an ox"—&c., &c. The set-to did not give satisfaction, and the public verdict was that Brown, after all, was nothing else but a strong countryman, yet a hard hitter with his right hand. Brown returned thanks, and challenged any man in England for £500 a side, but would accommodate Mr. Sampson for £300 a side.

Sampson informed the audience that he was to have a benefit on Monday next; and if he, who had been long known to the Ring, met with such patronage as Brown had done, he would not only fight Brown for £100 a side, but the whole of the money taken at the doors in addition.

At nine o'clock in the evening, after a sporting dinner at which Brown and his friends were the guests, Jem Ward and Sampson arrived at Tom Cribb's, in Panton Street, and the latter proposed to accede to Brown's challenge on the part of Ward, and to make a match for £500 a side. Sampson then said that Ward had not been able to see his friends, and had only £10 to put down; but he should be prepared to make that sum £50 at his (Sampson's) benefit on Monday next. Some surprise was expressed at the smallness of the deposit for so important a match. Brown at once said that he would throw no impediment in Ward's way, but would meet him in any reasonable manner he might suggest.

A gentleman present then proceeded to draw up the articles, in which it was proposed and agreed to by Sampson, on the part of Ward, that the fight should take place on a stage similar to that on which Ward and Cannon fought at Warwick; that the place of fighting should be named by Spring, upon the condition that he gave Ward one hundred guineas for that privilege; and that it should not exceed one hundred and fifty miles from London. On coming to the discussion of the distance, however, a difficulty arose. Ward said his friends would not consent to his fighting beyond a hundred miles from London, and therefore if he fought at all it must be within that distance. To this Brown objected. During considerable argument, in which Sampson, still labouring under feelings of irritation against Brown, gave way to a spirit of hostility altogether misplaced, he repeatedly offered to fight Brown for a hundred himself within a month, which Brown declined. At last Sampson said he would fight him for £10 in a room that night. To such a ridiculous offer Spring would not suffer Brown to accede; but at last Brown, in order to prove that he had no personal fears for Sampson, said he would fight him next morning for love. This proffer was hailed with cheers by his friends, but was not agreeable to Sampson, who reverted to his old proposition to fight for a hundred in a month, and this not being accepted he retired.

As an impartial historian we must state that about this period the nuisance of newspaper challenges, correspondence, defiance, chaff, scurrility, and braggadocio had reached an unendurable height. Three rival sporting papers opened their columns, or rather their reporters and editors lent their pens, to indite all sorts of epistles from pugilists, each striving to make itself the special channel by which the hero of the hour proclaimed in "Eccles' vein" and braggart buncombe his fearful intentions and outraged feelings, and scattered furious cartels among his foes or rivals.

Columns of letters purporting to be from Ward, Phil Sampson, Brown, and a host of minor celebrities—most of them in unmistakable Eganian slang—adorned the columns of the journals throughout 1826 and 1827. Ward's affair went off in smoke; but early in 1828 the newspaper controversy with Phil Sampson culminated in a match with Brown, for £500. This was decided on the 8th of April, 1828, near Wolverhampton, and resulted in the defeat of our hero in forty-two minutes and forty-nine rounds. The preliminaries to this defeat and the battle itself will be found in our Life of Phil Sampson, in the next Chapter.

Brown's defeat, though manifestly owing to the serious accident to his shoulder in the fourth round, had the effect of " an occultation of a star of the first magnitude " in the fistic firmament. But there was another big Boanerges, of fifteen stone, who kept the "Black Bull," in Smithfield; who, having doffed his white apron on the provocation of Stephen Bailey, and twice beaten the blue-aproned butcher, fancied that he could win further laurels by a tourney with the defeated, but not daunted, Champion of Bridgnorth. The public were accordingly edified by a challenge from Isaac Dobell, which was promptly answered by Brown's retort of the "Black Bull's" defiance.

The stakes agreed on were £300 on the part of Shropshire to £250 on behalf of Smithfield, in consideration of the battle coming off within five miles of " the cloud-capped towers " of Bridgnorth. Tuesday, the 24th of March, 1829, was the day appointed, and on the Saturday morning previous Dobell, who had trained at Hendon, Middlesex, under the care of Harry Lancaster, set out by the " Wonder " coach for Towcester, where he sojourned on the Saturday night. Here he excited the wonder of the yokels by his wonderful bulk, and the wonderful amount of the stakes which he declared his confidence of winning. On Sunday he reached Birmingham, and took up his quarters at the " Crown," awakening the curiosity of the natives of the " hardware village " by promenading through the streets. On Monday he arrived in Bridgnorth, and there patronised the " Royal Oak."

Brown had trained at Shipley, and had named Bridgnorth for two reasons—first, to oblige his fellow-townsmen and backers, and secondly, to exhibit to them how he would wipe out the defeat he had sustained at the hands of the " Birmingham Youth," which he maintained was solely owing to the accident hereafter mentioned. On Monday evening he returned to Bridgnorth, and put up at his brother's house, the " King's Head," where he was joined by Tom Spring, Tom Cribb, Ned Neale, and Harry Holt, with several other celebrated men of the London P.R. A rumour of a warrant, however, induced him to make a retreat from the town in a post-chaise, together with his seconds, and sojourn in a neighbouring village for the night. Deux Hill Farm being named as the rendezvous, thither the Commissary repaired with the ropes and stakes of the F.P.C. (Fair Play Club), and there in due time an excellent ring, with an outer circle of wagons and carriages, was formed. Some bets of seven to four and six to four were taken by the friends of Dobell, who, however, was reported to be feverish and unwell from a cold caught on his long journey. An attempt to arrest Brown was cleverly frustrated by Spring, who drove over the Severn Bridge in a post-chaise, accompanied by a portly friend well wrapped up. An order to halt was given at the tollgate ; the door of the chaise was opened, but Brown was not there, having meantime crossed the river in a boat some distance higher up. At half-past twelve, after Dobell and friends had waited more than half-an-hour, Brown and his party appeared, and were heartily cheered. The £50 to be paid to Dobell for choice of place were duly handed over, and the colours—crimson and white for Brown and a blue bird's-eye for Dobell—tied to the stakes. The men shook hands heartily at meeting, and the ceremony of peeling forthwith began ; Lancaster and Jem Burn attending on Dobell, Spring and Neale waiting on Brown.

On stripping, Brown looked thinner than when he fought Sampson, and had altogether an aged and worn appearance, but his eye was bright and his look confident. His arms were longer and his height superior to that of Dobell. Mine host of the " Black Bull " displayed a pair of brawny arms and most substantial understandings, which, with his round and portly body, gave him anything but the look of an active boxer. At three minutes to one all was in readiness. The men toed the mark and began

THE FIGHT.

Round 1.—Brown covered his front well, and throwing his arms across his face, looked smiling through them at his antagonist. Dobell seemed serious. He made first play with his left, but was out of distance, and was stopped. He tried the same hand again, but was again too far off to make an impression. Brown, seeing that nothing was to be done by acting on the defensive, made up his mind to begin. After a feint with his left, he popped in his right slightly on Dobell's mouth; he then drew back, but again advancing, quickly delivered his left on Dobell's eye, and his right on his cheek. The former blow filled Dobell's eye with water. Both now made quick play, and slight hits were followed by a tremendous smack on Dobell's nose, which drew claret, and dropped him like a sack of malt. (First blood and first knock-down blow announced for Brown, amidst the shouts of his friends, who offered ten to one in his favour. Neale, too, was in high glee, as it made him the winner of two fives, which he had bet on these events.)

2.—Dobell came up serious, but ready for the affray ; and Brown smiled good-humouredly, as if it were all his own. After a short spar Dobell tried his right, but Brown jumped actively away. Brown returned again to his man, and with great quickness planted his left and right on his phiz, and broke away. Dobell, somewhat annoyed, rushed in and delivered his right on Brown's cheek, and his left on the body, but did not seem to make much impression. Both now got to a rally, in which some heavy blows were exchanged. Brown then drew back, and Dobell, rushing after him, received two flush hits in the face, right and left. Dobell would not be denied, but rattled in, while Brown retreated, stopping and hitting with severity. Dobell was not idle, but his blows fell short, and at last Brown caught him a terrific hit over the right eye with his left, making a deep incision. Dobell stood it like bricks, and rushed to a close, when Brown slipped down rather questionably.

3.—Brown came up playfully, while Dobell's dexter ogle had an ugly appearance. Both stood quiet for a time ; but at length Brown, seeing his man inclined for reflection, rushed in with great rapidity, and catching poor Dobell a heavy slap on the left jaw with his right, dropped him again, amidst shouts and encouraging exclamations from Sampson. Few, in fact, seemed to think that the poor Londoner deserved any quarter. (Any odds on Brown.)

4.—Dobell found there was no use in outfighting, and therefore determined to rush to business. Brown, however, who was active on his legs, jumped back, and again caught the "Bull's Head" on the grinders, and downed him again. ("Bravo, Brown—it's all your own ! take him away !")

5.—Dobell, no way daunted or discouraged by the shouts of victory, rushed to work. Brown missed his right and left as he came in, and Dobell planted his right on his throat. ("Well done, Dobell !") This he followed with a slap from his right on Brown's scent-box, and drew blood for the first time from the Pride of Bridgnorth. This seemed to give Dobell new life, and in rushing in Brown went down.

6.—Brown ready—showed the superiority of length, and again jobbed heavily right and left, and broke away. This he repeated, when Dobell charged him courageously ; on grappling him, with intent to fib, Brown wouldn't have it, and went down—Dobell on him.

7.—Brown planted his left on the canister and his right on the body of the publican. Dobell took it bravely, without flinching ; he then rushed to in-fighting, but missed several of his blows, and after mutual but ineffectual attempts to fib, Brown got down. (This show of caution did not suit Dobell's

friends, and they cried out, "Fight fair !" Brown's friends, however, replied, "All right," "Nothing wrong." Indeed, Brown did not seem to keep his legs with certainty.)

8.—Dobell on the defensive, but not sufficiently quick to stop his antagonist, who jobbed him twice on the head. This long shooting did not suit Dobell, and he had recourse to his rush, and planted his right on Brown's jaw, and in the scramble which followed Brown went down.

9.—Dobell popped in his left unexpectedly, but made but little impression. Brown was not long in returning the compliment right and left. This he repeated, when Dobell bored in desperately, as the only chance. Brown retreated, fighting and meeting him as he followed. At last Dobell caught him round the neck, and fibbed slightly ; in the tussle which followed Brown fell ; and Dobell, in hitting, as Brown was on his knees, caught him with his right on the back. (Brown called "foul," and it was foul, but was not noticed by the umpires ; indeed, the blow was accidental.)

10.—Dobell again rushed in, hitting right and left, but Brown retreated, stopping and jobbing in turn. In the end he was bored down on his knees. (More chaffing from Sampson, and from Brown's friends.)

11.—Good stopping on both sides, but Brown succeeded in making two jobbing hits. Dobell again had recourse to his desperate rush, and a close followed, when both tried vigorously for the fall, but neither could get the lock, and in the end Dobell dragged Brown down, showing that his strength was still unimpaired.

12.—On getting to their seconds' knees, both piped a little, but Dobell most. Dobell came up as game as a pebble, and tried his left at Brown's body, but was out of distance. He then hit with his right, but was stopped. He found that nothing but close contact would do, and pursued the rushing system. Brown retreated round the ring before him, and actually turned round to avoid, but in again meeting his man he caught him with a flush hit with his left, and Dobell fell on his face. (Chaffing now commenced on the part of Stockman for Dobell. He swore that Brown's shoulder was out, and that all Dobell had to do was to go in and win it.) Brown had certainly hurt the thumb of his right hand, but no material mischief was done.

13.—Both now showed distress, but Dobell was most winded. Brown smiled, and, after a short pause, let fly right and left, planting both blows heavily, and repeating the dose till he hit his man down. Brown fell himself on his knees, showing weakness in the pins.

14.—Dobell now showed additional symptoms of weakness, and was slower than ever. After a short pause Brown rushed in, planted his left and right, and dropped him heavily.

15.—Dobell vindicated his courage by again

rushing in; but Brown met him with two terrific jobbing hits right and left, and again floored him all abroad, amidst the triumphant shouts of the Shropshire lads.

16.—Dobell evidently felt that his chance of winning was vanishing; still, summoning all his remaining energies, he rushed to in-fighting. He missed his right-handed hit, and was met with a terrific left-handed job in the muzzle. He would not be denied, how-ever, and fought away gallantly, making some wild hits. Brown was active, and had him at all points, till he fell almost exhausted. (Dobell's brother now endeavoured to per-suade him to give in, but he resolved to have another shy.)

17, and last.—Dobell once more rushed in, but Brown, retreating, met him as he came forward with a flush hit in the mouth, and dropped him for the last time. On again getting up he consented, though reluctantly, to say "enough," and the hat was thrown up amidst shouts of victory for Brown, who had thus regained the confidence of his Shropshire friends.

The fight lasted twenty-two minutes, and Dobell was taken from the ground much punished about the head. Brown showed but a slight scar under one of his eyes, and was so fresh that he seized a whip with intent to administer it to Stockman for his chaffing, but was prevented by Tom Spring. The chaffing on both sides was bad, and par-ticularly towards Dobell, who, as a stranger in that part of the country, ought to have been protected. It is but just to state, how-ever, that the old ring-goers were most to blame. Dobell was able to help himself to brandy after the battle was over.

REMARKS.—During this fight Brown had it all his own way, and showed the superiority of length and science over mere weight and muscular strength. Dobell, although the first to attack, almost invariably hit short, and was unable to plant his blows well home. At in-fighting neither was clever, and there was not a good throw throughout the contest. Brown, in getting away from Dobell's rushes, was deemed by some to be over-cautious; but the fact is, he was weak in the legs, and, under Spring's direction, would not wrestle, lest he might endanger his shoulder, which it may be recollected was put out in his fight with Sampson. With respect to Dobell, if not a good fighter, he has proved himself a game man; and with this praise he must be content, for he can scarcely hope for improve-ment in the fistic art. It was clear through-out that Brown was not in the best condition; but had he been less fresh, we think he understood his business too well, and was too good an out-fighter to give Dobell much chance. Brown remained at Bridgnorth, showing but slight marks of punishment; and Dobell arrived at his house in St. John Street on Thursday morning. He had a levee of condolence in the evening, at which it was proposed to match him once more against Brown, for £200 a side; but nothing definite was done. It seems that the knuckle-bone of Brown's right-hand thumb was broken; and, on reaching home, the hand was dread-fully puffed; the injury was done in the second or third round.

The friends of Dobell attributed his defeat to a severe cold and want of condition, and as mine host himself shared this opinion a second trial was agreed on, this time for £200 a side. Dobell went at once into training, but for some reason twice forfeited £5 deposit. At length the stakes were made good, and the day named was November 24th, 1829, the place of meeting being near Uckfield, Sussex, on the Crowborough Road. Dobell trained finally at East Grinstead, where he got off much superfluous flesh, but still drew little short of fifteen stone. Brown trained actively among the hills of his native county, and appeared in the ring in far better form than on the previous occasion.

On Monday Brown, accompanied by his brother and some Bridgnorth friends, Tom Spring, and Ned Neale, set out from Streatham for the "Shelley Arms," at Nutley, close to the residence of Sir John Shelley. On their way they passed through East Grinstead, where Spring had an inter-view with Dobell, who was surrounded by his friends, and attended by his chosen seconds, Tom Shelton and Peter Crawley. All was good humour, and each man seemed confident of the result of the approaching combat, no doubt booking himself as the victor.

The Commissary, Tom Oliver, and his coadjutor Frosty-faced Fogo, were among the throng at Nutley; and at an early hour in the morning they commenced forming a ring on a piece of the forest close at hand, but before they had commenced their labours orders arrived from Dobell to move to Crowborough, to which place they proceeded, across the country, by a most villanous road, and at the risk of being scattered like chaff before the wind, which blew a perfect hurricane.

In the interim Dobell, with his *cortége*—embracing two carriages and four and sundry chaises and pairs, gigs, horsemen, &c.—started from East Grinstead, and passed the "Shelley Arms" at a rapid pace, being obliged to take a circuitous route through Maresfield and Uckfield to get into the Crowborough Road. Brown's party were soon in their rear, their carriages being all prepared for the start, and in point of respectability of "turn-out" being upon an equality. The Dobellites, however, having the start by some minutes, reached the scene of action first, and it being then close upon one o'clock proceeded to the ring, which was not yet complete. Brown not having arrived, and one o'clock having passed, Dobell's party were at once for claiming forfeit, and "to this intent" spoke; but at five minutes after that time Brown and Spring were within the still incomplete arena. The storm at this time raged with unabated fury, and the stakes having been pitched on a hill, for the advantage of a good gate, the crowd and the combatants were exposed to its utmost severity. The consequence was that hats and umbrellas were seen driving across the heath in all directions—their owners in full chase—while those who were preserved from these casualties were only secured by the aid of cords, straps, and handkerchiefs, which were so applied as to resist the furious blasts.

The usual preliminaries of choosing umpires and referees were now arranged, and the men peeled for action, Brown attended by Spring and Tom Oliver, and Dobell by Peter Crawley and Tom Shelton. In point of condition they were, as we have said, much better than at their last meeting, Dobell looking much lighter in weight and firmer in flesh, but still too much of the Bacchus to suit our notions of the necessary activity for a milling hero. His arms were too short, and from the fleshiness at his shoulders he seemed to want that spring which is essential to effective hitting. Brown was thin as a greyhound, and had an obvious advantage in length, while his general appearance showed freshness and vigour. At this interesting moment a few of the friends of Dobell readily accepted some bets at seven to four and two to one.

THE FIGHT.

Round 1.—The men came up cautiously, both covering their points with judgment, and Brown evidently waiting for the attack. Dobell did not keep him long in suspense, but let fly with his right at the head, which was prettily stopped. He then tried with his left at the body, but was again stopped, and Brown jumped away active on his pins. A long pause ensued, neither making play, but both receiving strong pepper from Æolus, which imparted a bluish tint to their mazards. Dobell once more tried his left at Brown's body, but was out of distance. Sparring and position changed, when Dobell made a rush and attempted to catch Brown's right hand with his left, while he drew back his right to hit, but Brown jumped back, and the effort was fruitless as well as injudicious. Another long sparring bout, of which Dobell evidently got tired, for he dropped his hands and looked mortified; but Brown seemed determined to give him the lead, and wait for his assault. Dobell now put in a slight body hit with his left, while Brown made an over-handed chop with his right, but missed. Dobell became impatient, and making up his mind to mischief, tried his one two; but both were stopped, and Brown jumped back. Brown now, in turn, made a dart, and put in his left slightly on Dobell's collar-bone. Dobell tried to plant his left and right several times, but was stopped; at length he caught Brown slightly with his right on the mark; but the distance was ill-judged, and Brown smiled. Long sparring. Dobell stopped a well-intentioned visit from Brown's left to his nob. Again did Dobell drop his arms as if fatigued at holding them up so long, for fifteen minutes had now expired. "Go in, and get to work," cried Dobell's friends, and after a pause he followed their advice; he rushed to a rally, and delivered a slight tap on Brown's cheek with his right. This produced a quick return from Brown, who slashed away right and left with great force and quickness on Dobell's frontispiece, setting his eyes on the twinkle, and ultimately flooring him on his capacious base. (Loud shouts from Brown's friends, and five to two offered in all directions.) The round lasted seventeen minutes.

2.—Dobell came up considerably flushed in his upper works, but steady. "In to him!" cried Shelton; and obedient to the word of command, he instantly commenced operations; but he found the game not so safe. Brown was ready, and hit away right and left, meeting his man as he came in with stinging severity. Dobell felt the force of these visitations, and turned his back for a moment. Brown saw the advantage, and quick as lightning jumped in, and as Dobell came to the rightabout met him with a flush hit with the right on his mouth, and his left on his nose; this he repeated, and after a very slight return from Dobell, he was floored, the purple stream distilling from his mouth and proboscis. (Four to one on Brown, and no takers.)

3.—Brown now changed his tactics; and seeing that he had it all his own way, he made the beginning with right and left handed chops, but both were stopped; Dobell, however, was too much confused to play the saving game long, and in another second he found Brown's right and left slap in his physog. The hits were terrific. Dobell made some returns, and caught Brown under the right eye, but the rapidity and force of Brown's attack were irresistible; he again jobbed well right and left, and at last down went Dobell of his own accord; he found he was at the ropes, and sought refuge by dropping beneath them. (Shouts from Brown's friends in all directions, while Peter Crawley ran to the umpires and exclaimed "that it was made all right for Brown, and that Dobell wouldn't fight.") While he was thus raving, however, his man again got up.

The 4th and last round was fought. Dobell made a short but desperate effort; he tried one or two wild hits with his left, but in return napped it heavily on his canister, and was once more grassed. It was now clear that all was over, and, in fact, Dobell plainly indicated that he would not prolong what he felt was a useless struggle. On "time" being called Brown was proclaimed the conqueror in exactly twenty-one minutes. He was as fresh as when he commenced, and immediately shook hands with his antagonist, and dressed in the ring.

Attention was now paid to Dobell, who complained of considerable pain in his right forearm, which was much swollen and contused. He had evidently lost the use of it, and on being examined by two surgeons on the spot the small bone was pronounced to be fractured, and he was carried out of the ring to receive proper professional attention. Independently of the accident, however, which, it is believed, occurred in the third round, from his arm coming in contact with the point of Brown's elbow, he had not a chance of winning, nor had he himself a doubt on the subject from the first round, when, from the difficulty he felt at getting at Brown, he said to Crawley he was sure it was of no use—a declaration which naturally excited Crawley's suspicions, and led to the observations which he had made, and which, from Dobell's state, he subsequently regretted. He said he thought it was odd that Dobell should want to cut it so soon, and this it was which provoked him to say what he did.

REMARKS.—Considering the distance and the vicissitudes of weather encountered this was one of the most unsatisfactory mills that had been witnessed for some time. There were not above four minutes' actual fighting, and this all one way—for Dobell never had a chance—a result which all good judges anticipated; and the only surprise was that he could have been so imprudent as to make a match so obviously to his disadvantage. He seems to have been flattered, however, with the idea that had he been in better condition when he fought at Bridgnorth he could have given a better account of himself; and forgetting that Brown at that time was equally out of sorts, and capable of improvement, he resolved upon another trial, the issue of which must have satisfied him that his forte is not prizefighting, and especially with men superior in length, activity, strength, and science. With a commoner like Bailey, who is an old man, and who possesses little science, his slaughtering powers might tell, but when opposed by science these qualities lose their value, and, as in the present instance, if met by corresponding powers of punishment, are altogether set aside. The very first round, as he confessed to Crawley, evidently satisfied the host of the "Black Bull;" and finding he could do nothing when at his best, he naturally concluded the chances which followed were scarcely worth seeking. Upon the whole, we believe there was very little money won or lost on the match. Brown had greatly improved, both on his legs and in his style of setting to, and by out-generalling poor Isaac, and fatiguing him in the first round, rendered victory more secure.

Brown and his party returned to the "Castle Tavern," Holborn, the same night, while Dobell returned to East Grinstead, and was put to bed. His arm was set by Mr. Jones, of East Grinstead, assisted by the two surgeons who attended him on the ground. He arrived at the "Black Bull" on Wednesday night, which, instead of sparkling with illumination, looked as black as an undertaker's shop.

Brown, although he now announced his retirement from all claim to championship honours, was still from time to time made the subject of attacks and taunts in the newspaper outpourings of the boastful Phil Sampson. At length preliminaries, after nine months of chaffering, were settled, and at Doncaster, on the 19th of September, 1831, they met for the second time in battle array.

A number of disgraceful quibbles were made by the Birmingham party, and there seemed no probability of a fight, unless £50 was conceded to Sampson, and a promise that he should name the place within a certain distance of Birmingham. Finally, on the authority delegated to Mr. Beardsworth, the stakeholder, Doncaster was named as the rendezvous. The Town Moor was talked of, but the authorities intimated their intention of interfering, and Pegbourn Leys, four miles distant, was named as the spot; the fight to commence at the early hour of nine, so as not to interfere with the day's racing.

On the Monday morning the roads to the appointed spot bore much resemblance to the road to Epsom in the olden time. Thimble-riggers and

" prick-in-the-garter " men, gipsies, and all the motley toddlers of a race-meeting were gathered. There was, however, a very poor sprinkling of the upper-crust patrons of the Ring and of racing men.

At half-past eight Tom Oliver and Fogo had pitched their stakes and rove their ropes, and Brown threw in his castor, followed by Tom Oliver and Yorkshire Robinson as his seconds. Sampson, attended by Jem Ward and Harry Holt, followed. Brown was received quietly, with a slight murmur of applause, but the shouts when Sampson showed himself indicated to the observant the mob of partisans he had on the ground. Indeed, continual ruffianly threats towards Brown were uttered by many of these roughs. Brown, on Sampson's appearance, advanced in a frank manner towards him, holding out his hand, but Sampson, eyeing him with a savage and defiant look, withheld his, shook his head, and walked towards his seconds. The colours, crimson with a white border for Brown, and a deep crimson for Sampson, were tied to the stakes, and the men stood up. Brown's weight was stated at 14st. 11b., Sampson's at 12st. 4lbs. Brown's age (forty) was a counterpoise, Sampson numbering but thirty summers. At twenty minutes past nine the men were left face to face at the mark, and began

THE FIGHT.

Round 1.—The attitude of Sampson was graceful—indeed, elegant—that of Brown constrained and stiff. Brown moved his arms about as if intending to strike, Sampson watching him keenly, and never shifting his guard. Brown hit short, and was stopped, Sampson returning with the left, and being stopped in turn. More sparring, when Brown got in his left, but not heavily, on Sampson's collar-bone. He again hit over with his right, but Sampson shifting, he caught him on the back of the head. Sampson again tried his left, but was stopped neatly. Again he feinted, and then let go, successfully planting a sharp hit on Brown's head. Brown rushed to a close, and mutual fibbing ensued. Brown succeeded in throwing Sampson, falling on him, and leaving a large red mark on his breast-bone. This round lasted ten minutes.

2.—Brown all anxious to begin; Sampson waiting on the defensive. Sampson's left stopped, when Brown again hit over with the right, catching Sampson high on the side of the head, no mischief done. Sampson, who had been watching for an opening, got it, and sent in his left a smasher on Brown's left eye, which instantly swelled in sign of the force of the blow. First blood was claimed for Sampson, who again went in and visited Brown's left ear heavily.

Brown caught Sampson on the side of the head with his right, and in the close threw him. (The Sampsonites were now uproarious, and backing two to one—any odds —on Sampson.)

3.—Brown went in resolutely; Sampson hit up and tried to fib him, but got down quickly in the close.

4.—Sampson on the defensive, and retreating; Brown forcing the fighting. After one or two short exchanges Brown sent a fair hit with the right straight on Sampson's left ear, and floored him. (Shouts for Brown, but the Sampson party drowned them by cries of " Two to one," &c.) First knockdown to Brown.

5.—Sampson got in lightly on Brown's jaw. Brown caught him on the head with the right, and with the left on the breast. A sharp rally followed, in which hits were exchanged. Sampson fell on one knee, but although open to receive a blow, Brown withheld his arm and walked away, in his anxiety to avoid any appearance of unfair advantage.

6.—Sampson, after some sparring, caught Brown a tremendous smack in the right eye, balancing the favour to the left. Brown bored in, a desperate rally followed, and a close. Sampson hit up well, and put in a sharp hit as they were going down together.

7.—Brown's eyes were both in mourning, but he was strong and active. Seeing he had the worst of out-fighting he worked his way in, nobbing Sampson with some severity. In the close Brown tried to screw up Sampson for the throw, but he slipped through his arms, hitting up, and got down cleverly.

8.—Sampson exhibited signs of distress. He breathed heavily, while Brown, though most punished, was strong and firm on his legs. Sampson popped in his left, but Brown sent in a heavy one on his nob in return. Counter-hits—Brown on Sampson's throat, Sampson on Brown's damaged right eye. Brown closed, and threw Sampson a heavy cross-buttock, falling over him.

9.—Brown still forcing the fighting; Sampson on the defensive. Brown reached Sampson's head with each hand, but got it in return. In the close at the ropes Sampson got down. (Sampson's friends were ominously silent as he was taken to his corner.)

10.—Sampson's forehead exhibited a large bump, the effects of the nobber in the last round. In the exchanges which followed, Sampson was active, and several times planted on Brown. In a ding-dong rally Brown caught Sampson such a back-handed slap as he was going down that a spectator said, "A Shelton hit, by Jupiter!" alluding to the finishing touch in the fight of Brown and Shelton.

11.—Brown pursued Sampson vigorously, who hit up, catching him in the eye; Brown persevered, and finally Sampson went down in the hitting.

12.—Sampson popped in a facer, but it did not show. Brown took to weaving; a close. As Sampson was going down, Holt rolled himself down on the grass, so that his man partially fell on him, and was saved direct contact with the ground. (This was a common trick of seconds in old times, but is unfair. The seconds have no right to quit their corners until the end of the round.)

13.—Brown rushed in, and hit Sampson on the crown of his head. Sampson fell, weak.

14.—Brown's left eye was almost dark, and his right was damaged. A rally, in which Sampson hit straightest, and Brown was down from a slip.

15.—Brown, full of fight, worked away at his man—hit him with his left in the neck, and threw him.

16.—Brown pursued the boring game, giving Sampson no time for sparring. After a short bustle at the ropes, he got Sampson round the neck with the left and threw him a cross-buttock. Sampson, on being lifted, looked queer and stiff. (The outer ring was now broken in, and the inner-ring spectators

forced into and on to the ropes; it was, however, beaten out, and the fight proceeded.)

17.—Brown rushed in, hit over with his right, and fell from the overreach. Sampson stood up. (Cheers from the Brums.)

18.—Brown, still taking the initiative, hit Sampson on the head, who gave him, in return, a severe upper cut with the left, drawing the claret from his mouth and nose. Brown closed, but Sampson got down easy.

19.—Brown hit away right and left; Sampson retreating, exchange of hits; Sampson weak. Brown tried for the fall, but Sampson got down.

20.—Sampson came to the scratch bleeding freely from the olfactory organ. Brown again at work, Sampson popping in an occasional prop, but getting down to avoid a struggle. (Here the ring was again broken in, and great uproar ensued. Several robberies were effected, and the cries and denunciations of Brown were furious.)

21.—The interior of the ring was cleared. On coming to the scratch Sampson showed weakness. Brown lost not a moment in going to work; he hit away without hesitation. Sampson retreated to the ropes. Brown nailed him with the right on the ear; he fell across the ropes, where Brown hit him four or five blows, and he fell stupefied. (The uproar now became tremendous. A leader of Sampson's party pressed into the ring with a bottle in his hand; Brown was struck, and three minutes given to Sampson to recover. The referee was appealed to, but he escaped from the crowd and hurried to Doncaster, where he pronounced Brown to be the winner. Sampson's party bringing up their man, Brown's seconds allowed him to renew the fight, and the men met for round

22.—Brown fought Sampson down.

23.—General confusion. Sampson down in a scrambling rally.

24.—No time kept. Sampson brought up to face his man, who immediately fought him down. (The ring was here entirely broken in, and Brown struck more than once. He was kicked in the eye, and received a blow on the head from a stake.)

REMARKS.—Mr. Marshall, Clerk of the Course of Wolverhampton, seeing Brown's life in danger, withdrew him forcibly from the ring, whereon (after an interval) Sampson was brought to the mark, and proclaimed winner, amidst the shouts of his partisans. The stakeholder, Mr. Beardsworth, was loud in his condemnation of the violence used towards Brown. Yet when he returned to Doncaster he declared that Brown having left the ring, he "had given the money to Sampson. His friends had hunted him up, and there was an end on't."

Mr. Beardsworth, however, found that Brown was not so easily disposed of. At the Stafford Assizes in March of the following year was tried the action of Brown *versus* Beardsworth, in which the plaintiff sought to recover £200 (his own stake) paid into the hands of Mr. Beardsworth, of the Repository, Birmingham, on certain conditions set forth in the declaration. Mr. Campbell (afterwards Chief Justice and Chancellor) was for the plaintiff, Mr. Jarvis (afterwards Judge) for the defendant. Mr. Jarvis's defence (after an assertion that his client had paid over the money to Sampson) was a tirade against the Ring, gamblers, &c., and an appeal to " scout the case out of Court." Nevertheless the jury, by direction of Mr. Justice Littledale, were left to consider the "weight of testimony," and gave a verdict for £200 in favour of the plaintiff.

Brown now betook himself to his vocation as a Boniface in his native town, where he earned the respect of his neighbours and customers, justifying by his good conduct the axiom that " a man's profession never disgraces him unless his conduct disgraces the profession."

CHAPTER XIII.

PHIL SAMPSON ("THE BIRMINGHAM YOUTH")— 1819—1831.

PHIL SAMPSON, who was to the full as ready at chaffing and writing as at fighting, occupied at one period an undue share of newspaper space and of the public time. His milling career, though chequered, was not without brilliant gleams of success.

Sampson was born on the 27th of September, 1800, at Snaith, in Yorkshire; but when he was no more than a few months old his parents migrated to Birmingham and settled in the "hardware village," then rapidly rising in manufacturing prosperity as the metropolis of gun-making, cheap jewellery, and hardware. Pierce Egan tells us that Phil was "intended for a parson," but that "he preferred thumping nobs to a cushion." If so, and we remember him well, his acquirements in the *literæ humaniores* did not say much for his "college." Indeed, we have seen specimens of Philip's caligraphy which forbid belief in such a tradition. What we know, however, is that young Phil was a button-maker in a Brummagem factory at fifteen. We shall pass also young Phil's apocrypnal contests, in which he (and almost every other boxer in "Boxiana") fought and "polished off" men of all sorts, weights, and sizes, and come to his introduction to the Ring.

Gregson being at Birmingham on one of his sparring tours, the proficiency of Sampson, who put on the gloves with several countrymen, attracted the attention of that clumsy practitioner, who observed to him, "I think thee hadst better coom and try thy fortin in Lunnon, lad, 'moongst some o' t' loight woights." Sampson at that time had considerable scruples in his mind about fighting for a prize, although he was very fond of boxing, and declined the offer of Gregson. But, on his trade (button-making) failing badly from change of fashion, he determined to come to London to see his friend Bob. He found a hearty welcome from the latter at the

"Mare and Magpie," St. Catherine's, but, before Gregson could bring his *protégé* into the Ring, he left London for Dublin.   Sampson was now quite adrift, but owing to the good services of Mr. Baxter (brother to Ned Turner) he found a friend who enabled him to take a turn among the fistic heroes of the Metropolis.

Sampson's first appearance in the London Prize Ring might be termed little more than a turn-up.   He had been witnessing the battle, at Moulsey Hurst, on Tuesday, August 24th, 1819, between Cy. Davis and Boshell, and also Scroggins and Josh Hudson, and had crossed the water, on the point of returning to town, when he was unexpectedly brought into action owing to the following circumstance.   In the conversation which took place during dinner at Lawrence's, the "Red Lion," Hampton, it was mentioned by Ned Painter that a youth from Birmingham, about eleven stone and a half, had been on the Hurst to offer himself as a candidate, but none of the middle weights, much less the light ones, had fancied him, at which he was much disappointed.   An eminent brewer and a gallant captain immediately offered ten pounds if Dolly Smith, who was at hand, and who had fought Tom Cannon and Bill Abbot, would try what the new "piece of hardware" was worth.   Phil was sent for, and cheerfully accepted the task.

The combatants were informed that if anything like collusion or division of the stakes occurred not one penny would be paid over, and that the best man must win.   A select party thereon returned to the Hurst, and at six o'clock in the evening Smith stripped, seconded by Rolph and Ned Weston, Sampson being waited upon by Josh Hudson and Baxter.   The reporters having gone off to town, we are merely told that in fifteen minutes poor Dolly (who was decidedly out of condition) was defeated, being nobbed all over the ring and thrown like a sack by the new-comer.   The activity and slashing blows of Sampson astonished the amateurs, some of his right-hand deliveries appearing to completely stupefy Dolly, who behaved gamely and well, but had not even a chance turn throughout.

Phil, being an active, chatty, and certainly fast and bounceable young fellow, was at once in high favour with the "upper crust."

Accordingly, on Tuesday, October 26th, 1819, he was at Wallingham Common, when, Turner having defeated Martin, ten guineas was announced as a purse, in addition to ten guineas from the Pugilistic Club, for the best of two men of eleven stone and upwards.   Josh Hudson, ever ready, offered himself; and Phil Sampson, as the event proved rashly, challenged the prize from the John Bull Fighter. It was a tremendous fight for a short time, but at the end of forty minutes Sampson was defeated. (See *Life of* HUDSON, *ante*, Chapter IV.)

Sampson, after a short interval, was matched against Abraham Belasco, the scientific Jew, for fifty guineas a side. This battle took place at Potter's Street, in Essex, twenty-one miles from London, on Tuesday, February 22nd, 1819. The badness of the day did not deter the Fancy from quitting the Metropolis at an early hour, and the combatants entered the ring, which was well covered with sawdust owing to the wetness of the ground, at one o'clock. Belasco appeared a few minutes before his opponent, attended by Oliver and Josh Hudson; the Birmingham Youth was waited upon by Painter and Shelton. Belasco was the favourite at six to four.

THE FIGHT.

Round 1.—Sparring; Belasco let fly, but was stopped. Sampson put in a sharp hit under the Jew's arm. Both went in. Exchanges. In struggling Belasco down. ("Go along, my little youth.")

2.—Counter-hits; a pause; the Birmingham Youth rushed in, and got to the ropes. In the struggle to fib the Jew, he slipped down. (Two to one on Belasco.)

3.—The Birmingham Youth drew first blood, and, in a struggle, the Jew went down from a slip. (Great shouting in favour of the Birmingham Youth.)

4.—Belasco stopped and hit well; a good rally; Sampson received a heavy body blow and went down.

5.—The Jew went to work, bled his opponent, and sent him down on his rump, rather weak. The Jew also went down.

6.—Sparring, and the Birmingham Youth piping. The Jew put in two good hits. Sampson returned, till he was got to the ropes, where he got it sharply, and in the struggle went down, Belasco uppermost.

7.—Belasco slipped down, cunning, and the Youth stood looking at him. (Hissing.)

8.—This was a well-fought round, and Belasco hit Sampson away; but the latter, in game style, returned to the charge, and fought like a hero till both were down, the Jew uppermost.

9.—Sampson commenced this round in gallant style; but Belasco changed it by good fighting, and had Sampson down at the ropes.

10.—After a few exchanges at the ropes, Sampson went down, but a good round altogether. ("Well done, Belasco!")

11.—After a hit or two, the Jew got Sampson at the ropes, and was fibbing him in good style, till he dropped on one knee. The strength and skill of Belasco enabled him to hold up his opponent, and weave on, till he got Sampson down on both his knees.

In the last two rounds Sampson was getting weak, and, to escape from severe fibbing in the eleventh, he fell one knee, but Belasco kept holding him up and punishing till he was down on both of his knees. "Foul" and "fair" were instantly cried out, when Painter and Shelton took Sampson out of the ring, put him into a post-chaise, and drove off without appealing to the umpires on the subject. This was certainly wrong; and, owing to this circumstance, a fierce dispute arose. No man should be taken out of the ring till the umpires have decided upon the propriety of such a step. Both sides may dispute, but it is only the umpires that can set it right. The superior science of the Jew prevented the hitherto slashing hitting of Sampson, which was so heavily experienced by Josh Hudson. Belasco stopped many blows in good style, and gave the movements of Sampson the appearance of being slow. It was by no means a decisive fight, such as the "Ould Fanciers" are fond of witnessing; although two to one was betted on Belasco, and even a point further, on the round previous to Sampson's being taken out of the ring. It was generally asserted that the Birmingham Youth was the best man, owing to his youth, but as to knowledge of milling, Belasco had the advantage.

'The decision of the umpires being appealed to, the dispute was finally argued and determined before Mr. Jackson, in presence of several persons of experience. The judgment given was simply as follows—" That as no objection had been made to the umpires on their being appointed to their situations; and also both of them uniting in one opinion that Belasco's conduct was fair; and, further, no interference of the referee having been called for, their decision must be considered final." This decided the paying of bets; and as the battle-money was given up to the Jew, it was insisted upon, in sporting phrase, that bets follow the battle-money.

Sampson was not pleased with the termination of the fight, and accidentally meeting the Jew at a house in Bond Street, where some friends were arguing the subject, the men got suddenly in collision; but after fighting a few minutes, during which nothing was the matter, the friends of the Jew took him away, saying "it was no fun to fight for nothing."

At Richmond's benefit at the Royal Tennis Court, Windmill Street, Haymarket, on Tuesday, February 29th, 1820, on the announcement of " Belasco and the Birmingham Youth," curiosity was on the stretch. It was a regular glove fight for nine rounds, and Sampson appeared so determined to get the better of the Jew that he disdained allowing any time between the rounds, till he not only exhausted himself, but distressed his opponent to a standstill. The Jew seemed now satisfied, and, while in the act of bowing to the audience and pulling off the gloves, Sampson said he should not leave off, and hit Belasco on the side of his head. The latter immediately returned the compliment, but had the worst of the round, and was thrown. It was considered necessary to part them, and Cribb took Sampson away. It was in fact a discreditable display of bad temper on the part of the Birmingham Youth.

In consequence of a purse of £50 given by the Pugilistic Club, and a private stake of £25 a side, Sampson entered the lists with Jack Martin, at North Walsham, on the 17th of July, 1820. After a sharp battle Sampson was defeated. (See Life of MARTIN, ante.)

Sampson was now certainly " under a cloud." Chance, however, brought him again into notice. A man of the name of Tom Dye, known as " Di the Table-lifter," a public exhibitor of feats of strength, who could carry a mahogany dining-table seven or eight feet long with his teeth, tie a pair of tongs round a man's neck by way of cravat, and break a poker across his arm like a rotten stick, was chaffed about the strength of Sampson. He expressed his opinion that he could dispose of the modern wearer of the name in very summary fashion, to which " the Youth" demurred, and a purse of five sovs. was offered if "Di" would make the experiment. It turned out an easy job for Sampson. In eight minutes, during which six rounds were fought, "Di" was completely *hors de combat* when time was called. On coming to, the "strong man" declared he was not fairly beaten, on which "the Youth" told him to "take his own time," and "Di" again put up his hands. He soon repented, for Sampson milled him down so suddenly that poor "Di" forgot for a while all about tables and pokers. Sampson had not a mark, and presented the crestfallen table-lifter with half-a-sovereign "to wash his teeth with."

The ill feeling of Sampson towards Belasco again broke out, and the latter, it would seem, declared his intention of thrashing his late opponent wherever he met him. In consequence Belasco, at Tom Oliver's benefit at the Tennis Court, on Monday, December 21st, 1820, mounted the stage, and said that being thus continually threatened he would accommodate Sampson for £100 or £50 a side. Hereupon Sampson rushed on the stage intemperately and declared his intention to fight "if any gentleman, who is a gentleman, will hold the money. That is necessary," he added, "as I have been robbed of the last fight. I am also ready to set to with Belasco immediately." Belasco coolly replied by putting on the mufflers, and at it they went for

A GLOVE FIGHT.

Round 1.—Both cautious, and eyeing each other. Sampson plunged in, and some exchanges took place, when Belasco slipped down, and Sampson was also on the floor.

2.—Very short work; Sampson's temper got the mastery of his skill. Belasco caught him as he came in, got his head in the corner of the stage, and fibbed him down. (Hissing from some parts of the court. "Nothing unfair," was the cry from the other. "Never mind," said Sampson, "it's all right, Belasco, come along.")

3.—Milling without ceremony, till Sampson put in a most tremendous nobber on the Jew's temple that completely stunned him for the instant, accompanying it with "Where are you now?" If it had been in the ring, it must have proved a winning hit. Belasco caught hold of the rails to prevent going down, and said, "Never mind, I'll soon be ready for you." The Birmingham Youth waited till the Jew was ready to commence another round.

4.—Very severe; both down.

5.—The Jew displayed science, but the rush of the Youth was sharp in the extreme, and pepper was the result, till they separated.

6.—Each man appeared anxious to have the "best of it." This was altogether a fine round, but, in closing, both down, the Youth undermost. In separating, the Jew, on getting up, from the motions he made, seemed as if his shoulder were hurt. Belasco stretched his arm on the rail, and the Youth rubbed his shoulder, amidst much laughter.

7.—Both down again, when the Jew made a similar complaint, and rubbed his arm. Here a surgeon stepped up, examined the shoulder, and said it was not out.

8.—Sampson had the best of it; but in struggling and going down, they both nearly fell through the rails of the stage into the court.

9.—The Jew said his shoulder was now so bad that he could not use it; but, in order to prevent disappointment, he would continue the combat with one hand only, if Sampson would agree to it. The latter said he had no objection, and each of them pulled off one glove, and commenced this *nouvelle* exhibition. (Loud cries of "Leave off," "Go on," &c.) Belasco received some pepper, and went down.

10.—This round was well contested; the

Jew, however, used his arm in the rally; indeed, neither of their hands were idle.

11.—Again a rally, and Sampson fought with both hands, Belasco following suit.

12.—This was the finale. Belasco was hit down, or seemed to be so. He sat upon his nether end quietly, and thunders of applause greeted the success of Sampson, who threw his remaining glove on the floor. Belasco rose and immediately addressed the spectators. He said he would fight Sampson that day six weeks for £50. ("Bravo.")

Mr. Sampson's skill in letter-writing, and in avoiding making a match, was now in full play for some months, and nothing done *in re* Belasco. Charley Grantham (alias Gybletts), however, was backed against Sampson for £50 a side, and on Tuesday, July 17th, 1821, the men met on Moulsey Hurst. At one o'clock Sampson, attended by Tom Spring and Hickman (the Gaslight Man), threw his hat within the ropes. In a few minutes afterwards Gybletts, with Harry Harmer and Bob Purcell, entered the ring. Sampson was the favourite at seven to four.

"The Youth," who looked in good condition, in his usual thrasonical style informed his friends he should "win in twenty minutes." It was not, however, the "straight tip," for Sampson was defeated in one hour and twenty minutes, the "flash side" losing their money, and another "moral certainty" going wrong.

Bill Abbott, whose recent victory over Tom Oliver had given him a high position, offered himself to Sampson, and the men met at Moulsey on December 13th, 1821. Here again Sampson was beaten in forty-seven minutes, forty-three rounds having been fought in that time.

The current of adversity now ran hard against Phil. His nominal townsman (Phil himself was a Yorkshireman), Bill Hall, assuming to himself the title of "the New Birmingham Lad," challenged "the slashing and scientific Sampson," as Pierce Egan was wont to call him.

On Tuesday, July 30th, 1822, on Warwick Racecourse, in a roped ring, in front of the grand stand, the "countryman" beat Sampson, after a shifty tumbledown fight of ninety-one rounds; Josh Hudson giving in for him with odds of two to one in his favour. The contemporary reports intimate that Sampson had only "a small amethyst under his eye," and had hard work to "look like losing it."

Sampson was pathetically verbose in print and talk about "the cruelty" of charging him with a complicity in his own defeat. He also expressed his desire for another trial with Hall, attributing his failure solely to want of condition. Meanwhile, Bill Hall had been consummately thrashed by Ned Neale (see Life of NEALE), a fact which did not tend to the satisfaction of the backers of the boastful Birmingham Youth, who left London "disgusted at their desertion."

At length Phil, who had certainly improved in strength and condition, persuaded his Birmingham friends that if they would give him another chance with Hall he would dispose of him with ease and win their money to a certainty. So a second match was made for £50, and on Wednesday, March 19th, 1823, the old Hurst at Moulsey was the arena of encounter, after the ring had been quitted by Arthur Matthewson, who that day polished off Mishter Israel Belasco, brother of Aby of that ilk.

Sampson had good attendants; no other than Tom Spring, champion *in esse*, and Jem Ward, ditto *in posse*. Hall had behind him Josh Hudson and "a friend from Birmingham." Such, however, was the want of confidence in "the Youth," that six to four on Hall went begging. "We'll wait and see," said those who were asked to speculate. The spectators had not long to wait, as will be seen by our report of

THE FIGHT.

Round 1.—No sooner had the men shaken hands than Hall ran at his opponent like a mad bull. Sampson got out of the way of his fury like an agile toreador, and then, by a half-turn, put in so severe a blow on Hall's nob that he lost his legs in a twinkling. ("Halloo! What's the matter? Sampson will win this time!")

2.—Hall seemed furious at his unexpected floorer. He ran after Sampson, pelting away, without any regard to science, and making Sampson fight under the idea of reducing his strength. In a short rally at the ropes Sampson put in a right-handed hit on his opponent's left eye, after the manner of his agonistic namesake, and Hall fell like a log. On his seconds picking him up he was completely insensible. The battle of course was at an end. A medical man stepped into the ring, bled Hall, and paid him every humane attention requisite, but several minutes elapsed before a return of consciousness could be discerned. Hall was then driven off, nearly in a state of stupor, in a coach, accompanied by the doctor.

REMARKS.—Hall, not the "John," but the "mad," bull fighter, to the great surprise and satisfaction of his friends, appeared at the Castle Tavern as early as eight o'clock on the same evening, thus contradicting the alarming rumours of his death. It appears that his recollection did not return to him till after he had been twice bled, and twenty-five minutes had elapsed, and even then his ideas were in a very confused state, so tremendous were the effects of the blow. Hall informed the company he did not feel himself any the worse, except from the sore state of his arm, rendered so by the instruments of the surgeon. The latter thought Hall in fine condition. It was now evident to the amateurs that Sampson was an improved man; and this little slice of fortune increased his confidence so much that he returned to Birmingham with all the honours of war.

In January, 1823, we find Sampson inditing insulting letters on Israelites in general, and Belasco in particular, in the *Weekly Dispatch*, which were responded to in more parliamentary language in the columns of *Bell's Life*, and "these paper pellets of the brain," after five months of popping, assumed the form of "Articles of Agreement," dated June 19th, 1823, whereby Philip Sampson and Abraham Belasco mutually bound themselves to fight in a twenty-four foot ring, half-minute time, for £100 a side, on Tuesday, the 25th of August, 1823, Mr. Jackson to name the place. "On signing the articles," says the reporter, "Sampson poured out a couple of glasses of port, and, handing one of them to his opponent, gave the toast, 'May the best man win.' 'I hope he will,' said Belasco, tossing off his glass."

Crawley Downs, in Sussex, was the fixture, and such of the Fancy as respected their nags too much to give the animals some sixty-six miles in a day were to be seen on the Monday trotting through Riddlesdown, Reigate, and East Grinstead, stopping to bait, " blow a cloud," and enjoy a chaff with Boniface, whose jocund countenance bespoke his pleasure at sight of such good customers.

In the morning Crawley Downs were alive with arrivals from all quarters of the compass. Sampson came on the ground in a barouche and four, enveloped in a large blue military cloak ; while Belasco trotted over the turf behind eighty guineas' worth of horseflesh, driven by a well-known East-end sportsman. At a few minutes past one Sampson threw his white nob-cover into the ring, and taking his bright crimson kerchief from his throat handed it to Josh Hudson, who, with Ben Burn, were his chosen seconds. Belasco quickly followed suit, dropping his beaver quietly within the ropes, and his colours, " a yellowman," were also fixed to the centre stake. Peter Crawley, in a bright green Newmarket and Belcher tie, with Bill Richmond, in West End Corinthian costume, acted as " esquires of the body " to Aby, who said to Josh across the ring, " Now, let's have a quiet fight, let it go which way it will." The seconds concurred, and we must say we never saw a mill better conducted, as a whole, by all parties concerned. The betting opened at five to four on Belasco.

THE FIGHT.

Round 1.—Sampson never looked better. The appellation hitherto borne by him of the Birmingham Youth seemed a thing of the past ; the gristle had become bone, and the smoothness of limb laced and knotted with hard and well-marked muscle. In fact, he looked a model athlete. Belasco was also a picture of a man in fine health ; his bust, a perfect anatomical study, together with his black nob, penetrating eye, and Mosaic countenance, rendered the Jew an interesting object in this ballet of action. Confidence sat on his brow ; he was cool, collected, and evidently anticipated victory. Upon shaking hands it was the general opinion that Sampson would have attempted to slaughter Belasco, in order to win off-hand, as a long fight might prove dangerous to him. Not so ; Sampson was cautious in the extreme. Belasco placed his hands very high, convinced the spectators he was an adept in science, and appeared armed at all points against the slashing onset of his adversary. Considerable dodging occurred, and several slight offers were made on both sides, but neither of them was to be deceived by the feints of the other. Belasco's left hand told slightly on Sampson's body without a return ; it was soon after repeated. Both eyeing each other for a short period, when Sampson put down his hands and rubbed them on his drawers. Sampson still cautious. The left hand of Belasco again told slightly on his antagonist's body. A pause. Each combatant attempted to hit, but their blows fell short. (Four minutes had elapsed.) Sampson at length made himself up for mischief, and let fly at the Jew's nob with tremendous force, but Belasco stopped it in the most skilful style. ("Beautiful ! bravo !") Sampson again tried it on, when an exchange of blows occurred, and Belasco's right eye received a little damage.

The Jew got away cleverly from another well-aimed nobber; and, in closing at the ropes, Belasco had the best of the fibbing, till Sampson went down on his back, and his opponent upon him. (Applause on both sides. The Sheenies said "it was all right," and the Brums observed "nothing was the matter.")

2.—Sampson hit the Jew in the body, but Belasco soon afterwards put in a sharp facer, and followed his opponent to do mischief. Counter-hitters and nobbers were the result. A short rally followed, the left eye of Sampson received a touch. In closing, both down, Sampson undermost. ("First blood," exclaimed Joah; "look at the side of Belasco's nose." The claret was just peeping, as it were, between his ogles.)

3.—The fine science displayed by Belasco, in stopping the heavy hits of his opponent, was the admiration of the spectators. The Jew went sharply towards his antagonist, when, after an exchange of blows, Sampson got down.

4.—This was a pretty round, and fine fighting on both sides was conspicuous. In struggling at the ropes, Sampson went down rather awkwardly, and Belasco, being in the act of hitting, struck his opponent on the nob. "Foul, foul!" by the Sampsonites; "Fair, fair!" by the Sheenies. The referee said "nothing wrong had occurred; but he felt afraid that he had consented to take upon himself a very difficult situation, as the opposite parties did not appear to agree on the true principles of prize-fighting. However, he had not one farthing upon the fight, and he should do his duty if called on to decide."

5.—This round was decidedly in favour of Belasco. He not only got away from a nobber that might have proved a settler, but in turn gave Sampson so heavy a hit on his head that the latter turned round from the force of it, and went a yard or two away; but he soon returned to fight. In closing at the ropes, pepper was used between them till both were down, Belasco undermost. (The latter was much applauded, and, up to this period of the fight, continued the favourite.)

6.—The Jew was also the hero in this round. Sampson appeared rather distressed. Belasco proved himself a more troublesome customer than his opponent had anticipated; he was indeed very difficult to be got at. Some blows were exchanged, when they closed at the ropes, and ultimately the Jew had the best of it, planting a blow on Sampson's nob as he was going down.

7.—Sampson was on the look-out to put in a slogger on the nob of the Jew, but the science of the latter prevented him. In fact, Sampson, although rather evil-disposed towards his opponent, which he let escape now and then in words, was nevertheless cool in his conduct. The cunning of the Jew, and the firmness of his guard, pointed out clearly to Sampson that he must be careful to avoid committing mistakes when opposed to so accomplished a boxer as Belasco, which accounts, in a great measure, for the Birmingham hero altering his hitherto smashing mode of fighting. The Jew stopped well; and, after an exchange of blows, Belasco dexterously planted a heavy body hit about an inch and a half below the mark, which sent Sampson down on his latter end. (A great burst of applause from the partisans of Belasco, who now, without hesitation, offered £10 to £5—100 to 50—two to one, all over the ring. "It's ash right ash the tay, Aby; feel for his vind next time.")

8.—Sampson, however, did not appear a great deal the worse for his floorer, for he came to the scratch instantly at the call of time. This was a well-fought round on both sides; but the science displayed by Belasco extorted applause from all parts of the ring. He planted a body blow with his left hand, and protected his head so finely with his right as to stop a well-meant heavy hit. Counter-hitting, but Sampson's blows were most severe, from his length; still in closing at the ropes the Jew fibbed Sampson down and fell upon him.

9.—Sampson went in quickly to do mischief, but Belasco made as usual some excellent stops. The Jew, in making a body blow, hit rather low. "What do you call that?" said Sampson. In closing, Sampson went down.

10.—This round was against Belasco. The Jew stopped delightfully at the commencement, but in counter-hitting Belasco received a terrific blow in the middle of his head, which almost knocked him backwards; but he returned to the attack as game as a pebble, and in closing at the ropes had the best of it while hanging upon them, until Sampson, by a desperate effort, extricated himself, and, strange to say, placed the Jew in his own former situation, fibbing Belasco till he went down, bleeding profusely. (The faces of the Brums, which had hitherto been very grave, now assumed a smile, and "Sampson for ever!" was the cry.)

11.—The face of Belasco exhibited punishment. Sampson had also the lead in this round, but he determined not to give a chance away, and in closing he went down. (Murmuring from the Sheenies.)

12.—Belasco endeavoured to plant a hit, but Sampson got away. In closing, Sampson again went down.

13.—The Jew put in a heavy body blow, but one of Sampson's hard hits met Belasco in the middle of his head. The battle was now alive, all parties highly interested, and doubts and fears expressed on both sides. The Jew, full of game, tried to get the lead, obtained it, and Sampson went down.

14.—The length and height of Sampson enabled him to stand over his opponent, and this, added to his excellent knowledge of boxing and increased strength, rendered him no easy opponent for Belasco. (The Jew was irritated in this round from the expressions of Sampson, while they were sparring together, who observed, "I have got you now, Belasco, and I'll not only lick you, but drive your Jew brother out of Birmingham." "Be quiet," said Josh; "fight, and don't talk so." "You can do neither," replied Belasco, "but you are an illiberal fellow." "Keep your temper," urged Crawley.) Belasco ran in and planted two hits; and, in closing, Sampson went down in the best way he could, and received a hit in consequence, which occasioned cries of "Foul!" and "Fair!"

15.—Belasco displayed superior skill in stopping two blows, but in counter-hitting he received such a tremendous blow near his temple that he fell out of the ropes on his head quite stunned. ("It is all up," was the cry; and "Ten to one he does not fight again!") The Sheenies were alarmed, and none but the gamest of the game would ever have come again. Belasco might have left off with honour.)

16.—No sailor "three sheets in the wind" appeared more groggy at the scratch when time was called. In fact, Belasco did not know where he was—his eyes had lost their wonted fire, and it really was a pity to see him standing up to a fine, strong young man like Sampson. The latter, very cautious, did not make play, and the Jew had none the worst of the round. Both down, but Sampson undermost. Six to four on Sampson.

17.—Belasco, recovered a little, fought like a brave man till he was hit down.

18.—The Jew seemed better—he exchanged hits, and was again sent down. Two to one on Sampson.

19.—Against Belasco; but he held up his arms well, and, after stopping a hit or two, got down.

20.—The Jew had recovered considerably; and, although he had the worst of it, Sampson thought it prudent to fight cautiously. Belasco made play with great spirit; but, in counter-hitting, received another severe blow on his head, which sent him out of the ropes. If he had not been a truly game man when time was called he would not have paid attention to it. Three to one.

21.—The Jew resolved that "his people" should have no reason to complain. He commenced fighting, although sorely distressed. The result of the round was that Sampson received a hit, and went down on his knees. ("Bravo, Belasco, you are a game fellow," from Tom Owen, "but you are overmatched.")

22.—The finish of this round was in favour of Belasco, and he fibbed Sampson down. ("It is anybody's battle, now," cried an old sportsman; "a good hit would decide it either way." "I'll lay forty to ten," said Tom Oliver, "Sampson wins!" "Stake," said a gentleman from Houndsditch, "and I will take it." Oliver didn't.)

23.—The face of Belasco was piteous, and his right eye swelled prodigiously; but he came to the scratch determined to dispute every inch of ground while a chance remained. "A little one for Mother Melsom," said Josh, "and the battle is at an end." Sampson saw that conquest was within his grasp, and he was determined to win it without risk. He accordingly let Belasco commence fighting before he offered to return. The Jew went down from a straight blow, quite exhausted. ("Take the brave fellow away; he ought not to be suffered to come again." "I am not licked yet," said Belasco.)

24, and last.—It was evident the battle must be soon over, but Belasco answered the call of time like a man. The Jew was too distressed to protect himself with his usual skill, and he received a hit in the middle of his face that floored him slap on his back. He was picked up by his seconds, but in a state of stupor. When the half-minute had elapsed Belasco remained insensible, and Sampson was declared the winner. It was over in forty-two minutes.

REMARKS.—Sampson retired from the contest with very trifling marks upon his face. He is altogether an improved man; his frame is set, and his fighting eminently superior to the style he exhibited in his battles with Martin, Gybletts, and Abbott. We think that he ought to have won the last-named fight. Nevertheless, it confers honour upon his milling talents to conquer so accomplished a boxer as Belasco proved himself to be. To speak of the Jew as he deserves, or of one brave man that has surrendered to another, it is thus: It is true Belasco has been defeated, but he stands higher in the estimation of his friends than ever; let no more slurs be thrown upon him as to "a white feather"! He had to contend against height, length, weight, and youth, added to which Sampson was also a good fighter and a high-couraged man. He has not disgraced "his people." The Jew was brought into the ring in spirited style, but we applaud most the feeling manner in which he was supported out of it. Every attention that humanity could suggest was paid to Belasco. A medical gentleman, of his own persuasion, brought down from London solely for that purpose, had the care of him. We could, if necessary, mention a list of Israelites who were most assiduous on this occasion, but we feel assured the sporting world will appreciate such feeling, generosity, and gentlemanly conduct. The weight of Sampson was said to be twelve stone three pounds; his height, five feet ten-and-a-half inches—Belasco, in his clothes, eleven stone six pounds; his height, five feet seven inches. To the credit of both men it may be stated that they now shook hands and became friends; Belasco, as we shall see, becoming a zealous second to Sampson on several important occasions.

Phil now flew at high game. He challenged Jem Ward, then the most promising of the candidates for the Championship. Jem, nothing loth, accommodated him for £100 a side, and on Monday, June 21st, 1824, gave Mr. Sampson an indisputable thrashing in fifty minutes, as chronicled in the memoir of WARD (*ante*, p. 206).

One of the peculiarities of Sampson, which he shared with the renowned Blucher, was that of " not knowing when he was beaten." He had further the remarkable faculty of talking and writing other people over to his own opinion. Thus, in December of the same year, 1824, he got himself backed a second time against Jem Ward, and on this occasion it took " the Black Diamond " only thirty-seven minutes and a half to finally floor " the strong man," all the circumstances of which will be found fully written in the book of " Pugilistica," in the Life of WARD (*ante*, p. 207), to which we beg to refer the reader.

Phil's " vaulting ambition, which o'erleaps the lists and falls on the other side," had now a temporary check, and "My Uncle Ben," who was looking out for a job for his " Nevvy," Jem Burn, proposed a battle with Sampson for £50 a side. After much ink-spilling the articles were formulated, and Tuesday, June 22nd, 1825, fixed. Mr. Jackson named Harpenden Common, near St. Albans, and thither, on the day appointed, the Fancy repaired. Unfortunately on the previous evening a whisper had gone forth that it was to be a squared fight, in consequence of which unfounded rumour lots of gents made up their minds to turn their backs upon the thing altogether. Burn, of course, as he was to win, and nothing else, according to " the man in the street," was backed at six to four, seven to four, and sooner than go without a bet those wiseacres (a wonderfully numerous class at all times) who thought they were in possession of the secret laid two to one. A meddlesome man in office, " dressed in a little brief authority," also turned up, and forbade the mill taking place on the old spot at No Man's Land. The Fancy, always ready to obey the mandates of the authorities, accordingly toddled on a few miles farther, and the ring was formed at Shere Mere, in Bedfordshire. Sampson declared he had been ill-treated by these sinister reports, and hoped his conduct would soon give the lie to his enemies. Jem Burn, at one o'clock, attended by Randall and Uncle Ben, threw his hat into the Ring, and was received with loud cheers. Sampson soon followed, and planted his topper within the ropes, waited upon by Josh Hudson and Rough Robin,

THE FIGHT.

Round 1.—Young Jem looked well; he was highly fancied, and the general opinion seemed to be that the Young One would win it. The canvas of Sampson appeared to be the tougher, and with the utmost coolness he himself went and tied his colours to the stakes, over his opponent's, confidently observing, "These belong to me." The caution displayed by Sampson showed he was anxious to win; and the steadiness of Jem told the fanciers victory was the object he had in view. Two minutes elapsed in eyeing each other, when the Young One let fly, and touched Sampson's body. Sampson gave a grin. A long pause. (The John Bull Fighter was so tired that he laid himself down in the ring, observing, "We are all right; Phil will win at his leisure.") Sampson put in a small taste on Jem's cheek. ("Bravo, Samsy!") The caution observed on both sides was so tiresome to the spectators that "night caps" were called for. At length Burn went spiritedly to work, but Sampson skilfully stopped him right and left. Sampson planted one on the head of his adversary, which provoked Jem to rush in, when Sampson caught him with an up-handed-hit, and My Nevvy fell on his face. The blow was a stunner, and visible on his forehead; the umpires, however, did not decide this to be a knock-down blow. Thirteen minutes and a half.

2.—Jem appeared to be fighting according to "orders"—he was over cautious. ("Never mind," said Josh, "let them do as they like; it is the 'Rising Sun' against the 'Half Moon'—the Moon for my money!") Sampson had decidedly the best of this round, hitting his man right and left. In closing, Burn was hit down. This round decided first blood and the first knock-down blow. Five to four on Sampson.

3.—Jem was not deficient in pluck, and came to the scratch like a good one. Jem planted a nobber, but Sampson countered well. A rally, in which Jem was sent down. Seven to four on Brummagem.

4.—This was a fine round, and good fighting on both sides. Burn was troublesome; but the skill and coolness displayed by Sampson were the admiration of the spectators. Some exchanges that told on both sides, but Jem had the worst of it. The claret made its appearance under Burn's left ogle, and Sampson, by way of a finish, hit his antagonist down. Two to one on the Brum.

5.—Burn, full of spirit, tried to punish the Brum, but he was stopped, nobbed right and left, and thrown into the bargain.

6.—This was short but sweet to Phil. Sampson stopped capitally, and, in turn, planted two facers—botherers—so much so that Burn staggered, turned round, and fell on his face.

7.—The nob of Jem was changed, but his courage never forsook him. The coolness of Sampson enabled him to plant his blows with effect. Jem lost many hits by being on the blinking system; he rushed in to mill, but Sampson caught him as he came. In a sharp rally, Jem went down.

8.—A tiny bit of a change for Jem—he sent Sampson down at the close of the round. (Loud shouting for Burn. "Do that once more; Phil don't like it—you'll soon make his knees tremble." "Tremble, indeed!" replied the Brum. "Fetch a fiddle, and I'll bet a pound I dance a hornpipe.")

9.—Jem was piping, and Sampson a little winded. The latter planted a jobber over the left eye of his opponent, and got away. (Great applause. "Fighting such as this looks like a +, don't it?" said jolly Josh, rubbing his hands.) Some excellent stops on both sides, and sharp exchanges of blows, till Burn napped an out-and-out one on his nob, which dropped My Nevvy. Three to one on Brummagem.

10.—Forty-eight minutes had elapsed, and Sampson was as fresh as a four-year-old. Burn, notwithstanding the state of his face, was game as a pebble, and stood to his work like a man. Sampson received a note of hand on his conk, without giving the return. Sharp fighting, till Burn went down.

11.—This round was a fine specimen of the art of self-defence; and both combatants displayed great skill. The right eye of Jem was nearly in the dark, and he raised his hand to wipe it. Sampson, quick as lightning, endeavoured to take advantage of the opening, let fly with his left, but to the surprise of the spectators Burn stopped him. This circumstance produced thunders of applause for Jem. Burn again stopped several blows; but at the conclusion of the round he was floored like a shot by a tremendous hit on the mouth. Jem put his hand to his head as he lay on the ground.

12.—This round, by the decided manner in which he took the lead, and also in finishing it by a heavy throw, rendered Sampson the favourite at four to one.

13.—The friends of Jem still stuck to him, and were filled with hopes that, as he had displayed so much real game, he might be able to wear out Sampson; but the latter was cool and collected. Jem was countered, and, in a hard struggle at the ropes, severely fibbed down. ("The 'Half Moon' now," said Josh, "has nearly put the 'Rising Sun' into darkness. Very nasty, Mr. Broad Day, eh?")

14.—Jem went down from a left-handed blow.

15.—Burn was really mischievous, and in close quarters nobbed Sampson heavily. ("Keep off," said Josh, "don't give a chance away.") Sampson measured his distance well, and poor Jem again went down.

16.—It was booked that Jem could not

win; but the brave fellow had not the slightest notion of saying "No!" Sampson waited for an opportunity, and by a flush hit nearly took the fight out of Jem by a floorer. ("Take him away!")

17.—It was now lick or be licked with Jem, and he acted boldly on this determination. Notwithstanding his blinking state, he administered several heavy thumps on Sampson's nob when in close quarters. In closing, Sampson caught Burn's nob under his arm, fibbed, and dropped poor Jem with ease.

18.—A little turn in favour of Burn; the latter, by his boldness, planted some heavy hits, one of which made Sampson stagger, and he fell on the ropes. (A tremendous shout from the friends of Burn, who did not give up hopes of victory.)

19.—Jem came to the scratch, but he was nearly blind. He was soon thrown.

20.—It was piteous to see Jem throw his blows away; he could not see his opponent. Burn received a heavy blow on the nose, and fell on his back. Ten to one, but no takers.

21.—It was nearly "all up" with Jem; he appeared like a man groping in the dark. The humanity of Sampson is worthy of record; he scarcely touched him, and only planted a tap to put an end to the battle. Burn was sent down quite exhausted. ("Take him away.")

22.—Jem, like a drowning man catching at a straw, made a desperate effort, and in a rush at Sampson received another floorer. ("Don't let the brave fellow fight any more —take him away.")

23, and last.—It is worse than death to a man of true courage to experience defeat, and Jem had made up his mind not to pronounce the afflicting "No." Burn had scarcely arrived at the scratch when he was sent down by a trifling touch. ("He shall fight no more," said Uncle Ben, positively, stepping up to the umpires.) It occupied an hour and ten minutes. Sampson immediately shook hands with his fallen opponent. Burn was severely punished about the head, but scarcely any body blows were given throughout the battle.

REMARKS.—Burn fought according to orders. Had he adopted the milling style which characterised the last seven or eight rounds, even if he had not proved victorious, it might have rendered the fight a more even thing. Sampson in all his battles has proved himself a good fighter. Like Jem Burn, he began his career too young. This battle was a most honourable contest, and reflected credit on both the combatants. Jem Burn is a truly game man. Every person returned home well satisfied with the fairness and honesty of the battle.

Hall, of Birmingham, now declared himself anxious to try his luck in a third battle with Sampson; and Phil, with the utmost politeness, agreed to accommodate him without delay for £50 a side. This mill was decided on Tuesday, November 22nd, 1825. The fight was booked as a certainty; "if," as the chaff went, "it was not already made right." Sampson was the favourite at six to four.

Early on Tuesday morning the Fancy were on the alert at Birmingham, Worcester, Coventry, Lichfield, &c., to arrive at Basset's Pole, between Birmingham and Tamworth. Few of the London Fancy were present, as their "minds were completely made up," from the capital fight Sampson made with Ward at Stony Stratford, that Phil must win the battle in a canter; therefore "it would not pay" to undertake so long a trot.

The description of the fight between Sampson and Hall lies in a nutshell, one round having put an end to the contest. Sampson was in prime condition, and certain of winning. Hall was upon equally good terms with himself. Sampson was seconded by Ward and Holland, and Hall by two brothers. On setting to Sampson did not treat his opponent with indifference, but waited for him cool and collected. Three minutes had nearly elapsed in dodging about, when Hall planted a bodier. ("Bravo!"

from his friends.) Sampson returned the compliment with great activity; hit for hit soon took place, and a sharp rally was the result. The men separated, and a trifling pause occurred. Sampson made himself up for mischief, and with his left delivered a heavy blow under his opponent's ear which gave him the doldrums; by way of quietus he then planted with his right so severe a facer that Hall was floored like a shot. When time was called Hall was insensible, and remained in a state of stupor for several minutes. Thus Sampson was pronounced the conqueror in the short space of four minutes and three-quarters. The backers of Hall looked not a little blue on viewing their man so easily disposed of by Sampson, and the spectators in general were much disappointed at so short a contest. The winners, however, held a contrary opinion, and were in high spirits, observing "the fight was long enough for them;" and Sampson, with a smile upon his face, stated that "he should like to be paid for such another job, as £100 for under five minutes was not to be done every day, even in the highest professions." The "Sage of the East," in a discourse upon the event, declared Sampson's right-hander to be "a golden hit"!

Owing to a quarrel with Josh Hudson at the East End, January 31st, 1826, Josh being by no means *compos*, Sampson beat the "John Bull Fighter" in six rounds, not much to the credit of the former. As a *per contra*, on June 30th, 1826, his bounce and quarrelsomeness got him a *third* thrashing from Jem Ward, which was administered by the Champion in ten rounds, at Norwich, while on a sporting tour. Sampson also put out at this time a challenge to Brown, of Bridgnorth, to fight for £50 a side; but the "big one" replied that the price did not suit him, so Sampson wrote again and again to show that Brown *ought* to fight for that sum!

Paul Spencer, a native of Ireland, elegantly designated the "Mud Island Devil," having defeated Manning, of Manchester, felt anxious to obtain a higher situation on the pugilistic roll, and challenged Sampson for £50 a side. Phil approved of this match, observing at the same time, "No Irishman can lick me." The articles stated that the fight should take place on Tuesday, November 27th, 1827, between Birmingham and Liverpool; and Newcastle-under-Lyme was named as the rallying-point. During the Sunday and Monday previous to the battle the above town was filled with visitors from Liverpool, Birmingham, and Manchester. About two miles from Newcastle-under-Lyme the ring was made in front of the grand stand on the racecourse. A few minutes before one o'clock the men arrived on the ground. Sampson threw his hat into the ring, attended by Tom Oliver and Young Gas; and Spencer was waited upon by Donovan and Bob Avery. Both combatants were in excellent condition. Spencer was an object of great interest to his Irish friends. He was a fine strong young fellow, in height five feet eleven inches and a half, weighing thirteen stone one pound. The colours were a crimson fogle for Sampson, and a green with a yellow spot for Spencer. Six to four on Sampson.

THE FIGHT.

Round 1.—The men prepared for action in good style, Spencer adopting Ned Neale's mode of keeping up his left hand. Sampson was also on the alert. After a short time occupied in manœuvring, Spencer endeavoured to make his right and left tell, but Phil got out of danger. A short pause; both on the look-out for an opening, when the Mud Island Devil planted his right hand on Sampson's nob; the latter boxer returned left and right, and a brisk rally was the result. In closing Phil fell on his knee, and Spencer, in fibbing, hit Sampson as he was down. ("Foul!" "Fair!") The friends of Sampson claimed the fight, but the umpires ordered the battle to proceed.

2.—Caution on both sides. Spencer held his left still up, and let fly with his right. Sampson stopped him skilfully, and hit out right and left, delivering well on the nob. A desperate rally followed, in which sharp hits were exchanged. Sampson planted his right on Spencer's mouth as he was rushing in, when Spencer caught him on top of his canister with his right, and made a slight incision. Sampson then closed, and fibbed at the body with his right, while Spencer peppered away at his upper works, but without much effect. At length Spencer got the lock with his right leg, and threw Sampson a cross-buttock, falling heavily upon him. (The Liverpool blades in an uproar; and, "You are sure to win it, Pat.")

3.—Sampson showed blood from his nob, and Spencer from his mouth. Spencer looked a little flushed and dropped his left. Sampson saw the opening, rushed in, and hit him down with a straight one, two, right and left. ("Sampson for ever!" and "Phil, it's all your own!")

4.—Sampson again planted his right and left from the shoulder, cutting Spencer on the left eye. Spencer was not to be shook off, but instantly went to work, hitting out right and left, but wildly. Sampson met Spencer as he rushed in with a few flush hits—a close followed, and some good in-fighting ensued, Sampson feeling for the bread-basket, and Spencer at the nob. Spencer then tried for another cross-buttock, but Sampson was not to be had, and slipped down in time. (Two to one on Sampson.)

The fight was now stopped by the interference of a magistrate. "You cannot fight any longer," said he; "I will not permit it." "It won't be long," cried Sampson; "I'll soon finish him, so let us have it out." "No," said his worship, "I must not. I should have no objection myself, but I have been applied to in my magisterial capacity, and I am forced to act. I am sorry for it, but 'needs must.'" Submission was the order of the day; his worship retired, and the men adjourned back to Newcastle, there to deliberate on further proceedings, Sampson proclaiming to his friends that he was sure to win, and offering three to one on the issue. The men had fought just eight minutes.

On reaching Newcastle Spencer was put to bed, while Sampson remained up with his friends. At length it was agreed, according to the "articles," that the fight should be fought out, and the word was given for taking up new ground at a village called Woore, in Shropshire, on the borders of

Cheshire. The moment the signal was given, "The devil take the hindmost!" was the order of the day, and the rush of the motley group to arrive at the scene of action in time beggared description. It was half-past four, and quite dusk, before the cavalcade reached the "Horse and Jockey," at Woore, in a meadow behind which the ring was again pitched by Tom Oliver.

The best pedestrians were completely knocked up in the run, and several first-rate roadsters beaten to a standstill. The entire group, owing to the wretched state of the road, were nothing but mudlarks.

No time was lost, both men appearing " eager for the fray," and each feeling equal confidence. Sampson showed first in the ring.

SECOND FIGHT.

Round 1.—The eagerness of Spencer to go to work delighted his friends. He cut away right and left, but the superior science of Sampson enabled him to stop the Mud Island Devil's efforts. Still Spencer would not be denied ; he bored in so hard and fast that Sampson was a little bothered, turned round, and retreated to prepare himself for the rude attacks of his opponent. The strength of Spencer was so great that he caught hold of Phil by the neck, and, in going down, pulled Sampson on him.

2.—Phil let fly right and left, and produced the claret from Spencer's domino-box ; nevertheless Spencer peppered away with rapidity ; but Sampson's counters were heaviest, and in the close both were down.

3.—Sampson waited for his opponent and popped in his left with terrific force. Spencer was not to be deterred, but rushed to in-fighting, when Sampson hit him up severely. Spencer then closed and delivered some home thrusts, grappled for the fall, and Sampson slipped down.

4.—Sampson planted his left hand on Spencer's muzzle. Spencer fought wildly, and in closing Sampson went down to avoid being thrown. (Cries of "Foul!" answered by shouts of "Fair!")

5.—Spencer took the lead, and hit out right and left, making his blows tell. Sampson went to work, but missed a terrific right-handed blow, which went over Spencer's shoulder. A good rally followed, and Sampson fell on his knees, receiving a hit as he went down.

6.—Neale called to Spencer to keep his left hand up. Sampson waited, and at length popped in his left on the ear. Counter-hits followed, and Spencer, in closing, pulled Sampson down.

7.—Counter-hitting in a spirited rally. Sampson down.

8.—Sampson was mischievous with his left, Spencer rushed in, when Sampson went down cleverly.

9.—Sampson stopped well, and both fought to a rally ; heavy hits were exchanged, when Spencer seized Sampson round the waist and threw him.

10.—This was a capital milling round. Counter-hitting, and no flinching. Spencer planted right and left, but Sampson caught him dreadfully on the jaw with his right. In the close, Sampson would not be thrown, and got down.

11.—Sampson delivered heavily on Spencer's mug with his left, and broke away. Spencer rushed in, and some good in-fighting followed. In closing Sampson was thrown.

12.—Sampson again put in a dangerous nobber with his left. Spencer countered, but again received right and left, and in the close Sampson went down.

13, and last.—Sampson waited for his man and delivered heavily with his left. Spencer would go in vigorously, but Sampson met him right and left with punishing hits, and jobbed him down. Spencer was hit stupid ; he rolled about, and could not stand when "time" was called. Sampson was proclaimed the victor. The second mill lasted fifteen minutes, making the fight, in the whole, twenty-three minutes. Spencer was heavily punished about the head, but Sampson was not much hurt. Both men were re-conducted to Newcastle the same night.

REMARKS.—Spencer was the right sort of boxer for Sampson. Men that will go and fight with Phil stand a good chance to be polished off-hand. A rushing boxer like Spencer is a sort of gift to him. It is, however, but common justice to observe that Spencer proved himself a game man and a troublesome customer to the Birmingham hero. The amateurs pronounced it a good battle. The right hand of Phil is at all times dangerous, and his experience in the P.R. and his science united render him a fit opponent for any countryman, let him be as strong as Hercules.

After this slice of luck the friends of Sampson rallied round him, and he immediately sent forth all sorts of challenges to all sorts of boxers by means of his editorial amanuensis and his weekly paper. As, however, these epistles, from their bad grammar and attempts at rude wit, do not commend themselves as "elegant extracts," we pass them by. One, to Whiteheaded Bob (who was under articles to fight Ned Neale), was pure "buncombe;" others, such as those to Jem Ward, proposed ridiculously low stakes, and others were mere "gag." One to Big Brown, of Bridgnorth, however, had better fortune.

One of Phil's challenges having taken the form of "Brown giving me (Phil) £20 to make a match for £300 a side," the Big 'un thus replied in another weekly journal:—

"*To the Editor of* 'BELL'S LIFE IN LONDON.'

"SIR,—I apprehend that addressing Philip Sampson through the medium of your valuable paper will be to little purpose. There seems to have been a little bounce, but I wish I could flatter myself there was any reliance to be placed on what he has sent forth to the public.

"With regard to his proposal of my giving him £20 to fight me for £300, my intention was to propose fighting him £320 to £300; for be it remembered that he once got £20 of my money in a way not very satisfactory to myself; but it is not my intention that he shall have any more of it unless I am fairly beat out of time by him, which, if he should happen to do, he shall be most welcome to.

"I will fight him £320 to £300, half-way between Birmingham and Bridgnorth, and I will attend at the place he appoints—the 'Woodman,' Birmingham—on Monday the 24th inst., between the hours of eight and ten p.m., for the purpose of making a deposit and entering into the necessary articles.

"I remain, &c., yours respectfully,
"THOMAS BROWN.

"Bottle-in-Hand Inn, Bridgnorth, December 19th, 1827."

The hero of Bridgnorth in this instance was mistaken about the bounce of the thing; for Sampson's friends were at the place at the appointed time, at the "Woodman," and articles were signed without delay, Mr. Beardsworth, of the Birmingham Repository, being stakeholder.

This big affair was decided at Bishop's Wood, in Shropshire, one hundred and thirty-four miles from London, on Tuesday, April 8th, 1828; and, since the battle between Spring and Langan, no pugilistic event had excited more interest. It appears that Sampson had some difficulty in making up the battle-money, and had it not been for little Arthur Matthewson—who not only stuck to Phil during his training, but procured him the last £70—a forfeit might have been the result of a rash engagement.

The principal patrons of the Ring left London in considerable numbers, on the Sunday and Monday previous, for Birmingham and Wolverhampton.

The latter place was overflowing with company of every description, all the inns crowded to excess, and beds not to be had at any price. The towns and villages contiguous to Wolverhampton came in also for their share of visitors.

Wolverhampton Racecourse was named as the scene of action, in front of the grand stand, an erection capable of accommodating upwards of a thousand spectators, which had been pointed out as a most convenient arena; but a magistrate interposed his authority, and Bishop's Wood was chosen, a lofty eminence, commanding an extensive and delightful prospect. It is situated in Shropshire, on the borders of Staffordshire, twelve miles from Wolverhampton, and about the same distance from Bridgnorth.

On Tuesday morning vast multitudes were *en route* for the scene of action. Vehicles of all sorts were in motion; equestrians and pedestrians thronged the way from Birmingham, Walsall, Dudley, Wednesbury, Bridgnorth, and Stafford, Lichfield, Shrewsbury, and other towns. Brown cut a dash on his turn-out to the ground; he was seated, with his friend Spring and several others, in a landau, his own property, decorated on the panels with the sign of his house at Bridgnorth (a hand holding a bottle), and drawn by four fine horses, while a great number of well-mounted gentlemen formed, as it were, a body-guard. Both Sampson and Brown waited at the "Bradford Arms" till the time arrived for entering the ring. Arrangements on the ground had been made with much judgment. A circle of wagons, with a stage on a convenient spot, formed the external barrier; in front of these the spectators on foot were kept at a distance of several yards from the twenty-four feet ring by a strong circle of ropes and stakes. The ring itself was formed with posts of great thickness, deeply fixed in the earth, and three ropes (one more than the usual number) were affixed to them. The number of spectators could not have been less than 25,000—some persons guessed their numbers at 30,000; of these, at least 15,000 were unable to see the twenty-four feet ring, and were consequently continually pressing forward.

A few minutes before one o'clock, Brown, leaning on the arm of Tom Spring, threw his hat into the ring. He was received with a loud welcome. The appearance of the Bridgnorth hero was prepossessing; he was dressed in the then country gentleman's costume, a blue coat, white cord breeches, and top boots. Sampson appeared soon afterwards, and his friends, in their turn, rent the air with applause. Phil was also well got up. On the entrance of the latter boxer, Brown, who was sitting on the hamper containing the bottles, &c., rose up, and, holding out his hand with a good-natured smile, said, "Well, my boy, how are you?" Sampson gave him his hand, but turned another way with an angry scowl, and merely repeated, "How are you?" Harry Holt and Dick Curtis seconded Sampson, and never was man better attended to. Harry had sported his money on Brown, but he communicated that fact to Sampson's backers, and they at once decided on trusting to his honour to do the best he could for Phil, promising, at the same time, to make up his losses if Sampson won. Brown was seconded by his friend Tom Spring and by Bill Richmond. The toss for sides was won by Sampson, and at about twenty minutes after one the fight commenced. Colours—crimson for Sampson; and crimson with white stripes for Brown. Betting, two to one, and in some parts of the ring five to two, on the latter.

THE FIGHT.

Round 1.—Brown, when divested of his outer garments, looked extremely well, not to say gigantic, weighing, at the least estimate, fifteen stone. A smile of confidence embellished his mug, and he seemed to say to himself, "I shall lick this Sampson like fun." Phil was equally slap up in condition—in truth, we never saw him to more advantage in any of his previous encounters; he weighed nearly thirteen stone. His countenance indicated composure, calculation, and perfect preparation for the job he had undertaken. On setting to, Brown did not appear exactly "at home;" he put up his arms more like a pupil who had been taught the rudiments of the art of self-defence than as a pugilist acting from his own suggestions. He scarcely seemed to know whether he should commence offensive operations or wait for his active adversary to make the onset. The science displayed by Sampson was judicious, correct, and decisive; he crept in, as it were, to measure his distance, and having ascertained he was right, he let fly with both hands. The mug of Brown felt them; when Sampson, in the style of Curtis, stepped backwards, by which means Brown, in returning, did not reach his opponent. ("Well done, Sampson!") The Birmingham blade again tried on the manoeuvre with increased effect, and planted a heavy blow just under the temple of Brown. The latter now attempted to fight first, but his movements were slow, and his right hand did little more than touch the side of Sampson's nob. Some sharp exchanges occurred, but the hitting of the "big one" was round, while Sampson planted his straight facers with electrifying effect, and had the best of the rally. Brown, by his superior-strength, bored his adversary to the ropes, where he held Sampson, and en-deavoured to fib him with his right hand but not à la Randall. The "big one" kept pegging at Phil everywhere until he was down. (Great disapprobation, and loud cries of "Foul," "Fair," &c.) It was the general opinion that a foul blow had been given by the hero of Bridgnorth, but perhaps not intentionally; therefore the umpires did not notice the transaction. ("First blood!" said Curtis; "that's an event worth summut to me.")

2.—The skill of Sampson again was the admiration of the ring. He, as in the previous round, coolly measured his distance so correctly as to plant two facers, and stepped back out of trouble. Sampson repeated the offence without delay by another left-hander on the mug of the "big one," when the latter returned a blow on the side of Phil's head. Sampson kept a good look-out; when, at length, he saw an opening, he planted a precious teaser on the left peeper of Brown, which not only damaged it, but placed it on the winking system. ("Go in," cried the friends of Brown; "don't stand out to be punished.") The Bridgnorth hero rushed to a close, laid hold of Phil at the ropes, and would have made mincemeat of him if Sampson had not got down cleverly.

3.—Of no importance. Sparring for a short period, when Brown endeavoured to plant a right-handed hit on the upper works of Sampson, but Phil got away from mischief, and Brown, with the force of the blow, fell on his knees. The "big one" jumped up, ready to renew the contest; Sampson was also on the alert to hit; but Spring, considering the round at an end, drew Brown back, who immediately seated himself on the knee of his second.

4.—Phil took the lead, like a master of the art; his left hand told twice successively on the mug of his adversary, and he retreated from mischief. Sampson put in a tremendous blow with his right on the left cheek of Brown, the claret following profusely. ("He's winning it nicely," said the Bruma.) The hero of Bridgnorth, rather wild at such unexpected rough treatment, went to work desperately; but Sampson kept milling on the retreat—jobbing Brown, as he followed, with both his hands, until the "big one" closed, got the fall, and dropped on Sampson.

5.—The nob of Brown was considerably damaged; he was also piping. The "big one" made a good stop, but Sampson, undismayed, went to work, and had the best of a short rally. Phil, with a sneer of derision and ill-nature, observed, "You Champion of England!" then, planting a heavy blow on Brown's left eye, exclaimed, "There's a small taste for your Championship!" The hero of Bridgnorth, irritated at the taunts, went in to do mischief, but Sampson met his rush with two heavy blows in the front of his head, which floored the *soi-disant* Champion. (The applause was deafening. "Sampson for ever!" "Sampson for choice!" "He can't fight at all!" "Send him back to Bridgnorth!")

6.—Sampson, quick as lightning, went to work, and Brown fought with him; but the former took the lead and had the best of it. Brown, in his anxiety to punish his opponent, stumbled, and his head went against a stake.

7.—The weight of the "big one," enabled him to drive Sampson against the ropes. The situation was rather dangerous. Brown held him as if he had been screwed in a vice, and kept milling his ribs with his right hand. (The row was immense—applause by the friends of the "big one," and the Sampsonites hissing and hooting beyond description.) Phil shifted his arm, and changed his position, but still it was most distressing. ("Don't hang the man, Brown!") The struggle was terrible on both sides. Phil at length got down, Holt sticking to him closely, and giving him advice how to get out of the clutches of his powerful adversary.

8.—Sampson came to the scratch much better than could be expected after the severe hugging at the ropes in the last round. Phil put in two facers, but received in return a heavy blow on the side of his head. Brown closed, but, failing in a cross-buttock, he dragged Sampson off his legs and fell by the side of him.

9.—The left ogle of Brown was almost in darkness, and one of his listeners and his nasal organ much swelled and out of shape. Sampson, on the sharp look-out, planted another facer with his left. Brown bored in, and caught Phil at the ropes; here the latter not only got out of danger well, but faced his opponent suddenly, and sent in a couple of blows as he went down. ("Well done, Sampson; you are sure to win.")

10.—Short. Brown was again met in his rush in the middle of his nob; he nevertheless bored in and got Sampson down.

11.—Sampson commenced fighting, and took great liberties with the pimple of Brown, using it for a drum by repeated hits upon the face of the Bridgnorth hero; the latter rallied in the most decisive manner, until they were both down. (Here the outer ring was broken, and thousands of persons rushed forward to the ropes, which were trodden down, in spite of all the opposition of whips, sticks, blows, &c. It was "dangerous to be safe," and the combatants were compelled to fight in the midst of a mob. Sticks and whips were at work, even to get for the men the space of a yard. No description can be given of the confusion; the heat was intolerable, and the spectators jammed together almost to suffocation.)

12.—Brown could not protect his face from the repeated visits of Sampson's fists, and went in to bustle him, until they both went down.

13.—The right hand of the Bridgnorth hero told on Sampson's pimple, but not until the latter had planted two facers. In closing, Sampson down.

14.—Brown was of little use in this round. Sampson hit his nob as if he had a sack of flour before him. It was first a facer—ditto, ditto, and ditto. The hero of Bridgnorth went down covered with claret. ("Sampson for a thousand!" and rounds of applause.)

15.—Brown was distressed beyond measure when he appeared at the scratch, but he recovered and went to work. Sampson again nobbed him, but the strength of Brown obtained him the fall.

16.—The confusion within the ring was dreadful; in fact, it was a mob of persons pushing and hitting each other to keep out of the way of the combatants. The men were suffering severely under the deprivation of air, violent perspiration streaming down their faces. Sampson took the lead as to blows, but he was fought down by his opponent.

17.—The coolness displayed by Tom Spring in this round was the admiration of the spectators, and showed his desire that the battle should be fought out fairly. In all probability, had he returned a blow for the one given to him by Phil, the battle might have been prematurely ended, or at all events brought to a wrangle. In bringing Brown up to the scratch, Spring got before his man, observing Sampson was on the wrong side of the mark. Phil considered the conduct of Spring wrong, and without hesitation gave him a facer, pushed Spring out of his way, and suddenly floored the Bridgnorth hero like a shot.

18.—The "big one" showed game, and came up like a man. But he was of "no use to himself," and reduced to a bad lot for his friends. He napped it in every way, and a floorer finished the round.

19.—Sampson lost no time, but went to work as soon as he had got his adversary before him. Brown fought wildly, till the punishment was too much for him, when he drew back, and Sampson, catching him with an upright hit, dropped him on his knees, giving him a facer as he was going down. ("If that ain't doing him brown, I never saw anything like it before," said a Brum who had taken the long odds.)

20.—The heat of the weather and pressure of the crowd operated terribly on Sampson; so much so that froth came from his lips, and he seemed nearly exhausted; nevertheless he came to his work like a man determined to conquer. Phil only wanted room for the display of his milling capabilities. The Championship was completely out of the grasp of Brown, and he might now be registered as Receiver-General. He was hit to a standstill, and then dropped. ("It's all over!" was the cry.)

21.—The customers from Bridgnorth now began to look all manner of colours; the secret was told—Brown was beaten against his will. Sampson sent his adversary down like winking.

22-23.—The weight of Brown, in close quarters, enabled him, in closing, to roll Sampson down in both of these rounds.

24.—It was now clear to every spectator that Sampson must prove the hero of the tale. Brown, as a last effort, exerted himself to overwhelm his adversary, but he napped it right and left as he went in, and was sent down like a sack of sand.

25-28.—Brown down. Ditto. Repeated by Sampson. Of a similar description.

29.—Brown staggering like a drunken sailor three sheets in the wind until Sampson hit him down. ("Take him home—take him away; he's of no use!")

30-31.—It is true Brown answered the call of "Time," yet his appearance at the scratch was only to receive additional unnecessary punishment. Sampson sent him down almost as soon as placed before him.

32-42, and last.—The calls of "time"

were obeyed by the "big one" in the whole of these rounds, but he had not the slightest chance in his favour. Indeed, it was a pity he was permitted to contest them. At the conclusion of the forty-second round, when he was down, he complained of his shoulder, and was not able to come again. The battle was over in forty-nine minutes. The "big one" was reduced to a complete state of distress—his left peeper completely in darkness, his right severely damaged, and his face fearfully cut. His left shoulder was afterwards found to have been dislocated. His feelings, we have no doubt, were equally cut up, for he had flattered himself that the Championship was within his grasp. He displayed game of the first quality, and after a short period walked out of the ring to his carriage, assisted by Spring and Richmond. Sampson had scarcely a mark upon his face, except a touch under his left eye; but the same side of his nob was peppered a little, and several other contusions were visible. Sampson left the ring amidst loud and repeated shouts in honour of his victory.

REMARKS.—No person could dispute the bravery and game exhibited by Brown throughout the fight; he was out-fought by the superior skill and tactics of Sampson. The latter entered the ring with a confidence which surprised the oldest ring-goers; his conduct was decisive in every round, and he never lost sight of the idea of conquest during the battle. The broken state of the ring and the very confined space for the men to fight in were certainly great drawbacks to Sampson against so powerful an opponent as Brown. It was evident that Sampson had improved in strength, and he altogether appeared a better man than in any of his former battles; his right-hand blows were tremendous. The hero of Bridgnorth must have suffered severely from the injury to his shoulder, and none but a brave man would have contested the battle after so severe an accident against such precision and straight hitting as met Brown's repeated efforts to get on to his opponent.

The return was full of bustle and incident. Sampson's colours were flying in all directions, out of the windows of houses on the road, on the tops of the coaches, and "Sampson for ever!" to the end of the chapter. The roadside houses never experienced such a day for the return of the ready; and "success to milling" was on the tip of the tongue of every landlord in the county.

Sampson left the ground under the patronage of Mr. Beardsworth in style, and during part of his journey on his victorious return to Birmingham the carriage which conveyed Phil and his friend was drawn by eight horses. Through the streets of Birmingham his reception was enthusiastic; Sampson was loudly cheered by crowds, and drawn by six fresh horses, until he reached the house of Arthur Matthewson. Every room in Arthur's crib was crowded to excess, and the anxiety of the persons in the street to gain admittance, to get a peep at the conqueror of " Big Brown," defied description.

The Shropshire folks looked upon their champion as invincible, and accordingly dropped their money heavily. In no previous instance of a big fight was there such an unanimity on the side of the " talent " and the " professionals." Careful betting men laid rash odds and suffered the proper penalty, as the " knowing ones " were thrown out. This battle was followed by an epidemic of letter-writing in the newspapers, provincial and metropolitan. First came our old friend Thomas Winter Spring, who, favoured by the ablest writer who ever devoted his talents to ring reporting (we mean Vincent George Dowling, Esq., Editor of *Bell's Life* for upwards of thirty years), gave a graphic account of poor Brown's dislocated shoulder, which took place in the *fourth round*, and which fully accounts for Brown's incapacity to ward off Sampson's " nobbers." Spring was justly indignant at Sampson's blow, and thus, after commenting warmly on the " ruffianism " of Sampson's friends, he wound up with a formal challenge to Sampson to meet him for £200 a side, " as it is not my principle to submit to a blow without wishing, like a man, to return it." Sampson's reply was characteristic of the man and his wordy amanuensis—full of boasting, bombast, and scurrility. Spring was taunted with " not daring to fight Ward," beating " stale old men," Oliver and Painter to wit, &c., &c. Attack, reply, and rejoinder stuffed the columns of the *Dispatch*, Pierce Egan's short-lived weekly paper, *Life in London*, and *Bell's Life*. Spring was at last provoked by the repeated threats of Sampson, who boasted in all company how he would serve the " old woman," to retort with a promise of chastisement. He says :—

" Sampson accuses me of acting wrong in the ring, but he forgets to say in what respect. I defy him or any person to say I did wrong. He also says I wanted to bring it to a wrangle. If that had been my object, I had a very good chance when he struck me—not once nor twice, but thrice; had I returned the blows, it must have put a stop to the fight.

" I think, Mr. Editor, I have answered quite enough of Mr. Sampson's scurrilous language; but when he speaks of chastising me I pity his weakness, and would have him take care that chastisement does not fall upon himself; for, the first time I meet him, I will put the toe of my boot against his seat—not of honour, Mr. Editor, he has none about him—but where his sense of feeling may be readily reached.

" I hope, Mr. Editor, you will pardon me for taking up so much room in your valuable paper, but unless Mr. Sampson chooses to come forward with his money I shall not condescend to take the least notice of anything he may say after this.

" I am, Sir, your obliged,

" Hereford, April 24th, 1828."   " THOMAS WINTER SPRING.

All this gasconading, so foreign to Spring's character, came to a "most lame and impotent conclusion." Sampson could not get backed, and the affair fell through. Spring, meeting Sampson soon after at Epsom races, in Merryweather's booth, declared his intention to fulfil his promise, made under sore provocation, to have satisfaction or an apology for the blow received by him at the fight with Brown. Sampson began to argue the matter, but Spring threw off his coat and called upon Sampson to defend himself. Sampson set to with his coat and hat on. "The crowd and confusion," says *Bell's Life*, "were so great that we have not been able to learn who gave the first blow." The rally was, however, a determined one, and after being separated the belligerents got together again and fought four sharp rounds. Spring, it is well known, required room to show off his fine fighting, and thus Sampson had the best of the tussle, for such it was. The combatants were of course soon parted by their friends, neither having fulfilled his intent of giving the other "the value of a bating." Spring, it was stated, was struck by other persons besides Sampson. It ought to be mentioned that Spring proposed to Sampson to come out of the booth and meet him on the course in the open, but the latter declined the offer. The next evening, at the Castle Tavern, Holborn, Sampson declared himself ready to fight Spring for £300 a side, half-way between London and Bridgnorth. Spring accepted the challenge at Tom Cannon's benefit, at the Tennis Court, the very next day.

A meeting was appointed to take place at Harry Holt's, where the battle-money in Neale's fight with Baldwin was to be given up. Here, after some argument, mutual explanations took place. Sampson said that when he "challenged Spring for £300 he was rather fresh; that he would retract it, and declare he had no animosity against Spring." The latter said he would have an apology for the blows he had received, and Sampson, persuaded by his friends, expressed his regret. Finally Spring offered his hand to Sampson, who accepted it; and over a cheerful glass it was agreed to bury the past in oblivion.

Phil's next encounter was with Simon Byrne, the Irish champion, for £200 a side. The battle was fought on a stage at Albrighton, on the 30th June, 1829, when Sampson succumbed after a severe fight of forty-five rounds, occupying one hour forty-three and a half minutes. This, with the disgraceful draw with Big Brown, at Doncaster, in 1821, the details of which will be found in our memoir of BROWN (Chapter XII., p. 451), closed the chequered pugilistic career of Phil Sampson, "the Birmingham Youth."

APPENDIX TO PERIOD VI.

TOM REYNOLDS—1817–1825.

As a connecting link of two generations of pugilists and of the Irish and English P.R., Tom Reynolds deserves a niche in our gallery. He was best known in his latter days as the mentor of Jack Langan and Simon Byrne, as a sound adviser, a professor of the *ars pugnandi*, a patron of aspiring talent, and a jolly Boniface in the "swate city of Dublin," where he died on the 15th of May, 1832, much respected.

Tom was born on the 20th of January, 1792, at Middleton, in the county of Armagh, and early in life came to London as salesman to a relative, with whom he some time lived in James Street, Covent Garden, until, being grown to man's estate, he became a "murphy-dealer" on his own account.

Tom was decidedly, with the single exception of Henry Josiah Holt, the most erudite pugilist of his day. He had received a good education, possessed a strong mind, and could write as good a letter as any of the "scribes" of the time. Of this he was not a little proud, and the *cacoethes scribendi* with which he was occasionally afflicted often led him into epistolary contentions in the sporting papers, in which he invariably had the best of his competitors. His "Defence of Pugilism" proves him to have been a writer of no mean pretensions, and the view which he takes of his own profession affords the best apology for its adoption as well as for its encouragement.

About the close of the great Napoleonic wars Reynolds fell into difficulties and was arrested. Reverses in trade, combined with a love of company, at length led to his introduction to the once well-known "College" in what is now Farringdon Street, then called "The Fleet." Here he had time and opportunity for study, and, having long had a predilection for the science of milling, he attended a regular course of lectures, and became a perfect adept at the practice of fives, tennis, and the gloves, and a great favourite with his brother " Collegians." Being at the top of his class, and rising in fame, it was determined by some envious opponent to take the shine out of him, and for this purpose the celebrated George Head, one of the most scientific sparrers of the day, was introduced as a stranger, and, in a set-to which followed, Head found it necessary to try his best before he could convince Tom that there was a superior to himself. The trial ended in a friendly manner, but both having afterwards partaken rather freely of the " rum puncheon," some wag insinuated to Reynolds that Head had spoken contemptuously of his fistic talents. This roused Tom's ire, and he at once challenged Head to combat. Head, nothing loth, accepted the invitation, and a battle commenced on the " College Green" (so called upon the Horatian principle of there being nothing *green* on or around it), in which the " murphy-dealer " was down in every round. The "janitors," at length, interfered, and Head was expelled from the " College," but not till he had received a crack on the listener which considerably confused his senses.

Shortly after his emancipation from the thraldom of "College" duties, Tom commenced business as a professional pugilist, and on the 23rd of July, 1817, entered the lists on Moulsey Hurst with Aby Belasco, the Jew, whom he beat by his determined game in sixty-six rounds and one hour and twenty minutes. In September in the same year (the 9th) he fought and beat Church on the same ground; and on the 11th of November following beat the *Broom-Dasher* (Johnson), in Lord Cowper's Park, near Canterbury. Subsequent to these "slices of good fortune," he became a publican in Drury Lane, but having fallen through a trap-door his health became impaired, and he determined on a sparring tour in the country for the benefit of his health. He was accompanied by Jack Carter and Sutton the Black, and was well received in Manchester, Liverpool, and Dublin. While in the latter city he was matched against John Dunn, a novice, for £50 a side, and fought him on the 4th of July, 1820, in Donnelly's Valley, on the Curragh of Kildare. In twelve rounds and fifty-four minutes Dunn was completely done up, being hit to a state of insensibility, while Reynolds had scarcely a scratch.

In his way back to London our hero took Macclesfield in his course, where he was matched against Sammons, who had beaten all the Lancashire pugilists who had been opposed to him. On August 21st, 1820, the match came off within a mile of Macclesfield, and the Lancashire hero was disposed of in seven rounds. Tom now proceeded to London, but shortly after returned to Ireland to fight Cummins, but that fight went off in consequence of a forfeit.

Tom next took Jack Langan under his tuition and care, and was his mentor when he fought Tom Spring; acting the part of his secretary, and dipping his pen in gall, then much used in the composition of ink, in the course of his correspondence. His next *protégé* was Simon Byrne, to whom he afforded the most friendly assistance, and seconded him in his fights with Sampson, M'Kay, and Jem Ward. Previous to the last affair, which ended in the defeat of Simon, he opened a public-house in Abbey Street, Dublin, which he conducted with great regularity until " his sand was run out." He was decidedly a brave man and a scientific boxer, and left a wife and two children to lament his loss.

As a specimen of Tom's talent in the use of the pen we append his

DEFENCE OF PUGILISM.

" I must acknowledge the gentlemen of the Press are favourable to the cause of pugilism ; and it is not surprising when we consider that the persons conducting it are men, in general, possessing a liberal education, and blessed with a greater share of brains than the average of the community. Yet there is no rule without an exception ; for two or three of the London journalists, imitated by a few country flats, occasionally give us a 'facer ;' though I am confident it is not from conviction, but because they think a little opposition to generally received opinions may suit their pockets better than following the tide, where the brightness of their genius would not make them conspicuous. One of these worthies speaks of us as monsters that brutalise the country ; another describes our poor little twenty-four foot ring as the only place in the three kingdoms where rogues and blacklegs spring up like mushrooms ; a third says a pair of boxing-gloves debase the mind, and recommends the use of the foils as a preferable exercise ; and a fourth, after a most violent philippic against the Ring, blames Government for not immediately putting an end to pugilism, and recommends, as a substitute, that Government should take into their wise consideration the propriety of giving greater encouragement to dancing assemblies. This idea is ridiculous. Certainly, if the editor does fill up his leisure hours as a hop-merchant, I do not blame him for putting in a good word for the shop, but what the devil has dancing to do with fighting ? Can two men decide a mill by 'tripping on the light fantastic toe' ? The French dance every night in the week, and all day on Sunday, and what are they the better for that ? Are they better men ? Can they boast nobler feelings than Britons ? They certainly make graceful bows, and there is no doubt dancing has an effect on the heels, for Wellington has often scratched his head, and given them a left-handed blessing, for their quickness in giving leg-bail.

" Because the English are not considered a dancing nation, that is no reason they are brutalised. The most savage people dance ; the American Indian dances round his captive while he is roasting him alive ; the Italians dance, fiddle, and sing ; and, if they consider themselves offended, employ ruffians to assassinate the offender. The dancing Frenchman would shudder with horror at the sight of two London porters giving each other a black eye or a bloody nose, and say 'twas a brutal practice ; yet the same fellow, in his own country, would take snuff, grin like a monkey, and cry ' Bravo !' at seeing two poor devils boring holes in each other's hide with a yard of steel. So much for the consistency of the 'Grande Nation,' and the sense of the men who recommend dancing as a substitute for pugilism.

" I am no enemy to dancing ; in fact, I am passionately fond of music ; but there is a time for all things. With every inclination in the world to let every one ride his own hobby in his own way, I see no reason why a poor pugilist should take a facer from the wielder of the foil. Two hundred years ago, when the sword was worn, and decided quarrels in the streets, fencing was, without doubt, a necessary part of every man's education ; but, at the present day, though the foils may be very good exercise, I consider it the height of folly for any man to throw away his money and time in the attainment of an art that can never be of use. But we will suppose two pupils taking their lessons, the one with the gloves attaining a graceful method of drawing a cork, painting the margin of an ogle with some of the most beauteous tints of the rainbow, or directing a customer to the victualling-office; the other, with the foil, passes away his hours in attaining precision to pierce the centre of the heart, or in transfixing the ball of the eye, to cause instant death by perforating the brain. Let me ask in this mimic warfare which man's mind was most debased? Blacklegs are not the peculiar growth of our Ring. Wherever men will sport on chance events, there Mr. Blacksbanks will be found walking, and that, too, on shores where the fist is never used except by our brave tars, who often make them scamper by the mere flourish of their bunch of fives. Thieves may be found in the mob that surrounds our Ring; but where are they not to be found? A Radical assembly or Bible meeting is not exempt from their visits; and they will even be found at a charity sermon, praying they may have good luck when the jostling comes on, and may be considered as instruments of divine mercy, sent to deliver good men from the sinful dross of the earth.

"The only charge that can be brought against the Ring is crossing fights; and though the members of the Press growl, and very justly too, whenever a × takes place, yet none of them attempt to point out the cause or remedy. Fighting men are not all alike, neither are kings; for who would compare the British Sovereign with the scoundrel Ferdinand of Spain? There are men in our Ring with integrity that would adorn a more elevated situation: men that would sooner drop senseless under punishment, though fighting for little more than the colours that are tied to the stakes, than receive five hundred pounds to lose wilfully. I do deny most positively that pugilistic exhibitions debase, demoralise, or brutalise us as a nation; on the reverse, I am confident they introduce chivalrous (they may be rude) notions of honour, courage, fortitude, and love of manly fair play—characteristics so strongly indented in the British character that they are known and acknowledged from pole to pole. And who will be hardy enough to say the excitement to those feelings does not originate in the very same cause which our enemies say brutalises the feelings of the country?

"Even on the score of humanity pugilism ought to be encouraged; for, wherever it does not exist, murder, by violence and treachery, more frequently takes place. Without going to foreign countries for proof, a single glance at home will strike the blindest with the necessity of its encouragement. The men of Lancashire, twenty years ago, were up-and-down fighters: then murder was almost an every-day occurrence. Indeed, some of the old ones of that day took no little pride to themselves if they could boast of having stopped the 'smoke of a chimney' (choked a man), after the manner of Virginius. Since pugilism has been introduced, though the population is fourfold, yet murder seldom or never takes place. Compare the population of Ireland, where the stick has been thrown aside, and the fist used, to the other parts: the difference in the number of deaths by violence will strike conviction on the dullest. In fact, though chivalry did much to smooth down the roughness of the darker ages, 'tis only the boxing-gloves can give the true polish of civilisation to the world. And, I am confident, if Adam had been a Briton, he would have taught his sons to box; then the club would not have been used, and the first murder prevented. Cain would have given Abel a good milling instead of crushing his skull: and the brothers would have been found next morning supping porridge as comfortable as the Lord Mayor's sons on a more recent occasion.

"Greece, the birthplace of the arts and sciences, encouraged pugilism; and the first man of the day considered not only himself, but his family, honoured, if lucky enough to mill his man at the Olympic Games. Look at the effeminate beings that now parade the streets of Rome, once trod by the conquerors of England and the world; with them a boxing or a milling match would have had more charms than the finest strains of a Rossini. The Government knew the advantage of exhibitions that would excite an admiration of courage and fortitude. 'Twas this reason induced the Athenian General to stop his army, that they might look at a cock-fight—'tis this that has secured our Ring the patronage of the noblest blood, rank, and talent in the country; and long may we deserve the support of men that soar above the braying of asses or the cant of hypocrites!

"With all due submission and thanks to the ancients, as the inventors of boxing, I cannot help feeling pride at the vast superiority our Ring possesses over theirs; for death was too frequently the result, in consequence of the metal braced to their arms. When our Ring is formed the combatants are left to themselves without fear of interruption from a third person. Temperate, manly courage is loudly applauded—passion, cowardice, or foul play as loudly blamed; and should either of the men display any little act of humanity to his sinking opponent (of which I could state numberless instances), his gallantry is cordially praised; but the moment the dreadful word "ENOUGH" is uttered, hostilities cease and the conqueror, shaking hands with his fallen antagonist, wishes him better luck next time, and, in a kindly voice, expresses a wish that he may soon recover.

"Man is the creature of habit, and of the force of example; and, I again repeat, exhibitions of this kind have their good effects, which can be traced to us as a nation, and, independent of fighting, influence other actions of life. Show me the man completely opposed to pugilism, and you will find his character to be a bad neighbour and a tyrant under his own roof. The immortal Wyndham was the staunch advocate and patron of our Ring, and champion for the abolition of the slave trade. Have dealings with any other country—will you find them, in the mass, so honest or so honourable as Britons? In every part of the known world, who are more welcome than our merchants? What flag more respected or feared? Quarrel in the streets of any other country, you will have more than one to contend with. If an object of distress is pointed out, who is more ready to assist than a Briton? In other countries murder and robbery go hand-in-hand; in ours the most desperate men never dip their hands in blood, unless to protect themselves from ill-judged resistance. And who can boast an army or a navy so gallantly brave, or so ready to extend the hand to save, as Britons? Tell me a nation that could meet our brave sons on equal terms in the field or on the wave; yet, if conquered, which of them but would sooner become a prisoner to a British sailor or soldier than any other? Theirs is not the frenzied courage like that inspired by fanaticism, ferocity, or brandy, which, after the first gust of passion, leaves its helpless, hopeless, panting possessor; no, 'tis that kind of round-after-round courage which will admit of thinking and command, and knows no abatement till wearied nature or death closes the scene. Fair play is a Briton's motto; we would extend it to the extremities of the earth, no consequence what country, religion, or colour. The sable African, throwing aside the chains that levelled him with the beast, now walks erect, in the majesty of freedom and liberty, calling down blessings on the country that, in spite of all the world, burst his bonds asunder. If these are the symptoms that the country is brutalised by pugilism, long may she continue so! Long may she be the home for the exile—the defender of the oppressed—the best boxer—and the fairest arbiter of the world!

"TOM REYNOLDS."

With hearty approval we commend "Old Tom's" spirited "defence" to the careful perusal of Sir Wilfrid Lawson, Messrs. Bright, Agnew, Richard, the Stigginses, the saints and sinners of Exeter and St. James's Halls, and the Peace (at-any-price) Preservation Society.

DICK CURTIS ("THE PET")—1820–1828.

FOR skill, neatness, finish, straight, and therefore swift, hitting, no such boxer as Dick Curtis has appeared in the present century. His weight, nine stone, and his height, five foot six, as a matter of course precluded his appearance among the Champions; but, as Champion of the Light Weights, Richard Curtis has had no superior, if any equal, in the annals of pugilism.

He was decidedly the most perfect specimen of a miniature fighting man of modern times. His science was, we might almost say, intuitive, his judgment of time and distance extraordinary, his readiness in difficulty most remarkable, his change from a position of defence to that of attack instantaneous and astonishing, and his power of punishment, for so light a man, unparalleled. Curtis was patronised by the most distinguished admirers of pugilism of the period in which he lived, and throughout his long career was never defeated, with the single exception of his last battle, when with Perkins, of Oxford, to whom he was inferior by a stone and two pounds in weight, as well as in length and height, he fell before youth and stamina.

Richard Curtis was born in Southwark, on the 1st of February, 1802. He came of a fighting family, his brothers John and George having both figured in the ring. Young Dick's first public appearance was at the age of eighteen, on the well-known battle-field of Moulsey Hurst, where on Tuesday, June 27th, 1820, in the same ring in which George Cooper had just defeated Shelton, he entered the lists with Watson, a Westminster boxer, of about ten stone. Watson was game, and fought desperately for twenty-five minutes, when he cried " Enough ! " and Curtis was hailed the conqueror, almost without a mark. Curtis's skill was so remarkable in this *rencontre* that two months afterwards some Corinthians, previously to leaving town for the shooting season—which was then September—as railroads had not brought grouse and the Scottish moors within hail of the Metropolis, determined to see the smart young Bermondsey lad again show his prowess. A match for £40 was accordingly made for him with a well-known light weight, Ned Brown (the Sprig of Myrtle) ; and on Monday, the 28th of August, 1820, Brown, waited on by Jack Martin and Paddington Jones, tried to throw his hat into the ring on Wimbledon Common, in such a smart gale that it blew it over, and away across the heath. Shortly after, Curtis, attended by Josh Hudson and Tom Belcher, approached the ropes ; but his lily-white beaver shared the same fate, so that the omen was negative. Both men were in good condition. The colours—a canary yellow for Curtis, and a blue bird's-eye for Brown—being tied to the stakes, the men shook hands and began

THE FIGHT.

Round 1.—Brown, full of confidence, made an offer to hit, but Curtis was awake, and nothing was done. A long pause took place, each endeavouring to get an opening, when Brown rushed in to work ; a change took place in the struggle to fib each other, when both went down, Brown undermost. (Great shouting ; and Curtis for a trifle.)

2.—This round occupied thirteen minutes, and the amateurs were delighted with the science and manliness displayed on both sides. Curtis hit at a longer distance, and nobbed Brown in great style. Both of these little ones displayed as much caution as if a million of money depended upon the event. To describe the stop-hits and getting away would occupy a page : suffice it to say that Brown's right eye was nearly closed, and, after some desperate milling, Brown went down undermost. The great length of this round showed the good condition of both the combatants. Curtis appeared the weaker man.

3.—Brown proved himself a fine and game fighter, but Curtis out-fought him, put in nobbers with the utmost dexterity, and also damaged his other eye. (Tom Owen sung out, "Go it, my white topper ; it's as right as the day.") Both went down, Brown undermost. Two to one on Curtis.

4.—This was a short round ; in closing, Brown endeavoured to fib his opponent, but Curtis got down. (Any odds upon the latter.)

5.—Brown displayed good tactics, and at in-fighting was quite clever. Curtis made some good nobbing hits, and Brown went staggering away ; but the latter returned to the charge, and, in struggling for the throw, Brown dragged Curtis over the ring and downed him. (Brown for £20. Curtis seemed weak.)

6.—This was rather a long round. Fibbing on both sides. Both down, Brown undermost.

7.—Curtis not only stopped in good style,

DICK CURTIS (" THE PET ").

but nobbed Brown away. After some exchanges at the ropes, Curtis dropped Brown by a blow on the side of the latter's head.

8.—This was a famous round; and, in closing, Brown broke away twice with great activity. The punishment was severe on both sides. Brown was ultimately hit down, as if shot, from a tremendous blow on his forehead. (Great shouting. The "Sprigs of Myrtle" all drooping, and the denizens of Caleb Baldwin's dominions upon the fret. "It's all over.")

9.—Brown, however, came first to the scratch. A severe struggle took place at the ropes, each too game to go down. ("Go down, Curtis," from all parts of the ring.) Both at length fell, but Brown was undermost. (Here a near relative of Brown came close to the ropes, and told the seconds they were not doing right in not letting Brown "go in.")

10.—Brown recovered a little, made a rush, and the change was considered in his favour. Curtis got down cleverly.

11, 12.—Both combatants excited the admiration of the ring by their fine fighting. In the last round Brown was hit down from a severe hit in the ribs. (Two and three to one.)

13 to 15, and last.—Brown was floored in all these rounds on coming to the scratch; he was terribly punished, but the game he displayed was of the first quality. Here the patron of Brown stepped forward (a more gentlemanly, liberal, or distinguished character for humanity of disposition does not exist, nor a greater admirer of true courage is not to be found) and said, "My man shall not fight any more."

REMARKS.—A better battle has not been seen for many years; 57 minutes of complete good fighting. Brown has fought eight prize battles, and proved the conqueror in the majority of them. Curtis, although a mere boy, bids fair to prove a teaser to any of his weight; he is a cautious boxer and a severe hitter. The amateurs never expressed greater satisfaction at any fight. It was the general opinion that although Curtis appeared weak two or three times in the conflict, yet the scale of victory was always on his side. It is true that Brown had no other chance to win but "going in;" yet the clever defence of Curtis rendered that plan equally dangerous.

Curtis's next match was with Lenney, at Moulsey Hurst, on the 24th of October, 1821. "At one o'clock," says the reporter, "young Curtis, in a white upper-benjamin, which would have set off a Regent-street 'pink,' a brilliant canary round his throat, and a white beaver of the most fashionable mould, showed arm in arm with the President of the Daffy Club,* and threw his natty castor into the ring." Lenney soon after appeared, with the Gaslight man and Curtis's old opponent, the Sprig of Myrtle, and replied to the signal of defiance. Spring and Hickman seconded Lenney; Tom Belcher and Harry Harmer officiated for Curtis. The odds, within the previous two or three days, had changed in favour of Lenney, on whom five to four was laid. The colours were tied to the stakes by Spring and the President, who observed to the former, "I'll bet you a trifle that I take them down."

THE FIGHT.

Round 1.—The condition of Curtis was that of the finest racehorse; blood and bone were conspicuous, and he appeared as confident as if the battle were over. Lenney was equally fine; he commenced the fight with the most determined resolution of being declared the conqueror. Curtis was in no hurry to make play: Lenney was also on his guard. After some little manœuvring, Curtis let fly on the nob of his opponent, without return. This hit operated as a sort of stopper, and some little sparring occurred. Lenney endeavoured to go to work, and some blows were exchanged. The science displayed by Curtis was fine in the extreme, and he planted two sharp facers, right and

* At this time Tom Belcher bore that title.

left, that floored Lenney on his face, and the claret trickled down his cheek. (Loud shouting, and two to one all round the ring.)

2.—Lenney came to the scratch with a severe cut under his right eye. Curtis planted a severe body hit without a return; he also put in two severe facers. It was evident that Lenney could not protect his face from the out-fighting of his opponent, and to go in seemed equally dangerous. Curtis kept nobbing his man, and getting away with the utmost ease. In closing, Lenney was fibbed down, and Curtis fell upon him. (Thunders of applause, and " You're a pretty boy, Curtis.")

3.—This was a short round; a close took place, and the fibbing tactics went on till Lenney went down.

4.—The coolness of Curtis was the theme of the ring. He measured his distances with the accuracy of a mathematician, and nobbed his opponent with the severity of a hammer-man at an anvil. Lenney could make no impression on the mode adopted by Curtis. The latter followed Lenney up to the ropes, and, with his right hand, planted such a tremendous facer that it was heard all over the ring. In the struggle for the throw both combatants were hanging on the ropes; Curtis's nose touched them, as they both came to the ground; but previous to this he put in some heavy blows on his opponent's loins.

5.—Lenney came like a gamecock to the scratch; but his nob had undergone a strange alteration. Some exchanges occurred. Curtis, by a dreadful right-handed blow, sent down his adversary like a shot. (Three to one. " What a beautiful fighter!" exclaimed Randall.)

6, 7, 8.—Lenney stopped several blows with considerable skill; but his head was completely at the service of his opponent. Oliver made so sure of the event that he asked if any gentleman would oblige him by taking ten to two.

9, 10.—The fine fighting of Curtis now rendered the battle quite safe to him; so much so, that he could take his time about it without danger. Curtis astonished the ring with his execution as well as his science: he put such a tremendous blow on Lenney's mouth that his ivories were on the chatter like dice in a box, and he felt it so seriously that his left arm dropped for an instant. (" It's all safe now—it's the Bank of England to a screen," was the chaffing throughout the crowd.)

11, 12.—Lenney received so much punishment about the nob that he was quite groggy. Twenty to one was offered.

13, 14, 15, 16, 17.—All these rounds were nearly similar to the preceding ones. Any odds.

18 to 29, and last.—Lenney was game to the backbone, but he had not a shadow of chance. He ought to have been taken away several rounds previous to the last. He was hit out of time; and remained in a state of stupor for a short period. The battle occupied thirty-eight minutes and a half.

REMARKS.—A more elegant or scientific fighter than Curtis was never seen in the Prize Ring. He could have won in half the time if he had wished, but he was determined not to give half a chance away, consequently no long rally took place in the battle. Curtis also proved the stronger man, and left the ring without a scratch upon his face; but his hands were much bruised from the severe punishment he had administered to his opponent. Lenney was carried out of the ring and put to bed. The attitude of the latter was not a judicious one; he leaned too far back. not only to do execution, but such a position must have distressed him much: in fact, Lenney could not reach Curtis with any degree of certainty. It seemed to be the general opinion of the Fancy that no one on the list of Curtis's weight can beat him.

DICK AT EPSOM RACES.—Although it was nearly five o'clock before the last race—the Maiden Stakes—was over, on Thursday, May 26th, 1822, and most excellent sport had been afforded, yet numbers of the sporting fraternity seemed to think the day was not exactly complete—that it wanted a sort of finish. As some of the lads from the Metropolis were upon the look-out for a little job, a mill was proposed by way of dessert, and a subscription purse of £16 was collected in a very short time. Little Dick Curtis, with as much blood as any horse upon the course, made his bow to the amateurs, and said he had not the least objection to peel, more especially as he had been cleaned out of all his loose rag by backing Deaf Davis on the previous Tuesday. " You're a good lad," replied a swell; "and it is a thousand pities you should be suffered to remain idle." A gipsy pricked up his ears upon hearing these remarks, and offered himself to the notice of the "Pink of Society," just to have a small taste, for the amusement of the company, if his honour had no objection. "Why," said the pink, "you seem to have been a little bit about the hedges lately. By your looks you are a gipsy. What set do you belong to?" The brown-visaged hero, with pride, answered, "The Coopers." "That will do," replied the swell; "show yourself at the scratch without delay." Dick Curtis was seconded by Ould Tom Jones and Harry Holt; and Cooper was handled by Gipsy Cooper and another "traveller." Seven to four on Dick.

THE FIGHT.

Round 1.—The Gipsy stripped well, and was what the fair sex term rather a handsome young man. He seemed, by the attitude he placed himself in, to meet his opponent as if he knew something about milling. Dick measured the Gipsy from head to foot with much confidence; but he was in no hurry to go to work. The Gipsy at length let fly, and missed, when Dick, lively as a dancing-master, put in some telling hits, and in the struggle the Bohemian went down amidst thunders of applause. ("Two to one!" lustily roared out.)

2.—Dick came laughing to the scratch, as keen as a stockbroker and cunning as a fox, giving the wink to his friends it was all right. Still he would not hit first. The Gipsy was again gammoned to make play, when his domino box got as much slashing as if seven had been the main. The rattling of the ivories was repeated, and the Gipsy floored. (Five to one, and no takers.)

3.—This round took the conceit out of the Gipsy, who ran furiously at Curtis, but the latter, with the utmost ease, stopped him, by giving him the pepper-box on his sensitive plant. Dick now commenced fighting, and put in four such complete facers that they made the Gipsy all abroad; he went down like a log. (Ten to one, and the multitude chevying from one end of the ring to the other, "What a prime little fellow Dick is!")

4.—This was short and sweet to Curtis; he sent the Gipsy down to cool himself on the turf for half a minute. (Any odds, but no takers.)

5.—It was clear to the judges that it must be soon over, and that the Gipsy must be milled off-hand. Curtis again drew his cork, and the hero of the bush once more embraced his mother earth. It was all stuff to offer odds, for no person seemed inclined to take ten to one.

6.—The pepper-box and vinegar cruet were again made use of by Dick, till the Gipsy had nearly let it escape out of his mouth that it was no go. Gipsy down.

7, and last.—The Gipsy napped a rum one on his canister, and he went down immediately, saying "he would not fight any more, as he had not room enough for his strength." Curtis gave a jump, and pocketed the purse almost without receiving a bit, exclaiming, "Success to Epsom Races!"

REMARKS.—It is true it was a very bad ring, owing to the vast multitude that pressed in upon the boxers from all sides; but if the Gipsy had had the whole of Epsom Downs to shift in he would never have been able to defeat Curtis. The latter is decidedly one of the best boxers of the day; no commoners must think of having a turn with him, and first-rate fighters must make a pause before they enter the lists with Dick. Two bystanders gave Dick a sovereign each for winning, which he generously made a present of to the Gipsy.

It would unnecessarily swell the bulk of the present volume to reproduce the numerous ring encounters in which Curtis was engaged during the succeeding years, in which time he fought with Peter Warren no less than five times, defeating that boxer on four occasions, and on the second the contest terminating in a drawn battle. The dates and duration of these are here given:—

1. Beat Peter Warren, 20 min., 10 rounds, £30 a side, at Colnbrook, July 23rd, 1822.

2. Draw with Peter Warren, £25 a side, 16 min., Moulsey, April 16th, 1823. On this occasion a wrangle and riot ended in the stakeholder returning the stakes to each party's backers. A third contest was therefore arranged, for £50 a side.

3. The third battle was decided at Crawley Hurst, July 8th, 1823. On this occasion Warren was defeated in one round, occupying nine minutes only, having sprained his kneecap so severely as to put him at once *hors de combat.*

4. After defeating Dick Hares, as we shall presently detail, Curtis beat Warren (£20 a side) on Epsom Downs, in six sharp rounds, occupying eight minutes only, and finally—

5. Defeated his pertinacious opponent at Warwick, in 7 rounds, time 16 minutes, for a stake of £100 to £90, on July 19th, 1825.

Dick Hares was in the interim matched with Curtis, for £50 a side, to come off April 13th, 1824, but the affair was prevented by an information laid at Bow Street, and two officers were sent down to Moulsey to stop the fight. It will perhaps raise a smile if we state the "reason" assigned for this prompting of the magisterial energy. The information of the "impending breach of the peace" was laid by a theatrical manager, who, his house being shut up because it was "Passion week," did not see "why other public amusements should be tolerated"! *Hinc illæ lachrymæ,* the laying of the information, and the disappointment of the Fancy.

A new match was accordingly made, as neither party desired a "draw;" and on Tuesday, July 8th, 1823, on Moulsey Hurst, on the ring being cleared after Ned Neale had defeated Gaynor (see *ante,* Life of NEALE, PERIOD IV., CHAP. V.), Hares, attended by Peter Crawley and Tom Shelton, threw his hat within the ropes. Curtis followed, waited on by Josh Hudson and Tom Owen, the Sage of the East, whose admiration of Curtis as a boxer had been long loudly expressed. Curtis's hat was about to go over the ropes with the wind, when Bill Moss caught it cleverly in both hands, and dropped it within the enclosure. Curtis fought under a yellowman, and Hares sported an emerald green flag. Six to four on Curtis.

THE FIGHT.

Round 1.—On stripping, the condition of Hares was the admiration of every amateur present. He looked like a new man, instead of an old one. Such are the advantages of training, if an athlete is not absolutely used up. "Curtis must be licked to-day; he has not stamina enough to get rid of Hares," was the cry. We also heard Jack Randall express the same opinion. On setting to, Curtis appeared well in health; but he looked thin, boyish, and little compared to his opponent. The attitudes of both men were pretty, and the anxiety of Curtis to get the first advantage remarkable. Hares too was eager to let fly, but he could not get an opening. Not so with the Pet; he embraced the first opportunity that presented itself, and his left hand alighted very heavily on the nose of Hares. An exchange of blows followed, in which Curtis received a small grain of pepper on his left cheek; but Hares napped a full dose. Standing still for a minute, nothing to be done. Curtis again let fly his left hand, which nearly sent Hares's teeth on a journey down his throat. The men closed soon afterwards at the ropes, when the fibbing of Curtis was terrific—he spoiled the look of his man, got Hares down, and fell upon him. A deafening shout for Curtis, the "Bermondseys" nearly out of their senses with joy. Two to one on the Pet.

2.—Hares was bleeding at the nose, his face much disfigured, and Curtis a little distressed and winking. Hares made an excellent stop. ("Well done, Hares!") Dick put in another nobber, the claret following. Counter-hits, and Curtis received a heavy blow on his cheek. An exchange of blows, and no light play. Hares made another good stop Curtis slipped a little near the ropes, when Hares ran up to him, and planted a heavy body hit; the Pet endeavoured to retreat, when his opponent stuck close to him, and put in another blow. Curtis recovered himself, and let fly his left hand in the middle of his opponent's head. Counter-hits. Two more terrific, stupefying facers by Curtis, and no return. In closing, the fibbing administered by the Pet was tremendous, and Hares went down, Curtis uppermost. ("What an extraordinary little fellow! He hits as hard as Cribb. The other man has no chance; take him away.")

3, and last.—Hares came up game as a pebble; but his head was quite altered; and his seconds, with all their industry and attention, could not keep his face clean. Both offering, but nothing done. Hares stopped a tremendous nobber. Rather a long pause. "Go to work, Hares." The latter made a second and also a third attempt with great skill; but after this time the execution was so decisive on the part of Curtis that it was positively one hundred pounds to a farthing. The left hand of Curtis went flush into the middle of Hares's head; a profusion of claret followed. ("What a limner this Pet is!" said the Sage of the East to Josh. "I never saw such a painter before. Why, he is a master of colour! What an artist!") The succession of hits planted by Curtis in the middle of Hares's head, without return, was surprising. It was a nobber, and claret—ditto—ditto—ditto. "Take the brave fellow away," said his backer—"I will not suffer him to fight any more. He has no chance." But Hares, regardless of the humane entreaties of his friends, stood up to receive punishment till Nature deserted him, when he fell in a state of stupor. Curtis jumped for joy, but immediately ran up to shake the hand of the fainting Hares. He was at once carried off the ground, and medical advice procured. It is but justice to say that Shelton and Crawley deserve great praise for the humanity and attention they paid to the brave but fallen little man.

REMARKS.—We have no hesitation in pronouncing the execution of Curtis the most decisive thing we ever witnessed in the Prize Ring. He won the fight with his left hand only, as he never made but two blows with his right hand during the battle. The Pet is the very first of boxers, and we think all pugilists will accede to the remark. He won the fight in twenty minutes, but did not prove the conqueror without receiving some heavy blows. Three or four tremendous hits were made by Hares. Although Curtis won the fight in such superior style he was certainly overmatched in weight and strength. The position of Curtis was so extremely fine that he was guarded at all points. Curtis dressed himself immediately, and walked about the ring receiving compliments from his friends. His left hand, however, if not quite gone, was terribly damaged.

Barney Aaron, whose weight was 10st., and who had beaten in succession Ned Stockman, Lenney, Frank Redmond, and Peter Warren, now challenged Curtis, and articles were signed for £100 a side. The battle was to have been decided on Tuesday, November 23rd, 1824, on the stage at Warwick, after Josh Hudson and Cannon had settled their differences; but on this occasion Curtis received forfeit of the battle-money, under very suspicious circumstances as regarded some of the Israelitish speculators, who had calculated on "getting at Curtis" in such a way as to secure what was then called "a slice of ready-made luck."

Soon after the match was made, Curtis being the favourite, such eagerness was shown in certain quarters to take the odds, and subsequently to lay even as much as six to four on the Jew " rather than not do bishnesh," that strong suspicions were excited, and a ×, in which Curtis was to " chuck the fight," was publicly talked of. Alarm spread at the sporting houses, and on inquiry Curtis came forward and declared " that he had rather lose his life than his fame." Upon this declaration the odds veered about, and Curtis was the favourite at five to four, giving chance, at any rate, of hedging. Then the assertions of dishonest intentions became stronger, and Barney was declared a safe winner. Thus matters stood when, some days previous to the big fight, Barney Aaron and his backers left London for Leamington, and made their headquarters at the "Crown." In due time, also, Curtis and his friends arrived at Warwick. Still such doubts existed that betting was at an end, until some heavy stakes were sported on the night before the fight, at the "George," at Warwick, and Barney again taken for choice. At an early hour in the day a report was circulated through the Race Stand that "the fight was off." This circumstance created regret among the true sporting men. However, in a few minutes after Hudson and Cannon had left the stage, Curtis appeared, attended by Tom Belcher and his backers, and threw up his hat amidst loud cheers. Aaron was called for, but not showing himself, Curtis addressed the multitude. He said, " I attended here according to the articles, and I call upon Barney Aaron to face me according to articles." He repeated the challenge twice without reply being made. Curtis then declared that " he would wait one quarter of an hour, and if Aaron did not appear, he should claim the stakes, £100, as a forfeit." Previous to the quarter of an hour having elapsed, Curtis wished it to be known that he would fight any man of his weight in the world, for £200 a side, and give half a stone.

Tom Belcher said he was the stakeholder, and the forfeit being claimed, he considered it his duty to give the £100 to Curtis, according to the rules of sporting. (" Perfectly correct, Tom," from the spectators.) Belcher then presented Curtis with a new £100 Bank of England note, which the Pet smilingly deposited in his pocket. Belcher then took the nattily shaped " Pet " on his back, and lightly carried him, amidst laughter and applause, through the mud to the Grand Stand, where his health was drunk in sparkling " cham " by his friends, backers, and the admirers of straightforward honesty.

At Ned Neale's benefit at the Fives Court, two days after this fiasco,

Curtis and Aaron met in the most friendly manner. Curtis said : " I would rather have fought for the money ; but I am sure, Barney, it was not your fault."

Aaron then proceeded to explain. He said he was told the place was Oxford, and there he was taken by his backers in a post-chaise, contrary to his intention, which had been to meet Curtis. He had with him his drawers and shoes. "Had I been licked," said he, " which I don't think I should have been" (a laugh from Curtis), " I should have got some blunt ; but I have been regularly dished." " I hope you will get backed," replied Curtis ; "I know you're a brave man, and I hope next time we shall have a *comfortable* fight ! "

Some chaffering about the amount of stakes followed this interview ; Curtis proposing to fight for £200, and Aaron's backers modestly suggesting that Curtis (in consideration of the forfeit of £100—the forfeit was only £50) should fight Barney £200 to £100. The subjoined stanzas, conveying the challenge, seem of sufficient merit to deserve snatching from oblivion :—

THE PET'S INVITATION.

Richard Curtis to Barney Aaron—Greeting.

Come, Barney, 'tis Curtis, the Pet, who invites thee ;
  No longer to fight for two hundred refuse ;
For while all the pride of "the Peoplesh" excites thee,
  You can't need the needful, my star of the Jews !

Remember the glories of ancient Mendoza,
  And hard-drinking, hard-hitting, shifting Dutch Sam ;
Think on old Ikey Pig, and Big Bittoon, who knows thee,
  With the rush of a lion, yet mild as a lamb.

What though Mrs. Aaron thy mug may delight in,
  And thinking of black eyes, turns fretful and wan ?
She'll say, when convinced that you really mean fighting,
  " Mine husband, Cot plesh him, 's a brave little man."

I'll own that as good as e'er pulled off a shirt is
  The lad I now call to the old milling game ;
And remember, friend Barney, though challenged by Curtis,
  No *Cur-'tis* invites to combat for fame.

Then try all the good ones who live in the Minories,
  Kick the shins of the dwellers in Petticoat Lane—
Get blunt, which of all sorts of milling the sinew is ;
  Drop chaffing, and take to fair fighting again.

August 28th, 1825.

THE STAR'S ANSWER.

Barney Aaron to Richard Curtis—Greeting.

I come, Mr. *Cur-'tis* the Star of the Sheenies
  Who advances to pluck from thy brow the high crest,
With a *sufficit quantum* of courage—and guineas—
  To lower thy *caput*, my Flower of the West.

> You fought Peter Warren a hundred to ninety,
> 　　Then why not fight me for the first-mention'd name?
> But being all bounce you the scratch will not come to,
> 　　To show your much-vaunted pretensions to fame.
>
> You say that the ochre—the metal—the rhino,
> 　　Is flush 'mong the Sheenies of Petticoat Lane;
> 'Tish more scarsh nor you think—I vish it vash mine, oh!
> 　　I'd fight for my losht reputation again.
>
> Now hear! For one hundred, I'm ready to fight you,
> 　　Surely, out of mere fairness, you cannot refuse;
> You'll have to contend with no Warren, my Cur-tis,
> 　　But with brave Barney Aaron, the Star of the Jews!

DUKE'S PLACE,
　　September 3rd, 1825.

These poetic effusions, with a dozen prosy letters to boot, failed to bring the men to terms.

Curtis was now indeed " the Pet of the Fancy;" no sparring exhibition of any pretension was perfect in its programme without the Light-weight Champion displayed his skill in the art of which he was such a consummate master; and as Dick never hesitated to put on the gloves, and give away a stone or two and a few inches, the disparity of his opponents added a keener interest than usual to his demonstrations. The newspapers of the period are full of them. Curtis was now perforce idle, for there was no boxer near his weight who could get matched against him. Of course he was the object of envy to many of the fraternity, and as

> " Envy doth merit like its shade pursue,
> 　　And by the shadow proves the substance true,"

so with one Mister Edward Savage, whose anger at the want of appreciation of his own merits, and the favour lavished on " the Pet," carried him beyond all bounds of common civility. Edward Savage, an eleven stone man, was one of three Savages, the others named William and Cab. (or Jack) Savage, who were professed boxers. Ned Savage, on the evening of the 5th of August, 1825, entered the parlour of Tom Belcher's, the " Castle," Holborn, where Curtis and other friends were taking their whiff and their wet. The conversation turning upon pugilistic affairs, Mister Savage made some most insulting remarks upon the diminutive size of Curtis, coupled with regrets that he (Savage) could not get himself down to ten stone (Dick had challenged all comers and to give a stone), and concluded with a ruffianly threat of what he would do if Curtis would " give him a chance." The Pet was about to leave when Savage, true to his name, struck him severely in the eye. The return on Mister Savage's optic was made with lightning celerity, and the next instant the little one had his man round the neck, and delivered a succession of left-handers of such cutting severity that when Savage got down his head was a piteous spectacle. The company now interfered, but Curtis declared that he "must teach this Savage a lesson." Savage rushed in blind with rage, and it is charity to suppose somewhat upset by liquor, when he was met by one, two, three steadiers in the head, his returns being parried, until he fairly staggered down. The affair now became a regular battle. Curtis threw off his upper garments, and Savage did the same. Savage rushed at his man so fiercely that Dick, stepping aside, delivered his blow on the ear of a bystander, to the man's great astonishment and the amusement of the company, while Curtis simultaneously delivered alternately with both hands in such style that Savage turned away from the punishment. He was, however, game, if nothing else, and came up as receiver-general until the sixteenth round, when he was so completely cut up and beaten that he cried, "Enough!" Not more than sixteen minutes elapsed from the first assault to the close of this unexpected performance, the description of which by a few of the scientific spectators raised the fame of Curtis to a height hardly exceeded by that attained by his victories in the twenty-four foot. Tom Belcher's concluding remark when narrating this little episode used to be—"It wouldn't be lucky for some of us if Dick was twelve stone. There wouldn't be much chaff about who would be Champion then"—a remark in which the heavy weights present usually coincided, some of them perhaps with a slight mental reservation in favour of his own brave self.

A ridiculous encounter with Ned Stockman, on the day of the fight between Gaynor and Bishop Sharpe (Tuesday, May 16th, 1826) is recorded. In this affair Stockman, after challenging Curtis and offering to fight him, laid down like a cur after a single round, as recorded in the reports of the time.

This brings us to the match at length arranged, by the concession of Curtis, for £100 a side, with Barney Aaron. The battle came off on Tuesday, February 27th, 1827, at Andover, Hants, upon a stage erected in a field at the back of the "Queen Charlotte" public-house, opposite that where Spring defeated Neale, in 1823, one mile from the town. The stage was erected by the townspeople free of expense, and upwards of forty wagons were sent to form an outer ring by the jolly Hampshire farmers of the neighbourhood. The pugilistic division from London was in great force. Jem Ward, Tom Oliver, Ben Burn, Young Gas (Jonathan Bissell), Harry Holt, Ned Neale, with Fogo the Laureate and Joe Fishwick the Commissary, had joined the wagon-train. Curtis, valeted by Young Dutch Sam, took up his quarters at the " White Hart," and Barney Aaron and Gipsy Cooper at the " Catherine Wheel," opposite. Curtis was the favourite, at five to four. At one o'clock Barney, accompanied by Mr. Nathan and Jem Ward, ascended the stage amidst loud cheering. Curtis, attended by his backer, and Josh Hudson with Ben Burn, soon followed, and were welcomed with acclamation. The men then shook hands, and the colours were tied to the stakes; a bright yellow for Curtis and a deep red with yellow spots for the Israelite; and the battle commenced.

THE FIGHT.

Round 1.—The Pet, as he exhibited in buff, gave great delight and satisfaction to his numerous friends. His condition was acknowledged to be quite tiptop. He might have been compared to the finest racehorse for blood, game, and bone; in fact, the *tout ensemble* of the Pet was the picture of a fine-framed man in miniature. His arms were beautiful. The Star of the East was equally bright; he had done everything to improve his strength during his preparation, and he appeared at the scratch a robust, vigorous, athletic young man. In elegance, ease, and grace, Angelo, O'Shaughnessy, or Roland, with the foils, would not have exhibited more taste in the polite accomplishment of fencing than did the attitudes and arms of Curtis and Aaron exhibit in the art of self-defence. Both combatants were armed *cap-à-pie*; it was an eye against an eye, toe for toe, arm opposed to arm, caution matched with caution; if one was " down " the other was " up "—it was, " I won't have it ! " on both sides; in short, it was diamond cut diamond. Such were the boxers opposed to each other in this great trial of skill. Barney, unlike the character of his milling in his previous battles, preferred the "look-out" to the rush; he being well aware of the great talent, judgment, and finishing qualities of his opponent, and determined not to give the slightest chance away. The Pet, like an accomplished general, soon perceived that his adversary was nothing else but a difficult one, and not to be gammoned upon old suits: indeed, that nothing but the utmost skill was necessary to be with him upon any point. For several minutes the spectators were delighted with the extreme caution displayed on both sides, and at the same time the readiness which Curtis and Aaron displayed should any opening offer for the exercise of their fists. Curtis looked as it were into the " very soul " of his adversary, and the richness of the " Jew's eye " was of an equally penetrating description. Barney waited for the Pet to commence offensive operations, but Curtis, finding that nothing could be done without great danger to himself, retreated slowly towards the corner of the stage, the Star of the East following him leisurely. The interest of the scene was intense, and every peeper on the stretch to witness mischief. Barney, with great spirit and tact, went in, and gave Dick pepper with his right and left hands on his face. (" Beautiful ! " from the Sheenies.) The Pet countered slightly. Barney, in closing, endeavoured to fib his opponent, but Dick bolted (" Hallo ! what's the matter ? ") and cleverly got out of trouble. The Pet turned quickly, and again met his man; an exchange of blows followed, and in closing they tried each other's strength severely, when both went down, Curtis undermost. (Loud shouting for Barney, and " Where's your two to one ? ") The claret was seen on Dick's mouth. " First blood " was declared in favour of Aaron.

2.—Curtis had always entertained a good opinion of the milling qualities of his opponent, but he was now completely satisfied that he was not only a troublesome customer, but a better man than any who had previously stood before him. Slow and sure appeared the order of the day on both sides. Aaron was not to be had by any stratagem practised by Curtis. The latter, however, gradually retired to the end of the stage, Barney in attendance upon him. Counter-hits were given, and both told. The Jew went to work in the most manly style, and the counter-hits were admirable. In closing Barney endeavoured to fib his opponent, but the Pet returned hard and fast, and it was difficult to say which had the best of it. Barney was ultimately thrown, but Dick also went down. The Pet-ites now began to let loose their red rags, and Curtis was hailed with shouts of applause.

3.—This round was "as long as Paterson's Road Book." Each of their mugs exhibited the handiwork of the other, and Barney's peepers had been measured for a "suit of mourning." The Pet was cautious, and his face bespoke that he had all his work to do to change the battle in his favour. Barney was equally shy, and kept a good look-out. Curtis, finding that he could not make an impression, tried once more the retreating system, but Barney was after him, though his blows were skilfully stopped by the Pet. Counter-hitting, and Jack as good as his master. Curtis's right eye received a sharp taste, but the Jew had the favour returned with interest. A pause, and nothing like mischief for a short period. Barney at length let fly on the Pet's chaffing-box, and the claret followed, which appeared rather troublesome to Curtis. The admirers of scientific fighting had a perfect treat, both men being prepared at every point. Curtis seemed rather fatigued, put down his hands for an instant, and the Jew followed his example. The truth is, the conduct of Barney in not availing himself of his weight and length not only surprised all his friends, but astonished the backers of Curtis. The disinterested part of the audience viewed it as a doubtful thing. Barney at last went to work, and planted two successful hits. Some sharp exchanges. In closing, fibbing was the order of the day, and the pepper-box changed hands in rapid succession. The men broke ground, and Dick adopted his skilful mode of retreating. The Star of the East went after him, and in the corner of the stage planted a severe blow on his throat, which made Dick gulp again. In closing, after a severe struggle, Curtis went down undermost, and Barney upon one knee. ("Vell done, Barney!" from the Sheenies.) The backers of Curtis, although not positively afraid, yet candidly acknowledged they had hitherto thought too little of Aaron.

4.—The face of Dick did not exhibit his usual gaiety of expression. His mind was at work to attack his opponent upon a new system. In short, we never saw him so puzzled before in any of his contests. The pause was long, and nothing done. Jem Ward, who had hitherto been silent, now exclaimed, "It will be—'who'd ha' thought it?' We shall win!" Barney cleverly hit the Pet away, and some little workmanship took place between them, when the left mauly of Dick caught Barney's nob, and he went down partly on his knees. It could scarcely be considered a knockdown blow. The Pet-ites were again liberal with their applause, and seven to four offered.

5.—Those persons who had witnessed the severity of execution done by Dick in his fights with gloves expected that he would have nobbed the Jew off-hand. But the science and caution of Barney astonished the ring-goers. Sharp counter-hits. The fighting was good on both sides, and both nobs were damaged. The right cheek of the Star of the East napped a severe cut. In closing the struggle was great to obtain the throw, when the Pet, by a sudden impulse, gave Barney a hoist between the ropes. He would have fallen at least six feet to the ground, but fortunately for the Star of the East a wagon had been placed near the stage for the accommodation of the reporters, umpires, and referee. Pierce Egan and another scribbler caught hold of Barney by the arm and his leg, and rescued the Jew from his perilous situation. Like one of the gamest of the game Barney jumped up and exclaimed, "I am not hurt, it's all right," and reascended the stage amidst thunders of applause.

6.—Of course the agitation and shock sustained by the above accident, added to the shortness of the time, only half a minute, to return to the scratch, were considerably against him. Yet he set to in the most manly way, and gave Dick not a very light one on his pimple. The latter countered as quick as lightning. Milling on both sides for a short period, until they separated. Both careful, and upon the look-out for an opening. A rally occurred, in which Dick rather took the lead, and Barney's head received severe punishment. The Jew at length went down upon his hands. ("You have got him now, Curtis, only go to work!" said the boys of the Borough. "He knows better," answered a Sheeny; "Curtis will be in trouble if he does!")

7.—The countenance of Curtis now became cheerful, and he gave the "office" to his friends that the fight was his own. Dick was evidently improved, but Barney, game as a pebble, commenced fighting. The Pet retreated with advantage, and as Barney followed him he planted one, two, and a third facer in succession. The Jew, good as gold, would not be denied, went in to work, caught hold of Dick, and fibbed with all his strength; Curtis was not behindhand. In struggling for the throw Curtis went down easy, but was undermost. Two to one on Curtis, and lots of shouting.

8.—The Pet was decidedly getting the best of it, yet the strength of Barney was by no means so reduced as to indicate that the fight would soon be over. Barney went to work, and a sharp rally was the result. Some hard hits passed between them, and Curtis received a teaser on his jaw. In closing both went down. The Sheenies did not desert their man, and cheered him with applause.

9, and last.—Dick, though quite satisfied in his own mind he was now winning the fight, was as cautious as if he had yet all his work to do. The head of Barney was rather out of shape, and the nob of Curtis was a little changed. Sparring for a short time, when Dick made himself up for mischief, and mischievous he certainly was. With his left he put in a tremendous blow upon his opponent's throat. Barney went down like a shot—flat upon his back—his heels up, and was utterly insensible when time was called. Curtis so well knew that he had settled the business that he went up immediately to the timekeepers to wait for their decision. The Pet jumped for joy, and was proclaimed the victor, amidst the shouts of the surrounding populace. Josh Hudson hoisted the Pet upon his shoulders and carried him to his postchaise, huzzaing all the way. The fight lasted fifty minutes.

REMARKS.—Such a real, scientific battle on both sides has not been seen for many a long day: indeed, no lover of the Fancy would have thought two hundred miles any distance to have witnessed the superior tactics displayed by Curtis and Aaron. The Pet, high as he stood before on the roll of pugilists, raised himself to the top of the tree by this victory. Curtis has now proved the conqueror in eleven prize battles. As we have already said, we never saw Dick so puzzled before, and until he had reduced the Jew to his weight the first four rounds were of a doubtful character. Without exception the Pet must be pronounced the most effi-

cient boxer in the pugilistic world. We cannot say more. At the same time it is equally true that Barney Aaron, if not exactly at the top of the tree, is very near to it. That is to say, if Curtis ranks as number one, number two of the light weights belongs to the brave little Sheeny. He is still the Star of the East, and instead of having fallen in the estimation of his friends by this defeat, his fine fighting, manly conduct, and fair play must raise him in the eyes of the sporting world. Curtis did not weigh nine stone, and Barney just drew ten. The severity of the blow which Aaron received on his throat operated so strongly that he did not come to himself for nearly an hour. To use Barney's own words, he said, "I do not know that I could have won the battle, but had I not received that blow on my throat, which fairly hit me out of time, I am certain I could have fought for half-an-hour longer." Curtis, before he left Andover, called upon his fallen and brave opponent and presented him with a guinea, and acknowledged that he was the best man he had ever fought with. A subscription of six pounds was also made on the ground, collected by one of the backers of Curtis.

Curtis was next backed to fight Jack Tisdale for £120 to £100.

Staines, on the Windsor road, was the great rallying point, and Shirley's, the "New Inn," the house of call upon the above occasion. Every room was full of milling visitors. In the stables, although extensive, the prads were riding over one another, the yard filled with drags of all sorts, and lots of customers could not find the slightest accommodation. Such were the attractions of the two heroes, the Pet of the Fancy and Jack Tisdale.

Between nine and ten in the morning of Tuesday, October 9th, 1827, the men met according to appointment to ascertain their weight, as required by the articles. Curtis proved to be no more than eight stone nine pounds and three-quarters, and Tisdale eight stone eight pounds. Curtis, in the most confident style, betted two sovereigns to one with Tisdale, after which the men retired to their inns, Curtis to Shirley's and Tisdale to the Swan Inn, near the bridge, at Staines.

Curtis was decidedly the favourite throughout the whole of the match, at seven to four, two to one, and higher odds. Tisdale was always viewed as a good little man, but it was considered he had entirely left the ring, five years having elapsed since his last battle with Lenney. Tisdale was highly respected by his numerous friends. He had made up his mind to win and nothing else, and assured his backers that if he could but get at Dick, and he thought he could, victory would crown his efforts.

The heavy rain did not damp the ardour of the visitors, and the ring was surrounded by thousands of spectators. Within a mile and a half of the town of Staines, in a meadow in the county of Bucks, almost opposite the racecourse at Egham, was the spot of ground selected for action.

At the appointed time Tisdale made his appearance, and threw his castor into the ring, followed by two good ould ones, Jack Randall and Bill Cropley, as his seconds. He was well received. In a few minutes afterwards the Pet, in a military cloak, repeated the token of defiance, waited upon by the John Bull Fighter and Young Dutch Sam. Lots of applause for Curtis. Tisdale and Curtis shook hands together in the most hearty style. The colours, yellow for Curtis and blue for Tisdale, had been tied to the stakes by Hudson and Cropley. The hands were crossed together by all parties and the battle commenced.

THE FIGHT.

Round 1.—On peeling Curtis looked extremely thin, nevertheless he was quite well. He had reduced himself during his training nearly fourteen pounds, but he was lively, strong, and well to all intents and purposes. It was a dangerous experiment for a light man like Curtis, but to use his own words, he assured his friends he was never better in the whole course of his life. Tisdale was as good as he could be made by the wholesome effects of training, and also inspired with the highest confidence that success would crown his efforts. In point of youth the Pet had the best of it. The attitude of Curtis was a picture, and he appeared to the spectators a master of the art of boxing. The style of Tisdale was not so imposing as his accomplished fistic rival, but it was firm, calculated to receive the attack, and formed an excellent outline of a scientific pugilist. Dick measured his opponent from head to foot, keeping a good look-out for squalls, anxious to give, but not to receive. Tisdale was also leary, but his guard was low. The Pet viewed his rival as a dangerous customer, and like a skilful general was determined not to give half a chance away; he not only worked hard with his hands, but he was likewise perpetually on the move with his feet. Plenty of caution was exhibited on both sides. "Do not be gammoned," was the advice of Randall and Cropley to Tisdale. The interest was intense amongst the spectators to witness the lead taken on either side. Tisdale attempted to plant a blow, but Dick got away like a dancing-master. Tisdale repeated the attempt twice, when ditto, ditto, on the part of the Pet was the time of day. A sort of standstill followed, both keeping prime look-outs, like experienced pilots. Curtis made

an offer, but Tisdale was awake. The Pet, after manœuvring in his best style, at length let fly his right and left, when Tisdale, with admirable skill, parried both hits, amidst loud applause from the surrounding crowd. A short pause. "It will be a long fight," said the amateurs. Tisdale made another neat parry. Dick, as if it appeared to his mind he had got his opponent, hit out one, two, reached the canister of Tisdale, then rushed in to his work and fibbed away. Tisdale endeavoured to return the compliment, but without effect, was ultimately thrown, and undermost. (It might be said not much was the matter, but the Bermondsey boys let loose their red rags, and odds to any amount were offered. This round occupied nearly nine minutes.)

2.—Tisdale wished to go to work, but Dick would not have it. Curtis with great force put in a facer without return. ("Beautiful!" from his friends.) Tisdale slightly touched the body of his adversary. Both made themselves up for mischief, and two prime counter-hits were the result. The Pet planted a ribber, which made Tisdale blow for breath. Both on the look-out. Curtis hit out right and left with effect, but in return he napped a rum one on his ear. Some exchanges occurred, when Dick, with great impetuosity, planted two blows that were heard all over the ring, and Tisdale went down. The effect was so heavy that Tisdale for the instant scarcely knew where he was, and he put up his hand to keep Dick off.

3.—The handiwork of the Pet was visible to all the ring—a lump on Tisdale's forehead, and his left eye damaged. Dick soon planted a nobber. A pause. Dick got away from mischief. Tisdale endeavoured to plant some hits, but Dick retreated in the most masterly style. Tisdale again missed several hits, owing to the retreating jumps of Curtis. Dick also made some beautiful stops. Tisdale satisfied his friends that he was a brave little man, although he could not get the lead. The skill evinced by Curtis was much admired. He gammoned his opponent to come and fight, and then punished him for his temerity. Dick again made his one, two, good, which produced some severe in-fighting, decidedly in favour of the Pet. In closing, both down, Tisdale undermost. ("Odds?" cried Josh; "why, you may bet anything, and no mistake! It's one hundred to a rump steak, and I'll lay the hundred pounds.")

4.—The Bermondseys were all in high spirits. Tisdale made play without effect, Dick being ready for his opponent at all points. Tisdale, rather wild from the one, two, of his opponent, hit at random. In closing Dick got the best of the fibbing, and Tisdale was again thrown. ("Meat in Newgate Market must rise to-morrow," said the John Bull Fighter, "to cover the losses of the kill-bulls.")

5.—Upwards of a minute elapsed before anything was attempted between the combatants, so much caution was observed on both sides. Tisdale was on the alert to effect a turn, but Dick was up to his movements. The latter also neatly, and with great force, planted two hits without return. Tisdale at length got into work, and some sharp blows were exchanged. Tisdale showed "first blood," from the mouth, which was announced to the ring by Josh Hudson. In closing Tisdale went down.

6.—The steadiness displayed by Tisdale was much admired. He came cheerfully to the scratch, and tried to punish the Pet, but the latter stopped him with ease. The right hand of Curtis made a smashing hit on Tisdale's left ogle, but the Newgate Market hero quick as lightning countered, and produced the claret from Dick's ear. ("My eye," said Cropley to Randall, "that was a teaser!") Dick tried all his skill to draw Tisdale again into his clutches, but Jack was not to be had, and a long pause ensued. Curtis jobbed with his left hand, nevertheless Tisdale returned the charge like nothing but a good one. The men fought their way into a rally, and pepper on both sides was the order of the day, until they broke away. This round was decidedly the best that had taken place; and although it was the general opinion that Dick would prove the conqueror, it was admitted at the same time that he would have his work to do. Tisdale could not plant his hits effectually, the Pet was so good upon his legs. Curtis in great style stopped a rib-roaster, and patted his arm, laughing at Tisdale. A rally was the tie-up of this round, to the advantage of Curtis, and Tisdale fell with his back upon the ropes. Several bets were now lost that Dick won the battle in half-an-hour.

7.—This round was a touch of the polish.

Dick had it all his own way. He jobbed and jobbed again, without any return, and closed the round by throwing the hero of Newgate Market.

8.—Dick, although so much in his favour, was still cautious, determined to make his conquest complete. The left hand of the Pet in numerous instances operated like the kick of a horse on the nob of Tisdale. The latter retreated to the ropes, followed by Curtis, when Dick took the lead in weaving, and a severe struggle for the throw took place. During the time Tisdale was balancing upon the ropes, and apprehensive of the punishment he was about to receive from Curtis, he said, "Dick, don't hit me now." "I will not," replied Dick, and laying hold of Tisdale's hand he pulled him up, and led him into the middle of the ring, amidst tumultuous applause. The battle was now severe indeed, and Tisdale hit wide and wild; the Pet planted a facer, when they both went to work like out-and-outers. Give and take, and summat the matter on both sides; the nose of Curtis appeared as if it had been scraped with a knife. The face of Tisdale had now assumed an altered aspect, and, according to the phrase of the Ring, his uncles and aunts would have doubted his relationship, his frontispiece was so completely altered. To add to Tisdale's already damaged head, Dick again planted two jobbers, and Tisdale was floored. (Hats were thrown up, the Bermondsey coves shouting and dancing, and odds as extravagant as St. Paul's to a cockle-shell offered.)

9.—Short. Tisdale suffering under the severity of punishment hit at random. This sort of conduct suited Curtis; he took advantage of the mistake, and by a hit on the domino box sent Tisdale to his mother earth.

10.—A brave man will always claim admiration, and a braver or better little man was never seen in the twenty-four foot than Jack Tisdale. But his superior in tactics stood before him. The coolness which had previously distinguished the conduct of Tisdale was gone by, and the repeated irritating blows had excited his passion; at all events, he threw several blows away. He would not be denied, and he bored Dick nearly to the ropes. In stopping a sort of kill-bull blow Dick slipped down on his latter end. This circumstance gave a little bit of new life to his friends, and Tisdale was loudly cheered.

11.—A few persons seemed to think that Dick was weak, but he soon convinced his partisans to the contrary. Dick got away from mischief, but was exceedingly mischievous in the return, and the nose of the hero of Newgate Market received a hit enough to have satisfied any common glutton. Tisdale, undismayed, never flinched, and returned sharply on Curtis's chin. ("Hallo!" cried Cropley, "Master Dick, you have napped it.") Dick, waiting for a turn, tried every move on the board to have the best of it; he planted a facer, repeated the dose, then tried it a third time with success. ("Blow my dickey!" said Josh; "why, I never saw a footman knock at a door half so stylish as Dick is paying his respects to Mr. Tisdale!") The hero of Newgate Market stood up with the firmness of a brick, counter-hitting, and exerting himself to win, until Dick punished him in all directions at the ropes. In struggling for the throw Dick had the best of it, and Tisdale was undermost. (Curtis, during the time he was sitting upon the knee of his second, informed his backer he could put on the polish and win it in a canter. "No," was the reply, "take your time; it is all your own; win at your leisure.")

12.—This round had hardly commenced when a facer was planted by Curtis. Tisdale, quite wild, followed Dick over the ring, but Curtis put on another opera stop, and nothing was the matter. Tisdale again went to work, but the skipping back of Curtis made him all right. The Pet put in a jobber, ditto, and ditto, repeated. The gluttony displayed by Tisdale called forth not only admiration, but pity. The Newgate Market hero made himself up for mischief, tremendous counter-hits occurred, and the claret was seen from the nose of Curtis. Yet nothing could take the fight out of the Pet. Tisdale wildly following him received punishment at every step. In closing Tisdale underwent fibbing, and was also thrown.

13.—This round had nearly proved a *finale*. Tisdale now became desperate, and plunged headlong to work, regardless of consequences. Dick stopped him, got away with ease, and punished his opponent severely. A pause ensued, Dick as cautious as when he commenced the battle. The appearance of Tisdale was really piteous, but he still kept the game alive, and did his best for himself and friends to obtain victory. The Pet soon got an opening, and hit poor Tisdale to a perfect standstill; his hands dropped, he staggered, and fell down. ("Take him away," said Josh; "it is a shame to let such a brave fellow be punished without the shadow of a chance to win.")

14.—When time was called Tisdale answered it, but he was as groggy as a sailor three sheets in the wind—"yes, and worse than that 'ere," as the John Bull Fighter observed, Tisdale scarcely knowing what he was about—in fact, he was quite abroad, dealing his blows at random. Dick hopped out of the way of mischief, then planted a facer, which gave his opponent the staggers. Tisdale fell on his hand and knee, but being too game to consider the round at end, immediately got up to renew the fight, when the Pet ran up to him and sent him down. "Foul!" and Fair!" were the cries—the umpires disagreed, but the referee considered it fair. The conduct of Curtis might have been censured as not exactly polite or gentle-

manly, as Scroggins said, nevertheless it was perfectly fair, as Tisdale rose upon his legs to renew the battle. In the first instance Tisdale was about leaving the ring, but upon hearing the referee's decision he returned to renew the fight.

15.—The time gained by the wrangle was good for Tisdale. He put up his hands at the scratch, then recollecting himself said it was "foul conduct," left Curtis, went up to the umpires, and asked "what he was to do?" "Why, fight on," replied the referee, "if you do not mean to lose the fight." It is worthy of remark that Curtis never took any advantage of Tisdale's movements, which he might have done. Some of the spectators had now left their places in the outer ring, and all was glorious confusion.

16.—This round was all upon the bustle, and whips and sticks were at work to keep the ring clear. The battle was now reduced a horse to a hen; Tisdale was of no use, and Curtis hit him down. ("Don't leave the ring, Dick, till you finish the fight properly," observed his friends.)

17, and last.—Tisdale again appeared at the scratch, but it was only to receive additional punishment. Dick was at him without delay, and Tisdale was again down at the ropes. On time being called Tisdale did not appear at the scratch. Curtis went up to him, when Randall said, "It is all over," and Tisdale also added that "he would not fight any more." The John Bull Fighter, after putting the colours, the fruits of victory, round the neck of the Pet, hoisted him on his shoulders, and carried him in triumph to his drag, amidst loud shouting. The fight was over in fifty-eight minutes.

REMARKS.—From the beginning to the end of the mill it never appeared to us that Tisdale had a chance of winning. In observing thus much it is not meant to convey an opinion to our readers that Tisdale is not a good boxer—the contrary is the fact. He is one of the best little men of his weight in the kingdom; he stands well upon his legs; he can stop like a tactician, hits hard, and possesses a capital knowledge of boxing. His courage is of the highest order, and his game unquestionable. He is not disgraced in surrendering to Curtis, the irresistible Champion of the Light Weights. Many spectators felt disappointed that Curtis did not do more with Tisdale at the beginning of the battle, as the friends of Curtis declared that Tisdale would be polished off *sans cérémonie*. But Curtis was not to be led away by the high praises of his backers, and like a skilful general he treated his adversary as a dangerous opponent. Curtis did not escape without some sharp punishment about the head, but in comparison with Tisdale's it was trifling in the extreme.

Curtis, from his unbroken career of conquest in the Prize Ring, might now be compared to the celebrated Eclipse, who, having won all the King's Plates he went for, was "cried down;" for the Pet was so decidedly excellent in his tactics that he was left without an opponent.

Some injudicious persons at this period began an idle newspaper controversy on the comparative merits of Curtis and Jack Randall, full of vulgar personalities; and the latter boxer, in the month of October, 1827, allowed a letter to appear with his signature in *Pierce Egan's Life in London,* in which he offered to fight Curtis " in *four months* from the time of making the match, for £300 to £1,000 (!) either on a stage or the turf," "money always ready at the Hole in the Wall, Chancery Lane." To which Curtis replied that " his weight was nine stone," but he would "give half a stone, and fight Mr. Randall, or any other man, for £100 to £300." This buncombe of course meant nothing. Indeed, poor Jack was already doing battle with the universal conqueror, who gave him the finishing blow within six months of this ridiculous challenge.

Curtis took his leave of the Prize Ring at a benefit at the Fives Court, in November, 1827, by an open challenge for a month to any man in England, half a stone above his weight. No boxer had the temerity to come forward and " pick up the glove;" and Curtis in consequence retired from the scene of active pugilism. But although the Pet had given up prize milling, he had not given up the use of his hands to protect himself from insult. On Wednesday afternoon, January 2nd, 1828, as the Pet and his pal, Young Dutch Sam, were walking along Blackfriars Road, they passed a couple of sturdy coalheavers, one of whom, in swinging his whip round, struck Dick. The latter asked Coaly what he meant by striking him. The exact reply we must not mention—suffice it to say that Dick threatened to kick the offender on that part of his person to which he was referred for an explanation. Coaly, not knowing the Pet, threw a brave defiance in his teeth, and a set-to commenced, Sam seconding the Pet, and Coaly having his own companion to pick him up. Dick found himself engaged with a very strong fellow, who knew a little about fighting, and was moreover fully a stone and a half the heavier man. Coaly rushed in to bring his strength to bear, and Dick, as his custom was, broke ground— jobbing and retreating. One of the black diamond's eyes was soon in darkness, but he did not take without giving; almost at the very commencement of the fight, he planted a nobber that severely damaged the Pet's neat countenance, besides sending him back against a cart, with a force that raised a peal of bells in Dick's cranium. The spectators of all sorts were, of course, numerous, and some of them expressed considerable disapprobation at Dick's mode of getting away. Encouraged by this, the second coalheaver went behind Curtis and stopped him as he retreated; Young Dutch Sam instantly floored him, which at once took all conceit of either fighting or interfering out of that gentleman. A bystander soon after received a topper from Sam for placing his carcass where it ought not to be; he soon after came up behind the young Dutchman, returned the hit on the sly, and retreated among the mob; but Sam quickly pulled him forth and gave him three or four facers, whereupon he cried for quarter. During these proceedings the Pet was still engaged with his first antagonist, who proved himself a game man, and though told that he was fighting with the celebrated Dick Curtis, he refused to give in, but declared that he knew he could beat his man, saying, " let him be Dick or Devil, he'd sarve him out." At length a gentleman, not liking to see a good man cut up where he had little or no chance, took Coaly by the arm, and after literally begging him to leave off, strengthened his counsel by a *douceur* of half-a-crown, upon sight of which the brave, though saucy, coalheaver consented to say " enough." He was severely punished about the head— nor did Curtis escape scot-free; his nob was visibly marked.

A long letter professing to come from the coalheaver and signed " George Phillips" appeared the following week in the *Dispatch*, in which the writer, denying his defeat, and offering to fight Curtis for £5 (!), hoped that the Pet would meet him " for love, and the £5 as a sweetener." Mr. Whittaker, an oilman and ex-pugilist, its supposed writer, also went about offering to back " his man " against " the Pet."

Curtis now went on a sparring tour to Manchester and Liverpool; at the latter place, at the Circus, he was enthusiastically received. Young Sam, Jem Ward, and Ned Stockman were also of the party.

All doubts respecting the milling capabilities of Coaly were completely put to rest at Joe Fishwick's benefit at the Tennis Court, on Monday, March 17th, 1828. The sturdy black diamond having declared, in opposition to all the statements published of that affair, that he had the " best of it," Curtis chivalrously volunteered to put on the gloves with him. He had not the slightest chance with Curtis, who nobbed him at pleasure, drew blood from his razor-shaped nose, and knocked him down no less than six times. All he could do was, when not hit off his legs, to bore Dick against the rail by superior weight and strength; but in everything that belongs to fighting it was " all the world to nothing " on the Pet. The latter seemed at length ashamed to hit the man, and offered to cut it, but Coaly was foolhardy enough to wish for more, saying "he was not hurt." Curtis therefore accommodated him with additional punishment. On pulling off the gloves the coalheaver appeared quite chapfallen. Dick was so completely armed at all points that the violent attacks of Coaly were utterly frustrated, and it might almost be said that Curtis left the stage without receiving a hit.

Though retired as a principal, Dick's talents as a second were in constant requisition, and his name will be found, in that capacity, in many pages of our volumes. It would have been well indeed for Curtis had he adhered to his resolution of retirement; but it was not to be. A ten-stone man, Perkins, of Oxford, who had received the title of "the Oxford Pet," had so raised his name by rapid victories over Wakelin, Jem Raines, and Dick Price, in one year (1827), that a battle for £100 was proposed and accepted. In this overmatched contest Curtis was defeated on December 30th, 1828, at Hurley Bottom, Berks, as detailed under our notice of Perkins in an after-page of this Appendix.

From the period of his first and only defeat Curtis did not enter the Prize Ring again as a principal. As a second he was constantly called upon to exercise his talents, as our pages will show. On these occasions he displayed incomparable tact and judgment, often winning fights " out of the fire," where all hope of success had been abandoned. He was second to Owen Swift in the unfortunate battle between that accomplished master of the art and Brighton Bill, as is fully set forth in the memoir of YOUNG DUTCH SAM. For this he was tried at the Hertford Assizes on July 14th, 1838, and was sentenced to three months' imprisonment. In the later period of his life he was a martyr to the rheumatic gout, and was frequently laid up for weeks together. The life of the Pet shows no exception to that of other public favourites, theatrical or otherwise—chequered by vicissitudes, at one time in " full feather and fine song," and at another penniless—a state of things to be ascribed to his propensity to " a hand at crib," and other gambling practices. For a short period he was a publican, keeping the " Star," in Blackman Street, Borough; but he had not then " sown his wild oats," and the eccentricity of his disposition soon caused him to " retire from the business," or more correctly the business retired from him. Notwithstanding his temporary acquaintance with the interior of Hertford Gaol, he continued to be sought as a " trump card " at all fights, and those who succeeded in securing his services had never any reason to regret their confidence. A contemporary, the late Vincent George Dowling, Esq., thus bore testimony to his worth in an editorial obituary notice in *Bell's Life*, and the writer, from personal knowledge, can well endorse that testimony: "Long as we have known Curtis, we never heard of his having deceived a friend, and he was one of the few of his class upon whom reliance in matters of opinion could be implicitly placed. He was always grateful for obligations conferred, and in the hour of need had never-failing sources of relief, when his pride would permit him to confess his necessities. His last and fatal illness is attributable to having burst a blood-vessel, from which he never thoroughly rallied, and it has been our lot to hear him speak in terms of deep gratitude for the kindnesses he experienced whilst an inmate of Guy's Hospital, as well from his medical attendants as from those numerous old acquaintances who sympathised in his sufferings, among whom we may rank his early pupil and *protégé*, Owen Swift, who was enabled to raise and contribute to his wants within the last six weeks upwards of eighteen pounds, while we know from other sources that sum was doubled during the same period. This is the best refutation of a tissue of gross falsehoods foisted upon the editor of the *Morning Herald*, unfortunately but too ready to adopt any statement, however absurd, which he deems calculated to throw discredit on the manly art of boxing or its professors. Young Dutch Sam, who was also introduced to the Ring by the deceased, contributed his mite, and we can say, from the best authority, that the expiring 'King Richard,' while he died in peace with all mankind, was surrounded with every comfort his situation required, and in homely terms testified his perfect satisfaction with all that had been done for him. 'Tis true he left no 'stock purse' behind, but that circumstance did not restrain those who knew and respected him in life from taking the necessary steps to secure a becoming attention to the last sad ceremonies of the grave."

To this spontaneous testimony of the " Nestor of the Ring," we may add that Curtis breathed his last at his own house in Dover Street, Southwark, on Saturday, September 16th, 1843. We have been more precise on this point because an eminent sporting writer, misled by the paper once known as "My Grandmother," has left it on record, "And the once caressed Pet of the Fancy breathed his last unfriended and unattended, save by the hireling servitors of a public hospital." "King Dick," as his companions were wont to call him, was sensible to the last, and perfectly conscious of the approaching close of his career.

His memory and his widow he bequeathed to his friends, feelingly deploring the reduced state of his exchequer, and hoping that his old " pals " would liberally come forward to contribute something towards alleviating the sorrows and distresses of his widow, who had been to him a careful and kindly nurse throughout a long and painful illness. For some days previous to the final flicker of the vital spark, Dick had been occasionally wandering, and the scenes of his former pursuits seemed to pass before his mental vision. He talked of battles won and lost, of the merits of his compeers, and of the qualifications requisite for his profession. When visited by Owen Swift, and others his "companions in arms," he was cheerful, although he occasionally mistook one for another, and on reference to coming events gave his opinion pretty freely about those modern pretenders who stickled for half a stone. Turning to a friend, he observed, " My last round is come ! " and sinking into a state of insensibility, shortly afterwards expired.

The remains of the departed pugilist were carried to their " narrow home " in St. George's Churchyard, Southwark, on the Thursday next after his decease, in a manner suitable to the respect felt by his family and friends. Among the mourners who followed were his brother, a well-known veterinary surgeon, the Champion of England, Peter Crawley, Jem Burn, Owen Swift, Alec Reid, Young Reed, Ned Turner, Johnny Hannan, Johnny Walker, Reidie, Deaf Burke, *cum multis aliis*. His friend Young Dutch Sam was absent from illness (he died in six weeks afterwards), and such was the sympathy and public curiosity on the occasion that quite ten thousand persons lined the route of the funeral procession. While upon this subject, we may add that the proceeds of a sparring benefit at Jem Burn's, £25, were handed over to the widow by the editor of *Bell's Life in London*, with more than £50 of subscriptions from other sources, with which she was placed in a humble but profitable business in Fetter Lane, and where the factory was known as that of " Curtis's Premier Blacking." We therefore consider the rhetorical flourish of "Nimrod" as completely " polished off " as " King Richard " during his reign himself polished off those who disputed his " fistic " supremacy.

MONODY ON THE DEATH OF DICK CURTIS.

FAREWELL ! a long farewell ! renowned King Dick !
Well may we mourn that thou hast cut thy stick ;
Victorious still in many a sharp attack,
Stern Champion, Death, hath laid thee on thy back ;

Exhausted all thy bottom and thy pluck,
Thine arm lies powerless, and thy colours struck;
Rigid thine elasticity of limb,
Deaf are thy listeners, and thine ogles dim ;
Pale are those lips from which rich humour rush'd ;
Spun are thy spicy yarns, thy tongue is hush'd ;
Stripped are the laurels bright that girt thy brow
And dust to dust is all that waits thee now.

Yet long the Fancy's tears thy grave shall wet,
Star of the Light Weights, all-accomplished Pet !
For thy bold spirit soared on eagle's wing,
And shed a halo round the fighting Ring—
Acknowledged there the bravest and the best,
For craven fear ne'er harboured in thy breast ;
Conquest, proud conquest, was thine only aim,
Unrivall'd still in gallantry and game.
As lightning quick to dart upon thy foe,
And in the dust to lay his glories low,
The palm of victory forcing him to yield,
And sing "Peccavi" on the battle-field;
Adieu, thou pride and wonder of the age,
The brightest star on Fistiana's page,
Where records of your manly deeds are stor'd,
The pinks you've pepper'd, and the trumps you've floored !
Why should we mourn of Perkins the sad tale,
O'er which sad memory fain would draw a veil,
And while unfading thy brave deeds shall bloom,
Consign thine errors with thee to the tomb !

Well may we weep for these degenerate days,
As a sad trophy to thy fame we raise,
And mourn, since boxing hath become a trade,
Its honour tarnished and its flowers decay'd !
No hardy Cribb now throws the gauntlet down,
Nor brave Tom Spring, of unalloyed renown ;
No brawny Belcher now for victory strives,
Nor tough Game Chicken flourishes his fives ;
No Molyneux now rears his sable nob,
Nor rough-and-ready stout Whiteheaded Bob.
Well may we grieve, as we thy fate deplore,
The golden days of milling are no more,
Exclaiming, as fresh candidates appear,
"Oh, what a woeful falling-off is here !"

But Curtis prov'd a trump, and no mistake, ⎫
To every move upon the board awake,   ⎬
And staunch as e'er tied colours to a stake ! ⎭
When a mere boy, by two good men assail'd,
Beneath his prowess Brown and Watson quail'd ;
And after combat resolute and tough,
Lenney and Cooper, sorrowing, cried, "Enough !"
Thrice Peter Warren tried to do the trick,
But found his master in triumphant Dick ;
In a turn-up, from momentary heat,
Ned Savage was made savage by defeat ;
And bouncing Barney Aaron, Hebrew stout,
Look'd all abroad when Richard sarv'd him out ;
Tisdale our Monarch ventur'd to attack,
But all the shine was taken out of Jack ;
And lastly Dick, urg'd on by insult's goad,
Whack'd a coalheaver in the Surrey Road.

But his last fight is fought, and clos'd his reign,
And time is call'd to poor King Dick in vain ;
For Death, that ruthless monarch, gaunt and grim, ⎫
Hath cruelly hit out and finished him,   ⎬
Sent him to earth, and stiffened every limb.   ⎭

Flower of the Fancy, yet one more adieu !
Where shall we look to find a " Pet " like you ?
Sound be thy sleep, receive my last good night,
And may the turf upon thy breast be light,
For though in manhood's prime by fate unshipp'd,
Thou wert a boy as brave as ever stripp'd ;
Time shall fly forward, years shall wax and wane,
Ere "we shall look upon thy like again."

W.

BARNEY AARON ("THE STAR OF THE EAST").
1819—1834. DIED 1850

THE subject of this biography first opened his eyes on the bustling world in the populous Goshen of Duke's Place, Aldgate, on the 21st of November, 1800.

At an early age, as we are told by "Boxiana," Master Barney distinguished himself by taking his own part, and milling with the utmost impartiality either Jew or Christian boy who might forget the law of *meum* and *tuum* in the matter of marbles, tops, kites, balls, or such other personal property as to boyhood appertaineth.

In the year 1819 one Bill Connelly (whose nationality we may suspect to be Hibernian), having assumed the title of the Rosemary Lane Champion, we presume in virtue of his talent, promised the young Israelite a thrashing. To the execution of this promise the juvenile Maccabeus put in a demurrer, and to sustain it hurled defiance in the teeth of Paddy. They met, and after sixteen rounds occupying thirty-three minutes the Philistine was routed, and the children of Israel sang " See the Conquering Hero Comes " in honour of the youthful Jewish warrior.

Aaron next laid hands very heavily on one of "the tribesh," Manny Lyons, a heavier man by two stone, and superior in length. It was a hard battle for an hour and a quarter, when Barney, worn out by his own exertions rather than the hitting of his adversary, lost the battle from exhaustion, but not his character as a pugilist of high pretensions.

In a second battle with Lyons, Barney in half-an-hour got his opponent " down to his own weight," beat him in fifty minutes, and refreshed his laurels, scarcely tarnished by his first defeat.

Ely Bendon, a good fighter and a game man, challenged Barney, and they

BARNEY AARON ("The Star of the East").

To face page 504.

met on Bow Common.   As the P.C. ropes and stakes were not there the fight is not reported.   Barney defeated Bendon in three-quarters of an hour.

Samuel Belasco, a brother of Aby and of Israel Belasco, and therefore of the family of " the fighting Belascos," tried the quality of young Barney at the cost of defeat, as did Angel Hyams, a nephew of the celebrated Dan Mendoza.   But the latter affair being interrupted by a magistrate at the seventh round was never brought to a conclusion.

Barney was now " somebody," and anxious to earn a name, fame, and " monish," so he went down to see the fights between Arthur Matthewson, of Birmingham, and Israel Belasco, and of Phil Sampson and Birmingham Hall, which took place on Moulsey Hurst on Wednesday, March 19th, 1823.

A purse was announced for a third battle, when Tom Collins (a 10st. 7lbs. pugilist, who afterwards fought Harry Jones) offered himself. There was a pause, when young Barney modestly stepped into the ropes as a candidate.   The fighting was all in favour of Barney, who took astonishing liberties with the nob of Collins, so much so as to turn the odds from six to four against him to five to four in his favour.   After half-an-hour's sharp work Barney's left hand was injured, and he was reluctantly compelled to discontinue the fight.

The exhibition however gained him immediate friends, and he was at once matched against Ned Stockman for £25 a side.   The battle was decided on the 6th of May, 1823, at Blindlow Heath, Sussex, after Peter Crawley had conquered Dick Acton.   Stockman had for his seconds Eales and Dick Curtis ; Barney was attended by Jem Ward and Rogers.   The battle was gallantly contested for forty minutes and as many rounds, when Stockman gave in severely punished.   He could not resist the resolute and heavy hitting of the Jew, and declared he had never met so good a man of his weight.   This victory at once stamped Barney as a boxer of talent.

He was now backed against Lenney, who had seen some service in the P.R., and was known as as a good and game trial horse, for £50.   Their difference of opinion was decided on the 5th of August, 1823, on Harpenden Common, near St. Albans.   Barney threw his castor into the ring under the care of Josh Hudson and Peter Crawley, for he had already gained the favour of the big 'uns.   Lenney was advised by the learned and eloquent Harry Holt, while Davy Hudson followed on the same side.

THE FIGHT.

Round 1.—The attitude of Lenney was interesting ; and he displayed himself to better advantage than usual.   The Jew was in a great hurry to feel for his opponent's nob ; but Lenney said, "Wait a bit!" However, they soon went to work; Lenney had the worst of the milling, and also went down. (Six to four on Barney.)

2.—Lenney put in two such severe blows on the Jew's head that for an instant he was quite abroad, and turned round; but he recovered himself before the end of the round, and Lenney again went down.

3.—It was a horse to a hen, in this early stage of the fight. Lenney received six distinct nobbers on the middle of his head, and went down helpless.

4.—Lenney succeeded in drawing the Jew after him, by which means he was enabled to give Aaron two or three sharp facers. Lenney at the conclusion of the round was on the turf. Ten to one.

5.—The Jew slipped, and went down from a slight blow.

6.—Lenney put in a couple of facers; but nothing could stop the Jew's eagerness to be milling. ("Stand still," said Josh; "do not give your opponent an opportunity by drawing you off your ground.") Both down.

7.—The nob of Lenney was a complete drum for his adversary to beat. Three successive facers were got in, and Lenney floored.

8.—Nothing could be more decisive; Lenney received three facers, and was hit down.

9.—"Take him away; he has no chance." The Jew boy had it all his own way. Lenney, it is true, did not want for courage, and now and then put in some good blows; but the stamina and courage of the Jew were too good for him. The jobbing of Aaron spoiled Lenney till he went down. Any odds.

10.—It was a pity to see Lenney continue the battle. He was punished all over the ring, and ultimately measured his length on the turf. ("Take him away; it is too bad to let him fight any longer.")

11, and last.—It was ditto and ditto, repeated till poor Lenney was again on the grass. His backer, we are informed, who betted fifty pounds that he would not be defeated in half-an-hour, urged him to continue the battle for a few more rounds, as the chance might turn in his favour; but the answer of Lenney was, "I will not fight longer for any man." It was over in fifteen minutes.

Lenney was not exactly satisfied in his own mind as to his defeat, therefore another match was made, for £20 a side. This was decided on Moulsey Hurst, on Tuesday, November 11th, 1823, after Josh Hudson had defeated Jem Ward. Aaron, followed by Aby Belasco and Bill Gibbons, threw his hat into the ring; but a quarter of an hour elapsed before Lenney appeared, attended by Harry Holt and Peter Crawley as his seconds. Aaron five and six to four the favourite.

THE FIGHT.

Round 1.—Both the "little ones" appeared to have too much pride in their composition to throw away any time in stopping, so went to work like blacksmiths, till Lenney found himself hanging on the ropes, where he was milled down. Seven to four on Aaron.

2.—Full of pluck, and both pelting away sans cérémonie. At this instant, the outer ring was broken, and the confusion was so great that the battle was stopped until order was restored. The Jew napped a heavy hit on the head, but in return Lenney was punished down.

3-8.—Lenney was not deficient in pluck or science, but was evidently overmatched. He was severely milled in all these rounds. ("Foul, foul!" frequently occurred, during the time Lenney was balancing on the ropes, but the latter kept fighting all the while he was in such situations.)

9-11.—These were all fighting rounds, but Lenney had so much the worst of it that ten pounds to one were offered on the Jew.

12-18.—Aaron was so full of gaiety that he bored his man down with the utmost ease. Here some words occurred between Belasco and Lenney. The latter kicked Belasco violently on his leg, and also gave him a blow on his mouth, and said, loud enough to be heard by the spectators, "I will not fight any more." Belasco, with much propriety and forbearance, did not meddle with Lenney, which otherwise might have produced a wrangle. Aaron left the ring instantly, thinking he had won the battle. A great disturbance arose, and the umpire considered the battle at an end; but in consequence of Lenney's asserting "that what he had said was from passion, declaring that he would not fight any more if Belasco remained in the ring, who acted foul towards him," the umpire consented the battle should go on again. Aaron observed he did not wish to take advantage of a slip of the tongue made by his opponent, and would most readily fight it out. Order being restored, the boxers recommenced.

19.—It was all up with Lenney; after being milled all over the ring, and his face covered with claret, he was ultimately floored. Any odds.

20.—Aaron punished his adversary in all directions; and in closing at the ropes Barney fibbed Lenney till he went down quite exhausted. ("Take him away; he has no chance.")

21, and last.—Lenney had scarcely put up his hands at the scratch when Barney floored him like a shot. This was a finisher; and Lenney found it was of no use to continue the contest any longer. Making deductions for the loss of time, the battle occupied about twenty minutes.

REMARKS.—The remarks we have to make on this fight are short, but we are compelled to be severe. Great praise is due to the Jew for not throwing his "own people" over, and likewise in firmly refusing to sell those who had laid money upon him. Thirty pounds, he asserted, were offered him at Hampton to lose the battle, on the morning of fighting, and his backers were well assured of the fact.

Frank Redmond, a brave little man (see note on Redmond, Life of EVANS, *ante*, page 392) under the patronage of Dick Curtis, was backed against Barney Aaron for £25 a side. The battle was decided on Moulsey Hurst, on Tuesday, December 30th, 1823.

The amateurs were not so numerous as usual (in consequence of the fight between Abraham Belasco and Neale being postponed till the 7th of January); however, those out-and-outers who never miss anything in the shape of a fight were present. At two o'clock Barney, attended by "one of his own peoplesh" and Maurice Delay, threw his hat into the ring; about five minutes afterwards Redmond, genteelly dressed, arm-in-arm with Curtis and Harry Holt, threw his hat out of the ring. The president of the Daffy Club was the stakeholder; and in order to make "all right," fresh articles were drawn up at Lawrence's, the "Red Lion," at Hampton, to obviate the difficulty of fighting in the same ring with Belasco and Neale, as expressed in the original agreement.

THE FIGHT.

Round 1.—Redmond, a tight, well-made man, weighing ten stone, when stripped and in attitude, looked as if he could "do something," more especially under the guidance of the Pet of the Fancy and the eloquent and elegant *aide-de-camp* of the Commissary-General, by which he had the advantage of the combined knowledge of the West and East Ends. He was the favourite, five to four. Mister Barney came out of the scale nine stone twelve pounds, as lively as an eel and as spirited as a young colt; with a face full of confidence, in rare condition, with sparkling ogles (each "worth a Jew's eye"), and with a firm step, he was eager to commence the attack. Redmond faced him smilingly, fresh as a daisy and gay as a lark. Barney surveyed his opponent from head to foot with coolness, and Redmond likewise took measure of Aaron. At length Mister Barney, by way of the compliments of the season, a kind of late Christmas-box, sent his right fist very near Redmond's head, but Master Frank declined to accept it, and got away. After a short pause, Barney rushed in, caught hold of Redmond, and began the weaving system with some success. Frank endeavoured to fib too, and in the struggle and hammering both went down, Barney undermost. ("Go it, Redmond, never leave him!")

2-6.—These rounds were full of fibbing, and no lies. Barney the hero in all of them. In the latter round the claret appeared on Redmond's nose. (Six to four on the Jew.)

7-10.—Redmond proved himself nothing else but a good little man; but he had little chance as yet to win; that is to say, he had not changed the battle in his favour, and the odds had left him. In the last round Barney planted two good nobbing hits, right and left.

11.—Redmond had a little turn here, and gave Mister Barney two out-and-outers upon his Mosaic index. These made his eloquent second exclaim, in Chesterfieldian style: "Elegant! beautiful! and so handsomely done, too. These were immense hits, 'pon honour. Be so good as to repeat them, Mr. Redmond. About four more such elegant blows will win you the battle. That circumstance accomplished, I will take you under my wing, among the heavy ones, on Sunday next, in Hyde Park." "Yes," said Barney, "so you shall; but I must dress him well before you take him out, Harry.") The Jew tried the fibbing system, but ultimately was undermost when down.

12.—This was a sharp round altogether; and the finish of it was, Barney down. ("Reddy, my boy," said the Pet, "he can't hurt you now; his hands are gone; and if you are only half as game as your dog, you'll win it in a canter. Why, it's Bermondsey tan-pits to a leather apron in your favour!")

13-17.—Barney had decidedly the best of all these rounds. He fibbed his opponent with the nimbleness of a drummer practising the roll-call. The Jew behaved very manly in the last round; he let Redmond down, holding up both his hands, when he might have dealt out punishment. ("Bravo, Barney!" from Christians and Jews; and lots of applause.)

18.—The fight was now drawing to the finish, from the execution done by the Jew. He put in four desperate jobbers on Redmond's nob, and sent him down. (Seven to four and two to one.)

19-21.—Redmond's nose was clareted, and his face and right eye exhibited sharp punishment. Barney had it all his own way, driving his man over the ring till down.

22-24.—Redmond fought like a man, but was getting groggy. Both down. ("Vat a peautiful hitter!" said a Sheeny; "it's as shafe as the Bank. I shall vin my monish to-day. Look, Israel, look how he nicks him, as the man shaid about the jackdaw. Moses, Levy, Benjamin, Ikey, Sholomons, and David, only look at him—so help me, it's Dutch Sam come to life again!")

25.—It was three to one against Redmond. Poor Frank had no chance, and was sent down. ("Take him away.")

26.—Redmond would not listen to surrender, and endeavoured to fight, till he went down.

27.—Barney did as he liked, till Redmond measured his length on the ground. ("Take him away!" was now vociferated from all parts of the ring.)

28.—Redmond down in no time. (Twenty to one. It was now Fonthill Abbey to a cowshed.)

29, and last.—The game of Redmond was so good that he came staggering to the scratch to have another shy, but was floored in a twinkling. It was over in thirty-two minutes.

REMARKS.—Barney did not win without napping it sharply. In the twenty-second round, he exhibited the finishing traits of Randall. Barney, when tired of administering punishment to Redmond with his left hand, changed his adversary in his arms, and fibbed him down with his right. We hope Barney will listen to advice which has been often given to other pugilists who laughed at all cautions in prosperity, but who have had to lament their neglect in the day of trouble. Barney, remember to keep good company, take care of your health, but above all things never show yourself a fighting man, except in the P.R. Let not Mr. Lushington scrape acquaintance with you. Bear the above things in your mind, and if you do not make your fortune by following them you are sure to be respected, and never want a friend.

Mister Barney returned to town in first-rate style, and showed with all the honours of conquest at Howard's Coffee House, St. James's Place, Houndsditch. It was crowded to excess, and many West End swells were present. On the Thursday after the fight Frank Redmond, in true English style, offered his hand to Barney as the best man at Howard's, and they drank to each other's health, when Barney put his hand into his pocket and presented his brave opponent with a sovereign for "expenses."

Peter Warren having expressed his anxiety to try his luck with Aaron, a match was made between them for £50 a side. This trial of skill was decided on Tuesday, April 6th, 1824, at Colnbrook, seventeen miles from London.

The road was rather thin of company; but the Sheenies, who were numerous and full of fun, gave a life to the scene which otherwise it

would not have possessed. Barney and his backers got over the ground in
gay style, under the patronage of the president of the Daffy Club. An
open barouche conveyed the " little Dutch Sam" to the scene of action.
When time was called Peter Warren, attended by his backers, showed, and
followed by Maurice Delay and Jem Ward as his seconds, in the most
polite way introduced his castor within the ropes. Barney in a minute
afterwards threw his beaver up, waited upon by Nathan and Aby Belasco.
The colours—yellow for Barney and green for Peter—were tied to the
stakes. " Let us have a quiet fight," said Warren to the seconds of Barney.
"Certainly," was the reply. " I shall be as good friends as ever with you,
Peter, after the fight is over," remarked Aaron.

It would be waste of space to report *in extenso* this and some other battles
of the clever light-weight, whose claim to a page in the history of pugilism is nevertheless undeniable. The battle was simply a struggle of game,
endurance, strength, and obstinacy against skill, straight—and therefore
swift—hitting, and a ready recourse to those changes of tactics on the spur
of the moment which mark the skilful boxer, and almost reduce such contests to a question of time. On this occasion twenty-three minutes and twenty-
nine rounds sufficed to render poor Peter Warren deaf to the call of " time."

Barney was driven off the ground in style, and arrived at an early hour in
London. Warren was brought back to the " Magpies," at Colnbrook, and
put to bed for a few hours. Peter exhibited much punishment about the
head. A naval officer, who had lost an arm in the defence of his country,
stepped forward, and in the most generous manner ordered a post-chaise at
his own expense from Cranford Bridge, in which he had Peter conveyed to
his residence in Whitechapel. The gallant tar also visited Warren the
next morning and administered a golden solatium to his sores.

A " chant of victory," indited by " A Singer of Israel," deserves to be
rescued from oblivion :—

BARNEY AARON.

TUNE.—*Rose of Sharon, Rose of Sharon.*

HOUNDSDITCH and the Lanes rejoice,
 Where the mart for clothes is ;
Hebrew science lifts its voice,
 Aaron proves a Moses.

Barney Aaron ! Barney Aaron !
 Through the Sin-a-gog and streets,
Rabbis, with their oily air on,
 Shout his name and praise his feats—
  Milling—fibbing—
  Muzzling—cribbing—

Blood-letting like a doctor's lance—
  Setting teeth chattering,
  Christianity shattering,
And, Joshua-like, making the moon-eyes dance.

Cutler Street is like a fair ;
 Barney Aaron ! Barney Aaron !
All the little Jews declare,
 Rows his keel like Charon.
Old Mendoza—Young Mendoza—
 Both are known and famed in fight ;
But Aaron is a priest-like poser,
 A sacrificing Israelite.
  Science—defiance—
  Attitude—latitude—
In the *sanctum sanctorum* he marks the "points ;"
  In sackcloth and ashes,
  The shewbread he slashes,
And to Pentecost sends their uncircumcised joints.

Shibboleth among the tribes
 Is Barney Aaron ! Barney Aaron !
Some to bet have taken bribes,
 And even'd odds to share on :
Barney fights *against* "the Cross,"
 Like ancient unbelievers ;
"Flats " are "naturals" by the loss ;
 "Sharps " are gainers and receivers :
  And sweet Miss Sharon !
  And nishe Miss Aaron !
Eat veal so white in the fistic cause,
  And with Seager's Daffy
  Their tongues are chaffy,
For Aceldama's victory brings monish and applause.

Barney, by his conquests, had made way both in the opinions of the Christians and the Jews, and ranked high in the lists of pugilistic fame, as one of the best "light-weights." Aaron was matched for £100 a side against Arthur Matthewson, from Birmingham, a boxer of well-earned provincial celebrity, and no little London fame, from his victory over Israel Belasco. Matthewson had never been defeated.* The tourney came off on Monday, June 21st, 1824 ; Aaron being seconded by a well-known Israelitish sporting man, Mr. Nathan, and Aby Belasco, while Matthewson was seconded by the two Harrys, Holt and Harmer, the host of the "Plough," in Smithfield. Although the battle was waged with varying success until the fifty-sixth round, and ten to one was several times offered on Aaron, in the fifty-seventh and last round a desperate straight hit in the throat floored poor Barney like a shot, and he was picked up deaf to the call of "time," at the end of one hour and ten minutes from the first

---

* Arthur Matthewson, for many years known in fistic circles as a sporting publican, was one of the best little men of his day. His first reported battle was with David Barnes, whom he defeated in fifty-one rounds, for fifty guineas a side, at Basset's Pole, near Birmingham, July 15th, 1822. He beat Israel Belasco in forty-four minutes at Moulsey Hurst, March 19th, 1823, and Barney Aaron as above. Matthewson died in his native town, July 13th, 1840, generally respected.

round. In a few minutes Aaron recovered, and could hardly be persuaded he had lost the fight. But, "who can control the uncertain chance of war?" beaten he was, but not disgraced. On his arrival in town he addressed a letter to the editor of *Life in London*, in which, after a quantity of Eganian balderdash, he challenged Arthur Matthewson to meet him "for two hundred sovereigns, to fight on a stage, as I am determined," he said, "never to subject myself to a repetition of such treatment" (?), &c., &c. A business-sort of P.S. adds, "I shall be happy to meet the friends of Richard Curtis at my benefit on the 6th of July, to make an agreement to fight."

Nothing came of this at that time, as has been seen already in the Life of CURTIS. However, the gallant Dick Hares determined to try the mettle of Barney Aaron; £50 a side was posted. On Tuesday, March 21st, 1826, No Man's Land, near St. Albans, was the chosen battleground, whereon the Israelites mustered strongly in favour of the Star of the East. Hares too was not neglected by his patrons. Hares in all his battles had proved himself a brave man, but the youth of Barney made him the favourite at six and seven to four.

It was nearly two o'clock before the men entered the ropes, in consequence of a mistaken "tip" that the battle would take place on Colney Heath, where several persons had assembled to witness the contest. Barney first threw his hat into the ring, followed by the John Bull Fighter and his friend and patron, Mr. Nathan. Hares was seconded by Peter Crawley and Paddington Jones.

The fight was a one-sided affair. Youth, science, activity, were on the side of the Jew, and after forty-three rounds of lively fighting, in which poor Hares was receiver-general, a claim of a "foul blow" was raised on the part of Hares, who was taken from the ring, but the claim disallowed, and the referee accordingly awarded the stakes to Aaron.

A *jeu d'esprit* which appeared in the *Morning Chronicle* bears marks of being the production of a scholar. It is in the form of "An Epistle from Mynheer Van Haagen in London to Mynheer Van Kloppen in Amsterdam," and shall here find a place :—

"London, March 22nd, 1826.

"DEAR COUSIN,—Agreeably to my promise to write to you whenever I met with anything worth recording, I proceed to give you a description of an English fight, or, as it is here termed, a 'prize battle,' I witnessed on Tuesday last ; and in order that you may the better understand it, I present you with a few remarks on the system of pugilism as practised here, for which I am indebted to our mutual friend Mr. Boxer. The English are naturally a brave and courageous people, but less sanguinary in its fullest extent than their Continental neighbours ; hence nothing is more common than fights between boys of from ten to twelve years of age, and similar exhibitions in the public streets by men of the lower orders. The boy or the man who, from the want of sufficient physical strength, or lacking the appetite for a good beating, is obliged to succumb, soon gets tired of the sport; but he who, possessing a strong, muscular frame, and the courage of a bulldog, frequently beats his man, becomes vain of his powers, and probably for the want of better or more honourable employment, determines to exhibit himself at a sparring-match. Here then we have him in the university pugilistic; and as in a National school boys are taught to mark in sand before they write with a pen, so here the neophytes thump each other with gloves well stuffed before they exercise with their naked fists. It is here where the Fancy (i.e., those who have a gusto for smashed faces and broken ribs) judge of their qualifications, and if found worthy some of the Fancy make a match—that is, subscribe a sum of money for the pugilists to contend for. This, Mr. Boxer assures me, is the origin of most of the pugilistic heroes. Having thus prepared you, I shall briefly state the manner of the last fight. The combatants were a Christian and a Jew—the Jew about twenty-six years of age, and the Christian some ten years older. I shall not here trouble you with the art of betting on fights, but bring you at once to the ring, which is a square space kept clear by stakes and ropes for the combatants to engage in. The men appear stripped to their waists, attended each by seconds or assistants, whose business is to encourage the men, and pick them up when they fall; for here, when a man falls in fighting, his adversary immediately leaves him till he rises and puts himself in an attitude of defence, the time allowed for which is half a minute, at the expiration of which, if the man be not ready, he loses the fight. The Jew from the commencement had the decided advantage; it was also evident he felt confident of success; he hit his man with amazing force, and absolutely spoilt (for the time) every feature of his countenance, while he himself escaped with scarce a mark. My greatest surprise is how it was possible for a man to receive so much beating and still be inclined to renew the combat. Such was, however, the case; and after fighting three-quarters of an hour, a cry was raised of 'foul,' meaning that the Jew had struck his man when he was on the ground. The ring was immediately broken into; the combatants moved from the arena, each party claiming the victory; an appeal was, however, made to the judges, who decided the Jew was entitled to the stakes—viz., fifty pounds. Having thus given you a narrative of the fight, I shall, at my earliest leisure, send you my reflections thereon, and whether, in a moral point of view as well as national, these contests ought to be tolerated or suppressed.

> "Believe me to be, dear Cousin,
>   "Sincerely yours,
>   "JAN VAN HAAGEN."

A match, at length arranged for £100 a side, was made between Barney Aaron and Dick Curtis. This scientific battle was decided upon a stage, at Andover, on Tuesday, February 27th, 1827. Curtis was declared the winner in fifty minutes, Barney, by a blow in his throat, being again hit out of "time," for the details of which we refer our readers to the Memoir of CURTIS, ante, p. 492.

The friends of Barney after this defeat rallied round him, and his benefit, at the Coburg Theatre, on Saturday, March 18th, 1827, was a bumper. The set-to between Curtis and Barney was pronounced one of the finest things ever witnessed in the art of self-defence.

Frank Redmond was not satisfied as to his former defeat, and solicited another trial with Barney Aaron. This battle, for £50 a side, was to have been decided on Tuesday, August 21st, 1827. It however turned out no fight. Chertsey, twenty miles from London, was named as the rallying-point. At Moulsey Hurst the "beaks" were in sight, and prudence suggested it would be unwise to form a ring. The ring was made in a field near Ford-water Bridge, about a mile from Chertsey. About half-past twelve o'clock a violent storm of thunder and lightning, accompanied by sheets of water, compelled the people round the ring to seek shelter from the effects of the "pitiless pelting shower." The storm having abated, and the time of peeling arrived, Barney, followed by Mr. Nathan and Josh Hudson as his seconds, threw his hat into the ring. After waiting about ten minutes, and Mr. Redmond having been called for several times, Barney claimed the blunt, and retired from the ropes. Dick Curtis now came galloping up out of breath, and informed the disappointed assemblage that Redmond had been stopped by an officer with a warrant. The lads who had got over twenty miles of ground, and many of them received a precious wetting into the bargain, felt themselves not a little vexed at such treatment, but there was no help for it. The lads however would not be disappointed.

Redmond's friends refused to forfeit, on the plea that an officer, by the order of a magistrate, had prevented Redmond meeting Barney Aaron in the ring, which in the absence of evidence of collusion was a valid objection to forfeiture.

The stakes however were given up to Barney Aaron, which so displeased Redmond that he threw up his hat and offered Barney to fight upon the spot.

To put the question of mastery to rest, a third match for £50 a side was made. This battle was decided on Tuesday, October 23rd, 1827, at No Man's Land. Redmond entered the ring amidst loud applause. Barney was the favourite, at five to four; but Redmond was considered altogether a better man than at the period mentioned, and several of his friends not only took him for choice, but laid the odds upon him. Barney was attended by Josh Hudson and Nathan, and Redmond by Dick Curtis and Ned Neale.

THE FIGHT.

Round 1.—Both combatants appeared in excellent condition, and determined not to give half a chance away. The attitudes of the men were interesting—the *tout ensemble* of Redmond capital, and his friends strongly anticipated victory. Redmond tried to draw the Jew to work, but the Star of the East was not to be had. Barney at length perceived an opening, and hit out, but Redmond stopped him cleverly. ("Bravo!") The Jew went to work in right earnest, and planted some nobbers in excellent style. Redmond with the most determined courage fought his way into a rally; and give and take was the criterion, until they both went down, Barney undermost.

2.—Barney's frontispiece showed punishment. ("First blood!" exclaimed Jack Randall.) The nob of Redmond looked flushed and peppered. Cautious, but both ready to administer mischief. Redmond with considerable science stopped the efforts of Barney, and also put in a tremendous nozzler. The Jew never flinched, but returned like a good one. Hit for hit for a short period. In struggling at the ropes, Barney endeavoured to fib his adversary. Both down.

3.—A long pause. Dangerous customers to each other, therefore a look-out necessary. ("You hold your arms too low," said Josh to Barney.) Each made offers in turn, and then retreated. Redmond stopped a rum one in capital style. Barney crept in, as it were, and put in a noser. Barney took the lead, and bored Redmond to the ropes, and tried to fib, until his adversary went down on his knees.

4.—A pause. Barney went to work, but received a precious stopper on his dial. ("That's the way to do it," said Neale.) A short rally against the ropes, until both down.

5.—Redmond's face was red, and he was rather on the piping system. Barney went in on the bustle; but Redmond jobbed and jobbed again with great success. ("Frank will win!" was the cry.) Barney, on his mettle, did not seem "to like it at the price," and went resolutely in to his work; smashing on both sides, until the combatants were down.

6.—Redmond had now a little the best of it; at all events Jack was as good as his master. Redmond with his left hand planted a bodier. Barney careful; and Redmond put down his hands. ("To set the thing a-going," said Joah, "I'll bet £20 to £10.") The fight had now become extremely interesting—the attitudes of the men pretty, and both confident of success. A long pause, counter-hits. Barney caught hold of Redmond and fibbed him down. Redmond, with great gaiety, jumped up again as if nothing was the matter, receiving great applause from Curtis and his friends.

7.—Two minutes nearly elapsed, and no blow, so great was the caution on both sides. Redmond's left hand touched the body of Barney, but the latter returned it with interest on the left peeper of Redmond. Frank planted two heavy blows right and left on Barney's face (immense applause by the boys from Bermondsey), and got away in style. Barney did not like this treatment, and went in to do mischief, but again napped it on the dial. In closing Barney was undermost. This round was decidedly in favour of Redmond, and six to four was betted on his winning.

8.—Frank was a little out of wind by his exertions in the last round. Barney made an excellent stop. Redmond, not to be denied, was as active as a dancing-master, hopping all over the ring, and putting his antagonist a little on the fret, until he planted a severe facer. The Jew rather severely felt for Redmond's listener in return. Barney kept close to his work, and paid Redmond on his canister as he was going down. (The Sheenies began now to open their chaffing-boxes, and sing out, "Vat a peautiful hitter! Barney's ash good ash gold!")

9.—This was a short round, but peppery, both giving and receiving punishment. In struggling both were down.

10.—Frank was the hero of the round. He jobbed his opponent, and got away like a first-rate miller. ("The Jew's napping it in style," said the friends of Curtis.) Both went down.

11.—The Jew's head showed the handiwork of Redmond, but in this round the Star of the East took the lead. Some sharp counter-hitting; Redmond napped it in his ear, and the round was finished by Franky finding himself on the grass.

12.—Good fighting on both sides. Redmond went down to avoid punishment.

13.—The Sheenies were now all alive, and began to sport their blunt. Barney took great liberties with the head of his opponent, and followed Redmond close to the ropes, the latter fighting at points like a clever little fellow, but nevertheless he had the worst of it, until he was thrown.

14.—Barney now showed himself to advantage, as Redmond was a little bit winded. The Jew planted his blows right and left, yet Frank was determined to be with him. At the finish of the round Redmond became weak, and went down.

15.—Cut away, hit for hit, give and take, as fast as any brave fellows could, on both sides. Barney at length got the turn, put in a teaser, and also hit Franky down.

16.—The Jew, gay as a lark, commenced offensive operations, and cut away. Redmond, equally gay, was not behindhand. Barney napped one on his canister, but he still kept to his work, until Redmond got down at the ropes.

17.—Frank endeavoured to get out of mischief, but the Star of the East would not be denied. Fighting like fun, until Redmond was sent on the grass.

18.—This was a fine fighting round; and if Barney showed pluck, the courage displayed by Redmond was equal to his adversary. Counter-hits. In closing Redmond broke away. Milling was soon afterwards resumed, and Frank was hit down.

19.—Barney kept the lead. He planted his blows successfully, and also bored Redmond to the ropes. Here Frank caught it severely, but the Jew did not get off without summat. Redmond down.

20.—Weakness on both sides; in fact, the pepper-box had been handed from one to the other without any mistake. Barney had been considerably punished, and Redmond had taken lots of milling. Barney appeared the stronger man of the two, and Redmond retreated before his opponent to the ropes. In a struggle both were down.

21-37.—Merry milling, with varying success. The hitting in favour of Aaron, the throws occasionally to Redmond, making the superiority doubtful. In the 31st round, and again in the 35th, Aaron fought Redmond down on to his knees. In the 36th Redmond sent down Aaron. In the 37th Redmond, exhausted by his exertions, went down weak.

38.—Aaron was deliberate and cautious, although Frank was evidently on the totter. Redmond was ultimately sent down.

39.—(Frank would not allow his seconds to give in for him. Mr. Nathan crossed the ring to Redmond, as the latter was sitting on Joah Hudson's knee, and advised Redmond to leave off—a most improper proceed-ing. Frank rose indignantly to his feet and pushed him aside.) Exchanges, and Red-mond down, amid great confusion.

40, 41.—Redmond game, but unable to stop his adversary or return with precision; was down.

42, and last.—Frank would not say " No!" There was a short bustle, and Redmond was pushed rather than hit down. Time, one hour and ten minutes.

REMARKS.—This was not only a game, but in several rounds a scientific mill; and in the opinion of most of the admirers of boxing present, Redmond had profited much by his lessons from Curtis. His style of

fighting was evidently improved, and for a long time the contest was considered doubt-ful; indeed, by several persons Redmond was chosen as the conqueror. Barney is a cool and determined boxer; and after Curtis we place him next on the list of light weights. Barney exhibited terrible marks of punishment about his head—much more than when he fought Curtis. Redmond re-ceived several heavy body blows, and was carried out of the ring; but Barney did not quit the ropes in a very lively state. Upon the whole, we never witnessed a more manly fight. Aaron's forbearance when his man was helpless, and Redmond's game, were alike conspicuous.

Aaron's next subsequent battles were with Marsh Bateman, for £40, whom he beat on Landsdowne Racecourse, July 4th, 1828, and with Harry Jones, by whom he was beaten, November 21st, 1828, at the " Old Barge House," Woolwich, in fifteen minutes, eighteen rounds, being much overmatched. He afterwards, May 26th, 1829, beat Jem Raines, at Navestock Green, Essex, in thirteen rounds, occupying twenty-eight minutes. His last battle was with Tom Smith, the East End Sailor Boy, by whom he was defeated, at Greenstreet Green, Kent, April 1st, 1834, in twenty rounds, twenty-six minutes—youth against age, Smith being twenty-seven, Aaron thirty-four.

From this period Aaron retired from the arena, but for many years was an attendant at the ringside. He followed his trade of an East End dealer in fish, and was a frequent purveyor of edibles to the voyagers down the river on the then frequent pugilistic excursions. Barney died in Whitechapel, in 1850, being up to his last days an authority in all fistic matters among " the peoplesh " of Houndsditch.

HARRY JONES ("THE SAILOR BOY").
1822—1834.

THE claim of Harry Jones to a niche in our gallery of pugilistic celebrities is in a great degree of a negative character, from the eminence of some of the men whom he contended with and did *not* beat, rather than the number of second-raters whose pretensions he disposed of. Ned Stock-man (three times), Young Dutch Sam, Barney Aaron, Frank Redmond, and Perkins (the last three of whom he beat), entitle him to a place; we shall not, however, occupy space by the reports of his minor battles.

Harry Jones was born on the 4th of April, 1804, in Meadow Street, Bristol, a city eminent in fistic annals for the boxers it has given birth to. At an early age Harry chose a sea life, and was apprenticed on board the "Staunton," East-Indiaman, Captain Harris, with whom he made three voyages. The traditions of his birthplace, and the fame and profit which had been achieved by the Belchers, Pearce, and other champions, were among the Sailor Boy's early memories, and he determined to try his fortune in the P.R. This was in his eighteenth year, and bidding adieu to the service of the Hon. E. I. C., he made his way to Moulsey Hurst, on the day when Oliver and Abbot settled their differences, November 6th, 1821. Jones had already shown his skill with the gloves at the Fives Court, and when a subscription purse had been made for a second fight, the Sailor Boy threw in his hat, and was opposed by Latham, also known as a sparrer in the schools. Belasco and Tom Jones picked up the Sailor Boy; Dolly Smith and Phil Sampson did the like for Latham. It was an interesting battle for twenty-six rounds, occupying thirty-three minutes, when Latham floored Jones by a hit in the short ribs. Jones tried three more rounds, but he was unable to recover his wind, and gave in.

Undeterred by this stumble on the threshold, the Sailor Boy went in for a purse against Ned Stockman, then called "Bill Eales's Chicken." The fight was at Rutledge Common, Edgware Road, on 29th January, 1822. It was a remarkable battle on the part of Stockman, who, in thirty-eight rounds and forty minutes, compelled the Sailor Boy to haul down his colours.

Harry Jones could not consider that his defeat by Stockman was a real trial of his quality, and, on June 12th, 1822, after Jem Ward had defeated Acton at Moulsey, he entered the ring for a new trial. Peter Crawley and Ned Turner were counsel for Stockman, and Jones's interests were looked after by Jack O'Donnel and Abbot. After a few minutes' sparring Jones rushed in and endeavoured to fib his opponent, but in the struggle to obtain the throw Jones sprained his ankle so severely as to be unable to continue the fight.

After these unfortunate ring exhibitions Jones fought several by-battles with commoners. Watts (a butcher) and Riley (a Westminster boxer) were beaten by him, and Peter Brookery, the Fishmonger, beat him in three-quarters of an hour.

In consequence of some chaffing at Tom Cribb's benefit at the Fives Court, on Tuesday, June 1st, 1824, a match was made between Jones and

Brown (the Sprig of Myrtle). A patron of boxing having offered a purse for the winner, Jones proposed, and Brown snapped at the offer, to fight it out that day. Accordingly, with Jack Randall as timekeeper, Dick Acton and Gipsy Cooper as seconds for Harry, and Tom Oliver and Tisdale for the Sprig, the party started for Paddington Fields, where, in nineteen rounds, lasting thirty-three minutes, the Sailor Boy achieved his first ring victory. This raised the reputation of Jones considerably.

About this time an amusing anecdote of Jones appeared in the newspapers. One Jem Aldridge, known as "the fighting typo," backed himself for £5 against Jones. The Sailor Boy at this time, as "most people fall in love some time or other," was engaged to a Miss Evans, and not keeping an exact "note of time," his diary was in such confusion that he had fixed June 28th, 1824, for both matches. Not seeing how he could honourably put off either his bride or his challenger, he met both; and soon after he had sworn eternal fidelity, and the etceteras connected with the ceremony of "taking this woman to be thy wedded wife," Harry started off to fulfil the other engagement. It is said that so lightly did he value his opponent that he merely consigned the lady to the gent who had given her away, with the remark, "Take care of my wife, like a good fellow, till I come back," and bolted off to the field of battle, in Copenhagen Fields, near Pentonville. Arriving on the ground somewhat flushed and out of breath, the Sailor Boy shook hands with the typo, and to work they went. In twelve minutes Mr. Aldridge declined any further favours at the hands of Harry, who, pocketing the fiver, returned to the wedding party, and spent the evening in fun and merriment until "the throwing of the stocking, O!"—thus bringing off the "double event."

Dick Price, a well-known butcher at Oxford, weighing upwards of eleven stone, and five feet eight inches in height, had given so much offence among his brother kill-bulls by his boasting and quarrelsomeness that they determined to give him a turn. A Mr. Parker, of Oxford, brought down Jones in butcher's garb, and Price insulting him in the market, "Mr. Parker's plant," as he was called, proposed a fight. To this Price, with an expression of pity and contempt for the "Lunnon boy," consented. At six o'clock in the evening of Wednesday, July 28th, 1824, the ring was pitched in Picksey Meadow, near Oxford. The combatants met first in Port Meadow, but an authority of the University city showed his awful phiz, and the crowd was put to the rout. Jones, after "kidding" his man to come in, played his part so well that in the ninth round he had him down to his own weight, and ten to one was offered by the undergrads and others, but no takers. At the end of the fifteenth round poor Price was at no price, when lo! after turning to avoid, he slung himself round again, and with a chance backhander caught Jones such an almighty whack on the left ear that down he went, and was deaf to time! The affair lasted in all twenty-one minutes. Jones felt immensely mortified, and challenged Price to a second meeting, but the latter had discovered his customer, and refused any further dealings. "I insist upon your giving me another chance," urged the Sailor Boy. "I will," said Price, "before the beaks;" so he applied to the Bench for a summons for a threatened assault, and the Sailor Boy was held to bail to keep the peace towards the complainant for twelve calendar months. "It's lucky," said the Sailor Boy, "that the bond only extends to Dicky Price. I must bid farewell to Oxford and look elsewhere for a job."

Tom Reidie, so well known as "the Colonel" for many years afterwards, among the frequenters of the Leicester Square and Coventry Street "hells," as the gaming-houses were then entitled, was hastily matched with Jones. The men met in the fields at the back of the "Red House," Battersea (now Battersea Park), on the 4th August, 1824. The affair was a tiresome exhibition. Reidie, nimble as a harlequin, retreated, whereon his man advanced, and would not be forced to a rally, getting down so provokingly that Harry was several times well-nigh irritated into a foul blow. The bystanders, too—many of them West End swells—pulled up the stakes, and the ropes were soon missing. Accordingly, as a reporter says, "the men were fighting out of one field into another, and Jones could not get a chance of planting a successful hit." "Only stand still," said the Sailor Boy, "and see what will be the matter." "I'm not such a fool, although I may look one," replied the Colonel, and then with his thumb to his nose he executed a backward double-shuffle, nobbed Harry slightly, and slipped his heels from under his hams, dropping on his South Pole with a grin. After two hours and three-quarters, in which both men were but slightly punished, Reidie's tactics triumphed, and Jones was so exhausted and baffled that he resigned the contest!

On September 21st, 1824, Jones, for the third time, entered the lists with Ned Stockman, at the "Old May Pole," Epping Forest, for £25 a side. After seventeen rounds, twenty-three minutes, Jones was again defeated.

A week only after this defeat, after the bull-baiting on Old Oak

Common, on Tuesday, September 28th, 1824, Frederick Edwards, a coachman, of some pretensions to boxing, offered to meet Jones for a purse that had been subscribed. Stockman seconded Jones, Reuben Martin united upon Edwards. Jones's skill, combined with caution, enabled him to get over the ground in style, and in an hour and a half the coachman gave in, confessing that even a good amateur must knock under to a professional.

Mike Curtain was matched against Jones for a trifling stake, and in October, 1824, Battersea Fields being again the scene of action, Jones defeated him in seventy-five minutes.

After the disappointment with Young Dutch Sam and Lenney, at the " Old Barge House," March 25th, 1825, Harry Jones fought a horsekeeper, nicknamed Captain Corduroy. The battle, which is fully reported in " Boxiana," lasted twenty minutes, when the Sailor Boy was hailed as victor.

The following report, from the pen of a distinguished *littérateur*, then on the staff of the *Morning Chronicle*, gives a lively picture of an extemporised fight of the period :—

" Old Oak Common, six miles from London, on the Harrow Road, and formerly the scene of many a sturdy battle between men of high pugilistic character, was, on Thursday, September 8th, 1825, honoured by the presence of a select assemblage of the mobocracy, to witness a subscription mill between Harry Jones, the Sailor Boy, and a Westminster champion, well known by the poetical appellation of 'Tommy O'Lynn,' but whose name in the parish books stands as Jemmy Wilson. Jemmy, it seems, had long been the drake of the walk in Duck Lane ; and in the various *rencontres* in which he happened to be engaged with the heroic youths of that neighbourhood he invariably came off with *éclat*. This circumstance rendered him a great favourite among the 'donkey dragoons,' of which he is a member ; and they determined, when an opportunity offered, to afford him the means of distinguishing himself in a way which might do honour to the school from which he sprang. This opportunity happily occurred at the ' Coopers' Arms,' in Strutton Ground. A large party being assembled over their ' pots of heavy ' in that place of social resort, some remarks were made on the want of diversion among the operative classes of society, while the nobs were pickling their carcasses on the seashore. Various proposals were made for a day's fun. Some were for ' grabbing a bull,' and taking him out for an airing, a recreation not then obsolete ; others were for a dog-fight, and more for a duck-hunt; but to all these there were objections; and Mr. Martin's Act was mentioned as an ugly bar to such exhilarating amusements. At last a mill was suggested, as more congenial to all their feelings; and the Sailor Boy being present, it was resolved that he and Tommy O'Lynn should have a 'shy' for a subscription purse. Both men were agreeable, and Thursday was fixed for the outing. The hat went round at the moment, and about five pounds were collected, which, with what might be contributed on the ground, was considered a tolerably fair prize. At an early hour on Thursday morning the lads were on the move, and the avenues leading to the Harrow Road presented a lively succession of donkey equipages, while the banks of the Paddington Canal, and the fields from the Uxbridge Road, were covered with groups of motley characters, all directing their steps towards the appointed spot. At one o'clock the assemblage was very numerous. Among the throng we noticed many Westminster celebrities, particularly Bill Gibbons and Caleb Baldwin. The former was present merely as an amateur, while the latter, with a jar of 'blue ruin' (copiously diluted from the neighbouring canal), endeavoured to enliven the spirits of his patrons, and to furnish the pockets of his own inexpressibles. A long list of the Boxing School was likewise on the ground, Tom Oliver acting as master of the ceremonies, stakeholder, and otherwise dictator of the day.

"The Sailor Boy was early on the ground, having been brought in prime style by Tom Callas and a couple of his friends in a 'one-horse shay.' He looked well, and was confident of winning. Tommy O'Lynn was said to be at a public-house on the Harrow Road, under the care of a 'gemman' whose delicacy was such that he did not wish his name to be mentioned, and was therefore described as the 'Great Unknown.' At two o'clock notice was sent to the 'Great Unknown' to bring his man, and in a short time he arrived with his shay-cart, drawn by his celebrated trotter, and was received with as cordial a cheer as if he were Sir Walter Scott or the Right Honourable George Canning, of which honour he seemed deeply sensible, and 'blushed like a bone-boiler'—which, we believe, is the profession to which he belongs.

" All being in readiness the ring was beaten out and a commodious area formed. The men soon made their appearance on opposite sides of the ring, throwing in their ' castors ' with mutual good humour. On stripping, the Sailor Boy was evidently the heavier and stronger of the two, and the odds were announced at seven to four in his favour. Tommy

O'Lynn was regularly got up for the occasion. Unlike his great ancestor, Brian O'Lynn, who, as history informs us, 'had no breeches to wear,' he advanced in all the pride of a new pair of tapebound flannel drawers, high-low shoes, and new cotton 'calf-covers.' On pulling down his knowledge-box by the forelock of its thatch, he was rapturously welcomed by the cry of 'Tommy for ever!' while the 'Great Unknown' whispered in his ear the words of the favourite Scotch song—

> 'Now's the time and now's the hour,
> See the front of battle lour.'

Tommy grinned a grin, and prepared for action. He was attended by Charley Brennan and Young Gas, while the Sailor Boy claimed the kind offices of Alec Reid, and that bright ornament to gymnastics and lyrics Frosty-faced Fogo.

THE FIGHT.

Round 1.—The positions of both men were good. Tommy especially threw himself into a studied attitude. The Sailor Boy tried to bring him out, and made two feints with his right. Tommy was steady, but at last Jones let fly with his right and caught him on the nob. Tommy was awake, and returned on the cheek, when after a short rally they closed, and went down together, Tommy undermost.

2.—Jones, anxious to begin, made a feint, and then hit out with his left, but was well stopped. Jones, still busy, rattled in, and caught Tommy on the ivories; a spirited rally followed, in which Jones caught his man round the neck, and pegged at his belly with great effect. He at last closed and threw him. ("Vait," cried a costermonger, "only let Tommy give him a touch of his own, and you'll see!" "Ve'll vait," cried another, "but I'm blowed if I don't think ve'll vait long enough!")

3.—Tommy came up active, but received a jobber in the dexter ogle, and in getting away dropped. The Great Unknown began to look serious, and was seen to scratch his block in a most significant manner.

4.—Jones was now perfectly acquainted with his man, and resolved to finish him without delay. He went in boldly with his left, but was stopped by Tommy throwing up his right and pitching back his head. Jones, however, followed him with his right, and hit him severely over his left guard. A desperate rally followed, in which Jones administered severe punishment, and Tommy went down piping and bleeding. It was now a donkey to a tom-tit in Jones's favour, but nobody would take the odds.

5, and last.—Tommy planted a body blow, but with little force. Jones returned on his smeller, and another desperate rally followed, in which Tommy had it in all directions, and was at last hit down senseless by a straight right-hander, Jones winning without a scratch in six minutes.

REMARKS.—Tommy may shine among the street heroes in the back slums, but won't do in the Ring. He was too light, and not sufficiently fed, for Jones. Gibbons recommended, from his greyhound condition, that he should go into training for what he called a "natommy vivante," and travel the country as "own brother to the living skeleton."

Jones, who had been gaining ground in the sparring world, and also in the estimation of his friends, was backed against Young Dutch Sam for £25 a side. This battle was decided at Shere Mere, on the borders of Bedfordshire, on Tuesday, the 18th of October, 1825. Sam was seconded by Dick and George Curtis, and Jones by Alec Reid and Goodman. Jones was signally defeated in eighteen rounds, occupying fifty-three minutes. See Life of YOUNG DUTCH SAM, ante, p. 358.

At No Man's Land, four miles beyond St. Albans, on Tuesday, March 14th, 1826, after Donovan had defeated Jennings, a subscription purse of five pounds was collected, when a man of the name of Knowlan, known as the Tumbler, entered the ring against Harry Jones. Knowlan, as a specimen of his professional agility, threw two summersaults before he began to peel. The Tumbler had also the advantage of Harry Holt for his second. In the course of fifteen minutes the activity of the Tumbler was reduced to a standstill, Jones proclaimed the winner, and the five pounds in his pocket.

After Barney Aaron had defeated Dick Hares, at No Man's Land, on Tuesday, March 21st, 1826, a subscription purse of five pounds was collected for Mike Curtain and Harry Jones; and although only seven days had elapsed since his fight with Knowlan, Harry was determined not to let a chance go by him. Curtain was anxious for another shy with the Sailor Boy, having been defeated by him, after a severe struggle of one hour and three-quarters, as stated in a preceding page. Jones, upon this occasion, was seconded by Fogo, and the battle was considered above mediocrity; but at the expiration of half-an-hour "the Curtain was let down" a second time, and Jones pronounced the conqueror.

After Young Dutch Sam had defeated Tom Cooper, the Gipsy, at Grays, in Essex, on Tuesday, April 25th, 1826, a subscription purse was collected for a second fight, when Jones and Tom Collins entered the ring. Collins was the man who defeated Barney Aaron when the latter boxer was a novice, and was considered a scientific, sharp boxer. He was soon reduced to a mere nobody in the hands of Harry Jones. In the short space of four rounds, occupying only six minutes, Collins was severely punished and defeated, while Jones left the ground with hardly a scratch.

On Tuesday, September 5th, 1826, after Bishop Sharpe had defeated Alec Reid, at No Man's Land, in Hertfordshire, to make up a third battle, for a subscription purse, Jones, always ready to earn a pound or two, and Pick, a Bristol lad, equally anxious to obtain a small slice, stood up on the shortest notice. Dick Curtis and Young Dutch Sam seconded Harry Jones, and Bayley and Gipsy Cooper acted as seconds for Pick. Twenty-seven rounds were contested. In every round Jones took the lead, and ultimately he was declared the conqueror. Pick had not the slightest chance, and was severely punished. The Sailor Boy had scarcely a mark upon him. Jones won the battle in thirty minutes.

The Sailor Boy at this period was hardly ever out of "action." At

Figett Hall, one mile and a half from Newmarket, after Larkins had defeated Abbot, a second fight took place for a purse of five pounds, between Harry Jones and Reuben Howe, on Tuesday, November 28th, 1826—the former well known in the London circles, the latter a bustling, boasting yokel, weighing a stone and a half more than Jones. Howe was seconded by two of his own pals, and Jones by Oliver and Fogo. Thirty-one rounds were fought in thirty-four minutes, during the whole of which Jones took the lead both in hitting and throwing, and won the fight almost without a scratch. No man could have polished off a customer in a more workman-like manner. The defeat of Howe was much relished by the chawbacons, as he was a complete bully among his companions, and being thus "taken down a peg" probably tended to improve his manners.

After Peter Crawley had defeated Jem Ward, at Royston Heath, Cambridgeshire, on Tuesday, January 2nd, 1827, Harry Jones entered the ring with Gybletts for a subscription purse. In the course of ten minutes Jones was defeated. It was considered no match. The blunt was divided between them. Gipsy Cooper seconded Gybletts, and Ned Stockman and a pupil of Israel Belasco's attended upon the Sailor Boy.

The second battle between Larkins and Abbot, for fifty pounds a side, according to the articles, was to have been decided on Tuesday, March 13th, 1827, within sixty miles of London; but as many things happen between the "cup and the lip," the "authorities" interfered, and Larkins and Abbot slept in whole skins that night. After some little murmurings by the disappointed crowd "that there is no certainty in this here life," Peter Crawley arrived, and added to their discomfiture by avowing it was the intention of Larkins to forfeit on account of illness.

The little fight, as it was termed, now became the interesting topic of the day ; and Jones and Raines started for a new piece of ground, followed by a string of vehicles of every description, hundreds of horsemen, and toddlers out of number. The road had a pleasing appearance, by the bustle, life, and activity, for several miles ; the turnpikes napped lots of blunt by the change ; and the pot-houses met with a variety of unexpected customers. But the principal part of the toddlers who were compelled to ride Shanks's mare were beaten to a standstill long before the grand halt took place at Chesterford. During the rapid motion of the "gay throng" several upsets occurred; but the Fancy were too game to complain of broken panels, or being canted over the necks of their horses, contenting themselves with the old saying that "worse accidents occur at sea." At

Chesterford a parley ensued about making the ring, and "Haydon Grange" was named as a place beyond the possibility of an interruption. But the crowd, who had already been over twenty miles of ground, were too much fatigued to undertake another of ten, and preferred chancing it; accordingly the stakes were knocked into the ground without delay, in the parish of Chester-ford. An outer ring was immediately formed by the carriages, and the combatants called for. Raines appeared first, and threw up his nob-cover, waited upon by Stockman and a hackney dragsman nicknamed Whipaway, while Peter Crawley and the Poet Laureate officiated as seconds for the Sailor Boy. This time Fogo did not show himself habited as a collegian, although his toggery bespoke the outline of a "Fellow Commoner" who had not decidedly taken his terms, although he was upon "terms" with the ancient tribe of costermongers. He wore his "beaver up" when he was recognised by the M.A.'s, and received the nod from them as a student of *Brasen-nose.* The colours were tied to the stakes—the Sailor Boy the favourite.

THE FIGHT.

Round 1.—The Sailor Boy was in prime twig; in fact, he never was, in any of his preceding mills, anything like in such good condition. His arms were peculiarly fine, and attracted the general notice of the spectators. Raines did not appear so muscular a man as his opponent, but nevertheless his frame was manly, and he exhibited great strength. The Sailor Boy was in no hurry to commence the attack, and some minutes elapsed before any attempt at hitting was made. Jones made play, but Raines stopped well. A pause. The Sailor Boy, rather furious, was going to work, but was again well parried by Raines. It was observed by the London amateurs that Raines had evidently improved in his knowledge of the science. In setting to with the gloves the Sailor Boy had always had the best of it. Several minutes passed, and the stopping system was adopted by Raines, until the Sailor Boy went in, and slashed away like a new one. In closing fibbing was attempted on both sides. Jones broke away cleverly, and milled his opponent down. "First blood!" from the friends of Jones. Raines was piping a little, and the Sailor Boy received shouts of applause from his "larned" friends belonging to the "Univarsity."

2.—The claret appeared slightly on Jones's lips when he arrived at the scratch. The Sailor Boy fought well—that is to say, cautiously. Raines he looked upon as an ugly customer, although a tolerably good-looking fellow in person. The latter made several good parries, but did not try to plant any hits. Jones put in a heavy bodier with his

left hand. A pause. "Go to work," was the cry, and "Why don't you, Mr. Poet Laureate (Fogo), put them together?" Jones planted a facer. ("Bravo!") Raines made a blow, but the Sailor Boy was on the alert, and nothing was the matter. Exchange of blows passed between them, and the fighting was rather sharp, until they closed. In struggling for the throw Jones got his man down, but Raines threw him over, and the Sailor Boy rolled out of the ring. The Sailor Boy was decidedly the favourite with the Euclids, the Virgils, and the Homers. But the "drag and tumbler" sort of folk rather fancied Raines, and the odds were offered upon him by a few of them.

3.—The lads were just now upon their mettle, and the fight had become interesting to the whole assembly of Greeks, Latins, and yokels; in fact, all classes of society were in high glee. Raines got away from mischief, but not out of trouble. At this instant a gent stepped into the ring and made his way up to Peter, saying: "If you are the director of this sort of thing, I must insist that you desist. It is a breach of the peace!" Peter, mild as a lamb and polite as a Chesterfield, observed, touching his tile to the man in authority, "I hope, sir, you do not mean to stop the sport? You do not intend to be so cruel? But if it is your wish, why, why, ——. The second degree is now made out," said Peter; "this interruption, after the fight has commenced, is harder than the first baulk! Such an occurrence has not happened for the last twenty years." A noble lord, upon a fine prad, in the shape of a beak, in an agitated tone of voice, added: "Do not come into Essex; I will not permit it. You will therefore do it at your peril!" In this dilemma the Greeks, the Roman-y's, the mathematical admirers of the angle hitting of Harry, put forth all their lexicon of gammon to the unrelenting beaks, not to make three or four thousand gentlemen look like fools; but it was all U-P. "The Fancy," exclaimed the hero of the *Brazen-nose,* "have now acquired the third degree," on hearing the member of the Upper House say, "Beware of pitching your tents in Essex." "It is the hardest thing I ever heard, in my whole history of prose and poetry, not to let the mill be finished anywhere to-day. I shall remember him in my next epic." Singing psalms to a dead neddy would have been of the same service! The gents belonging to the Bench retired outside of the crowd, and a ring court-martial was held for twelve minutes, upon the propriety of "to mill or not to mill," when it was unanimously determined "that the fight between Harry Jones and Raines was no go." Thus, after the "bubble, bubble, toil and trouble," in the words of Shakespeare, it proved to be "Much Ado about Nothing"—the spectators out of humour and ill-natured, the nags tired, "Home, Sweet Home," a long way off, and the rain coming down nicely.

The ground was cleared in a few minutes. The stakes were drawn on the part of Raines, but his backer offered to increase the sum to £25 a side, so satisfied was he that Raines would have proved the conqueror.

On Saturday, the 14th of April, 1827, at Bulpham Fenn, Essex, about twenty-two miles from London, in an angle on the right of Brentwood and Romford, Harry Jones and Bob Simmonds, a well-known sporting "clergyman" (*anglicè,* a sweep), entered a twenty-four foot roped ring at one o'clock. Jones was attended by Peter Crawley and Fogo; Simmonds was seconded by Dav Hudson and Gybletts. Crawley won the toss. On setting to, Simmonds, with great eagerness, attacked the Sailor Boy, but the steadiness of the latter soon gave him the advantage. Jones, cool and collected, waited for an opening, when he planted a rum one on the right eye of Mr. Simmonds, which not only produced confusion of vision, but floored the man of soot. Simmonds wished to appear cheerful on commencing the second round, but the spectators found out that he was of " no service " against a fine young man like Harry Jones. In the sixth round, the poor fellow received so severe a cross-buttock that he puffed like a pair of asthmatic bellows; after this shaking he fell down almost without a blow in every succeeding round. At the expiration of thirty-five minutes, and seventeen rounds, Simmonds acknowledged he was " up the flue." Jones, he said, was too good for him, and that he could not get at the Sailor Boy. Jones won the battle without a scratch. Crawley and Fogo were extremely attentive to Harry. It was so hollow a thing on the side of Jones that not a sov. was sported upon the event. Upwards of a thousand persons were present.

In consequence of the interruption of the battle between Raines and Jones, a second match was made for £25 a side, which was decided on Monday, the 4th of June, 1827, Watford, the rallying point, was gained without meeting with any particular objects worthy of note. At this place the office was given for Chipperfield Common, a distance of twenty-two miles fro.n London; thither the disappointed Fancy repaired, but not without " lots of grumbling" at the long trot. However, the ride was delightful, and upon the whole it was pronounced a pleasant journey, and a tidy day's sport. At ten minutes to two o'clock the Sailor Boy, habited as one of the true blue fraternity, threw his hat into the ring, accompanied by the Poet Laureate Fogo and Jack Clarke; Raines was not long behind him, attended by his seconds, Ned Stockman and a dragsman of the name of Woolley.

THE FIGHT.

Round 1.—The Sailor Boy could not have been better as to condition, and Raines was also in good trim as to his training. It seemed as if the combatants were aware they had a long day before them, as neither Jones nor Raines were in a hurry to go to work. Ten minutes had elapsed in looking and dodging each other about, when Jones let fly with his left hand, whilst Raines cleverly put on the stopper. The latter boxer never commenced offensive operations, but always waited for the attack. Jones also well knew that great danger was to be apprehended by the countering of Raines, and therefore he was extremely cautious, and thus are we enabled to account for this precious long round. The seconds were at the four corners of the ring like hackney coachmen upon a stand waiting for a fare. Several of the spectators proposed to them to accept a cigar, smoke a pipe, take a hand of cards, &c. At length a slight rally, or rather exchanges, occurred, when stopping, dodging, offering, again took place. Jones let fly, but Raines would not have it at any price. Good stopping on both sides. "Go to work," from all parts of the ring, had not the slightest effect. The Sailor Boy made a hit with his left hand, which was sharply returned by Raines; a little milling took place, and both of them cried out " First blood," but it was a dead heat in this respect, a slight tinge of the claret appearing on both of their mugs at the same instant. It would be a waste of time to repeat all the stops, &c. The Sailor Boy at length went in like a jolly fellow, and the fibbing system was resorted to, hard and fast, on both sides, until they both went down, Raines undermost. Forty minutes had now passed in sparring.

2.—This round was altogether as short. Some little stopping occurred, until Jones went in as before, and finished the round by tipping it to Raines and placing him undermost.

3.—Little bumps were observed upon the foreheads of both combatants, but nothing like mischief had passed between them. The ear of Raines had napped a little pepper. The latter endeavoured to put in a right-handed blow, and, if it had told, summat might have been the matter. Raines stopped well; but he did not fight until he was compelled to defend himself. In closing, smart hitting on both sides was administered, and the Sailor Boy was thrown out of the ropes. (" Well done, Jem !" and lots of applause.)

4.—The nose of Raines looked red. For why? Jones's left had given it a sharp tap; he was also a little on the piping suit. At the ropes Raines was fibbed by his opponent, and ultimately thrown.

5.—This was a tidy round, but the wind of Raines was rather troubled; and both cautious in the extreme. Jones planted cleverly a conker without any return, and repeated the dose. Parrying on both sides, until Raines received a slight hit in the body, when he staggered backwards and fell out of the ropes. (Two to one on Jones.)

6.—The Sailor Boy always commenced milling, although cautious. He gave Raines another nose-ender which sent him rather backwards; Jones then went in, and had the best of it until Raines was thrown.

7.—It was clear to the spectators that Jones was now taking the lead; he cleverly put in a jobber that made the nose of Raines not only swell, but spoilt the shape of it. In closing Raines endeavoured to be busy, but the Sailor Boy was the quicker; Raines received the most punishment, and in going down was undermost. (Jones for a trifle; in fact, the friends of Raines began to perceive something was the matter.)

8.—Raines put in a sharp blow on the ear of Jones. (" Well done, Jem !") The Sailor Boy, however, returned the favour with interest—he nosed his opponent, ditto and ditto. (Laughing by the crowd, and " It is not fair to hit a man twice in one place.") Raines in the struggle was again down.

9.—This round was decidedly in favour of Jones. All his blows told. The nose of Raines again caught it, and he was ultimately hit down. (The Jonesites had now booked it that the Sailor Boy could win without a scratch upon his face.)

10.—Not last; but interrupted. Jem made play, and slightly touched the cheek of Jones; but the Sailor Boy returned another noser. They closed, when some blows were exchanged; and the Sailor Boy broke away. A long pause — both on the look out. Counter-hits. Jones was going to repeat the dose, when a gentleman on horseback rode up to the ropes, followed by a constable with a staff in his hand, and proclaimed, "In the name of the King I command you to desist." The assemblage immediately bowed submission and the combatants instantly "cut their lucky." The fight had lasted one hour and a quarter, but the yokels were sadly disappointed, and expressed their anger by loud hisses and groans. The motley group were soon in motion, and in less than ten minutes the ground was summat like the "baseless fabric of a vision;" not a cove was left behind. The nags soon felt the persuaders, and the toddlers, puffing and blowing, were compelled to put their best feet foremost in order to keep up with the drags. Watford was once more the rallying point; and after a few minutes' conversation as to finishing the thing, a gentleman offered his meadow near Bushey Lodge, within a mile and a half of the town, which was gladly accepted. Here the Commissary-General and his pal knocked up the ring almost before you could say "Jack Robinson," and at a quarter to six the men were again in attitude.

THE FIGHT (PART II.).

Round 1.—The Sailor Boy looked as fresh as a daisy, while Raines appeared none the better for the delay. He was rather stiff, and his right hand was a little swelled. Raines made some good stops; but Jones now seemed determined to finish the thing well, and went up to his man, fought with Raines, had the best of it, and downed him.

2.—The left eye of Raines had napped pepper in the last round; and Jones lost no time in polishing off his opponent. He closed, and fibbed Raines severely until he got him down; but the Sailor Boy held up his hand to show he would not do anything wrong. ("Bravo!" and Jones three to one.)

3.—Short; but all in favour of Jones. Raines down.

4.—The mug of Raines was covered with claret, and Jones again fibbed him off his pins.

5.—Jem was getting abroad, and he hit at random; however, it was a milling round on both sides, and Jones did not get off without some clumsy thumps. Both down, Raines undermost.

6.—Sharp work at the ropes. The Sailor Boy held his antagonist and tipped it him until he went down.

7.—This round decided the fight. Raines was punished all over the ring until he was down.

8-12.—It was as nice as ninepence to Jones. In the ninth round Raines was done, and time was called three times before he was brought to the scratch, and even then he was quite stupid; he, however, recovered, and fought the remaining rounds—or rather stood up to be punished—until Jones was declared the conqueror in twenty minutes.

REMARKS.—Raines never attempted to fight—that is to say, he always waited for the attack. He countered at times well, but showed himself more of a sparrer than a milling cove. The Sailor Boy did everything in his power to win; he fought with capital science, and likewise bravely. By the above battle he has risen in the estimation of his friends. Jones will not stand still for backers; and no doubt the Sailor Boy will soon throw up his hat again in the P.R.

After Reuben Martin had defeated "the Gas," on Tuesday, October 16th, 1827, at Westbourn Common, Sussex, Harry Jones and Ike Dodd entered the ring. To detail the rounds of this fight would be not only a waste of time but of paper. Dodd stood like a chopping-block, and was completely at the service of the Sailor Boy during thirty-four minutes and eighteen rounds. Jones took the lead, kept it, and finished off Dodd with the utmost ease. He won the battle without a scratch upon his face; while, on the contrary, the mug of Dodd exhibited divers blows in sundry places. Jones was seconded by Curtis and Stockman, and Ike Dodd by Joe Fishwick and Lewellin. The above battle was for only £10 a side and a trifling subscription purse,

After considerable chaffing, letter-writing, and even blows upon the subject, a match for £25 a side was made with Bill Savage and Harry Jones. The latter went into training at Shirley's, New Inn, Staines, and conducted himself like a man desirous to do credit to himself, and likewise to satisfy his backers. This match was decided on Tuesday, March 25th, 1828, in the same field, near Chertsey, in which Barney Aaron and Redmond were to have fought. A few minutes before one o'clock Jones entered the ring, attended by Young Sam and Ned Stockman. Some trifling delay occurred before Savage put in an appearance, during which time Dick Curtis, owing to some misunderstanding with the backer of Jones, turned round and took five to four for a good stake. This circumstance rather alarmed the betting men, it being previously understood that Curtis was to have acted as second to Jones. Savage threw his castor into the ropes, and Curtis and Alec Reid entered as his seconds.

THE FIGHT.

Round 1.—Jones was in tip-top condition, and armed at all points for his antagonist. The appearance of Savage did not indicate so much muscle and strength; nevertheless, he was considered up to the mark. He had also the advantage of a stone in weight and two inches in height. Some little time occurred in sparring, when Jones endeavoured to plant a facer with his left hand, but Savage stopped it skilfully, and got away. The latter retreated to a corner of the ring, and hit out; but it was "no go," Harry being too cunning. The science on both sides was admired, and the parries were excellent. Jones, eager to go to work, touched Mr. Savage's os frontis rather "nasty," when a close took place, and both combatants endeavoured to serve it out, until both were down.

2.—The Sailor Boy was too fast for Savage; the latter retreated, but napped two nobbers. In closing, Savage was bored to the ropes, and Jones tried on the fibbing system with success, until both went down.

3.—The Sailor Boy made good use of his science, but Savage stopped several hits like a pugilist. Jones went in, pelting away, and caught hold of Savage by the neck with one hand, and made some blows tell with the other. Savage was not idle in returning upon the body of Jones. Savage was thrown, and "First blood" called out by Young Sam, which was discovered upon the lip of Savage.

4.—Jones seemed quite confident that he had nothing to fear from his opponent, and commenced milling without delay, but Savage made several good parries. The Sailor Boy slipped down, but jumped up with so much gaiety as to floor his opponent,

("Harry, go it; that's the time of day - it is winning, and nothing else.")

5.—Jones, without ceremony, planted two nobbers; he also caught hold of his adversary and gave him a severe cross-buttock, shaking Savage, his nob coming on the grass and his pins in the air. ("There's a burster!" said the Lively Kid; and the friends of Jones were loud in their marks of approbation. Seven to four.)

6.—Savage showed game to the backbone, and rallying was the result; in closing, both were down.

7.—Jones's left hand was exceedingly troublesome, but Savage several times made skilful stops. In fact, this was a well-fought round on both sides, until the combatants were upon the ground.

8-10.—The gameness of Savage was the admiration of the ring in all these rounds; and he also satisfied the spectators that he was not deficient in science. Savage's left eye was in mourning and otherwise damaged, and his face exhibited severe marks of punishment. Jones took the lead, kept it like a master, and finished all the rounds in his favour. The mug of the Sailor Boy was as clear from blows as when he commenced the battle. (Two to one and higher odds on Jones.)

11-13.—All these rounds were decidedly in favour of Jones; and the latter showed himself also the best man in obtaining the falls. Savage was floored by a tremendous hit on his left peeper; and his pimple shook again from the violent effects of the blow.

14.—Savage was under good instruction, having the Pet of the Fancy at his elbow, and Bill endeavoured to profit by his advice;

nevertheless, the Sailor Boy could not be reduced, and he, in general, finished the round in his favour.

15.—Counter-hits, but Savage had the worst of the punishment. ("Long bowls," said Curtis to Savage, "will not answer; you must yardarm it with your adversary.") Savage endeavoured to do as Curtis wished him, and he resolutely went in to work; the Sailor Boy hit him right away, enough to floor an ox, but the Welshman was too game to go down. Savage continued the round in the highest style of courage, until he was thrown cleverly. ("Any odds," and "Jones, it is all your own.")

Any further detail of the rounds would be useless; enough has been stated to show that the Sailor Boy was completely the hero of the tale, and reduced conquest almost to a certainty. Jones had never lost the lead for a moment, but he now took it most decidedly. If Savage stood out he was jobbed—if he went in he was weaved and thrown. The fine fighting of Jones was the admiration of the whole ring, and the delight of all who had not risked their money against him. But Savage fully supported his character as one of the gamest of the game; though he had not the slightest chance of winning he refused to give in, and continued to obey the call of time, in spite of reiterated cries of "Take him away!" In the twenty-first round Harry planted a left-hander on Bill's nose, and also threw him heavily. In the thirty-second round Savage fought with amazing spirit and put in two or three good right-handed bodiers, but Jones finished the round by giving him a tremendous cross-buttock. In the thirty-fifth round Harry was winded and was troubled with sickness, no uncommon occurrence with him in a long fight. Savage, cheered on by Curtis, endeavoured to take advantage of this circumstance and some little alarm was in fact felt by those who were not well acquainted with Harry; but the efforts of Savage were entirely vain. Sick as he was, Harry had the best of the round, and in the half-minute's respite that followed Jones brought up the troublesome matter, and was soon "all right" again. In the forty-ninth round Jones threw Savage and fell on him, but under the able management of his seconds

he recovered sufficiently to obey the call of "Time." It was clear, however, that Savage could not see his man. Ned Savage entered the ring in the fifty-fourth round and threw up his hat, declaring that his brother should fight no more. Harry capered about the ring for victory, but to the surprise of all present Bill declared he would not give in. He fought or rather groped his way through a couple more rounds, when his seconds, seeing that he had not the "shadow of a shade" of chance took him away, and Harry Jones was declared the victor, after a most gallant fight of fifty-six rounds, in one hour and thirty-five minutes.

REMARKS.—Savage showed himself as brave a man as ever pulled off a shirt, and as being able to stop with considerable skill. His blows did not tell in out-fighting, his distances were incorrect, and when he closed he could not punish. He had hitherto been considered a good wrestler, but Harry almost always threw him. Indeed, poor Bill received more than twenty, perhaps we might say thirty, cross-buttocks, each of which was terribly effective. Harry Jones showed tactics of the very highest order. It is difficult to say which we had most occasion to admire—his out-fighting or in-fighting. He was evidently notwithstanding the disparity in size, much stronger than Savage, and, in fact, so fine was his science that he quitted the ring with hardly a mark on his face, and returned to Staines to dine so little "the worse for wear" that a stranger could not have discovered from his appearance that he had been fighting. His brave but unfortunate antagonist, on the contrary, was borne off the ground to the "Cricketers" public-house, where he was put to bed. The fight would have been brought to a conclusion much sooner had not Jones, in the early part of the action, sprained his left arm in one of the falls. The injury prevented the use of his left hand throughout the rest of the fight. Not the slightest dispute took place during the whole of the fight. Jones was often deservedly applauded for his forbearance in releasing Savage when he was entirely at his mercy, and, upon the whole, it was as fair, clever, and manly a battle as the best well-wishers to honest pugilism would desire to witness.

Jones had now given undeniable proofs of more than ordinary boxing qualifications. In fact by many fanciers he was declared to be the best ten-stone man on the list. Ned Stockman, however, "the Lively Kid," at that time a first favourite in sporting circles, strenuously denied this at all times and places, pointing to his early defeats of Harry, twice for purses (of course impromptu affairs), and later for £25 in the regular P.R., at Epping, in 1824. Mr. Stockman, however, had forgotten that Harry had been improving in bone and stamina (he was only twenty-one), while "the Lively Kid" had been "going the pace" in very fast company. Ned soon got on a match for £25 a side, and, all going smoothly, articles were signed, and he met Harry Jones at Shere Mere, on the 16th September, 1828. A clever fight on the part of Stockman, not without occasional game rallies, almost uniformly to the advantage of the Sailor Boy, in the forty-third round ended in Stockman's defeat, his chances being quite out some time before the finale.

Barney Aaron, whose victorious career we have just given, was the Sailor Boy's next opponent. In weight the men were about equal, but the fame of the "Star of the East" shone so brightly that the £100 staked were already "as good as won," and so discounted by the denizens of Duke's Place. But the soundness of Mark Twain's advice, "never to prophesy unless you know," received here another illustration. On the 11th of November, 1828, at the Barge House, Woolwich Marshes, the renowned Barney struck his colours to the gallant Sailor Boy, after eighteen sharp fighting rounds, lasting fifteen minutes only.

Tom Reidie, "the Colonel," conceiting himself upon his shifty perform-ance among the cabbages at Battersea, already noticed, having spoken disparagingly of Harry's victory as "a fluke," followed it up by express-ing a wish that "somebody" would back him for "half a hundred," and let him "stand in a tenner of his own." A patron of the "silver" or "copper hell," whereof the Colonel was for the time being "groom-porter," volunteered "the needful," and, in the short period of seven weeks from his victory over Aaron, the Sailor Boy was face to face with Reidie at Hurley Bottom, Berks, on the 30th of December, 1828, for £15 a side. This time the Colonel's "strategic movements to the rear" entirely failed him. The stakes and ropes enclosed him in the limits of twenty-four feet, and in less than that number of minutes (the fight lasted twenty-two minutes) down went Tom Reidie for the last time, at the close of the six-teenth round, perfectly satisfied that he had quite another "boy" to deal with than the lad he had tired out in Battersea Fields.

Frank Redmond, whose game battles with Barney Aaron we have already chronicled in these pages, proposed to try conclusions with the Sailor Boy for a stake of £100 a side, which Jones had now little difficulty in getting together. It was a game and, for a few rounds, a tremendous struggle, but Harry had "a little more left in him" in the last three rounds (there were only ten in all), and in thirty-six minutes he was hailed the victor of a well-fought field.

We should unduly extend the bulk of our volumes did we attempt to give the detailed rounds of all the fights of the minor celebrities to whom we have given niches in our gallery of pugilistic pen-portraits. We shall therefore summarise Harry's other battles by merely enumerating them.

On the 19th May, 1829, at Harpenden Common, he fought and beat George Watson for a stake of £50 a side. Time, thirty-nine minutes; rounds, thirty.

June 7th, 1831, beat Dick Hill (the Nottingham Champion), for £100 a side, at Bagthorpe Common, Notts, in sixty-nine rounds, eighty minutes.

Harry next met "the Oxford Pet," Perkins, whose victory over Dick Curtis had placed him on a pinnacle above his real merits as a boxer. On January 17th, 1832, Harry Jones disposed of "the Pet's" lofty pretensions in twenty-two rounds, occupying forty-six minutes only. The battle was fought at Hurley Bottom.

On April 2nd, 1833, Jones, who had just recovered from a long illness, fought Gipsy Jack Cooper for £25 a side, at Chertsey. It was a long and tedious battle, with heavy punishment on both sides, for two hours and ten minutes, twenty-six long rounds, when Jones was hailed as conqueror.

For some time Harry, who was suffering from a chronic disease of the lungs, caused by exposure, earned money by sitting at Somerset House as an artists' model; and we can well say a finer bust and arms for an athlete, or an exemplar of muscular development and symmetry, could rarely be met with. As poor Harry, too, was a civil-spoken and good-looking fellow, he had a numerous *clientèle*.

Another "Sailor Boy," with the prefix of the words "The East End," hight Tom Smith, was now in the field. He was ten stone four pounds; and having disposed of the nine-stone lad, Owen Swift, and also Jack Adams and Aaron, he challenged Harry. The match was made for £50 a side, and the two "Sailor Boys" met at Shrubs Hill, Bucks, on the 17th June, 1834. Harry was no longer the "Gay Sailor Boy." His heart was sound, but his breathing apparatus was rapidly going out of repair, and in five rounds, occupying only fourteen minutes, down went poor Harry for the last time, and his colours and the £50 were the prize of "the East End Sailor Boy."

Soon afterwards Jones became an inmate of the Westminster Hospital, where he died on the 14th April, 1835, at the early age of twenty-eight years,

JACK PERKINS ("THE OXFORD PET").
1827—1830.

AMONG the ten-stone boxers who ran a bright but brief career we note Jack Perkins, "the Oxford Pet," renowned chiefly for his victory over the theretofore unconquered Dick Curtis.

Perkins's first recorded battle, at the age of nineteen, with Bailey Wakelin, an Oxonian pugilist nearly a stone his superior in weight, spread his fame among the "gownsmen." The affair came off at Radley Common, on the 30th January, 1827, for £25 a side, "the Pet" polishing off his opponent in twenty-three active rounds, occupying thirty-two minutes only.

His next appearance in buff was with Godfrey, an Oxford waterman, at Henson. near the University City, on the 3rd of July, 1827. In the seventh round, after twenty-eight minutes' fighting, the referee awarded the fight to Godfrey (against whom two and three to one was current), on the ground that Perkins had got down without a blow. Godfrey refused a second trial.

Perkins's next match was with a well-known London man, Jem Raines.* The battle was for £25 a side, and came off at Penton Hook, near Staines, on the 21st August, 1828. The Londoner's skill was completely outshone by the provincial professor, who out-fought and in-fought, rallied, and sent down poor Jem for about a dozen of the twenty-five rounds which comprised the battle, lasting forty-four minutes.

Perkins was now voted a don in the "University of Fives," and was soon matched by some of his "undergrad" admirers with Dick Price, of whose qualifications a slight instance is given in the sketch of HARRY JONES, in a previous page of this Appendix. Perkins's fight with Dick Price, at Wantage, Berks, on October 15th, 1828, in which Price had for seconds Peter Crawley and Dick Curtis, from London, was a one-sided affair, the Oxford Pet knocking down the eleven-stone butcher in the second and

---

* Jem Raines, ten stone four pounds, fought a draw with Harry Jones, the Sailor Boy, at Chesterfield, March 17th, 1827. He was subsequently beaten by Harry Jones (see Life of the SAILOR BOY, page 526), Ned Stockman, and Barney Aaron, all, at that period, good men. and made in most instances a very creditable fight.

third rounds, and administering punishment *ad lib.* until the sixteenth and last, when the fight was over.   Time sixty-two minutes.

On this occasion some chaffing between Curtis and Perkins produced an ill feeling, and in the very next issue of *Bell's Life* we find " a friend from Oxford " was commissioned to stake for a match with Curtis for £100 a side, and articles were signed for a meeting between the two "Pets." Curtis forfeited on the second deposit, being matched to fight Edwards for £200 a side in the ensuing February. This match also ending this time in a forfeit to Curtis, the affair with Perkins was resumed.   We may here note that Curtis was at this period suffering from an attack of rheumatic gout, and that he stated this fact in reply to a challenge of one Joseph Hudson Gardener to fight for £300, in April, 1829. A "short-notice" battle was eventually agreed upon for £100 a side, and the day fixed for the 30th December, 1828.

In London and its vicinity, Curtis, who had pursued a long career of glory, and who, in all his battles, had never been beaten, was considered almost invincible ; and few, in the first instance, were disposed to lay against him, although seven to four and two to one were repeatedly offered. As the time of fighting approached, however, more minute inquiries were made respecting the merits of his opponent, and those who had had opportunities of judging described him as a customer of no ordinary stamp. He had been, like Dick, successful in all his contests, and was described by those who knew him best as a scientific pugilist—active on his legs, a straight and severe hitter with his left, a good getter away, and distinguished for sound bottom.   Independent of this, it was known that he was at least a stone heavier than Curtis, weighing when stripped ten stone four pounds, while Dick was booked at nine stone at most.   He was also five years younger than Curtis, being scarcely twenty, while Dick was twenty-five; and those who knew the habits of the latter were perfectly aware that they were not such—since he had been in the habit of " seeing the gas turned off "—as to improve his stamina or increase his muscular powers.

Both men went immediately into active training—Curtis to Hartley Row, and Perkins, first in Oxfordshire, and latterly to Mr. Shirley's, the New Inn, at Staines, whose system of training and unremitting care of the men entrusted to his charge placed him deservedly high in the estimation of the best judges.   It was observed that both men were uncommonly attentive to their exercise, and both were acknowledged to be in excellent condition. These were points to which particular attention was paid as the period of

the last deposit approached, and the friends of Perkins exhibited an increasing confidence, many boldly asserting that Curtis would find himself
mistaken in his estimate of the talent of his opponent, and others boldly
asserting that they thought he was overmatched—a stone being far too
much for any man to give away, where it was accompanied by a corresponding proportion of science and game. Still, such was the deep-rooted
prejudice in favour of Curtis, and such the confidence in his generalship
and cutting severity of punishment, that the great majority of the Metro-
politans considered it next to treason to harbour a thought of his defeat.
There were those, however, who were not quite so bigoted in their opinions,
and who, viewing the merits of the men dispassionately, were disposed to
think that Curtis, as well as many of his gallant contemporaries, might find
an equal, if not a superior, in the art which he professed. Among this class
were found ready takers of the long odds of two to one, and subsequently
of seven to four—but on the night of the last deposits the odds were taken
to a large amount at six to four.

On the Monday evening the road to Maidenhead, which was appointed
headquarters, was crowded with vehicles of all descriptions, and every
house which would receive such visitors was crowded to excess. Curtis
and his backers cast anchor at the "Sun," and Perkins, under the auspices
of the Oxford Dragsman, brought to at the "Dumb Bell," on the London
side of Maidenhead Bridge. Curtis was accompanied by Tom Reidie, who
had trained with him, and Perkins by Harry Jones.

Tuesday morning produced a numerous accession to the multitude, and
countless vehicles continued to pour in as the day advanced, embracing
some of the most distinguished patrons of the Ring, and giving ample
occupation to the postmasters.

At an early hour Tom Oliver and his assistant, Frosty-faced Fogo, proceeded to form the milling arena in the Parish Meadow, at Hurley Bottom,
Berks, thirty-four miles from London, and close to the banks of the
Thames—in summer no doubt a very desirable spot, but in the winter
season, from the marshy state of the soil, anything but eligible, especially
for those who had to travel in heavy vehicles. Several of these stuck fast
in the yielding soil, and the casualties which followed were of the most
ludicrous description—many of the inmates, who till then had escaped the
miseries of damp feet, being obliged to alight, and, ankle deep in mud, to
scramble to that portion of the turf which was still capable of bearing their
weight. Having encountered these dangers "by flood and field," they

reached the ring, which was admirably constructed, and surrounded by an ample supply of wagons, flanked by an immense number of carriages of every denomination. As a proof of the interest excited we may state that the crowd assembled was estimated at more than 5,000 persons.

At one o'clock the men had arrived on the ground, sporting their respective colours—Curtis a bright orange, Perkins a crimson. The bustle of preparation was soon visible. The whips were distributed to the men appointed by the Fair Play Club, and the stragglers were driven back to the outer ring of rope which had been constructed near to the wagons. Shortly after Dick Curtis approached the scene of action, accompanied by Josh Hudson and Young Dutch Sam, and was soon followed by Perkins, under the guidance of Tom Spring and Harry Holt. On meeting within the ring they shook hands, and immediately commenced stripping. Both looked well in health; but it was impossible not to observe that there was a rustic hardiness in the appearance of Perkins, very different from that of Curtis, who, nevertheless, had that sleekness and delicacy in his aspect which one is apt to ascribe to superior breed or higher blood. On stripping this contrast was still more apparent; for while Curtis showed that beautiful symmetry of person for which he was so distinguished, and which would have formed a perfect model for the sculptor, Perkins was rough, square, and muscular in appearance. His head, too, being stripped in patches of its hair, from the effect of ringworm in early life, gave him rather the cut of a ragged colt just caught upon the mountain wilds than the well-groomed nag coming from the stud of an indulgent master. Overcoming first impression, however, on seeing both men stripped, it was impossible not to discover at a glance the great disparity in point of size between the men. Perkins appeared to us to be at least two inches taller than Curtis, and every way larger in proportion. He was well pinned, with substantial thighs, and his shoulders and arms showed powerful muscle, though his loins were thin. His phiz, too, exhibited various scars, which were convincing proofs that he had been engaged in encounters of no trifling character. He evinced a great coolness in his manner, and, as throughout his training, booked victory as certain. Curtis looked to us light, but, nevertheless, in high favour with himself. Many old followers of the stakes did not hesitate on seeing the men for the first time stripped in fair comparison to exclaim, "Dick is over-matched," an opinion which had often been expressed before, but met with little attention. Everything being in readiness the men were conducted to the scratch and commenced

THE FIGHT.

Round 1.—The positions of both men were good. Curtis, his head a little advanced, his arms well up, and his eye measuring his man with the piercing look of the eagle. Perkins, his head rather on one side, and thrown a little back, his right hand well up, to stop Dick's left, and his left ready for a fling. Each manœuvred and changed ground. Dick made several feints with his left, but Perkins was not to be drawn from his caution. ("He's not to be kidded!" cried one of the Oxonians.) Dick crept in, tried to draw his man once or twice, but it would not do. Perkins stood well to his guard. Five minutes were occupied in this way, and not a blow struck; at last Dick plunged in with his left, which was stopped, but he delivered with his right. Good counter-hits were exchanged in a rally, Dick catching the left between his eyes, which made them twinkle, and the right on the tip of his conk. Perkins instantly stepped back and exclaimed, "First blood!" at the same time pointing to Dick's nose, and sure enough the purple fluid came gurgling forth. Dick, undismayed, bustled up to his man, and caught him heavily on the mouth with his left. Perkins got well away, but no time was lost in again getting to a rally; Dick would not be denied, and got close to his man. Perkins again put in a left-handed facer, but had a tremendous hit in return from Dick's right, which cut him over the corner of the left eye, and drew a copious stream of blood. Both again drew back, but Dick suffered no time to elapse, rushed in to deliver, and after two or three exchanges Perkins went down from a slight hit. The round lasted seven minutes, and the fighting on both sides was excellent, and acknowledged by the most sceptical to be better than was expected on the part of the Oxford Pet.

2.—Dick again came up in beautiful position, while Perkins seemed perfectly at home, and nowise dismayed by Dick's "ocular demonstration." Perkins waited; and Dick, after two or three feints with his left, made a good hit with his right, but was well countered by Perkins. A sharp and active rally followed, in which Perkins caught it on the nozzle, and was on a par with his opponent, for he too showed abundance of claret. In the end Perkins was down, though not a decided knock-down blow.

3.—Perkins came up fresh as a kitten, while Dick looked deeply intent on his work. Dick hit out with his left, but was cleverly stopped. Perkins made a similar effort, but was likewise stopped. Dick then rushed in to hit, while Perkins retreated and fell back at the ropes, half out of the ring. (Shouts for Dick.)

4.—Dick's face was now a good deal flushed, and the first hit between the ogles began to show its effects, as his right eye became discoloured. Dick, after a leary feint, rushed in to hit with his left; but Perkins, with great steadiness, parried the compliment, and smiled. Dick finding he could not plant his favourite nobbers, now tried the body, and popped in two or three pretty hits in the breadbasket with his left. Perkins was not idle, and caught him on the side of the head with his right. Both were again cautious, and Perkins covered his upper works in good style; he was always ready to counter with his left as he stopped with his right. Dick saw this, and repeated his body blows, leaving pretty obvious marks from his knuckles; Perkins did not return. Good counter-hits at the nob right and left, and both away. Again to manœuvring, when Dick's body hit was stopped; he then rushed in and hit Perkins open-handed with his left. Perkins returned with his left, catching him on the mouth, and a few slight exchanges followed. Dick again had him in the body with his left. After a short pause a fine slashing rally followed, and some jobbing hits were delivered on both sides, but little advantage was observable. The punishment received by Dick, however, was more obvious; in the end Perkins fell. This was a fine manly round, and excited general applause; and from Dick's steadiness, his friends' confidence increased.

5.—The symmetry of Dick's more delicate physog. was a good deal altered, while Perkins's only showed the cut over his right eye, and still preserved his coolness and self-possession. Dick again planted his left-handed body hit, but was idle with his right; in fact, Perkins was so well guarded as to bid defiance to his usual sharp and cutting jobs. A short rally, in which hits were exchanged, and both went down easy, Perkins under.

6.—Dick tried to plant his left on Perkins's nob, but he got well away, and succeeded in stopping a second attempt at his body. Perkins made two excellent stops right and left at his head, but napped it in the ribs; this did not seem to affect him, and he preserved his steadiness in a manner little expected from a yokel. Good stops on both sides, and an admirable display of science; Perkins stopped right and left, but his returns passed beside Dick's head, and were rather at random; hits were interchanged, though not of great moment, and in the close Perkins went down.

7.—Dick fought a little open-mouthed, and seemed somewhat crabbed at not being able to reach his man. He took a drop of brandy-and-water and again went to action. Perkins still steady and collected, and evidently as strong as a horse. Dick resumed his feinting system, and caught

Perkins cleverly with his left, while he delivered his right heavily on his collar-bone. Had this reached his canister, as was no doubt intended, it would have told tales, but Perkins's activity on his legs enabled him to step back in time. Dick put in three body blows in succession with his left, but they did not seem to tell on the iron carcass of Perkins. Dick then rushed in to punish, but Perkins, in retreating, fell, and pulled him upon him. (Dick's friends were still satisfied all was right, and booked winning as certain. But little betting took place, so intense was the interest excited by every move.)

8.—Dick tried his left-handed job, but was stopped, and with equal neatness stopped the counter from Perkins's left. In a second effort Perkins was more successful, and put in his left cleverly on Dick's nob, while Dick countered at his body. Perkins again stopped Dick's left-handed job, and showed great quickness in getting away. A fine spirited rally followed, in which mutual exchanges took place, and the blood flowed from the smellers of both. It was a fine, manly display on both sides, but in the end Perkins hit Dick clean off his legs with his right, catching him heavily on the side of the head. (Immense cheers from the Oxonians, and the Londoners looking blue.)

9.—Dick, a little abroad, popped in his left on Perkins's body, and then rushed in to fight. Perkins retreated, and got into the corner of the ring, when a desperate rally followed; Perkins jobbed Dick several times right and left, catching him heavily under the ear with his right, thus showing he could use both hands with equal effect. Dick fought with him, but the length of Perkins seemed too great to enable him to hit with effect. Finding himself foiled at this game, he closed, and catching Perkins's nob under his arm, was about to fib; but Perkins slipped down, by the advice of Spring, and evaded the punishment he would otherwise have received. Dick, on getting to his second's knee, was covered with blood, and looked all abroad; the right-handed hit under his lug in the last round was evidently a stinger.

10.—Both came up collected, but Dick did not seem disposed to lose much time in reflection; he hit with his left, but had it in return from Perkins on the nob. A lively rally followed, in which both got pepper; Dick rushed in hastily, and Perkins fell, Dick on him.

11, and last.—Dick now came up evidently resolved to make a desperate effort to put aside the coolness of Perkins, but he found his man ready at all points; good counter-hits were exchanged, and both fought with fury; Perkins threw in a heavy hit with his left on Dick's nob, and then on his body with his right; Dick fought with him boldly, but had no advantage, when Perkins again caught him heavily under the ear with his right, and he fell "all of a heap." He was immediately picked up, and his seconds tried every expedient to bring him to his senses, but he was completely stupefied, and on time being called was incapable of standing. The hat was immediately thrown up, announcing victory, and Perkins ran out of the ring as strong as ever. He was, however, sent back till the battle was pronounced won or lost. The decision was given in favour of Perkins, and in a short time Dick was conveyed to his carriage, and from the ground to Maiden-head. The fight lasted twenty-three minutes and a half.

REMARKS.—At the conclusion of the fight, which was certainly more quickly ended than we anticipated, most of the persons close to the ring seemed to be satisfied that Curtis had been outfought, and that, in fact, he had been, as was observed in the first instance, overmatched. The losers, however, soon began to state a different impression, and certain shrugs and twists gave indication of a feeling that all was not right "in the state of Denmark." It is certain that Dick did not do as much with Perkins as we have seen him do with other men; but then it must be considered that we never saw him opposed to so good a man as Perkins was on this day. In addition to his superior weight and physique, the Oxford man from first to last preserved a coolness and steadiness, and covered his points with a scientific precision, which few men of his age and experience have displayed in the Ring. This was admitted even by those who had most reason to lament his success. In our opinion Dick fought too quickly, and lost that presence of mind which with such an opponent was his only chance of success. From the undiminished strength which Perkins showed at the last, too, we are satisfied he could have continued the fight much longer. We agree with Sam (who seconded Curtis) that he was more of a match for him than for the Pet. It cannot be forgotten that from the first moment the match was made we expressed our fears that Dick was giving away too much weight, and the result has confirmed our judgment.

In a very few minutes after the fight Perkins entered the ring dressed, and little the worse for his engagement, beyond the cut over his left eye and a little puffiness in the mouth and nose; he must, however, have felt for some time the effects of his body blows, which were both heavy and numerous.   He expressed a strong desire to second Harry Jones in his fight with Reidie, but this his friends would not permit.

A challenge from Bob Coates procured for that boxer a thrashing in twenty-five rounds, occupying twenty-eight minutes, near Chipping Norton, on the 19th of March, 1830.

The defeat of Curtis, as we have already noted in cur Memoirs of ALEC REID and HARRY JONES, rankled in the memory of the London Ring, and consequently a more equal opponent for the fresh and hardy provincial was looked out in the person of Alec Reid, " the Chelsea Snob," the full details of which may be read in the tenth chapter of this volume, pp. 423-426.

This first defeat took place on the 25th May, 1830, and thenceforward, until 1832, Perkins remained without a customer.   Towards the close of 1831 a negotiation with Harry Jones, the Sailor Boy, was concluded.   The stakes, £50 a side, were tabled, and on January 17th, 1832, at Hurley Bottom, the scene of his victory over the London Pet, the Oxford man was defeated, after a gallant defence, in twenty-two rounds, time forty-six minutes.

With this defeat closed the Ring career of " the Oxford Pet," in three short years.

INDEX TO VOLUME II.

—◦❖❖◦—

LaVergne, TN USA
09 December 2010
208070LV00004B/318/P